'This book is an authoritative resource for students, researchers and practitioners. Written and presented in an engaging and accessible manner, it guides the reader through all the necessary material for understanding the catalysts and challenges of starting a new business. This will undoubtedly become the core text for entrepreneurship modules on undergraduate, postgraduate and MBA courses.'

Julian Campbell, Norwich Business School, University of East Anglia, UK

'This book is an insightful and informative read. It reflects current trends in the academic field and is written in a style that is accessible to students at undergraduate level. It is particularly suitable for business programmes that incorporate experiential learning into their curriculum. I would recommend it!'

Claire Baird, Business School, Manchester Metropolitan University, UK

'The book is full of inspiring case studies making the learning journey extremely relevant to the real world. All the theories will make sense to my students now!'

Yu-Chun Pan, School of Computing and Engineering, University of West London, UK

'Having used the previous edition, this is still my go-to core textbook. It is a comprehensive resource that combines theory with practical application, while maintaining its easy-to-read format that students find engaging. The range of case studies provided is excellent and together with the *Academic insights* further supports learning. *New Venture Creation* truly complements both undergraduate and postgraduate business venturing courses.'

Laura Jackman, Edinburgh Business School, Heriot-Watt University, UK

To my grandchildren

Amelie, Evelyn, Dylan and Robyn

The future is theirs to create – one of exciting opportunities and feather-light hope but also carrying with it the burden of uncertainty, framed by a history we created.

NEW VENTURE CREATION

A framework for entrepreneurial start-ups

Second edition

Paul Burns
Emeritus Professor, University of Bedfordshire

palgrave

First edition published 2014
This edition published 2018 by
PALGRAVE

Palgrave in the UK is an imprint of Macmillan Publishers Limited, registered in England, company number 785998, of 4 Crinan Street, London, N1 9XW.

Palgrave® and Macmillan® are registered trademarks in the United States, the United Kingdom, Europe and other countries.

ISBN 978–1–352–00050–4 paperback

This book is printed on paper suitable for recycling and made from fully managed and sustained forest sources. Logging, pulping and manufacturing processes are expected to conform to the environmental regulations of the country of origin.

A catalogue record for this book is available from the British Library.

A catalog record for this book is available from the Library of Congress.

Printed and bound in Great Britain by Bell and Bain Ltd, Glasgow.

Brief contents

Contents

Research phase   1

ENTREPRENEURSHIP

Academic insights

Case insights

BUSINESS IDEA

Academic insights

2.1 How to challenge market conventions
2.2 Symptoms of change
2.3 Measuring your creativity
2.4 Thinking outside the box – connectivity
2.5 Discovery skills
2.6 Thinking inside the box – Systematic Inventive Thinking

Case insights

2.1 Bizarre business ideas
2.2 Summly
2.3 Swatch
2.4 DUPLAYS
2.5 Bloom & Wild
2.6 TutorVista
2.7 Mamanpaz
2.8 OnMobile
2.9 Enabled Employment
2.10 Great Ormond Street Hospital
2.11 Swarfega
2.12 Henry Ford
2.13 The Million Dollar Homepage
2.14 Fetchr
2.15 Nikwax
2.16 Maggie's

Sofa-bed Factory

INDUSTRY AND MARKETS

Academic insights

3.1 Porter's Five Forces – assessing industry competitiveness

Case insights

3.1 Video gaming industry in India
3.2 Online dating
3.3 Temple & Webster
3.4 The internet market in China
3.5 Internet start-ups in Iran
3.6 Novo Nordisk
3.7 Bill Gates and Microsoft
3.8 Convergent US technology markets
3.9 Nuffnang

Sofa-bed Factory

Academic insights

Case insights

MARKETING PLAN

Case insights

Academic insights

7.1   Seven principles for communication
7.2   Integrated marketing communication (IMC)

Case insights

7.1   Huddle
7.2   BicycleSPACE
7.3   Instant Pot
7.4   American Giant
7.5   Good Hair Day
7.6   Clippy
7.7   Jack Wills – University Outfitters
Sofa-bed Factory

Academic insights

8.1   Sticking to the knitting

Case insights

8.1   Invoice2go
8.2   Ahmed Khan and McDonald's
8.3   Flying Tiger Copenhagen (2)
8.4   Figleaves
8.5   Zoobug
8.6   Mind Candy and Moshi Monsters
8.7   Crocs™
8.8   Brompton Bicycle
8.9   Reliance Industries
Sofa-bed Factory

OPERATIONS PLAN

Academic insights

9.1 Business failure
9.2 Learning from failure

Case insights

9.1 Trunki
9.2 Xmi
9.3 The English
     Grocer
9.4 Starbucks
     Australia

9.5 Alex Meisl
9.6 ZedZed.com
9.7 Cobra Beer
Sofa-bed Factory

Academic insights

10.1 The benefits of
      partnerships and
      strategic alliances

Case insights

10.1 Ice Cream Mama
10.2 Cotton On Group
10.3 Made.com
10.4 Smak Parlour
10.5 Richard Branson
      and Virgin (2)

10.6 Gordon Ramsay
10.7 Flying Tiger
      Copenhagen (3)
10.8 Kirsty's
Sofa-bed Factory

RESOURCES

Academic insights

Case insights

Academic insights

12.1 Sources of finance used by small firms in the UK
12.2 Agency theory and information asymmetry
12.3 Is there discrimination in lending?

Case insights

12.1 Hotel Chocolat
12.2 Lingo24
12.3 Solar Power Company Group (SPCG)
12.4 Grameen Bank
12.5 Purplle.com
12.6 Zopa
12.7 Kickstarter
12.8 Hamijoo
12.9 InSpiral Visionary Products
12.10 FarmDrop
12.11 Crowdcube
12.12 TransferWise
Sofa-bed Factory

Academic insights

13.1 Entrepreneurial optimism and forecast bias

Case insights

13.1 The English Pub (2)
Sofa-bed Factory

Academic insights

14.1 Do formal business plans really help?
14.2 Entrepreneurial strategy development

Case insights

14.1 wiGroup
14.2 audioBoom
14.3 Moonpig

Index of case insights

List of figures and tables

Figures

Tables

About the author

Paul Burns is Emeritus Professor of Entrepreneurship at the University of Bedfordshire Business School, UK. He has been Pro Vice Chancellor and for 10 years was Dean of the Business School, stepping down in 2011. Over his 40-year career he has been an academic, an accountant and an entrepreneur – giving him unrivalled academic and practical insight into the entrepreneurial process. As well as launching and running his own business, he has helped develop hundreds of business plans and has worked with entrepreneurs, small firms and their advisors, helping launch successful businesses.

For ten years he was Professor of Small Business Development at Cranfield School of Management, UK, where, in 1983, he launched the Graduate Enterprise Programme in England, which was offered at dozens of universities. Paul started his academic career at Warwick University Business School, UK, where he set up their first Small Business Unit. For eight years he was Director of 3i European Enterprise Research Centre researching small firms and entrepreneurs across Europe. He has been a Visiting Fellow at Harvard Business School, USA and for three years was Visiting Professor at the Open University Business School, UK, where he developed the multi-media Small Business Programme which was screened on BBC2. He is Fellow and a former President of the Institute for Small Business and Entrepreneurship (ISBE).

Paul qualified as a Chartered Accountant with Arthur Andersen & Co., where he worked with many growing businesses. He launched and ran his own business, Design for Learning Ltd., advising and training on entrepreneurship and growing firms where he worked with organizations such as the accounting firms Grant Thornton and BDO Stoy Hayward, venture capitalists 3i, and banks such as the Royal Bank of Scotland, Barclays and Lloyds. He has advised and consulted at various levels of government in the UK and overseas, and Margaret Thatcher wrote the foreword to one of his books, *Entrepreneur: Eight British Success Stories of the Eighties* (Macmillan, 1988).

He has authored dozens of books and hundreds of journal articles and research reports. *Entrepreneurship and Small Business: Start-up, Growth and Maturity* (Palgrave) was first published in 2001. The fourth edition, published in 2016, is described as 'one of the most comprehensive books in the area of entrepreneurship' – a 'masterpiece', 'highly engaging' and 'an exceptional treatise'.

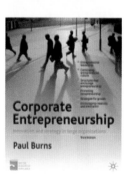

Corporate Entrepreneurship: Innovation and Strategy in Large Organizations (Palgrave) was first published in 2005. The third edition, published in 2013, was praised as a 'definitive guide' that 'combines a profound understanding of theory with practical guidance'. It shows how strategies for encouraging entrepreneurship and innovation might be embedded in larger organizations through the concept of 'architecture' – leadership, culture and structure. A fourth edition is planned for 2019.

Acknowledgements

I would like to thank all those who have helped me with this book, including the students and staff who inspired me to write it. Particular thanks go to Andrew Malvern, Isabel Berwick and Tiiu Särkijärvi at Palgrave, my editor Ann Edmondson and the (anonymous) reviewers from around the world for their pertinent comments and suggestions.

My thanks go to Tahseen Arshi at Majan College, Oman, for permission to use his two Case insights: Sadaf Gallery and Ice Cream Mama. I am grateful to Russell Manfield at University of Queensland Business School for providing web content on the legal and regulatory environment in Australia. Thanks also to my wife, Jean, who helps me with all my books, providing inspiration and insights. She insists that I write in plain English, avoiding jargon, and is an invaluable sounding board for new ideas. She also patiently helps with much-needed proofreading. Any errors or omissions, however, remain my own.

The publisher would like to thank Dr Russell Manfield from University of Queensland Business School for kindly creating the *Guide for Australian Entrepreneurs* on the companion website, as well as all the companies who have provided logos or photographs for the Case insights. We are also grateful to the following organizations for granting us permission to use their material:

The Boston Consulting Group (BCG), for Figure 8.3 Growth Share Matrix

CPP, Inc., for Figure 11.17 Thomas–Kilmann Conflict Modes. Copyright 1974. All rights reserved. Further reproduction is prohibited without CPP's written consent. For more information, please visit www.cpp.com

Design Council, for Design Council's Double Diamond, 2004 in Figure 5.3

Gulf Publishing Company, for Figure 11.15 Leader and task. Adapted from Blake, R. and Mouton, J. (1978) *The New Managerial Grid*, London: Gulf Publishing Company

Harvard Business Review, for Figure 11.1 Growth stages of a firm. Adapted from Exhibit II: The five phases of growth. From 'Evolution and Revolution as Organizations Grow' by Larry E. Greiner, *Harvard Business Review* 50(4) July–August 1972. Copyright © 1972 by Harvard Business Publishing; all rights reserved

SAGE Publishing, for permission to adapt and reproduce the questionnaire in Workbook exercise 11.6 Develop your leadership skills. From Sergiovanni, T. J., Metzcus, R., and Burden L. (1969) 'Toward a Particularistic Approach to Leadership Style: Some Findings', *American Educational Research Journal*, 6(1): 62–79. © Sage 1969. DOI: doi.org/10.3102/00028312006001062

Strategyzer and strategyzer.com, for Figure 4.4 The Business Model Canvas

Guided tour of the book

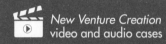

New Venture Creation video and audio cases

Video introductions by Paul Burns open each part of the book, discussing key questions and issues.

Laura Schwartz, Speaker, TV Commentator and Author
Website: lauraschwartzlive.com
Country: USA

Description:
Laura is a networking expert, having written and presented extensively on the subject. Author of the bestselling book, *Eat, Drink and Succeed: Climb Your Way to the Top Using the Networking Power of Social Events*, she believes wholeheartedly in the power of communication. Laura's vast experience includes working as The White House Director of Events, as a television presenter and as a speaker in her internationally acclaimed *Eat, Drink and Succeed* lecture series. Today, she travels the world working with businesses, industry associations, universities and non-profit organizations to teach others the art of success. In this interview, Laura discusses how she progressed from volunteer to Director of Events at The

Recommendation(s) to a start-up:
Don't undervalue your idea, your business plan or yourself. The better you know the value of your product, the more seriously you will be taken.

Questions:
1. What skills, knowledge and experience does Laura think you need to start a business?
2. How do you build social and human capital whilst in education?
3. Which discovery skills did Laura use to build this capital?
4. How important is networking? How do you build a network of contacts systematically? Do 'contacts' have to be friends?

Visit
www.macmillanihe.com/burns-nvc-2e to watch a video interview with Paul Burns.

Case insights with questions are woven throughout the book showing how real organizations and entrepreneurs address issues and apply the approaches explained in the chapters.

CASE insight 1.6 — Sahar Al Kaabi and Sadaf Gallery — OMAN

Influences on entrepreneurship

Sahar Al Kaabi is probably the best-known female entrepreneur in Oman. She is Chairwoman of Sadaf Gallery, a company providing luxury home accessories, gifts for special occasions and flower arrangement services. Sahar was the first woman to be elected to Oman Chamber of Commerce and Industry and, in 2015, she was appointed as a member of the advisory board for the National CEO Program established with the aim of developing the next generation of Omani leaders and entrepreneurs. However, Sahar's road to entrepreneurship was not straightforward, and Sadaf Gallery only succeeded second time around.

Sahar graduated in Arabic literature in 1993 and initially worked for Oman Air as an assistant manager in the purchasing department. After two years she decided to

leave her job because the working hours conflicted with her family and other obligations. She had just divorced and had three children to take care of. She also found that the job routine was not fulfilling her ambitions and she wished to acquire new skills. These circumstances created a number of social, financial and psychological difficulties for her, and her family arranged for her to go on holiday to the United Arab Emirates (UAE). While visiting the city she saw a shop selling gifts, flowers, home accessories, and toys with a gift wrapping service. This reminded Sahar of her childhood when as a 10-year-old, she was different from other children because of her interest in different types of accessories and antiques rather than toys. This inspired Sahar to start a similar business in Oman as soon as she returned. She worked on a feasibility study due to her lack of business experience. She found that

Learning outcomes

When you have read this chapter and undertaken the related exercises you will be able to:

- Critically assess the dimensions of your creative potential
- Develop your creativity and discovery skills
- Scan the environment for business opportunities
- Come up with a business idea by either creating or spotting an opportunity

Learning outcomes identify the key concepts covered in each chapter and the knowledge and skills you will acquire by reading the content and completing the exercises.

Academic insights present the research and theory underpinning the concepts.

ACADEMIC insight 14.1 — Do formal business plans really help?

Evidence about the positive effect of business plans can be mixed, particularly for early-stage businesses where the product/service may still not be well defined and the market uncertain. Based on her study of 27 successful US entrepreneurs, Sarasvathy (2001) observed that entrepreneurs do not like extensive, formal research and planning (Academic insight 4.1). Timmons (1999) claimed that the vast majority of *INC.* magazine's annually produced 500 fastest-growing US companies had business plans at

the outset. However, another study claimed that this figure was only 28% of a 'sample' of these companies (Bhidé, 2000), and this figure is closer to the 31% found in another survey of 600 US SMEs (Wells Fargo, 2006). Burke et al. (2010) asserted that the impact of business plans depends on their purpose, observing that in the UK firms with formal, written plans reported superior employment growth.

Entrepreneurs may not like formal plans, but they do seem to produce them, especially when they are

Quotes from entrepreneurs offer an inside view on starting, developing, launching and running a business.

Most successful businesses are started by teams. Solo entrepreneurs certainly succeed … but they are very much the minority. Even those who we think of as great individual entrepreneurs … all had co-founder partners in the early years.

Luke Johnson, Chairman Risk Capital Partners, Sunday Times 21 May 2017

A business requires many resources such as buildings, vehicles, machinery or stock. Most can be purchased for cash although, as we have seen, there are ways of minimizing the investment needed. The one thing every business needs if it is to grow is people. Nevertheless, many entrepreneurs try to minimize the cost of people by doing as many things as possible themselves, despite the fact that this is not always a good idea as they may not have the necessary expertise. People cannot be purchased in the same way as other assets. They have to be attracted to join the business as employees or partners. Of course many new ventures do not employ anybody to start with, preferring instead to subcontract as many operations as possible. However, the only way you will grow is by recruiting appropriate staff, including managers, to deliver your product/service to more and more customers. Selecting, developing and

Summary and action points recap the principal lessons from the chapter as a handy to-do list.

Summary and action points

13.1 Forecast your income statement: For a new venture to survive and grow it needs to be financially viable. This means it needs to be profitable and efficient, sufficiently liquid to pay its bills, whilst minimizing the risk that it faces. Start by forecasting your income or profit (sales or turnover minus total costs). This shows the growth in all the assets owned by a company, not just cash.

13.2 Estimate your breakeven point: Estimate your breakeven point. This measures the operating risk of the business caused by the amount of fixed costs it faces. The lower the breakeven point the lower the risk. To achieve this you should attempt to keep your fixed costs as low as possible and your contribution margin as high as possible.

13.3 Forecast your cash flow statement: Profit is not the same as cash flow. You can be profitable but illiquid, without cash to pay your bills. Forecast your monthly cash flow for your first year.

13.4 Forecast your balance sheet: The balance sheet is a snapshot at a point of time that shows the assets the business has and where the funds for these assets came from. You now have enough information to forecast your balance sheet at the end of the first year.

Key terms are highlighted in colour and defined in the glossary on pages 466–477.

Financial capital

The financial capital you bring comprises cash and other assets. Your financial may be limited, but it can probably go further than you think. The important remember is that you do not necessarily have to buy and own a resource to be ab it. Using resources that you may not own is called **bootstrapping**. Entrepreneur commit only limited resources themselves – the resources they can afford to lo

Workbook exercises

The New Venture Creation Workbook contains a digital version of these exercises that can be modified as your business model develops and builds into a draft business plan. It can be downloaded from www.macmillanihe.com/burns-nvc-2e.

14.1: Summarize your business model

Use the Framework Worksheet or the PowerPoint slide on the companion website to summarize the key elements of your business model. The table below tells you which Workbook exercises may be relevant to each element of your business model.

Business model	Relevant exercises
Market segment(s) and value proposition(s)	5.3; 5.5
Marketing plan	6.1; 7.4; 8.3; 10.6
Operations plan	9.1; 10.2; 10.4; 10.5; 13.6; 13.8
Resources	9.2; 11.3; 11.4; 12.1; 12.2; 13.7
Financial plan	13.1; 13.2; 13.3; 13.4; 13.5

Sofa-bed Factory

Piotr graduated from university in Krakow, Poland, with a degree in Business. He spoke excellent English so, when he was unable to find a job in Poland, he left to work in the UK. He quickly found a job as a salesman in the store of a large furniture retailer. He was a hard worker and good at his job. After only a year he became store manager and then quickly went to work in the store's head office as a management trainee. In this role, he rotated around jobs in the company's operating areas of purchasing, distribution, marketing and finance, learning how the company worked as well as making friends and developing a network of contacts as he progressed. His hard-working mentality and strong interpersonal skills made him popular with other staff. After two years he was appointed Regional Sales Manager. That was some five years ago.

Unfortunately, Piotr was not happy. He returned to Poland regularly to meet family and friends and longed to go back. It was not that he disliked the UK, just that Poland was where his roots were. He liked the lifestyle there and things were so much cheaper. His family was close-knit and his parents were keen to see him settle down in Poland. As a Regional Sales Manager Piotr had a good salary but he still could not afford to buy his own

but far less about business in general. He asked Piotr if he knew of any manufacturing opportunities – perhaps for products to be sold in the UK. Piotr started talking about the furniture his company sold. Because he had been a management trainee, he knew a lot about the business: the product range, where it was manufactured and even the prices the company paid for furniture. Gradually Piotr and Olek started wondering if there might be a business opportunity here for both of them. So they decided to have another drink and think it through a little.

This was the first time Piotr had thought about starting a business, so the first thing he did was to get some paper and jot down the pros and cons of working for himself:

Pros:	Cons:
1 A challenge;	1 No clear business idea;
2 Being your own boss (not taking orders);	2 Little capital;
3 Potentially earning more money;	3 Risk of business not working (but little to lose);
4 Based in Poland (but would it be?).	4 Will they generate a regular income?

A running case study shows how two young people might deal with the issues raised in the chapters by examining the choices they make for their fictional company Sofa-bed Factory.

Workbook exercises at the end of each chapter and on the companion website help you to find and develop a business idea by providing a clear, progressive structure to organize and write down your thoughts and ideas. They develop into a comprehensive business model and can be used to produce a business plan.

Other online teaching and learning resources

Visit www.macmillanihe.com/burns-nvc-2e

Additional digital resources can be found on the companion website (www.macmillanihe.com/burns-nvc-2e).

New Venture Creation
A Framework for Entrepreneurial Start-Ups, 2nd Edition
by Paul Burns

> HOME

> TEACHING RESOURCES

> LEARNING RESOURCES

> ABOUT THIS BOOK

A core textbook for creating a successful business plan which looks at everything a budding entrepreneur needs to consider to have the best chance of launching a successful new venture. It is a very practical text and progressively builds a roadmap towards the creation of an effective business plan.

Introduction to New Venture Creation

Contents:

» The Framework: Phase 1, Phase 2, Phase 3
» The Workbook
» Case insights
» Other online teaching and learning resources (www.macmillanihe.com/burns-nvc-2e)

The Framework

New Venture Creation sets out a systematic framework for creating a new venture – from idea generation to business launch and growth. I call this the *New Venture Creation Framework*, and the book takes you through the three phases involved in creating a new venture:

» Phase 1: Research
» Phase 2: Business model development
» Phase 3: Launch

The Framework forms the structure of this book. Each phase is broken down into a number of stages and each stage covers everything you need to know to start your new venture. At each stage of the New Venture Creation Framework relevant chapters explain what is needed to launch a successful new business, providing guidance and support throughout and building into a comprehensive business model and plan. However this is not just a 'how-to-do-it' book, it is also a 'why-you-do-it' book. **Academic insights** in each chapter outline the research underpinning the theories, concepts and practical advice given in the text.

Page xxxii shows the New Venture Creation Framework – the three phases comprising nine stages. Alongside this, page xxxiii shows how this relates to the fourteen chapters of the book.

Phase 1: Research (3 stages; 3 chapters)

The research phase is the groundwork for a new venture. It provides the foundations upon which all else is built. You need to decide whether entrepreneurship is for you; whether your personal character, skills and resources are well suited to launching and running your own business. If this is the case, you need to find a good business idea, one that will give you a good chance of success, help you fend off competition and create an appropriate income. It will involve looking at the industry and markets in which your business is based. These are the foundations upon which the next phase is built, as you move on to develop your business model. The research phase is iterative and circular, requiring as many iterations as are needed to provide you with the assurances necessary to move on to the business model development phase. However, this decision may not be a final one because, as you explore your business model, you may need to return to this phase to address issues raised. This is suggested in the 'feedback loop' arrows between Phases 1 and 2 in the Framework. The research phase is made up of three different stages, with a chapter devoted to each.

Entrepreneurship (Chapter 1)

Entrepreneurship is not an easy option. The first step is to decide whether it is right for you – and then to match your skills to a business opportunity. Chapter 1 will help you gauge whether you have the motivations, skills and overall entrepreneurial character traits that indicate you might be successful in starting a new venture. It will help you evaluate the human, social and financial capital you bring to the venture.

Business idea (Chapter 2)

Many people think entrepreneurship is not an option for them because they do not have a good business idea. However, finding a good business idea is not as difficult as many people think. Essentially it is about finding a solution to a problem that a sufficient number of people are willing to pay for and that you are able to deliver. That 'product' might be a physical or virtual (internet-based) product or service. And these days it can often be delivered through virtual as well as physical channels of distribution, opening up a global market. Chapter 2 will help you find a good business idea in a systematic way by highlighting market opportunities that exist and then matching them to your skills and resources. It will also help you understand its commercial potential and any difficulties or unknowns associated with it.

Industry and markets (Chapter 3)

Having found a good business idea you need to go about trying to make it as unique and attractive to customers as possible. To do that you need to look in more detail at the market you are entering. Chapter 3 will help you identify your key competitors and understand the characteristics of the market – the opportunities and threats that it poses. This should help you refine your idea and give you clues about how to combat competition effectively. Of course in doing this you may want to modify or change your business idea and question whether you have the appropriate skills to deliver it. This is all part of the screening process in this phase.

Phase 2: Business model development (5 stages; 10 chapters)

A business model describes how a business competes, uses its resources, structures its relationships, communicates with and creates value for customers, and in doing so generates profits for its founders. It is the strategic framework that gives the business direction. It is a framework that generates a common language and mechanism for communication as it is developed. The business model development phase is right at the core of the New Venture Creation Framework. A good business idea can fail because of a bad model and a poor idea can survive because it has a good one. A good model can provide competitive advantage. The challenge is to develop a model that is simple but attractive to customers, one that can be delivered by a start-up but is sufficiently robust to resist competition from existing players. As shown on page xxxii, this phase is broken down into five stages and within each stage there are a number of critical building blocks (highlighted on pages xxxiv–xxxv). Each building block is explained fully in the relevant chapter. Phase 2 also involves iterations – going back over the building blocks to ensure consistency and coherence in the model. It may even involve returning to Phase 1 if necessary. The Framework provides a coherent and consistent structure as well as a language to develop a business model that best suits your business idea. It allows you to ask 'what if?' questions and try out different hypotheses.

> 'A good organizational framework is minimalist – it is as simple as is consistent with illuminating the issues under discussion – and is memorable … [It] organizes and develops what would otherwise be a disjointed experience … [It] provides the link from judgement through experience to learning.'
>
> John Kay *Foundations of Corporate Success* (1998, Oxford: Oxford University Press)

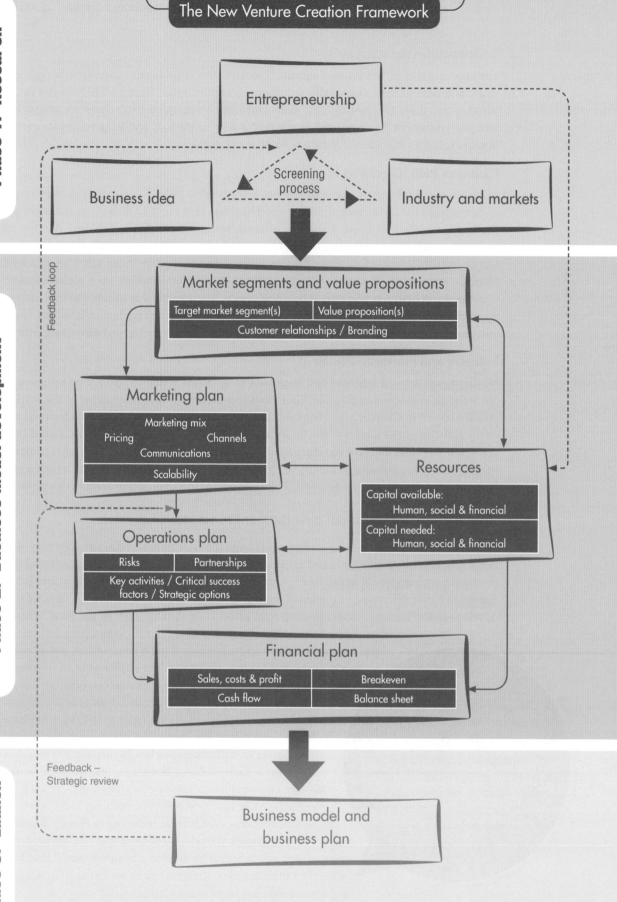

The New Venture Creation Framework

Phase 1: Research

Phase 2: Business model development

Phase 3: Launch

Entrepreneurship

Business idea

Screening process

Industry and markets

Feedback loop

Market segments and value propositions

Target market segment(s) | Value proposition(s)

Customer relationships / Branding

Marketing plan

Marketing mix

Pricing | Channels

Communications

Scalability

Resources

Capital available:
Human, social & financial

Capital needed:
Human, social & financial

Operations plan

Risks | Partnerships

Key activities / Critical success factors / Strategic options

Financial plan

Sales, costs & profit | Breakeven

Cash flow | Balance sheet

Feedback –
Strategic review

Business model and business plan

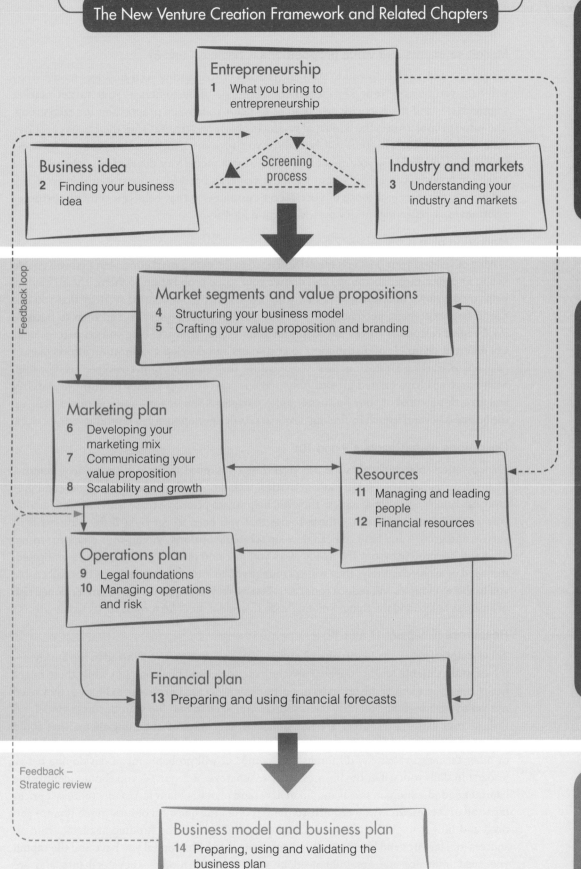

The New Venture Creation Framework and Related Chapters

Phase 1: Research

Entrepreneurship
1 What you bring to entrepreneurship

Business idea
2 Finding your business idea

Screening process

Industry and markets
3 Understanding your industry and markets

Feedback loop

Market segments and value propositions
4 Structuring your business model
5 Crafting your value proposition and branding

Marketing plan
6 Developing your marketing mix
7 Communicating your value proposition
8 Scalability and growth

Resources
11 Managing and leading people
12 Financial resources

Operations plan
9 Legal foundations
10 Managing operations and risk

Financial plan
13 Preparing and using financial forecasts

Phase 2: Business model development

Feedback – Strategic review

Business model and business plan
14 Preparing, using and validating the business plan

Phase 3: Launch

Market segments and value propositions (Chapters 4 and 5)

Chapters 4 and 5 will help you to start the process of structuring your business model. They will help you identify your key customers or groups of customers – your **target market segment(s)** – and their specific needs so as to tailor your value proposition for each group. The **value proposition** is the bundle of products or services that satisfies their needs or solves their problems. The chapters will introduce you to some generalized or generic business models and explain how you might test the business model you develop. The chapters also show you how you can enhance your business model and make it more sustainable by adding values – both yours and those of your target customers – that help you cement **customer relationships**, reflecting these values in a **brand** identity.

Marketing plan (Chapters 6, 7 and 8)

Having developed your business model you need to develop a marketing plan that will enable you to find your target customers and deliver your value proposition to them. These chapters help you develop a **marketing mix** that will form a coherent marketing strategy that you can use to find customers, persuade them to buy your product or service and then to become loyal, repeat customers – even advocates for your 'brand'. They will help you set **prices**, identify different **channels** of distribution to customers and develop a **communications** plan to get your marketing strategy across – cementing that all-important customer relationship. Many start-ups have limited growth potential but success really comes from the **scalability** and growth potential of your business model. Chapter 8 shows you how you might scale up the business beyond launch by finding new markets or developing related products or services.

Operations plan (Chapters 9 and 10)

The operations plan highlights the practical things you need to do to launch a new venture. These chapters help you identify **key activities**, including legal, intellectual property and pre- and post-launch operational issues. They will help you to prioritize these activities and identify your **critical success factors** – those things that you need to get right if the business is to survive and grow – and how you can develop **strategic options**, should your plans go wrong. They will help you tease out the major **risks** you face and plan how they might be mitigated, managed or avoided entirely. They will encourage you to look for **partnerships** that will enable you to share resources and reduce your risks. Finally, they deal with the often unmentioned risk of business failure and the things you might do to avoid it, or at least mitigate its worst effects.

Resources (Chapters 11 and 12)

These chapters help you identify the resources you (and your partners) bring to the business – the **capital available** to start the business: human, social and financial. But while these might have helped you identify the business opportunity you decided to pursue in Phase 1, they need not limit you. You should identify the resources you need to develop your business model and then, if your existing resources are not sufficient, find ways of obtaining them. That could mean recruiting people with the missing skills or experience, or partnering with individuals or other businesses that can do things you cannot. It will probably mean developing better leadership skills yourself as the business grows. Whatever is required, you should identify the **capital needed** – human, social and financial – and plan to obtain it. Usually there is a price-tag to all of the resources you require, so there is often the question of how much finance you need and how it might be obtained. Chapter 12 will explain the funding available from all sources for start-ups and how to go about accessing them. The capital you have and the capital you need influence and are influenced by your business model. They feed into and are informed by each stage of the Framework, which means that the whole process of developing this model is iterative and subject to alteration as circumstances change. The book will show you how you can use the Framework to 'try out' different options.

Financial plan (Chapter 13)

This stage pulls together the financial consequences of the decisions you have made in developing your business model. This chapter shows you how to draw up a set of financial forecasts that show your **sales, costs and profitability**. It will show you how to calculate your **break-even** point and explain what this means and how a simple knowledge of how costs behave can help you make important business decisions. It will enable you to develop a **cash flow** forecast and draw up your **balance sheet** at the end of your first year's trading. It will also explain how to interpret these financial forecasts and how they can be used to develop metrics that measure the performance of the business.

Phase 3: Launch (1 stage; 1 chapter)

Finally you get to launch the business, although even then the refinement of your business model will continue. You might even start with a 'lean' launch, limiting the resources you commit while putting in place processes to learn more about customer needs. This phase comprises a single stage to which Chapter 14 is devoted.

Business model and business plan (Chapter 14)

This chapter helps you pull together your business model and, after launch, to undertake a **strategic review** to see which elements are working and which need to be modified in the light of the realities of trading – whether you need to 'pivot'. It will also help you decide whether you need to draw up a formal, written business plan. It outlines what goes into that plan and how it can be used to obtain finance.

The Workbook

Each chapter explains the relevant stage of the New Venture Creation Framework, and exercises at the end of each chapter get you to apply the concepts in a structured, systematic way to find and develop a business idea. Unlike many academic books, this is a book you can write in and I encourage you to do so. We have left space for your notes and answers to these exercise questions. However, a version of these exercises is also contained in the digital Workbook that is available for download from the website accompanying the book (www.macmillanihe.com/burns-nvc-2e). Once downloaded the exercises can be undertaken at a pace that suits you.

If you record the answers to the exercises in the digital Workbook they can easily be modified as your business model develops and new information emerges. You can also try out 'what if?' scenarios that can help you to decide on the best possible business model. Taken together, they capture all the details of your marketing, operations and financial plan. The answers can also be 'cut and pasted' into a pro forma business plan, which is also available on the website, ready for editing.

The exercises can be undertaken on your own or in groups. It is something you can use at each stage of your journey in launching a successful new venture. They give you the opportunity to assess the viability of your business idea and to find out whether starting your own business is likely to suit you. They may also be used by your instructor to monitor your progress.

Case insights

New Venture Creation is practical, containing advice about how to do things as well as signposts to where resources can be found. However, entrepreneurship is a risky activity and anything you can do to reduce the risk of failure must be good. So you can learn from the successes and mistakes of other entrepreneurs. The book contains dozens of Case insights from around the world that show you how other entrepreneurs have navigated the choppy waters of starting their own business. Video links are available on the companion website (www.macmillanihe.com/burns-nvc-2e) featuring short clips about many of these companies and interviews with the entrepreneurs. There are also numerous quotes from entrepreneurs throughout the book, providing their own advice. In addition, the companion website contains video and audio interviews with six other entrepreneurs, with accompanying questions available on pages xxxviii–xliii of this book. Please note though that things move quickly in business, so by the time you read, watch or listen to the material, some things may have changed. Go to the company websites for updates.

To give you practice in using the New Venture Creation Framework some Case insights may ask you to apply the information given in the case to the Business model development phase in the Framework. To help you do this, there is a Framework Worksheet on the companion website (www.macmillanihe.com/burns-nvc-2e) that can be downloaded, printed and then written on (Figure 1). The companion website also contains a Microsoft® PowerPoint slide showing the Worksheet (Figure 2). This has simulated sticky notes that can be written on and posted onto the Framework (Figure 3). This can be downloaded, used for group discussions or class presentations. The slide can be used to summarize and report on your progress as you undertake the Workbook exercises and develop your own business model. The need to be succinct in writing to these sticky notes is a valuable discipline that will help focus your thinking.

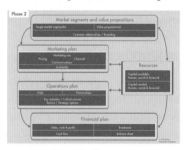

Figure 2 *PowerPoint version of Framework Worksheet*

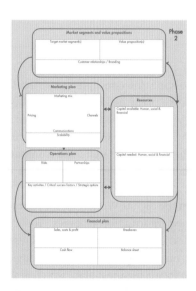

Figure 1 *Framework Worksheet*

Figure 3 *PowerPoint version of Framework Worksheet with sticky notes*

Finally, **Sofa-bed Factory** is a fictitious case that runs throughout the book at the end of each chapter. It shows how two young people deal with the issues raised in the chapter as they start up their own business.

Other online teaching and learning resources

Visit www.macmillanihe.com/burns-nvc-2e

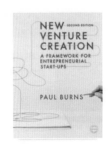

New Venture Creation
A Framework for Entrepreneurial Start-Ups, 2nd Edition
by Paul Burns

> HOME

> TEACHING RESOURCES

> LEARNING RESOURCES

> ABOUT THIS BOOK

A core textbook for creating a successful business plan which looks at everything a budding entrepreneur needs to consider to have the best chance of launching a successful new venture. It is a very practical text and progressively builds a roadmap towards the creation of an effective business plan.

Student resources

Students who purchase *New Venture Creation* have access to a range of additional resources, including:

- Interactive chapter quizzes
- Flashcards of the key terms highlighted in colour in the text and defined in the glossary
- A *Guide to UK Sources of Help, Advice, Information and Funding*
- A *Guide to UK Laws and Regulations for Business*
- A *Guide for Australian Entrepreneurs*, produced by Dr Russell Manfield.

Instructor resources

As an instructor who has adopted this book for your course, you can also gain access to a password-protected Instructor's Manual to help plan and deliver your teaching. The Manual contains chapter-by-chapter:

- PowerPoint slides
- Teaching notes
- Case insight notes (all cases come with questions)
- Group activities and discussion topics
- Weblinks to videos and other websites supporting Case and Academic insights.

Additionally, the Workbook exercises (described on page xxxv) can be undertaken by students individually or in groups. You can use them to monitor students' progress. If students use the digital Workbook, these exercises can be stored electronically and submitted online.

The downloadable New Venture Creation Framework Worksheet or PowerPoint slide with sticky notes (described on page xxxvi) can also be used by students to present case analyses in class as well as demonstrating progress in developing their own business model.

New Venture Creation
video and audio cases

Laura Schwartz, Speaker, TV Commentator and Author

Website: lauraschwartzlive.com
Country: USA

Description:

Laura is a networking expert, having written and presented extensively on the subject. Author of the bestselling book, *Eat, Drink and Succeed: Climb Your Way to the Top Using the Networking Power of Social Events*, she believes wholeheartedly in the power of communication. Laura's vast experience includes working as The White House Director of Events, as a television presenter and as a speaker in her internationally acclaimed *Eat, Drink and Succeed* lecture series. Today, she travels the world working with businesses, industry associations, universities and non-profit organizations to teach others the art of success.

In this interview, Laura discusses how she progressed from volunteer to Director of Events at The White House. She passes on some valuable lessons about communication, networking and work ethic, which can also help you as a budding entrepreneur.

Key lesson(s) learned:

Having a social foundation is as valuable as an academic foundation. You never know whether the next conversation will be the one that changes your life.

Recommendation(s) to a start-up:

Don't undervalue your idea, your business plan or yourself. The better you know the value of your product, the more seriously you will be taken.

Questions:

1 What skills, knowledge and experience does Laura think you need to start a business?
2 How do you build social and human capital whilst in education?
3 Which discovery skills did Laura use to build this capital?
4 How important is networking? How do you build a network of contacts systematically? Do 'contacts' have to be friends?
5 How do you build a relationship with your network of contacts? How important is emotional intelligence in helping to develop relationships?
6 What lesson do you learn from Laura about effective communication?

Relevant chapters: 1, 2

Cobi Bezuidenhout, Founder of Feather-light Accounting Solutions and Director of Ikgolela Informal Business Development

Country: South Africa
Date launched: April 2009

Description:
Cobi runs Feather-light Accounting Solutions, offering bookkeeping services to other local businesses. She is also the director of Ikgolela Informal Business Development, which offers training and workshops. Author of the book *Business is about Balance*, aimed at small business owners in the informal sector, she has a wealth of experience of entrepreneurship in a South African context.

Target market(s):
Feather-light Accounting Solutions targets local businesses which require bookkeeping services; Ikgolela Informal Business Development offers help to entrepreneurs in the informal business sector.

Value proposition(s):
Giving a very good service which encourages referrals from existing customers; providing basic training in a way that can be readily understood by people with limited education.

Major challenge(s):
Finding new clients in a crowded market can be difficult; you can't always control the flow of money and be sure when customers are going to pay you; on the business courses, the attendees often don't have proper equipment to do things like stock control.

Key lesson(s) learned:
Things seldom work out the way you anticipated! You need the ability to change and adapt constantly and quickly, and to be willing to learn.

Recommendation(s) to a start-up:
Be realistic – it's great to have a dream but it must be implemented; be aware of who you are as a person and how you are going to cope with the challenges that come your way; understand the value of personal relationships – they are vital!

Questions:
1. How easy is it to combine commercial and social objectives in a business?
2. Are the barriers to entrepreneurship really just about the risks the entrepreneur faces? Are these barriers greatest if the entrepreneur's motivations comprise 'push' or 'pull' factors?
3. What commercial risks does a start-up face? Are these increased by marrying them with social objectives?
4. How can you prepare for these risks when so much is unknown and might change after launching?
5. What help and support is there for start-ups in your country?
6. What are the benefits and costs of undertaking a start-up course?

Relevant chapters: 1, 9

Suzanne Noble, Founder of Frugl

Website: www.frugl.com

Country: UK
Date launched: March 2014

Description:

Frugl started life as an iOS app offering fun events and local activities for under £10. It then pivoted into a deals website covering thousands of experiences across the UK from art exhibitions and comedy clubs to massages and holidays. The company has won a range of awards, including Mobile Business of the Year in the Smarta 100 Awards 2014 and a commendation in The Good Web Guide Awards 2015.

Target market(s):

Urban residents who are looking for new things to do on a budget; businesses and organizations who want to advertise their deals.

Value proposition(s):

Providing deals that span a wide range of options in each city rather than covering one particular category; possessing a name which is instantly recognizable and fun.

Major challenge(s):

Driving new traffic to the website and ensuring repeat visits.

Key lesson(s) learned:

- It takes a while to understand your value proposition and how to communicate that to your audience.
- Remain lean for as long as you possibly can in order to maximize your learning.
- Keep abreast of your competition but don't obsess about them.
- Raising money is very hard so aim to generate revenue as early as you can or have some kind of side hustle/passive income stream to help keep you afloat.
- Having a good team is crucial and vital for the longevity of your business.

Recommendation(s) to a start-up:

The quicker you can generate revenue, the more likely you are to find investment.

Questions:

1. Describe Frugl's business model and how it generates income.
2. Describe Frugl's communication strategy. How does the company drive users to the website? What are the implications for Frugl's marketing strategy?
3. What barriers does Frugl have to competitors? How important is branding?
4. Why has Frugl been financed in the way described? What problems did it encounter?
5. What do you learn about how to finance an internet business from Frugl's experience?
6. What are the critical success factors for Frugl?

Relevant chapters: 4, 5, 6, 7, 8, 12

Hugh Thomas, Co-Founder of Ugly Drinks

Website: uglydrinks.com

Country: UK & USA
Date launched: April 2015

Description:
Ugly sell cans of fruit-infused sparkling water which contains no added sugar or sweeteners. Since the filming took place, their range of flavours has been expanded and includes Lemon & Lime, Triple Berry, Orange and Tropical. Conceived as a healthier alternative to traditional fizzy drinks, Ugly is sold through their own website and stockists including Amazon, Holland & Barrett, WHSmith and Selfridges & Co. Ugly will launch in the USA in early 2018.

Target market(s):
A young, urban audience who are looking to switch to healthier products; retailers who sell to this market segment.

Value proposition(s):
Offering a healthy, natural alternative to traditional drinks which is sugar-free, sweetener-free, zero-calorie and affordable; possessing a fun, lively brand which is reflected in the name, the packaging and all contact with the public.

Major challenge(s):
Growing the brand on a limited marketing budget; building a good team; continuing to innovate with the product; obtaining sufficient capital for growth; ensuring operational efficiency.

Key lesson(s) learned:
The obstacle is the way. Obstacles will stand in your path but you need to learn to use them to your advantage, much like a judo move. If you can be optimistic, and think around the challenge, then you will be able to keep moving forward in times of difficulty.

Recommendation(s) to a start-up:
Be patient. Take one step forward every day and keep working hard. There is no such thing as over-night success but there are plenty of start-ups who gave up or went too quickly too soon. Be patient and build things one step at a time.

Questions:
1   Describe Ugly's target markets and value propositions, distinguishing between consumers and customers. What are the implications for Ugly's marketing strategy?
2   How unique are Ugly's value propositions? What barriers does it have to competitors? How important is branding?
3   How important are channels of distribution for Ugly? What incentives are there for retailers to sell these drinks? How secure are these channels?
4   What role does pricing play in Ugly's marketing mix? Why does it aim at a retail price of 99p (£0.99), rather than £1?
5   How does Ugly try to stimulate consumer demand? What has been their promotion strategy (awareness – trial purchase – repeat purchase)? What role does social media play in this?
6   Where do economies of scale and economies of scope lie for Ugly? How important is it to achieve them?
7   What are the critical success factors for Ugly?

Relevant chapters: 4, 5, 6, 7, 8, 10

Vinayak Dalmia, Co-Founder of AMBER

Website: www.hiamber.com

Country: India
Date launched: September 2014

Description:
AMBER is India's first Emergency Management System. With the country lacking a comprehensive emergency response service, the AMBER app connects users to nearby emergency rooms, ambulances and other emergency services. Location, medical information stored in the app, and other relevant data is shared with the service provider to enhance their response, while family members are also alerted. The app is currently available to the public for free, but AMBER sells its related ambulance management software to hospitals and is partnering with insurance companies on the app.

Target market(s):
Insurance companies looking to build their digital offering; hospitals which lack the IT infrastructure they need to manage their ambulance fleet; members of the public who want an app that can offer assistance in an emergency.

Value proposition(s):
Solving the medical emergency response problem in India for individuals and hospitals; offering a service that can help life and health insurance companies improve their digital offering.

Major challenge(s):
Ensuring that the technology works flawlessly, since the consequences of failure are more severe for medical emergencies; ensuring adequate legal protection; innovating with the product.

Key lesson(s) learned:
As a result of creating the AMBER app, it became apparent that there was also a market for a backend system which could help hospitals manage their ambulance fleet – an accidental by-product of the original idea.

Recommendation(s) to a start-up:
The only way to really learn is to experience something yourself; be dispassionate – you need to think objectively about your business idea; focus on your team at an early stage because they can determine whether or not you succeed; do not be afraid to do unglamorous things!

Questions:

1   Are Indian health insurance companies customers or partners with AMBER? Are Indian hospitals customers or partners with AMBER? What is the synergy between AMBER and the insurance companies and hospitals? What are the strengths and weaknesses of AMBER in these relationships? What are the implications for AMBER's marketing strategy?
2   What is the role of the consumer in this multi-sided B2B2C relationship? How do they drive users to the app? What are the implications for AMBER's marketing strategy?
3   What are the implications of having to balance supply of ambulances for medical emergencies using AMBER (through hospitals) with demand from consumers/patients who have insurance?
4   How important to AMBER's business model is the fact that there is no standard procedure for dealing with medical emergencies in India? What are the implications of this?
5   What scalability options does AMBER have?
6   What are the critical success factors for AMBER?

Relevant chapters: 4, 5, 7, 8, 10

David Eales, Former Regional Business Development Director at NatWest

Country: UK

Getty Images/iStockphoto/chrisdorney

Description:

David Eales had a long career in banking at NatWest, working with a range of businesses and professionals. In this video he discusses the importance of a good business plan, what it should include and the key things that bankers are looking for when they make a lending decision. He offers useful advice for any businesses looking to obtain funding from a bank.

Recommendation(s) to a start-up:

Having trust and respect for each other is key to a banking relationship. If you tell your lender about a problem early on, steps can be taken to resolve it. If you approach them with a *fait accompli*, people start to fall out.

Questions:

1   What 'hard' commercial information are bankers looking for in a business plan?
2   Are they looking for anything else?
3   David Eales talked about the need to generate 'confidence' and 'trust'. How do you generate this in a written document like a business plan?
4   How do you maintain it once the bank has made a loan to you?
5   Would your answers to these questions be any different if the loan came from crowdfunding? Explain.
6   Would your answers to these questions be any different if the funding was in the form of equity? Explain.

Relevant chapters: 12, 13, 14

Visit
www.macmillanihe.com/
burns-nvc-2e to watch a video
interview with Paul Burns.

1 What you bring to entrepreneurship

Contents

- Taking back control
- What is an entrepreneur?
- The attractions of entrepreneurship
- Barriers and triggers to entrepreneurship
- Your personal drivers
- Your resources
- Character traits of entrepreneurs
- Factors influencing entrepreneurial character
- Summary and action points
- Workbook exercises

Learning outcomes

When you have read this chapter and undertaken the related exercises you will be able to:

- Understand your motivations for wanting to start your own business
- Critically assess the resources you would bring to your business
- Critically assess whether you have entrepreneurial character traits

Academic insights

1.1 Myths about entrepreneurs
1.2 Measuring your entrepreneurial tendency
1.3 Cognitive development theory
1.4 National culture

Case insights

1.1 Julie Spurgeon and Material Pleasures
1.2 Kiran Mazumdar-Shaw and Biocon
1.3 Angie Coates and Monkey Music
1.4 Ambareen Musa and Souqalmal
1.5 Adam Schwab and Lux Group
1.6 Sahar Al Kaabi and Sadaf Gallery
1.7 Lowell Hawthorne and Golden Krust (1)
1.8 Steve Jobs and Apple (1)

Sofa-bed Factory

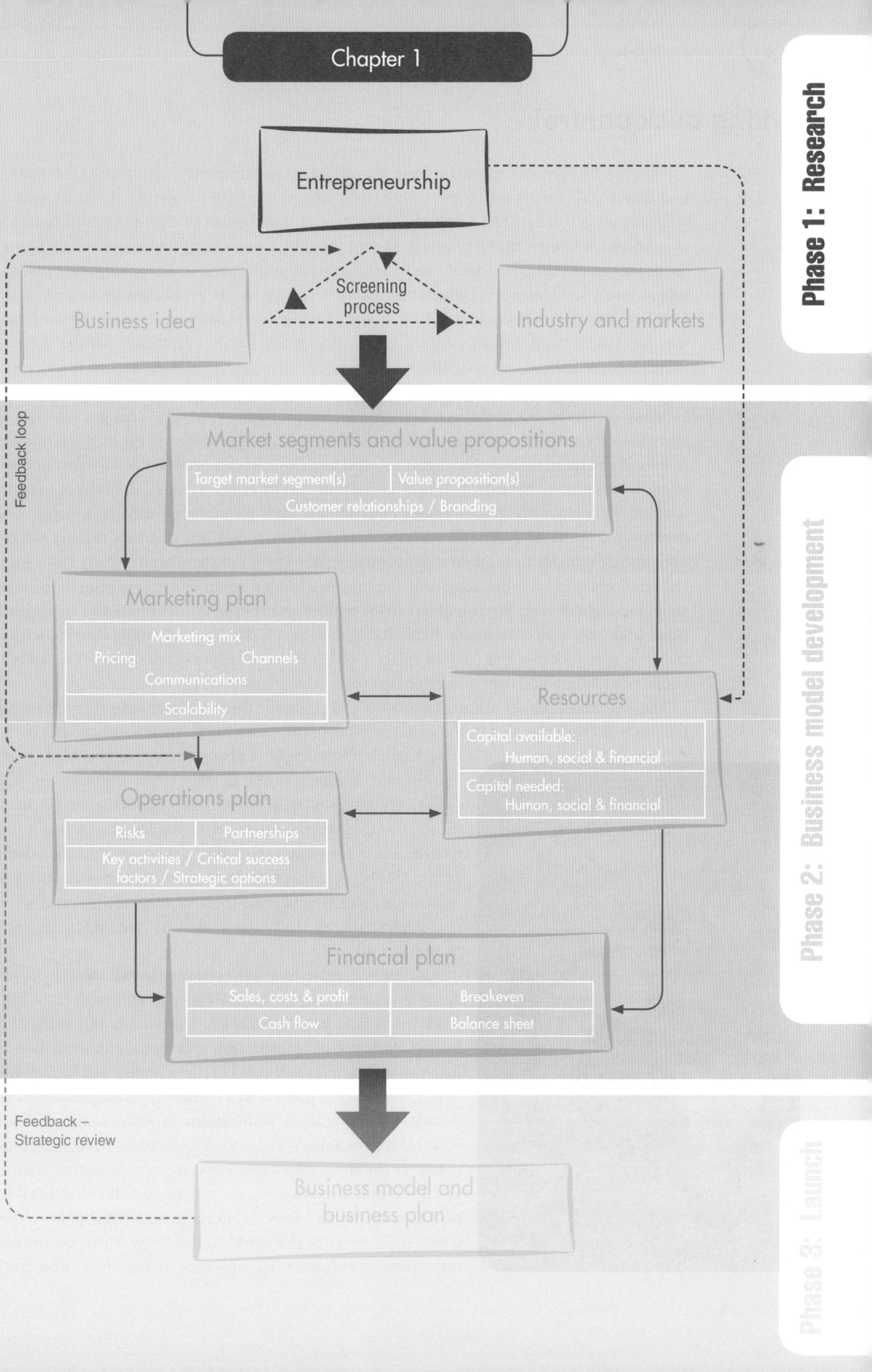

Chapter 1
Entrepreneurship
Screening process
Business idea
Industry and markets
Phase 1: Research
Feedback loop
Market segments and value propositions
Target market segment(s)
Value proposition(s)
Customer relationships / Branding
Marketing plan
Marketing mix
Pricing
Channels
Communications
Scalability
Resources
Capital available:
Human, social & financial
Capital needed:
Human, social & financial
Operations plan
Risks
Partnerships
Key activities / Critical success factors / Strategic options
Financial plan
Sales, costs & profit
Breakeven
Cash flow
Balance sheet
Phase 2: Business model development
Feedback – Strategic review
Business model and business plan
Phase 3: Launch

Taking back control

The twenty-first century has so far been characterized by turbulent and unpredictable change and disruption – a world of 'permanent revolution'. The rise of terrorism led to wars in Afghanistan and Iraq. The so-called Arab spring of 2011 led on to disruption and unrest in many countries in the Middle East, including the civil wars in Syria and Libya, which in turn led to the rise of ISIS. These led to increasing levels of migration into Europe, causing political unrest and even violence. And much of this volatility has been caused by business. The banking crisis of 2008 saw the failure of a number of banks such as Lehman Brothers and Citigroup in the USA and Royal Bank of Scotland (RBS) in the UK. It plunged the Western world into recession and saw disposable income in many countries shrink, particularly among the poorest and most vulnerable, leading to even more political unrest.

Many sectors of the global economy are facing profound structural change. Take the oil and gas sector where companies continue to invest some $700 billion a year in extracting and refining fossil fuels, with 40% of it going to fuel vehicles. Oil exploration has a 25-year or more investment horizon, but how will vehicles be powered in 25 years' time? The vehicle industry itself is changing with the advent of electric cars and autonomous driving systems. Will demand for oil-based fuels still exist in 25 years' time or will autonomous driving electric taxis or hire vehicles have taken over? Probably the biggest upheaval seen already has been in the retail sector where the advent of the internet has led to an enormous growth in home shopping and delivery. What will our town centres and shopping malls look like in 25 years' time? Many of these changes are being felt by business today. In 2016 public bankruptcies in the USA rose by more than 25%, a quarter of which were large corporations with assets in excess of $1 billion and over 40% in energy related businesses.

These winds of change are strong indeed, and alongside them we have seen corporate scandals such as those revealed in the Panama Papers (2017). But major corporate scandals have a

long history: for example, Enron (2001), Freddie Mac (2003) and Bernie Madoff (2008) in the USA; Parmalat in Italy (2004); Olympus in Japan (2013); and Volkswagen in Germany (2016). These scandals alongside the banking crisis might lead us to question corporate ethics. But at the same time the salaries of the CEOs of the world's largest corporations continue to increase at rates well beyond those of other employees, which is symptomatic of increasing income inequality in most Western countries.

Alongside this, we have seen unprecedented volatility in just about every market from commodities to exchange rates, from stock markets to bond markets. Underpinning this volatility is the development of globalization and global connectivity – an increasingly complex world full of interconnections formed by a truly global market place linked by new technologies that allow instant communication with almost anywhere. We all know what others are doing – instantly. Social media is replacing mass media as the most effective means of communication. Twitter and Facebook, for example, are providing 'echo chambers' for people with similar views, reinforcing both their political and commercial views of the world to the point where commentators question whether we are now living in a 'post-truth'

GETTY

society with 'fake' news read by more people than 'real' news. It has been estimated that up to 70% of people in the USA now get their 'news' exclusively from these news sources and nobody really knows whether they can be trusted. It is little wonder that the boundaries between 'truth' and 'lie', 'fact' and 'fiction' are becoming increasingly blurred. In these highly connected systems small changes tend to be amplified – whether in interpersonal relationships, politics or markets. Actions in one part of the world can have unexpected and rapid consequences in another part of it. And nobody, not even sovereign states, seems able to predict this, let alone control it. What is more, the pace of change has accelerated. Change itself has changed to become a continuous process, albeit often one of frequent discontinuous steps – abrupt and all-pervasive.

The new globalization has meant that nobody is safe from the chill winds of competition, a wind that is unforgiving of frailty and no respecter of past reputations. There may be ample opportunities, but they only go to those who can spot them first, are swift to adapt and are open and willing to change. Just as these opportunities have raised many people out of poverty in the East, they have fuelled increasing income inequality, and not only in the West. The 'collateral damage' caused by these winds can be huge, destroying whole communities and industries as jobs move around the world to where resources are cheapest. Only the so-called 'liberal elite' – the 'establishment' – are seen as benefiting. It is little wonder that ordinary people feel insecure and out of control. The old order may be changing but nobody really knows what the new order might look like.

The public backlash against this unprecedented period of change in the West has been resentment against 'the establishment' and in particular large, global corporations, especially banks. The old political orthodoxy of global neo-liberalism seems to be in decline and populist right-wing political parties are in the ascendency. Both the UK vote to leave the European Union and the election of Donald Trump in the USA demonstrate a mistrust of the established order and echo a cry to 'take back control', although, even if this is possible, by whom, from whom and to what purpose is less clear.

Increasing numbers of people see self-employment as one way of regaining control of their lives. Many large firms are slowly dying. They increasingly find it difficult to deal with the new order. Start-ups and smaller ventures seem to find opportunities in the changes that larger, more established firms find threatening. Even in this age of austerity new ventures seem to thrive, despite facing increasingly fierce competition. Never has it been easier to create a new venture. However, while the chances of success on a global basis have probably never been higher, many start-ups struggle to provide even a living wage for the founder. Based more on hope than realistic expectation, the truth is that most start-ups are born to stagnate and die, rather than to become the large corporations of tomorrow. To grow a business requires skill, hard work, perseverance and sacrifice. As the late Steve Jobs, founder of Apple, said:

Making an enduring company is both far harder and more important than making a great product.

Nevertheless many of today's most successful corporations have been founded since the 1970s, and there is no shortage of entrepreneurial role models. Bill Gates started Microsoft in 1975, Steve Jobs started Apple in 1976, Michael Dell set up Dell in 1984, Pierre Omidyar launched eBay in 1995, Larry Page and Sergey Brin launched Google in 1996, and Mark Zuckerberg launched Facebook in 2004. And this was not just happening in the USA. In the UK Alan Sugar launched Amstrad in 1968, Richard Branson started his Virgin empire in 1972, James Dyson started selling Dyson vacuum cleaners in 1976, the late Anita Roddick opened the first Body Shop in 1976, and Julian Metcalfe and Sinclair Beecham opened their first Pret a Manger in 1986. In India, Sunil Mittal started the business that was to become Bhati

Enterprises in 1976 and Kiran Mazumdar-Shaw started Biocon in 1978. These are now gigantic corporations that have made their founders into millionaires. And many new young millionaire entrepreneurs from around the world are featured as Case insights in this book, such as Jack Cator (Hide My Ass!), Nick D'Aloisi (Summly), Dale Vince (Ecotricity) and Taavet Hinrikus (TransferWise) in the UK; Arvind Rao (OnMobile) and Krishnan Ganesh (TutorVista) in India; Ben Silbermann in the USA (Pinterest); and Wandee Khunchornyakong (SPCG) in Thailand.

Over the last thirty years or so entrepreneurs establishing new ventures have done more to create wealth than firms at any time before them – ever! Ninety-five per cent of the wealth of the USA has been created since 1980. Young, high-growth firms (those achieving annual growth of over 20%) – called **gazelles** and/or **unicorns** (very high growth) – are few in number but have a disproportionate importance to national economies. In the UK a report in 2015 estimated they accounted for 20% of economic growth and one in three new jobs.[1] In the USA it has been estimated that the top performing 1% of all firms generate about 40% of new jobs.[2] Small, growing firms generally create jobs from which the rest of society benefits. They have outstripped large firms in terms of job generation, year on year. At times when larger firms have retrenched, smaller firms continue to offer job opportunities.

It has been estimated that in the USA small firms now generate half of GDP and more than half of exports come from firms employing fewer than 20 people. In the UK middle-sized firms represent just 1% of business but generate 30% of GDP.[3] No wonder our governments and media are so fascinated by gazelles and their role is now so lauded by society. Entrepreneurs have finally been recognized as a vital part of economic wealth generation. They have become the heroes of the business world, embodying ephemeral qualities that many people envy – freedom of spirit, creativity, vision and zeal. They have the courage, self-belief and commitment to turn dreams into realities. They are the catalysts for economic, and sometimes social, change. They see an opportunity, commercialize it, and in doing so might become millionaires themselves.

However, while millionaire entrepreneurs such as Richard Branson and Mark Zuckerberg make the headlines, most start-ups are nothing like as successful. In the UK almost 80% (4 million) are sole traders or partnerships, creating employment only for themselves. A report by the Resolution Foundation highlighted that the UK's self-employed earned less in 2015 than they did twenty years previously, with average weekly earnings falling from £300 in 1995 to £240 (£12,480 per annum) in 2015 – some 40% less than the typical employed person.[4] In reality there is no such thing as a typical entrepreneur. There are two tribes. The Resolution Foundation identifies a divide between the 'privileged' – typically with good educational qualifications and higher earnings – and the 'precarious' self-employed – with poorer educational qualifications, more likely to be young, immigrants, underemployed and in receipt of benefits. But classification of the self-employed is not pre-ordained at birth. The question is, which tribe do you want to belong to?

1. Octopus Investments (2015) *High Growth Small Business Report 2015*. Available on: www.scaleupinstitute.org.uk/research/high-growth-small-business-report-2015-2
2. Strangler, D. (2010) 'High-Growth Firms and the Future of the American Economy', *Kauffman Foundation Research Series: Firm Growth and Economic Growth*.
3. GE Capital (2012) *Leading from the Middle: The Untold Story of British Business*, London: GE Capital.
4. Resolution Foundation (2016) *Britain's Self-employed Workforce is Growing – But Their Earnings Have Been Heading in the Other Direction*, London: Resolution Foundation. Available on: www.resolutionfoundation.org/media/blog/britains-self-employed-workforce-is-growing-but-their-earnings-have-been-heading-in-the-other-direction/

Myths about entrepreneurs

Read et al. (2011) claim there are seven myths about entrepreneurs who supposedly 'see opportunities others don't, seize them faster, make better predictions and are brash risk-takers.' These lead to the usual objection to starting your own business – namely, 'I don't have an idea, money, entrepreneurial skills – and I'm afraid to fail.' The seven myths are:

- **Entrepreneurs are visionary** – Visions evolve as opportunities emerge. You define your own vision and measures of success. These will change over time and may expand beyond your current imagination. An unrealistic vision can be just an illusion.
- **Entrepreneurs have good ideas and you do not** – Ideas are easy to come by, but you never know how successful they will be, and that includes entrepreneurs.

- **Entrepreneurs are risk-takers** – They may be willing to accept risk but they do not like it, and limit and mitigate it in any way they can.
- **Entrepreneurs have money and you do not** – Just not true. Money does not guarantee success and many money-starved start-ups have blossomed.
- **Entrepreneurs are extraordinary forecasters** – They are not. They are just willing to live with uncertainty but then organize themselves to cope with, indeed influence, it.
- **Entrepreneurs are not like the rest of us** – They are, and entrepreneurial principles and skills can be taught.
- **I do not know how to take the plunge** – This may be true but hopefully books like this will show you how to do just that.

The message is simple: entrepreneurs are not special – find an idea, have a go but limit your losses. This book will show you how to do this.

Read, S., Sarasvathy, S., Dew, N., Wiltbank, R. and Ohlsson, A.V. (2011) *Effectual Entrepreneurship*, London: Routledge.

What is an entrepreneur?

The notion of **entrepreneur** has been crafted over many centuries, starting with the Irish-French economist Cantillon in 1755, and has seen many different emphases. In essence, entrepreneurs are best defined by their actions. Entrepreneurs create and/or exploit change for profit, even if they do not take it themselves. In doing so, they innovate and accept risk in order to move resources into areas where they earn a higher commercial or social return.

Notice that this definition makes no mention of starting a new venture or of being self-employed. Nor does it mention growing the business. Most new ventures do not grow to any size. More than 95% of small firms in Europe employ fewer than 10 people. The 80% (4 million) of sole traders or partnerships in the UK create employment only for themselves. Many people choose to start up **salary-substitute firms** – ones that simply generate an income comparable to what they might earn as an employee (e.g. plumbers, store owners etc.). Others start up **lifestyle firms** – ones that allow them to pursue a particular lifestyle while enabling them to earn an acceptable living (e.g. sports instructors, artists etc.). Both lifestyle and salary-substitute firms are the backbone of societies. In many cases self-employment is the conventional and accepted way of pursuing these life options. However, a growing number of people are being pushed into salary-substitute self-employment by larger companies seeking to subcontract rather than employ full-time staff. These workers

CASE
insight
1.1

Julie Spurgeon and Material Pleasures

UK

Lifestyle start-up

In her mid-forties, Julie Spurgeon graduated with a first in ceramic design from London's Central Saint Martin's College of Art and Design in the summer of 2008. As part of her final project to design a range of tableware she had to seek critical appraisal from retailers and industry experts. One of the firms she contacted was up-market retailer Fortnum & Mason and they were sufficiently impressed to commission a range of bone china tableware, called Material Pleasures, that was launched in August 2009.

The trademark Material Pleasures, which goes on the reverse of each piece, is registered (cost £200) and Julie joined Anti Copying in Design (ACID), which allowed her to log her design trail as proof against copying. Julie had to pay for tooling and manufacturing costs herself. The moulds cost £5,000 and the factory in Stoke on Trent required a minimum order of 250 pieces. The contract with Fortnum's involved exclusivity for six months. All this was funded with a £5,000 loan from the Creative Seed Fund and a part-time job.

In the future I'd like to continue creating specialist tableware, as well as handmade pieces. Material Pleasures stands for individual design, not big-batch production.

Sunday Telegraph 12 July 2009

Visit the website: www.materialpleasures.net

Questions:

1   Would you agree that this is a lifestyle business? Is it likely to grow to any size?
2   What are the pros and cons of society offering training, grants or subsidized loans to this sort of business – for the entrepreneur, the business and for society?

UK Container Maintenance Sunday Times 29 June 2014

You'll need passion, a belief in what you do and hard work to achieve it.

Emma Elston founder

seek temporary, short-term work with companies such as Deliveroo (food delivery), Uber (taxis) or Hermes (parcel delivery), obtained by searching out opportunities on smartphone-based apps. They have been called **gig-workers**. They form part of the **gig-economy**, and comprise people who may not necessarily want to be self-employed. They are employed in low-earning jobs, sometimes below the statutory minimum wage and usually without any form of employment rights or protection. Many would question whether these workers truly are self-employed. The paradox is that Deliveroo, Uber and Hermes are successful, recent start-ups that are using a novel business model to minimize their costs, risks and start-up capital. The truth is that there is a widening income gap for different types of ventures into self-employment.

You might argue that the people starting these sorts of businesses are not 'true' entrepreneurs. Truly **entrepreneurial firms** are the ones that bring innovative ideas and ways of doing things to the market. They are set up to grow from the start and are the ones with the potential to earn high rewards. But they require hard work and the risks associated with any new venture are high. One-third of businesses cease trading in their first year, although ceasing to trade does not always signify failure or the loss of money. And many of the challenges they face are similar. What is more, the business skills you need to survive can be applied to growth, so these distinctions are not absolute. Lifestyle and salary-substitute firms can become more entrepreneurial – with the right management and **leadership**.

But profit is not always the prime motivation for creating a new venture. For many people profit is simply a badge of success and the attraction of being an entrepreneur lies in being their own boss – 'taking back control' and doing what they want to do rather than what they are told to do. Some people spot a business opportunity – a product or a service that they do not see offered in the market or a way of doing something better or cheaper. Some people might be frustrated by the characteristics of current products or by being offered services that do not meet their needs. Some people, just a few, have a genuine 'eureka' moment when they come up with a new invention or have an idea that can revolutionize an industry. Whatever the source of their business idea, they feel motivated to do something about it – perhaps wanting to make a lot of money on the way. What defines the entrepreneur is their willingness to act upon the idea.

Entrepreneurs are creating all sorts of new ventures, not just their own commercial businesses. They are creating new ventures for established, larger firms while remaining in salaried employment, content for the profits (and risks) of their work to go to their employers. We call them **intrapreneurs**. Entrepreneurs are also creating new ventures for a range of non-profit motives. Some have social or civic objectives and are willing to invest their own time and risk their own capital for little or no financial return, with profits being ploughed back to meet these objectives. We call them **social** or **civic entrepreneurs**. Sometimes these entrepreneurial projects do not even result in the establishment of a new venture but are subsumed within an existing organization, to change it subtly over time.

> I wake up at 6am, work for a couple of hours then take a break, maybe work 12 hours a day; weekends, four or five hours a day, even on holidays.
>
> Adam Schwab founder Lux Group *Management Today* July 2014

The attractions of entrepreneurship

> Be fully aware that you are going to eat, sleep and breathe the business.
>
> William Morris co-founder Charlie Bears *Sunday Times* 23 April 2017

> A good entrepreneur doesn't just run a business; they live and breathe it.
>
> Martyn Dawes founder Coffee Nation www.startups.co.uk

While creating a new venture has never been easier, the risks are high. And running it can be hard work – an all-consuming, 24-hour, seven-day-a-week activity (at least until you have a management team you can rely on). So it helps enormously if you enjoy what you are doing. You need commitment and dedication. You need stamina – '90% perspiration, 10% inspiration'. Running a small business can break up relationships and split families. It is risky, without guaranteed results. So, you need to be able to bounce back from setbacks, because there will be many. You need determination and persistence. You need to be emotionally tough – self-employment can generate a roller coaster of emotions. You need to be self-sufficient – it can be lonely. You need to be task-orientated – motivated to deliver the best product or service to your **customers**. You need to be attuned to the opportunities generated by these customers and the market in which you operate. Most of all you need to be able to live with a degree of risk and uncertainty – you will always be the last one to get paid and then only if there is enough cash left over. If you crave certainty, routines and regular pay, entrepreneurship is not for you.

However, the rewards for being successful can be high, especially if you enjoy what you are doing. There is the freedom and independence you have on a day-to-day basis, the sense that you control your own destiny and that it is you who will benefit from your hard work. There is the sense of purpose that launching your own business brings and satisfaction that comes from your achievements. And for many of the most successful entrepreneurs, it can bring wealth and even fame.

CASE insight 1.2

Kiran Mazumdar-Shaw and Biocon

INDIA

Millionaire entrepreneur

Born in 1953 in Bangalore, India, Kiran Mazumdar-Shaw is one of the richest women in India. She is the founder of Biocon, a biotech company and India's largest producer of insulin. With a degree in zoology, she went on to take a postgraduate course and trained as a brewer in Australia, ahead of returning to India hoping to follow in her father's footsteps as a brewmaster. Despite working in the brewing industry in India for a couple of years, she never achieved her ambition, finding her career blocked by sexism. Instead, in 1978, she was persuaded to set up a joint venture making enzymes in India.

Kiran Mazumdar-Shaw started Biocon India with Irishman Les Auchincloss in 1978 in the garage of her rented house in Bangalore with seed capital of only Rs 10,000. It was a joint venture with Biocon Biochemicals, Ireland. The early years were hard. Eventually Kiran found a banker prepared to loan the company $45,000 and, from a facility in Bangalore making enzymes for the brewing industry, started to diversify. Biocon India became the first Indian company to manufacture and export enzymes to the USA and Europe. This gave her a flow of cash that she used to fund research and to start producing pharmaceutical drugs.

I was young, I was twenty five years old ... banks were very nervous about lending to young entrepreneurs because they felt we didn't have the business experience ... and then I had ... this strange business called biotechnology which no one understood ... Banks were very fearful of lending to a woman because I was considered high risk.
BBC News Business 11 April 2011

In 1989, Kiran met the chairman of ICICI Bank, which had just launched a venture fund. The fund took a 20 per cent stake in the company and helped finance its move into biopharmaceuticals. Shortly after this Unilever took over Biocon Biochemicals, and bought ICICI's stake in Biocon India, at the same time increasing it to 50 per cent. In 1996 it entered the biopharmaceuticals and statins markets. One year later Unilever sold its share in Biocon Biochemicals, and Mazumdar-Shaw bought out Unilever and was able to start preparing Biocon India to float on the stock market, which it did in 2004, with a market value of $1.1 billion.

Today Biocon has Asia's largest insulin and statin production facilities and its largest perfusion-based antibody production facility. It produces drugs for cancer, diabetes and auto-immune diseases and is developing the world's first oral insulin, currently undergoing Phase III clinical trials. It employs more than 8,000 people across its 10 subsidiaries and has a turnover in excess of Rs 26,000. It is listed on the Bombay and New York Stock Exchanges.

Kiran Mazumdar-Shaw has enjoyed many awards and honours. In 2010 *TIME* magazine included her in their 100 most powerful people in the world, in 2016 *Forbes* magazine featured her on the Asia 50 Power Businesswomen list. She has featured in 'The Worldview 100 List' of the most influential visionaries (*Scientific American* magazine), in the '100 Leading Global Thinkers' (*Foreign Policy* magazine) and was ranked second in Global 'Medicine Maker Power List' (*The Medicine Maker* magazine). Passionate about providing affordable healthcare in India, she has funded the 1,400-bed Mazumdar-Shaw Cancer Centre, a free cancer hospital in Bangalore. Every year, she donates $2 million to support health insurance coverage for some 100,000 Indian villagers.

Visit the website: www.biocon.com

Questions:

1 How typical is this story?
2 What are the chances of becoming a millionaire by starting your own business?

Barriers and triggers to entrepreneurship

For most people there are blocks or barriers that prevent them from creating a new venture, even if they have a good business idea. Some are real and some are psychological. Some people are just too risk averse. They fear the unknown and do not like uncertainty. If you have a family you might fear the consequences of not having a regular income or losing what little financial capital you have.

What many people need is some sort of 'trigger' that either 'pushes' or 'pulls' them into it. Some people are 'pushed' into setting up their own business because they are made redundant, they find they just do not fit into the company they work for or, simply, that they have no alternative. Typically these are situational factors that push you towards self-employment. Immigrants are often 'pushed' into being highly entrepreneurial. They have few alternatives. The USA, famed for its entrepreneurial culture, was built by immigrants and many millionaire entrepreneurs are first- or second-generation immigrants. Sergey Brin, co-founder of Google, emigrated to the USA with his family from the Soviet Union at the age of six. Steve Jobs' father was Syrian. In the UK, six of the most successful wholesale medicine and drug supply companies were founded by Kenyan Asians – pharmacists – who came to Britain in the 1960/70s as forced immigrants and are now millionaires (Navin Engineer, Bharat Shah, Bharat and Ketan Mehta, Vijay and Bikhu Patel, Ravi Kari and Naresh Shah).

> **Mark Constantine founder Lush RealBusiness 26 May 2009**
> We got the inspiration (for Lush) because we were broke. The previous business had gone bust. We had mortgages, three children and no money. So – make a living!

On the other hand, many people are 'pulled' into starting up a business for more positive reasons. They yearn for independence and recognition of their achievements. This gives them drive and determination. They look for personal development. And the prospect of becoming rich might be attractive. Pull factors are typically psychological – they derive from people's character traits and the influences on them. When 'push' and 'pull' factors combine it is little wonder that the result is a powerful trigger to potential entrepreneurs to create a new venture – as long as they have that all-important business idea. The combination of these triggers – the push and pull factors – and the barriers they face in setting up their own business are shown in Figure 1.1. It is no coincidence that the peak ages of entrepreneurs creating new ventures – in their early 20s or early 40s – match periods when barriers might be low because they have least to lose or have reducing family commitments as children leave home.

Situational and psychological barriers to entrepreneurship
- Need for regular income
- Fear of loss of capital
- No capital
- Risk averse
- Doubts about ability

Push factors
- Unemployment
- Disagreements
- Organizational 'misfit'
- No other option

Pull factors
- Independence
- Recognition
- Personal development
- Wealth

Figure 1.1 Barriers and triggers to entrepreneurship

Your personal drivers

The most important thing you bring to your new venture is you, which makes it important to understand what that means. You start by understanding your drivers – what motivates you to think about starting your own business? You need to understand your own motivations for being an entrepreneur. Why are you considering it (push and/or pull)? What are your barriers? What are your personal drivers? What do you want the business to become – a salary-substitute, lifestyle or entrepreneurial business? Or do you want it to achieve some social or civic objectives? In other words, what is your business purpose?

> Fun is at the core of the way I like to do business and has informed everything I've done from the outset. More than any other element, fun is at the core of Virgin's success.
>
> *Richard Branson founder Virgin Losing my Virginity (1988, London: Virgin)*

Of course, entrepreneurs often start out thinking they want to achieve one thing and then change it later as new opportunities emerge. Many people start with a business that appears to have no growth prospects but go on to seize opportunities as they present themselves. John Hargreaves is a docker's son who left school at 14 and started a market stall in Liverpool selling M&S clothing seconds (i.e. less-than-perfect clothing). He went on to found the Matalan clothing chain in the UK, a venture he sold for £1.5 billion in 2009. Alan Sugar, now famous for his appearances on *The Apprentice* TV show in the UK, founded the computer companies Amstrad and Viglen and is a millionaire. He started in business by boiling beetroot to sell from market stalls in London's East End.

Nevertheless, you need to match your personal motivations and drivers with the business you intend to set up now – not in ten years' time. There is no point in setting up a business that is intended to grow rapidly unless you are willing and able to make the additional time and resource commitment. And you certainly will need to enjoy whatever your venture entails. You will spend a great deal of time working in it.

You also need to consider any personal constraints (barriers) that might affect your venture. Are you short of money, time or skills? What are your fears about self-employment? Many of these may originate from family or other commitments. It is important that your business fits in with what you want from your life and lifestyle. You need to have a balance between work and personal life that suits you. Without an acceptable balance the stress and pressure may be too much.

Your resources

You need four things to start a business, all covered in this book:

1 A good business idea.
2 Sufficient **capital** to launch it and help it grow (human, social and financial).
3 An entrepreneurial character – temperament and motivation.
4 A plan as to how you will make it happen.

Considering capital first, you bring capital to your start-up, even if you are short of cash, because capital can take a number of different forms. There are three sorts of capital: financial, human and social (Figure 1.2 on page 14). The more capital – of any form – you bring to the business the greater your chances of success, but you can compensate for a lack of one by bringing more of another.

CASE insight 1.3

Angie Coates and Monkey Music

 UK

Motivation and risk

Angie Coates' mother was a teacher and her father owned a small engineering firm. At the age of 11 she won a scholarship to study the oboe at the Guildhall School of Music and Drama in London, graduating with a music degree in 1988. She went on to become Head of Music at Thomas's London Day Schools. So, when she had a baby daughter it was only natural that she would want her to share her love of music. However, she was not happy with the baby music classes she found locally, so in

Logo courtesy of Monkey Music Ltd

1993, with her daughter only a few months old she started her own business, Monkey Music, based in London. Monkey Music started out offering music classes to infants and pre-school toddlers from a church hall in Dulwich, southeast London.

I was a young mum and ready to change my lifestyle completely. I wanted to stop having to get up at 6am every day to then leave my baby with a childminder before travelling to work. I wanted to do something fresh and exciting, for my daughter and for me.

By 1998 she was struggling with the huge demand for her classes and was teaching more than 500 children a week, so, on the advice of her lawyer brother, she decided to franchise the music curriculum, taking a percentage of the fee charged by the franchisee (Chapter 8). The Monkey Music programme is divided into four stages, each tailored to a specific age group of babies and young children from 3 months: Rock'n'Roll, Heigh-ho, Jiggety-Jig and Ding-Dong. Each class will take up to a maximum of between 10 and 15 children. Class fees average around £7.50.

We take children through a very specific and progressive curriculum which comprises a vast repertoire of especially composed songs and musical activities. Our curriculum supports all aspects of child development and classes are led by highly trained Monkey Music teachers. We start children very young

so we support their social and emotional development as well as physical and language development ... Creativity is the most exciting part of Monkey Music.

Monkey Music is widely recognized by the British franchise industry as an award-winning business. It was winner at the British Franchise Association Franchisor of the Year Awards in 2005 and was a finalist in the same awards in 2010 and 2013. National parenting awards include winner of the Best National Pre-Schooler Development Activity in 2010 and 2013 and Best Toddler Development Class in 2008, with Monkey Music teachers winning numerous other parenting awards on a local level. Angie has decided not to dilute the product offering and to keep the product range simple and focused, with the website and teachers selling merchandise that extends the class experience: the soft Monkey and Baby Mo toys, class CDs and T-shirts.

By 2014 the business had nine staff based in Harpenden, just north of London. The network was generating sales of over £3m. There were around 50 franchises with more than 100 teachers running classes in more than 300 venues across the UK. The most successful franchise reported a turnover of £180,000 and profit of £70,000, and a significant number of franchises have remained under the same ownership for more than 10 years.

On top of all this, Angie now has five daughters.

Visit the website: www.monkeymusic.co.uk

Questions:

1 What was Angie's motivation in starting up Monkey Music?
2 How did she keep the costs of starting the business down?
3 How much of a risk did she face in starting and then growing the business?

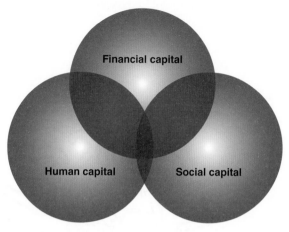

Figure 1.2 Start-up capital

Financial capital

The **financial capital** you bring comprises cash and other assets. Your financial capital may be limited, but it can probably go further than you think. The important thing to remember is that you do not necessarily have to buy and own a resource to be able to use it. Using resources that you may not own is called **bootstrapping**. Entrepreneurs often commit only limited resources themselves – the resources they can afford to lose. They find ways of using resources that they do not own by partnering with others – all techniques covered in Chapter 10. Actually, minimizing your ownership of resources reduces your risks and gives you more flexibility – it allows you to commit (and de-commit) quickly to new opportunities.

> Get as much professional training as you can before starting a business. Doing a MBA first really helped me.
>
> *Andrew Valentine founder Streetcar Sunday Times 15 November 2009*

Human capital

Capital is more than just financial. **Human capital** comprises your skills, abilities, education, training and previous managerial or industry experience. Knowledge and experience of a business or industry can be an invaluable source of business ideas. It can also give you an insight into the problems that you will face in business and it is always better to make mistakes at somebody else's expense rather than your own. If you do not have that experience then education and training can alert you to the problems and give you the skills to overcome them. That is why so many people take training courses before they actually start up in business – it improves their chances of success. Human capital in the form of education and a track record increases your credibility with financial backers. It counts for a lot if you can demonstrate achievements, particularly in the industry where you want to start up.

> Contacts are important but you have to get out there and meet people. It can be difficult when you are absorbed in running a business. But there is always something to learn from meeting someone new and a lot to learn from meeting someone old. The right contacts can become an invaluable source of learning as well as an inspiration and support.
>
> *Jonathan Elvidge founder Gadget Shop The Times 6 July 2002*

Social capital

There is also **social capital** – derived from access to personal networks of friends and commercial contacts. Social capital is about your ability to get on with people – your social skills. It is built on relationships and this is at the core of the

CASE insight 1.4

Ambareen Musa and Souqalmal UAE

The importance of social and human capital

Born in Mauritius, Ambareen Musa holds an undergraduate business degree from RMIT University, in Melbourne, Australia and a MBA from INSEAD, France. She started her first online business, a property portal for international students in Australia at the age of 21. Moving to London in 2004 to work for GE's financial arm, GE Money, she had various roles including marketing, financial literacy, customer advocacy and e-commerce. Ambareen led the first online financial literacy initiative in the UK, Moneybasics.co.uk. Moving to the Middle East in 2008, she worked as a consultant for Bain & Company Middle East and focused on financial services projects such as growth strategies for banks in the region. She moved on to set up the consulting arm of MasterCard Middle East and Africa, where she stayed for two years, before founding Souqalmal in 2012 in Dubai in the United Arab Emirates.

Souqalmal is Arabic for 'money market'. The online site says that its aim is to 'create a transparent market place and empower consumers'. It allows consumers to compare some 3,000 products online, including credit cards, car loans, insurance, SME loans, mobile phone plans, schools and nurseries in the UAE, Saudi Arabia and Kuwait. The site also has news and guides about the markets it covers. It has become the leading financial comparison website in the Middle East.

Visit the website: www.souqalmal.com

Questions:

1 What human and social capital did Ambareen Musa possess?
2 How did her education and experience help her in starting up Souqalmal?

> You're constantly reading business books and constantly meeting people, [taking] advice from all sorts of people. I would recommend that.
>
> *Mark Constantine founder Lush RealBusiness 26 May 2009*

entrepreneurial approach to doing business – relationships with customers, employees, suppliers, the bank and your landlord. It is social capital that enables you to build your credibility with all these stakeholders in your business. It is the personal touch that distinguishes entrepreneurs from the faceless, grey-suited managers of large firms. These relationships can build into an invaluable network of contacts and goodwill that can be used to generate knowledge and information on new opportunities or threats. Networks can therefore increase your flexibility and reduce, or give you early warning of, the risks you face. Networks might also yield up partners or ways of bootstrapping resources. They might provide you with your first customer, or provide you with low-cost or free office space. They might provide professional advice and opinion, often without charge. They might even provide you with the cash that the banker is so reluctant to provide. It is no surprise therefore that networking has been found to be one of the most important factors underpinning long-term business performance.

Character traits of entrepreneurs

Your personal drivers and fears about entrepreneurship derive from your personal character. This influences the importance you place on 'pull' factors and how you react to 'push' factors, as well as being the source of many of the barriers you place in the way of being an

An entrepreneur is unfailingly enthusiastic, never pessimistic, usually brave, and certainly stubborn. Vision and timing are crucial. You have to be something of a workaholic, too. You have to be convinced that what you are doing is right. If not, you have to recognize this and be able to change direction swiftly – sometimes leaving your staff breathless – and start again with equal enthusiasm.

Chris Ingram founder Tempus Sunday Times 17 March 2002

I was not a job type of guy. I think it's my personality. I've always liked to make my own decisions.

Henri Nyakarundi founder African Renewable Energy Distributor CNN African Start-up 9 August 2016

entrepreneur. We do not completely understand how character traits develop and whether some might be 'hardwired' into your personality. However, they are at least in part the product of the many influences that have shaped and developed you over your life; from your parents to your nationality, from your education to your career. They are influenced by the different groups of society in which you operate, their culture and norms of behaviour. And, while it might be possible to classify your character at a point of time, it can change over time and in different circumstances. Many researchers believe that entrepreneurs have certain identifiable character traits or personality dimensions that incline them towards setting up their own business and help them navigate through the uncertainties of entrepreneurship. What is more, some believe personality traits can be acquired or developed by individuals.

Research into the character traits of entrepreneurs is substantial and goes back some 40 years. While facing many methodological issues, it has thrown up a number of overlapping personality dimensions or character traits that might incline an individual towards setting up their own business and help them navigate through the uncertainties of entrepreneurship. Figure 1.3 summarizes the five main entrepreneurial character traits, harvested from numerous research studies. Each is a necessary but not a sufficient trait. What is needed is the combination of all of them to be present.

Figure 1.3 *Character traits of entrepreneurs*

Need for independence

Entrepreneurs have a high need for autonomy and independence. This is most often seen as the need to 'be your own boss' or an unwillingness to take orders. It has been said that, once you run your own firm, you cannot work for anybody else. This is the most often cited entrepreneurial character trait and supported by researchers and advisors alike. However, independence means different things to different people: doing things differently, being in a situation where you can fulfil your potential or controlling your own destiny.

Need for achievement

Entrepreneurs have a high need for achievement that gives them a drive and determination that is often lacking in others. However, people measure their achievement in different ways, depending on the type of person they are: for example, the satisfaction of producing a beautiful work of art, employing their hundredth person, or making the magic one million dollars. For many entrepreneurs, money is just a badge of success, validating their achievement. It is not an end in itself. What they are satisfying is their underlying need for achievement – recognition of their success. And while they may have a 'need' for achievement, that does not necessarily mean that they are actually high achievers, only that this 'need' creates a drive within them. If they have a high need but achieve little then they can be profoundly unhappy.

Internal locus of control

Entrepreneurs have a high 'internal locus of control' – a belief that they control their own destiny. They may believe in luck, but not fate. They believe that they can create their own destiny. This is underpinned by a high level of 'self-efficacy' – self-confidence (possibly unfounded) in their ability to undertake a task. In extremis, a high internal locus of control can also manifest itself in a desire to control everything and everyone around them. This can lead to a preoccupation with detail, overwork and stress, particularly if you feel you cannot trust those around you to complete the tasks delegated to them. This in turn can lead to a mistrust of subordinates, an unwillingness to delegate and an 'infantilization' of subordinates – an expectation that they will behave as incompetent idiots.

The combination of a high need for achievement and a high internal locus of control means that entrepreneurs, typically, have enormous drive and determination. They believe that their drive and determination will lead them to achieve the outcome they want. It explains why entrepreneurs tend to be proactive rather than reactive, and more decisive. They act quickly and can be task focused. However, they can also appear impulsive and easily diverted. They seem to work 24 hours a day and their work becomes their life with little separating the two. It is small wonder that this can place family and personal relationships under strain. Since they work so hard, putting in long hours themselves, they can often be impatient with the commitment and pace of work of others – unwilling or unable to tolerate disagreement or wait for other people to complete tasks The combination of these traits can often make them a difficult boss. For example, the late Steve Jobs, founder of Apple, was notoriously difficult to work for and was well known as a 'control freak' who was often accused of being rude,

Eddy Shah founder Messenger Group *The Times* 16 March 2002

> Entrepreneurs don't like working for other people … I was once made redundant by the *Manchester Evening News*. I had a wife who had given up a promising career for me, and a baby. I stood on Deansgate with £5 in my pocket and I swore I would never work for anyone else again.

Chey Garland founder Garlands Call Centres *Sunday Times* 27 June 2004

> As a child I never felt that I was noticed. I never felt that I achieved anything or that there was any expectation of me achieving anything. So proving myself is something that is important to me, and so is establishing respect for what I have achieved.

Wing Yip founder W. Wing Yip & Brothers *Sunday Times* 2 January 2000

> I am motivated by my success, not by money. But success is partly measured by money.

Elim Chew founder 77th Street *BBC News* 20 December 2010

> Being an entrepreneur is like being a juvenile delinquent … The more you tell us we can't do it; the more we want to prove you wrong … If we were to listen to people who keep telling us not to do it, then 77th Street would never have happened. Because in the early days everyone was telling us we would fail … Today we have proved everybody wrong.

abusive and even bullying in order to get his own way. He believed he knew best and wanted things done his way – quickly.

Creativity, innovation and opportunism

> I think as entrepreneurs we are driven by ideas … When I have my free time, I like to go onto the internet and really explore the different things that people are doing; what are the different ideas popping all over the world.
>
> *Elim Chew founder 77th Street BBC News 20 December 2010*

> I actually don't believe in luck … I don't know anyone who got anywhere without hard work.
>
> *Lyn Lee founder Awfully Chocolate BBC News Business 8 November 2010*

The ability to be creative and innovative is an important attribute of entrepreneurs. But creativity can mean different things in different contexts. For entrepreneurs creativity is focused on commercial opportunities. They spot an opportunity and then use creativity and innovation to exploit it. They tend to do things differently from the competition. As we shall explain in the next chapter, the more creative and innovative the entrepreneur the greater the growth potential of their business.

Acceptance of risk and uncertainty

> You have to be prepared to lose everything and remember that the biggest risk is not taking any risk at all.
>
> *Jonathan Elvidge founder Gadget Shop Sunday Times 17 March 2002*

Entrepreneurs are willing to take risks and live with uncertainty – things that can be very stressful for most people. They are willing to risk their money, reputation and personal standing if the business fails. However, that does not mean they are gamblers, and they will try to avoid or minimize the risks they face and insure against them. As we shall see later in this chapter, they have a distinctive approach to risk mitigation involving gaining knowledge and information from networks, partnerships and compartmentalization of risks. They have 'inside information' – real or imagined – that reduces the risk and uncertainty in their minds. They never really believe the business will fail and have complete faith that they will be able to affect the outcome – their high self-efficacy and 'internal locus of control'. They really do believe that they can succeed where others might have failed. The challenge is to ensure that the information on which this belief is based is real, verifiable and can be shared with others. The problem of different levels of knowledge is called 'information asymmetry' and is important when it comes to raising finance (see Chapter 12).

> You have to have nerves of steel and be prepared to take risks. You have to be able to put it all on the line knowing you could lose everything.
>
> *Anne Notley founder The Iron Bed Co. Sunday Times 28 January 2001*

There is at least one validated psychometric test to measure entrepreneurial potential. Called the **General Enterprise Tendency (GET) test**, you can take it online for free (see Academic insight 1.2). Results are analysed and a report automatically produced giving an analysis (and score) for your entrepreneurial character. Try the test and see what you score. The five character traits measured in the test are likely to show themselves in the behaviours summarized in Table 1.1. How many of these do you exhibit?

> We take risks – but they're always calculated.
>
> *Emma Elston founder UK Container Maintenance Sunday Times 29 June 2014*

There is one further quality that entrepreneurs with growth businesses seem to have, although not necessarily at the launch of the business. They have or quickly develop a vision for the business. This is part of the fabric of their self-motivation. They are able to see what the business might become despite the odds. It is an essential leadership quality and helps them to bring others with them – employees and customers.

> The secret is to have vision and then build a plan and follow it. I think you have to do that, otherwise you just flounder about … You change your game plan on the way, as long as you are going somewhere with a purpose.
>
> *Mike Peters founder Universal Laboratories Sunday Times 11 July 2004*

Table 1.1 Behaviours associated with entrepreneurial character traits

High need for independence	High need for achievement	High internal locus of control	Highly creative and innovative	High acceptance of risk and uncertainty
You are likely to be a person who:	You are likely to be a person who is:	You are likely to be a person who:	You are likely to be a person who:	You are likely to be a person who:
• Dislikes taking orders • Prefers to work alone and 'do their own thing' • Likes to make up their own mind and not bow to pressure • Can be seen as stubborn and determined • Prefers to do 'unconventional' things	• Restless and energetic • Proactive rather than reactive • Decisive and quick acting • Goal orientated, working hard to achieve them • Task and results orientated • Persistent and determined • Forward looking and self-sufficient • Optimistic rather than pessimistic • 'On the go' all the time	• Believes they control their own destiny and discounts fate • Believes they create their own luck by hard work and effort • Is self-confident and shows considerable determination • Is willing to take advantage of opportunities that present themselves	• Is curious and questioning • Is intuitive and imaginative • Is innovative with an abundance of ideas • Is a bit of a daydreamer • Enjoys change and the challenges it poses	• Makes decisions quickly • Can act on incomplete information, evaluating likely costs against benefits • Can accurately assess their capabilities and then set challenging but attainable goals • Is neither overambitious nor underambitious

ACADEMIC
insight
1.2

Measuring your entrepreneurial tendency

The General Enterprise Tendency (GET) test provides you with the opportunity to reflect on whether you have an entrepreneurial character. It is a 54-question, validated psychometric test of entrepreneurial character – high need for independence, high need for achievement, high locus of control, highly creativity and accepting of risk and uncertainty. The results are automatically analysed and a personal report on your character traits can then be printed out.

Caird (1991a, b) established the construct validity and reliability of the GET test by testing it on entrepreneurs and comparing it to results for occupational groups including teachers, nurses, civil servants, clerical workers and lecturers and trainers. Overall, entrepreneurs were found to be significantly more enterprising than the other groups, but they were not the only group to score highly on *individual* measures. Stormer et al. (1999) applied the test to 128 owners of new (75) and successful (53) small firms. They

concluded that the test was acceptable for research purposes, particularly for identifying owner-managers, but it was poor at predicting business success. Either the test scales needed to be refined for this purpose or the test did not include sufficient indicators of success, such as antecedent influences on the individual, or other factors related to the business rather than the individual setting it up.

The GET score needs to be looked at overall as well as individually in each of the five dimensions. To be categorized as 'entrepreneurial' you need to score above the entrepreneurial minimum level in every one of the five dimensions. Also, the score does not predict business success – that involves too many other factors. However, the test does provide an indicative, although not a definitive, measure of your enterprising tendency. As the website says, the test is best used 'as an educational aid to think about entrepreneurship'.

The GET test is free and takes only 5 minutes to complete. It can be taken online at: www.get2test.net

Caird, S. (1991a) 'Self Assessments on Enterprise Training Courses', *British Journal of Education And Work*, 4(3).

Caird, S. (1991b) 'Testing Enterprising Tendency in Occupational Groups', *British Journal of Management*, 2(4).

Stormer, R., Kline, T. and Goldberg, S. (1999) 'Measuring Entrepreneurship with the General Enterprise Tendency (GET) Test: Criterion-related Validity and Reliability', *Human Systems Management*, 18(1).

Factors influencing entrepreneurial character

Dale Vince founder Ecotricity Daily Telegraph 27 May 2011

> I thrive on adversity. I like it when the chips are down. When nobody believes that something can be done, I think, 'We are going to do this!'.

Cognitive development theory provides us with an insight into how the psychological factors that push, pull and restrain us from going into self-employment and form part of our character might have developed through our life experiences. It also gives us an insight into how and why entrepreneurs approach decision making using the mental models or dominant logic that they have developed over time based upon these experiences – even if the mental model is based upon relatively few experiences. It can make entrepreneurs seem overconfident about future outcomes. It also explains how they make extensive use of cognitive heuristics (simplifying strategies) based upon these mental models to help them make quick decisions (see Academic insight 1.3).

Cognitive development theory emphasizes the effect of situational factors on our character traits. And, while they are 'learned' through our individual experiences in life, they are also framed and influenced by the cultures and subcultures of the different groups that we operate within – such as nationality, family, religion, work background, stage of life and so on (Figure 1.4). Culture is about the prevalent norms, basic values, beliefs and assumptions about behaviour that underpin that group and press us to 'conform'. The major influences relevant to our entrepreneurial propensity seem to be nationality, education, family, gender, partnerships, immigration and ethnicity.

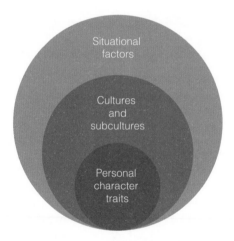

Figure 1.4 Influences on our character traits

Nationality – National cultures do seem to vary widely, reflecting underlying core values. However, measuring them in any meaningful way is extremely difficult. The most widely used study of dimensions shows that there are dominant, measurable cultures in particular countries (see Academic insight 1.4). This is especially interesting because it allows us to describe the culture of what we might expect to be the most entrepreneurial country of all – the USA; a competitive, achievement-orientated society that values individualism and material wealth and is not afraid of taking risks. We might assume that countries with similar cultures encourage entrepreneurship and those at opposite extremes of these dimensions probably inhibit

Cognitive development theory

Jean Piaget (1896–1980) is usually credited with the origination of cognitive development theory. He saw children's cognitive development as influenced both by biology and environmental experience. Children construct mental models (shortcuts or 'rules of thumb') of how the world around them operates, and these models change as they experience discrepancies between the real world and their mental models. Cognitive theory therefore shifts the emphasis from the individual towards the situations that lead to our behaviour. In particular, it seeks to understand how people think and react in different situations. It tries to understand the mental models or dominant logic (also called cognitive heuristics) that influence entrepreneurial behaviour and how they can be affected. Cognitive skills are an important part of human capital but, as we shall see in the next chapter, they can also constrain our thinking. Some strands of cognitive theory reinforce ideas about how traits may influence behaviour.

CORBIS

Chen et al. (1998) argue that it is **self-efficacy** that motivates entrepreneurs and gives them the dogged determination to persist in the face of adversity when others just give in. With this characteristic entrepreneurs become more objective and analytical but tend to attribute any failure to outside factors such as insufficient effort or poor knowledge. They argue that self-efficacy is affected by a person's previous experiences – success breeds success, failure breeds

failure. This is the entrepreneur using their mental model or dominant logic as a basis for decision making, even if the mental model is based upon relatively few experiences. Entrepreneurs appear to make extensive use of cognitive heuristics – simplifying strategies – in decision making (Delmar, 2000). Because of this, successful entrepreneurs can often be seen as 'overconfident' (Forbes, 2005), particularly with regard to predicting a future outcome, to the point of escalating their commitment to it (Baron, 1998). Many studies (e.g. Chen et al., 1998; Koellinger et al., 2007; Krueger and Dickson, 1994) observe that people who report overconfidence and high levels of self-efficacy are more likely to become entrepreneurs. Generalized self-efficacy is effectively the same as the locus of control trait observed in entrepreneurs.

Delmar (2000) outlines two other cognitive concepts. **Intrinsic motivation** suggests that people who undertake tasks for their own sake perform better than those motivated by external factors ('pull' factors compared to 'push' factors). This strong inner drive – type 'A' behaviour – amounts to almost compulsive behaviour. 'A' types tend to be goal-focused with high levels of drive, wanting to get the job done quickly. They also tend to try to proactively affect events (internal locus of control), focusing on the future when they are often not in control of the present. The second concept, **intentionality**, suggests that people who intend to do things are more likely to do them than people who do not. This is the result of entrepreneurs' internal locus of control and is what underpins their drive and determination.

Baron, R.A. (1998) 'Cognitive Mechanisms in Entrepreneurship, Why and When Entrepreneurs Think Differently Than Other People', *Journal of Business Venturing*, 13(4).

Chen, P.C., Greene, P.G. and Crick A. (1998) 'Does Entrepreneurial Efficacy Distinguish Entrepreneurs from Managers?', *Journal of Business Venturing*, 13.

Delmar, F. (2000) 'The Psychology of the Entrepreneur', in S. Carter and D. Jones-Evans (eds) *Enterprise and Small Business: Principles, Practice and Policy*, London: Prentice Hall.

Forbes, D. (2005) 'Are Some Entrepreneurs More Overconfident than Others?', *Journal of Business Venturing*, 20.

Koellinger, P. Minniti, M. and Schade, C. (2007) '"I Think I Can, I Think I Can": Overconfidence and Entrepreneurial Behaviour', *Journal of Economic Psychology*, 28.

Krueger, N.F.J. and Dickson, P.R. (1994) 'The Social Dimensions of Entrepreneurship', in M. Casson, B. Yeung, A. Basu and N. Wadeson (eds) *The Oxford Handbook of Entrepreneurship*, Oxford: Oxford University Press.

Adam Schwab and Lux Group

AUSTRALIA

Influences on entrepreneurship

Lux Group started life with just one employee, offering local deals in Melbourne through a single website. Launched by Adam Schwab and Jeremy Same in July 2010, DEALS.com.au sold everything from day spa to restaurant offers, based on the Groupon flash sales model (see Chapter 4). By 2017 the business had changed its name and grown to become one of the largest e-commerce businesses in Australia and New Zealand, comprising 13 websites with a turnover of more than AUD300 million annually. Key properties include Luxury Escapes – one of Australia's most popular travel websites with a turnover of more than AUD200 million in fiscal year 2017 (www.smh.com.au/small-business/managing/serial-entrepreneur-adam-schwab-on-stepping-back-from-luxury-escapes-20160830-gr4fnk.html), Brands Exclusive, Living Social, Cudo and TheHome.

Adam Schwab

Courtesy of Adam Schwab

Schwab is the son of a builder and an accounting teacher. His first experience with the business world came as an 11-year-old, when he realized he could exploit the captive market for lollipops by selling them to other children on his school bus. After attending Caulfield Grammar School with Same, the pair would later start a number of successful small ventures together, including DigiCat, which sold CDs containing copies of high-scoring assignments to students across Australia:

This wasn't a huge business but relatively speaking, it was a nice little earner for a couple of 18-year-olds.

After leaving school Adam studied Commerce/Law at Monash University where he also had a number of part-time jobs, including ripping tickets at a cinema, working in a supermarket and as a nightclub host. During university he set up a business called DigiLaw by replicating the DigiCat model, but selling notes to law students. Schwab managed to convince the law bookstore to sell the product, leading students to believe that it was somewhat more official than it actually was. Despite being successful, the business was forced to close when the Dean of the Law School banned students from using it.

After leaving university, Schwab started work as a corporate lawyer specializing in mergers and acquisitions with Freehills. However, in late 2004, he and Same spotted a commercial opportunity in the property market in Melbourne – renting and furnishing inner-city apartments, which they would then offer to 'high end' backpackers and travellers. With very little capital and borrowing an old trailer owned by his father, Adam scrounged cheap furniture to fit out their first apartment. The pair soon realized that they would be able to make a reasonable margin by offering the apartments to small groups for shorter periods. The model would later morph into offering apartments to corporate clients under the Living Corporate brand:

We could put one corporate client in an apartment instead of four travellers, which was a lot more popular with owners.

As the Melbourne property market was booming, Adam and Jeremy acquired six properties which would within a couple of years be sold for a profit of more than AUD1 million. This cash would allow them to fund a business that was scalable on an international basis without raising any external finance.

Searching for ideas from around the world, Schwab and Same noticed the success of the TopTable restaurant-booking business in the UK (now a part of global travel giant, Priceline).

In late 2009, they started working on MyTable, a similar discount-based restaurant booking site and, in parallel with DEALS.com.au, they developed their MyTable business into a takeaway food-ordering website before selling it to Catch Group. The business would eventually become part of MenuLog and was sold in 2015 to the UK-based giant Just Eat for AUD855 million.

Schwab continues to run Lux Group which grew strongly in 2017 and has expanded from Australia into New Zealand, India and Singapore. In August 2017, Lux Group launched its first retail concept store in the Melbourne City Centre, marking the online group's first foray into high street retail.

Visit the website: luxgroup.com

Questions:

1 Going from his history, what social and human capital does Adam Schwab possess?
2 What characteristics of the entrepreneurial character can you see in Adam Schwab?

entrepreneurship. Many academics and politicians believe that the impact of national culture upon aggregate levels of individual entrepreneurial activity could have significance for public policy. However, proof of any causal linkage has proved difficult because of methodological challenges.

ACADEMIC insight 1.4

National culture

The most widely used dimensions of national culture are those developed by Hofstede (1981), who undertook an extensive cross-cultural study using questionnaire data from some 80,000 IBM employees in 66 countries across seven occupations. Although the survey was conducted some 40 years ago, it remains one of the most authoritative studies on national culture. From his research, Hofstede established the four dimensions of national culture shown in Figure 1.5. This figure also shows the dominant culture he found in employees in particular countries. Although national cultures change only slowly, this will probably have changed since the 1970s.

Individualism versus collectivism: The degree to which people prefer to act as individuals rather than groups. Individualistic cultures are loosely knit social frameworks in which people primarily operate as individuals. In these cultures the task prevails over personal relationships and the atmosphere is competitive. Collectivist cultures are composed of tight networks in which people operate as members of groups, expecting to look after, and be looked after by, other members of their group. The atmosphere is cooperative inside the group but can be competitive with outside groups.

Power distance: The degree of inequality among people that the community is willing to accept. Low power distance cultures endorse egalitarianism – relations are

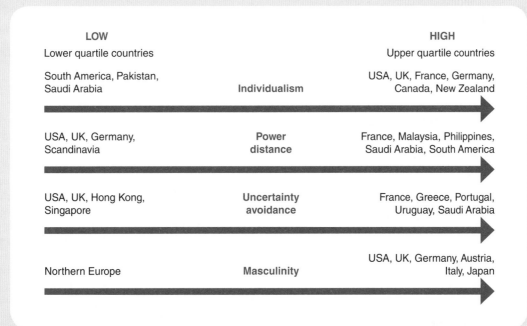

Figure 1.5 Dimensions of national culture

open and informal, information flows are functional and unrestricted and organizations tend to have flat structures. High power distance cultures endorse hierarchies – relations are more formal, information flows are formalized and restricted and organizations tend to be rigid and hierarchical.

Uncertainty avoidance: The degree to which people would like to avoid ambiguity and resolve uncertainty, and would prefer structured rather than unstructured situations. Low uncertainty avoidance cultures tolerate greater ambiguity, prefer flexibility, stress personal choice and decision making, reward initiative, experimentation, risk taking and team play and stress the development of analytical skills. High uncertainty avoidance cultures prefer rules and procedures, stress compliance, punish error and reward compliance, loyalty and attention to detail.

Masculinity versus femininity: This defines quality of life issues. Hofstede defined 'masculine' virtues as those of achievement, assertiveness, competitiveness and success. These cultures reward financial and material achievement with social prestige and status. 'Feminine' virtues include modesty, compromise and cooperation.

These cultures value relationships, so issues such as quality of life, warmth in personal relationships, service and so on are important. In some societies having a high standard of living is thought to be a matter of birth, luck or destiny, rather than personal achievement (an external locus of control – the opposite of internal locus of control).

At a later date Hofstede and Bond (1991) added a fifth dimension – short/long-term orientation. A short-term orientation focuses on past and present and therefore values respect for the status quo, including an unqualified respect for tradition and for social and status obligations. A long-term orientation focuses on the future and therefore the values associated with this are more dynamic. They include the adaptation of traditions to contemporary conditions, so these cultures have only qualified respect for social and status obligations. Clearly an entrepreneurial culture is one with a long-term orientation.

Hofstede, G. (1981) *Cultures and Organizations: Software of the Mind,* London: HarperCollins.

Hofstede, G. and Bond, M.H. (1991) 'The Confucian Connection: From Cultural Roots to Economic Performance', *Organizational Dynamics,* Spring.

CASE insight 1.6

Sahar Al Kaabi and Sadaf Gallery

 OMAN

Influences on entrepreneurship

Sahar Al Kaabi is probably the best-known female entrepreneur in Oman. She is Chairwoman of Sadaf Gallery, a company providing luxury home accessories, gifts for special occasions and flower arrangement services. Sahar was the first woman to be elected to the Oman Chamber of Commerce and Industry and, in 2015, she was appointed as a member of the advisory board for the National CEO Program established with the aim of developing the next generation of Omani leaders and entrepreneurs. However, Sahar's road to entrepreneurship was not straightforward, and Sadaf Gallery only succeeded second time around.

Sahar graduated in Arabic literature in 1993 and initially worked for Oman Air as an assistant manager in the purchasing department. After two years she decided to leave her job because the working hours conflicted with her family and other obligations. She had just divorced and had three children to take care of. She also found that the job routine was not fulfilling her ambitions and she wished to acquire new skills. These circumstances created a number of social, financial and psychological difficulties for her, and her family arranged for her to go on holiday to the United Arab Emirates (UAE). While visiting the city she saw a shop selling gifts, flowers, home accessories, and toys with a gift wrapping service. This reminded Sahar of her childhood when as a 10-year-old, she was different from other children because of her interest in different types of accessories and antiques rather than toys. This inspired Sahar to start a similar business in Oman as soon as she returned. She worked on a feasibility study due to her lack of business experience. She found that there was no direct competition and she could source the required capital through a family loan. She also selected Sadaf as the name for her business. It means an amalgamation of darkness and light, representing the period between night and dawn that was consistent with her psychological state at that time.

In 1996 Sahar opened Sadaf Gallery in Muscat. However, she was inexperienced and the business concept was new, which meant that she was unable to promote it well to the right customers. Her customer base was limited and her financial obligations increased. As a result she experienced financial problems resulting in a cash flow crisis, and she closed the gallery in 1998.

Sahar travelled to Egypt for higher studies and returned to Oman in 2000, but her attraction to entrepreneurship had not diminished. At a jewellery exhibition arranged by her aunt she met a Bahraini businessman, who offered her the opportunity to market his product: a 'Holy Quran', carved in 1.5 cm stone inlaid with precious stones. As a result Sahar started to prepare a list of the companies, banks, and governmental institutions to whom she might market the product. She started her promotion plan with the Diwan of the Royal Court, a high official in His Majesty's Palace where it might be presented as a gift for guests. She did not succeed in selling the product, but she came to know the kind of gifts such organizations find attractive. She came to realize that banks needed special promotional items at reasonable prices, whereas the Diwan needed luxury Arabic perfumes, jewellery and watches, and was willing to pay much more.

Sahar started looking for local dealers to provide souvenirs, luxury perfumes and jewellery. She arranged catalogues and provided prospective customers with samples in innovative packaging with customized designs, all subcontracted to a local designer who gave Sahar's products a unique appearance that provided a distinct competitive advantage. The first contract from a bank was worth Omani Riyals 1,900 (about £3,200) and the total cost was OR1,200, giving a profit of OR700. A few months later she secured her first contract worth OR7,000 from the Diwan of the Royal Court to supply them with perfumes, with a profit estimated at OR3,000. As she started to focus on the Diwan's needs, she shrewdly investigated global brands that were not available in the local market. As a result she travelled to Switzerland to visit watch exhibitions and to France to visit a perfumes exhibition in 2003. There she was able to build a strong business relationship with watch and perfume producers for the purpose of marketing their products, especially to the Diwan, and brought catalogues and samples of perfume back to Oman. She hired a Kuwaiti with experience in gift wrapping and flower arrangement, and within five months was joined in the business by her sisters. Sahar was able to re-open the gallery and this time sold a number of high-value gift items to a range of consumers from all walks of life. Sahar also came up with the innovative idea of opening a ladies' coffee shop as a part of the gallery. According to Omani culture, women do not accompany men in their social gatherings and on weekends they do not have the opportunity to socialize.

In 2004, Sadaf Gallery was awarded OR5,000 as the best new project in the 'Intilaaqah' competition – a program sponsored by Shell Oman to finance small projects. Since then Sahar has opened three more galleries in Oman, and one in Qatar, with a Qatari partner. In 2008 Sahar was selected as deputy president to lead the Oman Business Women Association. She became the first woman to be elected to the Oman Chamber of Commerce and Industry. In 2015 she was appointed as a member of the advisory board for the National CEO Program. Sahar continues to develop her business, upgrading the company website to enhance its competitiveness and building an online customer base.

When you want to start something, you should study and have a good plan.

omaninfo.com / *Times of Oman*

Questions:

1 What factors made Sahar become an entrepreneur?
2 What lessons did she learn that contributed to her success?
3 What is the importance of Sahar as a role model in Oman?

Education – One influence that comes through in many studies of both start-up and growth is educational attainment. This may be because education increases your social and human capital. It might also be because it makes you more likely to question the status quo and more aware of opportunities around you. Clearly there are problems with measuring educational attainment consistently over different studies. Nevertheless, particularly in the USA, many research studies show a positive association between the probability of starting up in business and high educational attainment. The educational attainment (degree level and/or MBA), experience and management skills of the founders of high-growth, often technology-based firms in the UK and USA, is typically high. You might indeed question this, given that Bill Gates, Steve Jobs and Michael Dell all dropped out of university. However, similar research in other countries tends to support this result, albeit less strongly and not consistently.

Age – Although entrepreneurial activity is spread across all age groups, research shows that mature (late 30s) or very young (early 20s) entrepreneurs are most likely to be associated with growth companies. What is more, the proportion of young entrepreneurs is increasing. Youth brings creativity. However, age brings experience and knowledge, and an invaluable network of relationships and contacts. Between these two stages of life, many people decide to bring up a family, with all the constraints that brings.

Family – Studies show that a family business background, such as having a parent who was an entrepreneur or having worked in a family business, increases the probability of starting up in business.

> **Wandee Khunchornyakong founder SPCG** BBC Business 12 July 2016
>
> We [women] don't have enough confidence ... You have to believe in your own thinking and if you don't believe your own thinking who else will believe you?

Partnering – Growth companies are more likely to be set up by groups rather than by individuals, and these groups share in the ownership and therefore the success (or failure) of the business. Partnering with groups to set up a business can bring the same advantages as age – knowledge, experience and networks.

Gender – Although it is changing quickly, across most of the world women are less likely to start a business than men. In the UK, self-employment rates for women are less than half those of men. Another consistent research finding is that businesses owned by women are likely to perform less well than male-owned businesses, however measured – turnover, profit or job creation. The reasons for these findings may be many and varied, sometimes self-determined (although influenced by 'mental models' and cultures), sometimes due to imposed constraints.

Immigration and ethnicity – Ethnic minorities tend to have high self-employment rates in most Western industrialized countries. What is more, observation tells us that migration to a foreign country is positively associated with entrepreneurship (a strong push factor). However, evidence about ethnicity is mixed, and self-employment rates among the UK's ethnic minorities are not uniform. Those for Asians (Indian, Pakistani, Bangladeshi etc.) and Chinese are higher than those for white males, while those for black African and black Caribbean men are lower, typically more comparable to white women. With some 200,000 Asian-owned businesses in the UK, Asians are recognized as the most likely ethnic minority group in the UK to become entrepreneurs, and are represented across all sectors of business.

Studies on the personality traits of entrepreneurs have focused on their propensity to start and maintain a business successfully. Increasingly, however, the debate on entrepreneurship is moving to consider not only what the entrepreneur 'is' but what they actually 'do'. And successful entrepreneurs have a number of characteristic approaches to doing business and managing that have implications for you. Many of these derive from their character traits, but they also derive from the circumstances they typically face in running a small firm. Entrepreneurs realize that they may have limited market influence, particularly if they cannot differentiate themselves from competitors. However, they want to minimize the risks they face while having to manage in an uncertain and changing commercial environment with a shortage of most resources, but particularly cash. We shall deal with all of these circumstances in subsequent chapters.

CASE
insight
1.7

Lowell Hawthorne and Golden Krust (1)

USA

Immigrant entrepreneurs

Lowell F. Hawthorne used to work with his family in his father's bakery in St Andrews, Jamaica. In 1981 he and many of his family emigrated to the USA where he joined the New York Police Department. Seven years later Lowell decided he wanted to start his own business, so he brought the family together and nine of them decided to start up what they knew most about – a bakery. However, the first problem was that they were unable to obtain any loan finance from the banks. Undaunted, the family pooled their resources (which involved family members having to remortgage their houses) to find $107,000, and Golden Krust was launched in 1989 on East Gun Hill Road in Bronx, New York.

Today Golden Krust is known for its Jamaican patties – flaky, yellow half-moon turnovers of dough filled with a variety of spicy meat or vegetables – and the sauces to go with them. However, for the first three years of its existence, while the company produced a range of Jamaican bakery products, it bought in the patties from a West Indian restaurant distributor. It was only when the supplier cut off supplies that Lowell was forced to find out about making patties himself – going to the UK, Jamaica, and US states of Wisconsin and Illinois (Chicago) to find out how to do it. Less than a year after the crisis, equipped with a baking method from Scotland, UK, a chef named Mel and a new machine, sales exceeded $2 million for the first time. By 1996, as well as a bakery, the company had seven restaurants.

> *As an immigrant, not understanding the system here made it more difficult … Had I lived there and understood how it worked I think we would have gone through it easier.*

Golden Krust remains a family business and has become the largest West Indian food chain in the USA. It still has its manufacturing base in New York, but it also operates as a franchisor and has a chain of more than 120 restaurants selling its patties in nine US states. Turnover exceeds $100 million. It now makes most of its money as a franchisor, which generates an upfront fee and a restaurant royalty of 5% on the turnover. The company also sells its patties wholesale to big distributors such as Wal-Mart and supplies the US military and New York's schools and prisons in an effort to expand the customer base beyond the West Indian communities.

Lowell Hawthorne

> *We have a 2020 vision: We want to make Caribbean cuisine mainstream by 2020.*
> BBC News Business 20 June 2012

Over the years, Lowell has won many prestigious awards including Ernst & Young's Entrepreneur of the Year Award in 2002, and The Order of Distinction, Commander Rank (Jamaica's highest national honour) in 2014 for his service to Commerce and Community Development. He is currently a Director of the Caribbean American Chamber of Commerce and Industry (CACCI).

We shall return to Golden Krust in Chapter 5.

Visit the website: www.goldenkrustbakery.com

Questions:

1 What were the motivations to launch Golden Krust?
2 How does being a family business help or hinder it?

CASE
insight
1.8

Steve Jobs and Apple (1) USA

Entrepreneurial character

Steve Jobs died on 5 October 2011, aged 56, of pancreatic cancer. He was the epitome of an entrepreneurial leader who revolutionized three industries – computing, music sales and cinema animations. With Steve Wozniak, he cofounded Apple in 1976. Apple revolutionized the IT industry through its innovative designs: the Macintosh computer with its mouse, the iPod with its click wheel and the iPhone with its 'user interface'. Apple also revolutionized how digital content, in particular music, could be sold rather than pirated. Through Jobs' animation studio, Pixar, films such as *Toy Story* (1995) completely changed our ideas about the use of computer-generated animations. And yet Steve Jobs was not an inventor. He was the bridge between the business idea and the market place – the entrepreneur. Not only did he start up Apple, he was also forced out of it in 1985 after an acrimonious boardroom battle. He returned in 1997 to turn it around from near bankruptcy and, by 2011, had created the second most valuable company in the world, measured by market capitalization, with a cash mountain of some $80 billion.

The story of Steve Jobs is the story of a Silicon Valley hero. Born to a Syrian father and an American mother in San Francisco, he was the adopted child of a blue-collar couple and grew up in Mountain View, a suburb of San Francisco close to what is now known as Silicon Valley. The fact that he was put up for adoption by his birth parents was said to have left a deep scar. While at high school, he met Steve Wozniak who was working on a summer job with Hewlett-Packard in Palo Alto. After high school Jobs reluctantly went to Reed, a liberal arts college in Portland, Oregon, but failed to attend his required classes and dropped out after one term. He grew his hair and did the sort of things that drop-outs at the time did, including visiting a guru in India. His engagement with Zen Buddhism, with a focus on stark, minimalist aesthetics and a belief in intuition, was to become ingrained in his personality. However, he never achieved the inner peace associated with Zen Buddhism, rather he was always driven by the particular challenges facing him at the time.

It was Steve Wozniak who had the talent for electronics and designing circuits with the minimum number of chips, and built the first Apple computer. At the time Wozniak was working for Hewlett-Packard and Jobs for Atari. Apple I was a hobbyist machine assembled by hand in Steve Jobs' parents' home and housed in a wooden box. The pair sold many of their personal possessions to get the start-up finance that was needed. Jobs' role was that of the businessman, the marketer who persuaded the local store to order 50, and then persuaded the local electrical store to give him 30 days' credit on the parts to build the computers. He also eventually persuaded Mike Markkula, a former Intel employee, to invest in the company and become its first chief executive. What followed was the beautifully designed, classic Apple II with its built-in colour graphics, easily accessible expansion slots and ability to connect to a TV set. Its simple design, understandable instruction manual and consumer-friendly advertising guaranteed it success until the launch of the IBM PC. Apple went public in 1980 with a market valuation of $1.8 billion only four years after being launched.

Steve Wozniak retired from Apple one year later following a serious plane accident. Jobs took over the development of the Apple II's successor, the Apple Macintosh. The Mac was intended to be the first mass-market, closed-box computer based on the now ubiquitous mouse and a graphic user interface. These ideas were not new. They were developed by scientists at Xerox Palo Alto Research Centre (PARC) and had been tried out in high-priced computers (Xerox Star and Apple Lisa) without commercial success. The launch of the Mac was the first of what became the signature Steve Jobs product launch. He appeared on stage with Bill Gates promising Mac versions of Word, Excel and PowerPoint. There were 20 full-page advertisements in major US magazines. However, it was the TV commercial that had the biggest impact: shown in the USA during the 1984 Super Bowl, it associated IBM with George Orwell's *1984* Big Brother. Despite the dramatic launch, the Mac failed to sell in the expected volumes, signalling the start of Apple's decline. In 1985 it closed three of its six factories, laying off 1,200 employees. In the same year Steve Jobs was forced to leave Apple, and by 1987 the Mac II was launched as a conventional three-piece computer system.

Jobs resented being thrown out of Apple, particularly by someone he had recruited two years earlier to the job of Chief Executive Officer – John Sculley, formerly president of PepsiCo. He took several Apple employees with him and set up another company (NeXT) to produce a powerful Unix workstation targeted at business and universities. It was very expensive and flopped, so the company switched to selling the operating systems, again without much success.

Steve Jobs bought the company that became Pixar in 1986 from Lucasfilm. Initially, the company produced expensive computer hardware. The core product was the Pixar Image Computer, a system primarily sold to government agencies and the medical market, but this was never particularly popular. The company struggled for years and, in an effort to demonstrate its capabilities, Pixar began producing computer-animated commercials. In 1991 this led to a deal with the Walt Disney Corporation to produce three computer animated films, the first of

MACMILLAN SOUTH AFRICA

which was the ground- breaking *Toy Story*. Until this point Pixar had been in decline, having already sold off its hardware operations. Released in 1995, *Toy Story* was an outstanding box-office success, which was just as well because, as late as 1994, Jobs had considered selling off Pixar. After a series of highly successful, award-winning films such as *A Bug's Life* (1998), *Toy Story 2* (1999), *Monsters Inc.* (2001), *Finding Nemo* (2003) and *The Incredibles* (2004), the Walt Disney Company eventually bought Pixar in 2006 at a valuation of $7.4 billion, making Jobs the largest shareholder in Disney.

Meanwhile the PC market was again transformed in 1995 by the launch of Microsoft Windows 95 which really popularized the mouse and the graphic user interface. Apple was struggling to survive and the new Mac OS software development was not working. It was managed by committees and had lost its innovative flair. Apple knew it needed to buy in a new operating system, and fast, so it turned to Steve Jobs and paid a much-inflated price for NeXT. In reality, this turned out to be a reverse takeover and Jobs took over as 'interim CEO' in 1997.

Jobs killed off weak products and simplified the product lines. He adapted NeXT's NextStep operating system to become the Mac OS X operating system. He also started the process of creating the distinctive eye-catching Apple designs with the teardrop shaped iMac, followed by the portable iBook. Explaining himself to the 1997 meeting of the Apple Worldwide Developers Association, Jobs said:

Focusing is about saying no ... and the result of that focus is going to be some really great products where the total is much greater than the sum of the parts ... One of the things I've always found is that you've got to start with the customer experience and work backwards to the technology and try to figure out where you are going to try to sell it. I've made this mistake probably more than anyone else in this room, and I've got the scar tissue to prove it, and I know that it's the case.

But Apple's fortunes were really transformed when Jobs completely changed direction and launched the iPod in 2001 and the iTunes music store in 2003. This transformed the music industry, which was facing a decline in CD sales because more and more music was being pirated through online sites such as Napster, by allowing music to be easily downloaded, but at a price. Apple started on its growth path, which was reinforced in 2007 by the launch of the iPhone – a clever but expensive combination of cell phone, iPod and internet device. This was followed in 2010 by the iPad – a tablet computer without a physical keyboard. By 2011 Apple was selling more iPads than Macintosh.

Jobs was, of course, in the right place at the right time to capitalize on developments in computing and the change from analogue to digital technologies. But he shaped these developments to appeal to customers. The distinctive feature about Apple products was never the innovation – that normally came from elsewhere – but rather the application of an innovation to make the product easier and simpler to use, whether it be the physical product design or applications such as iTunes. All Apple products also enjoy a distinctive, eye-catching design. And they are never cheap. They were also supported by massive marketing campaigns with Jobs, dressed in black turtle neck, jeans and trainers, launching products himself with carefully choreographed, pseudo-religious stage presentations (known as 'Stevenote') that attracted adoring fans and received massive worldwide press coverage. In many people's eyes Jobs enjoyed the status of a rock star. At the same time the Apple brand had become iconic.

Visit the website: www.apple.com

Questions:

1 What entrepreneurial qualities or characteristics did Jobs exhibit?
2 Why was he so successful? How much of this success was just good luck?

Sofa-bed Factory

Piotr graduated from university in Krakow, Poland, with a degree in Business. He spoke excellent English so, when he was unable to find a job in Poland, he left to work in the UK. He quickly found a job as a salesman in the store of a large furniture retailer. He was a hard worker and good at his job. After only a year he became store manager and then quickly went to work in the store's head office as a management trainee. In this role, he rotated around jobs in the company's operating areas of purchasing, distribution, marketing and finance, learning how the company worked as well as making friends and developing a network of contacts as he progressed. His hard-working mentality and strong interpersonal skills made him popular with other staff. After two years he was appointed Regional Sales Manager. That was some five years ago.

Unfortunately, Piotr was not happy. He returned to Poland regularly to meet family and friends and longed to go back. It was not that he disliked the UK, just that Poland was where his roots were. He liked the lifestyle there and things were so much cheaper. His family was close-knit and his parents were keen to see him settle down in Poland. As a Regional Sales Manager Piotr had a good salary but he still could not afford to buy his own home in the UK. He also liked his job, but he yearned for something more and felt that he was not fully using the business skills that he had learned at university.

It was on one of his visits to Poland that he ended up in a bar talking to an old school friend called Olek about his ambitions. Olek had not gone to university and had stayed in Poland, initially working as an apprentice in a small jobbing engineering firm. He was a practical man and had worked his way up within the firm, gaining a number of qualifications on the way. However, he too was dissatisfied. The company was a family firm and it had been made clear to him that there was no long-term future for him there because members of the owner's family were expected to take managerial roles. He was frustrated and felt that his skills were not valued. He also disliked being told what to do when often he considered that he knew more about the work than the owner or his sons. He wanted to leave and had started looking around for another job. Both Olek and Piotr felt that they were at a junction in their lives. Neither were happy in their jobs and both wanted a change. They both longed for a greater challenge, but at the same time both valued security.

It was Olek who said that he was thinking about starting his own business – manufacturing something, but he did not know what. He knew a lot about manufacturing but far less about business in general. He asked Piotr if he knew of any manufacturing opportunities – perhaps for products to be sold in the UK. Piotr started talking about the furniture his company sold. Because he had been a management trainee, he knew a lot about the business: the product range, where it was manufactured and even the prices the company paid for furniture. Gradually Piotr and Olek started wondering if there might be a business opportunity here for both of them. So they decided to have another drink and think it through a little.

This was the first time Piotr had thought about starting a business, so the first thing he did was to get some paper and jot down the pros and cons of working for himself:

Pros:	Cons:
1 A challenge;	1 No clear business idea;
2 Being your own boss (not taking orders);	2 Little capital;
3 Potentially earning more money;	3 Risk of business not working (but little to lose);
4 Based in Poland (but would it be?).	4 Will they generate a regular income?

Piotr and Olek quickly decided a start-up might be an attractive option – if they could find a good business idea. Both were dissatisfied with their current jobs and wanted to find something more challenging that could generate more income for them. They were young and were willing to spend a lot of time and effort on something that interested and motivated them – particularly if it made money. They decided to meet the following evening to talk some more about the possibilities.

The following evening they started talking about creating their own business straight away. Before they thought about the right sort of business to set up they decided to jot down their personal strengths – the things they could bring to the business:

1 Piotr had a degree in business. He had experience in sales and had been a good salesman. His management training in the UK had given him a good background and a network of contacts in the UK furniture market. His family was quite well off and he had a wide network of contacts through family and friends.

2 Olek was immensely practical. He loved making things and had amassed a number of practical qualifications

while working for a jobbing engineer in Poland. His business experience might be limited but he had a range of manufacturing contacts around Poland that might be useful if they were looking for suppliers.

After some discussion they each thought that they needed to earn about €30,000 per year to make it worthwhile (they would like more in the longer run). However, they realized that it might be some time before money came into any business they set up, so they might have to borrow money to start with. But were they the right sort of people to become entrepreneurs? They decided to

take the online General Enterprise Tendency test and were surprised to find that they both scored highly in each of the five character traits (although this was borderline for Piotr for risk aversion). Encouraged by this, they decided to get together again and see if they could come up with a business idea.

Question:

Why do you think it might be worthwhile for Piotr and Olek to consider entrepreneurship?

Summary and action points

1.1   Understand your personal drivers: Decide whether being an entrepreneur suits you. Define your personal drivers and constraints. These will influence what you want your business to become. It is important that your business fits in with what you want from your life and lifestyle. You need to have a balance between work and personal life that suits you.

1.2   Clarify your business purpose: Be clear about why you want to start up a business and what you want from it. Do you want to start up a salary-substitute, lifestyle or entrepreneurial business that will grow rapidly and you will be able to sell on? Or do you want a start-up that delivers social objectives? Do you want to work with your family or keep family life separate? Are you willing to commit time and resources to a growing business? If you want to sell on the business, within what time scale will this happen? These sorts of questions underpin the purpose of the business.

1.3   List your personal assets and liabilities: Identify the resources you bring to your start-up – financial, human and social capital. The more capital you bring, the more likely you are to succeed. You should also calculate the minimum amount of income you (and your family) need to live on, at least in the short term, and the maximum loss you are willing to accept if the start-up fails.

1.4   Understand your character traits: You need to find out and decide whether entrepreneurship really is something that you will enjoy, or at least be comfortable with. Most people who start up their own business have a range of entrepreneurial character traits: high need for independence; high need for achievement; high locus of control; high creativity and opportunity perception; willingness to take measured risks. Do you have these traits? Some traits are more difficult to manage around (e.g. low risk taking) than others (e.g. low creativity). Consider how you will deal with traits for which you have a low score (e.g. by finding a partner).

Workbook exercises

 The New Venture Creation Workbook contains a digital version of these exercises that can be modified as your business model develops and builds into a draft business plan. It can be downloaded from www.macmillanihe.com/burns-nvc-2e.

1.1: Understand your personal drivers

1 List the things that you enjoy doing, and the things that you do not enjoy doing (e.g. hobbies and pastimes, figure-work, selling, meeting people, etc.).

2 List the things that motivate and drive you and those that do not (e.g. family, money, social causes, green issues etc.).

3 List the things that you would want to avoid in a business at all costs (e.g. travel, too little free time, etc.).

4 List the major risks of self-employment for you.

5 Bearing in mind the answers to questions 1 to 4, list the implications for your venture and for yourself and your lifestyle. Decide what sort of business you want to start up.

1.2: Clarify your business purpose

1 Now you are clear about the purpose of the business, you need to consider what targets or objectives you might want to set yourself to achieve this. Your objectives should be quantifiable (and therefore measurable), bounded in time and realistic. We shall return to this when your business idea has been evaluated.

Write down what you want this business start-up to achieve for you. *[e.g. To provide an immediate and adequate income for my wife and me, while living above the shop.]*

2 Write down your business objectives for three years' time in ideal circumstances.

[e.g. Sales of £1 million by the third year, and profits before tax and my salary over those three years of £200,000.]

1.3: List your personal assets and liabilities

1 List your personal strengths and weaknesses.

2 Write down the financial capital you could invest in the business. Are you willing to lose all this if the start-up fails?

3 List the elements of human capital you will be investing in the business.

4 List the elements of social capital you will be investing in the business. Make a list of your network of contacts and how they might be able to help.

5 List the regular outgoings and the minimum expenditure that you (and your family) need to survive, at least in the short term. Add this up and add 10%. This is the minimum amount that you will need to take from the business.

6 Write down the maximum loss you are willing to accept if the start-up fails. Distinguish between the amount you are actually willing to invest [exercise 1.3 (2)] and how much might be lost in other ways, for example by providing personal guarantees.

1.4: Understand your character traits

Take the General Enterprise Tendency (GET) test: www.get2test.net

Review the results and reflect on whether you agree with the results by finding examples from your life that support or disprove them. Decide on the implications of this result and list the things that you want to do as a result of this analysis.

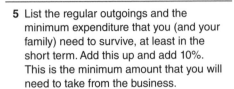

 Visit www.macmillanihe.com/burns-nvc-2e for chapter quizzes and other resources.

2

Finding your business idea

Contents

- Creating that 'eureka moment'
- New venture typologies
- Creating opportunity
- Spotting opportunity
- Nurturing creativity and innovation
- Active discovery
- Techniques for exploring change
- Techniques for exploring product inadequacies
- Summary and action points
- Workbook exercises

Learning outcomes

When you have read this chapter and undertaken the related exercises you will be able to:

- Critically assess the dimensions of your creative potential
- Develop your creativity and discovery skills
- Scan the environment for business opportunities
- Come up with a business idea by either creating or spotting an opportunity

Academic insights 📑

Case insights 💼

Sofa-bed Factory

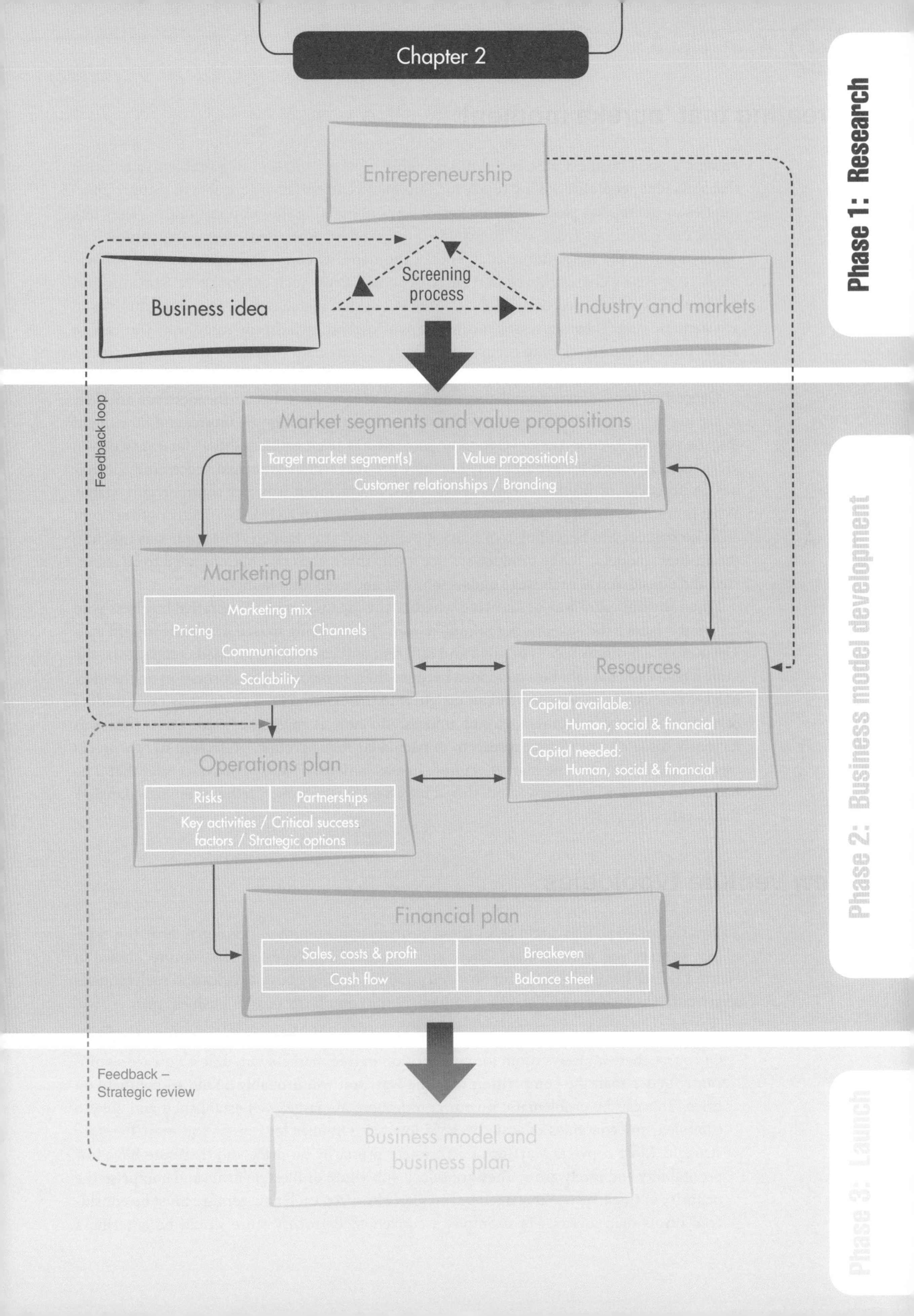

Chapter 2
Entrepreneurship
Business idea
Screening process
Industry and markets
Feedback loop
Market segments and value propositions
Target market segment(s)
Value proposition(s)
Customer relationships / Branding
Marketing plan
Marketing mix
Pricing
Channels
Communications
Scalability
Resources
Capital available:
Human, social & financial
Capital needed:
Human, social & financial
Operations plan
Risks
Partnerships
Key activities / Critical success factors / Strategic options
Financial plan
Sales, costs & profit
Breakeven
Cash flow
Balance sheet
Feedback –
Strategic review
Business model and business plan
Phase 1: Research
Phase 2: Business model development
Phase 3: Launch

Creating that 'eureka moment'

Finding a good business idea is about being able to find a solution to a problem, a solution that sufficient people are willing to pay for. Successful entrepreneurs are able to match opportunities in the market place with innovative ways of meeting those opportunities. They link opportunity with creativity and innovation. But which comes first: seeing the commercial opportunity or the innovation? That 'eureka moment', when a good business idea is born, rarely happens by chance. Successful entrepreneurial firms such as Google or Samsung also go about seeking out ways of developing innovations that match commercial opportunities in a systematic way. Their success is not just down to good luck. In the same way, you can go about finding and developing a business idea in a systematic way that gives you a greater chance of business success.

Generating good ideas is a numbers game: the more ideas you generate, the more you are likely to see the light of day. What are the problems we face, now and in the future, and how might they be solved? Even at the development stage, it has been estimated that for every eleven ideas starting out on the process only one new product will be launched successfully. It may not be practical, or insufficient market demand might mean it is not commercially viable. What is more, perfecting the idea can take time. The idea is unlikely to be exactly right straight away, so you need to be willing to modify it before and after launch. This applies as much to the business model as to the product/service itself. This means that options need to be generated and considered at each stage of development and even after launch.

Often the only sure way of knowing whether the idea will make a lucrative business is to try it out – launch the business but minimize your risks in doing so (see Academic insight 4.4). The more the business idea is original and different and without established competitors, the more a trial launch might be a good idea because there is incomplete information on the idea. Market research is unlikely to yield an insight into the demand for a completely new product or service because customers do not understand how it might be used. Steve Jobs was famously disdainful of market research, in particular focus groups, preferring to rely on his own insight about what the market wanted. Just as famously, Henry Ford once said that if he had asked people what they wanted, they'd have said 'faster horses', rather than 'new-fangled' things called cars.

New venture typologies

So how do you go about searching for these business opportunities? This depends on the 'type' of new venture you want to start. There are six generalized types of new venture, shown in Figure 2.1. Each has implications for how you go about finding a business idea and each requires a very different business model, which influences the complexity of your business plan.

1 **Copy-cat** – You can introduce the same product or service into an existing market. Of course there is always room for competition in free markets but, unless you are significantly better than the competition in some way, you will probably be left to compete on price. This can be problematic if your competitors are large, well established and able to capitalize on economies of scale because low price implies low costs. You may therefore struggle. Most copy-cat start-ups do compete primarily on price and therefore have low profitability and rarely grow. They are salary-substitute or lifestyle firms and comprise the majority of small, owner-managed businesses. However, each new venture must be considered on its own merits. For example, a convenience/grocery store would be entering a

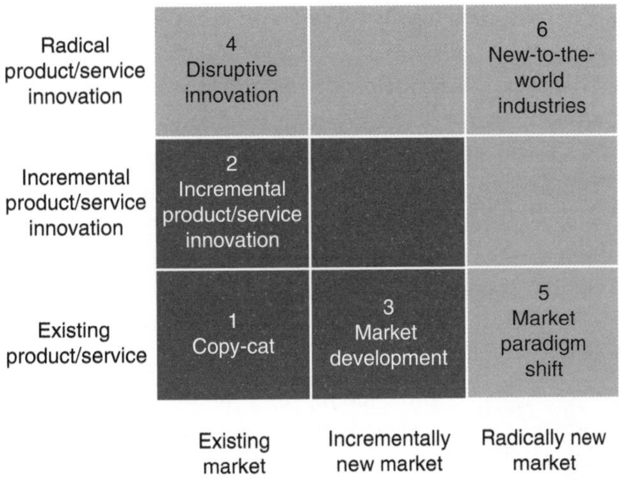

	Existing market	Incrementally new market	Radically new market
Radical product/service innovation	4 Disruptive innovation		6 New-to-the-world industries
Incremental product/service innovation	2 Incremental product/service innovation		
Existing product/service	1 Copy-cat	3 Market development	5 Market paradigm shift

Figure 2.1 New venture typologies

highly competitive environment where large supermarkets have enormous economies of scale and will be able to compete more effectively on price. However, if this is the only store on a new estate, with the nearest supermarket 10 miles away, then there is a good chance of making a healthy profit … that is until another copy-cat store starts up because there are no barriers to entry in this market.

2 **Incremental product/service innovation** – If you want your new venture to avoid competing primarily on price, the thing to do is to try to **spot opportunities** or gaps in the market, perhaps by altering the elements of the product/service in some significant way that adds value to customers. This avoids competing head-on with established businesses and should allow you to charge a higher price, at least until competitors appear. If you are able to safeguard your intellectual property on this innovation (Chapter 9) then you might sustain this strategy for longer. If you are able to create a market niche for your product/service, this could give you a sustainable **competitive advantage** and be very profitable – creating an entrepreneurial firm. Alternatively, it might allow you to establish a lifestyle business that lets you do the things you enjoy while generating an adequate income. The danger here is that you are, by definition, competing against established suppliers with recognized brands and distribution channels. Competition will be fierce and they may be able to copy your incremental innovation.

> Reinventing the wheel is risky and usually money and time-consuming – both of which would-be entrepreneurs normally lack. However, improving something that is already on the market means there is a demand for the product and you can just do it better with some lateral, creative thinking. That's not to say entrepreneurs should be discouraged from trying something revolutionary. But if you look through history, almost every super successful entrepreneur took an existing idea or business and made it better.
>
> Adam Schwab, founder Lux Group
> Business Review Australia.issuu.com July 2014

3 **Market development** – Another option is to find new customers not currently served by existing suppliers, for example in different geographical markets (both national and international) – another case of **spotting opportunity**. **Market development** offers considerable opportunities for new ventures because new products or services that originate in more developed markets find their way into developing markets at a later date. Timing and local knowledge can be crucial when new products or services are introduced into any market. However, the danger here is always that the established supplier in the original market eventually moves into this new market and has sufficient resources and market presence to out-compete

you. The challenge is therefore to move with sufficient speed that you dominate this new market before established suppliers try to enter it.

4 **Disruptive innovation or invention** – Introducing radically new products/services into existing markets will certainly confound the competition particularly if your innovation can be safeguarded, but it is not something that all of us are able to do. **Disruptive innovation** is an example of **creating opportunity** and is often linked to technological developments. While most companies are continually making improvements and incremental innovations to their products and services, invention can be risky and takes both time and money. Unlike James Dyson and his now ubiquitous cyclone vacuum cleaner, many inventors fail to make their invention commercially viable. For example, Thomas Edison, probably the most successful inventor of all time, was so incompetent at introducing his inventions to the market place that his backers had to remove him from every new business he founded. However, entrepreneurs are often able to make the connection between invention and market opportunity – the important link between creating and spotting opportunity. As we saw in Case insight 1.8, Steve Jobs never invented anything but he revolutionized three industries – personal computers, music and film animations – because he was able to find commercial applications for innovations.

> Innovation has more to do with the pragmatic search for opportunity than with romantic ideas about serendipity, or lonely pioneers pursuing their vision against all the odds.
>
> Nicholas Valéry 'Innovation in Industry', The Economist, 5 (28) 1999

5 **Market paradigm shift** – This is when you create radically new markets by challenging the paradigms or conventions upon which an industry bases its whole **marketing strategy** – creating opportunity. So, for example, the development of the low-cost airline industry involved no inventions or innovations, only different ways of doing things that involved minimizing the costs, and therefore the price, of air travel. In making this **market paradigm shift**, companies such as Southwest Airlines in the USA and easyJet and Ryanair in Europe created whole new markets for air travel that never existed before. Tony Fernandes copied this **business model** very successfully in different markets with AirAsia (market development).

6 **New-to-the-world industries** – And just sometimes, radical new inventions **create opportunities** by themselves creating radically new markets – with entrepreneurs capitalizing on the opportunities this brings. Tim Berners-Lee invented the World Wide Web in 1990, which in turn created new internet-based markets for information and changed the way we shop for many products and services. Like many inventors before him, the web did not make a fortune for Tim Berners-Lee. Others, like the founders of numerous internet or 'dot.com' firms, such as Larry Page and Sergey Brin of Google or Jeff Bezos of Amazon, created businesses and made their fortune out of his invention. Again, it was the entrepreneur who saw the commercial application for the invention. New-to-the-world industries have been created for centuries; water power, textiles and iron in the eighteenth century, steam, steel and rail in the nineteenth century, and electricity, chemicals and the internal combustion engine in the early twentieth century. These innovations are disruptive and difficult to predict, but cause enormous economic booms that eventually peter out as the technologies mature and the market opportunities are fully exploited.

The further you move away from being a copy-cat start-up (in either a vertical or horizontal direction in Figure 2.1) the higher the investment you are likely to need, but also the higher the profit you are likely to make. While copy-cat start-ups can be very risky because of the strong competition, the greater the product/service or market innovation the greater the risks you are likely to face. The 'dot.com' boom was rapidly followed by a 'dot.com' bust at the end of the twentieth century when many of the innovations were found not to have a viable market. Ideas that involve disruptive innovation or market paradigm shift are difficult to find and to launch as a business.

Good business ideas are usually based around finding a solution to a problem that somebody is willing to pay for. If you review the six new venture typologies you will see you have two options in finding this idea:

- If you are looking for **radical product/service innovation** or to create radically new markets, you must **create opportunity**, as it is unlikely that there is existing evidence of market need.
- If you are looking for **incremental product/service innovation** or to enter incrementally different markets, then you probably can **spot opportunity** that meets an unfilled current or future market need. Spotting opportunity is easier than creating opportunity and can be just as profitable.

The reality is that the most successful businesses are really just improvements rather than ground-breaking inventions. Apple's success is based upon good design and improving product ease of use rather than invention. Apple 1 was a big improvement on other computers with its graphic user interface and 'mouse', the iPod was a big improvement on MP3 players which had been available for years and the iPhone improved on mobile phones from Nokia

CASE insight 2.1

Bizarre business ideas USA

Bizarre business ideas

Some business ideas do come from serendipity and their success would confound most of us. Here is a selection of some of its weirdest real business start-ups from the USA. It all goes to show that you can make money out of most things.

- **HappyBalls.com** of Cumming, Georgia, makes foam balls with colourful faces to be placed on top of car aerials. Do not mock – this is a million-dollar company.
- **Afterlife Telegrams** of New Athens, Illinois, offers to contact the dead. For a fee, they arrange for terminally ill patients to memorize a message that can be relayed to loved ones who have died when they themselves pass on.
- **eNthem** of San Francisco writes full length corporate theme songs.
- **Lucky Break Wishbone** of Seattle sells plastic wishbones so that all the family can have one despite the fact there is only really one in a chicken or turkey.

MACMILLAN AUSTRALIA

- **SomethingStore** of Huntington, New York, will, for a payment of $10, send you something, anything – but no telling what.
- **WeightNags** of Austin sends mildly abusive weekly messages to dieters to encourage them to keep dieting.
- **Yelo** of New York City offers New Yorkers 20- or 40-minute naps in 'sleep pods'.
- **Throx** of San Francisco sells socks in packs of three – think about it.
- **Gaming-Lessons** of Jupiter, Florida offers video game lessons and coaching.
- **barefootlist.com** of Salt Lake City allows members to make up a list of things they want to do before they die, compare it to others' and track their progress.
- **Cuddle Party** of New York City offers 'structured, safe workshops on boundaries, communication, intimacy and affection … A laboratory where you can experiment with what makes you feel safe and feel good.'
- **Neuticles** of Oak Grove, Missouri, offers testicular implants for dogs that have been neutered.

and Blackberry. Google entered a crowded search engine market then dominated by AltaVista and simply created a better product by using an improved search algorithm. It became commercially successful after it introduced its AdWords bidding system – invented by Idealab. Facebook entered the market well after social networking sites such as Friendster and MySpace.

Creating opportunity

Creating a business opportunity that has not existed before involves radical product or market innovation and can lead to the development of new-to-the-world industries. It is more difficult and riskier than spotting an opportunity because there is no guarantee that the market need will finally materialize. It requires vision and self-belief aplenty, and is likely to take time and resources. It requires a high degree of creativity and innovation. However, the returns for success are likely to be high.

Disruptive innovation/invention – This is a step change in products, processes or the framing of markets. Generated by major inventions, they can have large-scale disruptive effects on markets, industries and even economies. For example, although Henry Ford did not invent the car, he did revolutionize the way cars were produced and sold, moving from craft-based to production-line methods and from wealthy customers to supplying an affordable car for everyman assembled on a production line. He created a new commercial market (Case insight 2.12). But where did Ford get his vision of the future from? How was he able to break away from the established thinking of how a car should be made and who it should be sold to? When disruptive innovation creates radically new markets, fortunes can be made (and lost) quickly. This form of innovation can be highly profitable but very risky. It requires a leap in creative imagination, from mere possibility to commercial reality. That can be difficult for many people. And to stand any chance of seeing the light of day most inventors need to partner with an entrepreneur.

If you are developing a completely new product or service, your business plan will need to explain what stage the development is at, and what further development is needed to take it to market. Basic ideas are unlikely to find funding. Even when there is a prototype, finding finance might prove difficult. The earlier the development stage, the more difficult this will prove. There is no guarantee the product will work and there is no guarantee that there will be customers for it. Even if it works, will you be able to stop competitors copying it? We outline the ways you can safeguard your intellectual property in Chapter 9.

Market paradigm shift – This happens when entrepreneurs challenge the conventional ways of marketing a product/service. In most sectors there are factors that managers believe are critical to the success of their business. These paradigms become part of the **dominant logic** of an industry. But circumstances and the environment can change and the managers running the industry may not adapt their way of thinking. For example, Microsoft arguably missed the internet revolution. It could have dominated the search engine market rather than Google, but new developments that threatened to cannibalize their main source of revenue – the Window Operating System and the Microsoft Office suite – were not allowed to surface. Instead all resources were targeted at defending Microsoft's existing dominance of the software market.

To see an opportunity for market paradigm shift you need to be constantly questioning the status quo. You need to ask the question '*why* are things done this way?' followed by the question '*why not* do them a different way?' This willingness to continually question the status quo is one of the five fundamental 'discovery skills' exhibited by successful entrepreneurs that we shall discuss later in this chapter. Sometimes doing things differently can add value for the customer without involving extra costs – indeed sometimes doing things differently can

CASE insight 2.2

Summly

UK
AUSTRALIA

Creating opportunity

Born in London to well-off parents but brought up in Australia for his first seven years, Nick D'Aloisio became adept at using the computer at an early age. It was his hobby. He used it to make animations and films, and even apps. Aged 15, he created an algorithm that formed the basis for an app called Trimit that summarized long articles down to tweet-lengths:

I was using Twitter a lot on my phone, and was realizing there was a massive gap between the link on the tweet and the full story. If you could come up with a summary layer to show in Twitter, that would be awesome.

Trimit enjoyed mixed commercial success but attracted good reviews, wide publicity and thousands of downloads. It was this that attracted the attention of Horizon Ventures, a venture company led by Li Ka-shing, a Hong Kong billionaire and Asia's richest man. Horizon Ventures decided to invest $300,000 in the venture. This allowed D'Aloisio to recruit a small team in London to develop a completely redesigned version of the app, which was launched as Summly beta in December 2011.

Summly summarizes news articles for mobile phone users. If they are sufficiently interested, they can then read the full article on the original website. The idea is that the app generates traffic for these websites from users of mobile phones and creates a market for this content with a wider, younger demographic.

There is a generation of skimmers. It's not that they don't want to read in-depth content, but they want to evaluate what the content is before they commit time. Especially on a mobile phone – you don't have the phone, or cellular data, or screen size to be reading full-length content.

The Guardian 29 March 2013

Less than a year later D'Aloisio secured funding of £1 million to further develop the app. Working with partners such as Stanford Research Institute, D'Aloisio also managed to obtain the help and support of a network of technology experts and celebrities such as Ashton Kutcher, Wendi Deng, Mark Pincus, Brian Chesky, Stephen Fry and Yoko Ono. The full Summly app was launched in November 2012. It reached number nine in the free iPhone app chart in the same month and within one year attracted more than one million downloads and more than 250 publishers, including News Corp.

In 2013, still aged only 17, D'Aloisio sold Summly to Yahoo, reportedly for $30 million (£19 million). Yahoo wanted to integrate the app into its own mobile services and Nick and his team joined Yahoo to help with this development. The first product using Summly, Yahoo News Digest, was launched by Yahoo in January 2014. D'Aloisio left Yahoo the following year.

Question:

What are the barriers to creating opportunity?

Strategies that Revolutionized an Industry (1999, New York: Harper Business)

> We learned the importance of ignoring conventional wisdom ... It's fun to do things that people don't think are possible or likely. It's also exciting to achieve the unexpected.
>
> Michael Dell *Direct from Dell:*

reduce costs – while still giving you the opportunity to charge a high price. You can approach the task of challenging market paradigms by systematically looking at sectoral, customer and performance conventions and continually asking the questions 'why?' – why are they like this and what value do they offer to the customer? – and 'why not?' – why can they not be something different that adds greater value to the customer? (see Academic insight 2.1).

Creating opportunity through market paradigm shift is probably easier than disruptive invention – and can be just as profitable. Both approaches need you to be able to think creatively 'outside the box'. You need to be able to generate new ideas and knowledge, a vision of the future that links market opportunities to your key capabilities. You need to be able to challenge conventions and be open to new ideas. You need to be able to deal with rapidly changing and disparate information in a wide range of new technologies and in diverse, fragmented and often geographically widespread markets. You need to be able to chart a way through often uncertain political and unstable regulatory environments. And in these circumstances knowledge and information are powerful sources of opportunity and innovation. But remember, creating opportunity can be risky because there is no guarantee that the market will agree with your vision of the future.

ACADEMIC insight 2.1

How to challenge market conventions

Based on a sample of 108 companies, Kim and Mauborgne (2005) estimated that, whereas only 14% of innovations created new markets, these innovations delivered 38% of new revenues and 61% of increased profits. So how might you go about creating completely new markets? Ian Chaston (2000) argued that you have to systematically challenge established market conventions and develop new solutions. Kim and Mauborgne call this 'blue ocean strategy' – market needs that are currently unrecognized and unmet. Companies creating blue ocean strategies never benchmark against competitors, instead they make this irrelevant by 'creating a leap in value for both the buyers and the company itself'. They create uncontested market space, creating new demand and making competition irrelevant. Kim and Mauborgne contrasted this to 'red ocean strategy' which involves gaining competitive advantage in existing, often mature markets. They acknowledge that 'red oceans' cannot be ignored, but criticize conventional marketing strategy as being too focused on building advantage over competition in this way.

None of this was new. Based upon a study of firms that had challenged established big companies in a range of industries, Hamel and Prahalad (1994) claimed that these firms had succeeded in creating entirely new forms of competitive advantage by asking three key questions:

- What new types of customer benefits should you seek to provide in 5, 10 or 15 years?
- What new competencies will you need to build or acquire in order to offer these benefits?
- How will you need to reconfigure our customer interface over the next few years?

Chasing 'blue oceans' involves questioning the dominant logic in an industry – challenging market paradigms.

Chaston's approach to this is simple: understand how conventional competitors operate and then challenge their approach by asking whether a different one would add customer value or create new customers – our 'why?' and 'why not?' questions. There are many conventions that can be challenged. Chaston suggests three categories.

1 **Sectoral conventions:** These are the strategic rules that guide the marketing operations of the majority of firms in a sector, such as efficiency of plants, economies of scale, methods of distribution and so on. Kim and Mauborgne talk about re-orientating analysis from *competitors* to *alternatives*. So, for example, in the UK insurance used to be sold through high street insurance brokers until Direct Line challenged the conventional wisdom and began to sell direct over the telephone, then on the internet. Now this is the norm.

2 **Performance conventions:** These are set by other firms in the sector and include profit, cost of production, quality and so on. Kim and Mauborgne argue that both value enhancement and cost reduction can be achieved by redefining industry problems and looking outside industry boundaries, rather than simply trying to offer better solutions to existing problems as defined by the industry. In the 1960s, Japanese firms ignored Western performance conventions en masse and managed to enter and succeed in these markets.

3 **Customer conventions**: These conventions make certain assumptions about what customers want from their purchases, for example, price, size, design and so on. Kim and Mauborgne talk about re-orientating analysis from *customers* to *noncustomers*. The Body Shop redefined the cosmetic industry's 'feel-good factor' to include environmental issues. Companies like Southwest Airlines, Ryanair and easyJet pioneered low-price air travel and redefined the airline industry.

Chaston, I. (2000) *Entrepreneurial Marketing: Competing by Challenging Convention*, Basingstoke: Palgrave.

Hamel, G. and Prahalad, C.K. (1994) *Competing For the Future: Breakthrough Strategies for Seizing Control of your Industry and*

Creating the Markets of Tomorrow, Boston, MA: Harvard Business School Press.

Kim, W.C. and Mauborgne, R. (2005) 'Blue Ocean Strategy: From Theory to Practice', *California Management Review*, Spring, 47(3).

CASE insight 2.3

Swatch — SWITZERLAND

Creating opportunity – market paradigm shift through design

Swatch created a whole new market for cheap watches by daring to be different. In the 1980s cheaper watches like Citizen and Seiko competed by using quartz technology to improve accuracy and digital displays to make reading the time easier. The industry competed primarily on price and functional performance. People usually owned just one watch. Swatch set out to change the watch market and make affordable fashion accessories that were also accurate timepieces. To do this they relied upon innovative design.

SMH, the Swiss parent, set up a design studio in Italy whose mission was to combine powerful technology with artwork, brilliant colours and flamboyant designs. For a start, Swatch had to be affordable so costs had to be kept low. Consequently it was designed with fewer components than most watches. Screws were replaced by plastic mouldings. It was made in large volumes in a highly automated factory, enabling labour costs to be driven down to less than 10% of the selling price. Swatch changed the reason for buying a watch from the need to tell the time to the desire to be fashionable. They differentiated themselves not on the function of the timepiece but on its design and also its emotional appeal – a lifestyle image that made a statement about the wearer. In doing this they encouraged repeat purchases because each watch was a different fashion accessory making a different statement about the wearer.

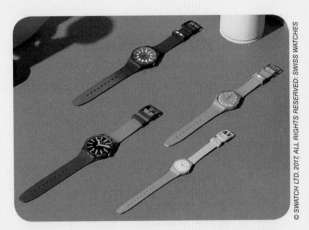

Because it was offered at an affordable price, people were encouraged to buy more than one watch. The company used innovative guerrilla marketing techniques (see Chapter 7) to bring the watch to the market under several different designs. Swatch has built up a core of loyal customers who repeat purchase their watches. New Swatch designs come out every year.

Visit the website: www.swatch.com

Question:

How difficult is it to change the way you think about a product or market?

Spotting opportunity

> As Darwin well understood, it is the species most responsive to change that is the best equipped for survival.
>
> Luck Johnson Chairman Risk Capital Partners Sunday Times 21 May 2017

Creating opportunity is hard to do. Spotting opportunity in a systematic way is easier and there are tools and techniques that can help you. This may involve incremental product/service innovation and market expansion. The main source of opportunity is change – changes in technology, law and regulation, market and industry structures, demographics, culture, moods and fashions all create market opportunities that entrepreneurs can exploit (see Academic insight 2.2). As already observed, the internet is an enormous source of business opportunity.

Reviewing the environment for change is therefore a prime source of business ideas, and a technique covered later in this chapter – PESTEL analysis – can help you with this.

Symptoms of change

The management guru, Peter Drucker (1985), listed seven 'basic symptoms' of change that can be used to search systematically for entrepreneurial opportunities.

1 **The unexpected** – be it the unexpected success or failure or the unexpected event. Nobody can predict the future but an ability to react quickly to changes is a real commercial advantage, particularly in a rapidly changing environment. Information and knowledge are invaluable.

2 **The incongruity** – between what actually happens and what was supposed to happen. Plans go wrong and unexpected outcomes produce opportunities for firms that are able to spot them.

3 **The inadequacy in underlying processes** – that are taken for granted but can be improved or changed. This is essentially improving process engineering – especially important if the product is competing primarily on price.

4 **Changes in industry or market structure** – that take everyone by surprise. Again, unexpected change, perhaps arising from technology, legislation or other outside events, creates an opportunity to strategize about how the firm might cope and, as usual, first-mover advantage is usually worth striving for.

5 **Demographic changes** – population changes caused by changes in birth rates, wars, medical improvements and so on.

6 **Changes in perception, mood and meaning** – that can be brought about by the ups and downs of the economy, culture, fashion etc. In-depth interviews or focus groups can also often give an insight into these changes.

7 **New knowledge** – both scientific and non-scientific. This amounts to the disruptive innovation and challenges to market paradigms that we discussed previously.

Drucker, P. (1985) *Innovation and Entrepreneurship*, London: Heinemann.

Of course, opportunity can also exist where markets are failing to meet customer needs – through laziness, ignorance or just because it takes time for the market information to be acted on (see Case insight 2.4). What is more, deficiencies in products or services can go undealt with for months or years, to the point where they are just taken for granted. Entrepreneurs are often closer to customers and listen to what they say, and they recognize and act on market opportunity more quickly than established firms. Again, there are systematic techniques that can help you spot these opportunities.

One way you can discover inadequacies in underlying processes or question market paradigms is by analysing the **value chain** of an industry. Behind this is the idea that real advantages in cost or product/service differentiation can be found in the chain of activities that a firm performs to deliver value to its customers. The value chain comprises five primary activities (see Porter, 1985):[1]

1 Inbound logistics (receiving, storing and disseminating inputs)
2 Operations (transforming inputs into a final product)
3 Outbound logistics (collecting, storing and distributing products to customers)
4 Marketing and sales
5 After-sales service

---

1. Porter, M.E. (1985) *Competitive Advantage: Creating and Sustaining Superior Performance*, New York: The Free Press.

and four secondary or supporting activities:

1 Procurement (purchasing consumable and capital items)
2 Human resource management
3 Technology development (R&D etc.)
4 Firm infrastructure (general management, accounting etc.)

CASE insight 2.4

DUPLAYS   UAE

Spotting opportunity – unmet demand

In many countries in the Middle East local people prize jobs in the public sector rather than in private business. It is not surprising therefore that many start-ups originate from the large expatriate populations. And where better to find a business idea than from the unmet needs of your own people? While working as expatriates in Dubai in the United Arab Emirates, Canadian-Indian-born Davinder Rao and Indian-born Ravi Bhusari wanted to make friends and play sport but found that most social activities revolved around going to bars or visiting shopping malls. They had already organized some 20 expatriate friends to play Frisbee on a regular basis and reasoned that if they wanted to do this, other expats might be interested as well. What is more, there might be a business opportunity. So, in 2007 they started DUPLAYS. From this small beginning, the company has grown and now organizes sports such as football (soccer), beach volleyball, basketball, touch rugby, netball, cricket, Frisbee and golf, often with related social events. They offer nightly league matches and weekend tournaments, organizing facilities, equipment, staffing and scheduling.

Most of the institutionalised activity seemed to revolve around shopping malls or going for drinks or brunches. We figured plenty of people like to play sport and so the secret was to meet that need and build a website and a business that helped people discover what was out there.

The notorious red tape in many countries of the Middle East can make it hard to start a new business. DUPLAYS' founders discovered that the bureaucracy can be especially difficult for expats to negotiate without local connections. However, while many countries require expats starting a business to have a local partner, Dubai has a free-zone system that gets round this requirement, meaning founders can own 100% of the business.

Nevertheless, DUPLAYS' founders still found that raising finance was difficult.

Attracting money can be harder as an expat. You can understand it from the investor's perspective. If an expat has a business and it goes belly-up, then they can walk away, go back home or to another country. They have less reputational risk, so for investors, that can be scary.
BBC News Business 14 April 2013

Since 2007 DUPLAYS has grown to over 100,000 members playing more than 29 recreational sports. It now has branches in cities in the UAE (Dubai, Abu Dhabi and Al Ain), Saudi Arabia (Riyadh and Jeddah), Qatar (Doha) and India (Delhi and Guraon) and claims to rank as one of the largest adult sport and social clubs in the world. In fact, much of its income now comes from organizing corporate events for international organizations such as Castrol, Gillette, Samsung and Volkswagen, as well as local companies. Being based in an international business hub has proved crucial to DUPLAYS' success in this market, while Dubai's tax-free status has not hurt either. The company has also expanded into what it calls 'corporate wellness', organizing events, leagues and complete wellness programmes for organizations to get employees healthy and active, using sport and activity to help with team building. Clients include Al Hilal Bank, Dubai Airport, Emirates Aluminium and First Gulf Bank.

We're proud that although we're expats, we're building a company that is good enough to export. That's a great feeling.
BBC News 14 April 2013

Visit the website: duplays.com

Question:
What are the barriers to spotting this sort of opportunity?

Each generic category can be broken down into discrete activities unique to a particular firm or industry. By looking at the costs associated with each activity and trying to compare them to the value obtained by customers from that activity, you can seek to identify any mismatches (see Case insight 2.6). It might be possible to reduce costs through new technologies, different sourcing or work efficiencies. The internet has given businesses the opportunity to look at disintermediation – reducing the use of intermediaries – in order to reduce costs. But equally, if customers value certain stages of the chain more highly than indicated by the resources allocated to them, it may be profitable to offer an improved product/service by increasing the resources allocated to these stages. In reality, it is difficult to do this with any precision, but often supply chains can remain unaltered simply because people fail to ask the

CASE insight 2.5

Bloom & Wild UK

Aron Gelbard

Spotting opportunity – reimagining the value chain

Started in 2013, Ben Stanway and Aron Gelbard took the inspiration for their online florist business, Bloom & Wild, from the inefficiencies they found when they researched the supply chain for cut flowers. Cut flowers typically wilt after 14 to 16 days. And yet the supply chain from field to customer can involve four middlemen – exporter, auctioneer, wholesaler and retailer. Each middleman can take a couple of days to move the flowers on, which means that their life in the home is reduced to only a week or so. Not only do these middlemen add costs to the flowers but they also reduce their value to customers.

Bloom & Wild's business model involves customers ordering flowers online a few days in advance, so that growers can cut them to order. They are then placed in small vials of water to keep them fresh and inside a net to keep the size down and then finally inside a specially designed box that can fit through a standard letter box. Sending the flowers by post in this way means that customers do not have to be at home to receive them and they should last twice as long as flowers bought in shops. There is one final advantage – the costs of the middlemen are cut out, making flowers from Bloom & Wild generally cheaper. So, at a stroke the new model solves issues of price, longevity and convenience. Videos on the company's website give ideas about flower arrangement. The company can even deliver flowers in London within two hours.

Visit the website: www.bloomandwild.com

Question:

What do you need if you are to reimagine a value chain?

question: 'why are they like this?' Industries can be prone to this sort of 'dominant logic' when things have not changed for a long time (Academic insight 2.1).

Entrepreneurial opportunities exist when customers might derive greater value by changing the value chain, even if this involves increasing costs, or if costs can be reduced without affecting the value to the customer. For example, low-cost supply may be linked to proximity to a key supplier of raw materials or labour (see Case insight 2.7). Another example might be a high-quality product that was let down by low-quality after-sales service – the value to the customer not being matched by sufficient investment. Entrepreneurial firms can add value to the customer in a number of ways, not least by developing the close relationships they offer to both customers and suppliers. A particularly effective entrepreneurial strategy is to identify a sector in which the relationships are weak, and to create value by tightening them up.

Other major sources of inspiration are new business ideas introduced in other parts of the world. Good ideas take time to spread, and the window of opportunity to exploit an idea is not the same around the world. You might be offered the opportunity to become a sales agent or a franchisee for a successful company based in another country. These opportunities can be attractive but also present risks (see Chapter 8). However, what might be a good idea today in one market might only be viable in another some years later. You need to be in the right place at the right time to be successful (see Case insights 2.8 and 2.9).

The spread of the internet makes the immediate exploitation of global markets a real possibility for many start-ups. Real and virtual products can be sold easily through virtual distribution channels and shipping can be subcontracted. At the same time some countries help

---

CASE insight 2.6

TutorVista INDIA

Spotting opportunity – developing the supply chain

Based in India, Krishnan Ganesh launched TutorVista in 2006. It offers a very twenty-first-century service. The company uses the internet to connect students in high wage-cost countries such as the USA and Britain with private tutors from low wage-cost countries such as India. It is completely dependent on the internet and the widespread availability of home computers. TutorVista is an intermediary. The part-time tutors are mainly employed full-time as teachers in schools and work from home for TutorVista – a remote business model that allows the company to keep capital and running costs to a minimum and to minimize risks. Teachers are vetted and quality is monitored. The company markets the service directly using Google search advertisements. When somebody searches for tutor support in any subject an advertisement for TutorVista comes up. When they click on the website they can talk to staff about the service.

And yet Krishnan had no experience of the education sector. He got the idea when he was travelling around the USA and was shocked to hear a media debate about 'the crisis in the US school education system'. He investigated (asking the question 'Why?') and realized that personal tutors in the USA were charging $40–$60 an hour and were regarded by most people as unaffordable. That got him to ask the question: 'Why not link teachers from India, where wage rates are lower, to the market demand in the USA?'

In 2011, the publisher Pearson increased a smaller stake in TutorVista to a 76% majority stake, paying $127 million. It acquired the remaining shares in 2013.

Visit the website on: www.tutorvista.com

Question:

What are the barriers to spotting this sort of opportunity?

CASE insight 2.7

Mamanpaz IRAN

© Mamanpaz

Spotting opportunities – ideas from other countries

If you have been to Mumbai you may have come across the 'dabbawallah system' that delivers hot, home-cooked lunches to workers in their offices around the city. For reasons of taste and hygiene, most office workers prefer to eat home-cooked food in their workplace rather than eat outside at a food stand or at a local restaurant. The meals might come from central kitchens, work-from-home women or from home itself. It is estimated that the 'dabbawallah system' delivers 250,000 lunches each day using bicycles and the railways.

Mamanpaz (meaning 'food like mother makes') is an Iranian online equivalent of the 'dabbawallah system'. It offers Iranian meals cooked by housewives working from home to customers who prefer home-cooked meals to canteen food or takeaways. It was founded in 2014 by Tabassom Latifi who worked for a corporate bank before she started the business. Originally she did everything herself, but within a year she had employed four office

Photos © Mamanpaz

staff and five motor-bike delivery people. She posts menus and photos of the meals every day and has a network of about 100 women cooking them. To maintain quality she undertakes snap inspections of kitchens and requests texted customer food-ratings and feedback. She currently supplies more than 1000 orders a day.

Visit the website: www.mamanpaz.ir

Question:

Why is it important to adapt ideas from other countries to suit local circumstances?

CASE insight 2.8

OnMobile INDIA

Spotting opportunity – the right time, right place

Arvind Rao was working in the financial services sector in New York when he tried to launch a business developing value-added services for mobile phones – ring tones, wallpapers and apps. Called OnMobile, it was originally incorporated in the USA in 2000, but failed to find a market. Not to be defeated, Arvind approached telephone operators in India with his ideas and found that his timing was perfect. India's mobile phone market was expanding

rapidly. He quickly found one customer, then another and by 2011 OnMobile had become India's largest value-added services provider. Based in Bangalore, India, it now has offices around the world.

Visit the website: www.onmobile.com

Question:

What lessons do you learn from OnMobile?

CASE insight 2.9

Enabled Employment

AUSTRALIA

Spotting opportunity in adversity

Following the birth of her first child, Jessica May developed a problem with her thyroid gland that greatly exacerbated a pre-existing anxiety disorder. Nevertheless, with the agreement of her doctor, she returned to her civil service job. However, having revealed her mental health problems to her employer she found that her managers and colleagues 'started to make negative assumptions about her capabilities, and began to exclude her from projects', which only made her anxieties worse:

I've had anxiety my whole life. The [thyroid] condition meant that my anxiety got out of control ... Because of how I was treated ... I didn't really get better.

However, the experience gave Jessica the idea and the determination to set up a business to help other people with mental or physical disabilities. In 2012 she decided to leave her job and, with a small grant and help from a local start-up initiative, launched Canberra-based Enabled Employment. Enabled Employment works with employers to find job opportunities for skilled people with a disability. The online, for-profit service now employs six staff. The site connects employers with people with a disability or Australian Defence Force members with post-traumatic stress and other injuries. It maintains an online listing of jobs, and acts as a mediator between prospective employees and companies. However, as a point of difference with normal employment agencies, it offers 'accessibility brokering' – trying to ensure that the companies are able to offer prospective employees the working conditions they need to perform at their best, such as remote working or flexible working hours and ensuring that offices have disabled access and toilets. It derives its income from employers who are charged a one-off fee for finding suitable employees, typically equivalent to 10% of the person's annual salary.

I knew there needed to be something for people with disabilities who just need a little bit of flexibility from their employers ... There's 4.2 million people in Australia with a disability. Many of these people are very competent, it is really about trying to break down their barriers to work ... We charge businesses for our services because you should be paying for amazingly qualified people, and you should also be paying for the diversity that it brings.
BBC News Business 20 March 2017

The company practises what it preaches: four of its seven full-time employees have a disability and work within a flexible schedule. The company and Jessica have also won a number of Australian awards, including start-up of the year in 2015, and a National Disability Award.

Visit the website: www.enabledemployment.com

Question:
What can you learn from Enabled Employment?

start-ups by placing local restrictions on potential foreign competitors. In China, the Google equivalent is Baidu and in Russia it is Yandex. The Facebook equivalents in China are Qzone, RenRen, PengYou or Kaixin. All these businesses benefited from restrictions placed on established Western competitors.

As outlined and seen from all the Case insights, good business ideas are based upon commercial opportunities underpinned by market need. You can *create opportunities* through radical or incremental, product or market innovation, but when you do so there is probably little or no evidence of market need. Your innovation creates a need that did not exist before. However, you can *spot opportunities* by looking for situations which leave some, or all, customer needs unmet or where the value to the customer can be improved in some way. If you can introduce product or market innovations to meet this unmet need or enhance customer value, you may have a viable business opportunity. To be successful both approaches must be linked to customer needs, as shown in Figure 2.2.

Figure 2.2 *Generating a business idea*

Nurturing creativity and innovation

Innovation is the prime tool entrepreneurs use to create opportunity. It is underpinned by the entrepreneur's character trait of creativity. Just like the GET test outlined in Chapter 1, there are a number of tests you can take to measure your general creativity. The AULIVE test can be taken online and is free (see Academic insight 2.3). Results are analysed and a report automatically produced giving an analysis (and score) for your creativity, measured in eight dimensions. Try the test and see what you score. While this is a test of general creativity, entrepreneurial creativity is used in a specific context – as an essential tool to seek out business opportunity, find unmet needs in the market place or innovative ways of meeting these needs – avoiding the pitfall of starting a copy-cat business.

ACADEMIC insight 2.3

Measuring your creativity

Creativity means different things to different people. The GET test provides only a limited insight into your creative character. The AULIVE creativity test provides you with the opportunity to reflect on your general creativity. It is a 40-question instrument that assesses you on eight dimensions against answers from others with similar backgrounds.

The creative dimensions are:

Abstraction – the ability to apply abstract concepts/ideas.

Connection – the ability to make connections between things that do not appear to be connected.

Perspective – the ability to shift one's perspective on a situation in terms of space, time and other people.

Curiosity – the desire to change or improve things that others see as normal.

Boldness – the confidence to push boundaries beyond accepted conventions. Also the ability to eliminate the fear of what others might think of you.

Paradox – the ability to simultaneously accept and work with statements that are contradictory.

Complexity – the ability to carry large quantities of information, and to manipulate and manage the relationships between such information.

Persistence – the ability to force oneself to keep trying to find more and stronger solutions even when good ones have already been generated.

The AULIVE creativity test is free and can be taken online at: www.testmycreativity.com

A prerequisite of all creative processes is the generation of knowledge and the awareness of different ideas – curiosity. Most people are constrained in their thinking by their prior knowledge and experience. Therefore, to be creative, you need to find ways of expanding this knowledge and awareness. You need to proactively seek it out. However, all too often we are unaware of the knowledge and information that is being generated around us. We then need time to mull over that knowledge and information. This subconscious 'incubation period' happens when you are engaged in other activities and you can let your mind work on the problem. The best activities are those that are instinctive and do not require 'left-brain' dominance (the part of the brain that is logical and analytical). Interestingly, sleep happens when the left brain gets tired or bored and during this time the right brain (the part that is more creative) has dominance. Incubation therefore often needs sleep. The old adage, 'sleep on the problem', has its origins in an understanding of how the brain works. It is little wonder that so many people have creative ideas when they are asleep – the problem is trying to remember them. Creativity, therefore, can take time and needs 'sleeping on'.

Manish Agarwal CEO Reliance Games The Guardian 22 April 2015

That's how we learned: by travelling, meeting people, setting up appointments, it's a continuous process.

Connectivity – an awareness of what is going on in the world in general and an ability to connect or link elements to the task in hand, in this case finding your business idea – is also an essential element in the creative process (see Academic insight 2.4). Awareness generates new ideas, knowledge and information. Reading newspapers, magazines, journals and books and surfing the web are passive forms of connectivity. But essentially it is a social process involving talking to people with different views of the world. Active connectivity means meeting a diverse range of people – networking. This might entail attending meetings, clubs, seminars and conferences. It is likely to involve travel. It is not just about being aware of different approaches or perspectives on a problem, but also about getting the brain

ACADEMIC insight 2.4

Thinking outside the box – connectivity

Stephen Johnson's thought-provoking book *Where Good Ideas Come From* does an excellent job of dispelling the myth that good ideas come from a 'eureka moment':

[Good ideas] come from crowds, from networks … You know we have this clichéd idea of the lone genius having the eureka moment … But in fact when you go back and you look at the history of innovation it turns out that so often there is this quiet collaborative process that goes on, either in people building on other people's ideas, but also in borrowing ideas, or tools or approaches to problems … The ultimate idea comes from this remixing of various different components. There still are smart people and there still are people that have moments where they see the world differently in a flash. But for the most part it's a slower and more networked process than we give them credit for.

Johnson's central thesis is that new ideas rarely happen by chance. They take time to germinate and mature. Often the big idea comes from the collision of smaller ideas or hunches, and the chance of these 'accidental' collisions is increased with the exposure you have to more people and different ideas. This can come from many sources – reading, meetings, your network of contacts, the internet etc. – the more diverse the better. The more you are exposed to these influences the more likely you are to be innovative. Indeed, the driver of innovation over time has been the increasing connectivity between different minds. As Johnson puts it:

Chance favours the connected mind.

Johnson, S. (2010) *Where Good Ideas Come From: The Natural History of Innovation*, London: Allen Lane.

to accept that there are different ways of doing things – developing an open and enquiring mind. As Albert Einstein said: 'Conventional wisdom is the source of many problems and is ill-suited to solving them'. Many people almost have to give themselves permission to be creative – to be unconventional, to think the unthinkable.

Connectivity extends beyond any industry or market context. Steve Jobs' interest in calligraphy is claimed to be the source of Apple's early development of a wide range of fonts on its computers. Some of the best business ideas have social origins, linking social need to commercial opportunity. Similarly, solutions to commercial problems or opportunities can come from unrelated disciplines. The ubiquitous Velcro fastening was conceived in 1941 by Swiss engineer, Georges de Mestral. He got his inspiration from nature. After a walk, he observed that there were burrs of the burdock plant sticking to his clothes and his dog's fur. He looked at them under a microscope and observed they had hundreds of tiny 'hooks' that caught onto 'loops' on clothing or fur. From this he conceived the possibility of two materials being bound together.

> I believe opportunity is part instinct and part immersion – in an industry, a subject, or an area of expertise … You don't have to be a genius, or a visionary, or even a college graduate to think unconventionally. You just need a framework … Seeing and seizing opportunities are skills that can be applied universally, if you have the curiosity and commitment.
>
> Michael Dell Direct from Dell: Strategies that Revolutionized an Industry (1999, New York: Harper Business)

In other words, ideas that are commonplace for one group can spark insight for another. It is all about being open to ideas from all and every source and not being inward looking. Companies like LG and Hallmark have active programmes to encourage staff to expose themselves to ideas from a wide, and sometimes unusual, range of sources. This is one reason why partnering with other people can be so useful in stimulating innovation. One person exposes the other to different ways of doing things or different ideas, and from this comes the spark of creativity.

CASE insight 2.10

Great Ormond Street Hospital UK

Connectivity – transferring ideas

Ideas for innovations can come from unusual sources. The Great Ormond Street Hospital for children in the UK took its inspiration from watching the McLaren and Ferrari Formula 1 racing teams take only six seconds to turn a car around at a pit stop. Doctors at the hospital were concerned by the time they took to move patients from the operating theatre to the intensive care unit where they recovered. Delays in an emergency handover could cost lives, so they contacted Ferrari to see how the process might be improved. Ferrari explained that their pit-stop procedure was kept simple, with minimal movements all planned in advance. In fact, it was so simple that it could be drawn on a single diagram. From that plan, every member of the Ferrari team knew exactly what they had to do and when to do it in a coordinated fashion. Ferrari videoed the hospital's handovers. When the doctors watched it they were shocked at the lack of structure. Ferrari concluded that, with an ever-changing team and unpredictable demand, the hospital's handover teams needed a simple formula they could understand and work to – just like a pit stop. And Ferrari helped the hospital to design it.

Question:

What are the barriers to developing discovery skills?

Active discovery

However, discovering entrepreneurial opportunities is not just about knowledge, awareness and even connectivity. While it involves being generally aware of and engaged with the world about you, it also means being questioning and willing to experiment. It is about developing and actively practising a set of five **discovery skills**.

> Network.
> Meet people. Show a genuine interest in others. Don't talk too much. Listen more.
>
> *Raoul Shah, founder Exposures The Observer 29 September 2013*

1 **Networking** with a wide range of people so as to be exposed to new ideas and be able to sound out ideas with others. Commercially, networks are important structures that can provide you with information about markets, professional advice and opinion, often without charge. Formal networks, such as Chambers of Commerce and Business Links in the UK and the Small Business Development Centers in the USA, and trade associations can be invaluable for this. Networks can also provide opportunities to form partnerships, either formally or informally, so as to better exploit an opportunity.

2 **Observing** others, particularly potential customers, so as to be exposed to the widest possible influences.

3 **Questioning** common wisdom or dominant logic, asking the questions 'why?' and 'why not?'

> There is always something to learn from meeting someone new and a lot to learn from meeting someone old. The right contacts can become an invaluable source of learning as well as an inspiration and support.
>
> *Jonathan Elvidge founder Gadget Shop The Times, 6 July 2002*

4 **Experimenting** and trying things out so as to see how things can be done differently. Sometimes this might even involve trying out a business idea by starting up in a low-cost way – an approach called 'lean start-up' that we shall look at in Chapter 4.

These four skills are used in conjunction with the fifth key skill that involves greater creativity:

5 **Associating** seemingly unrelated things – connectivity – so as to find novel solutions to problems or ways of doing things. For example, Larry Page's idea for PageRank, which underpins Google's search engine, stemmed from an unrelated project he was working on called Stanford Digital Libraries. James Dyson was able to see that a cyclone system for separating paint particles could be used (less obviously?) to develop a better vacuum cleaner. Similarly doctors at Great Ormond Street Hospital were able to see how the efficiency of Formula 1 pit stops could be used to improve patient care (see Case insight 2.10). If there is a 'eureka moment' this is when it happens – the realization that there is a solution to a

CASE insight 2.11

Swarfega UK

Connectivity – reusing ideas

Not all ideas find a commercial application in the way they were originally envisaged, and observation and connectivity can change the direction of an invention. Swarfega is a coloured gel that is a dermatologically safe cleaner for the skin. It is now widely used to remove grease and oil from hands in factories and households. But the original product, developed in 1941 by Audley Williamson, was not intended for degreasing hands at all. It was intended as a mild detergent to wash silk stockings. Unfortunately, the invention of nylon and its use for stockings and tights rendered the product as obsolete as silk stockings.

© Swarfega

© Swarfega

Watching workmen trying to clean their hands with a mixture of petrol, paraffin and sand which left them cracked and sore led Williamson to realize that there was a completely different commercial opportunity for his product. He *observed* a need to help clean grease from workmen's skin and *associated* the characteristics of Swarfega with the ability to solve that problem.

Visit the website: www.swarfega.com

Question:

How difficult is it to associate the characteristics of a product with the solution of a problem in a completely different context?

problem you have been facing – and it often comes from the most unexpected of sources. But this only happens if your mind has a 'library' of thoughts and experiences to draw from – to come together to spark a new thought or idea. As Steve Jobs said: 'Creativity is just connecting things.'

As shown in Figure 2.3, connectivity links with these discovery skills and combines to help make you more creative and innovative. These are the elements that will help you find a good business idea and sustain your competitiveness through innovation.

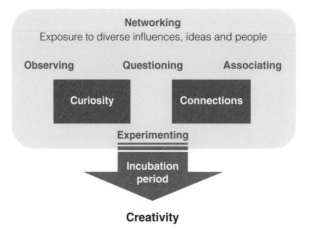

Figure 2.3 *Creativity through active discovery*

Discovery skills

I n a six-year study of more than 3,000 US CEOs, contrasting 25 well-known entrepreneurs (such as Steve Jobs of Apple, Jeff Bezos of Amazon, Pierre Omidyar of eBay, Peter Thiel of PayPal, Niklas Zennström of Skype and Michael Dell) with other CEOs who had no track record for innovation, a research study found five 'discovery skills' that made these entrepreneurs particularly adept at linking market opportunity and innovation.

1 **Networking**: Innovative entrepreneurs spend time finding and testing ideas with a network of diverse individuals in different countries. They do not just network with like-minded people. Networking in this context is just another aspect of observing and is therefore a prerequisite to associating.

2 **Observing**: Innovative entrepreneurs observe common phenomena and people's behaviour, particularly that of potential customers. They scrutinize these phenomena, noticing fine detail and gaining insight into new ways of doing things. Ratan Tata observed a family of four perched on a moped and asked why they could not afford a car. In 2009, after years of product development which involved new modular production methods, Tata Group launched the lowest-priced car in the world – the Nano. Effective observing requires the ability to handle complexity and shift one's perspective – abilities also measured in the AULIVE test. Observing is a prerequisite to associating. It is part of how associations or connections are made. You need to observe detail to be able to associate it across boundaries.

3 **Questioning:** Innovative entrepreneurs have the curiosity to challenge conventional wisdom, asking 'why?', 'why not?' and 'what if?' The iconic Apple iPod was developed at a time when MP3 players were well established. Staff developing Apple's iTunes software for use with MP3 players formed such a low opinion of their ease of use that they decided to do better. Most of the entrepreneurs were able to remember the specific question that inspired them to set up their business. They were also able to imagine opposites – apparent paradoxes including some different future state – and to embrace real-world constraints so that they became opportunities if they could be overcome. Questioning links the attributes of curiosity, paradox and boldness measured in the AULIVE test.

4 **Experimenting**: Innovative entrepreneurs actively try out new ideas, creating prototypes and launching pilots. Where these do not work, they learn from any mistakes and try to use the learning in different projects. The Apple iPod started life as prototypes made out of foam-core boards, using fishing weights to give them the right feel. All the entrepreneur CEOs engaged in some form of active experimenting, ranging from 'intellectual exploration' to 'physical tinkering'. One of their most powerful experiments was visiting, living and/or working in overseas countries. This was all part of being exposed to new ideas and mixing with people from diverse backgrounds. Experimenting is one aspect of curiosity.

5 **Associating**: Innovative entrepreneurs connect seemingly unrelated questions, problems or ideas from many different fields. This often comes from mixing with people from diverse backgrounds and disciplines. The minds of the entrepreneur CEOs in the study were able to make connections between seemingly unrelated things, transferring questions, problems or ideas from one discipline to another. They capitalized on apparently divergent associations. What is more, this ability to associate seemed to be something that could be encouraged through stimulation.

The more frequently people in our study attempted to understand, categorize, and store new knowledge, the more easily their brains could naturally and consistently make, store and recombine associations.

It is the associating skill that links the attributes of connection, abstraction and perspective in the AULIVE test.

Dyer, J.H., Gregersen, H.D. and Christensen, C.M. (2009) 'The Innovator's DNA', *Harvard Business Review*, December.

Discovery skills require you to be aware of and engaged with the world about you. They also require you to be questioning and willing to experiment. They are active skills that need to be practised. Essentially, the process of generating novel business ideas involves three stages.

1   Ensure that you are exposed to as many diverse and different ideas, influences and people as possible, and that you are aware of and alert to these influences. A general sense of openness to ideas from all directions is also important. Even when exposed to diverse influences, most people walk through life as if on auto-pilot, blinkered to what is happening around them. You need to consciously (as opposed to subconsciously) *see* things.

2   Recognize market opportunities by observing how consumers go about their daily lives and questioning whether their needs can be met 'better' (or at all) in a different way. You need to practise the skills and techniques outlined in this chapter that encourage you to question ('why?' and 'why not?') and experiment. You need to think about things that are happening around you and how they might affect the future. Just *seeing* things is not enough. You need to question why they are like that – question the status quo and ask why things cannot be done differently.

3   Finally, formulate and reformulate your business idea so that there becomes a commercially viable business model. Not all products work to start with, and not all ideas are commercially viable to start with. Howard Head, the inventor of the steel ski, made some 40 different metal skis before he found one that worked consistently. Recognizing market opportunities by observing how consumers go about their daily lives and questioning whether their needs can be met 'better' in a different way is an important first step, but experimenting with the connection so as to perfect the product/service and the business model is vital.

All of this takes time. You need time to think and ponder, time to incubate ideas. Incubation time happens when you are engaged in other activities, including sleep, and you can let your subconscious mind work on the problem. Time is also needed to make the connections or associations between opportunities and your capabilities. There is an element of serendipity here. But the longer the time and the more the potential connections, the more likely the ideas are to germinate. This process of reformulation of the business idea is one that repeats itself well into the concept phase of product development, even to the point where you develop your business model, and the use of discovery skills facilitates this process.

Techniques for exploring change

There are many techniques designed to help explore change and generate new commercial ideas. Generating ideas is a numbers game – the more ideas you come up with, the more likely you are to find one that is viable. So it is worth distinguishing between those techniques designed to generate volume and those designed to improve quality. Some techniques are more applicable to spotting opportunity, others to creating opportunity.

Brainstorming

Brainstorming is one of the most widely used, basic techniques, designed to generate volume for either spotting or creating opportunity. It is practised in a group. In the session you do not question or criticize ideas. You suspend disbelief. The aim is to encourage the free flow of ideas – divergent thinking – and to come up with as many ideas as possible. Everyone has

CASE insight 2.12

Henry Ford   USA

Creating opportunity – market paradigm shift using discovery skills

Henry Ford did not invent the car, but he did revolutionize the way cars were produced and sold in the 1900s, moving from craft-based to production-line methods and from wealthy customers – a strategy all other firms were pursuing at the time – to supplying an affordable car for everyman – a vision he had to turn into a reality. He created a new commercial market for

Getty Images/SuperStock RM

motor cars – a market paradigm shift that changed the rules of the game. And yet this involved only incremental changes, albeit on an extensive scale, to products and processes, component and factory design and in the way labour was organized in his factories. This disruptive innovation created the mass market for cars that we know today. But where did Ford get his vision of the future from? How was he able to break away from the established thinking of how a car should be made and who it should be sold to?

Henry Ford never believed in market research. He once said that if he had asked people what they wanted, they'd have said 'faster horses', rather than 'new-fangled' things called cars. And his vision led him away from car designs that reflected the old ways coachmen led the horse-drawn carriages of the wealthy – chauffeurs separated from the wealthy that they drove – to the driver being part of the group in the car. But Ford had to find ways of making his vision a practical reality and developing a business model that would make it commercially viable. So where did he get his ideas from? Henry Ford was an 'active discoverer'. Firstly he *questioned* why it was that only the wealthy could travel by car and came up with an alternative reality or vision. This all revolved around finding ways of producing cars cheaply – a low-cost business model with business strategies that reflected the need to mass produce and

sell cars in high volumes. He *connected* this vision with a number of other situations he had *observed* through his *networks*.

Ford's key idea was to get workers to undertake repetitive tasks on a moving assembly line, rather than craftsmen being responsible for much of the assembly within a static garage. This idea came from observing how a slaughterhouse worked and connecting this to his vision. He implemented a system of profit sharing with front-line workers in order to motivate them to do this quickly (time was money) – a concept that had been used by a French printing company decades earlier. His strategy of making one standard product in one colour (the black Model T Ford) was designed to make the assembly line operate as fast as possible – and he knew through *experimentation* that black paint dried faster than any other colour. Finally, to get the volumes of cars coming off this production line sold quickly he started a novel network of car dealerships, partly paid on a commission basis – just as Isaac Singer did to sell his sewing machines nearly half a century earlier. Henry Ford started with a problem, made new connections that led to novel solutions, and wrapped a successful strategy around the big idea – the moving assembly line. As he said:

I invented nothing new. I simply assembled the discoveries of others.

Questions:

1 From the examples given, which discovery skills did Henry Ford exhibit, and how were they used to make his vision a reality?
2 What do you have to do to develop these discovery skills?

CASE insight 2.13

The Million Dollar Homepage

 UK

Brainstorming for business ideas

The Million Dollar Homepage is a single web page that is divided into 10,000 boxes, each 100 pixels in size. Space was sold to advertisers at $1 for each pixel, providing a montage of company logos. Advertisers were promised that the page would remain online for at least five years. The idea for the page came to Alex Tew, a Nottingham Trent University student in the UK, in 2005. He had brainstorming sessions before he went to bed each night, writing ideas down on a notepad. The site took just two days to set up and cost £50. Alex sold the first blocks of pixels to his brothers and friends, and used the money to advertise the site. He never targeted any advertisers in particular, just 'anyone who wanted to buy pixels' but the site address began to appear in internet blogs and chat rooms and, following a press release, a BBC technology programme ran a short feature on the page in September 2005. Tew dropped out of university and by January 2006 was a millionaire.

> *I had literally no money, and I was worried about university. I just brainstormed this kind of crazy, get-rich-quick scheme that then took on a life of its own.*
> BBC Capital 15 September 2016, www.bbc.com/capital/story/20160914-the-man-behind-the-million-dollar-homepage

Fast-forward to 2017 and, after a number of start-up attempts that did not work out, Alex is CEO of a San Francisco start-up called Calm. Along the way there was Pixelotto, a spinoff of the Homepage selling advertising space; PopJam, a social network sharing funny content; and One Million People, similar to Homepage but with photos instead of advertisements. Calm was started in 2012 with Michael Acton Smith (founder of Mind Candy – see Case insight 8.6). Originally it was a website but it is now a mobile app of spoken relaxation and meditation programs, featuring visuals and audios of streams, rainstorms, waves and other calming influences. The app is free, but users can upgrade to a monthly, yearly or lifetime subscription, which gives them access to more relaxation and meditation options. The company went through three rounds of funding that generated $1.5 million to get off the ground and already has six million users.

Visit the websites: www.milliondollarhomepage.com and www.calm.com

Questions:

1 Why did the Million Dollar Homepage get off the ground?
2 Was it just good luck?

---

thousands of good ideas within them just waiting to come out. But people inherently fear making mistakes or looking foolish in front of others. Here making 'mistakes' and putting forward ideas which don't work is not only acceptable, it is encouraged. You might start with a problem to be solved or an opportunity to be exploited. You encourage and write ideas down as they come – there are no 'bad' ideas. All ideas are, at the very least, springboards for other ideas.

PESTEL analysis

PESTEL analysis is a widely used tool to aid thinking about future developments in the wider environment. This in turn can be used to spot commercial opportunities that these developments generate. PESTEL stands for:

Political changes such as local or central government elections, and political initiatives, for example, on price competitiveness, new or changed taxes, merger and takeover policy and so on.

Economic changes such as recession, growth, changes in interest rates, inflation, employment, currency fluctuations and so on.

Social changes such as an ageing population, increasing inequality, increasing work participation (often from home), 24-hour shopping, increasing crime, increasing participation in higher education, changing employment patterns, increasing number of one-parent families and so on.

Technological developments such as increasing internet bandwidth, the coming together of internet technologies, increasing use of computers and chip technology, increasing use of mobile phones, increasing use of surveillance cameras and so on.

Environmental developments such as climate change, waste and pollution reduction, species reduction and so on.

Legal changes such as health and safety, changes in employment laws, food hygiene regulations, patent laws and so on.

The technique is often shortened to **PEST** by dropping the 'legal' and 'environmental' elements of the acronym, or **SLEPT** by dropping just the 'legal' element.

The trick is to brainstorm about how these developments might create business opportunities that are not currently being met. Take, for example, the development of the internet. The ability to download films and music has questioned the viability of shops selling DVDs and CDs, but created opportunities for new devices (netbooks, tablets, smartphones etc.) and services (particularly niche services) linked to the internet. The development of internet shopping generally might cause developers to rethink the purpose and structure of our town centres. It might cause individual shops to re-engineer the way they meet customer needs – most shops now have websites and many offer internet shopping alongside conventional shopping.

Futures thinking

This is another technique that is often used to think about the future, and follows on from a PESTEL analysis. **Futures thinking** helps develop further insight into the change that has been identified, ahead of defining the commercial opportunity. It tries to take a holistic perspective, developing a vision about the future state after the change has taken place. From this the commercial opportunities can be identified, again using brainstorming. Current constraints to action are ignored and in this way the barriers to change are identified. Some barriers may indeed prove to be permanent or insurmountable, but many might not be. Objections are therefore outlawed and disbelief suspended at the initial ideas stage. Only later on might options be discarded, once the barriers are considered. The key to thinking about the future is not to assume it will necessarily be like the past. Change is now endemic and often discontinuous.

So, for example, you might start thinking about the state of a particular form of retailing in five years' time, given the impact of the internet and smartphone. Will bricks-and-mortar retailing continue to exist? If so, how will it combine with these technological developments? What will it look like, where will it be located and what services will it need to offer? How will it attract customers? These and many more questions might help to 'flesh out' a picture of how it might look and what you need to do to survive and prosper in the future.

Mind maps

This is simply a map of related ideas from one original idea. It helps develop and refine a business opportunity, whether it is spotted or created. It can be used by individuals or in a group. As with brainstorming, you have to suspend disbelief and simply generate related ideas that might not have been encapsulated in the original. It can help you to 'think outside the box' and generate relationships that might not initially have been apparent. Creativity is about making connections between apparently unconnected things, and this technique can be particularly helpful. A simple example related to the opening of a shop is shown in Figure 2.4. This illustrates how **mind maps** can be used to look at complex activities that need to be undertaken in order to launch a new venture.

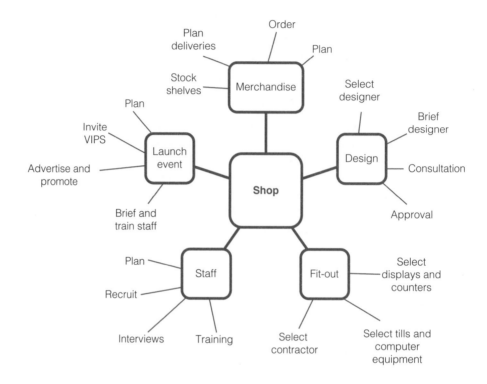

Figure 2.4 *Mind map for a shop opening*

Figure 2.5 shows a simple four-stage, systematic process for spotting a commercial opportunity and generating a business idea based upon the techniques covered so far: PESTEL analysis, futures thinking, brainstorming and mind mapping.

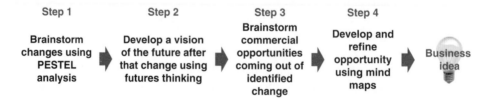

Figure 2.5 *Technique 1: spotting a commercial opportunity arising out of change*

Techniques for exploring product inadequacies

Sometimes there may be problems for which no solutions – or solutions that are commercially viable – have been found. More often perhaps, existing products or services can be improved, providing better solutions to existing problems. The question is how to explore these inadequacies?

Analogy

Analogy is a product-centred technique that attempts to join together apparently uncon-nected or unrelated combinations of features of a product or service and benefits to the customer to come up with innovative solutions to problems. It is therefore designed to provide more focused ideas that create opportunity out of unsolved problems for customers. Analogies are proposed once the initial problem is stated. The analogies are then related to opportunities in the market place. It works in a similar way to brain-storming. Georges de Mestral's connection between the properties of burdock seed and the need to stick and unstick things is an example of analogy that led to the development of Velcro.

In building an analogy you need to ask some basic questions:

- What does the situation or problem remind you of?
- What other areas of life or work experience similar situations?
- Who does these similar things and can the principles be adapted?

Often the analogy contains the words '... *is like* ...', so you might ask why something 'is like' another. For example, why is advertising like cooking? Answer: because there is so much preamble to eating. Anticipation from presentation and smell, even the ambience of the restaurant you eat it in, are just as important as the taste and nutritional value of the food itself. They 'advertise' the food to be eaten.

CASE insight 2.14

Fetchr UAE

Spotting opportunities – solutions to problems

Joy Ajlouny was raised in the USA by Palestinian parents. Before starting Fetchr she ran an e-commerce business called Bonfire that specialized in luxury footwear, and became frustrated by the number of packages returned from customers in the Middle East marked 'Address not found'. In many emerging markets delivery of goods can be a problem because of the absence of a physical address. Joy discovered that delivery companies were sending the driver out with a piece of paper containing telephone numbers to call the customers one at a time to find out where to deliver the package. Joy met Idriss Al Rifai at a technology conference in San Francisco in 2014. Idriss was born in Iraq and raised in France, and had experienced similar problems as head of operations of the Dubai-based e-commerce company Markavip. They started discussing the problem and identified a technology-based solution.

Idriss and Joy came up with a novel mobile technology-based solution – a patented app that allows pick-up or delivery of merchandise to an exact GPS location based on the customer's smartphone signal. It means that there is no need for delivery directions. As a result, they launched their pick-up and delivery firm, Fetchr, in 2015 in Dubai, UAE, and quickly rolled it out to Saudi Arabia and Bahrain. Their plan is to be an aggregator between couriers and customers, but to prove that the concept saved time and money the company has been using its own fleet of vans in Dubai. Fetchr raised $11 million in venture funding in 2015, making it the first early-stage investment in an Arab start-up by a top US venture capital firm.

Visit the website: fetchr.us

Question:

What problems might you foresee with this business idea?

Attribute analysis

Sometimes a product can be inadequate and simply not work properly, presenting a fairly obvious opportunity for a new, better product. However, sometimes the deficiencies can be more subtle. **Attribute analysis** is another more focused product-centred technique designed to evolve product improvements and line extensions – used as the product reaches the mature phase of its life cycle. Therefore it can be useful in spotting opportunities arising from inadequate existing products or services. It uses the basic marketing technique of looking at the features of a product or service which in turn perform a series of functions but, most importantly, deliver benefits to the customers. An existing product or service is stripped down to its component parts and then you explore how these features might be altered, using brainstorming. You need to focus on whether those changes might bring valuable benefits to the customer. Nothing must be taken for granted. You can then develop and refine these changes using mind mapping.

So, for example, you might focus on a domestic lock. This secures a door from being opened by an unwelcome intruder. The benefit is security and reduction/elimination of theft from the house. But you can lose keys or forget to lock doors, and some locks are difficult or inconvenient to open from the inside. A potential solution is to have doors that sense people approaching from the outside and lock themselves. You could have a reverse sensor on the inside – one that unlocks the door when someone approaches (which could be activated or deactivated centrally). The exterior sensor could recognize 'friendly' people approaching the door by means of sensors they carry in the form of 'credit cards' or the sensor could be over-ridden by a combination lock. The lock could be linked to a door that opens automatically.

Figure 2.6 shows a simple three-stage, systematic process for spotting a commercial opportunity and generating a business idea based upon analysing the attributes of an existing product or service and using brainstorming and mind-mapping techniques.

Figure 2.6 *Technique 2: spotting a commercial opportunity arising out of an inadequate existing product or service*

Thinking inside the box – Systematic Inventive Thinking

Boyd and Goldenberg observe that there are many opportunities for innovation based upon existing products or services that do not adequately meet customer needs or where customer value can be enhanced through changes.

The traditional view of creativity is that it is unstructured and doesn't follow rules or patterns.

That you need to think 'outside the box' to be truly original and innovative. That you should start with a problem and then 'brainstorm' ideas without restraint until you find a solution. That you should 'go wild' making analogies to things that have nothing to do with your products, services, or processes. That straying as far afield as possible will help you come up with a breakthrough idea. We believe just the opposite … that more innovation – and better and quicker innovation – happens when you work inside your familiar world (yes, inside the box) using what we call templates.

Boyd and Goldenberg's template, which they called 'Systematic Inventive Thinking', involves five approaches.

1 **Attribute dependency:** Bringing together or correlating two or more apparently unrelated attributes of the product can add value for customers. Examples include smartphones that provide information that depends on your geographic location; and in cars, windscreen wiper speed or radio volume that varies with the speed of the car, and headlights that dip automatically for oncoming cars.

2 **Task unification:** Similarly, bringing together multiple tasks into one product or service can add value for customers. For example, sunscreen products added facial moisturizers (and vice versa) to unify a task. Samsonite used this principle to redesign the shape of straps on backpacks so as to press softly at 'shiatsu points' on the back and provide a soothing massage sensation rather than causing back and neck strain due to the weight of

their contents. The heavier the contents, the deeper the sensation and the more stress-relieving for the wearer, thus using the heavy load carried as a comfort advantage.

3 **Multiplication:** By way of contrast, duplicating some product feature or characteristic that may enhance customer value can be of value to customers. For example, 'picture-within-picture' TVs allow people to watch more than one programme at a time. Pearson Education used this principle to create a new course designed specifically for students who failed algebra exams and needed a different approach to studying the subject.

4 **Division:** Alternatively, dividing out the functions of a product might add value for some customers. For example, dividing out the control features of many electronic products and placing them into a remote control provided more convenience and allowed the products to become smaller, cheaper and easier to use.

5 **Subtraction:** Finally, subtracting product features not valued by some market segments. This was the approach taken by low-cost airlines.

Boyd, D. and Goldenberg, J. (2013) *Inside the Box: A Proven System of Creativity for Breakthrough Results*, London: Profile Books.

Gap analysis

Gap analysis is a market-based approach that attempts to produce a 'map' of product/market attributes based on dimensions that are perceived as important to customers, analysing where competing products might lie and then spotting gaps where there is little or no competition. Depending on scale, this can be used to spot or create opportunity, particularly in the form of redefining market paradigms. Because of the complexity involved, the attributes are normally shown in only two dimensions. There are a number of approaches to this task.

- **Perceptual mapping** places the attributes of a product within specific categories. So for example, the dessert market might be characterized in a **perceptual map** as hot vs. cold and sophisticated vs. unsophisticated. Various desserts would then be mapped onto these two dimensions. This could be shown graphically (Figure 2.7). The issue is whether the 'gap' identified is one that customers would value being filled – and means understanding whether they value the dimensions being measured. That is a question for market research to attempt to answer.

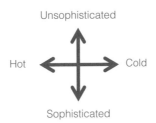

Figure 2.7 *A perceptual map for desserts*

- **Non-metric mapping** places products in generic groups that customers find similar and then tries to explain why these groupings exist. A classic example of **non-metric mapping** would be its application to the soft drinks market where products might be clustered and then described simply in terms of the widely used generic groups, 'still' vs. 'carbonated' and 'flavoured' vs. 'non-flavoured'. The key here is also finding the appropriate dimensions that create opportunities for differentiating the product. The mapping of soft drinks on the two dimensions of a perceptual map is unlikely to reveal any gaps in the market.
- **Repertory grid** is a more systematic extension of this technique using market research. Customers are asked to group similar and dissimilar products within a market, normally in pairs. They are then asked to explain the similarities and dissimilarities. The sequence is repeated for all groups of similar and dissimilar products. The explanations are then used to derive 'constructs' which describe the way in which people relate and evaluate the products. These constructs form a **repertory grid** that can be used to map the products, using the words used by the customers themselves.

Figure 2.8 shows a simple four-stage, systematic process for spotting or creating a commercial opportunity and generating a business idea based on mapping the attributes of an existing product or service, using brainstorming and identifying gaps in the market.

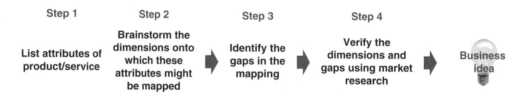

Step 1	Step 2	Step 3	Step 4	
List attributes of product/service	Brainstorm the dimensions onto which these attributes might be mapped	Identify the gaps in the mapping	Verify the dimensions and gaps using market research	Business idea

Figure 2.8 Technique 3: spotting or creating commercial opportunity using gap analysis

CASE insight 2.15

Nikwax 🇬🇧 UK

Spotting opportunity – inadequate products

Born in 1954, Nick Brown was a keen hiker who walked regularly in the Peak District and Scotland. However he was unhappy with the waterproofing products available in shops, because they just did not keep the water out of his boots. He was also a bit of a chemist, doing A-level chemistry at school. Consequently as a teenager he used to mix together various ingredients from his shed and the local hardware store in a saucepan to form a boot wax. He would then use it to coat his boots before going hiking. And it worked. He had dry feet and the boots did not soften up and lose their essential supportive feature.

However, it was a prolonged period of unemployment after leaving university with a third class degree in anthropology at the age of 22 that forced Nick to turn his invention into a business. In order to earn some money he boiled up the boot wax he had invented in his north London flat and sold it to a local shop at twice what it cost to produce. He produced the wax in a discarded tea urn, using a primus stove, a jug and materials bought from a local store. The wax was then poured into tins which he silk screened by hand.

> It was a low point for me. I stepped back and asked myself what I had done. I had done nothing well … I had already supplied a local store with a few pots of it. When they sold out quickly I realised this was something I could do.

Sunday Times 25 May 2014

Nick used a £200 overdraft to buy a van and travelled around selling the wax directly to stores during the day, returning to make more product at night. He focused on exports early on, travelling to Europe on an InterRail card to sell directly to shops and going to trade shows to push his product. Turnover grew quickly and he started employing staff, but the banks refused to provide finance, believing he was overtrading (see Chapter 13). He therefore financed the growth of the business internally through retained profits. Nikwax was so effective that it set the standard for a range of aftercare products under the Nikwax brand. Nikwax was the first company in the world to produce a range of water-based products for restoring waterproofing in the home. The range grew to include products for many other uses where waterproofing was required, from ropes to tents.

Today Nikwax, founded in 1977, employs 114 staff and has a turnover of £10 million. Nick still owns 92%, with the rest owned by employees. Seventy per cent of sales come from abroad and it has offices in the UK, USA, Australia and Poland.

Visit the website: www.nikwax.com

Question:

How easy is it to explore the adequacy or inadequacy of an existing product?

CASE insight 2.16

Maggie's UK

Spotting opportunity in social enterprise

Every year, more than 300,000 people are diagnosed with cancer in the UK alone. Maggie's, or to give it its formal name, the Maggie Keswick Jencks Cancer Caring Centres Trust, offers free practical, emotional and social support to people with cancer and their families and friends. It was set up by Maggie Keswick Jencks, a landscape designer with an international reputation, just before her death from breast cancer in 1995. Maggie lived with advanced cancer for two years before her death. During that time she used her knowledge and experience to create a blueprint for a new type of care. Maggie's Centres are built around her belief that people should not 'lose the joy of living in the fear of dying'.

The first centre was built in Edinburgh in 1996. Since then Maggie's has grown rapidly and by mid-2017 it had 21 centres in the UK and abroad, including Hong Kong and Tokyo, with a further nine planned. The centres are based upon ideas about cancer care originally laid out by Maggie around the principle that design affects how we feel. All of the centres are designed by leading architects. Each is unique, being built around a kitchen on an open-plan basis – no closed doors – and designed to be

MAGGIE'S
Everyone's home of cancer care

© Maggie's

friendly, welcoming and full of light – calming spaces. Each centre is staffed by health professionals, including a cancer nurse and a psychologist, and a fundraiser. Each UK centre is located next to a NHS cancer hospital. In 2016, Maggie's Centres were visited more than 200,000 times by people with cancer and their family and friends. Maggie's now also provides online support for cancer patients. This offers the same kind of support offered by the centres, with blogs and online advice managed by professional psychologists.

Maggie's programme of support has been shown to strengthen the physical and emotional well-being of people with cancer. Since 2000, the work of the Centres has been commended by the NHS Cancer Plan, NICE and the Cancer Reform Strategy. In 2013 it was highlighted as 'best practice' in the UK National Cancer Survival Initiative Report by the Department of Health.

Visit the website: www.maggiescentres.org.uk

Questions:

1 Can the approaches outlined in this chapter develop an idea for a social enterprise?
2 How would you apply them to Maggie's Centres?

Sofa-bed Factory

iStock.com/creativesunday2016

Piotr started thinking through the possibilities even before he got home from his meeting with Olek. It was expensive to live in the UK and he had realized that most of the furniture he sold was imported from countries where labour was cheaper. Those countries included Poland, which had a plentiful supply of skilled labour. Poland, like Britain (at least for the moment), was in the European Union, which meant that transporting goods from Poland to Britain was easy and there were no tariffs.

When he met Olek the next evening Piotr explained that things could be manufactured in Poland more cheaply than in the UK, and that he knew at least one company that bought quite a few manufactured products from East Europe. This was at least a spark of an idea for a business opportunity. Piotr said that when he got back to the UK he would investigate the furniture market further to see what opportunities there might be. He was surprised by the lack of enthusiasm shown by Olek and asked why this was. Olek explained, saying that furniture was made from wood and fabric or leather whereas his real skills lay with manufacturing or assembling mechanical things made from metal. What was more, he felt that he really did not know enough about where or how to sell the things he might be able to manufacture.

Piotr came back to the UK with mixed feelings. On the one hand Olek seemed not to be keen on the opportunity that Piotr had identified because he did not feel he had the necessary skills, but on the other hand Piotr knew this industry. In the next few weeks he found out more about the suppliers to his company. Most were not based in the UK. While he knew nothing about the costs of producing furniture, he discovered that his company tried to sell the furniture to customers with a mark-up of 200% (i.e. something costing £100 was sold for £300) – although stocks were often offered at 'sale' prices with discounts of up to 50% on these prices (still giving a retail mark-up of 50%). Despite the high cost of renting retail property and employing staff in the UK, his company was still very successful.

Piotr talked to the buyer for his company who confirmed that the main reason for buying from countries other than the UK was because their prices were lower – presumably because they faced lower costs. He said that most of the company's furniture was 'own-brand' (sold under their name), which meant that they could source from multiple suppliers. They did all the marketing to customers, so that the only extra cost borne by suppliers was delivery. He also gave Piotr a copy of the company's normal terms of trade, which Piotr was surprised to find included buying in euros (€) rather than sterling (£). The company provided the specification for the furniture and therefore guaranteed them minimum call-offs. The buyer said they had some long-term suppliers who he trusted to supply good quality products. The buyer also confirmed that most of the furniture they sold was wooden, with sofas and beds being upholstered in different materials. Hard wood like oak was used for facing but cheaper soft wood was used internally for sofas and beds. There was some metal furniture, mainly tables and chairs, but these were not particularly big sellers. Almost in passing, he said that sofa-beds – sofas that converted into beds – were particularly popular and that he was having trouble finding a good supplier, somebody the company could trust to work with.

Piotr went back to one of his stores and looked at a sofa-bed. He opened it to form a bed, realizing that the sofa had a complicated sprung steel frame that folded out to form the bed. The bed seemed to have quite a flimsy mattress. He looked in the catalugue and noted that sofa-beds were upholstered in a limited range of fabrics. Piotr began to wonder whether this was something he and Olek could produce in Poland and sell to his company in the UK. Later that night he talked to Olek on Skype, having earlier sent him copies of the relevant pages from the company's catalogue. Olek said he would investigate how sofa-beds were made and see whether the materials could be sourced easily in Poland. He also asked Piotr to find out more about the market in the UK, rather than just relying on the things the buyer had told him. But there was one more important piece of information he wanted Piotr to get from the buyer, and that was the price the UK company were paying for their sofa-beds at the moment.

Question:

What additional information would you need to take this idea further as a potential business opportunity?

Summary and action points

2.1 Evaluate your creativity potential: Spotting and developing an original business idea requires creativity. You can improve this by developing your discovery skills: networking, observing, questioning, experimenting and associating (connectivity). It is one skill that training can enhance and one that a business partner can supplement.

2.2 Generate a business idea: Good business ideas come from creating opportunities or spotting them. You can create opportunities by creating change. You can spot opportunities by analysing change.

Creating change involves product or market innovation – changing the product/service or its market either incrementally or radically. Radical market innovation involves challenging industry paradigms by questioning sectoral, performance and customer conventions (e.g. the value chain). This is less risky than radical product innovation.

Spotting change involves a systematic analysis of the environment to highlight changes (e.g. using PESTEL) and then developing an understanding of what commercial opportunities they might generate (e.g. using mind mapping, futures thinking).

You can also spot opportunities by finding innovative solutions to existing problems (e.g. using analogy) or highlighting inadequacies in existing products or services (e.g. using attribute analysis, gap analysis).

Workbook exercises

The New Venture Creation Workbook contains a digital version of these exercises that can be modified as your business model develops and builds into a draft business plan. It can be downloaded from www.macmillanihe.com/burns-nvc-2e.

2.1: Evaluate your creativity potential

Take the AULIVE test: www.testmycreativity.com

Review the results. Are they consistent with the GET test results? Reflect again on whether you agree with the results of both tests by finding examples from your life that support or disprove them. Decide on the implications of these results and list the things that you want to do as a result of them.

2.2: Generate a business idea

To work through the rest of this book you need at least one business idea. Subsequent chapters will help you to evaluate and modify your business idea(s) and, if you end up with more than one, evaluate which is the one you want to pursue.

1 If you already have a business idea or ideas, go to Step 5.

2 If you have identified an inadequate existing product or service, go through the processes outlined in Figures 2.6 or 2.8 to arrive at your new business idea. This is best done in a small group. Go to Step 4.

3 If you do not have a business idea, go through the four-stage process outlined in Figure 2.5 until you have at least one. This is best done in a small group. Go to Step 4.

4 Eliminate any ideas that do not meet any of the following three, simple criteria:

- Practicability
- Your ability to undertake the business idea
- Whether it is likely to fit with your personal drivers and business purpose (Exercises 1.1 and 1.2)

If none meet these criteria, repeat steps 2 and/or 3 until you have another idea.

5 Expand on the product or service idea(s) (e.g. using mind maps).

Write down as clearly as possible a description of it. What are its features or characteristics? What customer demands will it meet? What problem will it solve for them? What further development work still needs to be undertaken? Which new venture typology (Figure 2.1) does it most closely approximate to? What are the implications of this for the business?

6 Describe as clearly as possible the types of customers (groups or segments) who you think will buy your product or service. Why do you think each group will buy your product or service, rather than that of your competitors?

7 Write down the names of the competitors you might face. How does your product or service differ from theirs?

We shall return to this in Chapter 5 and define things in more detail, but you need to jot down these expectations about your original idea before you start to modify them. In the meanwhile get feedback on your idea(s) from your network of family, friends and any experts. This may take time, but it is part of the 'incubation' process. You may have a good idea but it may need to be modified in some ways to be viable.

Visit www.macmillanihe.com/burns-nvc-2e for chapter quizzes and other resources.

3

Understanding your industry and markets

Contents

- The importance of research
- Describing your market/industry
- Market/industry life cycle
- Market/industry concentration
- Market/industry geographic extent
- Market research
- Estimating your market size
- Identifying your competitors
- SWOT analysis
- Industry futures
- Screening and go/no-go decisions
- Summary and action points
- Workbook exercises

Learning outcomes

When you have read this chapter and undertaken the related exercises you will be able to:

- Define and describe your market or industry
- Assess the degree of competition in your market/industry and the likely effect on profitability
- Undertake a SWOT analysis on yourself and your competitors
- Review future trends in your industry and assess how they might affect you
- Critically evaluate whether your business idea matches your aspirations

Academic insights

3.1 Porter's Five Forces – assessing industry competitiveness

Case insights

3.1 Video gaming industry in India
3.2 Online dating
3.3 Temple & Webster
3.4 The internet market in China
3.5 Internet start-ups in Iran
3.6 Novo Nordisk
3.7 Bill Gates and Microsoft
3.8 Convergent US technology markets
3.9 Nuffnang

Sofa-bed Factory

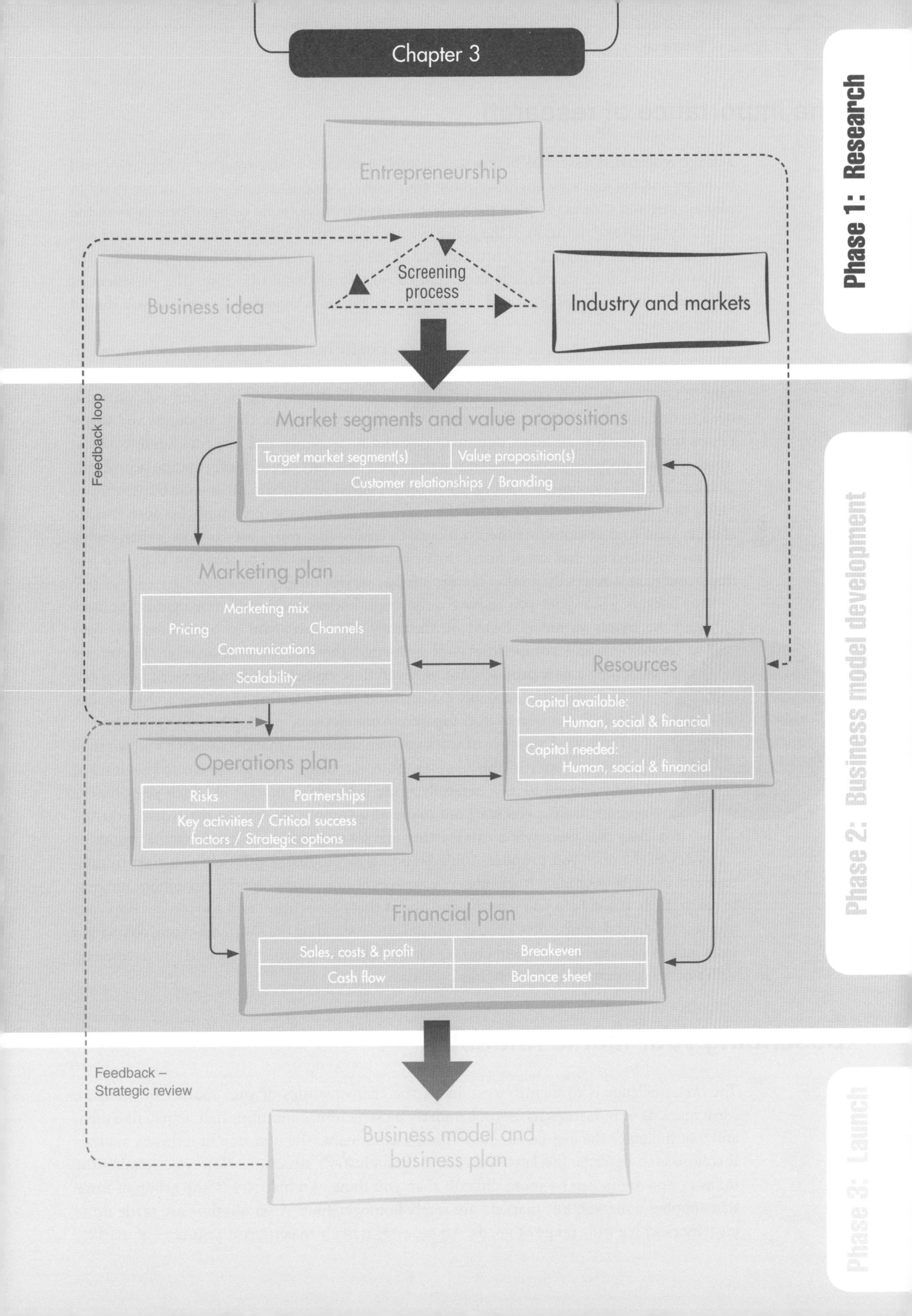

Chapter 3
Entrepreneurship
Business idea
Screening process
Industry and markets
Feedback loop
Market segments and value propositions
Target market segment(s)
Value proposition(s)
Customer relationships / Branding
Marketing plan
Marketing mix
Pricing
Channels
Communications
Scalability
Resources
Capital available:
Human, social & financial
Capital needed:
Human, social & financial
Operations plan
Risks
Partnerships
Key activities / Critical success factors / Strategic options
Financial plan
Sales, costs & profit
Breakeven
Cash flow
Balance sheet
Feedback –
Strategic review
Business model and business plan
Phase 1: Research
Phase 2: Business model development
Phase 3: Launch

The importance of research

Market research is essential before you launch a business. Just imagine being a football manager and not knowing anything about your team (your customers), who you are about to play against and how many players they are allowed to have (your competitors) or even the size of the pitch and duration of the game you are about to play (the nature of the market and industry). And then there is the little matter of the rules of the game (the laws affecting the industry). In such circumstances your chances of success would be slim. The President of Harvard Business School once said that if you thought knowledge was expensive, you should try ignorance.

As we have seen, you can either create opportunity or you can spot opportunity, but in both cases your creative skills must be linked to a market need. So, you need to find out about market need – who your customers might be and why they should buy from you. You also need to find out about your competitors – who they are and what their strengths and weaknesses might be. This all helps minimize risk and uncertainty and provides some basis on which to make decisions about marketing strategy. For a start-up, any information is probably of value, but the key question that needs to be answered is: why should anyone buy from you rather than from your competitors? If the answer to that question is simply because you are cheaper than your competitors then you need to ensure that your costs are lower than theirs. It is no coincidence that small firms thrive in markets where economies of scale are less important to customers than other factors such as service quality.

Your backers will expect you to have a thorough understanding of your market/industry and the trends within it. Based on this they will expect you to have identified your customers and competitors and estimated the size of your market. If you are launching a new product, not only will they expect it to actually work as you say, but they will also probably expect some market testing (field research) to gauge customer reaction to it, compared to competitors' products.

There are a number of ways you can undertake market research and we shall cover them later in this chapter; however, before you get down to this level of detail you need to look carefully at the industry or market in which you propose to operate. Unless you start out to create a completely new-to-the-world industry, it is likely that there will be an existing market or industry that sells similar goods or services to the ones you propose. Understanding this industry will help you start to fine-tune and evaluate your idea. It will give you an insight into your potential customers and how to reach them. It will help you identify and assess that competition and start to develop your business model and competitive strategy. Indeed, understanding the shortcomings of companies in an industry can sometimes yield new business opportunities which may lead you to come up with a better or completely different business idea.

> The Guardian Media Planet May 2015
>
> **Before you approach anyone with an idea you must do the research.**
>
> Peter Jones, serial entrepreneur

Describing your market/industry

The first challenge is to identify and define the characteristics of your market or industry. Most markets or industries have some underlying structural conditions that help define them and that influence the degree of competition within them. The first step in industry analysis therefore is to describe the key elements of the industry's structure. However, defining the industry you are in can be more difficult than you think. An industry is any group of firms that supplies a market, but markets are rarely homogeneous. After all, they are made up of customers with a wide range of needs. An industry is likely to comprise a number of markets or, more accurately, **market segments**. The competition within these segments can be very different, and as a result the profitability of individual companies within an industry can vary widely.

For example, the car industry comprises many market segments – hatchbacks, family cars, luxury cars, sports cars, SUVs etc. Do cars in each of these sectors compete against each other? Is Jaguar, a UK producer of luxury sedans and sports cars, a competitor of Honda, a Japanese producer of hatchbacks and family cars? There are clear market boundaries between segments and there is the question as to what extent a car and a car producer in one segment competes against another. Similarly, a local convenience or grocery store located, say, 10 miles from the nearest similar shop might not be competing directly against supermarkets, despite being in the food retail industry, because of its location. So, geographic boundaries to a market might also apply. The criterion here again is substitutability – are customers willing to travel to the supermarket? However, to some extent, markets and industries can overlap. For example, does the ready availability of communication apps such as Skype, WhatsApp and Facetime mean that it is somehow substituting for travel – and the computing industry therefore competing with the travel industry?

So, an industry is likely to comprise a number of markets. Drawing the boundaries of your industry and the market segments within it is therefore a question of judgement. It is an important judgement that will define who you think you compete with and, probably, the marketing strategies you then put in place. The judgement rests on an accurate identification of your customers, which we cover in the next chapter, and their willingness to buy similar products or services. This chapter outlines three commonly used ways of describing markets or industries, called typologies: life-cycle, concentration and geographic extent. All have implications for the firms within them and the opportunities they generate for newcomers.

Market/industry life cycle

The first set of typologies refer to the five stages in the **life cycle** of your market or industry (Figure 3.1).

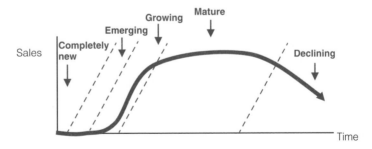

Figure 3.1 Market life cycles

1 Completely new (market paradigm shift)

This is the new market resulting from a market paradigm shift or radical innovation. The market is not proven and demand is very difficult to estimate. Processes and procedures are yet to be developed. There are no competitors.

Implications:

- High risk, but also potential for high returns
- Customers difficult to identify

- No competitors
- Gaining first-mover advantage very important
- Opportunity to dominate the market
- Likely to be high marketing costs (customers may not understand product/service benefits).

2 Emerging

This is a market where there is proven demand but the size of the market is still uncertain. The market is growing. Processes and procedures have still not become fully established. There are still no dominant brands or market leaders.

Implications:

- Few competitors
- Customers starting to be identified
- First-mover advantage still significant
- Opportunity to redefine processes and procedures that are not operating effectively
- Still opportunity to dominate the market
- Marketing costs still likely to be high
- Barriers to entry probably in the process of being established.

3 Growing

This is a market where there is proven and growing demand – market research would show it to be attractive. Processes and procedures are still developing as new competitors enter the market. Competition is fierce as companies battle to penetrate the market and gain market dominance. Dominant brands and market leaders are beginning to emerge at the same time as some companies are going out of business.

Implications:

- Growing number of competitors
- Product/service extensions likely to be emerging
- Buying patterns becoming established
- Aggressive marketing strategies in a fiercely competitive market
- Dominant brands beginning to emerge
- Competitive pricing
- Market looks good on paper, but entrants may be too late unless their product/service is based upon significant innovation.

BBC News Business 3 November 2011

It's always an opportunity when you see a big market that hasn't changed much.

Ning Li, founder Made.com

4 Mature

This is an established market with well-documented characteristics. It is large but growth is slow or non-existent. There are established processes and procedures, buying and repeat-purchasing patterns. Few new customers are entering the market. Competitors are established. There is limited innovation. Industry might be fragmented or consolidated (see page 75).

Implications:

- Well-established competitors (market might be fragmented or consolidated)
- Defensive pricing possible (meeting or beating new entrants)
- Difficult to break into market, competition strong

- Opportunity to innovate based upon existing product/service
- Opportunity to innovate based upon process or after-sales service
- Opportunity to innovate based upon established marketing processes.

5 Declining

This is a well-documented, declining market with established processes, procedures and buying patterns. There are declining numbers of customers and competitors. Product range is narrowing as weak lines are dropped. There is no innovation. Industry might be fragmented or consolidated (see below).

Implications:

- Market has a limited life expectancy
- Declining range of products
- Opportunity to consolidate market by becoming a dominant player (probably by buying out competitors)
- May be opportunity to establish niche if reducing competitors means demand is still high
- May be opportunity to cut costs by re-engineering production process to reflect reducing market demand
- May be opportunity to buy stock at 'distress prices' from companies going out of business and sell on at a profit
- Opportunity for radical product/service innovation.

It is usually easier to sell in an emerging or growing rather than a declining market, but it can be hard going if your market is completely new. Backers may tend to prefer emerging rather than completely new markets simply because it proves that demand does exist.

Market/industry concentration

The second set of typologies overlap with life cycles and refer to the concentration of competitors.

1 Fragmented

In a **fragmented market** there are a large number of competitors of about the same size, usually in a mature or declining industry.

Implications:

- Well-established competitors
- Competitive pricing, limited profitability
- Opportunity to consolidate industry and become market leader (probably by buying out competitors).

2 Consolidated

In a **consolidated market** there are a few, large competitors, usually in a mature or declining industry.

Implications:

- Well-established competitors
- Defensive pricing possible (meeting or beating new entrants)

- Barriers to entry are likely to be high
- Few entrepreneurial opportunities other than radical product or market innovation.

It is far easier to start up in a fragmented rather than a consolidated market. However, consolidation often happens as industries mature and decline, when some opportunities for mergers or acquisitions start to emerge. Start-ups are best advised to avoid consolidated markets, particularly when the established companies are competing primarily on price, because a new venture is unlikely to have either the experience or the economies of scale that established competitors have. What is more, the market may well be contracting. It is no coincidence that small firms tend to be few and far between in stable, mature, highly consolidated markets – unless they are introducing disruptive innovation that changes the nature of the market (see Chapter 2).

> Don't bother trying to compete in a busy market unless you can be the very best.
>
> *Gabriel David founder Luscombe Drinks Sunday Times 21 May 2017*

Market/industry geographic extent

The final set of overlapping typologies refer to the geographic extent of the market/industry.

1 Local, regional or national

This is often a new or emerging market; it may become global in time.
Implications:

- Gradual geographic roll-out allows the **marketing mix** to be fine-tuned, but at the expense of first-mover advantage
- Market dominance is easier in smaller geographic markets
- Some markets (e.g. technology-based) can spread geographically over time from developed to developing countries.

2 Global

This is a market that is international from the start. We look at it in greater detail in the next chapter.
Implications:

- Competitors quickly become established in foreign markets
- Opportunities exist for foreign start-ups where others have followed a local, regional or national strategy
- Internet-based new ventures have the opportunity to 'go global' at start-up
- 'Going global' at start-up can be very expensive
- Opportunity to expand on a country-by-country basis, varying product/service offering as appropriate.

It is traditionally easier to start up in a local market and gradually spread your market, but global start-ups are becoming easier to establish because of the internet, allowing products or services targeted at very specific, small customer segments to be sold globally. Sometimes thinking locally can also mean losing the window of opportunity for a good business idea by allowing competitors to gain a national or global foothold.

CASE
insight 🧳
3.1

Video gaming industry in India INDIA

Market research – identifying opportunities and challenges

India may now be a technology giant with its own billion-dollar companies such as Tata Consultancy Services (TCL), Wipro and HCL, and it is also home to big development centres for multinational companies such as Microsoft, Nvidia, Ubisoft, Zynga, Electronic Arts, Disney, Playdom, Sony and Digital Chocolate, but until recently it had not developed much of a home-grown video gaming industry. However, things are changing rapidly. It was in the late 1990s when companies like Dhruva Interactive and Indiagames started developing video games, mainly for the large multinationals who would subcontract specific graphics tasks, such as modelling racing cars, to local studios in India. These worked like factory production lines, exploiting India's cheap but skilled labour force. There were probably only a couple of dozen firms then, but by 2015 India had more than 250 video gaming companies, mostly recent start-ups with about half employing fewer than five people. The industry was worth about $890 million and growing rapidly. Inspired by the success of hit games such as *Doodle Jump*, *Angry Birds* and *Cut the Rope*, Indian companies are now both developing and marketing entire games themselves for local and international markets. The focus is on developing intellectual property rather than subcontracting.

> *In the last two years it has changed, mostly because of the emerging start-up community. We have Flipkart, which is India's Amazon, we have OlaCabs, which is India's Uber – these companies have shown that technology-driven concepts can flourish here. That has trickled down to the game development community, so we're seeing a lot of small studios springing up and taking risks. India has traditionally been a risk-averse society; we were told: 'if you don't take a job in a big company, you probably won't get married.' But the tech sector has opened up really quickly. Studios are now saying: if other tech start-ups are doing well, why can't gaming?*
> Abhinav Sarangi co-founder All In A Day's Play
> *The Guardian* 22 April 2015

This change is not only related to the culture within India, it is also to do with the democratization of game publishing and smartphone penetration. Today you can publish a game simply by becoming a developer registered with Apple or Google. And with an Android smartphone costing about £50, the increase in smartphones has been meteoric:

> *We took eight years to reach an installed base of 80 smartphones, and then this year we're adding 100 million more … We have the cheapest 3G in the world, and it's going to get cheaper because 4G is coming. We have very cheap Android smartphones coming in … Last year, India had about 1.2 billion downloads on Android. It's the fourth-largest market for Android.*
> Rajesh Rao http://venturebeat.com/2014/ March 2014

Founded in 1997, Dhruva Interactive is one of the early companies in this rapidly coming-of-age industry. The company still undertakes subcontract work on many well-known games that are published mainly by Western companies. However, it has also created its own games such as *Bazzle* and *Conga Bugs*, and its founder, Rajesh Rao, has started his own separate incubator, the Game Tantra Incubator, to invest in new game start-ups. Dhruva has two studios in Bangalore and employs more than 300 people. Founded in 2007, Yellow Monkey Studios has developed many games, including the tile-sorting puzzler *Socioball*, which features a map editor that allows players to create their own levels and then share them via Twitter. Founded in 2008, Gamiana Digital Entertainment publishes *Vinashi*, a multiplayer online strategy game based on Indian history. Launched in 2011, Reliance Games is already an international developer and publisher of games, specializing in movie licences such as *Hunger Games: Catching Fire* and *Pacific Rim*. 99Games, based in Udupi, has developed 15 games for both the domestic and global market, including *Star Chef*, a fast-moving cooking action game with 40,000 daily users. On The Couch, a small firm based in Mumbai, produced *Rooftop Mischief*. Other prominent gaming start-ups include HashCube Technologies, MadRat Games, Moonfrog Labs, Hashstash Studios, Rolocule Games, Octro, Growl Studios and All In A Day's Play.

Foreign giants are also starting to make games in India. The French company Ubisoft has been in Pune since 2008 with a large studio of more than 300 employees. Once just a subcontract studio, it is now making its own games such as the Indian smartphone music game *Just Dance Now*, tying up endorsement deals with Bollywood stars.

Easy-to-play arcade and casual games such as *Angry Birds*, *Candy Crush* and *Temple Run* dominate the Indian mobile market at around 85%. The market is driven by the growth in the mobile network. Games are targeted at this market because of the low entry cost for the value-conscious Indian customer. This gives smaller firms an edge because they can monitor user ratings and then alter the games quickly to reflect their interests. There are currently three constraints to the growth of the industry.

1 Payment methods – Barely 8% of Indians have credit cards and over 90% of mobile users are on prepaid contracts, meaning that the Western model of relying on customers to make seamless in-app purchases through online app stores does not work. Credit card remains the sole payment mechanism for iOS and Android systems. Also, the networks would struggle with the data load, because much of India's mobile infrastructure is still operating at 2G speeds; however, there are third-party wallet companies such as Paytm and MobiKwik that could be used to overcome the problem. Direct-operator billing is another answer to the problem, and Google has been trying to set up deals with Indian telecom companies, but so far without success. Yet another possibility would be to integrate direct-operator billing into in-app purchases, but all of this begs the second question.

2 Pricing – The average disposable income in India is low and the minimum Google in-app purchase threshold of £0.55 is just too high for the market – perhaps by a factor of 10! As a result, the ad-funded business model dominates the Indian gaming market, at least until a game becomes a 'hit' with customers. If a game is successful, income can also come from distribution

deals, selling the intellectual property of a game to a publisher and from brand licensing.

3 Funding – Like the movie industry, gaming is hit-driven, which means unknown start-ups have problems raising finance, with venture capitalists often expecting them to be profitable with a single game. They still tend to depend on subcontract work to finance the development of their own games. Founder of Hashstash, Sunil Kinshuk, started the company in 2011 with £1,000 of his own money and only by 2015 was in talks with venture capitalists to raise a further £50,000. However, in contrast, Gamiana raised just under $1 million in 2011 from the Indian Angel Network on the back of its successful *Jamia* and *Vanashi* games.

The video gaming industry is high risk but high reward, and India has a substantial knowledge infrastructure and a skilled, low-cost workforce to exploit it. If these three constraints can be removed, it may well explode.

Questions:

1 Using the typologies outlined above, how would you describe the Indian video gaming industry?
2 What are the strengths and weaknesses, threats and opportunities facing the industry?
3 Under what circumstances might this be an attractive market for a start-up?

CASE insight 3.2

Online dating GLOBAL

Market research – identifying opportunities and challenges

Mintel estimate that the online dating industry in Britain alone grew by 73.5% between 2009 and 2015, when it was thought to be worth £165 million, growing to more than £300 million in the next four years (*Sunday Times*, 8 February 2015). The market in the USA is far larger, estimated to be £1.3 billion ($2 billion), and the international potential is huge, with market growth in Eastern Europe, Russia, Asia and South America highlighted as being particularly attractive as the market

reaches the mature phase of its life cycle in other countries. It is little wonder then that there are hundreds of new websites and apps trying to cash in on this emerging market, raising large amounts of venture funding. It was estimated that in 2015 there were already more than 1,400 dating websites and apps. The trouble is that, with so many entrants, competition is fierce and the drop-out rate in terms of business failures is large.

Matthew Pitt, operations director at Global Personals, which is involved with more than 7,500 dating sites globally, warned:

If you are thinking of joining the industry now, you are very unlikely to be successful – unless you have very deep pockets and a differentiated dating offering. Nowadays it's a mature industry with a few large players dominating the mainstream markets and smaller independents doing OK because they've got a strong brand. The latter will find it increasingly tough going forward because they cannot match the investment in technology and resources that the larger sites can to keep their sites at the forefront.

BANANASTOCK

Huffington Post (UK) 26 October 2012

Typically, sites ask you to upload details of yourself, with photos and perhaps videos. They also ask you to submit a profile of the person you are looking for. They then match couples using computer algorithms that may allow for factors such as location, age, social demographics, religion, sexual orientation and so on. Some sites use psychometric personality tests to help match people; for example, Match.com uses the Myers-Briggs test. In recent years, niche sites have been set up to cater for particular groups of people. The range of niche characteristics is wide, for example, disabilities, professions, sexual orientation, lifestyle activities, even dietary requirements. However, the sites are driven by volume of traffic, and the more specialist the niche, the smaller the community being served.

Internet business models will be outlined in more detail in the next chapter. The dating industry uses three of them to generate income. The most common is a subscription or fee-based model. Others use the 'freemium' model, offering free sign-up but a subscription or fee (perhaps using prepaid virtual credits) to contact other people. Many sites also generate income from advertising. The sites may also offer additional services for a fee, such as sending real or virtual gifts or undertaking background checks.

Established companies in the industry include Tinder, Match.com, eHarmony, Plenty of Fish and Zoosk, and niche sites such as Mature Dating and Christian Mingle.com. Despite established competitors, there are still new entrants to the industry. The challenge they face is to find how they can be different from their competitors. One such entrant is Happn, which was launched in France in

2014 by Didier Rappaport. It raised $8 million venture funding from DN Capital to allow it to open sites in the UK, Spain, Italy, USA and Mexico within a year of its launch. Happn's USP (unique selling proposition) is that it locates nearby potential partners and allows members to track them in real time – for example, somebody passing close by, using the same roads on their daily commute to work or regularly visiting a particular cafe or bar – and ask them for a meeting. It uses a 'freemium' business model (which is free to women) with a charge for getting in touch. Another 2015 US entrant to the industry was Whim, which raised $200,000 from the founders' family and friends, and the seed fund 500 Startups. Founded by Katey Nilan and Eve Peters, this app aims to speed up the process of dating and eliminate the need for messaging, waiting and planning. Users indicate who they like and when they are free, and the app then arranges times and places for the various meetings. A third US entrant in 2015 was Bumble, whose USP is that only female users can start conversations with prospective partners.

Only time will tell whether any of these new online dating sites and apps will succeed. That will depend on a number of factors. For example, how significant is their USP to customers? How easily is it copied and how will the major competitors react if they are successful? How important is market scale and brand? But with the industry already fragmenting and consolidating, the competition is fierce. Although the potential rewards are high, so are the risks.

Questions:

1   How important is geographic location in the online dating market?
2   Under what circumstances might this be an attractive market for a start-up?
3   What do you think are the important things these start-ups need to do in their first year of existence?
4   If the three new companies highlighted are successful, what might be the competitive reaction they face? How might they combat or react to this?
5   Would you like to have been the founder of these businesses? Give the reasons for your answer.

Market research

I would have spent more time researching my idea. Although I couldn't afford it at the time, it would have saved me a lot of effort if I had recognized that customers wanted top quality gourmet coffee through machines rather than the instant product that was part of my original business plan.

You need to find as much relevant information as you can about your markets, your industry and your customers and competitors. There are two ways you can do this – desk research and field research. Desk research provides valuable general background information, while field research provides specific information. You should be able to obtain all of the market and industry information discussed so far through desk research, although you may have to use your judgement to analyse it in the way you want. The main characteristics of desk and field research are summarized in Table 3.1.

Desk research

Desk research is what it says – research that you can do from a desk, at home or in a library, using the computer and internet or journals and so on. Desk research is cheap, quick to do, and is usually good for getting background information. However, it will not be specific to your business, can be incomplete or inaccurate and may well be out of date. Information on markets, sectors and industries is published in newspapers, trade magazines, industry surveys and reports, trade journals or directories, many of which will be available on the internet. There are websites that provide all sorts of information but ultimately the prime source of information in the UK is the British Library, where most national and regional economic and business data and information is housed. Desk research can provide information on product developments, customer needs or

Table 3.1 *Characteristics of desk and field research*

	Desk research	Field research
Uses	Background information on: • Industries and markets • Environmental and market trends • Competitors • Customers • Distribution chains • Supply chains • Product development • National and regional economic data	Specific information on: • Customer/consumer needs, causes for satisfaction and dissatisfaction • Consumer reaction to products in development • Direct trial of competitors' product/service performance • Customer reactions to competitors' product/service performance • Premises investigation
Sources/techniques	• Newspapers and magazines • Trade magazines, journals and directories • Industry surveys and reports • Government reports • National statistics	• Observation and discussion • Face-to-face interviews • Focus groups • Telephone interviews • Text, email or postal questionnaires
Advantages	• Cheap • Quick • Good for background information, particularly on industries and markets	• Reflects your needs • You control quality • Up to date
Disadvantages	• Not specific to your business • Can be out of date • Can be incomplete or inaccurate	• Can be expensive and/or time consuming • Competitors may find out what you are up to • Can be complicated (e.g. sampling, question structure)

characteristics, competitors and market trends. However, for many start-ups local information is of far more importance than regional or national information, and that might come from Chambers of Commerce and other local sources of help and advice.

 The *Guide to UK Sources of Help, Advice, Information and Funding* is available on the companion website: www.macmillanihe.com/burns-nvc-2e. An additional guide for Australian readers, produced by Dr Russell Manfield, is also provided.

> If you ask me how we find new markets, the answer is research, research, research ... For us research is critical when it comes to opening new outlets. We put a lot of work into demographics and social indicators and really know our business. But they can fail: we put a store in Dewsbury, West Yorkshire, four years ago, everything looked good, we did the groundwork, but what the figures didn't show was that our site was in the middle of the town's devoutly Muslim centre. They ate only halal meat, and they certainly weren't eating pizza. We got it wrong and we had to shut the store.
>
> Stephen Hemsley CEO Domino's Pizza Sunday Times 23 May 2004

Clarifying who will be your customers should enable you to better focus your promotion and marketing efforts. It might also help you to identify both new customers and, eventually, new products or services. Desk-based market research should help you to estimate the size and growth of your market. You might intend to sell your product/service to private or business customers. It should help you to understand the profile of both these types of customers. A private customer profile might include personal characteristics (demographics) such as age, gender, socioeconomic group, occupation, geographic location and other characteristics of the home, stage in family life cycle, and so on. Similarly, an industrial profile might include the type of business, size, sector/industry, location, nature of technology, creditworthiness and so on. It might involve understanding why, where and when customers buy, the structure of established distribution channels and the nature of economic and other environmental trends that might affect the industry. Remember, you need to understand what the conventions in a market or industry are – even if you intend to try to change them. Clearly, while you might be able to find this information for an established market/industry, it is far more problematic for new or emerging markets.

It is just as important to know who your competitors are. Desk research should provide not only names but also information on competitors' product/service offerings, size, profitability, even their operating methods (e.g. whether restaurants are takeaway, self-service etc.). However, judgement is always needed. For example, a pizza restaurant may face competition from a whole range of other local restaurants, not just those offering pizza. Understanding why customers buy from competitors gives a further insight into the needs of customers and ideas about how you might combat competition.

Field research

Field research involves going out and collecting new information about customers and competitors that is not publicly available. Informal field research can be invaluable, particularly for start-ups dealing directly with the public. Visiting competitors at their place of business, perhaps buying their product or service and talking to other customers, will give an insight into how they operate. For retailers, location is obviously very important. Once prospective premises have been identified, check out the local trade. Find out how many and what type of customers pass by the location. Are shops in the immediate vicinity an advantage or a disadvantage? The world's biggest retailer, Walmart, was founded by Sam Walton who famously went to rival K-Mart stores with a notepad and pencil to note down exactly what they did and how they did it, and then improved on it. Location can be important for other businesses, for example, proximity to customers or a workforce. Many start-ups locate where the owner-manager happens to live. Some locate where the owner-manager wants to live. Neither is a positive decision unless there are sufficient customers.

Field research can provide a lot of valuable and unique information. Simple observation and discussion will go a long way without costing much other than time. However, its informality means that the samples of people you approach may not be representative of your customer base and your questioning may be less than precise. To be more reliable, you have to ensure that your respondents represent your potential customers. You also need to structure your questions so that the subject areas are covered comprehensively and consistently, so that there is no ambiguity and you can compare answers from one respondent to another. More detailed field research can involve conducting face-to-face individual or group interviews, telephone surveys or administering text, email or postal questionnaires. The main characteristics of these techniques are summarized in Table 3.2.

Table 3.2 Techniques for field research

	Personal interview and focus group	Telephone interview	Questionnaire
Quality of information	Very good	Good	Good
Quantity of information	Good	Fair	Good
Speed of collection	Good	Very good	Poor
Likely response rate	Good	Good	Poor
Cost (money and/or time)	High	Fair	Fair

Questions should be in a logical sequence, moving from general to specific, from factual to opinion or behaviour based, from least sensitive to most sensitive. They should try to influence respondents as little as possible. Questions should not 'lead' respondents by implying an answer to the question. And the design of your questionnaire should facilitate interpretation and possible data processing. A very simple piece of advice is to always test out a questionnaire before using it 'for real'.

The construction of questionnaires in field research involves using different types of questions for different purposes. There are four basic types of questions.

- **Closed question** – This requires a specific yes/no answer (often by ticking a box) and is best used where factual information is required. It can be used to build quantitative data on responses. For example, 95% of respondents said 'yes'. It takes little time for respondents.
- **Multiple choice question** – This is where the respondent has a number of options from which to choose. It is also best used for factual information. For example, 'Select the frequency of your monthly visits to this shopping centre' (respondents would then normally be presented with options and asked to tick the appropriate box).
- **Scaled question** – This is where respondents are asked to evaluate or rate some characteristic on a quantitative scale. For example, 'Rate the quality of service on a scale of 1 (very poor) to 5 (very good)' (often by ticking a box). It takes relatively little time for respondents, but predefines the dimensions of measurement.
- **Open question** – This requires the respondent to amplify an answer, often expressing an opinion. It is frequently used in conjunction with a closed question to provide some insight or depth to quantitative data, such as when seeking a better understanding of buyer behaviour. It takes time for respondents to answer.

However, sometimes, as we observed in the previous chapter, the only sure way of knowing whether the idea will make a lucrative business is to try it out – launch the business but minimize your risks in doing so. The more original the business idea, the less likely market research is to yield an insight into demand, simply because customers do not understand how the product or service might be used. For some start-ups the easiest and cheapest way to undertake market research is to test-market, for example, using focus groups or trying a pop-up shop. Another approach is called **lean start-up** (Academic insight 4.4), where start-up costs are kept to a minimum and customer reaction is closely monitored. However, this can still be an expensive way of doing market research if things go wrong, and some basic market research is probably essential for just about any start-up.

CASE insight 3.3

Temple & Webster

AUSTRALIA

© Temple & Webster

Spotting gaps in the market

Temple & Webster was founded in 2011 by Mark Coulter, Adam McWhinney, Conrad Yiu, and Brian Shanahan, all former colleagues and senior executives at eBay Australia and Newscorp Australia's digital division. The four shared the same ambition of business ownership and, unlike many people, decided to do something about it, starting with researching opportunities in online retail. According to Telsyte, a specialist e-commerce research house, online retail sales were expected to exceed AUD30 billion by 2016 – twice the level in 2011. At the time, existing online retailers such as eBay and Amazon tended to be 'horizontal providers' – offering everything but not specializing in any particular category. The co-founders had done a lot of research into these shopping categories during their time at eBay, and discovered that there was significant demand in the homewares category but very few providers. Only some 3% of retailers had migrated to online sales. The four decided that this was the market they would target. And so, homeware and furniture retailer Temple & Webster was born in 2011.

They decided that the company would be the 'expert' in this category and set about creating a brand that represented this characteristic: one that was a little old fashioned and concerned with attention to detail, showing customers the care they wanted to provide. The founders wanted a brand name that was Australian and spoke to Australian heritage and came across the names of William Temple and John Webster, two furniture designers who were commissioned in the 1820s to design two

© Temple & Webster

ceremonial chairs for the governor of New South Wales, Lachlan Macquarie. They developed that brand image using 'beautiful' print advertising, television and online video that attempted to create an emotional link with existing and potential customers.

The website would offer high discounts on premium exclusive products using a subscription model – a members-only site. The idea was to create an element of exclusivity and capture people interested in the homewares category, rather than just a particular product. Temple & Webster operated under this model with great success, going on to acquire the Australian subsidiary of online US homewares retailer Wayfair and Australian furniture manufacturer and retailer Milan Direct in mid-2015. In December 2015 the company was listed on the

Australian Securities Exchange as Temple & Webster Group.

By April 2016, the company had merged all brands and operations under the Temple & Webster banner and moved to an open e-commerce platform, doing away with its previous membership model and becoming Australia's largest online furniture and homewares retailer with around 130,000 products. CEO Mark Coulter says that at the time Temple & Webster began, no one was doing what the founders had in mind.

When the four of us started Temple & Webster, none of us came from retail. We knew the power of content in engaging audiences and we noticed that no-one was really doing homewares well. Homewares are emotional – you want your home to be beautiful. No-one was tapping into that, so we thought, 'How do we do it online'? From day one the focus was on the experience customers have when they visit the site and about taking beautiful products and making Australian homes more beautiful.

He attributes the success of the business to hard work, but says there are still growth opportunities to explore.

We want to push ourselves. We are thinking about the next horizon of growth with things like showrooms, our trade and commercial division and online education. Those things will push us to the next horizon and truly make us a national household name for beautiful furniture and homewares solutions.

www.sparke.com.au 16 October 2014

Visit the website: www.templeandwebster.com.au

Questions:

1 What do you think was the reaction of established bricks-and-mortar furniture retailers to the success of Temple & Webster?
2 What strengths and weaknesses does Temple & Webster have compared to them?
3 How might the company combat this competitive reaction?

Estimating your market size

Estimating the size of a new market created by disruptive innovation or market paradigm shift can be almost impossible. However, as we have just observed, even estimating the size of a segment of an existing market can be difficult. The market itself might be growing or declining and within it some segments might be growing while others are declining. Market research can provide only so much data. If you wish to introduce a new smartphone app, the fact that there are over 1 billion smartphones worldwide is not entirely relevant. That market is growing rapidly. However, your app might be in English, which limits the market size, and it might be developed for only one operating system. Then there is the question of the channels through which the app will be sold. All of these factors limit the market that you are attacking – even before the question of whether you are likely to achieve your target market penetration.

You can measure a market size in either value or volumes (units), but you need to distinguish between the different types of market shown in Figure 3.2.

1 **Potential market** is the size of a general market that might be interested in buying a product (e.g. one billion smartphones);
2 **Total available market (TAM)** is the size of your prospective market – those in the potential market who might be interested in buying your particular product. This reflects the total sales of competing products (e.g. English apps for a particular operating system);
3 **Served available market (SAM)** is the size of the **target market segment** you wish to serve within the TAM (e.g. particular app function);
4 **Penetrated market** is the size of the SAM you capture.

You can probably estimate the size of the first three markets using desk research. Your served available market is the market segment(s) of the total available market you are targeting,

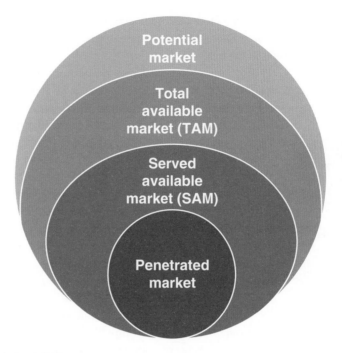

Figure 3.2 *Market size definitions*

given any restrictions such as demographics, geography, language, technology etc. However, in estimating SAM do consider adjacent markets from which customers might be persuaded to switch if your product/service proves successful. Your market share is therefore your penetrated market divided by SAM. If you are seeking funding, your backers will expect you to try to describe both your TAM and SAM and estimate their size and the trends within them. They will expect you to be able to explain and justify how you will achieve your penetrated market.

Identifying your competitors

The identification of your competitors is of equal importance to estimating your market size. You should be able to name them. There are three types of competitors.

- **Direct competitors** – those offering similar or identical products or services. These are the most important because they compete directly. You need to understand just how you are different and better than them, and how you will convince their customers to switch to you.
- **Indirect competitors** – those offering close substitutes. Where you have an innovative product or service you may have no direct competitors but will still need to persuade customers using the 'inferior' competitor offering to switch.
- **Future competitors** – those who could enter your market in the future. If your new venture is successful it will attract competitors. You need to think who they might be and how they might be countered.

Desk research might enable you to evaluate existing competitors in terms of their product/service offering, size, profitability, operating methods and distribution channels. You need to form an assessment of the strengths and weaknesses of competitors' products/services compared to your own. Ultimately you will have to make some judgements about whether they are attacking the same customer segments as you and the quality of their value proposition. How are you different? How sustainable is your competitive advantage? We shall return to these issues in the next chapter.

You should also assess the influence competitors have over the market – the level of industry competitiveness. Porter's **Five Forces** can be a useful vehicle for looking at an industry's structure, assessing the degree of competition in it and, hence, its profit potential (see Academic insight 3.1). Central to this is the rivalry between competing firms. This is based upon the number of competitors (fragmented vs. consolidated), industry growth (point in life cycle) and the degree of product differentiation. The relative power of your customers (the fewer there are, the higher their buying power) or your suppliers (the fewer there are, the higher their power) in your market is important. If you are selling to the big supermarket chains they will squeeze your margins. Can competitors set up easily in your industry or are there barriers to entry? As well as the threat of new entrants to a market, there is also the threat of substitute products. How likely are customers to stop buying your product/service?

Jeff Weiner CEO LinkedIn Sunday Times 14 July 2013

The ability to play your own game rather than playing the game of a competitor is exactly where you want to be as a company.

Two important points stand out from Porter's analysis. Firstly, the higher the degree of differentiation and inbuilt **switch costs** – the costs of switching to another similar product/service – the more likely your business is to succeed. Secondly, there is the question of the number of competitors you face (concentration). Typically, the fewer competitors you face, the more likely you are to succeed – although this might mean there is a very limited market for your product/service. However, this generalization depends on the market power of these competitors. If you are entering a market where there are few competitors, they might combine to deter your entry. You need to think very carefully before entering a market dominated by a few big companies because they will have well-established market positions and the resources to fight off new entrants.

With disruptive innovation or market paradigm shift it may just be that there is no real, direct competition – at least until new entrants appear in the market. This brings us to looking at the barriers to entry in the market and, in particular, the legal protection your product/service might enjoy (Chapter 9). Again, if you are seeking funding, your backers will expect you to have a thorough understanding of your competitors (real or otherwise) and their strengths and weaknesses compared to yours. After all, you will be battling against them in the market.

ACADEMIC insight 3.1

Porter's Five Forces: assessing industry competitiveness

Porter (1985) developed a useful structural analysis for looking at an industry, assessing the degree of competition within it and therefore its profit potential. He described five forces at play.

1 **Competitive rivalry** – The competitive rivalry of an industry is central to the analysis. Rivalry will depend on the number and size of firms within an industry and their concentration (fragmented vs. consolidated), its newness and growth (point in life cycle) and therefore its attractiveness in terms of profit and value added together with intermittent overcapacity. Crucially important is the extent of product differentiation, brand identity and switch costs. The greater the competitive rivalry, the less the ability of a firm to charge a high price.

2 **Threat of substitutes** – How likely are customers to stop buying your product/service? This revolves around the relative price performance of substitutes, the switch costs and the propensity of the customer to switch, for example, because of changes in tastes or fashion. The greater the threat of substitutes, the less the ability of the firm to charge a high price. So, for example, a small firm selling a poorly differentiated product in a price-sensitive fashion market would find it difficult to charge a high price.

3 **Threat of new entrants** – Barriers to entry keep out new entrants to an industry. These can arise because of legal protection (patents and so on), economies of scale, proprietary product differences, brand identity, access to distribution, government policy, switch costs, capital costs and so forth. Switch costs are the costs of switching to another product. A firm whose product is protected by patent or copyright may feel that it is relatively safe from competition. The greater the possible threat of a new entry to a market, the lower the bargaining power and control over price of the firm within it.

4 **Power of buyers** – This is determined by the relative size of buyers or customers and their concentration. A few large buyers/customers will have higher buying power than many small buyers/

customers. It is influenced by the volumes they purchase, the information they have about competitors or substitutes, switch costs and their ability to backward integrate or develop their own source of supply. The extent to which the product they are buying is differentiated in some way also affects relative buying power. The greater the power of the buyers, the weaker the bargaining position of the firm selling to them. So, for example, if buyers are large firms, in concentrated industries, buying large volumes with good price information about a relatively undifferentiated product with low switch costs, they will be in a strong position to keep prices low. Thus, if you are selling to the big supermarket chains they will squeeze your margins.

5 **Power of suppliers** – This is also determined by the relative size of firms and the other factors mentioned above – the fewer there are, the higher their power. So, for example, if suppliers are large firms in concentrated industries, with well-differentiated products that are relatively important to the small firms buying them, then those small firms are in a weak position to keep prices, and therefore their costs, low.

Porter, M.E. (1985) *Competitive Advantage, Creating and Sustaining Superior Performance*, New York: Free Press.

CASE insight 3.4

The internet market in China CHINA

Market research – identifying opportunities and challenges

Despite its recent slowdown, the Chinese economy grew at just under 10% a year for over 30 years, overtaking Japan in 2010 to become the world's second-largest economy. It is expected to overtake the USA within the next five years. New ventures and the SME sector have fuelled a significant part of that growth, and nowhere has this been more evident than in trade conducted on the internet. The internet has exploded in China, and with it the opportunity to do business in new ways with customers who have been inadequately served in the past. It is estimated that the e-commerce market in China is now well over £300 billion, rivalling the USA's in size

and many times larger than Britain's and Japan's, even combined. But the relatively underdeveloped nature of China's existing markets has meant that, rather than being a disruptive innovation as in the West, in China these internet companies have frequently filled a void, with relatively little competition. Western companies entering China have often been impeded by legal and cultural constraints. The Chinese internet companies began by copying Western models, but soon started to adapt to local needs and develop their own characteristics. And highly educated, overseas returnee entrepreneurs, often scientists and engineers trained in the West, have been at the forefront of starting up technology ventures.

As many Western firms have found, doing business in China is not easy. They have faced many bureaucratic institutional barriers in a country where there is heavy state intervention. China was ranked 91 out of 181 by the World Bank in terms of difficulty of doing business (World Bank, 2012). The report stated that it takes Chinese entrepreneurs on average 13 procedures and around 33 days to start a business, compared to an OECD average of 5 procedures and 12 days. Although Chinese entrepreneurs may be able to navigate China's institutional environment more easily than Westerners, they can still be hindered by the weak property rights and need good 'connections' at the right level in government.

The e-commerce industry in China is now dominated by three internet conglomerates: Alibaba, Baidu and Tencent. China has a high degree of state intervention and control, and these companies work closely with state agencies. The state regulates much of the internet in China, and these companies are able to spread the costs of regulation over a broad revenue base. This means that the nature of their market dominance is different to the internet market in the West. They seem to be able to easily resist foreign competition within China. What is more, they seem to prefer to build their own versions of popular new internet services (often copied from the West), rather than buying out competitors, as tends to happen in the West. It is feared that this will discourage innovative Chinese start-ups, not least because finance might be hard to come by.

Alibaba Group was founded by Jack Ma in 1999. It is China's equivalent of eBay or Amazon, whose combined turnover it now exceeds. However, Alibaba is simply a merchant connecting buyers with suppliers on the internet. It has no warehouses and does not operate a logistics network. Merchants arrange shipping through independent couriers. Alibaba's shares are now traded in the USA. The Group includes online retail sites, shopping search engines, payment systems, e-commerce businesses, business-to-business portals and cloud computing services. The original Alibaba continues as a global business-to-business site – now the largest in the world – that is often used by overseas businesses to tap into China's manufacturers. Alongside it is Taobao (similar to eBay), China's largest consumer-to-consumer and business-to-consumer online shopping platform. It also offers services that allow others to trade – instant messaging, payment systems and logistics. Profits mainly come from advertising. Its sister site, Taobao Mall, or Tmall, (similar to Amazon), is a huge online 'shopping mall' where only professional sellers are supposed to be allowed. However, in 2016 the US government put it on a blacklist of sites known for the sale of counterfeit goods and the violation of intellectual property rights. The Alibaba Group also has Juhuasuan, a shopping website specializing only in 'flash sales', and launched eTao,

a comparison shopping site. Alibaba acquired China Yahoo! through an exchange of shares in 2005, enabling it to offer a portal with news, email and search facilities (Yahoo! remains a major shareholder). As a direct result of competition from Alibaba, eBay withdrew from China in 2006.

Tencent was founded in 1998 by Ma Huateng and Zhang Zhidong and is the fourth-largest internet company in the world, after Google, Amazon and eBay. It started life as a copy of the ICQ chatroom, targeting young people, but has expanded into other areas, including social networks, web portals, e-commerce and multiplayer online games. It also sells virtual goods, such as dresses for avatars or weapons for online games, that are bought with virtual money (Q coins) that account holders buy for real money. It is rapidly expanding into smartphone services with offerings such as WeChat. Tencent derives income from a wide range of sources including advertising, products (real and virtual) and virtual and mobile services.

Baidu was founded in 2000 by Robin Li and Eric Xu (both returning Chinese nationals) and offers a range of web services such as Chinese-language search engines for websites, audio files, images and videos, similarly to Google, as well as hosting an encyclopaedia that is similar to Wikipedia. It claims to be the number one search engine in China. Importantly, it offers search services for government information and laws. Baidu Youa is a shopping and e-commerce site and Baidu Movies allows TV programmes, videos and movies to be downloaded. It also has a social networking service called Baidu Space, as well as offering cloud computing facilities. Baidu derives its income mainly from advertising models such as pay-for-placement and pay-per-click.

There are, of course, many other Chinese internet companies, many which copy Western businesses. Sina Weibo is a copy of Twitter but it allows users to attach comments, pictures and videos to their messages. Like Twitter, it has recruited thousands of celebrities to use its service. Sina Weibo worked closely with regulators when it was set up and, as a result, it can quickly stop certain users from logging on and blocking posts containing certain terms. Youku is a copy of YouTube, but mixed with Hulu and Netflix. While individuals can post videos, much of its content is made professionally by television companies or the company itself. Youku needed several licences to start up and has had to develop its own 'monitoring system', with editors viewing all clips before posting. However, it is interesting, but perhaps not surprising given the level of state intervention and control, that the dominant Western internet companies such as Google, Amazon, eBay and Twitter have not been able to secure the Chinese market. The question is whether there is space for more local start-ups.

Questions:

1 How and why is the Chinese internet market different to that in the West?

2 What opportunities exist in the Chinese market for internet start-ups? What are the threats?

3 Explain when and why global, national, regional and/or local market structures and conditions might be important to a start-up.

4 What level of industry or market analysis should you undertake for your start-up?

Source: World Bank (2012) *Doing Business 2013: Smarter Regulations for Small and Medium-sized Enterprises*, Washington, DC: World Bank Publications.

CASE insight 3.5

Internet start-ups in Iran   IRAN

Market research – identifying opportunities and challenges

In 2013 *The Economist* said that the most promising overseas markets for e-commerce would be 'low-trust, underbanked emerging economies' (*The Economist*, 23 March 2013). On these criteria the internet market in Iran must rank high for opportunity. In 2011 it had extremely slow internet and only patchy 3G coverage. By 2017 there were three 4G providers. Because of religious restrictions and international sanctions having been lifted relatively recently, doing business in Iran can be difficult, but it has not stopped a spate of e-commerce start-ups. Internet and smartphone usage is now very high in Iran, with more than half of its 80 million population having access to the internet and smartphones, and some 70% of its population under 35 years old. Indeed, *Internet World* estimates that there are 46 million internet users in Iran – representing almost half the total number in the entire Middle East. Internet speeds can still be a problem because of restricted bandwidths, and there is still online censorship blocking social media sites such as Facebook, Twitter and YouTube, on which most apps rely. Like China, Iran has set up its own national internet and search engine to try to control access to the web and communications are monitored and filtered by the Supreme Council of Virtual Space. Most Western sites remain blocked. However, Iranians can get around blocked addresses by using virtual private networks (VPNs) such as Hide My Ass! (Case insight 4.12). E-commerce can also face the problem that Iran is isolated from the outside world financially and Iranians do not have access to international credit cards; however, they do have Iranian bank debit cards, which work online within Iran.

The Rouhani government now offers grants to knowledge-based companies. It has seen the potential for internet start-ups to help solve the country's dependency on oil and help provide jobs, particularly for Iranian youth who face an unemployment rate of 30%.

Many Iranian internet start-ups are clones of western ones. **Digikala** is an online Iranian e-commerce site similar to Amazon. Founded by two brothers, Hamid and Saeid Mohammadi, in 2007, it has become the biggest e-commerce platform in the Middle East with some 750,000 visitors each day and over 2.3 million subscribers. Almost 90% of Iran's e-commerce takes place on the site. It was launched from a small rented office in Tehran with a group of seven people, offering only two products – mobile phones and digital cameras. Today, it has 760 employees and is operating in more than 20 Iranian cities, shipping more than 4,000 orders a day. One of Digikala's local competitors is **Bamilo**, a joint venture between South Africa's MTN telecom company and Germany's Rocket Internet, which also started a site similar to eBay called **Mozando**. As sanctions are lifted, Hamid Mohammadi does not see Amazon as a threat, as Digikala is too well established:

I don't think Amazon is a threat to us. Even if they do see Iran as so big a market, they would have to establish a Persian-language Amazon. I think lifting sanctions would be more of an opportunity for people like us than a threat … The situation in Iran is quite exceptional, there is a huge market for start-ups, something you can't easily find in other countries, and maybe that's why so many of the Iranian diaspora are returning to Iran.

Another western clone is called Snapp. This is an Iranian version of Uber. Founded in 2014 by Shahram Shahkar, a graduate of Manchester University, UK, it now has some 10,000 drivers and five million registered users in Tehran and two other cities. Shahkar recently launched Snapp One, offering a female-only driver service and Snapp VIP, offering Maseratis and Porsches for richer clients.

> *I knew what I was coming back to. We have restrictions but, at the same time, we have ways to access pretty much everything.*
>
> *Sunday Times* 21 May 2017

Aparat is an Iranian version of YouTube. Five million videos a day are watched on the site and it gets about 150 million hits a month. It recently introduced a new free-of-charge service called Filimo, a version of Netflix. Founded by Mohammad Javad Shakouri Moghadam in 2005, it is part of **Sabaldea**, a company that is also behind a number of other successful internet projects, including **Cloob.com**, a Persian-language social networking site with over 3 million users, and **Mihanblog.com**, a free blog hosting service. Sabaldea was launched with a staff of 3 and now has some 65 employees. As sanctions are lifted, Shakouri Moghadam hopes that many of its users will stay loyal:

> *Of course the absence of YouTube here has helped us to grow, but even if the filtering were lifted our emphasis on original content means we will be less affected.*

Takhfifan is an Iranian version of the deal-of-the-day website Groupon, offering discounts on a range of products

Nazanin Daneshvar

and services, from restaurants and coffee shops to theatres and concert tickets. Takhfifan claims to have over a million email subscribers and offers 20 to 25 deals a day. Founded in 2011 by Nazanin Daneshvar, who left her job in a German investment bank to return to Iran, together with her sister, it now has some 60 employees:

> *Four years ago, people in Iran didn't know what start-ups were or they associated them with fraud, but now they are taken seriously and people show trust.*
>
> *The Observer* 31 May 2015

NetBarg is Takhfifan's main local competitor. It was founded by Ali Reza Sadeghian, a graduate of Colombia Business School, USA. He sees the potential for internet start-ups in Iran as huge.

> *Other countries have far less challenges but we have less competition.*
>
> *Sunday Times* 21 May 2017

Questions:

1   Why is Iran an attractive market for internet start-ups? Explain.
2   How and why is the Iranian internet market different to the market in the West? How is it different to China's?
3   What are the challenges facing an internet start-up in Iran?
4   What might be the effect on these businesses if or when Western competitors enter the Iranian market?

SWOT analysis

Once you have looked at the market and industry you will be entering you can start to assess the strengths and weaknesses of your product or service against those of competitors. You can extend this to look at the strengths and weaknesses of your business compared to your competitors. Ultimately, however, your interest in market and industry analysis is about trying to predict the future – the threats and opportunities you might face. This is the classic **SWOT analysis** (strengths, weaknesses, opportunities and threats), which seeks to identify the overlap between the business environment and a firm's resources: in other words, a match between the strategic or core competencies, capabilities and resources you and your business have and market opportunities and threats that you face.

The process therefore starts with the identification of your own strengths (competencies and capabilities), matching them to the opportunities that you have spotted in the market. You also need to identify your weaknesses and plan for how they will be countered. Some of these will be more serious than others and some you will have more control over than others. Your market/industry analysis should inform you of the strengths and weaknesses of competitors as well as the opportunities and the threats that you face. Most opportunities also carry associated threats. Threats are part of the risks any business faces. They may be classified according to their seriousness and probability of occurrence (Chapter 10). A view of the overall attractiveness of a market is based upon the opportunities it offers balanced by the threats that it poses, given your strengths and weaknesses.

One of the outcomes of this analysis is that it may get you to question your original business idea and its viability, simply because you do not have the competencies and capabilities to take it forward or because the threats posed by competitors are too great. The whole process is an art rather than a science. There is no prescriptive approach. To undertake a SWOT analysis brutal honesty is required. And it means listening to people with different opinions about you and the market/industry you are thinking of entering.

Industry futures

The weakness with the SWOT analysis is that it can focus too much on the current market and industry situation. It does not provide you with any tools to help you look at the future, which is where your real interest lies. Unless there are structural reasons, current levels of profitability in an industry are unlikely to be a good predictor of the future because competitors are likely to enter an attractive industry. So, you need to understand the current industry and market structures and then look at how they might change in the future.

Some of the techniques we used to find a business idea in the previous chapter can equally be applied to how your industry might look in, say, five years' time, after you have entered the market.

- The PESTEL analysis can be used to identify the future influences on the industry (you might have already done this).
- You can then apply these influences to the broad trends you have identified through research into the industry. Is the industry expanding or contracting? Is it consolidating or fragmenting? Is competition intensifying or are products becoming more differentiated?
- The futures thinking or scenario planning technique can then be used to build up a scenario of how direct and indirect competitors might react to your entry into the market and where future competitors might come from. How will all this affect the industry? How will this affect you?
- You can then brainstorm to explore how you might react to these trends and competitors. What strategies might you adopt? Will you need to modify or change your product/service idea? Will you need to identify and enter new markets?

CASE insight 3.6

Novo Nordisk

DENMARK

Scenario planning

In 2006 the Danish multinational Novo Nordisk, the leading provider of diabetes treatments in the world, commissioned the Institute for Alternative Futures to produce four scenarios for what was seen as a looming twin epidemic of diabetes and obesity in the Western world.* At that time, 20.8 million Americans had diabetes. The study estimated that this number would more than double to 50 million by 2025 unless action was taken. The scenarios were designed to show the impact of various courses of action: to show how serious this twin epidemic could become if the West stayed on its current path, to illustrate the range of options available for averting the crisis, and to demonstrate how learning to meet the challenge of diabetes and obesity could play a major role in the evolution of the healthcare system. Starting with a scenario that assumed a continuation of the status quo (which would result in 50 million diabetics in the USA by 2025), each of the subsequent scenarios progressively incorporated more diabetes control factors and laid out the consequences of these actions, with the fourth scenario showing the most comprehensive approach to control.

* *Diabetes & Obesity 2025: Four Future Scenarios For the Twin Health Epidemics*, Institute for Alternative Futures, June 1 2006.

© Novo Nordisk

Visit the website: www.novonordisk.com

Question:

What are the best- and worst-case scenarios that might affect your business idea?

Scenario planning is another technique that tries to assess how possible future situations might impact on a firm. Trends and drivers of change are identified from the PESTEL analysis and built into scenarios. These situations must be logically consistent possible futures, usually an optimistic, a pessimistic and a 'most likely' future, based around key factors influencing your firm. Optional courses of action or strategies can then be matched to these scenarios. In effect, the scenarios are being used to test the sensitivity of your start-up strategies. They also allow assumptions about the status quo of the environment to be challenged. After the financial crisis of 2008, Lego started using scenario planning as part of its annual budgeting process, allowing it to build contingency plans for each 'crisis' scenario that it identified.

This review of the future should generate a series of opportunities and threats (or risks) that you may face in five years' time. You need to think through how you might deal with them. Your review should start to identify a series of **critical success factors** – things you need to get right to ensure your survival and success. They might come out of your scenario planning and will certainly be amplified and developed as you develop your **business model**. The sort of questions you are seeking to answer are:

- What drives competition?
- What are the sectoral, performance and customer conventions that competitors adhere to, and how important are they to customers?
- What are the main dimensions of competition?
- How intense is competition?
- How can you be different and obtain competitive advantage?

These in turn generate **strategic options** – actions you might undertake if the risks or opportunities actually materialize. The more strategic options that you can identify, the more flexibility you have. They are sources of real value to you and potential investors. Companies that present many options and/or opportunities are more attractive than those with fewer. In the same way, resources that can be used in a number of different ways are more attractive to own, as opposed to rent or buy in, than those with limited use. We discuss other ways of identifying critical success factors and developing strategic options in relation to the risks you face in Chapter 10.

CASE insight 3.7

Bill Gates and Microsoft USA

Looking to the future

In 1995, five years before he stepped down as CEO of Microsoft, Bill Gates wrote an internal memo that has become increasingly pertinent:

Developments on the internet over the next several years will set the course of our industry for a long time to come … I have gone through several stages of increasing my views of its importance. Now I assign the internet the highest level of importance. In this memo I want to make it clear that our focus on the internet is crucial to every part of our business. The internet is the most important single development to come along since the IBM PC was introduced in 1981.

PhotoDisc/ Getty Images

By 2014, Microsoft had only just started to focus on the importance of the internet and was falling behind competitors. With sales of Windows and Microsoft Office falling sharply, it had been forced to announce a 'far-reaching realignment of the company' to enable it to respond more quickly to change, 'focusing the whole company on a single strategy'. This involved disbanding product groups, making redundancies and reorganizing itself into functional lines such as engineering, marketing, advanced strategy and research. Will this work or will it be too little, too late? Only time will tell.

Visit the website: www.microsoft.com

Question:
How difficult is it to 'predict' the future?

CASE insight 3.8

Convergent US technology markets USA

Scenario planning – identifying competitors in an emergent market

The boundary between markets/industries can become very blurred in the fast-moving technology-driven world of the internet, making the identification of competitors difficult sometimes. This is particularly the case when the real fight is for an emerging market that, as yet, is not formally defined. This is the case with the battle currently under way between the five US giants of the digital age: Amazon, Apple, Facebook, Google and Microsoft. In the past these companies have provided hardware, software and various products and services, each content to 'stick to the knitting' and focus on its core market. However, new hardware, such as smartphones and tablet computers linked by Wi-Fi and 4G networks, and new software, in the form of apps, are breaking down these barriers and forcing old markets to converge.

The battle now is to become the sole provider of all our digital requirements, offering a vast range of services tailored to our 'needs', all day, every day, anywhere, from the best online platform – a kind of 'digital utility' offering of 'universal internet services'. The more services these companies offer, the more customers they are likely to attract, and the more advertising revenue they are likely to earn. But the reward is not just the profit from the goods or services that may be purchased but also the digital footprint of users (identified by their IP address) – their internet surfing and buying habits, likes and dislikes, times of day on the internet and even their location. All of this is collected automatically in real time. It is very valuable to advertisers and salespeople alike, allowing them to offer targeted advertising at particular times of day in particular geographic areas. This already exists and has been popularized as:

- Amazon knows what you read.
- Apple knows what you buy.
- Facebook knows what you like.
- Google knows what you want.
- Microsoft knows where you live.

However, each of the Big Five is coming to this new market from different existing markets with new products and services and very different strengths and core competencies.

Amazon started life selling books online and now sells almost everything. However, with the introduction of the Kindle, which allows the purchase and reading of books online, it entered the hardware market (it subcontracts production). The touchscreen Kindle Fire, usefully preloaded with your Amazon account details, not only

makes this easier, it comes with social networking that connects you to others who purchase the same books and films. Amazon also offers an app shop, online payment system, TV and film streaming and cloud computing facility. Amazon is a fierce acquirer of smaller companies to help it grow and achieve market dominance.

Apple started life designing and manufacturing computers and has become an iconic designer brand offering premium-priced electronic gadgets ranging from computers to the iPod, iPhone and iPad (see Case insight 1.8). Twitter is integrated into all its devices. Apple redefined how music was sold through iTunes. It sells books through iBooks. It also offers a wide range of apps for its devices. Web-enabled Apple TV sells films and TV programmes through iTunes. Apple also has its own cloud computing facility. Apple is sitting on $100 billion of cash, more than any of the other four companies. However, unlike other companies, Apple has a track record of working on its own to grow.

Facebook, the ubiquitous social network site, is the newcomer to this group. It is constantly improving itself and now offers many of the features of Google+. It has its own email system and even has Facebook credits, a virtual currency used to play computer games. It offers a search service based on the data provided by Facebook subscribers rather than computer algorithms. In a strategic alliance with Netflix (the film and TV website), Spotify (the music streamer) and Zynga (the computer gamer), it intends to launch Facebook TV, Facebook movies, Facebook music and Facebook games. Facebook's stock market launch in 2012 was estimated to have raised over $5 billion – small change compared to Apple, but still a substantial nest egg.

Google has become not only the name of a search engine and company but also the name for what we do when we search the internet for information. As well as information searches, it offers maps, images and many other services, including its own internet portal. Google also has Gmail, which is well established in the market, and Gmail+ is designed to make this more social, in direct competition with Facebook. Google has its Chrome internet browser. By 2012, its Android smartphone operating system had more users than Apple's iPhones and accounted for well over half of worldwide smartphone sales. It now sells smartphones and tablet computers under its own brand, although manufacturing is subcontracted to partners. It has Google Music offering music downloads and owns YouTube, where you can watch and rent TV programmes and films, and has plans to launch Google TV. It has its own online payment system called Google Wallet. Google has a history of partnering with others and using acquisition to help it grow.

Microsoft predates the other four companies, starting as the supplier of the ubiquitous Windows Operating System and then the Microsoft Office suite of software. It also has the internet browser Internet Explorer and email system Outlook Express. Many computers come with Microsoft software already installed, including the internet browser – which has been the subject of some anti-trust actions. It offers server applications and cloud computing services. It has entertainment systems including the Xbox video gaming system, the handheld Zune media player, and the television-based internet appliance MSN TV. Microsoft also markets personal computer hardware including mice, keyboards and various game controllers such as joysticks and gamepads. Arguably, it missed the internet revolution, and since then it has been playing catch-up by expanding, often by acquisition, into search engines such as Bing. It purchased the video communications company Skype, and has entered into a strategic alliance with Nokia to produce smartphones with its own Microsoft operating system. It is also imitating Apple and starting to open its own retail outlets.

So, Amazon started life as an internet retailer, Apple as a hardware supplier, Facebook as a social network, Google as an internet search engine and Microsoft as a software developer. But the questions are: Where will this convergence of competition lead? What will be needed to gain competitive advantage? Will there be only one winner? Will the winner(s) have a monopoly? If so, will they be more powerful than governments?

Questions:

1. Why are these industries/markets converging?
2. How might you describe this new industry/market, using the typologies outlined in this chapter?
3. These companies are in the same industry as the Chinese firms Alibaba, Tencent and Baidu. But are they competitors in the same market? How do the markets differ? How might this change in the future?
4. What opportunities exist in this new market for start-ups? What are the threats or risks they face?

Screening and go/no-go decisions

This is the point to take stock of whether you actually do want to launch a new venture. You start by asking yourself whether this is what you really want to do and whether you are well suited to being an entrepreneur. Does being an entrepreneur fit with your aspirations for your life at this time? We looked at the typical character traits of entrepreneurs in Chapter 1. Do you have these traits? Does being an entrepreneur fit with your aspirations for your life at this time? Do you have the skills and capabilities needed, and are you confident that you can assemble the resources you need (human, social and financial)? Most important of all, are you willing to take the risks involved in starting a new venture? Sometimes the business idea might be good, but you might not be the right person to take it to the market. If this is the case, you might need to find a partner or you might be able to sell on the idea. Whatever your motivations, you need to undertake an honest evaluation of your personal viability as an entrepreneur. Do you believe you can be an entrepreneur?

Most people base their business upon skills, experience or qualifications that they have already gained from a previous job or through a hobby. Do your skills match your business idea? Business ideas may (and often do) emerge from experience of an industry because you believe that your employer is not making the most of some opportunity. You might have an idea but cannot persuade your employer to take it up. You may have contacts in the industry that you believe can help you exploit this opportunity. These are positive factors that might 'pull' you into entrepreneurship, but you need to believe that the business idea itself will be viable. And at this stage that is difficult. Nevertheless, you need to decide whether you want to commit more time and effort and go to the next step in investigating the business idea. This is the first of two 'go/no-go' decision points – points at which you need to reflect on your motivations and perhaps rethink elements of your original business idea.

The next step is to look at the practicality and viability of the idea. You may have a business idea but the product or service concept probably needs to be developed; it needs to be specified in more detail and then tested – a series of trial-and-error iterations. Is it technically feasible to produce the product or service at a cost that allows adequate profits to be made? You may have to prepare a product prototype, although in the case of a service this is likely to be the same as a detailed product specification. Developing a prototype is a process of experimentation in which numerous iterations of an idea are created and tested to see whether they provide the desired result. Prototypes used to be complicated and expensive to produce but now can be developed relatively inexpensively in the early stages using computer simulations. (Google even provides a tool called Sketchup.) All the time, practicality must be weighed against what you believe the market needs and what competitors are currently offering. Eventually, however, a physical prototype will have to be built, not least because often only by seeing, touching and using the product can the potential consumer make judgements about it. But even here there may be a 'minimum viable product' that minimizes your costs, while giving you the maximum of information – a concept covered in the next chapter. At some stage you need to think about whether you can safeguard the 'intellectual property' (IP) of your business idea (Chapter 9).

Feeding into this is research into the market or industry you are entering – the need to check the way other businesses may be approaching the market. Is your approach viable? Who are your competitors? What is their supply chain? How will you compete against them? How are you different? Is this gap in the market real? Who might be your suppliers? Will you be able to capitalize on this idea as quickly as competitors? Can you learn from the way competitors operate? The practicalities of producing the product or service must be weighed against the needs of customers and the commercial viability of the concept. Commercial viability is never certain, particularly at this stage, but studying the market and industry should give you some clues.

Underpinning the process is the constant need to check the commercial viability of the business idea. This check, together with market/industry research will influence the form of the prototype product or service you develop. You need to assure yourself that there is a viable market for it. Who are your customers and why will they buy from you? And at some point you will have to make the decision about whether this product or service is really what customers will buy *at the price you want to charge*. You might be able to assess viability through focus groups or various forms of market testing, for example, trying out a retail idea as a 'pop-up' stall. Market testing can take different forms. We look at low-cost market testing through limited launch in the next chapter, once we better understand the form your business model might take, but all the time we are trying to gain information so as to limit the risks you face. The information feeds back to influence the final form of your product or service and the business model you develop.

A good business idea has a window of commercial opportunity. Too early or too late and it is unlikely to be successful, and it will only have a finite life cycle. Will your business be profitable? Commercial viability usually hinges on the profits the firm makes compared to the risks it faces. This will determine whether it can be funded. Even if you intend to launch a social enterprise, you need to know the costs and revenues and assure yourself that these are 'satisfactory'. At this stage you know very little about these things. You probably only know that there is likely to be a demand for your product or service for which some customers might be willing to pay. Based upon this limited information you are then faced with the second go/ no-go decision – whether to move into the next phase and develop a business model.

Figure 3.3 shows this screening process, taking you into the business development and launch phases. It is iterative. Even when you are into Phases 2 and 3, you may decide that you need to go back and modify your product or service as you find out more about your customers and their needs. As explained in subsequent chapters, developing a business model involves producing detailed plans about how the product or service will be produced, operated, marketed and financed. And the detail involved in developing this might lead you to alter some elements of the product or service and, in extremis, even abandon it. All the elements of your business model are interconnected. Change one and you may need to change another. Alter how you produce or deliver a product or service and you may have to alter the price, which in turn affects how it is marketed. This is a continuous process of refinement. Throughout the development of your business model you may want to go back and alter elements of it. So, even at this stage a preliminary 'go' decision does not mean that this business idea is viable – just that 'a priori' it seems so. Only after you have developed your final business model will you know whether it is viable. And, because plans are rarely 100% accurate, even once you have launched you should continue to monitor the effectiveness of your business model against customer reaction and be willing to modify it to better fit the realities of the market place. All you can do before this is maximize your chances of success through planning and minimize your risk of failure through a technique called 'lean start-up' that we shall outline in the next chapter.

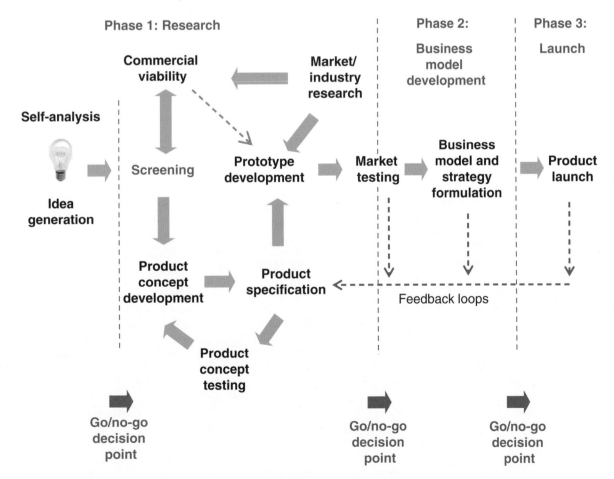

Figure 3.3 The screening process ahead of the go/no-go decision

CASE
insight
3.9

Nuffnang

SINGAPORE

Matching opportunity with skills

When he graduated from the London School of Economics, Cheo Ming Shen wanted to use his newly acquired skills to set up a new venture in his home country of Singapore, taking advantage of Asia's underdeveloped online market:

I look for business opportunities that I think can work in the internet space and then I go develop it, and then market it and sell it as a business.

Cheo applied his business and internet skills in his home country where he had more local knowledge. His first venture was based upon his observation that there were a lot of blank spaces on blogs:

In Asia there are hundreds of thousands of blogs … it's a fad that has taken off in such a way that … the West hasn't seen … This was a big chunk of internet space that wasn't being monetised. It represented a huge audience collectively but nobody could … effectively

put them together … The blogs are a very interactive medium so it's a very personal medium as well … When someone sees advertising … they're more likely to click.
BBC News Business 16 November 2010
www.bbc.co.uk/news/11757735

Founded in 2007 by Cheo and his partner, Timothy Tiah Ewe Tiam, Nuffnang acts as an intermediary between advertisers and bloggers. Bloggers are paid for each unique visitor and Nuffnang takes a percentage. The simple idea required little capital to establish as a business and it became profitable within its first year. It has proved so successful that it has expanded to countries throughout Asia. Cheo and Tiah now have four internet-based businesses in Singapore.

Visit the website: www.nuffnang.com

Question:

What skills do you have and how will that influence the business ideas that you explore?

Sofa-bed Factory

Piotr quickly discovered that finding out about the furniture market was time consuming. He visited numerous business libraries before a trade contact gave him a copy of an industry report that normally costs over £1,000. Piotr was glad he had not paid for the report himself, since its contents seemed so general. Nevertheless it did give him some valuable general background, confirmed some things he already knew and alerted him to some things he needed to find out.

The report said that the UK domestic furniture market was 'highly fragmented and complex'. It estimated its size at £9.8 billion at retail prices in 2013. The upholstered

furniture and beds sector dominated the overall furniture market, making up 46% of sales. This market had been growing at a steady rate of about 3–4% per annum through to 2015, with a similar increase expected in 2016 and 2017, although fears about the UK leaving the EU clouded the horizon beyond this. Sales of three-piece suites had declined with combinations of two-piece sofas now more popular. Often one of these two-piece sofas was a sofa-bed. The popularity of leather was declining. Sales of the divan sets that form the base of beds had also fallen but sales of mattresses continued to grow, largely because of an emerging replacement market.

Interestingly, the greatest increase in sales had been for mattresses with higher value pocket springs or for those made with other materials such as memory foam. Sales of single sofas and convertible sofa-beds were an important and growing part of the upholstered furniture market.

The report said that the supply structure of the upholstered furniture market had not changed much over the previous decade. There remained numerous small suppliers, although the major suppliers had increased their market share. Some 35% of upholstered furniture in the UK is imported, mainly from Eastern Europe and the Far East. Retail furniture multiples such as DFS, ScS and Sofology, and general furniture multiples, such as IKEA, Harveys and Furniture Village account for 49% of sales in the upholstered furniture sector and 46% in the beds sector. The report confirmed the high level of price competition in a mature industry and painted the picture of a highly competitive market with many suppliers and a number of large buyers with strong buying power. There were few barriers to entry or exit in the market and the high level of competition also reflected itself in the relatively high rate of business failure in both the manufacturing and retail sectors.

Commenting on the future, the report stated that 'design innovation should provide some opportunities for product differentiation and margin protection', but failed to say what this might entail. It did say that the trend was towards 'alternative furniture combinations' – flexible and modular – rather than the traditional three-piece suite. It also commented on the growing importance of the internet on the sales process in the sector. Customers are increasingly using it to shop around for designs and low prices, although they seem to want to actually see the furniture in-store before purchasing. Commenting on prospects for the future, the report concluded that, while the sector was mature and the UK economy might falter after leaving the EU, the growing demand for housing should stimulate market growth.

Questions:

1 Do you agree with Piotr when he said he was glad he had not paid for the report himself? Explain.

2 What is your assessment of the industry? Does it contain any clues about gaining competitive advantage?

Summary and action points

3.1 Understand your market/industry: Be able to identify and describe the characteristics of the market or industry within which you will operate. Commonly used typologies include life cycle, concentration and geographic extent. However, drawing the boundaries of your industry can be difficult and is a question of judgement.

Your total available market (TAM) is the size of your potential market – those who might be interested in buying your particular product. This reflects the total sales of competing products. Your served available market (SAM) is the size of the target market segment *you* wish to serve within the TAM. Your penetrated market is the size of the SAM you actually capture. Your market share is your penetrated market divided by SAM.

3.2 Understand the degree of competition you face: Porter's Five Forces can be used to assess the degree of competition you face in an existing market/industry and hence the threat to your profitability. However, there are things you can do to counter this threat, in particular the marketing strategies you adopt.

3.3 Evaluate the market/industry future: Your industry analysis is primarily about trying to predict the future – the threats and opportunities you might face. You can use techniques such as PESTEL analysis, brainstorming, futures thinking and scenario planning to help you do this. This analysis should generate a series of threats and opportunities and strategic options that you might undertake if they actually materialize. It should also generate a series of critical success factors – things you need to get right to ensure survival and success.

3.4 Develop your prototype and undertake initial screening for viability: This is where you decide whether entrepreneurship is for you and whether you have the skills to produce and deliver the product or service at the heart of your business idea. Does the idea look commercially viable, and are you willing to spend more time developing a business model?

Workbook exercises

The New Venture Creation Workbook contains a digital version of these exercises that can be modified as your business model develops and builds into a draft business plan. It can be downloaded from www.macmillanihe.com/burns-nvc-2e.

3.1: Understand your market/industry

1 Research your general market/industry and your TAM at a macro level. Find out as much as you can about the size, growth and structure of the market, market trends, customer demographics, buying patterns, established channels of distribution etc.

2 Describe the particular market you are targeting, your TAM (e.g. local vs. national, other characteristics). Repeat the exercise for your SAM. Explain any differences.

TAM characteristics	SAM characteristics

3 In the light of your answers to Workbook Exercise 2.2 (7), list your direct and indirect competitors and their strengths and weaknesses as companies.

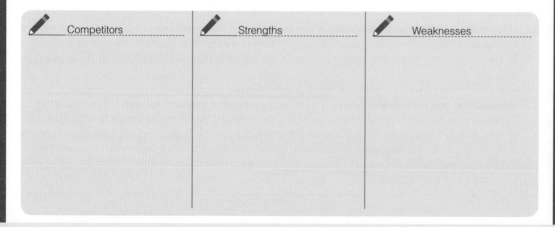

Competitors	Strengths	Weaknesses

3.2: Understand the degree of competition you face

Using the table, for each of Porter's Five Forces:

1 Assess the threat to industry profitability.

2 Note the implications of this for you.

3 List the actions you need to take to ensure that you can avoid or lessen the effect of high threats to profitability.

4 List the actions you need to take to create a sustainable position that means others cannot copy these actions.

If there are no actions you can take in an industry with a high degree of competition, you may want to reconsider whether you want to enter it and return to the exercises in Chapter 2 to find another business idea. However, if there is a low degree of competition you may equally need to consider why this is the case and whether it will stay the same after your entry. How will existing companies react to your entry? If the threat of new entrants and/or substitutes is low, how will you be able to enter the market?

Competitive Force:	Threat to industry profitability			Implications	Actions to lessen/ avoid threats	Actions to sustain position
	Low	Medium	High			
Rivalry among existing firms (e.g. number of competitors, industry structure, degree of product differentiation etc.)						
Threat of substitutes (e.g. degree of product differentiation, switch costs etc.)						
Threat of new entrants (e.g. barriers to entry, switch costs, economies of scale, access to distribution channels, degree of differentiation, capital requirements etc.)						
Bargaining power of suppliers (e.g. switch costs, supplier concentration, attractiveness of substitutes etc.)						
Bargaining power of buyers (e.g. switch costs, buyer concentration, product differentiation, buyers' costs etc.)						

3.3: Evaluate the market/industry future

Using the table below:

1 Undertake a PESTEL analysis on your market/industry to identify key influences or events that might affect it over the next five years.

2 Using this analysis and your conclusions from the previous exercises, construct three scenarios – 'best', 'worst' and 'most likely' cases – that reflect how these influences or events might impact upon the trends in your market/industry. Remember to factor in the existence of your firm.

- Will the industry expand or contract? Will it consolidate or fragment?
- Are the main dimensions of competition changing and what is driving this change?
- Will sectoral, performance and/or customer conventions change?
- Will competition intensify or will products become more differentiated?
- How will direct and indirect competitors be affected?
- How might they react to your existence?
- How will their reaction affect you?

✎ PESTEL influences on market/industry	✎ Worst-case effects and your reaction	✎ Best-case effects and your reaction	✎ Most likely effects and your reaction

3 Brainstorm to explore how you might react to these trends and competitors.
- What strategies might you adopt?
- Will you need to modify or change your product/service idea?
- Will you need to identify and enter new markets?

4 In the light of this brainstorming exercise, list the critical success factors for your business – the things you need to get right to ensure your survival and success.

✎ ....

3.4: Develop your prototype and undertake initial screening for viability

1 Review Exercise 3.1 and decide whether entrepreneurship is for you.

2 Building on Exercise 2.2 (5), flesh out your product/service concept, specifying in detail as much as possible. If this is a product, develop a prototype. Decide whether your product/service works and can be produced and delivered.

3 Decide whether you have the skills to produce and deliver the product/service at the heart of your business idea. List any skills gaps and decide whether they might be filled by other people who you might recruit or partner with.

4 Building on Exercise 2.2 (6) and the information you have gained from the exercises in this chapter, decide as best you can whether this idea could be commercially viable. You need to consider issues such as whether there is a clearly identified customer need, whether there is a gap in the market to meet that need, the size of that market, the nature of the competition you face and whether your idea can be easily copied. What risks might you therefore face? List the questions that remain unanswered at this point. We shall return to the issue of viability in the next chapter.

Visit www.macmillanihe.com/burns-nvc-2e for chapter quizzes and other resources.

Phase 2   Business Model Development

Visit
www.macmillanihe.com/
burns-nvc-2e to watch a video
interview with Paul Burns.

Photo source: PhotoDisc/Getty Images

4 Structuring your business model

Contents

- Bringing your idea to life
- Using the New Venture Creation Framework
- Generic business models
- Generic business models and critical success factors
- Generic business models and competitive advantage
- Niche business model
- Internet business models
- Low-cost market testing
- Characteristics of a good business model
- Summary and action points
- Workbook exercises

Learning outcomes

When you have read this chapter and undertaken the related activities you will be able to:

- Understand the meaning of the terms 'effectuation' and 'lean start-up'
- Understand the importance of developing a planning framework for your new venture and how a business model is developed and used for this purpose
- Understand the different sorts of business models that have been developed
- Understand the characteristics of a good business model

Academic insights

4.1 Effectuation

4.2 Business Model Canvas and Lean Canvas

4.3 Generic business models and competitive advantage

4.4 Lean start-up

4.5 The customer development process

Case insights

4.1 MOMA

4.2 Streetcar (now Zipcar)

4.3 African Renewable Energy Distributor (ARED)

4.4 easyJet (1)

4.5 Quad Electroacoustics

4.6 Morgan Motor Company

4.7 Escape to the Cape

4.8 Web 2.0

4.9 Pinterest

4.10 Amanti Cupcakes

4.11 TruffleShuffle

4.12 Hide My Ass!

Sofa-bed Factory

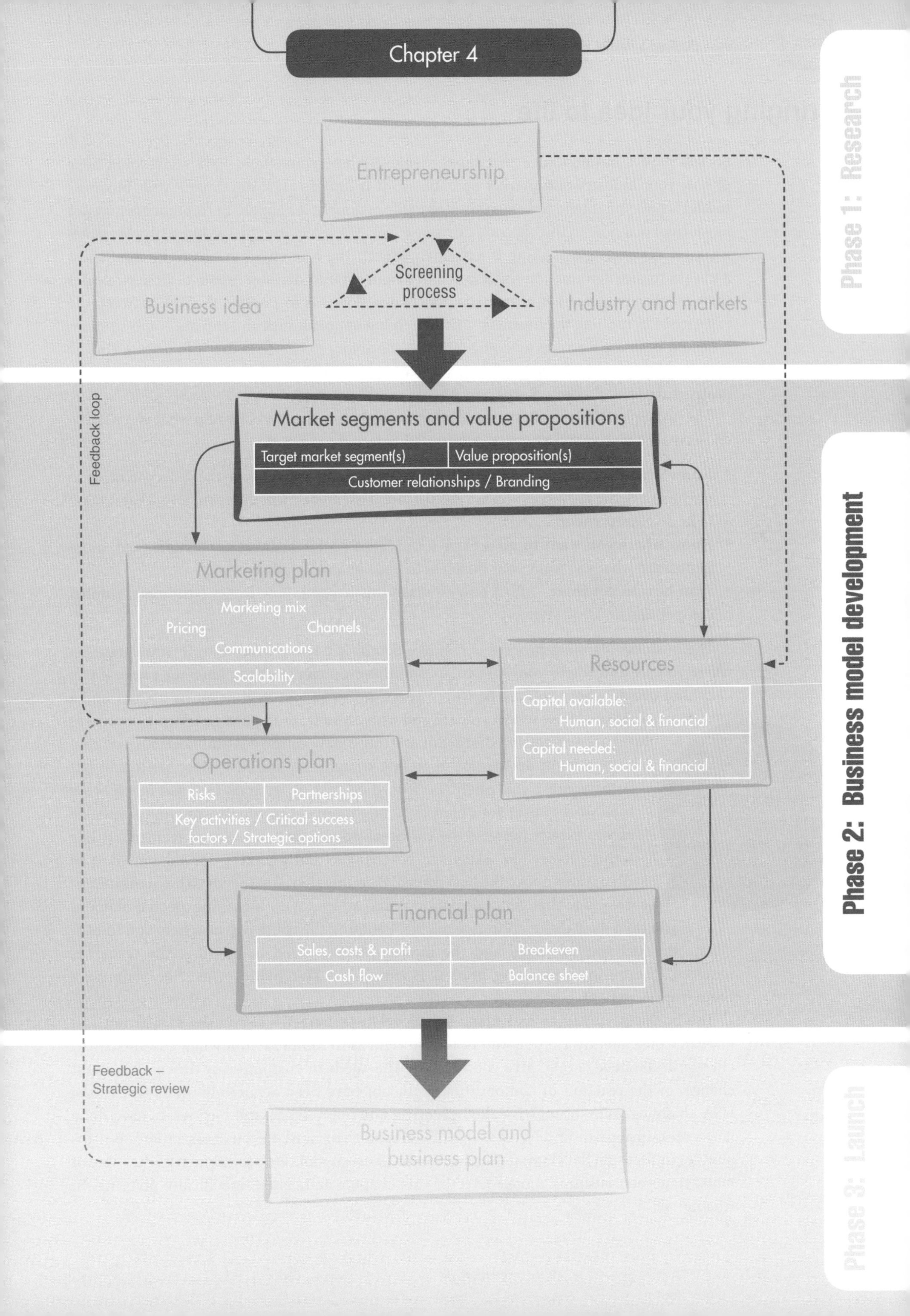
Chapter 4
Phase 1: Research
Entrepreneurship
Screening process
Business idea
Industry and markets
Phase 2: Business model development
Feedback loop
Market segments and value propositions
Target market segment(s)
Value proposition(s)
Customer relationships / Branding
Marketing plan
Marketing mix
Pricing
Channels
Communications
Scalability
Resources
Capital available:
Human, social & financial
Capital needed:
Human, social & financial
Operations plan
Risks
Partnerships
Key activities / Critical success factors / Strategic options
Financial plan
Sales, costs & profit
Breakeven
Cash flow
Balance sheet
Feedback – Strategic review
Business model and business plan
Phase 3: Launch

Bringing your idea to life

So you have a business idea that looks viable. By now you should have some knowledge of how your industry and market operates, so it is time to start developing your **business model** – how you intend to bring this idea to life and make it happen. Entrepreneurs may not like formal planning in the big company sense (see Academic insight 4.1) but a simple framework for developing a start-up is extremely useful. The framework needs to be minimalist and easy to use, illuminating the issues and helping you to develop broad, flexible strategies that can change as market circumstances change. It needs to provide the link between the experience of running the business – the emerging opportunities and threats – and strategy. It should facilitate learning by doing and also the ability to translate this into action. For the less practised, such a framework helps organize and develop what would otherwise be an unstructured and disjointed experience.

The principles of planning are straightforward and translate directly into what you need to do to create a new venture.

- **Know where you are** – Understand your strengths and weaknesses, the skills you bring to the business, the resources you are able to mobilize, indeed whether you have what it takes to be an entrepreneur.
- **Know where you want to go** – Have a clear idea of the business opportunity and, more important, what you want your business to become in the future.
- **Plan how to get there** – Plan how to make this happen, how to get customers, combat competition and lead staff.

The business planning process is just like planning a route from A to B: you decide on where you are and where you want to go, and then you can start to plan your route. If you cannot decide where you are or where you want to go, you will never be able to find a route. If you know where you are and where you want to go, a good route increases the chance of getting there. But starting a new venture is an uncertain exercise. So, you might decide not to go in a straight line because there are longer but faster routes; you might be forced to take diversions because unexpected road works upset your plans; you might not get to your destination as quickly as you expect because the car breaks down or you have an accident. While nothing is certain, plans can be changed and planning should provide you with options about the best routes. Planning therefore needs to be a continuous process, one that generates options and alternatives. If the unexpected happens you then have those options available. Planning the route will also help you to estimate the fuel you will need and the money you will need to buy it – the resources required. The business planning process is simple but systematic – just like planning a route from A to B.

> You jump off a cliff and you assemble an airplane on the way down.
>
> Reid Hoffman founder LinkedIn BBC News Business 11 January 2011

The business strategies and plans you develop to launch your business will not last forever. Consequently, they should not be so rigid as to inhibit action when circumstances change, and indeed should give you options. The needs of customers or the market might change, or the reaction of competitors might not have been accurately predicted. In the USA changing your strategy is called **pivoting** and many successful businesses have done it. Twitter, Instagram and WhatsApp all changed their start-up business model. But for now, let us focus on developing our start-up business model. We shall return to the topic of modifying your business model later in this chapter and, more specifically pivoting, in Chapter 14.

Effectuation

Sarasvathy (2001) undertook a study of how 27 successful US entrepreneurs approached business decisions. The entrepreneurs all had at least 15 years of entrepreneurial experience, including successes and failures, and had taken at least one company public. They were presented with a case study about a hypothetical start-up with the founder facing 10 decisions. The rationale for these decisions was then explored in more detail. Sarasvathy (2001) also reported the results of the same research, which was conducted some years later, on a group of successful professional executives in large organizations, allowing contrasts and comparisons to be made between the entrepreneurs and the executives.

Her conclusion was that the entrepreneurs came to decisions based upon something that was christened **effectual reasoning** or **effectuation** (making something happen), which was contrasted to the causal or deductive reasoning used by the professional executives. Sarasvathy came to five main conclusions about how successful entrepreneurs approach decision making in their uncertain, rapidly changing environment.

1 While the executives set goals and sought to achieve them sequentially and logically, the entrepreneurs' goals were broad and evolved over time based on whatever personal strengths and resources they had, creatively reacting to contingencies as they occurred. Entrepreneurs start with the resources they have and go to market quickly. They do not wait for perfect knowledge or the perfect opportunity. They learn by doing. This observation is supported by earlier research. It was Mintzberg (1978) who first coined the phrase **emergent strategy** development (in contrast to 'deliberate') to describe this: 'the strategy-making process is characterized by reactive solutions to existing problems … The adaptive organization makes its decisions in incremental, serial steps.'

2 While executives wanted to research opportunities and assess potential return before committing resources, entrepreneurs were far more inclined to go to market as quickly and cheaply as possible and to assess market demand from that. This approach was labelled **affordable loss**, representing the maximum amount they could afford to lose in the

event of failure. They set this affordable loss by evaluating opportunities on the basis of whether that loss was acceptable, rather than trying to evaluate the attractiveness of the predictable upside. The concept was expanded later in a book by Read et al. (2011). We explain the concept in more detail in Chapter 10.

3 The entrepreneurs did not like extensive, formal research and planning, particularly traditional market research. This was explained in terms of them not believing that the future was predictable (and that the upside could be evaluated), preferring instead to believe in their own ability to obtain the information needed to react quickly to changing circumstances. They believed that while they could not predict the future, they could control it, or more precisely, 'recognize, respond to, and reshape opportunities as they develop' – a character trait recognized by cognitive development theory (Academic insight 1.3) which results in successful entrepreneurs often being seen as 'overconfident' with regard to predicting future outcomes (Forbes, 2005). They use uncertainty to their advantage by developing contingencies and remaining flexible rather than slavishly sticking to existing goals. However, it was significant that they adopted more formal structures as their businesses grew; as the study put it, they became both 'causal as well as effectual thinkers'. Research by McCarthy and Leavy (2000) showed that strategy development changed from emergent to deliberate as firms went through recurrent crises followed by periods of consolidation.

4 Also prominent was the entrepreneurs' propensity to partner with stakeholders – customers, suppliers and advisors – to help them shape the business – reflecting the importance of building relationships. New ventures rarely have the resources to undertake all the tasks required to make the business work, so partnering gives them an important extra resource (Sorenson et al., 2008). They use networks of partnerships to generate knowledge, leverage resources and make the future become the reality. By way of contrast, the executives tended to know exactly where they wanted to go and then follow that set path without seeking partnerships.

5 It was noticeable also that the entrepreneurs were less concerned about competitors than the executives. This might be explained in terms of their inherent self-confidence (Forbes, 2005), but the study explained it in terms of them seeing themselves as on the fringe of a market or creating an entirely new market through some

sort of disruptive innovation. They believed they were different or better than competitors in a way that gave them a differential advantage.

There are lessons to be learned from this research. Firstly, an entrepreneur's approach to developing strategy and decision making is subtly different to traditional frameworks. Because of the uncertain and unpredictable environment they face, they prefer to make incremental decisions and let strategies 'emerge' as situations (and markets) become clearer.

This does not negate the need for strategic frameworks that can help with decision making and strategy development, whether emergent or deliberate. Secondly, although the entrepreneurs in the study did not like extensive, formal research, we have already seen that there are many quick, cheap and less 'formal' ways of finding out about your industry and market. The ultimate test, however, is the market place itself. And the challenge is to launch your business and test your idea within your 'affordable loss'.

Forbes, D. (2005) 'Are Some Entrepreneurs More Overconfident than Others?', *Journal of Business Venturing*, 20.

McCarthy, B. and Leavy, B. (2000) 'Strategy Formation in Irish SMEs: A Phase Model of Process', British Academy of Management Annual Conference, Edinburgh.

Mintzberg, H. (1978) 'Patterns in Strategy Formation', *Management Science*.

Read, S., Sarasvathy, S., Dew, N., Wiltbank, R. and Ohlsson, A.V. (2011) *Effectual Entrepreneurship*, London: Routledge.

Sarasvathy, S.D. (2001) 'Causation and Effectuation: Toward a Theoretical Shift from Economic Inevitability to Entrepreneurial Contingency', *The Academy of Management Review*, 26(2).

Sorenson, R.I., Folker, C.A. and Brigham, K.H. (2008) 'The Collaborative Network Orientation: Achieving Business Success Through Collaborative Relationships', *Entrepreneurship Theory and Practice*, 32(4).

CASE insight 4.1

MOMA  UK

Bringing an idea to life

Tom Mercer is a Cambridge University graduate whose first job was as a management consultant with Bain & Company in London. Before going to work, he would blend a mixture of yogurt, oats and fruit for his breakfast in his flat in London. But it took time and he was often late for work. Then it suddenly struck him that his problem was actually a good business idea – pre-prepare the blend so that people could eat it at home or as they travelled to work. So he decided to try out the idea, with the help of friends, by giving it to commuters arriving at Waterloo station, London, to try to get their feedback. He stayed up most of the night before, cutting up fruit, blending it with oats and yogurt and then pouring it into water bottles he had picked up from Tesco. The feedback was positive and Tom left Bain & Company to start MOMA in 2006.

The original idea was to sell the yogurt, oat and fruit mix – now called 'Oatie Shakes' – to early-morning commuters from colourful carts at high footfall points such as stations around London. The first MOMA cart opened at Waterloo East station, and by 2008 there were nine carts, employing mainly students wanting to earn extra money. MOMA also sold into a number of London offices and shops, including Selfridges. The breakfast mixes were prepared in Deptford, South East London, then driven to central London to be sold from MOMA's carts in the early morning.

After the 2008 recession, MOMA started to refocus its marketing away from selling directly to customers from its carts and onto selling via retailers. It now sells through supermarkets such as Waitrose and Tesco as well as being available in trains, planes and coffee shops across the UK. The product range was also broadened to include bircher muesli and porridge. By 2015 the MOMA brand had gone through two redesigns and three London-wide marketing campaigns. The company now sells a range of products such as Oaties – smoothies and oats (relaunched in 2014 as Oatie Shake Take 2), Jumbles – oats soaked in apple juice and mingled with low-fat yoghurt and fruit, and Hodge-Podge – a layer of fruit cooked with spices, yoghurt and a packet of granola. It also sells on-the-go pots and sachets.

Visit the website: www.momafoods.co.uk

Question:

What do you learn about bringing an idea to life from this Case insight?

Using the New Venture Creation Framework

Phase 2 of the New Venture Creation Framework is centred on business model development. The **business model** is the plan for how a business competes, uses its resources, structures its relationships, communicates with customers, creates value and generates profits (see Academic insight 4.2). It is your route to taking your business idea to market and it will have a very large impact on whether your business succeeds or fails. The New Venture Creation Framework breaks the business model down into five stages, designed to facilitate start-up planning in the sequential manner indicated by the arrows. However, each element of the model is dependent on other parts. They must be consistent, each reinforcing the others. For example, even if your business idea has merit, unless you find and then persuade customers to buy it and can then deliver it to them, you do not have a viable business. Even then, you have to persuade them that your product/service is so good that they want to buy it again and again. To do this you need marketing, operations and financial plans, based on the resources you need and have access to. You also need to identify and minimize the risks you face.

> Innovation matters, but it isn't everything. You need an economic model that makes sense – it's no good being original if there is no demand for your product or service at a price that generates a surplus.
>
> Luck Johnson Chairman Risk Capital Partners Sunday Times 21 May 2017

To help you develop your business model there is a Worksheet that replicates the five stages at the heart of the New Venture Creation Framework. This is available as a printed copy that can be written on (Figure 4.1) or as a Microsoft® PowerPoint slide (Figure 4.2) which has simulated sticky notes that can be written on and 'posted' onto the Worksheet slide (Figure 4.3). These can all be downloaded from the companion website, www.macmillanihe.com/burns-nvc-2e. The Framework Worksheet can be used for group discussions or class presentations. It can be used to summarize and report on your progress as you undertake the Workbook exercises and develop your own business model. You can use the Framework to help you identify patterns, ensure consistency and develop the processes needed to deliver your business model. You can alter elements of the model and ask those all-important 'what if?' questions, working through the likely consequences without necessarily preparing a formal business plan. For example, you will need to operationalize your marketing plan, and to do that you will need the appropriate resources. Some may already be available to you while others may need to be sourced externally. However, if you cannot obtain the resources you need, you may have to adapt your original plan. Similarly, the results of your market segmentation will probably influence the development of your **value proposition(s)**, and this could well cause

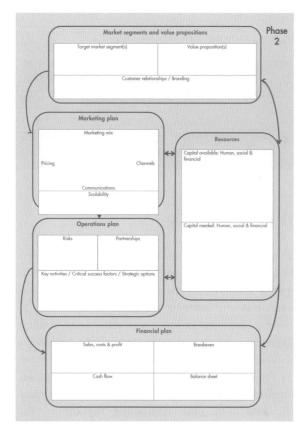

Figure 4.1 *Framework Worksheet*

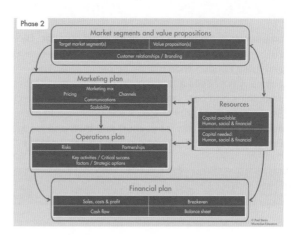

Figure 4.2 *PowerPoint version of Framework Worksheet*

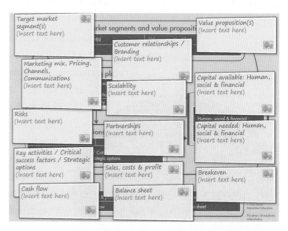

Figure 4.3 *PowerPoint version of Framework Worksheet with sticky notes*

Visit www.macmillanihe.com/burns-nvc-2e to download the Framework Worksheet and PowerPoint slide.

> As a start-up your core leadership qualities need to be adaptability and flexibility – you need to be continually looking at the business and responding and enhancing things until you get to an operating model that works for you.
>
> David Packham co-founder Samba Swirl *The Times* 25 February 2014

you to adapt and improve your original business idea. If you decide to target a number of different market segments each may require its own, slightly different, business model.

Using the New Venture Creation Framework in this way can help you develop new business ideas and modify target markets, value propositions and your marketing, operations and financial plans. It should lead to a series of strategic options, each option contingent upon different environmental circumstances, using information to modify strategies to reflect the reality of these uncertain situations. The more options that you can identify, the more flexibility you have in formulating, or indeed changing, your strategy. However, it is important that not all these options are constrained by your current resources or your current competitive position. Sometimes your vision might generate options that transcend these constraints, but may or may not be realistically attainable at the moment. The great entrepreneurs of our time never felt constrained by resources when they set up their businesses.

Business Model Canvas and Lean Canvas

Business models have a long history. Osterwalder and Pigneur (2010) developed the **Business Model Canvas** – a generic business model that provides a pictorial structure to aid understanding and development of business models. As shown in Figure 4.4, it comprises nine interlinked building blocks, each influencing the other. Maurya (2010, 2012) reworked the Canvas for web-based start-ups, but retained its overall structure. At the core of Osterwalder and Pigneur's model is the *value proposition* [1]. On the right are the four blocks of the business model that are driven by value to customers: *customer segments* [2], *customer relations* [3], *channels* (of distribution) [4] and the resulting *revenue streams* [5]. The four blocks on the left are driven by business efficiencies: *key activities* [6], *key resources* [7], *key partnerships* [8] and the resulting *cost structures* [9].

The idea is that you can use the canvas to sketch out (literally) and then develop your business model. As with the New Venture Creation Framework, when you change one block, you may need to change another. What is essential is that all the elements of the canvas are consistent and deliver the all-important value proposition to the target customers. Using real business examples for companies such as Apple, Google, Skype and Amazon, Osterwalder and Pigneur show how different business models – none of which is 'best' per se – can be sketched onto the Canvas so as to identify predictable patterns.

- Unbundling the core business types or disciplines into what we have called 'generic business models' – product innovation, customer relationships and infrastructure management (low cost).
- The long tail – whereby a company offers a large number of small-volume, niche products at a relatively high price, what we have called a niche marketing strategy.
- Multi-sided platforms – bringing together different market segments that derive value from the presence of the other, called the network effect.

8 Key partnerships (Problems): The network of suppliers and partners that make the business model work	6 Key activities (Solutions): The most important things you need to do to make the business model work	1 Value proposition: The product/service bundle that creates value for each customer segment	3 Customer relations (Unfair advantage): The types of relationships you aim to have with each customer segment	2 Customer segments: The different groups of people or organizations you aim to reach
	7 Key resources (Key metrics): The most important assets required to make the business model work		4 Channels: How you communicate with and reach each customer segment	
9 Cost structures: All the costs that you will incur to operate your business model			5 Revenue streams: The cash generated from each customer segment	

Figure 4.4 *The Business Model Canvas*

Note: Maurya's terminology is given in brackets.

Source: reprinted with permission of Strategyzer and strategyzer.com

- Free products/services – where non-paying customers are financed by other parts of the business model or other customer segments.
- Open business models – where value is created through collaboration between partners.

Osterwalder and Pigneur's model was intended mainly for larger, established businesses and Maurya (2010, 2012) modified the canvas to better suit web-based start-ups. He called this his 'Lean Canvas' in which he modified or replaced four of the nine original blocks:

- Box 3: *Customer relations* – became *Unfair advantage*. This is just another name for competitive advantage, which is what your marketing plan should seek to address. Maurya justified the exclusion of 'customer relations' on the ground that it was covered in the 'channels' box (as it is in the New Venture Creation Framework).
- Box 6: *Key activities* – became *Solutions*, which were the solutions to the problems that Maurya added to the Canvas (see Box 8). He justified the exclusion of 'key activities' on the ground that it was too 'outside-in' – 'helping outsiders looking in to understand what the start-up did'. In this book, key marketing and operating activities are considered to be vital to help you identify your critical success factors and remain an important separate box in the New Venture Creation Framework.
- Box 7: *Key resources* – became *Key metrics*, which Maurya explained as 'the few actions that matter'. These are really just the critical success factors discussed above. He justified the exclusion of 'key resources' on the ground that 'we need fewer resources than ever to get a product to market'.

While resources are rarely a barrier for a good business idea they are a worry for many entrepreneurs, and only when you identify what is needed can you start to plan how to obtain them. Therefore they have been retained as a separate element in the New Venture Creation Framework.

- Box 8: *Key partnerships* – became *Problems*, which were the key problem(s) that the value proposition seeks to solve for customers, and should underpin your business idea (Chapter 2) and your value proposition, and Chapter 6 explains how problems and solutions are communicated to customers. Maurya admitted that Key partnerships was the hardest block to remove. Because partnerships remain an important way of identifying an approach to solving the problems of risk and resources faced by entrepreneurs, as well as signalling a way of working in the future, they have been retained in the New Venture Creation Framework.

While Osterwalder and Pigneur developed their canvas for larger, established businesses, Maurya developed his for internet or web-based start-ups and acknowledged that 'it may have been easier to lay out a new canvas differently'. The New Venture Creation Framework is a more generalizable framework for business model development in start-ups, which can then be used to develop a formal business plan. All three models cover similar ground and are therefore consistent. Work through the differences between The New Venture Creation Framework Worksheet in Figure 4.1 and both versions of the Business Model Canvas in Figure 4.4, noting where different elements of the business model are located in the Canvas and the Framework. While this book is written around the New Venture Creation Framework, it can be used with whichever model you find the easiest and most natural.

Maurya, A. (2010) 'Why Lean Canvas vs Business Model', https://blog.leanstack.com/why-lean-canvas-vs-business-model-canvas-af62c0f250f0

Maurya, A. (2012) *Running Lean: Iterate from Plan A to a Plan That Works*, The Lean Series (2nd edn), Sebastopol, CA: O'Reilly.

Osterwalder, A. and Pigneur, Y. (2010) *Business Model Generation: A Handbook for Visionaries, Game Changers and Challengers*, Hoboken, NJ: John Wiley & Sons.

The advantage of developing a business model in this way is that it is (relatively) quick to develop and easy to change. It allows you to explore in a structured way innovative alternatives and options – always trying to understand the linkages and implications of different/product market offerings, while allowing you to test new models against established ones. You can experiment with different versions to see which critical assumptions are most realistic (revenue model: pricing, sales, costs etc.). Only when you are satisfied with the model created in this way would you go on to 'fill in' more of the details and write a formal business plan. The real challenge, of course, is to develop an innovative business model and then implement it effectively.

CASE insight 4.2

Streetcar (now Zipcar) UK

Developing a business model for market paradigm shift

Andrew Valentine studied modern languages and anthropology at Durham University. While there, he and a friend set up a student radio station, Purple FM. After graduating he joined the shipping company P&O and worked for them for six years, doing a part-time MBA. But in 2002 Andrew got itchy feet and, together with a friend, Brett Akker, decided he wanted to set up his own business rather than work for other people. The problem was that he did not have a business idea. So he and his partner set about searching systematically for the right business. They spent 18 months researching many ideas from organic food to training courses, meeting twice a week, before coming up with the final idea:

> We looked at hundreds of ideas. We were basically trying to identify gaps, so we were looking at how society was changing and what was missing. Our business had to have potential, be capable of being scaled up and play to our strengths. We kept looking until we found something that matched our criteria.

The final idea came from something Andrew read about in the USA – a car sharing club, but one with a commercial orientation. It piggybacked on environmental concerns about pollution and the problems city dwellers face in driving and parking in their cities. The idea is that members of the car sharing club can rent a car for as little as half an hour, replacing the need to buy. There is a one-off membership fee with an annual renewal charge and members then rent the cars by the hour. Cars are parked in unmanned, convenient locations just off residential streets and are ready to be driven away using a smartcard to open the door and start – thereby eliminating the need to go to an office to collect and return keys. Members can make car reservations online or by phone at any time and cars are available 24 hours a day. The cars are kept clean, serviced and fuelled – ready to go.

> I read about a similar business overseas and immediately thought what an amazing idea. There were a couple of other companies already running this kind of service in Britain but they weren't doing it the way we imagined we would be able to do it. We thought we could be more effective.

Once they had the idea, Andrew and Brett spent four months holding market research focus groups to test out the business model and developing financial projections to estimate the resources they would need.

> We were satisfying ourselves that not only would it work but that there was enough demand for it … Brett and I share a healthy level of permanent dissatisfaction with the service. This means that we are constantly working at making it better and improving everything. I really enjoy the creativity of growing a business.
>
> *Sunday Times* 15 November 2009

Initially called Mystreetcar and based in Clapham, South London, the business was finally launched in 2004 on the back of their savings, £60,000 of outside finance and £130,000 of lease finance to purchase the first eight cars. They did not see their competition as car rental companies, but rather car ownership. The scheme turns car ownership (a product) into a service and is seen by many as a 'greener' alternative because it encourages less road use. The business model challenges the basic paradigm of having to own a car to be able to use it at short notice, even for the shortest journey.

Andrew and Brett started by doing everything themselves, working almost a 24-hour day. They handed out leaflets at train and tube stations in the early mornings, eventually getting family and friends to help. They answered the phone and signed up members, meeting them to show them how to use the cars. They even washed and maintained the cars themselves. They offered a 24-hour service to members so, to start with, one of them had to be near to a phone all day, every day. After three months they had 100 members, each having paid a membership deposit and an annual joining fee, so they went out and leased 20 more cars at a cost of £300,000.

The company changed its name to Streetcar and, in 2007, Andrew and Brett gave up 43% of the business to Smedvig, a venture capital company, which invested £6.4 million. By 2009 Streetcar had a turnover of £20 million, with some 1,300 cars based in six UK cities. In 2010, the US company Zipcar (a company launched in 2000) bought Streetcar for $50 million (£32 million), giving the founders $17 million (£11 million). Zipcar subsequently purchased similar businesses – Carsharing in Austria and Avancar in Spain. In 2013 Avis, the third-largest car hire firm in the world, bought Zipcar for $500 million (£307 million) – a 50% premium on its share value.

By combining Zipcar's expertise in on-demand mobility with Avis Budget Group's expertise in global fleet operations and vast global network, we will be able to accelerate the revolution we began in personal mobility.
Scott Griffiths chair and chief executive Zipcar
The Guardian 2 January 2013

By 2016 Zipcar had more than one million members and the development of electric cars, needing their batteries to be recharged and designed specifically for urban use moving from charge-point to charge-point, is expected to accelerate this membership in coming years.

Visit the website: www.zipcar.co.uk

Questions:

1　Which customer segments do Streetcar/Zipcar target, and what is their value proposition?
2　How were these different from car ownership and traditional car rental? Why is this business model different?
3　Why will the development of electric cars improve the attractiveness of this business model? What other environmental trends might impact on Zipcar?
4　Why did Zipcar buy Streetcar, and why did Avis buy Zipcar?

Generic business models

There is no 'best' business model, no 'one-size-fits-all' solution and a Google search will reveal that there are dozens of different models. However, the oldest business model of all is to sell simply on low price. This is consistent with an economist's perfect market in which supply by many businesses and demand by rational buyers determines the price that achieves optimal efficiency, which usually means at the lowest costs.

Low price (low cost)

Where customers value low price more than anything in the **marketing mix** it is important to think carefully about how that low price might be achieved. Usually low prices can only be achieved through low costs, and if there are economies of scale to be had, a firm must achieve them quickly to survive in a competitive market. Operational excellence is usually needed to achieve this. These sorts of products are virtually commodities, undifferentiated and not tailored to specific customer needs, perhaps because these needs are too homogeneous. However, new flexible manufacturing technologies with just-in-time scheduling and the internet allowing customers to 'design' or configure products to their own specification mean that efficiency can often be combined with variety, making more products than ever 'homogeneous'. In markets that value low price fierce competition for market share is likely to lead to a market with a few dominant big players that are both efficiency and cost focused. You enter an established market like this at your peril because a new venture is unlikely to have either the experience or the economies of scale that established competitors have. Nevertheless, there may be an opportunity to create ancillary revenue streams alongside the low-priced product/service that make this business more viable.

There are, however, two strategic dimensions to business models that combine to affect the price you are able to charge (and therefore the profit you are likely to make) and have implications for how your operations are organized. These are **differentiation** and **customer focus or intimacy**. The more your product or service is different to competitors' and the closer and more focused you are on the needs of customers, the higher the price you are likely to be able to command. These dimensions are important and can be applied to a wide range of businesses to produce fundamental ways of creating sustainable **competitive advantage**.

A highly differentiated product or service offering, targeted at a focused market segment is called a niche business model. For a start-up this offers the best chance of success. At the other extreme, undifferentiated selling to anybody – an unfocused market – is virtually a commodity. This sells mainly because of the price charged – the lower the better. These business models are shown in Figure 4.5.

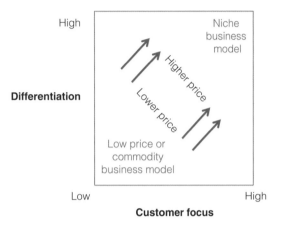

Figure 4.5 *Generic business models*

High differentiation

High differentiation is where customers value the other elements of the marketing mix more than price and are therefore willing to pay a premium. Often the key elements of differentiation are the ability to offer the best quality or most innovative products (e.g. Apple or Rolls-Royce), but the more product/service benefits you offer, the more ways you will be different to competitors. The more different you are, the more able you are to charge a high price, but you need to differentiate yourself from competitors in ways that are important to and valued by customers. If you have a strongly differentiated product/service you should move quickly to establish yourself in the market, developing the brand and making extensive use of its reputation. Differentiation is easiest when it is combined with a focused target market because it is easier to tailor the product or service offering more precisely to the needs of a smaller market. However, if sales increase and your market expands it is possible that your ability to maintain that customer focus will diminish. At the same time your success will attract imitators who may attempt to re-segment your market, thereby achieving greater customer focus.

> When you've got single-digit market share – and you're competing with the big boys – you either differentiate or die … The idea of building a business solely based on cost or price was not a sustainable advantage.
>
> *Michael Dell founder Dell Corporation Direct from Dell: Strategies that Revolutionized an Industry (1999, New York: Harper Business)*

High customer focus or intimacy

High customer focus or intimacy is where knowledge of customer needs is greatest, allowing the product or service to be more closely tailored to their specific needs. The key to having a high customer focus is the ability to have a close relationship with them. It goes hand in hand with effective market segmentation. It is often based on good customer service. Customer loyalty is likely to be high and there is the opportunity to develop a strong brand image. Small companies can thrive with this strategy because the smaller the market size, the more

> If you set up a company selling widgets like the bloke down the road and the only difference is that yours are cheaper, you'll make a living but that's all you'll achieve. If you can be truly differentiated and unique, then you've really got something.

effective the segmentation, and hence the customer focus, is likely to be. It can be particularly effective when combined with a highly differentiated product or service offering that gives the company a niche market (see Case insights 4.5, 4.6 and 4.7). The danger with customer focus is that the size of the market segment may be too small to be viable.

Both differentiation and customer focus provide significant opportunities to achieve **economies of scope** – also called **synergy**. This arises when the costs of an intangible asset such as product development or market research, or the cost of establishing a strong brand image (e.g. Apple, Mercedes Benz) can be spread over a range of products or services.

Different business models can exist successfully side by side in the same industry if it is sufficiently large and heterogeneous. For example, the business model for low-cost airlines like Southwest Airlines, easyJet (Case insight 4.4) and Air Asia is very different to that of flagship carriers like Delta, British Airways and Emirates. Yet both business models survive, appealing to different **target market segments**. Dell and Apple coexist in the personal computing market but with completely different business models serving different market segments with different value offerings. There is certainly no golden formula for success.

Competitors will, however, usually try to copy successful business models and today's novel business idea can often prove to be tomorrow's norm. So the question is: for how long can competition based on price, differentiation or focus be sustained? Your performance against competitors needs to be continually monitored and your value proposition continually reinforced and improved. It might also need, eventually, to be changed, and doing this goes to the core of the skills, capabilities and competencies a company has and the strategies it should employ.

CASE insight 4.3

African Renewable Energy Distributor (ARED)

RWANDA

Developing a business model – spotting opportunity

Born to refugee parents, Henri Nyakarundi is a Rwandan who studied computer science at Georgia State University, USA. He always wanted to run his own business but also hoped to go back to Rwanda to create opportunities for others.

> I was looking to do something that would not only solve a problem but also had a social impact by creating micro businesses for people.

Returning to Rwanda for holidays, he noticed that while many people had cell phones they often struggled to charge them. He checked his facts and found that,

although an estimated 70% of the population had cell phones, only 18% had access to electricity. He coupled this with the one thing Rwanda had plenty of – sunshine. And so his idea of a small solar-powered kiosk that could recharge cell phones was born. He sketched the first designs on paper and went on to build prototypes, refining them so that they could be produced relatively easily. The mobile kiosk, which could be towed by a bicycle and provides simultaneous charging for around 30 phones and other small electronic devices, was born at very little cost. Henri returned to Rwanda in 2012 to roll out his idea.

However, solving a problem does not always mean that there is a commercial opportunity. Henri had to develop a business model that created sufficient income to support the idea in a low-income country like Rwanda. His company, African Renewable Energy Distributor (ARED), decided on a 'business in a box' model, where kiosks were leased to agents (aggregators) under a micro-franchising system and they in turn recruited, trained and monitored kiosk operators (the micro-franchisees). But Henri also realized that phone charging alone would not sustain the business. ARED went on to design a software platform and mobile app, and in 2016 the company released a 'smart' version of the kiosk which offered Wi-Fi.

© ARED

Under ARED's business model, kiosk operators keep all the revenue they generate from charging electronic devices. However, secondary and tertiary revenues are shared between the operator, the aggregator and ARED. These are raised through selling additional services, such as internet access, phone credit, prepaid electricity, insurance, money transfers, tax payments and digital products, with the final revenue stream coming from advertising, online surveys and digital campaigns. Working with corporate partners in this way is critical to ARED's business. Selecting the right aggregators and micro-franchisees is vital for ARED, so a strict vetting process is in place.

When we offer a free opportunity, it becomes very important to have strong monitoring and evaluation. If they make money, we make money. So we want to make sure that people who are not performing get replaced immediately.

By 2016, some 40,000 customers were served in ARED's kiosks and many of these were in rural areas where the population is dependent on cell phones for communication and money transfers. Through his social enterprise, Henri hopes to solve key issues affecting parts of the African continent. Firstly, he aims to reduce unemployment and empower vulnerable people, particularly women and the disabled. As he notes:

Women don't have access to funding the way men do, and people with disabilities have even less opportunity.

Henri's second goal is to increase access to digital services and information. In East Africa, for example, fewer than 15% of the population currently have access to the internet. However, through ARED's Smart Solar Kiosks up to 50 users in a 100-metre radius can log on to the web or access free resources, such as health and educational content, through a local intranet.

A lot of people don't utilize their smart phone because they can't afford internet. Why not build our own intranet – our own network of content on the kiosk to serve our community?
CNN African Start-up 9 August 2016

Finally, Henri hopes to enable development in a sustainable way, with his ultimate goal being to build the largest solar-powered Wi-Fi network on the continent. The next stage of the company's ambitious plan is to increase the number of kiosks in Rwanda and beyond to between 50,000 and 100,000 within 10 years.

Our vision is to implement the best one stop shop for our customers in rural and semi-urban areas and to disrupt the existing informal sector in Africa.

Visit the website: www.a-r-e-d.com

Questions:

1 Would this business model work in a developed economy? Is it sustainable? How might it be developed?
2 Although ARED is a commercial business, it is one with strong social objectives. What problems does this pose in developing a business model?

Generic business models and critical success factors

Each of the generic strategies has different **business imperatives** which are shown in Table 4.1. Business imperatives are the things that you need to keep on top of, or risk failing to deliver your value proposition. Business imperatives can become the **critical success factors** for your business – the things you must get right to survive. The distinction is a matter of judgement.

Table 4.1 Generic strategies and business imperatives

High differentiation	High customer focus	Low price/cost
• Understanding the basis for the differential advantage • Building on the differential advantage • Building barriers to entry • Building the brand • Continuous innovation • Encouraging creativity and innovation	• Maintaining close relationships with customers • Keeping in touch with and understanding changes in customer needs • Maintaining customer loyalty • Maximizing sales to existing loyal customers (economies of scope) • Building the brand	• Maintaining cost leadership through economies of scale • Continually driving down costs • Achieving high sales volumes • Improving efficiency • Standardization

These imperatives can sometimes be conflicting, particularly between low cost/low price and the other two propositions, and also need the application of judgement. For example, a low-cost/low-price airline would never want to compromise on safety, despite it being an easy way to cut costs. However, usually the conflict is not so dramatic and there are ways of resolving it. For example, some large companies with product ranges based on different value propositions have unbundled their activities and set up separate organizations focused on those products with similar core value propositions. In this way, managers of these organizations have clear imperatives.

Generic business models and competitive advantage

You might ask whether the research tell us which strategies are most likely to deliver sustainable competitive advantage and hence maximize the chances of success for a start-up. The answer is that all of them have that potential – there are many examples of successful firms following any of them. However, the potential or odds are not the same. All the evidence points to high differentiation having a greater potential for success than low cost for a start-up (see Academic insight 4.3) and this is more easily achieved when applied to a focused target market. However, the bigger that target market the more vulnerable it is to further segmentation based upon even greater customer focus.

> Be very sure you have something unique that can't be replicated easily.
>
> *Angie Coates founder Monkey Music Sunday Times 30 November 2014*

The competitive advantage of a business stems from its core competencies or capabilities. For a start-up these will revolve around the skills and capabilities of the founder, the opportunity they have identified and the uniqueness of the way they intend to service the market they have identified. The more unique these competencies are, the more difficult they are to copy and the more successful the start-up is likely to be. They can be combined with other valuable or unique assets the business might have, such as equipment, trademarks, patents, brand and so on (called strategic assets) that allow the business to differentiate itself, and it is this that leads to sustainable **competitive advantage**. The more unique the core competencies and strategic assets of the firm, and the more difficult they are to copy, the greater the potential to differentiate its product/service, and thereby the greater its ability to create sustainable competitive advantage. It is therefore the strategy of high differentiation that has the greatest potential for success, so long as it is based upon a real, honest understanding of these competencies and strategic assets.

Generic business models and competitive advantage

A number of academic authors have claimed that there are only three **generic business models** that form enduring, core-value propositions. Michael Porter (1985) called them generic marketing strategies. Treacy and Wiersema (1995) called them **value disciplines**. There is little difference between the two descriptions. The three models are outlined in the text and are consistent with the fundamental ways of creating sustainable competitive advantage. To achieve this, Treacy and Wiersema say there are four questions that you need to answer:

1 For each dimension, what proportion of customers focus on it as their primary or dominant decision criterion? In other words, how important is each value discipline to each market segment?
2 Which competitors provide the best value in each of these value dimensions? In other words, who is your major competitor in each discipline?
3 How do you compare to the competition on each dimension?
4 If you fall short of the value leaders in each dimension of value, how can this be remedied? Of course, if you do fall short the real question is whether you can compete at all, or whether you have constructed a sufficiently different value proposition to create a new market not currently catered for.

The strategy of differentiation seems to have the greatest chance of success for a start-up. Competitive advantage stems from core competencies or capabilities. In a longitudinal study Rassmussen et al. (2011) showed that the more unique these were, the more difficult they were to copy, hence the greater the firm's ability to differentiate itself and the more successful it was likely to be. In his review of the literature, Grant (2015) also concluded that all the evidence points towards differentiation having a greater potential for success than low cost.

Grant, R.M. (2015) *Contemporary Strategic Analysis*, 9th edn, Chichester: John Wiley.

Porter, M. (1985) *Competitive Advantage: Creating and Sustaining Superior Performance*, New York: Free Press.

Rasmussen, E., Mosey, S. and Wright, M. (2011) 'The Evolution of Entrepreneurial Competencies: A Longitudinal Study of University Spin-Off Venture Emergence', *Journal of Management Studies*, September, 48 (6).

Treacy, M. and Wiersema, F. (1995) *The Discipline of Market Leaders*, Reading, MA: Addison-Wesley.

easyJet (1)  UK

Developing a low price/cost business model

One firm that has successfully followed the low price/cost business model is easyJet. It was founded by Stelios Haji-Ioannou, a MBA from London Business School, in 1995 with £5 million borrowed from his father, a Greek shipping tycoon. easyJet copied the business model of the US carrier South Western Airlines, changing the marketing paradigm for the industry, and in doing so created a whole new market for low-cost airline travel in Europe. The company has transformed the European air travel market and has beaten off many rival imitators. Today it is a leading European airline. easyJet was floated on the Stock Market in 2000, making Stelios £280 million profit. Only seven years after founding the company and still owning 29 per cent, Stelios realized that he was not suited to managing a public company and was better suited to being a serial entrepreneur, so in 2002 he resigned as Chairman, aged only 35.

A central strategy of being low price is being low cost, and that has a number of implications for the way the operations of easyJet are organized. Aircraft are leased rather than owned. Low costs

Getty Images/ groveb

come from two driving principles: firstly 'sweating' or making maximum use of the assets and secondly high operating efficiency. easyJet flies 'point-to-point' (average trip length about 1,000 kilometres), without the connecting flights and networks that the heritage carriers, like British Airways (BA), have to worry about. easyJet flies its planes for 11 hours a day – 4 hours longer than BA. Their pilots fly 900 hours a year, 50 per cent more than BA pilots. In terms of operating efficiency, it means:

- Aircraft fly out of low-cost airports. These are normally not the major airport serving any destination and can be some distance from the destination;
- Aircraft are tightly scheduled. Rapid turnaround is vital. Low-cost airlines aim to allow only 25 minutes to offload one set of passengers and load another, less than half the time of heritage rivals;
- Aircraft must leave and arrive on time (they will not wait for passengers), and delays can have horrendous knock-on consequences for the timetable. Nevertheless punctuality is varied, with the low-cost carriers just as good as full-fare airlines on some routes;
- There is no 'slack' in the system. easyJet admits to having 'one and a half planes' worth' of spare capacity compared with the dozen planes BA has on stand-by at Gatwick and Heathrow. If something goes wrong with a plane it can lead to cancellations and long delays;
- There are fewer cabin crew than full-fare rivals and staff rostering is a major logistical problem;
- All operations and processes must be slimmed down and made as simple as possible.

In terms of customer service, it means:

- Ticketless flights;
- A single class, therefore with more seats on each plane, with no 'frills' such as complimentary drinks, meals or assigned seats – all additional services must be paid for;
- Baggage allowances are lower than heritage carriers' and there is no compensation for delays or lost baggage;

- Transfers not guaranteed because the planes could be late;
- Aerobridges for boarding and disembarking are generally not used because these add cost;
- Concentration on point-to-point flights whereas the full-fare, heritage airlines tend to concentrate on hub-and-spoke traffic.

One of the fears about low-cost airlines has been that they will be tempted to compromise on safety for the sake of cutting costs. The British Airline Pilots Association has claimed that pilots of low-cost airlines have been tempted to cut corners to achieve flight timetables. The industry is all too aware that the low-cost US airline, Valuejet, went bankrupt after one of its planes crashed in 1996, killing all 110 people on board. However, by partnering with some of the best known maintenance providers in the industry, easyJet makes safety its first priority. In common with other low-cost operators, it operates a single type of aircraft. This offers economies of purchasing, maintenance, pilot training and aircraft utilization.

easyJet has started moving away from being the lowest cost carrier and adding customer value, for example by flying to airports nearer to major cities. AirAsia is now generally regarded as the lowest cost airline in the world with Ryanair, a competitor of easyJet, not far behind. Interestingly Ryanair has so little faith in its timetable that it advises passengers not to book connecting flights.

easyJet is generally regarded as having an excellent branding strategy, which was originally based on PR around its founder, and having one of the best websites in the sector. It is aggressive in promoting its brand and running advertising promotions that maximize seat occupancy. It realizes that planes must have high seat occupancy to be economic. To this end it is particularly inventive with pricing, encouraging real bargain hunters onto the less popular flights during the day and promoting early bookings with cheaper fares. easyJet has been at the forefront of the use of the internet for virtual ticketing, and now sells all of its tickets online. This means it does not have to pay commission to travel agents and check-in can be quicker and more efficient. Its website has been held up as a model for the industry and many have copied it. easyJet also tries to get more sales from every passenger visiting their website and sells other services such as airport car parking, car hire and hotel bookings.

The industry in Europe has seen some fierce price wars as competitors battled for market share in a fast-growing market where there were economies of scale to be had. easyJet has been aggressive in purchasing new routes and landing rights, which can be difficult to secure, giving it a comprehensive European network and securing the economies of scale that it needs. These days the low-cost airline industry is well established and far more difficult to enter. AirAsia entered the market in 2002, copying the successful low-cost model but in a new market without competitors.

Visit the website: www.easyjet.com

Questions:

1 From the information given in this case, use the Framework Worksheet or the PowerPoint slide to complete as many elements as you can of the New Venture Creation Framework.
2 What are the operational imperatives for easyJet – the things it needs to get right to enable it to deliver the value proposition? Which of these are critical for its success in this market?
3 How important is low cost compared to other elements of the value proposition?
4 How do you go about compromising the core value proposition? If you start to compromise your core value proposition, how far do you have to go before it is no longer core?

Visit www.macmillanihe.com/burns-nvc-2e to download the Framework Worksheet and PowerPoint slide.

Niche business model

Companies that offer both high differentiation and high customer focus are said to have a **niche business model**. Market focus involves understanding in depth the needs of relatively few customers, and therefore there is more scope for differentiation. It often involves targeting smaller markets, and therefore there are more opportunities for smaller businesses. This is the strategy that research tells us is most likely to succeed for a start-up because it can charge higher prices and is more likely to sustain its differential advantage because the smaller market segment does not attract competitors, at least initially. What is more, as discussed earlier, the internet has meant that market niches can be global and that means that while there may be a clear identification of the needs of a few customers, the global size of this market segment could be quite large. And once the start-up dominates one market niche it can move on to another.

Troy Collins founder Endource Sunday Times 5 March 2015

You need to figure out how you can be better or different. What are you doing that hasn't been done before?

There is usually a trade-off between price and the other elements of the marketing mix. The stronger or more distinctive and different these other elements, the higher the price you are normally able to command. Too many small firms compete primarily on price because they do not understand how the other elements might add value to the customer and they believe the other elements of their marketing mix are insufficiently different from their competitors'.

One small firm producing motor components found itself competing unsuccessfully against a large multinational that consistently undercut it on price. It decided that it could not survive with a value proposition relying on operational excellence/low cost and decided it needed a rethink. It researched its customers and the market and found there were many opportunities for products manufactured to a high technical specification in which quality and supplier reputation were more important than the price charged – a product leadership/differentiation value proposition – so it decided to switch its strategy. Low volumes and high price for specialist products proved to be a more sustainable strategy and, over time, it was able to develop close relationships with a few of its regular customers and became an established niche player in what otherwise might be seen as a highly competitive industry.

Following a niche business model involves maximizing your value proposition to a closely defined target customer group. It involves understanding the needs of this group – the benefits they are really looking for – and translating that into a marketing mix. The smaller the group, the more homogeneous their needs are likely to be. So you may want to look again at your original target market to see whether it can profitably be broken down into smaller market niches. Meeting the needs of each new niche may involve either adding costs, by adding more valued product features, or subtracting costs, by eliminating less valued features. For each niche there is the question of the price they are willing to pay for this improved and differentiated product – a topic we shall cover in the next chapter. This iterative process is likely to have implications for the resources you need and some of the needs of the different market niches you identify may not be profitable to target. It is all a question of judgement.

CASE insight 4.5

Quad Electroacoustics UK

Developing a niche business model

One Huntingdon-based family company that has been very successful in differentiating its products and selling to a small but lucrative market segment is Quad Electroacoustics. Originally founded in 1936 by Peter Walker as an 'acoustical manufacturing company' to produce 'public address' systems, today its silvery-grey, bizarrely sculptured audio equipment looks like no other. It sounds superb as well. While Japanese 'competitors' bring out new models every year, Quad's stay the same and last forever. Its original electrostatic loudspeaker was in production for 28 years. 'Quad' is a byword for quality, reliability and design originality – but the equipment is not cheap. Current models sell for over £3,000, and still 70% of Quad's sales are exported, especially to Europe, USA and Japan.

Visit the website: www.quad-hifi.co.uk

© Quad

Questions:

1 Why is Quad a niche business?
2 What are the pros and cons of this business model for Quad?

CASE insight 4.6

Morgan Motor Company UK

Developing a niche business model

One company that arguably could make even higher margins by charging a higher price for its products is the Morgan Motor Company. Founded in 1909, it is the world's oldest privately owned car manufacturer, making a quintessentially British sports car. Every Morgan is hand-built and looks like it came from the 1930s. Each car is different, with a choice of 35,000 body colours and leather upholstery to match. It takes seven weeks to build a car, and customers are invited to the factory to see the process. Morgan sells only about 500 cars a year, half overseas, and demand exceeds supply, cushioning the company from the vagaries of demand. Morgan is a unique car manufacturer in a niche market.

Visit the website: www.morgan-motor.co.uk

Questions:

1 Why is this a niche business?
2 What are the pros and cons of this business model for Morgan?

CASE insight 4.7

Escape to the Cape SOUTH AFRICA

Developing a niche business model

Escape to the Cape is a venture set up by Shaheed Ebrahim in 2010 in South Africa. The tourism industry is a fiercely competitive business in South Africa, but the company offers guided tours with a difference around Cape Town. Shaheed spent about $4,000 to register his company and get a website, and then took out a mortgage of $32,000 to buy his 7-seater bus which he equipped with the latest internet technology. As well as having an expert guide, the bus is equipped with Wi-Fi and clients can borrow a complimentary tablet computer that then allows them to go online to email, Facebook or Tweet their family and friends with emails, photos or videos of their tour. They can even talk to them using Skype. Every seat has a facility to charge any mobile device. The bus has its own fridge offering a range of drinks including complimentary chilled

Bo-Kaap, Cape Town
iStock.com/ JoRodrigues

water. Shaheed won the Emerging Tourism Entrepreneur of the Year award in South Africa for 2011/12.

> *There are hundreds of tour operators out in Cape Town but the difference is that we've taken technology that's available and put it onto our tours, thereby enhancing the tours.*
> BBC News Business 31 January 2013

Visit the website: www.escapeto thecape.co.za

Questions:

1 Why is Escape to the Cape a niche business?
2 What are the pros and cons of this business model for Escape to the Cape?

Internet business models

Because of their general applicability, we have looked in some detail at the generic business models. However, numerous other models can be just as successful and have been used successfully by internet businesses, although most are variants of the generic models. You are only limited by your imagination. Some new business ideas, particularly those involving internet-based virtual content ('knowledge products'), require considerable ingenuity to develop business models that generate income rather than just users (see Case insight 4.8). There is the issue of how to price this sort of 'product'. Once developed, it is available for downloading again and again at virtually zero cost to the producer (a problem to which we shall return in the next two chapters). On the other hand, online content can often be easily accessed and copied by end users, even if access is restricted. It can take time to 'monetize' a new internet-based business idea – longer than it does to design the product or service itself. Novel internet business models can generate income quickly and some have led to market paradigm shifts, creating whole new markets (see Case insight 4.2). Nevertheless, it is often the case that users have to be found first in order to prove the concept, and only afterwards can ways of monetarizing it be found – hence the idea of the **lean start-up** (Academic insight 4.4).

Publishers shouldn't be so dependent on anyone else's platform. It's a bad business decision. You don't own your audience, you're renting your audience – and that can turn off any time. When the algorithm shifts, everybody feels it.

John Avlon, Editor-in-Chief of The Daily Beast, Sunday Times 7 May 2017

Here are just some of the better known and more established ways of monetarizing your internet business model. They are not mutually exclusive. Often more than one model is used alongside another – called a **multi-sided market**:

- **Direct sales model** – where products or services are sold directly online and delivered by post (e.g. Amazon);
- **Bricks-and-clicks model** – where traditional retail is combined with the direct internet sales model either with postal delivery or customer collection (e.g. most large retailers such as John Lewis);
- **Affiliate model** – where you help sell a product or service, without necessarily taking ownership, in return for commission (e.g. Amazon);
- **Auction model** – where online shoppers bid for products (e.g. eBay);
- **Flash sales model** – where daily deals are offered to registered customers (e.g. Groupon);
- **Advertising model** – where the internet firms are paid for ads being placed on their website (e.g. YouTube, owned by Google). To persuade advertisers you need to have high levels of focused website traffic. This therefore works particularly well for popular niche sites, although it is becoming increasingly competitive with more and more websites but most of the revenue going through just two internet giants. It is estimated that in 2016 99% of the US and 89% of the UK growth in digital advertising expenditure went through two companies – Google and Facebook. Examples such as YouTube illustrate how hard it can be to monetize free content even when you have significant website traffic. Advertising can restrict screen content for your own product/service. What is more, increasingly internet content has to be tailored for mobile devices where the opportunity for advertising is even more limited. It is estimated that 90% of Facebook's turnover comes from mobile ads;
- **Pay-per-click model** – where clicks onto an advertiser's link are paid for (e.g. Google). This is just a variant on the affiliate and advertising models;
- **Subscription model** – where customers subscribe for the online product or service (e.g. newspapers such as *The Times*). This requires specialist content that is of real value to the

online customer and is often coupled with some sort of free trial usage to demonstrate its value. Because of the surge in 'fake news' in 2017, many newspapers saw a resurgence in their subscription levels;

- **Freemium model** – where the business gives away something for free such as a 'basic' service but extras or premium services are charged for (e.g. Spotify). This is most common in service-based businesses where the marginal cost of an additional customer is very small;
- **Bait and hook model** – where special deals are offered that lock customers into buying a particular product or service because the costs of switching are high (e.g. smartphones);
- **Open business models** – where value is created through collaboration between partners (e.g. price comparison websites);
- **Pay-as-you-go model** – where you pay for what you use or consume (e.g. some smartphone contracts).

CASE insight 4.8

Web 2.0 USA

US high-growth, web start-ups

Some of the fastest and highest-growth start-ups over the last two decades have been based on the development of interactive websites, where users can generate their own content and interact with each other to form a virtual community – called Web 2.0. This contrasts with websites that limit the user to viewing the content. Examples of Web 2.0 include social networking sites, wikis, blogs, video hosting sites, hosted services, mash-ups and so on. Fast-moving, high-growth start-ups face particular problems, not least how to develop a business model that generates income (see section above) for what is, essentially a zero-cost product (see page 192). Because of the uncertainties surrounding their market acceptance and their accelerated development these start-ups need to plan for growth, particularly because they often need to raise considerable finance at inception. At the same time they face considerable commercial uncertainty because of their unproven business model. Often the business model they start with has to be changed early in their existence as they find out more about customer needs and how usage of this new medium can be monetarized. The Lean Start-up techniques outlined later in this chapter can help mitigate the risks Web 2.0 start-ups face by trying out the new market with minimum risk. There are many examples of highly successful Web 2.0 start-ups that have made their founders into millionaires.

Facebook

This is arguably the best known Web 2.0 start-up. Founded by **Mark Zuckerberg** in 2004, it is a free online social networking site based in Menlo Park, California. Its famously oversubscribed initial public offering in 2012 raised $16 billion, although the share price subsequently slumped. It now has almost two billion active users and revenues in 2016 were some $27.6 billion.

LinkedIn

This is another social networking site but one targeted at professional occupations. Now headquartered in Mountain View, California and Dublin, Ireland. It was founded by **Reid Hoffman** in 2002 and launched in 2003. Its initial public offering in 2011 was also oversubscribed but shares subsequently doubled in value. It now has over 414 million members and revenues in 2015 were some $2.9 billion.

Twitter

This is a social networking and microblogging site that enables users to send and receive text messages called 'tweets' – famously used by the US President, Donald Trump. Based in San Francisco, it was launched by **Jack Dorsey** in 2006. It has 313 million active monthly users and revenues in 2016 were some $2.5 billion, although to date it has not made a profit.

Dropbox

This is a file hosting service founded by **Drew Houston** in 2007 and launched in 2008. It is based in San Francisco. It allows files to be stored 'in the cloud' – free up to a certain size and for a fee beyond this. It is a private company and when it last raised private capital in early

2014 it was valued at $10 billion, based on revenues of some $240 million. Revenues for 2016 are claimed to be over $1 billion.

YouTube

This is the well known widely used video-sharing website based in San Bruno, California. It was launched in 2005 by **Steve Chen, Chad Hurley** and **Jawed Karim**. The venture-funded start-up was purchased by Google only 22 months later, in 2006, for $1.65 billion.

Questions:

1 How easy is it to predict markets, sectors or industries that will enjoy this sort of growth?
2 What are the challenges in trying to construct a business model for this sort of business?

Generally, the more novel your business model the more likely you are to have some form of competitive advantage, at least in the short term. The question is how easy it is to copy that novel business model and therefore how sustainable your competitive advantage might be. Unlike inventions or innovations, you are unlikely to be able to safeguard the intellectual property around a new business model. And the more successful your business model is, the more likely it is to be copied. You have three major weapons to help secure sustainability:

1 The speed you get to market. There is a lot to be said for **first-mover advantage**;
2 The speed with which you dominate that market. Market dominance gives you market power, so it is generally better to dominate a small market than to be a small player in a big market;
3 The strength of your brand within that market. This is the marketing tool that will help you carve out that dominance.

Low-cost market testing

The idea that speed of market entry can be important creates a dilemma for many businesses that may have novel products or business models because any form of market testing can take time, might disclose valuable intellectual property to the public and, in some cases such as new inventions or internet-based services, may not be possible. However, it may be possible in some cases to try out products or services in the market ahead of a major launch, enabling you to at least fine-tune elements of your business model. A number of academics have recommended small-scale, low-cost market entry and trial where possible, in order to gain market information prior to a full product launch (see Academic insight 4.4). But there is always a tension. Launch a product too early and you risk being ill prepared, too late and you lose first-mover advantage.

There are many low-cost ways of testing market demand for a product. In the UK there are 'car-boot sales', in the USA 'garage sales', in Canada 'trunk sales', and in many countries, products are just sold by the side of the road. Indeed you can make a living by selling things in this way. In the UK you can find out where your

> We fully believe that the cost of inaction is greater than the cost of a mistake. So we move quickly and learn through trial and error. Trial, test, analyse. Then repeat.
>
> Brian Shanahan founder Temple & Webster www.sparke.com.au 16 October 2014

CASE insight 4.9

Pinterest USA

Developing a business model for a radical innovation

Founded in 2010 by Ben Silbermann, Paul Sciarra and Evan Sharp, Pinterest has attracted investments that value the company at $12.3 billion, despite the fact it has only just begun to generate revenue. Pinterest is a visual discovery app that helps people discover and save creative ideas. Users save (or 'pin') ideas they find on Pinterest or the web to themed digital boards – for example, fashion, photography, cooking, home or garden improvements and so on. The site is highly visual, unlike many other text-heavy social networks. 'Pinners' are given recommendations for Pins and boards that may interest them, based on what others with similar interests have saved. There are more than 175 million monthly active users on Pinterest.

© Pinterest

The inspiration for the idea came when Silbermann and Sciarra were working on a failed idea for a shopping app called Tote. They noticed that instead of buying through the app, users emailed pictures of products to each other. People liked pictures and they wanted to get ideas and inspiration from them. The challenge was to turn this into something that made money.

> *There has been so much remarkable work on search – on making it so that you can find what you're looking for and you can retrieve it really quickly. But there has been little work done on helping people discover things when they may not know exactly what they are looking for … From very early on with our investors, we were clear that the goal of the service was to help people discover things that were meaningful to them. That motivation falls closely in line with the goals of lots of businesses and advertisers.*
>
> *Sunday Times* 6 July 2014

Because Pinners have an obvious hobby interest, advertising can be highly relevant and targeted, thus commanding a premium price. Because Pinners browse Pinterest for attractive images and ideas, it has a very

different feel to conventional search engines, such as Google, that are designed to deliver specific information. Sites like Google build profiles of their users by mining the data they generate. But that means that their targeted advertising can often feel intrusive and therefore counterproductive for advertisers. People come to Pinterest to plan the things that they would like to do in the future, whether it is something they would like to buy, a recipe they would like to make, or a place they would like to visit. They just click on the pins they wish to investigate further. Therefore, it is a huge opportunity for marketers to be a part of the process in helping Pinners take action on the pins that they find online. And, while Pinterest also has pins promoted by companies, they look just like any other pin in the system with the exception of a note that says 'promoted', making a Promoted Pin less obtrusive than other ads. Companies have been pinning for years, setting up their own pinboards on Pinterest to showcase their own products. In 2014 the company launched a self-serve platform that enables companies to create their own Promoted Pins that can be posted to other boards.

With more than 175 million regular users, Pinterest has caught not only the attention of investors but also the big advertisers. However, now that they have devised a revenue-generating business model, the question is: how will the search engines from which they hope to take revenue react? In the past these companies have often bought up the best new ideas.

Visit the website: www.pinterest.com

Questions:

1 Which business models would you apply to Pinterest?
2 The inspiration for Pinterest came from a failed idea for an app called Tote. What are the potential effects on an entrepreneur of a failure like this?

Lean start-up

Ries (2011) coined the phrase 'lean start-up' for new ventures that minimize the lead time as well as their investment in a new product/service launch. The idea is that the product/service is not launched in a 'perfect state', but rather in its 'minimum viable' state. This **minimum viable product** (MVP) is one with just enough features to satisfy early customers. Customer feedback is then used in an iterative fashion to further tailor the product/service to the specific needs of customers – a process Ries calls **validated learning**. In this way, no valuable time and money are invested in designing features or services that customers do not value. This approach gives the company first-mover advantage and minimizes costs while, importantly, reducing market risks when the product/service finally reaches a wider market.

The key to the approach is close customer relationships and developing mechanisms to receive their feedback. Ries gives the example of the start-up strategy of Nick Swinmurn who founded the US online shoe retailer, Zappos. Instead of building a website and a large database of footwear, he tested his business idea by taking pictures of shoes from local stores, posting them online and selling them through his website, buying the shoes from the stores at full price. Although he did not make a profit, this method quickly validated his business idea, with minimum cost and risk.

The concept of lean start-up is associated with the concept of **pivoting**, defined by Ries as a 'structured course correction designed to test a new fundamental hypothesis about the product, strategy, and engine of growth'. This is where a company makes radical changes to its business model based upon the learning gained in its start-up phase, and is a process to which we shall return in Chapter 13 when all the elements of your business model are complete.

The lean start-up idea was originally developed for high-tech businesses, based upon the way companies like Google develop new products, but has gained popularity generally. It reflects the **parallel new product development model** – where product development and concept/market testing go side by side, as shown in Figure 3.3. It also embraces elements of the **lean manufacturing** philosophy – an approach that minimizes costs and waste in manufacturing without sacrificing productivity.

The lean start-up approach mirrors entrepreneurs' incremental approach to decision making – gaining knowledge as they proceed – and the way they limit their financial exposure as much as possible. The idea works well for some products – for example, software and web-based products – where new features can be trialled on the back of the core product. This is an approach often taken by Google. However, if the core product does not function you risk customer rejection. For high-investment (often disruptive) innovations, the product must be substantially right first time. Imagine asking Apple if they would have been happy to launch a 'minimum viable' iPhone.

Based upon this approach, Maurya (2010 and 2012) modified the Business Model Canvas to accommodate the information loops needed to monitor customer feedback on a MVP (Academic insight 4.2). The process he highlighted was a learning cycle of turning ideas into products, measuring customers' reactions to those products, and then deciding whether to persevere or pivot the idea. It could be repeated as many times as necessary. The process was:

Idea → **Build** → *Product* → **Measure** → *Data* → **Learn**

Maurya later (2016) highlighted the problems of firstly selecting the right **metrics** to monitor and secondly finding the time and resources to gather and analyse them. Even then, the link between cause and effect and any corrective actions needed may not be clear. Like Ries, Maurya was very much focused on internet start-ups and advocated the use of a metric that monitored 'traction' – 'the rate at which a business model captures moneterizable value from its users' – in essence, linking them to some target financial milestone(s). For example, an online magazine or newspaper could consider web-page views to be a key operational metric because they are directly linked with advertising revenue. All too often internet start-ups have focused on users rather than the income they generate, and a number of well-known companies achieved a listing on a stock market without having made any profit.

The idea of small-scale market entry and trial in order to gain market information prior to full product launch for a start-up is not new (Chaston, 2000). Nor is the idea that risk is related to the time taken to launch a new product/service – too early and you risk being ill-prepared and turning customers against it, too late and you lose first-mover advantage (Burns, 2005). Launch timing is critical.

But when do you have a MVP to launch? If the product/ service is so underdeveloped that customers reject it, even a limited launch might spell disaster later. And, even if you have the resources, how quickly can you modify the MVP to better meet the needs of customers? If you take too long you risk losing first-mover advantage. While these studies provide a valuable blueprint for many start-ups and emphasize the undoubted importance of monitoring customer information, they provide few answers to these questions.

Maurya, A. (2010) 'Why Lean Canvas vs Business Model', https://blog.leanstack.com/why-lean-canvas-vs-business-model-canvas-af62c0f250f0

Maurya, A. (2012) *Running Lean: Iterate from Plan A to a Plan That Works*, The Lean Series (2nd edn), Sebastopol, CA: O'Reilly.

Maurya, A. (2016) *Scaling Lean: Mastering the Metrics for Startup Growth*, London: Penguin.

Burns, P. (2005) *Corporate Entrepreneurship: Building an Entrepreneurial Organization*, Basingstoke: Palgrave Macmillan.

Chaston, I. (2000) *Entrepreneurial Marketing: Competing by Challenging Convention*, Basingstoke: Palgrave Macmillan.

Ries, E. (2011) *The Lean Startup: How Today's Entrepreneurs Use Continuous Innovation to Create Radically Successful Businesses*, New York: Crown Publishing.

local car-boot sale is taking place by simply looking on the internet – www.carbootjunction.com. More recently, as the high streets have more and more vacant shop sites, we have started to see 'pop-up', temporary shops (and even restaurants) testing out new marketing concepts.

The internet allows you to reach a far wider group of customers than these physical markets and at a relatively low cost. Sites like Amazon, eBay and Alibaba can be used to sell goods and offer a low-cost way of testing market demand. They also offer to host 'storefronts' for small merchants where 'buy-it-now' goods can be offered. This allows you to achieve visibility and brand loyalty which was previously only gained through traditional advertising or local shoppers. However, while these sites can offer an international reach, the fees they charge are increasing and the growth of social media means that new lower-cost outlets are now emerging. For example, there are thousands of Facebook pages dedicated to buying and selling products. The FaceBay community page (known as Fbay) was launched in 2010 and now has tens of thousands of members. To join you simply 'like' the page and then you can trade with members. These sites can be geographically based, thus facilitating the exchange of goods and services for cash.

Indeed, there are likely to be a number of locally based internet trading sites around where you live: simply Google 'for sale' and your postcode or zip code to find them. For example, in Bristol in the UK there is a site where some 500 mothers buy, sell and give away things like clothes, toys or furniture, mainly for children. This, like many groups, is open only to members, so you need to join before you can participate. Twitter is also an increasingly popular and free way of trading: simply enter '#forsale#', followed by the place you live. You can find anything from properties to computer games offered for sale in this way. Many classified ads websites now also have their own official Twitter accounts. The important thing with all these low-cost ways of buying and selling is that there is no official system of vetting and it really is a case of 'buyer beware' – hence the importance of location.

You can find other sites where you can buy and sell goods in the UK by visiting www.ebay-alternatives.co.uk. The site is updated regularly and lists alternatives to eBay including auction sites, some being more suitable for large volume business. These include www.preloved.co.uk, where you can advertise second-hand goods with no selling fees and www.gumtree.com, where you can advertise certain types of goods for free. There are also apps such as 'Shpock' (a UK app launched in 2014) that enable users to buy and sell goods

CASE
insight
4.10

Amanti Cupcakes UK

Low-cost market testing

Tina Katsighiras started Amanti Cupcakes in 2013, selling sweet treats like cupcakes, brownies and scones through the social networking site Facebook – a low-cost way of testing out a business idea. Working from her home in Prudhoe in the north of England, she takes orders online

and bakes them on the day they are ordered for, delivering them to local residents at night. She also supplies a number of shops and cafes after free samples she gave them quickly sold out. The mum-of-two decided to leave her clerical job and start up her own business after her father suffered a stroke.

Tina Katsighiras

I just got up one morning and realised that my life wasn't going to change unless I did something about it. I'm half Greek and come from a long line of successful chefs. I even trained in catering after leaving school. I had always enjoyed baking and people had always come to me for birthday and Christmas cakes, so I decided to follow that route.

www.hexhamcourant.co.uk 16 October 2013

Visit the website: www.facebook.com/AmantiCupcakes

A new product – the Cupcake Cornet

Questions:

1   What are the motivations behind this start-up? How would you describe it using the typologies in Chapter 1?
2   What are its prospects for growth? Does this say anything about this form of market testing?

through a virtual boot sale. This is particularly useful for local sales. You upload details of the sale item, including pictures and wait for buyers. Another app called 'Zapper' buys DVDs, CDs, games, mobiles or electronic devices. You scan in the bar codes using a free-to-download app, Zapper gives you a price and, if you accept the offer, you can send the goods to Zapper free of charge and they will forward payment.

These low-cost ways of market testing can also be low-cost ways of market trading. They avoid the high fixed costs of bricks-and-mortar retailers and often piggyback off the popularity of larger internet storefronts. And, while the sales at any one location or in any one storefront might be limited, if you have a number of them they can soon generate substantial income.

CASE insight 4.11

TruffleShuffle UK

Lean start-up

In 2004, Pat Wood's retro Dukes of Hazzard T-shirt, bought from a US website, aroused so much interest at his local pub that he wondered whether it might form the basis of a business. He bought another for £10, listed it on eBay and sold it within 24 hours for £20. And that was how the business was born. He bought the domain name truffleshuffle.co.uk and started selling retro T-shirts online from his one-bedroom flat.

Every time I sold a T-shirt I'd buy two more. I thought if I could make a couple of hundred pounds a month I would be happy.

The website attracted a lot of interest and within months he was receiving 30 orders a day. However, Wood kept his full-time job in IT, packing T-shirts in the evening with his girlfriend Claire, who was studying law at university.

I'd get all my mates to come over on a Friday night to put T-shirts in envelopes and I'd pay them in pizza, while Claire and I coped with demand by just not sleeping.

Wood finally decided to leave his job in 2005 when turnover reached £100,000 a month.

I didn't want to put all my eggs in one basket, so I stuck it out as long as possible, but in the back of my mind I knew I had a business that was able to provide me and Claire with a salary, so I took the leap.

Sunday Times 27 July 2014

Pat Wood

© TruffleShuffle Retail Ltd. Photographer: Simon Western

Wood generally bought T-shirts from the USA and resold them in the UK. If a T-shirt did not exist for a TV show, he would obtain a licence to use particular images. And gradually the proportion of own-made T-shirts grew. He also started selling to retailers such as Topshop and Next. He developed a second website for band T-shirts and now sells a range of clothing as well as novelty and gift items. In addition to selling on his own website, he also sells worldwide through Amazon and eBay. Although the business was cut back for a couple of years following the 2008 recession, today it takes approximately 30,000 orders a month and has a turnover of £4.5 million. Based in Avonmouth, UK, it employs 20 staff.

Visit the website: www.truffleshuffle.co.uk

Questions:

1 What are the advantages of lean start-up?
2 What is the link with the discovery skill of experimentation?

ACADEMIC insight 4.5

The customer development process

Building on the concept of a 'lean start-up', Blank and Dorf (2012) outlined four steps to bring a product or service to market.

1 **Customer discovery** – This is where the entrepreneur starts the discovery process, turning their vision into a series of business models that can be tested against customer reactions – defining the 'problem' and the possible 'solution'.

2 **Customer validation** – This is where the entrepreneur tests whether the resulting business model is repeatable and scalable. Each of these first two steps are iterative, requiring the entrepreneur to go back and repeat

elements of the process should they prove impractical or unable to be validated.

3 **Customer creation** – This is the start of execution; the process of building customer demand by developing and executing a marketing plan – the start of the customer journey outlined in Chapter 7. Different start-ups entering different markets will require different plans but, whatever the plan, building in customer feedback is important in validating a final business model.

4 **Company building** – This is the transition from building demand to creating loyal customers. It requires effective, systematic execution of the final, validated business model. It is the point where the business starts to take on many of the characteristics of larger firms and entrepreneurs find out whether they have the necessary leadership skills.

Blank, S. and Dorf. B. (2012) *The Startup Owner's Manual: The Step-By-Step Guide for Building a Great Company*, Pecadero, CA: K&S Ranch Press.

Characteristics of a good business model

No amount of detailed research, planning or market testing can guarantee 100% success. All you can do is stack the odds in your favour. Nevertheless, we know that the most successful business ideas generate high profits and involve low risk. Unfortunately very few such opportunities exist. Here is a checklist of 15 characteristics of a good business model against which to judge yours:

1 **Identified market need or gap** – the idea must meet a clearly identified market need to be commercially viable.

2 **No or few existing competitors** – the more innovative your product/service and markets, the fewer competitors, and the higher the price you are normally able to charge. However, remember it is always possible that there are no competitors because there is no viable market for the product/service.

3 **Growing market** – it is always easier to launch a business into a new or growing rather than declining market. Of course it may be that you are launching a business that will create a completely new market.

4 **Clearly identified customers and a viable business model** – if you don't know who you are selling to you won't know how to sell to them, which means you probably will not succeed. You need to go about building your business model systematically. And remember you may be selling to more than one market segment.

5 **Low funding requirements** – the lower the funding requirement, the easier it is to start up and the less you have to lose if the idea does not work.

6 **Sustainable** – the business must be built on solid foundations so that it has longevity.

7 **High profit margins** – the more innovative your product/service and your market, the higher your margin is likely to be.

8 **Effective communications strategy** – once you know who you are selling to, and why they should buy from you, you need to be able to communicate a persuasive message to them and build a loyal customer base.

9 **Not easily copied** – if it can be, protect your intellectual property. However, often getting to the market quickly and developing a brand reputation is the best safeguard.

10 **Identifiable risks that can be monitored and mitigated** – the future of a start-up is, by definition, uncertain. Identifying risks is the first step to understanding how they can be monitored and then mitigated. The more options you have identified the greater your chance of success.

11 **Low fixed costs** – low fixed costs mean lower risk should volume reduce. It gives you flexibility. A combination of high profit margin and low fixed costs (high profit, low risk) is always very attractive.

12 **Controllable** – putting in robust operating and financial controls increases your chances of survival and success, and ultimately will add value to the firm. The major imperative in the early years is to monitor and manage cash flow.

13 **Management skills that can be leveraged** – you need to have the appropriate management skills and, if you do not, you need to acquire them or recruit or partner with others with the appropriate skills.

14 **Scalable** – small projects can usually get off the ground easily but bigger projects can be problematic because they are just 'too big'. In that case, you need to see whether the project can be broken down into smaller projects that can be implemented when the original idea is proved – scalability. The idea is to avoid as much risk as possible for as long as possible – but make sure you do not miss the window of opportunity completely. This is all a question of judgement and changing market conditions, so you need to remain flexible and think through how you might scale up the project when it proves successful.

15 **Financeable** – if you do not have sufficient resources yourself, the project needs to be able to attract finance.

Many of these characteristics will only become apparent as you develop your business model. In doing this you need to be flexible and develop strategic options as you go through the process. If the preferred option turns out to be unattractive or impossible, you can then return to consider the other options you have come up with. Chapter 14 will show you how this can be achieved.

CASE insight 4.12

Hide My Ass! UK

Lean start-up and developing a business model

Hide My Ass! (HMA!) began as a free proxy service created by Jack Cator. He originally created it as a way around school rules about using the internet. He wanted to unblock sites that were popular at the time such as MySpace and online games sites. The original HMA! masked the user's IP address by using proxy sites. By replacing their online identity it allowed users to access sites that might be restricted from their home IP address, although it only worked on a site-by-site basis. It soon developed into a way people could get around censorship and access otherwise forbidden internet sites by appearing to be based in another country.

Jack enjoyed working with computers from an early age. He left school in 2005, aged 16, to enrol on a two-year technology course at college, where he developed HMA!. He worked from his bedroom at home and used income from advertisers to set up the service, employing freelancers in eight countries. HMA! went online in the same year and, because it was a free service, rapidly gained users. In 2008, still running the business from his parents' house, Jack added a low-cost subscription-based virtual private network (VPN) to the otherwise free service. This protects the user's entire internet connection – including browser, online games and Skype – rather than simply their activity on individual sites. Because the free proxy service was so popular, the business did not have to convert many of these visitors into paying customers to start generating substantial profits. What is more, regular professional users became more frequent. Because it offers users anonymity, the service is now used by professional security firms tracking down hackers and virus writers. In 2011 Jack opened company offices in London.

By 2014 Jack had built HMA! into an expert VPN service with the widest international server network of any other VPN company in the world. The parent company, Privax – of which Jack was CEO – provided VPN services to over 10 million users and 250,000 paying subscribers worldwide using over 700 servers in some 130 countries. It generated profits of £2.3 million on turnover of £11.5 million and employed more than 80 people based in London. That year it also launched an app, Hide My Phone!, which allowed users to rent mobile phone numbers temporarily, masking their country of origin.

In 2014 Jack was a guest speaker at the *Wired* Next Generation Conference. He gave these ten 'top tips' based on his success in launching and growing the business:

1   Exploit your age
2   Go out and get the experience
3   Understand your audience
4   Branding is everything
5   Get it out there
6   Make use of free marketing
7   Engage with users
8   Don't delegate too early
9   Outsource your staff
10 You don't need financing

In 2015 Jack sold HMA! for £40 million ($60 million) to AVG Technologies, a New York-listed Dutch company specializing in online privacy and internet security. One-third of the price was performance dependent. Not bad for a 26-year-old, one-time rebellious school boy!

Visit the website: www.hidemyass.com

Questions:

1   What lessons do you learn from Jack Cator and HMA!?
2   Explain the meaning of Jack's 'top tips'. Do they apply only to technology-based start-ups or can they be applied to any business? Do they reconcile with the characteristics of a good business model outlined in this chapter?

Sofa-bed Factory

Piotr and Olek got together again a few weeks later. By that time Piotr had decided that there was a potential business opportunity around the manufacture of sofa-beds. It was one of the few categories in the UK domestic upholstered furniture market where demand was growing and the existing suppliers were not keeping up with it. He also reflected on how complicated the folding mechanism seemed and how poor the actual mattress was. Piotr had discovered that there was only one existing supplier, that they were unreliable and that there had been complaints about the quality of their sofa-beds. Indeed, his friend said that the company was keen to find an alternative supplier. He also found out that the company thought that sofa-beds faced a retail price ceiling in the UK of about €1,000, which meant that the wholesale price would need to be €300–340.

Olek had been equally busy. In his garage he had disassembled the folding mechanisms from five different sofa-beds. In one corner was a new mechanism mounted on a steel, as yet un-upholstered, frame that Olek had designed and built himself. Not only did it open easily and smoothly but it looked robust and sturdier than the other mechanisms in the garage. Olek explained that it was not only better than the others, but it was also made from fewer parts, which meant that it should be cheaper. Piotr tried it out and agreed that it was certainly better than the one he was selling in his shop in the UK. Olek had asked the company he worked for whether they could manufacture it and how much they would charge. They replied that it would depend on the size of the order and it could be anywhere between €100 and €150.

Piotr and Olek decided that if they were to start a sofa-bed manufacturing business, based in Poland, they would sell directly to retail furniture outlets in the UK. They would try to get the retail chain that Piotr currently worked for as their first customer, because they were currently looking for a new supplier. If they could not get an order from them they would not proceed with the idea. Large retail chains handled all the marketing to consumers, which meant that margins would be tight. However, it also meant that all the costs and risks of marketing to the consumers would be taken by the retailers.

The two were excited. They had come a long way since they first sat down in a bar complaining about their jobs. However, there were still many questions that needed to

be answered before they could decide whether to go ahead. The first was whether they could actually manufacture the sofa-bed at a profit. The second was whether they could really find that first customer. More research was needed.

Questions:

1 Which generic business model best fits this business idea?
2 From the information available, does this look like a good business idea?
3 What other information do you need?

Summary and action points

4.1 Identify your business model: The New Venture Creation Framework provides a framework to help you find, explore, develop and refine your business idea. At the core of the framework is a holistic business model.

There are three well-understood business models: high differentiation, high customer focus and low price/cost. These models are consistent with the fundamental ways of creating sustainable competitive advantage. However, there are many variants that can be used for novel, often technology-based, products. Different business models can exist happily side by side in the same industry, appealing to different target markets. You should decide which model(s) best fit your business idea and then tailor your marketing strategy appropriately.

4.2 Low-cost market testing: Low-cost market testing (lean start-up) involves minimizing your investment and lead time in launching a new product, ensuring only that it is in a 'minimum viable state' and then using customer feedback to better tailor the product to customer needs. You must decide whether this approach is one that suits your business idea.

4.3 Evaluate your business idea: The best business models – ones that generate the highest profits with the lowest risk – have certain identifiable characteristics. You should check to see how many of these characteristics your business idea has.

Workbook exercises

 The New Venture Creation Workbook contains a digital version of these exercises that can be modified as your business model develops and builds into a draft business plan. It can be downloaded from www.macmillanihe.com/burns-nvc-2e.

4.1: Identify your business model

Reviewing the different business models outlined in this chapter, identify which of the three generic models best fits your business idea and what elements of other models you might use to monetarize your idea. Jot down the implications of the model(s) for the business.

Business model(s)	Implications

4.2: Low-cost market testing

Reflect on whether there is a low-cost approach to testing the market demand for your product or service, whether this is needed and how you might build it into your business model and plan. Jot down the implications.

4.3: Evaluate your business idea

1 Building on Workbook Exercise 3.4, use the 15 characteristics of a good business model to evaluate the attractiveness of your business idea on a scale of 1 (not attractive) to 5 (very attractive). You can add your own criteria to the list if you wish. If you have more than one idea or are working in a group repeat the exercise for the other ideas. Total the scores for each idea. The maximum score possible is 75. At this stage some of these judgements will be based upon incomplete information. We shall return to this exercise in Chapter 13.

Characteristic	Idea 1 Score	Idea 2 Score	Idea 3 Score
1 Identified market need or gap			
2 No or few existing competitors			
3 Growing market			
4 Clearly identified customers and viable business model			
5 Low funding requirements			
6 Sustainable			
7 High profit margins			
8 Effective communications strategy			
9 Not easily copied			
10 Identifiable risks that can be monitored and mitigated			
11 Low fixed costs			
12 Controllable			
13 Management skills that can be leveraged			
14 Scalability			
15 Financeable			
TOTAL SCORE			

2 Reflect on the scores you have given. If you had more than one idea or were working in a group, reflect on why the idea with the highest score was so attractive. Is this the idea you are taking forward? If not, why?

Get feedback on your scores from your network of family and friends and note any insightful comments. Do any cause you to adjust your business model in any way? If so, make the changes.

Decide on the business idea that you will be taking forward to work on in subsequent exercises.

3 Reflect on the individual characteristics of this idea. Where you have not given a score (presumably because you have insufficient information) or for those characteristics with low scores (say, below 3), jot down the things you need to find out to make a judgement or the things you need to do to improve these scores.

Visit www.macmillanihe.com/burns-nvc-2e for chapter quizzes and other resources.

5

Crafting your value proposition and branding

Contents

- Your values and vision
- Identifying your target customers
- Defining your value proposition
- Creating value through values
- Differentiation through branding
- The role of design in branding
- Branding your values
- Sustainable entrepreneurship and social responsibility
- Private or social enterprise?
- Building the brand
- Your mission statement
- Summary and action points
- Workbook exercises

Learning outcomes

When you have read this chapter and undertaken the related exercises you will be able to:

- Identify the values on which your start-up is based
- Develop a vision for your start-up and write its mission statement
- Identify and describe your target customer segment(s)
- Understand the importance of values-driven marketing and the social and commercial benefits of CSR
- Develop a value proposition for your product or service, appropriate for each target market segment
- Understand how to develop a brand identity consistent with your value proposition
- Decide whether your business is to be a commercial or social enterprise

Academic insights 📑

5.1 Strategic intent and *kosoryoku*

5.2 Service-dominant marketing logic

5.3 Values-driven marketing

5.4 Design thinking

5.5 Creating competitive advantage through design

5.6 Environmental sustainability and waste reduction

5.7 Commercial value of CSR

Case insights 💼

5.1 Ferrero

5.2 Apple MacBook Pro

5.3 Dell Corporation

5.4 Apple iMac

5.5 Zound Industries

5.6 Ecotricity

5.7 Goodone

5.8 Richard Branson and Virgin (1)

5.9 easyJet (2)

5.10 Golden Krust (2)

5.11 Adrenaline Alley

Sofa-bed Factory

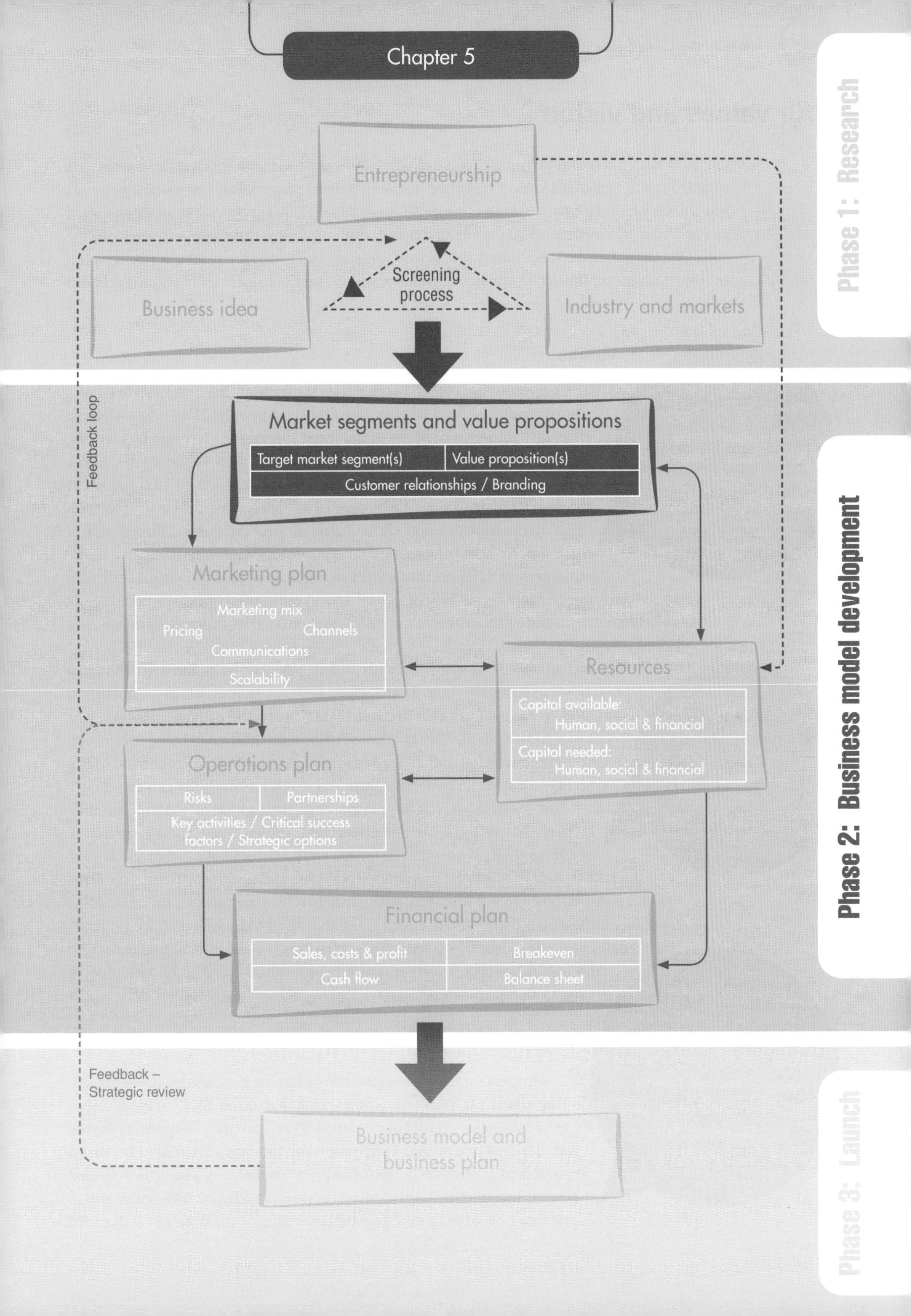

Chapter 5
Phase 1: Research
Entrepreneurship
Screening process
Business idea
Industry and markets
Feedback loop
Phase 2: Business model development
Market segments and value propositions
Target market segment(s)
Value proposition(s)
Customer relationships / Branding
Marketing plan
Marketing mix
Pricing
Channels
Communications
Scalability
Resources
Capital available:
Human, social & financial
Capital needed:
Human, social & financial
Operations plan
Risks
Partnerships
Key activities / Critical success factors / Strategic options
Financial plan
Sales, costs & profit
Breakeven
Cash flow
Balance sheet
Feedback –
Strategic review
Phase 3: Launch
Business model and business plan

Your values and vision

Just as it is important that you understand why you want to start a business and what you want from it, it is also important that your business reflects your **vision** and **values**. After all, you will be spending much of your time developing it and, in many ways it is an extension of you and your personality. Most people find it very difficult to live their lives within organizations that do not share their values and beliefs. Indeed, this is often a reason for starting up your own business. The vision you have for the business and the values upon which it is based will help shape your business model.

Our values are things that help us get in a state of mind and motivate us to get the results we want. You want something that attaches emotionally to each person in the team.

Barbara McNaughton founder Elements The Times 25 February 2014

Values

Values are core beliefs. The values you set for your business create expectations regarding how you operate and treat people. They may well have an ethical dimension. Many of the most successful Victorian businesses, such as Cadbury, Barclays Bank or John Lewis, were based upon Quaker values and many Victorian entrepreneurs went on to become great philanthropists. Values form part of the cognitive processes that will help shape and develop the culture of your business. Shared values form a bond that binds the organization together – aligning and motivating people. Organizations with strong values tend to recruit staff who are able to identify with those values and thus they become reinforced. They also help create a bond with customers and suppliers alike that can underpin a strong brand identity.

Reach for the stars and you will get there – or at least close. Aim low and you'll get there too.

Elizabeth Gooch founder eg solutions Launch Lab (www.launchlab.co.uk) 13 January 2009

You articulate values not only with words but also by practising what you preach – 'walking-the-talk'. It therefore follows that it is very difficult to pretend to have values that are not real. You will be caught out when you fail to practise them. Values are not negotiable and need to be reinforced through recognition and reward of staff. They need to be embedded in the systems and structures of your business, so that everybody can see clearly that you mean what you say. Every organization develops a distinctive culture that reflects certain underlying values, even if they are never made explicit. If you do not make your values explicit there is always the risk that they might be misunderstood and you end up with an organizational culture that you are unhappy with. This is why many successful companies actually write down their values. Your values also need to be reflected in the strategies you adopt when you launch the business – your ethical underpinning and social policies. In other words, your values need to be reflected in your value proposition.

I am often asked what it is to be an entrepreneur … If you look around you, most of the largest companies have their foundations in one or two individuals who have the determination to turn a vision into reality.

Richard Branson founder Virgin Group from Anderson, J. (1995) Local Heroes, Scottish Enterprise, Glasgow

Vision

It is important to create a vision for what the business might become – important for your motivation and that of all the stakeholders in your business – customers, employees, partners, suppliers, investors, lenders and so on. Your vision for the business should be based around and grounded in your business purpose. A vision is a shared mental image of a desired future state – an idea of what your enterprise can become, a new and better world. It must be attractive and aspirational and one that engages and energizes people, including yourself. However, it must be sufficiently realistic and credible that it is believable – stretching but achievable. It is usually qualitative rather than quantitative (that is the role of the objectives). Vision is seen as inspiring and motivating, transcending logic and contractual relationships. It is more emotional than analytical, something that touches the heart. It gives existence within an organization to that most fundamental of human cravings – a sense of meaning and purpose. It can be intrinsic, directing the organization to do things better in some way, such as improving customer satisfaction or increasing product innovation. It can be extrinsic, for example, beating the competition.

CASE insight 5.1

Ferrero ITALY

Values and beliefs

Ferrero Spa is a private company owned by the Ferrero family. Now headed up by Giovanni Ferrero, it employs some 22,000 workers and has a turnover in excess of €8 billion. It was founded by Pietro Ferrero and his wife Piera in the Italian Alba region in Piedmont in the immediate post-war years. They produced a chocolate bar which included nougat and hazelnuts and called it *pasta gianduja*. The same basic recipe is used for its Nutella chocolate spread, to which Pietro's son, Michele, added liqueur to make the famous Ferrero Rocher chocolate. Other brands owned by the company include Kinder and Mon Cheri.

The family are obsessively secretive. It has never held a press conference and does not allow media visits to its plants. Ferrero's products are even made with machines designed by an in-house engineering department. However, Reputation Institute's 2017 survey ranked Ferrero as the 17th most reputable company in the world. The company produces an annual CSR report and has sponsored the Ferrero Foundation since 1983. As well as sponsoring cultural activities, the Foundation offers health and social assistance to ex-employees. The company follows a number of core principles, which are outlined on its website and include 'loyalty and trust', 'respect and responsibility' and 'integrity and sobriety'. Every 29 June, Ferrero executives attend church in San Domenico to honour the day the company was founded. Every three years Ferrero organizes a pilgrimage to Lourdes for all its workers.

Visit the website: www.ferrero.com

Question:

Why are values and beliefs important?

ACADEMIC insight 5.1

Strategic intent and *kosoryoku*

Hamel and Prahalad (1994) studied firms that had successfully challenged established big companies in a range of industries. They said that to reconcile the lack of fit between aspirations and resources the successful firms used **strategic intent**. This necessitates developing a common vision about the future, aligning staff behaviour with a common purpose and delegating and decentralizing decision making. They argued that 'the challengers had succeeded in creating entirely new forms of competitive advantage and dramatically rewriting the rules of engagement'. The challengers were daring to be different. Managers in these firms imagined new products, services and even entire industries that did not exist and then went on to create them. They were not just benchmarking and analysing competition, they were creating new market places that they could dominate because it was a market place of their own making.

Ohmae (2005) used the Japanese word *kosoryoku* to describe what is needed to develop entrepreneurial strategy in an uncertain environment. He explained that it meant something that combined 'vision' with the notion of 'concept' and 'imagination', but unlike imagination, it has no sense of daydreaming but is rather an ability to see what is invisible and shape the future so that the vision succeeds:

> It is the product of imagination based on realistic understanding of what the shape of the oncoming world is and, pragmatically, the areas of business that you can capture successfully because you have the means of realizing the vision.

Hamel, G. and Prahalad, C.K. (1994) *Competing For the Future: Breakthrough Strategies for Seizing Control of Your Industry and Creating the Markets of Tomorrow*, Boston, MA: Harvard Business School Press.

Ohmae, K. (2005) *The Next Global Stage: Challenges and Opportunities in our Borderless World*, Upper Saddle River, NJ: Pearson Education.

Identifying your target customers

The first step in structuring your business model is to identify your target customers, what they want and why they will buy from you. A business will only succeed if it offers customers a value proposition that meets their real needs or solves real problems for them. The initial target market should also be the group of customers that most need your solution to their problem because other solutions are less satisfactory. While customers are all individuals, it is usually possible to group them in some way that is useful in terms of targeting, for example, by identifying their different group needs or problems. These are called **market segments**.

Normally, it is only possible to communicate with customers economically through these groups. The key for a start-up is to identify and focus limited resources on just three or four clearly defined, important and sizable market segments. The marketing mix, marketing and communications strategy can then be tailored to the needs of customers in these different segments. Of course you will not turn away customers who do not fall into these segments; it is just about focusing your limited resources where they are likely to have the greatest return.

There are many ways of segmenting markets and there are no prescriptive approaches. Market segments match groups of customers with their product/service wants or needs – the benefits they are looking for. The segment can be any one, or a combination of, descriptive factors. The descriptive factors for private customers might include personal demographics (e.g. age, gender, socioeconomic group, occupation, stage in family life etc.), geographic location (particularly important for retail start-ups) and channels of distribution used to get goods to the customers and so on. For business markets, they might include type of business, size, location, nature of technology and so on. You are looking for groups of customers with similar needs that can be identified and described in some meaningful and useful way. You are looking for a gap in the market, where the needs of a particular segment are not being met as well as they could be.

To be viable a market segment should be:

1 Distinctive with significantly different needs from other segments. Without this the segment boundaries are likely to be too blurred.
2 Sufficiently large or willing to pay a high enough price to make the segment commercially attractive. It may be that a gap in the market exists because it is not commercially viable.
3 Accessible. The gap in the market might not exist in reality because the segment cannot be reached – through communication or distribution channels.
4 Defendable from competitors. If the segment is not defendable, for example, because you are selling a copy-cat product, prices and profits will quickly reduce as competition increases.

Vary your markets. Think about how your product could fit into different markets. Clippykit works for retail, the promotions industry and education.

Calypso Rose founder Clippy Daily Telegraph 6 February 2009

Market segments vary in size. The slimmer the market segment that the product or service is tailored to suit, the higher customer satisfaction is likely to be, but so too is cost – and therefore price. We all like personal service and the ultimate market segment comprises just one customer. However, this might not be a commercially viable segment. The trend is towards slimmer and slimmer market segments, particularly since the internet has made it easier to link customers with similar needs in different geographic areas. The danger facing firms selling to slim market segments is their overreliance on a small customer base. If tastes change, the segment might disappear.

Defining your value proposition

Your value proposition is why customers should buy from you rather than from another company. Customers buy a product or service because it provides a benefit or solves a problem for them. The features or characteristics of the product or service must combine to deliver that benefit to the customer, or they will not buy it. And different market segments might be looking for different benefits. The features of a car combine to provide the benefit of transport, but different customers are looking for more than just transport – which is why there are numerous types of cars and many producers. Products and services often have other related benefits compared to competitors such as: saving time or money, producing more of the result, undertaking the task more safely or with less risk, or in a more innovative way.

It has been argued that customers essentially purchase services rather than goods, and goods should therefore be viewed as a medium for delivering or 'transmitting' services (see Academic insight 5.2). If all industries are service industries, it becomes vital for them to understand the service – or benefits – that consumers are really seeking. You need to understand the core benefits a customer is looking for when they purchase goods or services, and then engineer the features to deliver those benefits. And these features can take many forms, both physical and psychological. They can then deliver additional forms of benefit such as conveying status, or being more ethical or environmentally friendly. Focusing on the benefit needs of your market segments and delivering distinctive, differentiated value propositions to each of them is at the very core of developing your marketing strategy. Unfortunately, many owner-managers like to define their products in physical terms and therefore think they are selling one thing, only to find that customers are buying something else.

Service-dominant marketing logic

In their award-winning paper, Vargo and Lusch (2004) seem to have changed the dominant logic of marketing academia. They argued that customers valued and purchased services rather than goods, and goods should therefore be viewed as a medium for delivering or 'transmitting' the firm's services. They defined service as 'the application of specialized competences (knowledge and skills) through deeds, processes, and performances for the benefit of another entity or the entity itself'. In this way companies manufacturing cars are not in the business of selling cars but in the business of providing 'mobility services' through the cars that they manufacture – a concept adopted by Andrew Valentine with Streetcar (Case insight 4.2). Thus, all industries are service industries and it therefore becomes vital for firms to understand the service that consumers are seeking from them. It requires a shift in focus from the product to the consumer and an understanding of their needs and how these translate into a service they value.

Vargo, S.L. and Lusch, R.F. (2004) 'Evolving to a New Dominant Logic for Marketing', *Journal of Marketing*, 68(1).

Features can be translated into benefits by exploring their meaning, as shown in Table 5.1.

Table 5.1 Features and benefits

Feature		Benefit
Our shop takes credit cards	*Meaning…*	You can budget to suit your pocket
Our shop stays open later than others	*Meaning…*	You get more choice when to shop
Our shop is an approved dealer	*Meaning…*	You can be guaranteed that we know and understand all technical aspects of the product
Our shop is a family business	*Meaning…*	You get individual, personal attention from somebody who cares

Listing the features of a product or service can be the start of the process of understanding the benefits that the customer is seeking from them. The features form part of the 'marketing mix' you put together as part of your marketing strategy – a topic to which we return in the next chapter. However, it is more convincing to start with the benefits that customers are looking for and then construct features that provide those benefits. Which actually comes first is a little like the chicken or the egg question. Once you start looking at benefits, you start thinking like a customer. You also realize that some of the benefits customers might be looking for are intangible. As we shall see later, they could be psychological, even emotional benefits.

Your value proposition should therefore state three things:

1 How your product or service will solve a problem for your target customers.
2 The benefits they can expect – tangible and intangible (as we shall see later, you may have to offer proof of this in your marketing message).
3 Why they should buy from you rather than from your competitors.

It is important that you understand precisely what the value proposition(s) of your product(s) or service(s) is/are, and the target market(s) you are aiming for. The discipline of expressing this in a few, specific words is extremely valuable and one that you will be able to refer back to again and again as you develop your marketing campaign. To help you do this you might find this template useful:

> Because our product/service has *(features and other differentiating and provable attributes)* it will *(problem solution)* for *(target customer segment)* meaning that *(customer benefits)*.

Often the value proposition forms the basis for the 'straplines' (short one-line sentences) you see describing what products or companies do or what they represent. For example the cosmetics firm Lush (Case insight 6.7) leaves no doubt about what it does by using the simple strapline 'Fresh handmade cosmetics'. The computer equivalent of Post-it® notes, Evernote, is equally clear: 'Remember everything' but adding 'Inspiration strikes anywhere. Evernote lets you capture, nurture, and share your ideas across any device'. Skype uses the strapline: 'Skype makes it easy to connect with your loved ones', but if you go to their website the front page states very clearly what it does (helps you share, message, and call), how it does it (on phone, tablet, and desktop), and who it does it for (the whole world.).

CASE insight 5.2

Apple MacBook Pro   USA

Value propositions

Many products or services make effective use of value propositions in their marketing, often as 'straplines'. For example, if you went to the front webpage for the Apple MacBook Pro in 2017 you saw a slick photo of an open, thin MacBook from the top down showing its bright screen and its gleaming aluminium. This was headed up with 'MacBook Pro – A touch of genius'. The brief value proposition below claimed:

> *It's razor thin, feather light, and even faster and more powerful than before. It has the brightest, most*

colourful Mac notebook display ever. And it features the Touch Bar – a Multi-Touch-enabled strip of glass built into the keyboard for instant access to the tools you want, just when you want them. MacBook Pro is built on ground-breaking ideas. And it's ready for yours.

Visit the website: www.apple.com/macbook-pro

Question:

Why is this an effective value proposition?

Creating value through values

Your values and vision are tools that create *identity* for your business – an identity that should be reflected in your value proposition. And if this identity is attractive to customers it can create value. At the very least, a clear identity for the business means that customers know what they are buying and, if they like it, facilitates a repeat purchase. But identity can do more than this. It is also about *reputation*. As we have seen, customers buy a product/service because it provides them with a range of benefits that they value. Reputation assures

CASE
insight
5.3

Dell Corporation

 USA

Changing your value proposition

Michael Dell

When it launched Dell offered both a low-price/low-cost and a customer focus value proposition (selling direct and allowing customers to configure their own computers). Dell became market leader in the provision of value-for-money computers in the 1990s because it integrated its supply chain with its online retail operations. Its fully integrated value chain – a business-to-consumer-to-business (B2C2B) business model – meant that customers could configure their own computers and order online while suppliers had real-time access to orders and deliveries, so that Dell could receive stock information on a just-in-time basis, keeping the assembly line moving while minimizing its costs. It underpinned their low-cost/low-price business model.

Dell patented many of the innovations in this integrated value chain. Nevertheless, over the years competitors were able to copy many of these technological developments and integrate their own supply chains so as to achieve similar cost savings, thus eroding the basis for the low-price/low-cost element of their value proposition. Consequently the question has arisen as to whether Dell's direct relationship with customers is now of higher value than its low-price/low-cost proposition. If it is, then Dell might also want to sell other digital consumer electronics and office automation equipment direct to customers. And why should it not subcontract more of its assembly, focusing rather on the core strength that the customer values – the direct relationship? Again, this is something it has started doing. This raises many questions about the scope of Dell's activities and the nature of its business domain.

Visit the website: www.dell.com

Questions:

1 What are the advantages and disadvantages of relying on the physical features of a product or a low-cost business model for your value proposition?
2 How easy is it to change your value proposition?

customers that this will be delivered every time they purchase the product or service. It reduces their risk and is therefore of value to them.

However, benefits can be psychological as well as physical. For example, a successful sole trader might offer a reliable, friendly service that differentiates them effectively from the competition. The personal *relationship* they establish with their customers epitomizes the reliability and friendliness of the service they deliver. And this relationship underpins the customer loyalty that is generated. The challenge is to extend it beyond the single-person business. Just as with a sole trader, establishing a reputable brand for your product, service or business should therefore help create value by doing three things:

1 Establish an *identity*
2 Help build a *reputation*
3 Help develop a *relationship*

The development of a relationship with customers reflects a move away from seeing the customer as someone with whom to have an arm's-length transaction – just somebody to sell to. It is part of the development called **relationship** and **values-driven marketing** that seeks to actively engage with customers and use them to help sell existing products/services and develop new ones. This is based

> You and your rival have access to virtually all the same resources. Only by constantly thinking of new ways to reorganize these factors can you differentiate yourself. It's like poker. Everyone has the same number of cards. It's how you play your hand that matters.
>
> Zhang Ruimin, CEO Haier Group Strategy + Business, Issue 77, Winter 2014

upon establishing a good relationship with customers – one that is underpinned by mutual self-interest, where there is something in it for both the customer and the company with each helping the other in certain ways. Relationships are built on good communication – a topic to which we shall return in the next chapter – and technology has made this easier on a mass basis. Indeed, the development of the internet and social media has made it possible and affordable on a global scale.

There are therefore four questions you need to ask:

1 What are the values you wish your business to embody?
2 Do these values differentiate you from competitors?
3 What values are attractive and of value to your customers (i.e. they might find attractive and be willing to pay for) and can they be reconciled with those of your business?
4 Can these values be incorporated into your value proposition? If so, how?

Your values should be reflected in your value proposition. But doing this is only part of the challenge. The next stage is communicating this 'values-enhanced' value proposition to customers and consumers. This can be complicated. One way of shortcutting the process is to develop a brand that encapsulates the value proposition and everything you and the company stand for. In this way the customer's script is written for them and articulation is easier.

ACADEMIC insight 5.3

Values-driven marketing

Piercy (2000, 2001) was one of the first academics to observe that, as customers become increasingly sophisticated, marketing will move away from just relationships to values-driven strategies that reflect customer priorities and needs:

> *Achieving customer loyalty with sophisticated customers is the new challenge and we are only just beginning to realize what this means. It will mean transparency. It will mean integrity and trustworthiness. It will mean innovative ways of doing business. It will mean a focus on value in customers' terms, not ours. It will require new types of organization and technology to deliver value.*

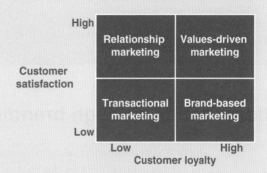

Figure 5.1 *Values-driven marketing*

Piercy characterizes marketing strategy and the search for customer loyalty as a progression from transactional and brand approaches to relationship and values-based strategies. These are illustrated in Figure 5.1.

Values-driven marketing (also called Marketing 3.0) has been characterized as a holistic approach to marketing based upon combinations of segmentation approaches. It places a *participative* customer at its centre – a customer that is not only king, but also market research head, R&D chief and product development manager – for example, through open

source innovation. Customers are actively involved as advocates of the product/service, for example, through social network sites. In this way the customer's involvement is leveraged far beyond the simple purchase of the product/service. This only happens if the organization is continually engaged in dialogue with customers through as many media as possible.

Piercy suggests that the sources for this values-driven strategy are:

- **Management vision** – clarity in direction and purpose, effectively communicated through a wide range of communication media.

- **Market sensing and organizational learning** – understanding and responding to the external world using all possible networks and channels of communication.
- **Differentiating capabilities** – using core competencies to build differential advantage.
- **Relationship strategy** – managing the network of relationships and channels of communication used for market sensing to achieve superior performance.
- **Reinventing the organization** – changing the organization's form and processes to sustain and renew this strategy.

Kotler et al. (2010) are keen advocates of values-driven marketing. Rather than seeing values as an 'add-on', they envisage marketing and values as being integrated, without separation. They say companies need to focus on creating products/services and entire organizational cultures, which are driven by the values of customers at a more multi-dimensional, fundamental level, starting with the vision, mission and values of the company. Customers are looking for products/services that not only satisfy their consumer needs, but also address their spiritual needs, appealing to their head, their heart and their spirit. The key to this is customer participation and involvement, using all the channels of communication created by internet-based social media. Kotler et al. argue that to thrive in this interlinked world companies must collaborate with each other, with their shareholders, channel partners, employees and customers.

Kotler et al.'s book concludes with ten principles that the authors claim integrate marketing and values:

1 Love your customers and respect your competitors.
2 Be sensitive to change and ready to change yourself.
3 Guard your name, and have a clear identity.
4 Customers are diverse; first find those who benefit most from your product/service.
5 Always offer a good product/service at a fair price.
6 Always make yourself available and spread the news about your product/service.
7 Find your customers, keep and grow them.
8 Whatever your business, remember it is a service business.
9 Continually refine your business processes – quality, cost and delivery.
10 Continually gather information, but be wise in making your final decisions.

Kotler, P., Kartajaya, H. and Setiawan, I. (2010) *Marketing 3.0: From Products to Customers to the Human Spirit*, Hoboken, NJ: John Wiley & Sons.

Piercy, N.F. (2000) *Tales from the Market place: Stories of Revolution, Reinvention and Renewal*, Oxford: Taylor & Francis.

Piercy, N.F. (2001) 'The Future of Marketing is Strategizing', in S. Dibb, L. Simkin, W.M. Pride and O.C. Ferrell, *Marketing: Concepts and Strategies,* Boston, MA: Houghton Mifflin.

Differentiation through branding

The first step in creating sustainable competitive advantage is to clearly differentiate yourself from competitors in the eyes of customers and consumers – create an identity and reputation through your brand. It is what companies like Apple have achieved with their brand identity. Apple is a lifestyle brand that stands for design excellence, simplicity and ease of use. It identifies the owner of its products as part of the exclusive Apple 'tribe' and therefore builds a relationship of loyalty with them. Their advertising reflects not only the product value proposition but also the company's identity (see Case insight 5.2). Values-based marketing involves having a strong brand identity which includes good customer relationships. It uses these things to the mutual advantage of both customer and company. The advantages of branding to both customers/consumers and product/service providers are shown in Table 5.2.

Differentiation means setting out to be unique in the industry along some dimensions that are widely valued by customers. These can be based upon the product or service and can be tangible (observable product/service characteristics such as function, quality, design, performance or technology etc.) and/or intangible (customer needs such as status, exclusivity,

The Guardian Media Planet May 2015
Richard Branson founder Virgin Group

Customers relate to a brand and the values it stands for more than the tangible aspects of a product.

Table 5.2 Advantages of branding

Advantages to customers/consumers	Advantages to product/service producer
• Clear product/service identity • Clearer communication of value proposition • Aids with product/service evaluation • Reduction in risk when purchasing (homogeneity of offering) • Can create additional interest or character for the product/service	• Conveys emotional aspects of the value proposition and helps develop relationships • Promotes product/service loyalty • Helps target marketing • Defends against competitors (creates differential advantage) • Allows higher prices to be charged • Increases power in distribution channels

care for the environment etc.). Both elements can be reflected in the product or service identity and reputation. Often differentiation is more sustainable when based not just on tangible factors, which can often be easily copied, but also on intangible factors, which are not. So, for example, Mercedes-Benz cars and Dom Pérignon champagne differentiate themselves through product quality and status in the respective sectors. The UK retailer Lush differentiates itself through its bright, fun, shopping environment, novel products and ethical values (see Case insight 6.7).

Even companies competing primarily on price attempt to differentiate themselves not just through brand recognition. Dell may no longer have differentiated products but it attempts to differentiate itself on speed of delivery, uniqueness of personal systems configuration and other elements of service, while still maintaining a competitive price. McDonald's has a very recognizable brand associated with value-for-money meals but also tries to differentiate itself, in part, through consistency and quality of service (speed, cleanliness and so on). You can differentiate yourself therefore by 'bundling' these things in different ways – so long as the customer values the 'bundle' and cannot create the 'bundle' easily themselves. This 'bundle' is often called the marketing mix.

> When you've got single-digit market share – and you're competing with the big boys– you either differentiate or die … The idea of building a business solely based on cost or price was not a sustainable advantage.
>
> *Michael Dell Direct from Dell: Strategies that Revolutionized an Industry (1999, New York: Harper Business)*

Michael Eisner, CEO Disney, said that 'a brand is a living entity – and it is enriched or undermined cumulatively over time, the product of a thousand small gestures'. It should be the embodiment of the product or service value proposition to customers. Not only should it tell you what you are buying (the physical product or service) but also what you want from the purchase (the psychological benefits). So, for example, the Mercedes-Benz, Jaguar and BMW brands tell you that you are buying a car but, more importantly, all convey quality and status. Virgin is the embodiment of Richard Branson: brash, entrepreneurial, different, anti-establishment. Effective brands, therefore, are emotional, appealing to the heart as much as the head. However, many so-called brands fall far short of this instant recognition of values and virtues, being little more than expensive logos allowing recognition of the physical product or service but conveying little else. What do the Barclays, Shell or the BT brands convey, other than the knowledge of what the firm sells? Do they have a reputation? Do they try to develop a relationship? Brands should be more than just logos that identify the products sold. They should represent the very identity – the persona – of the product. And, just as you are more than a head, body, two arms and legs, so too any product/service should be more than the sum of its parts. The challenge is to create that brand identity.

The role of design in branding

Design is an important way of identifying and differentiating a product. Design can be an important tool in both radical and incremental innovation. It is also an important weapon in the branding armoury. Good design can help not only improve the functional performance of a product, but also make the product distinctive. Good design is aesthetically pleasing and conveys emotions that functionality cannot. SMEs may not have the money to spend on design that big companies have, but, nevertheless, design is not something that can be ignored, particularly if it is part of your value proposition.

Apple has a track record of using outstanding design to create competitive advantage. Like the Swatch that created a paradigm shift in the markets for watches (Case insight 2.3), the launch of Apple's iconic iMac in 1998 did the same for desk-top computers (Case insight 5.4). Apple still combines high quality with easy-to-use product functionality and elegant design. This even extends into the packaging of Apple products. The design features of their products are promoted as part of their marketing strategy to create a fashionable, distinctive and desirable brand that allows them to charge high prices for their products (Case insight 5.2). For Apple, all the elements of this marketing mix, including design, must be consistent, mutually reinforcing the brand identity and the value proposition of individual products. Design and branding add extra layers to a differentiated product – shown in Figure 5.2. The functional qualities of the product/service can be enhanced through the aesthetics of design and reinforced by the emotional values associated with the brand. The more points of differentiation from competitors you have, the more sustainable your competitive advantage.

> Branding is valueless if consumers get home and are disappointed with the product.
>
> The Observer 29 September 2013
> Simon Smith, Head of Brand The Saucy Fish Co.

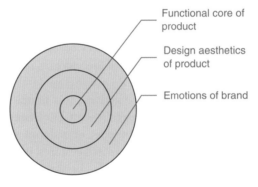

Functional core of product

Design aesthetics of product

Emotions of brand

Figure 5.2 Layers of differentiation

CASE insight 5.4

Apple iMac USA

Creating opportunity – market paradigm change through design

The original Apple iMac (G3) with its teardrop or gum-drop shape was designed by Jonathan Ive, a bathroom designer who rose to become Chief Design Officer at Apple. It was launched by Steve Jobs in 1998 less than a year after his return to Apple. It was the first Macintosh computer to have a USB port but no floppy disk, allowing other hardware

STOCKBYTE

manufacturers to make peripherals compatible with the Mac. But more importantly its friendly, translucent candy-colours and futuristic form made it stand out from other desk-top computers of the time with their pervading beige colours. It quickly became a design icon, a 'futuristic home appliance' rather than an office machine. It was something to be admired – a bold statement and talking point that started to influence the things the home-owner surrounded it with, items such as lighting and furniture. And, like

Swatch and watches (Case insight 2.3), it changed how people perceived computers and created demand because of its form rather than just its function. For once, design was driving innovation and creating new markets.

Question:

Why and how did the original iMac change customers' views about home computers?

'Design thinking' is a term used to explain the creative process of finding solutions to problems using a holistic approach and 'thinking outside the box' (see Academic insight 5.4). It is user-focused and in many ways it is an approach to thinking that resembles those outlined in Chapter 2, employing skills similar to the discovery skills outlined in Academic insight 2.5. 'Design thinking' is just that – a way of thinking rather than a clearly defined set of processes. The UK Design Council uses a simple four-stage model to represent the design process that is not inconsistent with 'design thinking' but a little more straightforward. The 'double diamond' graphic in Figure 5.3 represents the alternately divergent and convergent modes of thinking in the four phases of the process:

Phase 1   **Discover** – the stage when, as outlined in Chapter 2, the initial idea or inspiration needs to be found, based on identifying user needs.

Phase 2   **Define** – when these needs are interpreted and aligned to business objectives, resulting in the definition of the design project.

Phase 3   **Develop** – when design-led solutions are developed, iterated and tested. This will involve multidisciplinary prototype development and testing.

Phase 4   **Deliver** – when the resulting product is finalized, approved and launched, followed by evaluation and feedback.

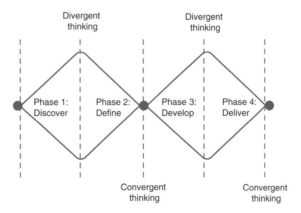

Figure 5.3 *The double diamond design process*
Source: Design Council's Double Diamond, 2004

Good design may cost money but it is not just for large companies like Apple. A small up-market restaurant understands that the design of its restaurants – its décor, layout and ambience – is just as important as the quality of its food and service, making it able to charge higher prices than other restaurants. The important thing is that all the elements that contribute to the brand image are consistent – and that includes the product or service itself. If you have ever bought something because of fancy advertising or packaging and then been disappointed by the functionality of the product itself, you will realize that this can turn customers against a brand. They feel cheated and lied to. Good design, however, can be expensive and it is therefore important that it can be seen to provide tangible benefits (to both the company and to its customers) that outweigh the additional costs.

Design thinking

Design thinking (also called customer-centric design) is a loose set of holistic concepts that approach design from the perspective of solving complex problems for people, rather than just creating distinctive objects or shapes. Design thinking is evident in the design of some high-tech products where software and hardware are integrated and made intuitive, simple and even pleasurable to use. And for this it needs to meet both people's practical and emotional needs, what is often called 'the user experience'. Companies that follow this approach develop value propositions that not only offer a promise of utility but also one of feeling or emotion. Kolko (2015) gives the example of automotive design which might offer not only 'safe and comfortable transportation in a well-designed high-performance vehicle' but also a promise that 'you will feel pampered, luxurious and affluent'. But design thinking is not just confined to product design and value propositions, it is holistic and seeks to integrate all the 'touch-points' a customer might have with the company rather than dealing with fragmented elements. In this way Apple takes as much care over the design of its packaging as it does with the product itself.

Getty Images/Hero Images

The approach involves a number of principles, which are consistent with developing a coherent, integrated business model.

- Empathy with users – goes to the core of any new venture – understanding customer needs and finding solutions to problems they face and, as explained in this chapter, these needs are both functional and emotional (heart and head). Companies like Samsung achieve this, in part, by sending designers out to see how customers use their products.
- Discipline of prototyping – espouses the use of prototypes to explore the effectiveness of potential solutions to problems. Kolko (op. cit.) says companies following this approach 'aren't shy about tinkering with ideas in a public forum and tend to iterate quickly on prototypes'.

- Tolerance of failure – innovation is risky and, as with brainstorming, generating new ideas is a numbers game – the more you have, the more likely it is that one will be a good one, but that involves having many that are not. Failure is therefore to be expected in an organization that is innovating. The trick with a failing project is to limit your exposure, terminate it quickly and learn from it – all principles used in a lean start-up (Academic insight 4.4). As Thomas Edison, the inventor of the light bulb, said: 'I have not failed, not once. I've discovered ten thousand ways that don't work.'

The origins of design thinking can be traced back to Simon (1969). Although there are many versions of a 'design thinking' process with numerous stages, Simon talks about it being a seven-stage process:

1 **Define** – identify the real problem to solve, not necessarily the obvious one, and define the design brief in a way that is unconstrained by existing solutions.
2 **Research** – observe how people deal with the problem and how similar problems in different contexts are handled.
3 **Ideate** – think outside the box – look at the problem from different perspectives and come up with as many different ideas and options as possible. This may involve a multidisciplinary approach and periods of divergent and convergent thinking. Do not close down options too early.

4 **Prototype** – experiment with prototype solutions to see which work.

5 **Choose** – this is a process of synthesis which helps select the one that works best or the *ones* that work best. Different solutions might be used to solve slightly different problems or meet the needs of different groups of people.

6 **Implement** – try out the solution(s) and monitor effectiveness. Prototype solutions – both products and services – need to be tested, iterated, and refined.

7 **Learn** – always learn from both success and failure.

These are characteristics and processes that any entrepreneur should be able to identify with and, using slightly different terminology, were covered in Chapter 2 as ways of finding a business idea. Underpinning this approach is a customer focus: a willingness to learn from their needs – the benefits they are seeking, both physical and emotional – and constantly refine a product/service offering to better meet them.

Kolko, J. (2015) 'Design Thinking Comes of Age', *Harvard Business Review*, September 2015.

Simon, H. (1969) *The Sciences of the Artificial*, Cambridge, MA: MIT Press.

CASE insight 5.5

Zound Industries SWEDEN

Differentiation by design

Zound Industries was founded in 2008 by eight individuals with different backgrounds in design, product development, finance, marketing, sales and business. It is making its mark in the technology industry by bringing distinctive design to bear on headphones, merging the function of a sound source with fashion accessories targeted at different markets. It is one of the fastest-growing companies in Sweden, with offices in New York and Shenzhen, where most of the equipment it sells is manufactured. Co-founder and President Konrad Bergström explained:

Eight years ago, when you were choosing your sneakers and the right shirt and then you just put on your ugly headphones. You didn't think about it, because the headphones showed that you liked music. And then when someone started to work with it and then make nice headphones that were more in line with design ... then all of a sudden everybody started to say 'oh, I can't wear these headphones because they don't look cool' ... It's not only about technology, it's a combination of technology and brand and design.
The Guardian 25 September 2014

The big dinosaurs of headphones or electronics still look at headphones as a technical product. If you
search on the web, they are seen as a technical product. What we try to do is be the best in other aspects. Be best in design, be best in functionality but also be best when it comes to sound. What we are working really hard on is building these soft values, that if you use our products it says something more than just functionality. You are connecting in some way.
www.highsnobiety.com 3 May 2013

Zound's mission is 'making electronics fashionable and fashion electronic'. Not that long ago it was the brand of trainers you wore that defined your lifestyle and 'tribe'. Today it is your headphones, and Zound has helped to create this. Zound produces four brands of headphones and mini-speakers, each range targeted at a different market, although you can only really appreciate these different products by viewing them on the website.

• **Urbanears:** Launched in 2009, this is the biggest brand. It is fashion-orientated, quirky and fun at a mid-point price range. It was voted one of the 'CoolBrands' of 2014/15 in the *Sunday Times* annual survey. These headphones feature many useful functional design details as well as using a range of materials and textile wrap cords that give them a feeling closer to a garment than a technological product. There are also distinctively designed mini-speakers.

- **Coloud:** Targeted at the young and active, this range offers a colourful, cheaper alternative to Urbanears. It is a headphone equivalent of a Swatch watch. Zound has partnered with Nokia to make these headphones from a smaller number of components and keep costs low. Triangularity is a distinctive theme that runs throughout the Coloud range, from the logo to the packaging to the angles in the headphone design.
- **Marshall:** Launched in 2010, this is a brand licensed from the much-respected amplifier company. It is a quality range of headphones and speakers that sells to the high end of the market. It mirrors the distinctive look of Marshall amps and, by working with Marshall Amplification, also mirrors the distinctive sound quality.
- **Molami:** Launched in 2011, this is an ultra-high-end, female-focused fashion range, distinctively angular and incorporating materials like leather and silk. Zound boasts that the range can be worn as a stylish fashion accessory that complements any outfit, whether or not it is being used as a headphone. It was launched in cities around the world in the same way as a fashion house might show off the latest season's designs. It is regularly featured in fashion magazines.

To support and promote its products Zound hosts high-profile 'Swegie' events showcasing Swedish design, culture and creativity that coincide with fashion weeks in cities around the world, making certain they all have a 'celebrity' feel.

Zound set its sights on going global from its very beginning. Its vision is 'to be the world-leading lifestyle headphone manufacturer'. The company's strategy has been thought through systematically. Its distinctive design-led products are targeted at specific markets: 'From the time a product is developed to the day it is sitting on a store shelf, it has been strategically thought through how to create, market, and distribute it and which brand the product will be sold under. This way, multiple demographics are reached'. Zound has developed new products and new markets with relentless effectiveness.

Zound's success has also been based on its ability to partner with others, starting at the very beginning: the founders had a range of skills and experience. They describe themselves as a 'collective'. It has sought additional capital systematically at different stages of its growth, starting in 2009. It has partnered with different distributors in different countries and even produced joint-branded products with the retailer H&M. In 2014 Zound announced a partnership with Swedish telecom operator TeliaSonera, which acquired a stake in Zound. The aim is to bundle fashion headphones, audio speakers and device accessories together with TeliaSonera's mobile telecommunications.

The company had sold more than 10 million pairs of headphones in over 20,000 stores globally, including Apple, Best Buy, HMV, Target, Urban Outfitters, Colette, FNAC, Media Markt, Telia, Deutsche Telekom, Orange and Tesco. Thousands of articles have featured the company's products in publications such as *Vogue* (US), *Elle* (US) and *Time*.

Visit the website: www.zoundindustries.com

Questions:

1 Describe who you think is the target market for each of the four brands.
2 What is the value proposition for each target market?
3 How are the company's products differentiated from those of competitors?
4 If this is a fashion brand, is it sustainable? If so, how?

Creating competitive advantage through design

ACADEMIC insight 5.5

Studies have shown that for every £1 invested in design, businesses can expect turnover to increase by more than £20 and profit by more than £4 (Design Council, 2012). A report by Warwick Business School and the Design Council (2014) explored how business uses and benefits from design. It found that design can add value to any organization but it benefits most when design is customer-centred and related to solving customers' problems. It works best when culturally embedded with strong support in the organization.

The report made eight recommendations.

1 Design is about making an organization stand out from the competition, and is therefore valuable in any sector and for any size of company.
2 The focus should be on the needs of customers and how these might be better met in ways that differ from what is currently offered by competitors.
3 Design is successful when it embodies and reinforces the brand, and speaks a language that is consistent with it.
4 Design processes need to be clearly structured, strongly led with a clear vision, but collaborative, involving all key stakeholders and functions.
5 Design innovation needs support at the highest level in the organization so as to engender trust among those involved in the process.
6 Problem-solving design needs to be embedded in the organization's culture.
7 Design should be present in the work environment, enabling collaboration, exchanges of ideas and teamwork.
8 For strategic design to work, designers have to be able to work in cross-functional teams and act as influencers who champion design. They have to be capable of using and understanding different languages and perspectives and to be fully aware of commercial considerations.

Design has a role in a market paradigm shift (Chapter 2). Much of the literature on innovation has focused either on radical innovation pushed by technology or incremental innovation pulled by the market. Verganti (2009) made the point that not all 'design-driven innovations' come from the market, making existing products better, easier to use or more distinctive. They can also create whole new markets by giving products 'new meanings', emotional, psychological and sociocultural rather than just utilitarian reasons for purchasing them (see Case insights 2.3 and 5.4). Customers come to view the product in a different light. Verganti argued that for truly breakthrough products and services, you must look beyond customers to those he calls 'interpreters' – 'experts who deeply understand and shape the markets they work in'. Although in advance of their markets, they are absorbed in them, understanding trends, styles, materials and technology. However, they are able to rise above the dominant logic by recognizing and questioning it (see Academic insight 2.1). They are also able to influence the market through their insight, powers of persuasion and marketing skills. Like Steve Jobs and Jonathan Ives at Apple, they have a vision and they take that vision to customers, persuading them that this new 'meaning' has value.

Verganti, R. (2009) *Design-Driven Innovation: Changing the Rules of Competition by Radically Innovating What Things Mean,* Boston, MA: Harvard Business School Publishing.

Micheli. P. (2014) *Leading Business by Design: Why and How Business Leaders Invest in Design,* London: Warwick Business School and Design Council.

Design Council (2012) *Design Delivers for Business A Summary of Evidence from the Design Council's Design Leadership Programme,* London: Design Council.

Branding your values

It is a common misconception that only large companies can have 'brands'. The name of local tradesmen is often their 'brand' and that name may stand for many things, such as quality of service. They will place great store on their local reputation. What is more, good tradesmen will take time to develop personal relationships with their customers – something big companies have difficulty doing – and those relationships will be based on trust that they provide 'value-for-money' and respect that they will do a good job. When customers have a good relationship with a reputable tradesman they will often recommend them personally to friends. And all of this costs infinitely less than the expenditure large companies make in developing their brand.

Consumers tend to form relationships with brands in much the same way as they form relationships with people. A recognizable brand that resonates with customers can outlive its founder and can be a vehicle for growth for the company that has real commercial value. However, differentiation of any form usually adds costs, even if it is just taking time to talk to customers, and branding can be expensive. It is therefore essential that branding not only succeeds in creating an identity for the product or service that is seen as different to that of competitors, but that the benefits to the customers are seen by them as outweighing the costs. In other words, customers are willing to pay the extra costs involved in conveying the reputation and developing a relationship. The value of reputation to the customer is about risk reduction – the assurance that the product/service offering will be consistent or homogeneous. The value of the relationship is about trust, that the reputation is accurate, but also about other psychological benefits that we humans derive from any form of relationship.

Relationships are based on trust, which develops over time, and respect for the other person, usually based upon the values they hold. And while these may be just professional and commercial values, there are other values that might be attractive to customers, values that many are increasingly willing to pay for. These can be broadly categorized as ethical, social and environmental and have now been subsumed in the corporate world within what is called **corporate social responsibility (CSR)**. If they are effectively incorporated into the product offering, including design, this can provide added or sustained 'meaning' to the brand.

> One of the most important aspects of any business is its ethical code, a statement of the principles governing the way it operates and its employees behave.
>
> Duncan Bannatyne serial entrepreneur *Daily Telegraph* 5 August 2009

There is a long history of socially motivated entrepreneurs – from the chocolate maker J. Cadbury & Sons with its Quaker values, to the jam maker Wilkin & Sons. More recently companies like Lush and Timberland have managed to combine business and social values successfully – and in the process enhance their brand image and make substantial profits. Another approach to this issue in recent years has been the emergence of what has become known as **sustainable entrepreneurship** – where issues of CSR, sustainability, ethics and good corporate governance are at the core of the commercial enterprise. It is said to be about meeting the needs of today through profit without prejudicing the future. Entrepreneurship that emphasizes only economic and ecological value creation has been called **environmental entrepreneurship, eco-entrepreneurship** and **eco-preneurship**. In all cases the prime objective is to develop a profitable business that adheres to certain principles, usually emphasizing them as part of its branding.

Sustainable entrepreneurship and social responsibility

Ethical values in the corporate world translate not only into the culture of an organization and its brand, but also into strategies and actions that have an ethical and social, rather than just a profit, dimension. It is now widely accepted that many business practices can have negative social and environmental side effects. There is a hierarchy of virtue for companies practising what is broadly called CSR, shown in Figure 5.4. At its base is CSR that delivers profit to the company. Next is CSR that comes through compliance with the law. Finally, there is CSR that is discretionary, based upon ethical norms and a desire to do the best thing for the community and society as a whole. Fortunately this hierarchy is not always as rigid as Figure 5.4 suggests, and there can be commercial benefit in many forms of CSR.

> More than ever, consumers expect brands to be environmentally aware. They want to invest financially and emotionally in a product and, at start-up, you can't ignore that.
>
> Chris Holmes founder Woodbuds *Sunday Times* 28 June 2015

CSR can offer both commercial and social benefits. The two are not necessarily mutually exclusive. And the more a firm can benefit from CSR, the more it is likely to integrate it on a strategic decision-making level, simultaneously increasing its effectiveness in promoting its CSR causes. Looked at strategically, CSR can be used to bring both social and economic goals into alignment and to leverage capabilities and relationships in support of charitable causes. This can create additional value for both the company and the causes it supports. As well as helping to achieve altruistic aims, strong CSR policy can have three sound commercial benefits.

Figure 5.4 *Hierarchy of virtue*

> We're really noticing people's perceptions changing. More than ever they want products that are sustainable but without sacrificing style or quality.
>
> *Heather Wittle founder Beyond Skin Sunday Times 28 June 2015*

> You can be eco-aware without being boring. It is really important that small businesses consider sustainability, and doing it without compromising the end product is crucial.
>
> *Chris Holmes founder Woodbuds Sunday Times 28 June 2015*

1 **Increased sales, brand identity and customer loyalty** – While any product must first satisfy the customer's key buying criteria (quality, price etc.) a strong CSR brand can increase sales and customer loyalty by helping to differentiate it. Customers are increasingly drawn to brands with a strong CSR profile and CSR has become an element in the continuous process of trying to differentiate one company from another. A strong CSR brand can even create its own market niche for an organization. For example, the Co-operative Bank in the UK has a long history of CSR. It has set itself up as an ethical and ecological investor with an investment policy that is the most frequently cited reason that customers choose the bank. On the other hand, a bad CSR image can severely damage sales, as BP found after the 2010 oil spillage in the Gulf of Mexico.

2 **Reduced operating costs and productivity gains** – One aspect of sustainability concerns the measurement and control of inputs, and many environmental initiatives therefore also reduce costs (e.g. reducing waste and recycling, having better control of building temperatures or reducing the use of agrochemicals). Yahoo saved 60% of its electricity costs simply by opening windows where servers are located so as to let the hot air out. General Electric started a programme of becoming more sustainable ('greener') in 2004. By 2008 this initiative had yielded $100 million in cost savings. Waste-reducing cost savings can come from looking at raw materials usage, the manufacturing process, packaging requirements, transport needs, maintenance and the use of disposal methods. Actions to improve working conditions, lessen environmental impact or increase employee involvement in decision making can improve productivity. For example, actions to improve work conditions in the supply chain have been seen to lead to decreases in defect rates in merchandise. Many social initiatives can increase employee motivation and cut absenteeism and staff turnover. An increasing number of graduates take CSR issues into consideration when making employment decisions.

3 **Improved new product development** – A focus on CSR issues can lead to new product opportunities. For example, car manufacturers are striving to find alternatives to fossil fuels, while developing conventional engines that are more and more economical. Innovation linked to sustainability often has major systems-level implications, demanding a holistic and integrated approach to innovation management. As well as reducing costs, General Electric's sustainability programme yielded 80 new products and services that generated $17 million in revenues between 2004 and 2008.

Environmental sustainability and waste reduction

Many academics and business people have observed that what is good for the environment can also be good for business. Sustainability means doing more with fewer resources, and that reduces costs. Scott (2010) gives the example of Walmart, which demanded that its 60,000 suppliers reduce packaging by at least 5%. As a result, Walmart expected to reduce solid waste by 25% and shave $3.4 billion off of operating costs. General Electric decided to become 'greener' in 2004. By 2008, 'green' practices had reduced costs by $100 million and yielded a portfolio of 80 new products and services that generated $17 billion in annual revenues. Here are Scott's 10 guidelines to reduce product waste:

1 Carefully design the product to minimize resources so it can be reused in a closed-loop system.

2 Design products so they can be disassembled easily.
3 Reduce the use of hazardous inputs.
4 Switch to non-hazardous manufacturing methods.
5 Reduce the amount of energy required in manufacturing and use sustainable energy.
6 Use newer, cleaner technologies.
7 Use sustainable, re-manufactured, recycled or scrap materials in the manufacturing process.
8 Improve quality control and process monitoring.
9 Find ways to get the product returned for disassembly and harvesting of parts.
10 Reduce packaging or use recycled materials.

Scott, J. (2010) 'The Sustainable Business', *Global Focus*, Vol. 04, EFMD.

Richard Branson www.hrmagazine.co.uk 13 July 2010

I think every business needs a leader that does not forget the massive impact business can have on the world. All business leaders should be thinking 'how can I be a force for good?' What I see is demand from our people to be a business that is good, makes a profit, but also does something for the planet and humanity. I think this is a trend we will see more of … CSR in my mind is defunct now. Compartmentalizing the social responsibility is not the way to go. I think the model for starting employee engagement activities has to be embedded in everything you do.

If you want to find out more about CSR in the UK, The Institute of Corporate Responsibility and Sustainability (ICRS) should be able to help. It is a not-for-profit professional membership body established in 2014 by a number of leading companies to help promote CSR and sustainability through seminars and other events. Of course it is one thing to claim to be socially responsible and quite another to prove it. Indeed, if your claims prove to be unfounded, it is likely that there will be a backlash from your customers, as BP found to its cost with the Deepwater Horizon oil spill in 2010. The Planet Mark is a mark that assures customers that the organization from which they are purchasing is active in improving its environmental and social performance. Established in 2013 by the Eden Project and the sustainability consultancy Planet First, businesses achieving the mark are then helped to monitor their environmental impact and lessen it, as well as encouraging their employees, customers and stakeholders to take action.

Information on corporate responsibility and sustainability, including how to contact these organizations, can be found in the *Guide to UK Sources of Help, Advice, Information and Funding* on the companion website: www.macmillanihe.com/burns-nvc-2e. An additional guide for Australian readers, produced by Dr Russell Manfield, is also provided.

ACADEMIC insight 5.7

Commercial value of CSR

Is there evidence that CSR adds any commercial value? The quest to link corporate CSR directly to financial performance and/or share price performance spans some 40 years and the results have often been contradictory and confusing. Nevertheless, in a review and assessment of 127 empirical studies, Margolis and Walsh (2003) concluded that there is a positive relationship between CSR and financial performance, a result supported in a meta-survey by Orlitzy et al. (2003). Looking at investment portfolios, Ven de Velde et al. (2005) concluded that high-sustainability-rated portfolios (ones that integrated environmental, social and ethical issues) performed better than low-rated portfolios. What is more, an Economic Intelligence Unit Survey in 2008 showed that the vast majority of US business leaders and their boards of directors now accept a clear relationship between CSR and financial performance (Business Green, 2008).

In a 2010 review of the literature Carroll and Shabana concluded that on the whole a positive relationship exists between CSR and financial performance, 'but inconsistencies linger'. This is because financial performance is affected by many other internal and external variables, not all controlled by the firm. What is more, 'the benefits of CSR are not homogeneous, and effective CSR initiatives are not generic'. They concluded that CSR activities need to be part of a coherent and consistent strategy that is directed at improving both stakeholder relationships and social welfare. They talk about 'a convergence between economic and social goals' – where social good is crafted into creating economic value. Kurucz et al. (2008) summarized the four ways CSR can add value:

1 Reducing costs and risk (waste, hazards etc.).
2 Strengthening legitimacy and reputation, particularly through branding.
3 Building competitive advantage through reputation and branding.
4 'Creating win–win situations through synergistic value creation' – linking economic and social goals.

Business Green (2008) 'US Execs: CSR Initiatives do Boost the Bottom Line', www.BusinessGreen.com.

Carroll, A.B. and Shabana, K.M. (2010) 'The Business Case for Corporate Social Responsibility: A Review of Concepts, Research and Practise', *International Journal of Management Reviews*, www.academia.edu.

Kurucz, E., Colbert, B. and Wheeler, D. (2008) 'The Business Case for Corporate Social Responsibility'. In A. Crane, A. McWilliams, D. Matten, J. Moon and D. Seigel (eds), *The Oxford Handbook of Corporate Social Responsibility*, Oxford: Oxford University Press.

Margolis, J.D. and Walsh, J.P. (2003) 'Misery Loves Companies: Rethinking Social Initiatives by Business', *Administrative Science Quarterly*, 48.

Orlitzy, M., Schmidt, F.L. and Rynes, S.L. (2003) 'Corporate Social Performance: A Meta-Analysis', *Organization Studies*, 24.

Porter, M.E. and Kramer, M.R. (2006), 'Strategy and Society: The Link between Competitive Advantage and Corporate Social Responsibility', *Harvard Business Review*, 84.

Ven de Velde, E., Vermeir, W. and Corten, F. (2005) 'Corporate Social Responsibility and Financial Performance', *Corporate Governance*, 5(3).

Private or social enterprise?

So far we have talked about using the broad area of CSR to enhance the profit potential of your business while also benefiting some (undefined) ethical, social or environmental issues. The discussion has always placed the commercial objective first, assuming that the entrepreneur would decide on any social mission and how it was to be met. However, the distinction between a private enterprise with strong social objectives and a social enterprise is not always clear.

A social enterprise operates in a commercial way to achieve its social objectives, and any profits it generates are ploughed back to help achieve them. It is often also about creating social change at a community level, normally through voluntary or community groups. The social objectives come first and the commercial objectives second. Profit is a means to a social end. In the UK this has a long history, from Victorian hospitals to the modern-day hospice movement.

CASE insight 5.6

Ecotricity UK

Mablethorpe, UK

All photos courtesy of Ecotricity

Environmental opportunities and value enhancement

Born in 1961, Dale Vince was once a New Age hippie. He dropped out of school aged 15 and at the age of 19 toured Britain and Europe for a decade in a peace convoy. These days he is better known as a millionaire entrepreneur who owns Britain's greenest energy company, Ecotricity. Founded in 1995, Ecotricity generates electricity from its wind turbines and sun parks around the UK, as far apart as Dundee and Somerset, and sells the 'green' energy to domestic and corporate customers, including Lush, Universal Studios and Ford.

Vince used to mend vehicles and improvise mobile shelters from scrap in his hippie days. He also built wind turbines to take to music festivals to power sound systems. The idea for large-scale turbines came to him on a hill near Stroud in Gloucestershire where his home – a former army lorry – was powered by a small wind turbine. He thought, why not build a full-sized, permanent wind turbine in the field?

All us hippies used to say 'Why don't they build big wind turbines?' One day I thought, who are 'they'? So I dropped back in to build windmills.

Originally he planned only to build turbines for other people, but, having failed to get backing from his local electricity company, he decided to build a turbine for himself on adjacent land and connect it to the national grid. However, the electricity company wanted to charge him £500,000 to connect it. He persisted and negotiated the price down to £27,000.

It took a long time to get that down. And I still had to borrow some money. The big banks here in Stroud looked at me like I was crazy.

He borrowed some of the money from a 'green' bank, Triodos, but had also raised funds by selling wind monitoring masts.

I thought about going to people with a good cause and asking for funding as a charity. But having a business model was better.

Daily Telegraph 27 May 2011

Ecotricity is still based in Stroud and employs almost 800 staff. It is a private company 100% owned by Vince and is very much a family business, with a number of his family employed by the company. The company operates a 'not-for-dividend' model, reinvesting income directly into new sources of renewable energy. In 2010 it raised funds directly from the public by offering 'EcoBonds' with a preferential rate of interest for customers, and has replicated that offering with three further Ecobonds since, which have raised more than £50m. It has also diversified into other sustainable energy areas such as battery storage and developing green gas using grass in an anaerobic digester.

Visit the website: www.ecotricity.co.uk

Question:

Is Ecotricity anything other than a commercial business? If so, how does it differ?

The simplest legal form of social enterprise is an **unincorporated association**, an informal association of individuals that can form (and re-form) quickly. This is similar to sole traders or informal partnerships. While this enjoys great freedom because it is not regulated, it cannot own assets or borrow money because an association has no legal status. Other legal forms of a social enterprise can be cumbersome and carry with them many restrictions, the primary one being that *all* the profits of the venture must be ploughed back into its activities. This can make raising capital difficult unless you obtain finance specifically offered to social enterprises. There are other pragmatic advantages to remaining a sole trader or private company, such as the avoidance of public accountability for decisions made by the founder. Remaining a commercial, for-profit entity ensures that the founder can decide on the balance between commercial and social objectives without interference. We cover this in more detail in Chapter 9. Whichever form of enterprise you decide on, CSR generally can play an important part in giving an identity to your brand – one with which an increasing number of customers identify.

CASE insight 5.7

Goodone UK

Private or social enterprise?

Nin Castle and Phoebe Emerson met at Brighton University in 2001 where both were doing fashion courses. They talked about setting up a fashion business but were uneasy about some of the ethical and environmental issues relating to the industry. Two million tonnes of clothes are sold annually in the UK, of which one million will end up in landfill sites when half of it is reusable. It was while at a nightclub in 2003 that they came up with the idea of Goodone. The idea was to design and produce innovative, quality, one-off clothing which was made from hand-picked, locally sourced, recycled fabrics. They called it 'up-cycling', 'innovatively combining new British and sustainable fabrics with reclaimed textiles'. They wanted to change perceptions of what recycled clothing can be by creating garments that did not look recycled.

Starting with only £1,000, in 2005 they made a deal with a local charity shop that allowed them to go through all the bags of textiles that were being sent to the rag factory at the cost of £1 a bag. They also acquired a disused car showroom in Brighton – a large open space into which they put two makeshift beds and a couple of second-hand sewing machines – and started their business:

We had no funding, were living on housing benefit and doing part-time jobs to try and get the business up and running. In 2006 our first customers were local boutiques. We were full of enthusiasm and rather naive as we really thought that our tiny business could make an impact on the huge fashion industry.
Nin Castle *Daily Telegraph* 5 February 2009

Nin did the design work and Phoebe looked after the business side, both working on the manufacturing. Within a few months they decided to go on a three-day 'Creative Business' start-up course run by the National Council for Graduate Entrepreneurship (NCGE) and registered Goodone as a company. After a year in the car showroom, they relocated to Hackney in London so as to be in the 'fashion hub' of the UK. They also set up their own online shop.

In 2007 they won a £15,000 prize from NCGE, much of which was spent on repairing the sewing machines. However, the prize also generated free PR, and articles about the company appeared in the national press. These stimulated sales – Goodone fulfilled orders for clothes from the cult shop 'Side by Side' in Tokyo, Japan – and created more opportunities. They exhibited at the 'Fashion Made Fair' sale in Brick Lane, London, 'The Clothes Show Live' in Birmingham and the 'Margin' trade show in London, and started giving presentations to the London School of Fashion. They were awarded Manufacturing Advisory Service funding to develop the Goodone product line and brand, and a London Development Agency SME Innovation Award, which gave them a manufacturing consultancy from the London College of Fashion. Normally, lengths of cloth are sent to the manufacturer, but with recycled fabric every piece is different and that creates special problems. Goodone also began outsourcing some manufacturing to HEBA Women's Project, a London charity.

In January 2008 Phoebe amicably left the company to work in other areas of social enterprise and since then has become a lawyer working in the human rights field. Nin then went on to produce charity T-shirts by recycling old campaign T-shirts from Greenpeace, Shelter, Amnesty, Liberty and WWF. She spent August 2009 in South Africa working for the Tabeisa Project, designing and producing clothes in a township outside Cape Town for sale in the UK. Goodone's mission statement sets out their aims:

Goodone design and produce innovative, quality, one-off clothing which is made from hand-picked, locally-sourced, recycled fabrics. We aim to exceed people's expectations of what recycled clothing can be by creating garments which don't look obviously recycled. Instead of 'reworking' or 'customising' existing pieces we design for production. Using our specialist knowledge in the deconstruction and reconstruction of garments, sustainable sourcing and production we are able to create a limitless amount of new clothing from old, which, dependent on the combination of coloured, patterned and textured fabrics chosen, will inherently always remain unique. This means we are able to mass-produce the one-off.

By using these recycled materials we are not only providing a creative and sustainable solution for waste reduction but also minimising energy use and the damage to the environment caused by the production of new clothing. It is our goal to continue to build a reputable brand which is internationally recognised for pioneering the production of high-quality, innovative 'recreated' clothing, secondly,

provide specialist consultancy, working with, instead of against, existing brands and retailers to solve their own waste issues, consequently impacting the industry on a bigger scale, and thirdly, to educate the next generation of fashion designers, entrepreneurs and consumers on the urgency and methods for designing, producing and consuming sustainably.

Goodone's collections have been shown at London Fashion Week and offered at Topshop's website and flagship Oxford Street store. In 2010, Claire Farrell joined the Goodone team as co-designer. By 2016 Goodone was supplying outlets in London, Manchester, Brighton and Glasgow in the UK and internationally in Germany, USA, Switzerland, Canada and Spain. They were also selling from their website, although the turnover is modest. Goodone employs part-time staff and makes use of interns. Both Nin and Claire also teach at fashion colleges and Goodone's income gets ploughed back into the business. Goodone is an example of a business with social objectives and one that has made the most of grants and support that are available to young enterprises.

Questions:

1   Is this a social enterprise or just a socially ethical business?
2   Is Goodone successful? How do you measure this? What does money measure in this business?
3   Was it right that Nin and Phoebe should have been able to make so much use of grants and support?

Building the brand

As we have seen, in a world where products and services are all too often homogeneous, a good brand is a powerful marketing tool that must be the cornerstone of any strategy of differentiation. It also helps to cement customer loyalty. The brand must reflect the promise of your value proposition and the personality of the organization that offers it. Support for social and ethical causes can reinforce this, as well as often making good commercial sense. Building a brand takes time. It is built up through effective use of communication media and is recognized through the brand or company name and logo.

At this stage you may not have a recognizable brand like the ones cited, but you do have yourself and that can start to shape the identity of your start-up. In many ways shaping the identity of a start-up is easier the fewer people you have working with you. You have your personal values and beliefs to build on, underpinned by what the big companies call CSR. The trick is to understand what these values and beliefs are, and to make them explicit and clear in order to ensure that they are reflected not only in what you do, but how you do things. They need to be clear to customers, employees, distributors and suppliers alike. And they need to be sincerely felt values and beliefs; otherwise you will be quickly found out and any trust you may have built up will disappear.

The key thing is never to do anything which discredits the brand, like ripping off the public or doing something which you'd feel uncomfortable reading about.

Richard Branson founder Virgin Group The Observer 14 September 2014

The identity of your business should reflect the culture within it – its personality. You create the culture of your business through your leadership and you need to ensure that you create the culture and identity you want. This involves being consistent in words and actions. It requires an emotional intelligence that does not always come naturally but can be nurtured. It will take time to develop, but you need to start immediately. We discuss these leadership skills and how they can affect the culture of your business in Chapter 11. Your brand should reflect the identity of your business, and one of the best ways to do that is to use yourself to promote the brand. In Britain, probably the best known proponent of this is Richard Branson. His companies, under the Virgin name, are closely associated with him and what he stands for personally.

Brand name and logo

Brand and company names need to be distinctive and easy to remember, say and even spell across different cultures and nationalities. This implies short names are best. It is important that they do not have negative associations or that names do not mean bad things in other languages. Names should be supportive of your value proposition. This is not always easy or straightforward. 'Freeserve' was a good brand name for one of the first UK internet service providers – it was free. However, in 2004 it was changed to 'Wanadoo' because the name was easier to market across Europe. In 2006 it was again changed to 'Orange' as the company's product offering was expanded to include internet and telecommunications.

Because it adds value to the company, your brand name and logo can and should be trademark protected if possible (Chapter 9).

There are no hard and fast rules about using the company name as a product name. Sometimes this works, particularly when it is a one-product company, but there are examples of successfully using different company and product names alongside each other. 'Burger King' is a successful company brand that describes at least the major part of the company's product range. It is associative – suggesting some characteristic or benefit of the product, albeit sometimes in an indirect way. In this way 'iPhone' is another associative product brand name, but this time is used alongside the company name 'Apple', which has a different set of brand associations. This is a freestanding name that has built brand value over a number of years. Some company names have been less successful in transferring across product ranges. For example the Dyson brand name is based upon the inventor/entrepreneur James Dyson, but is still very much associated with vacuum cleaners, although the company now offers a range of electrical products.

Your mission statement

By this stage you should have a good idea of what your venture intends to achieve, for you and for its target customers. So it is time to write your **mission statement**. This is a formal

CASE insight 5.8

Richard Branson and Virgin (1)

 UK

Building the brand

Richard Branson is probably the best known entrepreneur in Britain today, and his name is closely associated with the many businesses that carry the Virgin brand name. He is outgoing and an excellent self-publicist. He has been called an 'adventurer', taking risks that few others would contemplate. This shows itself in his personal life, with his transatlantic power boating and round-the-world ballooning exploits, as well as in his business life where he has challenged established firms such as British Airways and Coca-Cola. He is a multimillionaire with what has been described as a charismatic leadership style.

Virgin is probably the best known brand in Britain with 96% recognition and is well known worldwide. The Virgin name has found its way onto aircraft, trains, cola, vodka, mobile phones, cinemas, a radio station, financial services, fitness studios and the internet. It is strongly associated with Sir Richard Branson – 95% can name him as the founder. Virgin believes their brand stands for value for money, quality, innovation, fun and a sense of competitive challenge. They believe they deliver a quality service by empowering employees and, while continuously monitoring customer feedback, striving to improve the customer's experience through innovation. According to Will Whitehorn, director of corporate affairs at Virgin Management:

> At Virgin, we know what the brand name means, and when we put our brand name on something, we're making a promise. It's a promise we've always kept and always will. It's harder work keeping promises than making them, but there is no secret formula. Virgin sticks to its principles and keeps its promises. (1)

The brand has been largely built through Branson's personal PR efforts. He recognized the importance of self-publicity very early in his career when the BBC featured him in a documentary called 'The People of Tomorrow' because of his first venture, *Student* magazine. Since then he has become known for his often outrageous publicity stunts, such as dressing up as a bride for the launch of Virgin Bride. According to Branson:

> Brands must be built around reputation, quality and price... People should not be asking 'is this one product too far?' but rather, 'what are the qualities of my company's name? How can I develop them?' (2)

As to what these qualities are for Virgin, Branson gives us a candid insight into at least one of them:

> Fun is at the core of the way I like to do business and has informed everything I've done from the outset. More than any other element fun is the secret of Virgin's success. (3)

Virgin has a devolved structure and an informal but complex culture based upon the Virgin brand. It is the brand that unifies the different companies in the group. Branson believes that finding the right people to work with is the key to success and the Virgin brand is so strong that it helps to attract like-minded staff. He believes that it is not qualifications that matter in people, rather their attitude. He calls them 'Virgin-type' people – staff who will enjoy their work and are customer focused. And their enthusiasm for the brand rubs off on the customers. As Branson says:

> Our brand values are very important, and we tend to select people to work for us who share these values ... For as much as you need a strong personality to build a business from scratch, you must also understand the art of delegation ... I started Virgin with a philosophy that if staff are happy, customers will follow. It can't just be me that sets the culture when we recruit people. I have a really great set of CEOs across our businesses who live and breathe the Virgin brand and who are entrepreneurs themselves. (4)

Visit the website: www.virgin.com

Sources:

1 *The Guardian*, 30 April 2002.
2 Branson, R. (1998) *Losing my Virginity*, 1998, London: Virgin.
3 Andersen, J. (1995) *Local Heroes*, Glasgow: Scottish Enterprise.
4 *www.hrmagazine.co.uk*, 13 July 2010.

Questions:

1 What is the essence of the Virgin brand? Why is it important to the company?
2 How is it developed and maintained?
3 How important is Richard Branson to the brand? What might happen when he retires?

statement of business purpose. The mission statement says what the business aims to achieve and how it will achieve it. It therefore usually defines the scope of the business (what areas of activity it is engaged in) by including reference to the product/service, value proposition, customer groups and the benefits they derive. This stops you straying into markets where you have no competitive advantage, clarifies strategic options and offers guidance for setting objectives. Often it encompasses the values upheld by the organization. Like a vision statement, a mission statement should be short and snappy. Mission statements can take many forms. The template below is a suggested basis for arriving at a statement that includes all these elements:

> To provide *(business scope)* to satisfy the *(customer needs)* of *(customer segments)* by offering *(value proposition)* using our *(basis of competitive advantage)* to achieve *(vision)*. In doing this we will uphold *(values)*.

The mission and vision of your business must be consistent with your values. All three go hand in hand, each reinforcing the others. You can then start to build the strategies that enable you to achieve your vision. This includes your business model and your marketing strategies. Finally, the tactics are the activities you conduct day to day, such as promotion or sales campaigns. As shown in Figure 5.5, while strategies and tactics might change rapidly in an entrepreneurial firm, mission, vision and values are more enduring. Together, they form the 'road map' that tells everyone where you are going and how you might get there, even when one route is blocked in the short term.

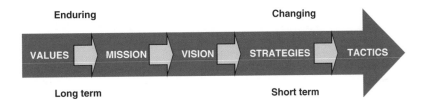

Figure 5.5 *Values, mission, vision, strategies and tactics*

CASE insight 5.9

 easyJet (2) UK

Mission statements

easyJet is the low-cost airline we looked at in Case insight 4.4. Its mission statement is:

To provide our customers with safe, good value, point-to-point air services. To effect and to offer a consistent and reliable product, and fares appealing to leisure and business markets on a range of European routes.

To achieve this we will develop our people and establish lasting relationships with our suppliers.

Visit the website: www.easyjet.com

Question:

Is this a good mission statement?

CASE insight 5.10

USA

Golden Krust (2)

© Golden Krust

© Golden Krust

Blending vision, mission and values

We looked at Golden Krust in Case insight 1.7. Here are its vision, mission and values.

Vision:
Golden Krust exists to provide the taste of the Caribbean to the world.

Mission:
- To provide consumers with authentic, tasty Jamaican patties and relevant Caribbean cuisine in convenient settings and sizes;
- To provide customers with outstanding customer service and reliable predictability at every touch-point;
- To provide employees with an environment that is rewarding, fun and aspirational;
- To provide communities in which we operate with a corporate citizen of which they can be proud;

- To provide stakeholders with a superior return on their investment.

Values:
- Our customers are at the core of our success;
- Integrity, value and fun are hallmarks of our approach to business;
- All stakeholders should benefit from their association with Golden Krust.

Visit the website: www.goldenkrustbakery.com

Question:

Are the vision, mission and values of Golden Krust consistent?

CASE insight 5.11

UK

Adrenaline Alley

Blending vision, mission and values in a social enterprise

Based in Corby in Northamptonshire (UK), Adrenaline Alley is Europe's biggest urban sports park. Although it is run as a commercial business, it is a charitable social enterprise established to benefit the local community and to act as inspiration for others. Here are its vision, mission and values:

© Adrenaline Alley

leading provider of urban sports using a range of partnerships to become a sustainable social enterprise.

Values:

Delivering our mission as a team, we strive to be:

- *Approachable and honest – always willing to listen and learn;*
- *People focused – operating for the benefit of our community and participants;*
- *Accessible – willing to go the extra mile to ensure everyone can participate;*
- *Versatile – adapting the business to the needs of our customers.*

Visit the website: www.adrenalinealley.co.uk

Vision:

To expand our thriving centre for urban sports and community use, bringing change that makes a real difference to people's lives, and provide opportunities for other communities to develop social enterprises in the same way.

Mission:

To provide safe, secure and manageable facilities addressing the needs of local communities and to be recognized as a

Question:

Are the vision, mission and values of Adrenaline Alley consistent?

Sofa-bed Factory

Piotr and Olek decided that initially they would sell their sofa-beds unbranded through the large UK retailer where Piotr has a friend who is the buyer. This decision had been a pragmatic one, dictated by the chance friendship that had highlighted an opportunity, market conditions in the UK and the reality that the partners had little money to spend on marketing. As a result they expected that their margins would be lower than otherwise, not least because they had no market track record. Nevertheless securing this customer would give them access to the UK market and they could then look for additional customers.

However, while this retail chain might be their direct customer, they realized that, ultimately the end user of their product would need to be satisfied with it. They understood that consumers would have to find their sofa-beds attractive, comfortable and robust – at least more so than their competitors'. The folding steel frame had been developed by Olek and was lighter, stronger and more easily opened to form a bed than other sofas he had seen

– a definite competitive advantage. The foam mattress was often the weakest point of these sofa-beds. They tended to be thin and low density, which made them uncomfortable and not very durable. Piotr and Olek decided that they wanted to make their sofa-beds better. They had heard of 'memory foam' – a polyurethane with additional chemicals that increase its viscosity and density so that it softens in reaction to body heat, allowing it to quickly mould to a warm body and making for a more comfortable mattress. They decided to investigate the use of this. They are also aware that they need to make the sofas look contemporary through the design and use of distinctive fabrics and probably needed to quickly develop other modular units to fit alongside the existing sofa-bed.

The pair decided that three features – quality, comfort and ease of use – were the distinctive characteristics of their sofa-bed and should remain the feature of any new products. After a little discussion, they decided that the sofa-bed features and benefits should include:

- A robust, sturdy frame – that is easy to unfold into a bed;
- A comfortable mattress – that ensures a good night's sleep;
- Contemporary, modular design – that fits in with different styles of modern furniture;
- A competitive price – that enables a retail list-price of below €1,000 but delivers a good margin to the retailer.

They also decided to call their business 'Sofa-bed Factory', because it stated clearly what the company did, sounded reassuring (being manufacturers rather than sales people) and was relatively short (useful if they eventually were to sell on the internet). They also thought they might be able to use the phrase 'straight from the manufacturer' if they decided to sell directly to the public in the future. Piotr thought for a moment and joked that they had a motto to go with their logo: 'Manufacturer of dreams – quality, comfort and ease of use'. Maybe it sounded better in Polish.

Questions:

1 For each target market, what is the value proposition for Sofa-bed Factory? What do you think of it?
2 What are the advantages and disadvantages of selling through this large retail chain?
3 What do Piotr and Olek still need to do or find out? Do you have any concerns at this stage?

Summary and action points

5.1 Develop your values, beliefs and vision: Understand your values and beliefs and make sure they underpin the business. They set expectations for how to operate and treat people – customers, employees, partners and suppliers – and should be reflected in your value proposition.

Develop a vision for the future of your business.

5.2 Understand customer benefits: Understand the benefits that customers are looking for in purchasing your product/service rather than just focusing on its features.

5.3 Develop your target markets and value proposition: Develop a value proposition for each of your target markets that is consistent with your own values. This summarizes how it will solve a problem for them, the benefits it offers (supported by its features, underpinned by the marketing mix) and the reasons why they should buy from you rather than from your competitors.

5.4 Develop your mission statement: Develop a mission statement that sets out the purpose of your business and how it will achieve your vision.

5.5 Create your brand identity: Develop a clear identity for your product/service and business. You can differentiate your product/service through its features, its design and its branding.

5.6 Decide how your brand identity is best communicated: Branding identifies your product/service offering to customers, communicates your value proposition and should also encourage loyalty by developing a relationship with them.

Workbook exercises

 The New Venture Creation Workbook contains a digital version of these exercises that can be modified as your business model develops and builds into a draft business plan. It can be downloaded from www.macmillanihe.com/burns-nvc-2e.

5.1: Develop your values, beliefs and vision

1 Building on Exercises 1.1 to 1.4, list details about your (and your group's) personality, values, beliefs, social concerns, philosophies about life and other characteristics that you wish the business to adopt. Reflect on how these might be evidenced.

2 Building on Exercise 1.2, write down your (and your group's) vision for the business.

5.2: Understand customer benefits

Building on Exercises 2.2 (5), 2.2 (6) and 2.2 (7) for the idea selected, and bearing in mind the answers to Exercise 4.1, list the features of your product/service and, alongside this, the benefits to each of your target market segments.

Product/service features	Benefits Target market 1	Benefits Target market 2	Benefits Target market 3

5.3: Develop your target markets and value proposition

Building on Exercise 5.2, write down your value proposition for each target market segment. Ensure that your values and beliefs are reflected in your value proposition(s). Use the template below, if it helps.

> Because our product/service has *(features and other differentiating and provable attributes)* it will *(problem solution)* for *(target customer segment)* meaning that *(customer benefits)*.

Target market segment(s)	Value proposition(s)

5.4: Develop your mission statement

In the light of the previous exercises, write down your mission statement. Use the template below, if it helps.

To provide *(business scope)* to satisfy the *(customer needs)* of *(customer segments)* by offering *(value proposition)* using our *(basis of competitive advantage)* to achieve *(vision)*. In doing this we will uphold *(values)*.

5.5: Create your brand identity

Based upon Exercises 5.2 and 5.3:

- Write down words that convey the message you want your brand to convey – its identity.
- Brainstorm how these words can be crafted into a simple, coherent message by linking the words to associated images and actions. Draw the images. Can any of these images be used to promote the brand?
- Redraft the words into a single sentence that conveys your brand message.

5.6: Communicate your brand identity

1 Brainstorm how you might best:

- Communicate this identity to customers.
- Provide evidence to customers of the reality of this identity.

Write down the actions you need to undertake to do this.

2 Brainstorm whether there is an appropriate name and/or logo for your business that is consistent with this identity.

6

Developing your marketing mix

Contents

Learning outcomes

When you have read this chapter and undertaken the related exercises you will be able to:

- Understand the difference between features and benefits, and how features might be engineered to provide valued benefits for customers
- Understand how to develop a marketing mix that supports your brand identity and delivers your value proposition to your target customer segments
- Decide on your channels of distribution
- Set your selling price(s)
- Use profit data to make commercial decisions

Case insights

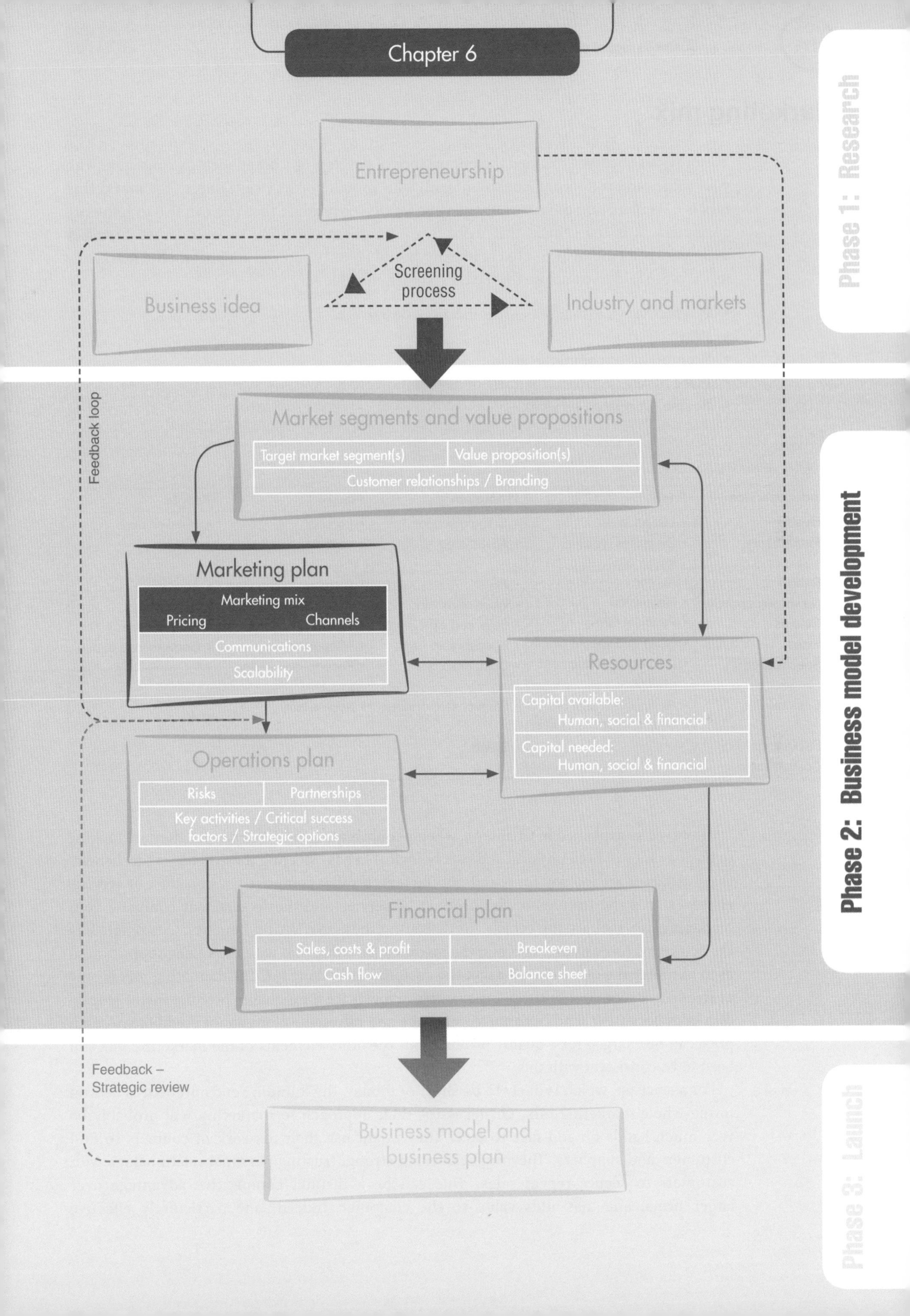

Chapter 6
Entrepreneurship
Screening process
Business idea
Industry and markets
Feedback loop
Market segments and value propositions
Target market segment(s)
Value proposition(s)
Customer relationships / Branding
Marketing plan
Marketing mix
Pricing
Channels
Communications
Scalability
Resources
Capital available: Human, social & financial
Capital needed: Human, social & financial
Operations plan
Risks
Partnerships
Key activities / Critical success factors / Strategic options
Financial plan
Sales, costs & profit
Breakeven
Cash flow
Balance sheet
Feedback – Strategic review
Business model and business plan
Phase 1: Research
Phase 2: Business model development
Phase 3: Launch

Marketing mix

The previous chapter explained the importance of developing a brand identity consistent with your value proposition, and consistent with your product or service features. The **marketing mix** is a combination of factors about your service or product that you can use to influence customers. It is the vehicle that delivers your value proposition to your target customer segments. It should help you to create your brand identity and will support it. The marketing mix is often said to comprise the 'Five Ps' shown in Table 6.1:

- **P**roduct/service (functional specification, design etc.);
- **P**rice;
- **P**romotion (or communication);
- **P**lace of sale (location, channels of distribution etc.);
- **P**eople (or related service).

Table 6.1 Marketing mix

Product/service	Price	Promotion	Place	People
• Quality	• List price	• Communication	• Location	• Relationships
• Performance	• Discounts (volume, loyalty etc.)	• Advertising	• Layout	• Service
• Design	• Auction	• PR	• Distribution channels	• Advice
• Newness or novelty	• Negotiated	• Word-of-mouth	• Retail/wholesale	• Support
• Colours	• Payment terms	• Fairs and exhibitions	• Internet	• Partnerships
• Sizes	• Sales and special offers	• Sponsorship	• Telephone	• Convenience of use
• Specification	• Differential or segment pricing	• Competitions	• Face-to-face selling	
• Customization	• Reduction in cost of other products/services	• Point of sale displays	• Accessibility	
• Packaging		• Brand		
• Convenience				

However, as explained in Chapter 5, when people buy a product or service they are looking to meet a range of both physical and psychological needs. Meeting these needs is the 'benefit' that customers are looking for – and not the features that comprise your product or service. However, it is the features of the product or service and the factors that comprise your marketing mix that are the vehicle for delivering these **marketing benefits**. Customers buy the marketing mix as a package, and the mix must be consistent with the value proposition so as to reinforce the overall benefit that the customer is looking for. The marketing mix is only as strong as its weakest link. So, for example, a low price for a quality product might jeopardize sales because it sends a confused message and raises questions about credibility. A high price can be charged for a quality product, but the other elements of the marketing mix still need to be consistent with this.

For a start-up, which is likely to be short of money, the founding entrepreneur is central to the whole marketing mix. Of necessity, their approach to marketing will probably be very much hands on and face to face. They might use their network of contacts to find customers and suppliers. They might develop strong, trusting personal relationships with customers to secure repeat sales. This can be a distinct competitive advantage over larger firms, one that adds value to the customer. Indeed, one particularly effective entrepreneurial strategy is to identify a sector in which customer relationships are weak and to create value by tightening them up. In the longer term, this relationship can evolve into a distinctive brand. Customer relationships are an important part of the marketing mix and marketing strategy.

While any individual element of the marketing mix may not be unique and can often be easily copied, elements of the mix can be combined to produce something unique and distinctive. It is the combination that is unique, not the individual elements, and this can provide a differential advantage over competitors. If the combination is sufficiently unique, it may challenge existing market paradigms. Establishing a brand that captures the elements of uniqueness can itself add value to the value proposition. And building switch costs for customers into the value proposition – costs of changing supplier – can also enhance your competitive position by discouraging them from buying from competitors. Rather than building costs into your proposition you might offer additional benefits for customer loyalty that would reduce the cost of other products or services.

CASE insight 6.1

The English Pub* (1) UK

Linking value propositions, market segments and marketing mix

You might think that a pub (a bar selling food and alcoholic and non-alcoholic drinks) is a very English institution. However, it faces all of the challenges facing any retail outlet. In particular, it faces high fixed costs related to its physical location and its serving staff. These costs need to be paid even if there are no customers. To compensate for this, gross margins can be high – 60–70% – so the operational imperative is to attract customers throughout the day.

To meet this challenge, an English high-street pub chain developed a two-tier marketing strategy. One at the corporate level outlined how it planned to expand and grow. The second, at the English pub level was designed to help local pub managers.

Each of these pubs was located in a prime, high-street, town-centre location, close to shopping centres and offices. Each was large, with different seating, lighting and so on in different areas, allowing it to change the ambience and target a number of different market segments. The English pub chain needed to maximize the number of customers it attracted throughout the day –

spreading its high fixed costs as far as they might profitably go. That meant targeting different market segments at different times of the day.

The local pub strategy is summarized in Table 6.2, as it appeared originally on one page of A4 paper. It was designed to target different market segments at different times of the day. It highlighted the value proposition for each segment in each time slot and the main elements of the marketing mix needed to deliver that proposition. Finally it told the English pub manager the critical factors they needed to get right at each of these times.

*The English Pub is a real company, but the name is fictitious.

Questions:

1 What is this marketing plan designed to do? Does it convey the key activities needed to deliver the marketing mix effectively? Why is this important? Outline any details you think might have been omitted.

2 Why is the location and size of the English pub important for this marketing strategy to work?

Table 6.2 Local-level marketing strategy for a pub

Segments	Shoppers	Office workers	Pensioners and unemployed
– Time – Male/female	11.00–17.00 10/90%	12.00–14.00 40/60%	14.00–17.00 90/10%
Value proposition	A comfortable, safe, value-for-money place to eat and drink	A quick, value-for-money place to eat lunch	A comfortable, value-for-money place to spend time
Marketing mix – Main products	Coffee, tea, soft drinks and food	Food, range of drinks	Alcoholic drinks
– Service	Friendly	Fast	Low priority
– Price	Value-for-money	Competitive	Low-price beers
– Ambience	Safe, clean and comfortable	Clean and comfortable	Warm, TV, newspapers
– Importance of location	High	High	Low
Critical success factors	Safe, clean and comfortable environment	Rapid service Value-for-money food	Low-price beers

Linking features and benefits with marketing mix

The challenge is to engineer the features of your product or service so as to deliver distinctive benefits that customers value, and craft these into some sort of marketing strategy. But, as we have seen, features can be many and varied, covering all the elements of the marketing mix, and combined in almost endless variations. It is therefore important that you understand the real benefits – both physical and psychological – that customers are looking for when they purchase your product or service.

Let us take as an example the simple pen. One type of pen is the cheap, disposable ballpoint, bought simply as a writing implement. Clearly, its core value proposition to end-use customers is based upon low price/cost, and the pen manufacturer needs to drive down costs and drive up volumes. Pens of this sort sell for a few cents in volumes of 100+, but for more when sold individually (although still very cheap). These pens typically have a low-cost, functional plastic shell, usually with a cap. Two end-use market segments might be private customers and organizations with employees needing pens. The characteristics of these segments and the routes to market are shown in Figure 6.1 on page 180. Our pen manufacturer needs to understand the benefits these two segments are seeking. They are looking for a pen that writes satisfactorily and can be conveniently purchased, but is also cheap and therefore disposable (although doing this in an environmentally friendly way may also be important). If new technologies produce cheaper, more

Office workers	Students	Regulars	Young, pre-clubbers
17.00–19.00 60/40% A lively atmosphere to meet friends after work	Any time 50/50% A relaxed, value-for-money place to meet friends	19.00–22.00 60/40% A welcoming place to meet friends for value-for-money food and drink	21.00–24.00 60/40% A fashionable, lively place to meet friends
Wide range of alcoholic drinks	Alcoholic drinks	Food, range of drinks	Wide range of alcoholic drinks
Friendly Attractive 'happy hour' Up-beat, lively	Low priority Value-for-money Relaxed, safe	Friendly Value-for-money Friendly, home away from home	Fast Low priority Lively, up-beat with music and promotions
High	Moderate	Moderate	High
Up-beat, lively ambience with 'happy hour'	Relaxed, safe environment with other students	Friendly service and ambience Value-for-money food. Recognition as 'regulars'	Lively, up-beat ambience with music and promotions

convenient ways of writing or passing messages, these customers may stop purchasing pens altogether – which is happening because of smartphones and computers.

Our pen manufacturer also needs to understand the routes to market, shown in the lower part of Figure 6.1. **Channels of distribution** are important for this product and each channel will be looking for different benefits – typically profit and product availability. If they do not get the benefits they are looking for, the end-use customers may never be offered the product, no matter how good it is.

Consider the route to market for the single-purchase private customer (segment 1A). Convenience of purchase is their primary consideration. No advertising or promotion is expected and service is non-existent, as pens are probably sold on a self-service basis. Other elements of the marketing mix are relatively unimportant, so there is strong price competition from manufacturers of similar pens. These customers purchase the pen through retailers like newsagents or stationers. Retailers buy in bulk through wholesalers. The benefit that retailers, like wholesalers, are looking for is profit – which means the higher the margin to them, the more attractive the product and the more prominent they are likely to display the pen. Indeed they may be persuaded to stock only this pen rather than those of competitors (called **supply-push**). The margin must however be sufficient to satisfy both wholesaler and retailer. The retailers might be encouraged to purchase the pens because of 'free' point of sale displays. At the same time, just-in-time deliveries, with increased delivery reliability and improved distribution times, may allow wholesalers to both decrease their inventory costs and at the same time reduce stock-outs – real benefits that help differentiate this manufacturer from others.

Private customers buying in large volumes (segment 1B) and organizations buying for their employees (segment 2) may buy these pens in bulk from wholesalers. They expect lower prices than those offered by the retailer, as well as speedy, reliable delivery. Pens selling

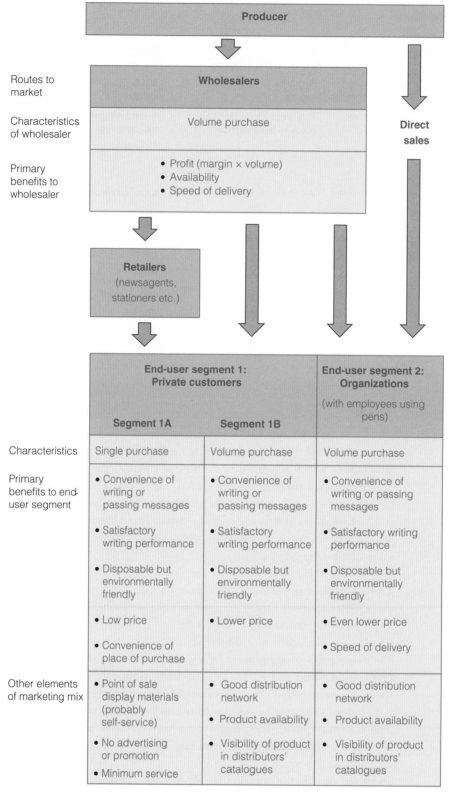

Figure 6.1 *Features, benefits and marketing mix for pens*

through this distribution channel will not need point of sale display materials but may need different packaging. Discounts may be offered, based upon volumes purchased. The wholesaler may need to invest in a catalogue, website, advertising and a direct sales force. The pen must be prominently displayed, or at least easily found, in the catalogue or website. The pen manufacturer might also decide to sell direct to these end users, but it would have to invest in a catalogue, website, advertising and a direct sales force – things that may not be its core activities.

One way of stimulating end-user demand is to advertise directly to the end user and persuade them to seek out the product from the distributor (called **demand-pull**). This only works if the product they are seeking is highly differentiated (e.g. through branding), so it is unlikely to work for this sort of pen. The less differentiated the product, the more likely this strategy is to work. However, an innovative start-up may decide to bypass the established distribution channels and sell directly to the end customer. But this is likely to involve extra costs (advertising, distribution, delivery etc.), which may not be commercially viable.

Channels of distribution

This disposable pen example underlines the fact that customers buy benefits, not features, and you need to understand the benefits offered to both end-use customers and distributors. You must tailor your marketing mix to suit the needs of customers and **consumers** at each stage in the chain. This is what your marketing strategy should articulate in a coherent, consistent way. Each element of the marketing mix needs to be consistent with the others. And your marketing strategy will have implications for other elements of your business model, from the operations plan to the resources you will need. It will determine costs and revenues and have implications for the risks you will face.

Whether you are selling physical or virtual goods your channels of distribution need careful consideration. Using retailers, wholesalers or agents for physical goods or app stores and referrals for virtual products may extend your market reach, but each link in the chain is important and is looking for benefits, of which profit is probably the most important element. You do not control your distribution channels directly, you influence them – and they eat into your profits. On the other hand, if you decide to sell directly to customers, your revenues may be higher but so too are your costs. For a physical product selling direct to customers your direct sales costs might include your own direct sales force, costs of developing your website, online and/or telephone sales team, advertising and mail/delivery costs. For a web or mobile product sold through web or mobile channels of distribution sales may come from your own website either directly or by referral or through an app store, with a cost attached to the last two sources. Remember that many products sell through a number of different distribution channels, each with a different profit margin. This is called a **multi-sided market**. Figure 6.2 shows the typical channels of distribution for a physical, consumer and business-to-business product. Figure 6.3 shows the distribution channels for a typical web or mobile product sold through web or mobile channels. Although multi-sided markets might get your product/ service in front of more customers, there is a cost and every link in your chain will typically add costs to your business model, which need to be weighed against the increase in sales revenue.

There is no one 'best' way to distribute a physical or virtual product or service and, as we have seen in the previous chapter, deciding to do it differently than the competition can prove profitable if the customers value the difference, and if you can keep competitors from copying you for a sufficient length of time. Low-cost airlines such as easyJet changed the way

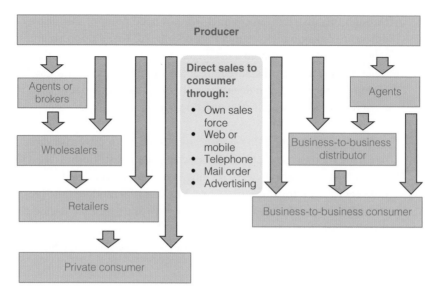

Figure 6.2 Typical distribution channels for a physical product sold through physical channels

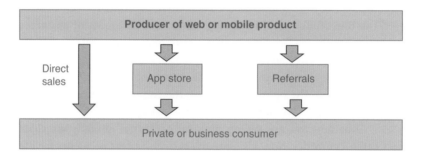

Figure 6.3 Distribution channels for a web or mobile product sold through web or mobile channels

passengers bought their tickets by insisting they could only book their flights online or by telephone, thus cutting out any intermediaries and the margin they might expect. Of course, other airlines have now copied this direct route to market.

Understanding customer and consumer benefits

Not all pens are the same and not all customers are consumers of the product/service. Some pens are bought by a customer as a gift for the ultimate consumer. And, again, we need to offer benefits to both the customer and the consumer. While a gift pen must perform the basic function of writing, it is likely to look very different and to have a very different marketing strategy, with a value proposition based upon high differentiation rather than low price. Two market segments and the benefits they are looking for are shown in Figure 6.4. The routes to market are likely to be the same as the disposable pen, although in this case retailers are likely to be gift shops or department stores. Smaller gift shops might go through a wholesaler, while department stores might purchase direct from the manufacturer. As in the previous example, retailers and wholesalers are looking for profit, but in this case from smaller volumes at a higher price.

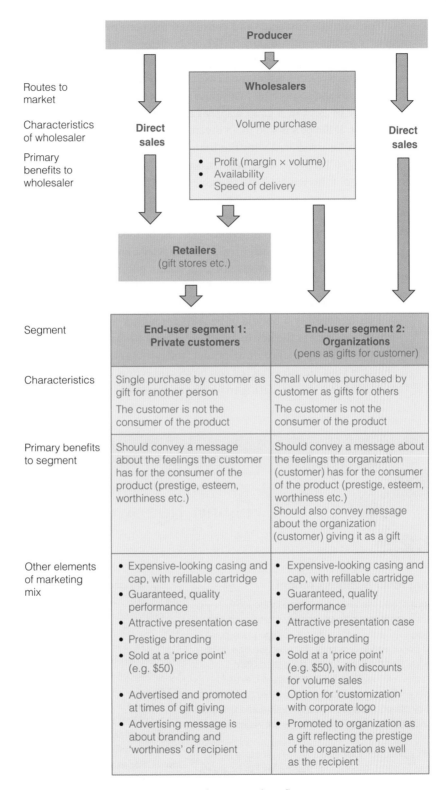

Figure 6.4 The difference between customer and consumer benefits

For both the customer and consumer, the pens must be functional and well made, high quality and elegantly designed. The other elements of the marketing mix are also important. The pen will have prestige branding with guaranteed quality performance. It will come housed in an attractive gift presentation case and is advertised and promoted at times of gift giving as prestigious and something that values the 'worthiness' of the recipient. If sold in a shop, it will probably be kept in a glass display case that can be accessed only with the help of a shop assistant. If the pen is sold to an organization, the organization will probably want the opportunity to be associated with the brand by having its name put on the pen, although it will probably still expect a discount if ordering in bulk.

The point here is that the customer wants to spend, say, $50 on a prestigious gift for the consumer – one that conveys a message to them about the feelings of 'worthiness' the customer has for them. The brand and what it conveys, reinforced by the design, are probably more important than the functionality of the pen itself. This is the benefit they are looking for. A low price is not consistent with the message and the benefit sought. And a box of 500 cheap, disposable ball pens is not a substitute gift, even though they are likely to last longer than the expensive pen. They just do not provide the right benefits. Competition comes from other gifts costing the same that convey a similar message.

Putting together a bundle of benefits through a consistent marketing mix for each target market segment is the key to an effective marketing strategy. It is not easy. There is no blueprint to work from since most products/services and their markets are different. And, while studying your industry can tell you how competitors currently do things, this is no guarantee for the future. Indeed, daring to do things differently can be very profitable.

CASE insight 6.2

Flying Tiger Copenhagen (1)

DENMARK

Price-point retail business model

The price-point retail model was invented in the USA. Typically it is a model operated by variety stores, selling a range of inexpensive household goods. Single price-point means that goods sell at one price, for example one dollar, pound or euro. And the name of the store then often reflects its value offering. The UK's Poundland claims to have introduced the concept to Europe in 1990 and is still the largest single-price discount retailer. Value and discount retailers have seen a boom in sales since the recession of 2008.

Lennart Lajboschitz opened the first Tiger store in Copenhagen in 1995. The story is that he left his brother's girlfriend in charge and she could not find the prices so he told her to sell everything for 10 kroner (about £1). Since then it has grown to some 680 stores in 29 countries, employing more than 3,500 people. Sales in the UK alone in 2015 were £62 million.

Flying Tiger Copenhagen – or just Tiger as the shops are called – is a Danish version of price-point retail concept. It sells a quirky, ever-changing range of products such as toys, stationery, hobby and craft goods like knitting needles and glitter glue. The products are own branded, simple and colourful, and most retail at less than £5. Global best-selling lines include low-value items like popping candy, pencil sets and soap bubbles, but the store also sells a few items at higher prices, such as a record player at £100. Tiger taps into seasonal occasions like Christmas or Halloween. For example, in 2016 it offered an inflatable Santa suit. It also taps into lifestyle trends. For example, when the trend for crafting took off it started offering knitting needles and brightly coloured wool.

Tiger stress their Scandinavian, functional but aesthetic design. Some 50% of new products are now designed, or have quirky design elements like packaging added, in house. Tiger recently received a Red Dot award for its pink and green food containers. The store itself is light, colourful and fun – laid out to be appealing to passers-by and to encourage impulse buys once inside as shoppers negotiate their way through the maze of stalls. It has been likened to an Ikea market place. In the UK, Tiger has been called the 'posh-Poundland': whereas you might go to Poundland for necessities, you would go to Tiger for 'affordable indulgences'.

> When we opened our first store in Basingstoke in 2005, some press called us a cool Scandi company. We hadn't seen ourselves like that. We were just a Danish store selling cheap items. It was a game changer because then Lennart hired the first in-house designer. The vision was to make design affordable.
> Tina Schwarz Brand Director *The Observer* 18 December 2016

Business model

The price-point retail model is basically a low-cost/low-price one, enhanced by other elements such as location. Tiger's website says that its business model is based on four elements: value proposition, assortment, store and customer experience.

- *Value proposition:* 'To deliver everyday magic by providing a unique and playful experience in our stores, where customers discover a world of products that we carefully select and design. Flying Tiger Copenhagen stores are designed and curated to give our customers creative, fun and useful products. Our mission is to engage with people's lives, to help them live out their values and ideas and connect to the people that matter to them. While our products are offered at affordable round-price points, it is a key objective that the quality should meet or exceed the

customer's expectations as well as Zebra's corporate social responsibility requirements.' (taken from Tiger's website)
- *Assortment:* Tiger's value-for-money products are continually changing. Up to 300 new products can be introduced in any one month. They are primarily proprietary 'inspired by Danish heritage' items, often with a quirky twist.
- *Store experience:* Stores are located in high-footfall locations on high streets and in popular shopping malls. Store size is between 150 and 250 m². The clean Scandinavian décor is a differentiating characteristic. The maze-like floor layout leads customers through pallet tables displaying products with discreet price signs. The warm lighting creates stylish but unpretentious product presentations.
- *Customer experience:* Tiger wants to provide a 'fun' customer experience derived partly from the shop and its products (which often just make you smile) but also from the attitude of the shop workers.

We shall return to Tiger in Chapter 8 to look at their growth model and in Chapter 10 to look at their operations model.

Visit the websites: flyingtiger.com and corporate. flyingtiger.com/about

---

Questions:

1 From the information given in the case, use the Framework Worksheet or the PowerPoint slide to complete as many elements as you can of the New Venture Creation Framework.
2 Is Tiger's marketing mix consistent, with each element reinforcing the other? Does it reflect the value proposition?

 Visit www.macmillanihe.com/burns-nvc-2e to download the Framework Worksheet and PowerPoint slide.

Prices and costs

The more valued the brand to customers and consumers, the higher the price you will be able to charge. Setting price is a crucial element of the marketing strategy, but it is an art rather than a science. You may have one list price for your product or different prices for different market segments. Alternatively, you may operate an auction or negotiate the price of your product. You may offer discounts for some types of purchases, such as volume or loyalty and even prompt payment. There may be special offers at sales times.

The underlying principle is that the price charged for a product or service ought to reflect the **value-to-customer** of the package of benefits. The value can be different to different customers and in different circumstances. Take, for example, the price charged for emergency, compared to routine, plumbing work. A premium price reflects the benefit to the customer of preventing the house from being flooded. However, the features of that emergency service, as echoed in the marketing mix, must reflect the benefits the customer is looking for; for example, ease of telephone call-out, 24-hour fast and efficient service, clear-up, facilitation of insurance claims and so on. Similarly, a low-cost airline like easyJet is able to charge a range of different prices for what is essentially the same service, transportation from one place to another, for example, by offering early booking or off-peak fares. However, there is usually a **going rate** charged by competing firms for a similar product or service.

One factor in the pricing decision is the costs you face. Many people use what is called **cost+** or **full-cost pricing**. This takes the total cost of producing a product or delivering a service and divides it by the predicted number of units to be sold, to arrive at the average cost, to which a target mark-up is then added. Some costs, often called overheads, are fixed, and do not change with volume (e.g. depreciation of equipment, rent and some salaries). So what happens if predicted sales volumes are not achieved? The same fixed costs have to be spread over smaller volumes; implying that you need to charge a higher price to recover the overheads – a strategy that itself is likely to lead to falling sales. The reverse is true if volumes are greater than predicted.

Another benchmark is the **variable cost** of the product or service – the cost of producing one additional unit (e.g. the costs of materials or components and piecework labour). You cannot charge just your variable cost because you are not recovering those fixed overhead costs. Unless price is above variable cost, there is no incentive to produce, because each additional unit sold would incur an additional loss. However, if you want to charge a range of prices to different market segments, these can be as low as your variable cost, so long as the average price you charge is above your full cost. The lower your variable cost, the greater discretion you have in pricing. This is why off-peak tickets on low-cost airlines can be so much lower than peak fares. The extra variable cost of taking a passenger off-peak, when the plane is not full, is very low.

Pricing is therefore a question of judgement. Figure 6.5 shows the pricing range. Minimum short-term price is set by the variable cost, but long-term viability is set by the full-cost price. However, these ignore the customer. To make a profit, the average value-to-customer price needs to be above this. However, this can be made up of a range of prices to different segments, some of which might be below full cost (segments A, B and C).

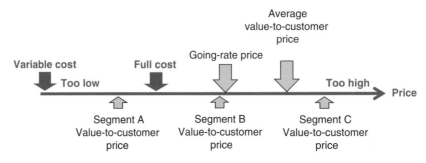

Figure 6.5 The pricing range

Setting your prices

PhotoDisc/Getty Images

Since it is always easier to lower prices than to raise them, it is important not to underprice your product/service. The price you charge should reflect the value-to-customer (Figure 6.5). The problem is that value-to-customer is not always obvious and can vary according to circumstances. The important point is that it is not *necessarily* linked to your costs. Nevertheless most consumers, including business consumers, associate high price with high quality, which implies higher costs. So, charging too low a price can mean that your customers associate too low a quality with your product or service. It sets assumptions and expectations about price and quality that may be difficult to change.

If the product or service is novel or unique or even just fashionably desirable you may be lucky enough to be able to charge a **premium price** at its launch. Demand may outstrip supply. This is usually only the case with 'big-ticket' (high-price, infrequent purchase) products or services and is most often seen at the launch of new technologies (e.g. 4K HD televisions) or branded goods (e.g. the latest iPhone). It may take some pricing encouragement to persuade customers to make an initial trial purchase of 'small-ticket' (low-price, frequent purchase) products or services that are less unique and repeat purchases are significant. Even after launch, if your offering proves attractive to customers, competitors may start to price more aggressively and you may be forced to do the same.

In trying to establish the value-to-customer price of your product or service, the principle is never to charge too low a price, and this can involve an element of trial and error. If customers show resistance to a higher price you can always offer a one-off, introductory discount. Indeed for 'small-ticket' items offering an 'introductory discount' can be part of your launch strategy – encouraging trial purchases. This might be coupled with discount and/or loyalty vouchers that encourage repeat purchases. In this way you have established the market price and can remove the discount in due course. If you can do this on a customer-by-customer basis, it should help you establish the actual value-to-customer. When you then try to remove the discount, you can reappraise the effect on demand. It is always easier to reduce prices if you start off too high, than to increase them if you start off too low. As we shall see in the next section, this all depends on how customer demand reacts to changes in prices. For most product/services, the lower your price the higher your sales are likely to be. The question is whether that will lead to higher profit – and that is not always the case.

Prices and volumes

How demand reacts to changes in price is determined by the **cross elasticity of demand**. The more the product or service is a commodity, the more price will be elastic – sales volumes will be affected by price changes. The more differentiated the product or service, the more price inelastic is demand – the volume sold does not vary greatly with changes in price. Price elasticity may sound a highly theoretical concept, but the practical applications of it are important.

Table 6.3 shows the increase in sales volume required to maintain the same level of profitability as a result of a price reduction. This depends on the **contribution margin** (sales price minus variable cost, expressed as a percentage of the sales price) before the price cut. If the contribution margin is only 20% and you were tempted to cut prices by 15%, you would have to increase sales volume by a massive 300% – a quadrupling of sales – just to generate the same profit as before. The higher the margin the less the effect, but even at 40% margin, you would still have to increase sales by 60%.

Table 6.3 The effect of price reduction on profit

		Contribution margin		
		20%	**30%**	**40%**
Price reduction	**–5%**	+33%	+20%	+14%
	–10%	+100%	+50%	+33%
	–15%	+300%	+100%	+60%

In contrast, Table 6.4 shows the decrease in sales volume that could sustain the same level of profitability in the face of a price increase. The same 20% margin could see a reduction in sales volume of 43% if prices were to be increased by 15% and would still generate the same level of profit. Of course the effect is less the higher the margin, but even at 40% margin, you could afford to lose 27% of your sales volume. However, if you cut overhead costs at the same time (why maintain the same level of staff with less work?) you should see profits actually increase. Alternatively, you might decide to improve the level of service offered by redirecting these overheads so as to justify the higher price. Either way, lower volumes might mean that stocks/inventories as well as other capital expenditures can be reduced – an important consideration if cash is scarce.

Table 6.4 The effect of price increases on profit

		Contribution margin		
		20%	**30%**	**40%**
Price increase	**+5%**	-20%	-14%	-11%
	+10%	-33%	-25%	-20%
	+15%	-43%	-33%	-27%

As you can see from Tables 6.3 and 6.4, if you are working on slim margins, lowering prices may well lead to increased sales volumes, but it may also lead to lower profits. On the other hand, increasing prices may lead to increased profits, despite lower sales volumes. The tables show that the lower your contribution margin, the less able you are to reduce your price and the more vulnerable you are to price competition. In contrast, the higher your contribution margin, the lower the increase in volume needed to justified a price reduction and therefore the greater your discretion in terms of offering discounted prices. This can make differential pricing particularly attractive (segments A, B and C in Figure 6.5).

These calculations underline the importance of understanding the costs related to your business. They affect your business model, the risks you face and the funding you may need.

CASE
insight
6.3

Property Fox SOUTH AFRICA

Linking low price to low costs in the business model

Property Fox is a company that facilitates the buying and selling of property in South Africa. Founded by Crispin Inglis and Ashley James in 2016, it uses a low-cost business model that threatens to disrupt the real estate market in that country by charging commission of only 1.5% compared to the more normal 5–7%.

Getty Images/Caiaimage/Chris Ryan

To do this it offers a 'stripped-down' but consistent service and an online market presence. As Ashley James explains:

> We saw a gap in the market to help people sell their house for a fraction of the cost, while simultaneously offering more exposure in the market … Our research showed that unreliable viewings, expenses involved, agent frustrations were among the most common challenges in selling a house.

Unlike conventional estate agents, Property Fox does not have any agents on the ground, relying instead on centralized services. This, together with the help of clients, partners and technology, enable it to cut the costs of a traditional sale. Crispin Inglis explains:

> Existing high street property agencies have a tiered hierarchy – agent, franchisee and franchisor – while we operate from a centralized operations centre. This saves us money, the benefit of which is passed along to our customers.

Property Fox offers a one-week free trial, at the end of which, sellers who want to continue must select a payment option – either a one-off, upfront payment of R25,000 (regardless of sale price) or 1.5% commission on selling price. Sellers can, if they wish, use other estate agents at the same time. Sellers sign up with Property Fox online, after which a professional but freelance photographer will visit their homes to take pictures. Property Fox's pre-sales team visit the property, produce a floor plan, and draft an advertisement. They also supply a 'for sale' board.

Lightstone Property, a leading online property market intelligence company in South Africa, provides a valuation of the property.

Once approved by the seller, the advert will 'go live' on Property Fox as well as other online property portals in South Africa such as PrivateProperty.co.za and Property24.com. Analytics are used to regularly show customers how many views their property advertisement has received, and how many resulted in property viewings. Crispin Inglis explains:

> We need to impress our potential customer base within seven days, and show them how our services are not only the best but also the most affordable. This allows us to not only review the selling price if necessary but ensures full transparency for the seller.
> SA Real Estate Investor August 2016

One of the key differences with conventional estate agents is that the sellers host their own viewings, although, if preferred, the company can undertake this for an additional fee. The company has partnered with online verification service thisisme.com for verification of the identity of potential buyers prior to any viewing and purchase. Customers are supported by telephone, email and live online chat throughout the sales process. The company also offers conveyancing and bond origination services by partnering with the Dykes van Heerden Group as well as OOBA in South Africa.

Visit the website: www.propertyfox.co.za

Questions:

1   From the information given in the case, use the Framework Worksheet or the PowerPoint slide to complete as many elements as you can of the New Venture Creation Framework.
2   As a start-up, what are the risks Property Fox faces and what does it have to do to address them?

 Visit www.macmillanihe.com/burns-nvc-2e to download the Framework Worksheet and PowerPoint slide.

CASE insight 6.4

Abel & Cole UK

Pricing high and creating differential advantage

Abel & Cole may be the UK's largest organic food delivery, but that was not how it started. In 1985 Keith Abel was studying history and economics at Leeds University, and selling potatoes door-to-door to make some money. He was a good salesman and that meant he could charge more for the potatoes than the supermarkets. Keith went on to City University, London, to study law. Unfortunately he failed his bar exams and decided he might as well team up with a friend, Paul Cole, and start selling potatoes to make some money – no notion of organic food, just making money. A Devon-based farmer, Bernard Gauvier, approached them to sell his organic potatoes. They cost more, but after a week of selling them Keith realized that nobody asked the price. He decided to investigate the differences between organic and non-organic products, and went to see what his regular supplier was spraying on his potatoes. Keith was 'pretty appalled' at what he saw. The organic idea slowly started to creep into his consciousness and he started to 'push' the organic side of the business. After all he was good at selling, and he was delivering the produce to the door of the customers. The customers responded by buying more and asking for other things. Bernard persuaded Keith and Paul to start putting together organic vegetable boxes and by 1991 Abel & Cole converted to selling only organic vegetables, buying them directly from farmers.

Sales took off in the 1990s and they started to employ people. Unfortunately, while sales increased, the result was mounting losses. Things came to a head when unpaid debts caused the Inland Revenue to threaten them with bankruptcy. Paul decided to leave and set up his own wholesale company, while Keith decided to retake his bar exams – and passed. Then Keith realized that he could not practise law if he was declared bankrupt. When Keith was threatened with losing the family house, his father-in-law, Peter Chipparelli, then chairman of Mobil Oil in South America, decided to bail him out. This may have focused Keith's mind because he started taking advice, first from his father-in-law then from social entrepreneur, Alan Heeks, who introduced him to his 22-year-old daughter, Ella. She stayed to do work experience and went on to become Managing Director only three years later.

Getty Images/EyeEm/ Manuela Schewe-Behnisch

The success of the company is due to the consistency of its marketing mix. Its ethical, eco-conscious profile is assiduously nurtured. Vegetables are organic, local (never air-freighted), seasonal, and ethically farmed. They are delivered in a recycled cardboard box by a yellow bio-fuel van, together with a newsletter which includes lively vegetable biographies and hints on how to deal with some of the more obscure vegetables in the box. The company prides itself on employing the formerly long-term unemployed and offers them bonuses for cutting waste. It gives to charity. Customers can deposit keys with the company so that vegetable boxes are left safe and sound indoors. Prices are high, but not outrageously so since the 'middle-man' has been cut out of the distribution chain. Customers are middle class and shopping from Abel & Cole is definitely fashionable.

In 2007 the private equity firm Phoenix Equity Partners bought a stake in the company, valuing it at over £40 million. However, the recession of 2008 took its toll and, as consumers tightened their belts, sales slumped dramatically. In 2008 Abel & Cole made a loss of £13.8 million. This led to the main holder of company debt, Lloyds Bank, taking control in a debt-for-equity swap. Keith Abel remained in managerial control and bought back into the company shortly afterwards. By 2011 it was again making profits: £2.5 million on sales of £9.3 million and in 2012 the company was bought by the William Jackson Food Group, a 180-year-old family business that makes Aunt Bessie's Yorkshire puddings. Keith remained in managerial control.

Visit the website: www.abelandcole.co.uk

Questions:

1 Describe Abel & Cole's target market and their value proposition.
2 How does the marketing mix contribute to the value proposition?
3 Why can Abel & Cole charge relatively high prices? Do prices reflect costs?
4 What dangers does a company like this face?

Pricing high fixed-cost products

The contribution margin a product or service typically commands varies enormously from product to product, market to market, sector to sector. This is not just because of market demand, but also because of the high fixed overhead costs that some businesses need to cover in order to make a profit. Margins in the bricks-and-mortar retail or leisure sector are likely to be high because of the high fixed overhead costs they face in staffing and running their buildings. Just think of the costs you face to lease and run a prime-site, high-street store before you make a single sale. Many retailers try to operate with contribution margins of over 60%, allowing them considerable price flexibility for regular store 'sales'.

High fixed-cost businesses face the risk that these costs might not be met by the income generated from sales. Consequently, there is an increasing trend to try to 'share out' these fixed overhead costs as far as possible by partnering with other businesses such as suppliers, for example, having just-in-time supplies which cut down stock-holding costs. Similarly, using established distribution channels rather than establishing your own will reduced your fixed costs, although the distributors will extract something to make a margin on their sales. While you might not be able to share costs with a customer, you might be able to get them to guarantee a certain volume of purchases in return for that lower price. This is why suppliers will often offer lower prices to the large supermarkets and retailers in exchange for volume guarantees, and why subscription-based business models might be attractive.

If you own the intellectual property rights of your product (see Chapter 9) you are in a much better position to recoup the fixed costs involved in developing it. For example, new drugs cost huge amounts to develop but relatively little then to manufacture and distribute. The intellectual property in the invention is protected through a patent, in effect giving a monopoly on the sale of the product for up to 20 years. This allows the drug to be sold at higher prices, allowing the fixed costs of development to be recouped over the 20-year period.

CASE insight 6.5

Mobike CHINA

Business models and competitive advantage

Invented in 1817, bicycles used to be the most common means of transport in China but these days they have been overtaken by cars, which leaves China's roads, particularly in its cities, heavily congested. This heralded the return of the bicycle. Many Chinese cities started municipal bike-rental schemes years ago, allowing users to pick up and drop off their bikes at designated stations, similar to hundreds of programmes around the world. However, Mobike is different. It uses mobile technologies and targets China's 700 million mobile phone users.

Mobike was the idea of David Wang who left his job as General Manager of Uber in China to start the venture. It was launched in Shanghai in 2016 and brings mobile technologies to the bicycle. For customers Mobike is a bike-sharing app that allows them to pick up and leave a bike wherever they need to go. It is the world's first cashless and station-free bike-sharing platform. It uses a unique patented bike design and smart lock system combined with the smartphone app. Every Mobike has GPS tracking and comes with an internet-controlled electronic wheel lock that automatically unlocks but requires manual locking after use. The bikes are powered by a small generator installed on the rear wheel hub to power the lock. Mobike shares a time-lapse graphic that, using its GPS system, tracks customer rides. Mobikes are very distinctive with fashionable modern design, clearly setting them apart from 'normal bikes'. They are also built for durability and low maintenance. They have a shiny aluminium V-shaped chassis, with puncture-proof tyres and a shaft transmission system. The wheels have five sets of double metal, bright orange spokes making them very distinctive.

Mobikes are intended for short urban trips, solving the 'first-mile/last-mile' problem of moving to or from public transport points. A one-hour journey can cost as little as 1 yuan (about 15 cents). The app requires customers to register using their mobile number and identification or passport number. They must open an account and make a prepaid, refundable deposit against deliberate damage. The software automatically disallows users under the age of 14 and tracks not only where customers go but also 'how they behave', giving them a 'credit score' which penalizes things like forgetting to lock the bike after use. Once the fee is paid it allows customers to locate the nearest bike not in use. Customers then unlock the bike by scanning a code, which is displayed at the base of the handle as well as on the smart lock. They can then use the bike and leave it where they choose. The distance travelled, time spent, energy used and cost of using the bike is then displayed on the bike, which will be deducted from the customer's account.

Mobike's big rival is Ofo, which was launched in 2015. However, the two companies are targeting different market segments. Mobike has gone for high-end branding with bikes that cost as much as 3,000 yuan (about $440) to build and have fashionable, modern and distinctive styling combined with GPS satellite navigation. Ofo is targeting students with cheaper, far more conventional and basic, bright yellow bikes, that are much cheaper to rent out. Ofo tracks the smartphones of riders and sends a code to unlock the bike, rather than using GPS.

After less than two years Mobike has some 1.5 million customers taking 500,000 bike rides every day. However the company has international ambitions. It raised $110 million of venture capital in 2016 and the following year raised a further $215 million from Chinese internet giant Tencent (Case insight 3.4) and a group of other venture capitalists to allow it to roll out the concept to some 100 cities in China and globally. In early 2017 it launched in Singapore.

Visit the website: mobike.com

Questions:

1 From the information given in the case, use the Framework Worksheet or PowerPoint slide to complete as many elements as you can of the New Venture Creation Framework.
2 Mobike faces high fixed costs but charges a premium price compared to its main rival. How is it able to do this?
3 How is its business model unique? What distinctive features give it a competitive advantage?
4 Is this advantage sustainable? What does the company have to do to maintain any advantage?

Visit www.macmillanihe.com/burns-nvc-2e to download the Framework Worksheet and PowerPoint slide.

Pricing zero-cost products

Zero-cost products are becoming increasingly common. These are most likely to be 'knowledge products', often internet-based – like software, other web or mobile products such as apps, recorded music or videos – where no additional variable cost is incurred by producing one additional unit. Once developed (incurring a fixed cost) the content can be downloaded again and again, at virtually zero (variable) cost. However, the fixed costs for development could be high and still need to be recouped and reflected in the price. So how do you set your price? If you set it too high, sales might not be as good as you hope and total contribution might not even meet your fixed coats, let alone generate a profit. There is also the problem that the product itself might be easily copied, so that if you charge too high a price there will be an incentive to copy it.

The first thing to do, unless you wish to offer your product as 'open source' (e.g. like Wikipedia or Linux), is to ensure that you have secured your intellectual property rights as best you can (see Chapter 9). If you need to charge for your product in order to recoup your fixed costs and make a profit you need to think about how many copies of the product you are able to sell. The next thing is to be clear about who are your intended customers and the benefits they derive from it.

If you do not expect to sell many copies and your fixed costs are high, the only way to make a profit is by charging a relatively *high price*. Whether you can do this depends on the benefits derived by the customer. For example, you might charge a large corporate client a high price for software that saves them a lot of money by streamlining their processes. You might go on to sell similar software to another corporate client at an equally high price, despite the fact that the additional costs involved in modifying the software for them are low. This is an example of differential pricing. The fact that you are selling a complex product to a few clients means that they are unlikely to copy it, and you can more easily assert your intellectual property rights since you know precisely who it has been sold to.

If you expect to sell many copies of the product you can afford to charge a *low price*. The total contribution must then cover your fixed costs and make a profit. Sales volume is the key to success, so you must have good distribution channels – probably through referrals and app stores. For example, recorded music is a zero-cost product – once a song is recorded, the cost of downloading it is zero (although there is the fixed cost of the distribution network). Apple sells its iTunes globally for just a few cents through its iPod and iPhone networks. Apple makes a profit from selling both the music and the device. If your business idea involves smartphone apps or music then selling it through the Apple and/or Google networks may be a good strategy. However, there still remains the problem of copying. Apple's approach is to make purchase so cheap and easy that the customer will not be tempted to illegally copy the material, with all the extra time and risk involved.

Whether you sell few or many copies of the product, you may be able to price differently for different target customers or markets (e.g. country). Similarly, the 'brand' is likely to be an important influence on price since this guarantees a certain quality (see Chapter 5). 'Brand' means not just the name of the organization producing the product (this could be a consultancy, a software house or even a band), but also the values behind it that enable customers to trust in it.

Another option is to offer your product *free* and instead generate income indirectly. For example, a free-to-use website might show related advertising or offer related products to purchase on a click-through basis (e.g. Google). Often successful websites address multi-sided markets, with multiple income streams from one of the internet business models outlined in Chapter 4 (see also Case insight 6.6). With this model there is no incentive for consumers to copy the product, and your major effort needs to be directed towards generating the alternative revenues that build your profit. This means having a two-sided marketing strategy: firstly, attracting a large volume of users together with views per page, click-throughs etc.; and secondly, it means signing up sufficient advertisers and retailers for your website at rates that generate adequate income.

CASE insight 6.6

Zaytouneh (now Atbaki)

JORDAN

Monetarizing website content

Fida Taher's family laughed when she decided to launch a website, called Zaytouneh (meaning olive), showing recipe videos in 2011. By her own admission, her cooking skills were not great and she had no business experience, although she did work for a video-production company. However, the website attracted many hits. The key to its initial popularity was simplicity. The video clips lasted only a few minutes and showed only the ingredients and the hands of the cook, so they could be easily followed.

As the website grew in popularity Fida turned it into an income-generating business. Now called Atbaki and based in Amman and Beirut, it attracts some 1.5 million users per month. Atbaki now offers thousands of free short video recipes, kitchen tips, and cooking articles on its website, social media networks, YouTube channel and through its apps. It even features some of the most acclaimed chefs from the Arab world. Users can also create their own profiles on its social platform and upload recipes for the community.

The content can still be viewed for free, so how did the company monetarize the idea? It got going by attracting financing from a satellite broadcaster, which also aired the videos. But the answer was really to open up as many revenue streams as possible. Most income comes from advertising on the website, social media and videos, and through content licensing to third parties such as Yahoo!, MSN Arabia, Layalina and Alghad. Product placement and sponsorship generate additional income. The company also launched a revenue-share model for mobile users and, with the growth in popularity of apps based on both IOS and Android, mobile content is now the company's primary focus for revenue growth.

Visit the website: atbaki.com

Question:

What particular problems do internet businesses face in developing an income-generating business model?

Changing your prices

An understanding of your product or service contribution can also be used to help you decide whether to change your prices in the face of competition. Suppose that your product sells at $20 wholesale and your competitor starts price cutting, selling a similar product at just $16 wholesale. The question is whether to match the price reduction or to seek a more profitable alternative strategy. Look at the calculation in Table 6.5. Column 2 shows the effect on profits if prices are maintained, with the result that there is a one-third fall in sales. Column 3 shows the effect on profits if prices are reduced in order to maintain the level of sales.

As we see from column 3, the business will actually lose money ($4,000 per month) if it follows the price lead of the competitor. If it maintains its prices, the position is rather better, although it will still not make a profit (column 2). However, there may also be the opportunity in this situation to reduce overheads to reflect the lower sales, or even to spend more on advertising to persuade customers that your product is better and worth more than $20. Despite the evidence that an analysis of this kind can reveal, many start-ups automatically cut prices as a 'knee-jerk' reaction to competitive pressures, without evaluating the alternatives.

Table 6.5 Changing prices

	1 **Current position**	2 **Competitor lowers price but we hold ours**	3 **Competitor lowers price and we follow**
Price per unit	$20	$20	$16
Variable cost per unit	$12	$12	$12
Contribution per unit	$8	$8	$4
Sales volume per month (units)	3,000	2,000	3,000
Total contribution	$24,000	$16,000	$12,000
Fixed costs per month	$16,000	$16,000	$16,000
Profit/(loss) per month	$8,000	nil	$(4,000)

Allocating sales effort across a product portfolio

If you intend to produce or sell more than one product or service one of the questions you face is which one(s) you decide to 'push' the sales of? Let us start with the situation where the resources are not limited. Here the decision may seem straightforward. You might expect to 'push' the sales of your most profitable product – the one with the highest contribution margin. But examine the situation in Table 6.6, where you produce or sell three products: A, B and C. Product C has the highest price contribution ($), but product A has the best contribution margin (%). So which is the one that you should 'push'?

Table 6.6 Allocating sales

	Product A	**Product B**	**Product C**
Price per unit	$25	$32	$50
Variable cost per unit	$10	$16	$30
Contribution per unit	$15	$16	$20
Contribution margin (%)	60%	50%	40%
$ contribution per $1,000 of sales	$600	$500	$400

The answer depends on whether the markets for each product are independent or not.

- Where the products or markets are independent, for example if product A is sold to one customer or market segment, B to another and C to a third, *and selling to one does not affect the budget available for other customers to buy the other products,* then you should 'push' sales of the product with the highest $ contribution: product C first, product B second and finally product A. This will generate the highest $ profit. This is the logic of differential pricing.
- Where the products or markets are not independent, that is, if the total $ budget to purchase these products is fixed (e.g. because the market is limited or you are selling to just one customer) and increasing the $ sales of one product simply reduces the $ sales of the others by the same amount, then you should 'push' the sales of the product with the highest % contribution – product A. As can be seen from the calculation, for every $1,000 spent, you will make a higher profit than from any of the other products.

Allocating scarce resources

If you intend to produce or sell more than one product or service and face limited resources, one of the questions you face is where to allocate these resources. Which product or service makes the most profitable use of these limited resources? In the case of the customer with a limited budget, the firm has to take account of a limiting factor: the amount of money available to buy their products. In fact, many start-ups face internal limiting factors, such as a lack of skilled labour, limited machine capacity, shortage of raw materials, lack of management expertise, or shortage of money. Retailers often regard available shelf space as being their main limiting factor, and make decisions about its allocation based upon contribution analysis. Here the 'rule' is more straightforward – you should 'push' the sales of the product(s) with the highest $ contribution per unit of limiting resources (machine hours, shelf space, etc.).

In the example in Table 6.7 there is a shortage of machinery, which reflects itself in availability of machine hours. You need to decide how to use the machine hours available to maximize profits. As can be seen, the contribution per machine hour is highest for product B. The company should therefore 'push' sales of product B, followed by product A and finally product C until all the available machine hours are used up.

Table 6.7 Allocating resources

	Product A	Product B	Product C
Price per unit	$25	$32	$50
Variable cost per unit	$10	$16	$30
Contribution per unit	$15	$16	$20
Machine hours needed to produce 100 units	1.0	0.5	2.0
$ contribution per machine hour	$1,500	$3,200	$1,000

As always, the real world doesn't behave quite like a mathematical formula. If a supermarket filled its shelves entirely with small, high-$-contribution products it might find it had a lot of dissatisfied customers who were unable to find bread, sugar and washing powder. Similarly, a manufacturer may prefer to sell to reliable large customers rather than to take greater risks selling to small traders, even though the $ contribution per sale may be higher in the latter case.

 Lush

Target markets, value propositions and the marketing mix

If you walk down any high street in the UK – and many in a wide range of overseas countries – you might suddenly have your attention taken by a very distinctive, honeyed smell that causes you to look around and notice the bright,

inviting shopfront from which it emanates: a shop called Lush. In 1994 Lush was a start-up. Today it has more than 1,000 stores in over 50 countries, and its founder, Mark Constantine, has become a multi-millionaire. It remains a privately owned family business and all seven shareholders work for Lush.

The story of Lush is intimately bound up with another very similar retailer called The Body Shop. In fact, you might, in passing, think that the shop front (if not the smell) bears more than a passing resemblance to The Body Shop, originally founded by Anita Roddick in 1976 and sold by her to the multinational L'Oréal (part of the Nestlé group) in 2006 for £652 million. And you would be right; not only the look but also the culture and ethics of the business are similar to The Body Shop, at least in its early years.

The link is the founder of Lush – Mark Constantine – and his is a very entrepreneurial rollercoaster of a story. Born in 1953, Mark was thrown out of his home by his mother and stepfather at the age of 17 and initially lived rough in the woods in Dorset, UK, before moving to London. He got a job as a hairdresser but started developing natural hair and skin products in his small bedroom. His ambition was to turn this into a business making and selling natural cosmetics, but it was not until he was 23 years old that he stumbled on his first success. He had read about The Body Shop in the press and sent Anita Roddick some samples, including a henna cream shampoo 'which looked a bit like you'd just done a poo'. She had just opened her second shop. They met, got on well together and she placed her first order for £1,200 worth of products. At the age of 24 this was the real start of his first company, Constantine and Weir, set up with his wife, Mo, and Elizabeth Weir, then a beauty therapist and now retail director and shareholder of Lush. The company became The Body Shop's biggest supplier of cosmetics and Mark is credited for many of the elements of the company's ethical brand image, in particular its opposition to animal testing, that The Body Shop and Anita Roddick built up over those early years.

However, The Body Shop became uncomfortable with the formulations of many of its products being owned by another company and, in 1988, it bought Constantine and Weir for £6 million. Mark put the money into a new company, Cosmetics to Go, a mail-order company he had already started. The company never made a profit in any of its years of trading and went into bankruptcy in 1994. Faced with no money and a family to maintain, Mark started selling the bankrupt stock from a shop in Poole. This was the start of Lush.

As the business grew, new finance was injected by Peter Blacker, of British Ensign Estates, and Lush's finance director, Andrew Gerrie, who now sits on the board. They put in 'modest sums' but, cleverly, Mark set the exit value of these investments at the time, so that they could be bought out. Mark never forgot these ups and downs, and part of the firm's mission statement (prominent on the wall of its shops) states that 'we believe in the right to make mistakes, lose everything and start again'.

Lush does more than just make and sell cosmetics through its own shops. The distinctive elements of the marketing mix might be small individually but add up to give it a uniqueness that differentiates it from competitors. And, while cosmetics have always delivered a 'feel-good' mood, Lush has added an environmental and social responsibility dimension to this value proposition. Its range of hand-made soaps, shampoos, shower gels, lotions, bubble bath and fragrances are 100% vegetarian, 83% vegan and 60% preservative free. They are made in small batches based upon shop orders from fresh, organic fruit and vegetables, essential oils and safe synthetic ingredients in factories around the world. Stores do not sell products that are older than four months. In addition to not using animal fats in its products, Lush is also against animal testing and tests its products solely with human volunteers. Moreover, Lush does not buy from companies that carry out, fund or commission any animal testing.

Lush shops are located in high footfall retail locations. They are very distinctive with simple, bright window displays. But it is the particular smell of a Lush shop that first announces its presence. This is caused by the lack of packaging on its products – which is environmentally sound – and Lush offers a free face mask for returning five or more of their product containers. The aim is to have 100% of their packaging recyclable, compostable or biodegradable. The store itself looks unlike any other store selling cosmetics. Some products, like 'bath bombs', are stacked like fruit and others such as soap are sold like cheese, wedges stacked on shelves and sold by weight wrapped in greaseproof paper. These attractive, bright displays give Lush shops the feel of old-fashioned market stalls or sweet shops.

Lush shops are also fun places, often with promotions and campaigns going on inside and outside. The company supports many campaigns around animal welfare, environmental conservation, human rights and climate change. The shops are staffed by enthusiastic young people who are trained not to 'sell' but to help people select products by providing comprehensive product information, which includes who at Lush made the product.

Lush donates around 2% of its profits to charity, supporting many direct action groups such as Plane Stupid, a group against the expansion of UK airports, and Sea Shepherd, a group that takes action against Japanese whaling ships. Often it launches products specifically to support these groups. Profits from the sale of 'Guantanamo Garden', an orange foaming bath ball, were donated to the human rights charity Reprieve, which helped Binyam Mohamed, a British resident who was held at Guantanamo Bay. It launched a Charity Pot moisturizer, giving the entire proceeds to charities such as the Dorset Wildlife Trust and the Sumatran Orangutan Society.

The founders of Lush have some strong ethical beliefs that are reflected in their lifestyle and the values of the company. These values are stated on their website:

iStock.com/ ghoststone

- We believe in buying ingredients only from companies that do not commission tests on animals and in testing our products on humans.
- We invent our own products and fragrances, we make them fresh by hand using little or no preservative or packaging, using only vegetarian ingredients and tell you when they were made.
- We believe in happy people making happy soap, putting our faces on our products and making our mums proud.
- We believe in long candlelit baths, sharing showers, massage, filling the world with perfume and in the right to make mistakes, lose everything and start again.
- We believe our products are good value, that we should make a profit and that the customer is always right.
- We also believe words like 'Fresh' and 'Organic' have an honest meaning beyond marketing.

Lush never advertises. Its growth has been organic. It owns its businesses overseas in various joint ventures, including the USA, Japan and Australia. In 2001 Lush tried to buy The Body Shop, but the Roddicks turned down the offer. It is listed regularly in *Sunday Times* 100 Best Companies to work for. The business is still based in Poole, Dorset, and run from a small office above the first shop. Mo still designs cosmetics. One son, Simon, is head perfumer, and

another, Jack, does the online marketing. Daughter Claire works for the charity Reprieve, to which Lush donates. The Constantines have lived in the same house for more than 25 years. Mark does not hold a driving licence and has never owned a car. He often cycles to work. His hobby is bird songs and he has published a book on the subject. Mark is proud of Lush:

Lush has been the most lucrative and successful thing I have ever done. There have been some innovative products that have helped propel the business, including bath bombs and the dream cream. The fact that the products don't have packaging helps boost profits. It is both an environmental and economic decision. The model is that if you don't package, you have enough money to put into your product and can give better value to the customer.

Sunday Times 20 April 2014

Visit the website: www.lush.com

Questions:

1 From the information given in the case, use the Framework Worksheet or the PowerPoint slide to complete as many elements as you can of the New Venture Creation Framework.
2 What does the Lush brand represent and how does this reflect the value proposition?
3 Is this reflected in Lush's marketing mix?
4 How does the company seek to differentiate itself from competitors? How real and sustainable are these elements of competitive advantage?

Visit www.macmillanihe.com/burns-nvc-2e to download the Framework Worksheet and PowerPoint slide.

Sofa-bed Factory

The next thing Piotr and Olek decided to do was estimate the cost of producing their sofa-beds. However, this was almost impossible to calculate accurately without knowing the numbers they would produce and sell. They had been told that the frame would cost between €100 and €150 to manufacture, depending on volumes. Piotr checked out the cost of suitable mattresses. The memory foam he was interested in trying was expensive, and when he tried it out he realized that, while it might be easily folded, it tended to retain that shape when unfolded, making it lumpy and uncomfortable. Reverting to ordinary foam he found that a small increase in cost secured a much better and more comfortable mattress than the one he had originally seen. This could be bought in, already cut and covered, with price depending on volume. Olek found out that skilled labour for manufacturing furniture was traditionally paid on a piecework basis (i.e. a set rate based on the units produced) and he estimated this would work out at only €30 per sofa. They decided to add €20 to their estimates as a contingency and jotted down their estimates:

Frame	€100 to €150	per unit
Mattress	€60 to €100	per unit
Labour	€30	per unit
Contingency	€20	per unit
Total	€210–300	

With a target wholesale price of €300 to €340, this meant profits could be anywhere between zero (€300 – €300) and €130 (€340 – €210), giving a contribution margin of between zero and 38% (€130 ÷ €340). This seemed a wide variation – and that was before any fixed costs, which depended on the volumes they would produce. They quickly decided they would subcontract the manufacture of the frame to Olek's employer. They were reliable and this option would be the least complicated and need less capital. However, they would still need a small factory to assemble the sofa-beds. The local council offered suitable factory space at €1,000 per month with a rent-free period of three months. There was a plentiful supply of local skilled labour willing to work

at the piecework rates. They concluded that the factory could be up and running in only a couple of months.

The low contribution margin (between zero and 38%) worried Piotr. He knew from his university days that the lower the contribution margin, the more vulnerable the business to reductions in selling price or increases in variable costs. Costs had to be kept under tight control. Prices might be guaranteed but the least he needed was a better indication of the price his employer would be willing to pay for a sofa-bed of this quality and, equally as important, the volume of orders that they expected to place.

Olek and Piotr decided that, if they wanted to take this idea any further, they needed to produce a number of sample sofa-beds. This would tell them whether their idea really was viable. It would give them a more realistic idea of costs and give them something that they could take to buyers so as to find out what price they might be willing to pay, and hence the profits they could make. Only then would they know whether this business was really viable.

Within a couple of months they had five sample sofa-beds that they were happy with. The sample sofa-beds looked good and were comfortable. All used the same folding mechanism, designed by Olek and manufactured by Olek's employer. Each was in a slightly different style, and each could be covered in a range of different fabrics. Olek's employer had turned out to be cooperative and enthusiastic about the prospect of Olek becoming a new customer for him. He produced the sample batch without charge (Olek did much of the work), on the promise of an order for large volumes if the business idea was successful. Having produced the samples, he guaranteed a price of €110 per frame if they placed orders of over 1,000 units a year. This gave Piotr and Olek a target to aim for.

Questions:

1 What do you think of the progress of Pietr and Olek so far? What do they still need to do or find out?
2 Should they be concerned about leaving the marketing of their sofa-beds to the large retail chain? What can they do to facilitate this?

Summary and action points

6.1 Set your price(s): Estimating your best selling price is not a precise science. It involves judgement, based upon information from an iterative process. For each customer segment, decide on the price for your product/service. This should reflect the value to customers, rather than just your costs, but it will reflect the 'going rate' in the market.

6.2 Develop your marketing plan: Marketing strategy is made up of elements of the marketing mix as they relate to the customer segments they are targeted at. It delivers the value proposition to these target market segments. For each customer segment, decide on the elements and relative importance of your marketing mix.

6.3 Assess your performance against competitors: Decide on the critical success factors in your marketing mix. They will largely determine the strength of your value proposition. Assess them against your competitors. At this point you may decide to alter your business model or other elements of your marketing mix.

Workbook exercises

 The New Venture Creation Workbook contains a digital version of these exercises that can be modified as your business model develops and builds into a draft business plan. It can be downloaded from www.macmillanihe.com/burns-nvc-2e.

6.1: Set your price(s)

1 Reflect on the results of Exercise 3.2 for the idea selected and complete the table on the next page for each market segment for which a different price will be charged:

- Insert either the 'going-rate' or 'value-to-customer' price per unit (**A**) and multiply by the estimated sales volume (**B**) at this price to give you total estimated sales value (**B × A**).

- Estimate your variable cost of producing/selling one unit (**UVC**). Multiply this by the sales volume to give your total variable costs (**B × UVC**). Deduct this from your total estimated sales value to give you your contribution towards fixed costs [(**B × A**) − (**B × UVC**)].

  Variable costs might include: material costs, direct, variable wage costs (e.g. staff on piecework rates), commissions, delivery charges etc.

- Estimate your total fixed, overhead costs in the first year (**FC**). Deduct this from your contribution to give you your estimated profit [(**B × A**) − (**B × UVC**) − **FC**].

  Fixed overhead costs might include: rent and rates, fixed wages and salaries, depreciation of fixed assets, gas and electricity, transport and travel, repairs and renewals, telephone, postage and stationery etc.

- Estimate the effects on sales volumes of increasing your prices by 10% and then decreasing them by 10%, and repeat the calculations.

	Segment 1 price	+10%	−10%		Segment 2 price	+10%	−10%
Unit selling price (£/$) **(A)**							
Estimated sales volume (#) **(B)**							
Total estimated sales value (£/$) **(B × A)**							
Total variable costs (£/$) **(B × UVC)**							
Total contribution (£/$) **(B × A) − (B × UVC)**							
Fixed overhead costs (£/$) **(FC)**							
Profit (£/$) (B × A) − (B × UVC) − FC							

2 If the profit you generate from the last exercise is not what you expect, the calculation below shows you how you might arrive at your profit target by either altering your estimated sales volumes or your estimated selling price.

- Insert the profit target you have set (**TP**) and add your fixed costs (**FC**) to arrive at your contribution target (**CT**).

Profit target (£/$) **(TP)**

Fixed overhead costs (£/$) **(FC)**

Contribution target (£/$) **(CT) (TP + FC)**

In the exercise on the next page:

- Calculation 1 assumes the price you wish to charge is fixed or set and cannot be changed. It shows you the volume sales you need at this price to achieve your profit target. Deduct the variable cost per unit (**UVC**) from the fixed unit sales price (**P**) to give the unit contribution (**UC**). Divide your contribution target (**CT**) by your unit contribution (**UC**) to give you the sales volume targets (**CT ÷ UC**).

- Calculation 2 assumes the volume sales you will achieve is fixed or set. It shows you the sales price you need to charge to achieve your profit target. Divide your contribution target (**CT**) by your fixed sales volume (**V**) to give your contribution per unit sales (**UC**). Add this to the variable cost per unit (**UVC**) to give your sales price target (**UC + UVC**).
- If you have more than one product/service or are charging a different price for different customer segments repeat the calculation for each one.

1: Price fixed

Fixed unit price (£/$) **(P)**

Unit variable cost (£/$) **(UVC)**

Unit contribution (£/$) **(UC) (P – UVC)**

Required sales volume (#) **(CT ÷ UC)**

2: Volume fixed

Fixed sales volume (#) **(V)**

Unit contribution (£/$) **(UC) (CT ÷ V)**

Unit variable cost (£/$) **(UVC)**

Required unit sales price (£/$) **(UC + UVC)**

3 Reflect on the results of this exercise and decide on the price(s) that you will be charging.

6.2: Develop your marketing mix

Build on the results of Workbook Exercise 5.3 to complete the exercise below (see Case insight 6.1):

1 List and describe the customer segments you intend to sell to.
(If you have more than two target markets copy the template.)

2 Alongside each segment list the main elements of your marketing mix (e.g. for 'product' it could be quality, functionality, design etc.; for 'place' it could be that you sell through distributors and that speed and reliability of delivery to them is also an element).

3 Estimate their relative importance to each customer segment (1 = low, 10 = high).

4 For each market segment decide what the critical success factors are (those that are most important to delivering your value proposition).

	Customer segment 1	Relative importance (max 10)	Customer segment 2	Relative importance (max 10)
Value proposition				
Marketing mix (list elements)				
– Product				
– Price				

– Promotion				
– Place				
– People				
Critical success factors (CSF)				

5 Compare the critical success factors above to those from Workbook Exercise 3.3 (4) for the idea selected. Combine the lists to produce one set below. Jot down your thoughts so far on how you intend to market your product/service and combat competition in each market segment.

✏ Critical success factors	✏ Notes

6.3: Assess your performance against competitors

Using the table on the next page, for each target market segment:

1 List the critical success factors from Exercise 6.2 (5).

2 Estimate their relative importance to the customer in percentage terms (adding to 100%).

3 Give your product/service a score (1 = low, 10 = high) for each factor.

4 Multiply the score by its percentage importance and divide by 100 to arrive at a weighted score out of 10. Add these to arrive at a total weighted score.

5 Repeat steps 3 and 4 for the product/service of your major competitors, identified in Exercise 3.1 (3).

A comparison of simple, unweighted scores with competitors' gives an informative map of different value propositions being offered in the market place. A comparison of the weighted scores gives you an indication of how your product or service might be perceived by each market segment, compared to competitive products or services.

Reflect on the scores, in particular any implications for your marketing strategy. In which market segments is your competitive advantage greatest?

If you do alter your marketing strategy in any way as a result of this exercise, make sure you reflect the changes by reworking Exercise 6.2.

Critical success factors [Exercise 6.2 (5)]

	Importance (%)	Score (1–10)	Weighted score	Competitor 1 Raw	Competitor 1 Weighted	Competitor 2 Raw	Competitor 2 Weighted	Competitor 3 Raw	Competitor 3 Weighted
1.									
2.									
3.									
4.									
5.									
6.									

Total weighted score

Visit www.macmillanihe.com/burns-nvc-2e for chapter quizzes and other resources.

7 Communicating your value proposition

Contents

Learning outcomes

When you have read this chapter and undertaken the related exercises you will be able to:

- Understand the customer buying process and how the marketing mix can be used to encourage customers to become repeat customers and advocates of your product/service
- Understand how to find prospective customers throughout your distribution chain
- Enhance your face-to-face sales skills
- Write a press release
- Draw up a communications campaign that helps launch your business
- Develop a marketing strategy that launches the business

Academic insights 📓

7.1 Seven principles for communication

7.2 Integrated marketing communication (IMC)

Case insights 💼

7.1 Huddle

7.2 BicycleSPACE

7.3 Instant Pot

7.4 American Giant

7.5 Good Hair Day

7.6 Clippy

7.7 Jack Wills – University Outfitters

Sofa-bed Factory

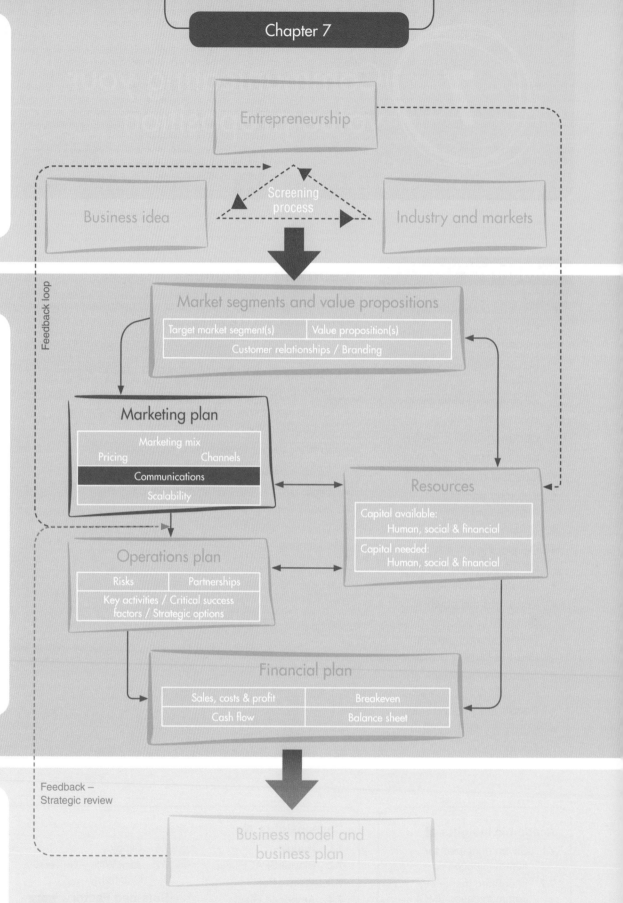

Phase 1: Research

Phase 2: Business model development

Phase 3: Launch

Entrepreneurship

Business idea

Screening process

Industry and markets

Feedback loop

Market segments and value propositions

| Target market segment(s) | Value proposition(s) |
| Customer relationships / Branding | |

Marketing plan

Marketing mix	
Pricing	Channels
Communications	
Scalability	

Resources

| Capital available: Human, social & financial |
| Capital needed: Human, social & financial |

Operations plan

| Risks | Partnerships |
| Key activities / Critical success factors / Strategic options | |

Financial plan

| Sales, costs & profit | Breakeven |
| Cash flow | Balance sheet |

Feedback – Strategic review

Business model and business plan

The customer journey

A good business idea and a persuasive value proposition do not guarantee success on their own. Customers will not queue up at the door of a start-up if they are unaware of its existence. Indeed, even if they are aware, they still might take some persuading to try a new, unproved product or service. As a newcomer to the market, you have little or no credibility or reputation. Even if you have a brand, customers will not initially recognize it. And then you still need to persuade them to purchase it again, and again. Your brand should help them do this, but building the relationship that underpins an effective brand will take time. You need to attract the customer segments you are targeting and persuade them to start the journey to become the valuable loyal customers we discussed in the previous chapter. It is not easy or straightforward, even if you have the best product/service in the world. To do this you have to use all the tools in your marketing armoury – product, price, promotion, place and people – and in different ways, at different times and in different circumstances. How you go about this all depends on who your customers are.

In a similar way to the product/market life cycle (Chapter 3), the journey a customer takes in becoming a regular customer can be broken down into the four-stage process shown in Figure 7.1.

> *Jay Conrad Levinson Guerrilla Marketing (1984, London: Piatkus Books)*
>
> In order to sell a product or service, a company must establish a relationship with the customer. It must build trust and support the customer's needs, and it must deliver a product that delivers the promised benefits.

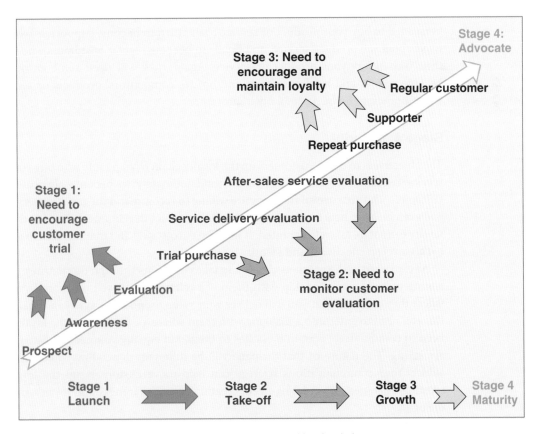

Figure 7.1 The customer journey – the buying process and loyalty chain

Stage 1: Launch

The objective at this stage is to encourage the customer to try the product or service. Once your prospective customers become aware of your product they will evaluate the value proposition it offers. They need to be made aware and encouraged to make that all-important first trial purchase. Often characterized as a buyer-behaviour model, this can be broken down into a three-stage process: firstly, the cognitive stage, where the customer needs to be made aware of your product; secondly, the affective stage, where they need to have their interest stimulated and a desire to purchase generated; and, finally, the behaviour stage, where action to buy needs to be triggered.

Stage 2: Take-off

The objective at this stage is to monitor customer evaluation and then, if possible, alter any elements of the value proposition that they are unhappy with. Once they have purchased your product/service, customers will naturally evaluate whether you have delivered the value proposition that you promised before deciding whether they might purchase the product or service again. Remember, it will be the whole marketing mix that they evaluate, including service delivery and after-sales service, all at the price you charge. And while they will be evaluating your offering, you should be checking to see if they are happy with it.

Stage 3: Growth

If the value proposition that is delivered meets their expectations then customers may be persuaded to buy your product or service again, then to become supporters who think positively about the product/service, and finally to become regular customers who will go out of their way to buy your product or service. Again, they will need some encouragement to become regular and loyal customers and not try competitors' products or services. This is where branding can be particularly important.

Stage 4: Maturity

The objective is to move customers up the loyalty chain from people who buy your product or service regularly to become supporters and ultimately to become advocates. These are customers who are so loyal that they are willing to recommend the product/service to others, and even bring in new customers or help with product development. Even at this stage their loyalty cannot be taken for granted. It must be encouraged and maintained. To get customers to this level an effective brand identity is vital.

As explained in the previous chapter, to take customers through this journey you should be aiming to build a relationship with them – a relationship based on shared values and one where they can trust that you will deliver your value proposition again and again. To achieve this you need to enter into a dialogue with them wherever they are on the loyalty ladder. You need to communicate certain messages to them, but equally you need to listen to what they are saying. The nature of that dialogue will be different, depending where they are on the ladder. Your communications strategy can help move customers up the loyalty ladder – creating awareness, stimulating need, creating brand awareness and loyalty and facilitating dialogue.

Ideally, relationships are based upon one-to-one and face-to-face interactions, but they can be influenced by various media. Indeed, in today's interconnected, knowledge-based society you can use a range of mass communications media to initiate, develop and maintain these relationships. And mass media becomes vitally important in communicating with mass markets, where the logistics of communicating face to face are problematic. Nevertheless, whether you are selling face to face or to mass markets, the objective is to build a long-lasting relationship with customers, rather than just selling them something on a one-off basis.

Finding your first customers

Finding the first customer is crucial, and if your network of contacts includes prospective customers or family or friends who might introduce you to them and use your network, it can short-circuit the problem you have with a lack of credibility. It all depends on who your prospective customers are and how you get to them. The first customers to buy a radically new or different product/service – such as Tesla cars or the new edition of an iPhone – have been characterized as **innovators** – people who think for themselves, like novelty and try things. Promoting your product/service by playing to these desires is likely to be most effective for this group. Innovators constitute only 2 or 3% of the market. They are followed by second-wave customers characterized as **early adopters** – people with status in their market segment and opinion leaders. These constitute about 14%. They choose new products carefully. They adopt successful products, making them acceptable and respectable and they can be influential, particularly if encouraged to share their opinions, for example through social media. Promoting your product/service by playing to these desires and using these media is likely to be most effective for this group. So, deciding on your promotion strategy – the message and the media – depends not only on who your target customer segment is, but also their motivations for buying early in a product/service life cycle.

Much of business-to-business selling is face to face, particularly when you are looking for that first order. Selling into distribution networks also often involves face-to-face selling. You start by identifying who specifically in the company you need to sell to. You need to find out the name of the buyer of your type of product/service and make an appointment to see them. Even this requires a degree of 'selling', just to get an appointment, because these are busy people with established suppliers. They need a reason to see you. And then you need to master some basic selling skills to turn these prospects into customers.

Face-to-face selling can be necessary for mass consumer markets but, because there are so many people, finding prospective customers that meet your marketing segmentation profile can be extremely time consuming. Of course you can sometimes buy in lists of prospects that meet your marketing segmentation profile and contact them directly – by phone, email or text. You may need to 'qualify' these leads – assess their real potential – before you commit too much time to trying to sell to them. You might be able to obtain referrals. This can be particularly valuable once you are established and satisfied customers are willing to help. However, you need to persuade these prospective customers to show some interest in your product/service so they can be sold to. And this is particularly the case if you are counting on prospects contacting you rather than the other way round. There are many communications techniques you can use and there is a wide range of communications media. What media to use depends on the target market you wish to reach and the product/service you are offering. For example, if your target market is young males, digital media, using the internet and smartphones, can be very effective and good value. However, if your target market does not use the internet or consume online content, this approach will not work. Sometimes

CASE insight 7.1

Huddle 🇬🇧 UK

Getting noticed, getting used and getting customers

Huddle is a cloud computing system that allows documents, music and other data to be securely stored and accessed via the web. Its collaborative software allows users to share documents online and across multiple devices securely (on desktops via Microsoft Office applications, on the move with Android, iPhone and iPad apps), making it suitable for use by any organization where security is a concern. In fact, since its inception in 2006 it has become the global leader in cloud collaboration and content management, being used by more than 100,000 organizations – ranging from NASA to Beats by Dre – in over 180 countries. Huddle now employs over 170 staff in London, San Francisco, New York and Washington, DC, has raised nearly $90 million in funding and has seen sales double year on year.

Huddle's co-founder is serial entrepreneur Alastair Mitchell. Born in 1977 and a graduate of Southampton University, his first start-up was an online media business and his second was an online commodities exchange. Both were reasonably successful. He started Huddle with Andy McLoughlin, a Sheffield University graduate and friend with whom he played badminton. It was financed from £25,000 of savings and venture capital.

The company grew rapidly through users inviting colleagues either in the same workplace or from other organizations to work with them collaboratively using Huddle. Any individual could join for free but companies were charged a fee. This worked so well that most of the departments in the British civil service found themselves using the system extensively to share data and work collaboratively, resulting in a large British government contract. Since then Huddle has repeated its success in the USA and is now also working with the Department of Homeland Security and the National Geospatial-Intelligence Agency to further develop its software.

Visit the website: www.huddle.com

Questions:

1　What are the advantages and disadvantages of Huddle's early approach to generating customer awareness and purchase?
2　Would you continue to use the same model once you had gained established users?
3　Can this model be applied to other types of products? If so, give some examples.

old-fashioned media such as flyers and posters can be more effective. Once you have identified the media, you need to decide on the message. Why should the prospect contact you, even if they see your message?

Developing your sales skills

While marketing involves understanding your customers and their needs, selling skills involve tailoring them to specific customers, communicating them effectively and being able to address their specific concerns. Most entrepreneurs will have to sell face to face at some stage – either to other businesses or to consumers. This might be at a trade fair or in a real sales situation. Ideally to sell face to face you need to identify the prospective customer by name and then be able to meet with them. This is easy to say but usually more difficult to arrange. Corporate buyers have busy schedules and established suppliers. Personal buyers often try to avoid salespeople. They need a reason to meet you – a hook that offers them something that they need.

It sounds obvious, but your first action is to thoroughly understand your value proposition and make certain you have identified the benefits this specific customer is looking for. A face-to-face meeting gives you the opportunity to tailor these to the *specific* needs of this customer. You must do some basic research on the prospect and, if relevant, the company they represent. The larger the potential sale, the more important the research and the longer you should spend on it.

If this is a chance meeting, for example at a trade fair, you need to ask questions to find out who they are and make judgements about what their specific needs might be. If you are visiting a prospect, send them information on your company and your product/service in advance if possible. A brochure can be very useful. At the meeting you want to build a relationship. Knowing a few personal details about the prospect and sometimes spending a little time on 'small talk' can help break down barriers quickly. But a professional relationship is based on mutual self-interest – you both want something – and trust that you both can deliver what you promise (in your case the value proposition and in their case cash payment). You need to establish what they want – the 'problem' they have – and how your product/service can solve it for them. You need to be able to:

- Ask questions and listen to the answers;
- Be clear about how your product/service will solve their specific 'problem' and be able to demonstrate its features either directly or with the help of photographs or brochures;
- Back up the claims you make about your value proposition with proof, for example, by providing references or testimonials from satisfied customers;
- Handle objections and concerns;
- Close the sale.

Dealing with objections

Buyers are unlikely to eagerly buy your product or service on just your say-so. They will have doubts. How will the product or service really perform? Why should they trust what you claim? Ultimately this will boil down to a question of trust. And the bigger the expenditure you are asking them to make, the greater this barrier will be. However, there are techniques that can help you deal with 'objections' and persuade customers to buy and try your product or service. Some objections are fundamental – the customer does not want your product/service. But some are just raising other problems that you might be able to solve. There are six other types of objection or concerns, some of which can be dealt with.

1 **Feature objection** – Some of the features do not meet the customer's approval. This might be overcome by emphasizing the positive reasons for these features.
2 **Information-seeking objection** – The customer wants more information about the product/service, often about proving your claims for it. This gives you the opportunity to provide that information.
3 **Price objection** – This might be fundamental or a buying signal and the start of negotiations. If they are seeking a lower price, try stressing the product benefits compared to competitors' and value-for-money. If this does not work, try offering a discount only in exchange for something else such as a larger order.
4 **Delay objection** – The customer wants to put off making a decision. This is difficult if the delay is genuine and you need to find out the reason. If necessary, arrange a return visit.

5 **Loyalty objection** – The customer may have an established relationship with a competitor. Stress the benefits of the product; do not 'knock' the competitor but try to find reasons why they should change supplier, for example, because they are not receiving the service they ought to. Always keep in contact as it may just take time to convince them to try you.

6 **Hidden objection** – The buyer prevaricates for no obvious reason. It is important to get to the unstated objection and deal with it, so ask questions.

Closing the sale

Even when you have overcome these objections, some people have problems recognizing buying signals from customers and can continue relentlessly through a sales meeting long after the customer actually wanted to buy the product or service. They just need an invitation to do so. Buying signals can be many and various: the customer becoming interested and animated, positive body language such as leaning forward or wanting to pick up or try the product. If interest is confirmed by asking a few questions, the whole process can be short-circuited and you can go to the most important stage of all – closing the sale. Again, there are six techniques that help you do this without appearing too 'pushy' or impolite.

1 **Trial close** – You can try this one as soon as you see a buying signal. This close uses the opportunity of an expression of interest to ask a further question which implicitly assumes a sale. For example, 'It is the quality of the product that has convinced you, hasn't it?' The trial close ends with a question, and if the answer is positive then you can proceed straight to closing the sale.

2 **Alternative close** – This forces the customer to a decision between options. For example, 'Do you want an initial order of 1,000 or 2,000?' or 'Can we deliver next month or would you prefer next week?'

3 **Summary close** – This is useful if the buyer is uncertain about the next step. It summarizes what has been said and sets out the next steps. For example, 'So those are the advantages our service offers over the one you are using at the moment, and I think you see that we are better in every respect. Do you agree?'

4 **Concession close** – Concessions are usually on price. They may secure orders but should not be given away too early, only at the end of the meeting when you judge it necessary to tip the balance in your favour. Always try to get something in exchange for a price concession. For example, 'And if you place an order this month, there is a special 5% discount.'

5 **Quotation close** – Often you have to provide a formal quote at the end of the sales interview. If this is the case, then it should be followed up with another visit to the customer to clarify the main points, answer any queries and secure the sale.

6 **Direct close** – Sometimes it is necessary to ask for the order directly – and then remain silent and listen to the answer. If the answer is 'no', a follow-up question should illicit some objections that you might be able to overcome.

Selling to well-informed customers can be particularly difficult. They may have sought out online reviews or gathered expert advice from independent sources rather than relying on what you might tell them. They come to a sales meeting with a decision already half made and, after clarifying a few points that confirm they want to buy your product, often try to go straight to a price negotiation. The approach to take here is called **insight selling** and involves trying to disrupt these pre-meeting decisions. Firstly, it involves trying to establish relationships with prospective customers well ahead of the meeting in their 'learning' phase so that you are seen as an expert consultant with valuable knowledge. Secondly, it involves using this position to disrupt and 'reset' customer thinking by challenging their assumptions, perhaps

Personal recommendation still counts for a lot. As my first boss told me: 'Make one person happy and they'll tell four others. Make one person unhappy and they'll tell seven others.' Never underestimate the power of word of mouth.

I believe that one of the most important things is to spread the word in your personal network. Get your personal network working for you. A personal recommendation is so much more valuable than any kind of advertisement you can make.

by identifying undisclosed problems they might face. In this way, the buying decision is a joint one, with the salesperson adding value by action as an expert consultant in the process.

Communications media

This brings us back to the importance of building relationships with prospective customers – not an easy task for a brand new start-up. And you can use a range of mass communications media to initiate, develop and maintain these relationships. Indeed, there has never been a greater choice of communications tools, and it grows every year. The most basic of these, one practised by most small business is word-of-mouth recommendation. This is spread through your relationships and networks and can be a very effective way of promoting a local start-up. It is a low-cost option that involves personal time and effort. It is extremely effective because, essentially, you are using advocates to promote your business. Family and friends might be able to help you initially but, once you are established, unpaid customer recommendation is very powerful. However, word of mouth even through networks of family and friends has a limited reach.

Table 7.1 on the next page lists a range of communication tools that you might consider. Each has its pros and cons and some are more appropriate to particular stages in the customer journey than others.

ACADEMIC insight 7.1

Seven principles for communication

Kotter (1996) said that a leader should adhere to seven principles to communicate their values and vision for a business. I think they apply equally to the problem of communicating brand values:

1 Keep it simple – Keep the message focused and jargon-free.
2 Use metaphors, analogies and examples – Engage the imagination.
3 Use many different forums – The same message should come from as many different directions and use as many different media as possible.
4 Repeat the message – The same message should be repeated again, and again, and again.
5 Lead by example – You need to prove what you say. Trust has to be earned.
6 Address small inconsistencies – Every aspect of your value proposition must be consistent. Small changes can have big effects if their symbolism is important.
7 Listen and be listened to – Work hard to listen to customers, it pays dividends.

Kotter, J.P. (1996) *Leading Change*, Boston, MA: Harvard Business School Press.

Table 7.1 Communication tools

Word of mouth	Newspaper advertising	Posters
Relationships and networks	Radio advertising	Flyers
Social networks and media	TV advertising	Hoardings/billboards
Blogging	Internet advertising	Direct mail
Guerrilla marketing	Sponsorship	Email
Publicity and public relations	Telephone	Texting/tweeting

Social networks and media

Where word of mouth works well within a limited geographic location, **social networks and media** can take over to spread the word to a wider audience. This is a term that covers any communication hosted on the internet or on smartphones, such as texting, tweeting or blogging. It includes social networking sites such as Facebook, Instagram, Twitter and YouTube. Social media can spread word-of-mouth recommendations very cheaply. It is extremely fast and can 'go viral' – reach enormous audiences very quickly. For consumer goods, word-of-mouth promotion using web-based social media networks – viral marketing – has been found to be more effective in developing brand identity through what is sometimes referred to as 'shared values', 'tribal identity' or 'emotional dialogue' rather than traditional mass-market advertising that focuses on product characteristics (see Case insight 7.7). It is therefore a powerful tool for any start-up – relatively cheap and effective.

> Even if you have all the money in the world to spend, the best way to market your business and get eyes on your product is to establish a social media presence.
>
> www.virgin.com/entrepreneur/richard-branson-making-most-social-media-entrepreneur
>
> Richard Branson founder Virgin Group

Social media sites can be used in a number of ways, for example, by establishing a presence and creating a community around your product/service. Usually linked to your own website, it can be used to establish a dialogue with customers, solicit feedback from them, build brand awareness and even generate sales leads. If used effectively, it can help harness the 'advocate effect' by building a 'community' of interest around your product/service. You can generate interest by constantly providing new topics for discussion or by organizing events or contests. The key to success is getting people to 'talk about' your site or share resources such as videos that you produce.

Blogging is one way of familiarizing people with your product/service and building an emotional bond with them. You can set up a blog for free through Wordpress.com. For it to work, a blog must be constantly refreshed with new content. It must be interesting, informative and fun. It must deal with more than just your company's product/service and reach out to address other lifestyle or industry issues of more general interest. It is unlikely to work if used as a medium for straightforward advertising. Instagram and Twitter can also be cheap ways of developing relationships with customers. You might even email friends and family and ask them to promote your business. Many larger organizations now expend considerable resources on developing an internet presence through blogging and other social networking sites, generating artificial excitement and web traffic around their message.

Another approach to using social media to promote your product/service is to offer a free phone app that is useful or entertaining. This might be offered on a trial basis, after which the app can be purchased or subscribed for, or it can be offered as part of a Freemium business model (see Chapter 4). If an app is something your target market uses this can be extremely effective because it will be shared and talked about. You might even get some

CASE insight 7.2

BicycleSPACE USA

Using social media as a retailer

Erik Kugler and Philip Koopman opened their BicycleSPACE cycle store in Washington, DC in 2010. But with so much competition, this set out to be a cycle store with attitude, indeed passion, aiming to build 'a cycling community' around the shop using social networks. The retailer organizes regular group maintenance workshops and bike rides, such as the monthly 'full-moon' rides and a recent Halloween 'night of the cycling undead' attended by hundreds of cyclists. These are organized as social outings and are accompanied by music and food and refreshments.

Image Source/Johannes Kroemer CM

People can find all the products we sell online, and are often so well-read and knowledgeable. They've looked up every detail and come in knowing so much. To sell to those people you have to appeal to something greater – we're selling a lifestyle and an experience. People want to be part of something and come to a place where they'll be taken care of. We're really a social gathering spot and an essential place to learn about bikes, use them and have a good time.
BBC News Business 3 March 2013

Visit the website: www.bicyclespacedc.com

Questions:

1 What role does the internet play in building customer relationships for BicycleSPACE?
2 Does it replace face-to-face relationship building for BicycleSPACE?

recommendations. Consider the example of Volkswagen's US launch of its Golf GTI in 2010. It decided to use exclusively a mobile platform, targeting young males, and offered a free gaming app for featuring the car. Within five days the app had been downloaded 800,000 times and had become the number one free app download on Apple's iTunes App Store in 36 countries.

Guerrilla marketing

Guerrilla marketing is a term that refers to any low-cost approach to creating awareness of a product/service using any of the media in Table 7.1. It relies on time, ingenuity and novelty, rather than cash, to get the message taken up and passed on. It might adopt unconventional ways to do this, such as publicity stunts, graffiti, flash mobs etc. For example, notoriously, BMW attached a styrofoam copy of a Mini Cooper to the side of a skyscraper in central Houston, Texas, as part of a guerrilla marketing campaign. Restaurants and shops have the opportunity to create a visually compelling centrepiece outside their premises. This might be changed regularly. Similarly they might organize 'events' designed to get people to notice them.

The idea is to get noticed and to create a 'buzz' around the business or the product/service so that potential customers want to find out more.

iStock.com/ Andrushk

This human ribbon is a low-cost way to raise awareness of cancer charities

They are eager to enter the shop or restaurant or to search out where the product/service can be seen and/or purchased. Encourage onlookers to take pictures or videos on their smartphones and share them with friends – they can then do your marketing for you. The more extraordinary the stunt the more likely they are to do this, and there is just the possibility it might also be picked up by the mainstream media.

One approach to guerrilla marketing is to encourage the spreading of rumours related to your product/service. The campaign might use social networks and mobile technologies to encourage the buzz or the rumours to spread – to 'go viral'. You only have to look at Donald Trump's pre-election tweets to see how effective this can be. To be effective the rumours must be exciting and different, something people will find interesting and unusual enough to pass on to friends. The whole idea is to involve prospective customers in promoting the product/service, at the same time building a relationship with them.

CASE insight 7.3

Instant Pot | CANADA

Using social media as a manufacturer

Instant Pot is a multi-cooker that does the job of a slow cooker, electric pressure cooker, rice cooker, steamer, yogurt maker, sauté/browning pan, and warming pot. It has attracted a cult following, selling through social media and word of mouth rather than the more traditional forms of advertising and promotion. Developed through brainstorming sessions for business ideas by Robert Wang and his friend Yi Qin in 2008, the first version was finally launched in 2010. They saw it as a way to cook healthy family meals quickly and affordably.

> We have tried to automate cooking as much as possible and tried to simplify the cooker. One press of the button can cook the meal for the family.

Initially they thought the product was so good that customers would flock to buy it. Promotion was typically low key, through word of mouth. But the Pot suffered from an image problem of being seen as old fashioned because of its function as a pressure cooker, and one early challenge was designing a foolproof product and persuading customers that it was safe. However, Wang and Qin remained convinced that people would love their Instant Pot, if they could just be persuaded to try it. Sales were steady but unspectacular until 2013 when they started to sell the Pot on Amazon. At that time the product started to get noticed by food bloggers who wrote enthusiastically about it and started sharing recipes with their followers. Realizing the effect this was having on sales, the company started to give Pots to bloggers and launched its own Facebook page, encouraging the development of an Instant Pot community that shares recipes, photos and tips online: tips for making anything from soups, stews and chilli, to poached eggs, popcorn and cheesecake in the appliance. They recognized that cooking is a social and emotional activity that creates relationships and one that people like to talk about. All they needed was the spur to do so and a medium to communicate through. As Robert Wang explains:

> If you look at the Amazon reviews, one common word is 'love'. Americans are very open with their emotions. Love is all over the place. Another one is that 'Instant Pot changed my life'.
>
> BBC News Business 6 March 2017

In 2016 Instant Pot featured on Amazon Prime Day, the online retailer's global 24-hour annual sales event, and became an instant bestseller, selling 215,000 in the USA alone. Instant Pot's website carries help videos, blogs and recipes and Instant Pot now has over 400,000 followers on Facebook, who often share their like for the Pot with a friend. There are also a number of versions of the Pot, with development often having been initiated by feedback and ideas submitted by users. The latest Pot can even be operated via a mobile phone app. The company launched by Robert Wang and Yi Qin remains a small business with just 25 employees. It contracts out the manufacture of its Pots to a factory in China.

Visit the website: instantpot.com

Question:

What do you learn from Instant Pot?

Publicity and public relations (PR)

PR involves getting media to recognize what you are doing and write news articles or record radio or TV features about it. It is therefore likely to reach a wider audience than your network of relationships. The key is to find something that is newsworthy or interesting. You must create press releases and be prepared to give interviews. A major advantage is that PR is free, and because you do not pay for it, these articles or programmes will have greater credibility than advertising, which is often seen as self-serving and simply trying to increase sales. However, the problem is that you do not control the content of the article or feature, and prospective customers may be left interested in the product/service but not knowing how to purchase it or contact you. Worse still, there is a danger that the published article or feature might be negative or critical. And sometimes your story will not be run because other, more newsworthy events have happened on that day. If you have the cash, one option is to hire a professional PR company to manage your message.

You can get PR from the human interest story associated with your start-up, promoting yourself as a successful local entrepreneur. The combination of an interesting personality and a 'David and Goliath' story of taking on larger competitors can be irresistible. Richard Branson has been particularly good at this, ever since he launched his first magazine – *Student* – at the age of 18. He used PR to establish the Virgin brand. As we saw in the previous chapter, Branson's exuberant personality and newsworthy publicity stunts mean that he often grabs the headlines. He launched Virgin Atlantic by identifying himself with the brand and positioning himself as the entrepreneur competing against the established competitor British Airways, a 'national carrier' that had government backing and a near monopoly on transatlantic air travel.

You might be able to get PR because of the novelty of your new product/service. Another approach is to have a celebrity launch the product or open new premises. You might also get specialist media to review your product by sending them a free sample. Apple used PR by getting respected computer and technology experts to review their new products prior to launch.

CASE insight 7.4

American Giant USA

Using PR

Established in 2012 and only eighteen months into business, everything was going according to plan for the online clothes retailer American Giant. The San Francisco-based company was founded by Bayard Winthrop and sells better-quality sweatshirts and other items of clothing produced in the USA from US cotton. With limited resources, the company had relied upon word-of-mouth marketing and had estimated it would take at least two years before growth really started. It had built this into its business plan. It only took pre-orders on its most popular styles, like the zipped hooded sweatshirt, while recognizing that it was not possible to restock the other less popular styles quickly. It bought and stocked prudently so as to manage its cash flow.

But success can cause as many problems as failure. It was December 2012 and the firm was actually a little overstocked, when the online magazine *Slate* ran an article saying that the company's hooded sweatshirt was 'the greatest hoodie ever made'. Within two days the company received over half a million dollars of extra orders, clearing out the stocks of hoodies. The company had neither the manpower nor the materials to meet demand. Because the company's supply chain went all the way back to cotton fields in the USA, with fabric specially woven and dyed for American Giant, it could not simply pick up a phone and order more material. At the same time the factory was set up to make hundreds of sweatshirts – not thousands. Since the company was not willing to change some of the founding principles on which it was based and source elsewhere, all it could do was to contact customers to apologize and hope they would be patient and wait for orders to be fulfilled. The company issued a press release commenting openly on its 'problem':

> *Commitment to quality comes first ... we're going to ask our customers to be patient because we believe in the quality and the pay-off is worth it ... it's an acceptable thing for a customer to fall out of the queue.*
> BBC News Business 10 March 2013

Some customers agreed to wait but many did not. Nevertheless the open and honest way the company dealt with the problem was appreciated by customers. And running out of stock proved to be good PR – everybody likes to have something others cannot. American Giant survived the crisis and sales continue to increase, although they have never peaked in the same way again.

Visit the website: www.american-giant.com

Question:

What lessons do you learn from American Giant?

Advertising

Getty Images/retales botijero

While having a presence on social media these days may seem essential, there is still a role for more traditional forms of advertising – even if it is on the internet. Advertising a new product/service launch can be achieved through a range of media such as the internet, particularly search engines like Google, as well as newspapers, magazines (print and virtual), radio, TV, flyers, posters, hoardings, direct mail, emails etc. Some advertising media such as radio and TV might guarantee a wide audience but they can be expensive. However, if they can be focused in a small geographic area, for example, with a local newspaper or radio station, these can be very effective for local shops or restaurants. Low-cost advertising such as posters and flyers, delivered to homes or placed under car windscreen wipers, can also be extremely effective for locally based businesses. They can create product/service awareness and tell customers where you are located and, if combined with a message or discount coupon that encourages a trial purchase, can quickly stimulate sales (covered later in this chapter).

For retailers with shops in high footfall areas, the shop window offers geographically focused, prime-space advertising at zero extra cost. For traders on the internet their home page is their shop window and search engine optimization (SEO) can drive customers to it (see Chapter 10). For businesses using trucks or vans, these are all opportunities to advertise without charge – and yet white vans remain the norm. For local tradesmen undertaking work in a location, the time taken to put up an advertising sign or post a few flyers through adjacent letterboxes might be minimal.

Some social media sites also take advertising, which can be a useful way of reaching your target market. For example, Facebook allows start-ups to deliver targeted advertisements based upon key words in personal profiles and geographic location. Similar paid-for advertising is available on Google, Reddit, Twitter, LinkedIn and StumbleUpon. But remember, if you are using the internet to promote your business, you need to have an attractive website and one that customers can navigate easily around.

Highly focused advertising allows you to target your message more precisely and can be cost-effective, for example, trade press, themed magazines or the pay-by-click advertising offered by Google and Bing. Pay-by-click allows you to advertise on the screen only when certain search words are used. It also allows you to place adverts on other people's websites that offer related products or services. With pay-by-click you only pay when your advertisement is clicked on.

You might also consider sponsoring an event if the target audience coincides with your target market. Not only might this give you the opportunity to advertise, it might also give you an opportunity to give out samples or discount coupons that encourage people to try your product or service. Another approach is to produce short videos (which these days can be cheaper than you might think) which are placed on YouTube and your website and then encouraging people to share them with friends. In fact, your sponsored events can be the backdrop to your video. Companies like Jack Wills use this to great effect (see Case insight 7.7).

Finally, it might be worth considering collaboration with other organizations targeting similar markets but not selling competing products or services, so that media costs can be shared. There are many examples. World Wildlife Federation WWF persuaded Whiskas cat food to support their global Tigers Alive protection programme. Genealogy website www.findmypast.co.uk collaborated with Grant's Whisky to give consumers the opportunity to research their own family history. Onesie designer OnePiece collaborated with Virgin Atlantic to trial a limited edition OnePiece onesie for Upper Class passengers. Finding partners in different sectors with whom to collaborate can involve some lateral thinking. They must have a mutual but non-competitive consumer interest. However, it can work well in any form of media for the mutual advantage of the partners.

Developing a communications campaign

You need to develop a communications campaign as part of your launch strategy. This can be aimed at your end-use customers as well as your distribution channels. Your campaign needs to be slightly different at each stage in Figure 7.1. However, underpinning it is the need to develop sustainable customer relationships and create a clear brand identity. Your strategy must both deliver and receive communications with customers, but ultimately it should be designed to open up a dialogue. Listening to customers is important at all stages. The major aims at each stage are listed below.

Stage 1: This is the launch stage of the business, where creating awareness of the product/service and persuading your first customers to purchase it are important. You need to get customers to understand what the product/service does for them and create a desire to at least try it. It is about:

* Creating brand awareness – getting customers to recognize that your brand, among others, meets their needs and should be considered;
* Stimulating brand purchase – persuading customers to buy your brand because, in some way, it offers a better value proposition than others.

Stage 2: This is the take-off stage of the business when you are still trying to persuade more customers to try your product/service at the same time as persuading those who have tried it to repeat purchase. It is about:

* Creating brand attitude – getting customers to recognize how your brand is different to others;
* Facilitating brand purchase – having decided to buy your brand, the customer needs to know where the product can be purchased and at what price.

Stage 3: This is the growth stage of the business. This stage is about continuing to facilitate brand purchase and restating brand attitude and identity, reinforcing your value proposition so that regular customers are convinced that they are making the right purchase decision.

Stage 4: This is the final stage of creating brand advocacy. It is about cementing the relationship with the customer, involving them in prospecting, encouraging new customers and product/service development.

You need to develop a communications campaign that integrates with your overall launch strategy and moves customers through these four stages. Remember that, while there may be short-term objectives at each stage, the longer-term aim is to develop close customer relationships based on shared values. Developing such a campaign involves six steps:

1 Identifying the target market you wish to communicate with.
2 Identifying the media that reach this target market.
3 Defining your communications objectives.
4 Developing and refining your communications message – words and images.
5 Setting the budget (money and other resources). Deciding whether the media that reach your target market are appropriate for your message and within your budget.
6 Preparing your communications plan – media, dates, times etc.

If your communications campaign is expensive, you would be well advised to test it out through focus groups before you launch it. And once the campaign is over you should evaluate it against the objectives you set in step 3.

ACADEMIC insight 7.2

Integrated marketing communication (IMC)

IMC as a concept emerged in a book by Schultz et al. (1993) as a result of the increasing pace of technological change in media platforms that gave companies more opportunities for promotion, but also made customers more aware of competing or contradictory messages that might be sent out across this myriad of platforms. IMC involves integrating all promotional tools including the marketing mix. Taken together, the marketing mix and marketing communications are often referred to as part of the marketing plan. The American Marketing Association defines IMC as 'a planning process designed to assure that all brand contacts received by a customer or prospect for a product, service, or organization are relevant to that person and consistent over time'.

In essence IMC is a simple, common-sense concept designed to ensure that all forms of communications and messages to prospects, customers, consumers and other target audiences are consistent and carefully linked. IMC starts by focusing on the customer – their preferences, buying patterns, media exposure and so on – and then offering a product/service that meets their needs,

promoting this through a mix of communication methods that the customer finds credible and attractive (called the 'outside-in' approach). This all requires a good knowledge of prospective and/or existing customers. Ultimately IMC seeks to develop a relationship with target customers by promoting a consistent brand message at all contact points so that the brand becomes more credible and appealing to them.

Research indicates that most customers make their buying decision based on perceived value and not on the information a company chooses to present to them. They are influenced more by networks of family, friends and even 'outside' networks than by mass media (Dahlen et al., 2010). This is particularly the case when 'outside' networks involve 'opinion formers' (experts) or 'opinion leaders' (individuals perceived as having higher social status). Therefore, the ability to use an 'outside-in' approach and to portray a consistent brand image to target customers can be a critical success factor in competitive, information-rich markets (Jin, 2003/2004). Other claimed benefits of IMC are greater consistency among the various communication messages and functions, cost savings and a better use of media and promotional mix (Pickton and Broderick, 2005).

Dahlen, M., Lange, F. and Smith, T (2010) *Marketing Communications: A Brand Narrative Approach*, Chichester: John Wiley & Sons.

Jin, H.S. (2003/2004) 'Compounding Consumer Interest', *Journal of Advertising*, 32 (4), 29–41.

Pickton, D. and Broderick, A. (2005) *Integrated Marketing Communications*, Harlow: Prentice Hall.

Schultz, D.E., Tannenbaum, S.I. and Lauterborn, R.F. (1993) *Integrated Marketing Communications: Putting it together and making it work*, Lincolnwood, IL: NTC Business Books.

Creating awareness

While all start-ups need to create awareness, how you approach this will depend on the type of business you are launching. Refer back to the start-up typologies in Figure 2.1 (page 37). The more radical the product/service innovation, the more likely the start-up is to create genuine public interest. You are also likely to be able to use PR when you are introducing a product/service that exists elsewhere into a new market. Such developments are newsworthy in their own right and mean that you can use PR to your advantage. But even here, few companies would trust the public to beat a path to their door on the back of a news story. There is no guarantee that it will be accurate, nor is there any guarantee that they will explain where potential customers can buy the product/service. So it is important that you provide the media with information on what the product/service is and why it is newsworthy. This involves producing and distributing a press release and possibly organizing a press conference or launch event. This can be supported by a range of other activities that utilize as many of the communication media as time and money permit.

Few product launches enjoy the level of anticipation and pre-ordering of Apple products – and certainly Apple plans these launches meticulously. Even before the launch of a new product Apple ensures that there is promotion of the product, normally through a mix of free PR (pre-launch feature leaks, pre-launch product reviews etc.) and a theatrical launch event supported by media advertising. But then Apple has a brand recognized for design and innovation that has an established band of loyal customers and advocates – something that takes time to create and is not an option for a start-up. So you need to be creative in organizing such events and motivate customers and press to attend. And the lesson is clear – you need to create awareness of your product or service before the customer will even consider purchasing it – and you do not leave it to chance. You need to consider all the communications media discussed in the previous section.

With any product/service launch it is important to get the right message to prospective customers. The message you want to convey to your target market segment is that you have a value proposition that meets some, as yet unmet, need they have or meets it better than other products or services. They need to be told about your product/service, what it can do for them – the benefits – and where they can buy it. However, if your product or service is entirely novel you may have to limit the awareness message to what the product does, explaining the benefits offered. In both cases you want to create sufficient curiosity that prospective customers will consider purchasing it when they see the product or service on sale.

For those start-ups where the product innovation is incremental, the job of creating awareness is more difficult because the launch is less newsworthy. That means PR is less likely to bear results and you might focus more on the other communications media. However, you still have options that might get results. Some businesses are lucky enough to be able to have a celebrity to launch their product/service – sometimes free and often found through their network of contacts. Celebrity launches can be extremely effective, particularly for shops because they attract potential shoppers. A celebrity might also be persuaded to endorse the product/service, but do remember that they are putting their reputation on the line. Alternatively, never underestimate the newsworthiness of your personal entrepreneurial story. Many newspapers run regular small business pages and are looking for inspiring stories to fill them.

As we have already discussed, social media can be a very cheap way of generating interest in a new business, but you need to have a 'hook' to get people interested even with this medium, and you need to find a way of finding the addresses to send your message to. Posters and flyers can do the same thing for local businesses. One way to short-circuit the early stages in the process outlined in Figure 7.1 is to get customers to jump straight to the evaluation or

CASE insight 7.5

Good Hair Day UK

Start-up marketing strategy

Good Hair Day (GHD), part of Jemella Group, was started by Martin Penny in 2001. Based in West Yorkshire, the company has revolutionized the hair industry with an iron that straightens hair between two heated ceramic plates. But when Martin first took the idea to his bank, asking for a £50,000 loan, the bank manager was sceptical, seeing the product as 'just another set of hair tongs'. Martin got the money on the strength of his track record running an environmental consultancy. But Martin decided on two important strategies that were to underpin the subsequent success of his business:

1 Not to manufacture the product himself but to have it manufactured in Korea where costs were lower. This way, he could focus on sales and keep his fixed costs to a minimum.
2 Not to sell through the high street but to target firstly up-market London West End hair salons and then salons across the UK. The 'hair styling irons' were sold both for salon use and to customers by the salons themselves. Customer prices were high but so too were the margins for the salons. Despite product costs being relatively low, using this route to market differentiated GHD tongs

from 'just another set of hair tongs'. It was seen as professional, special and up-market.

Since they used hair stylists, many celebrities such as Madonna, Victoria Beckham, Jennifer Aniston and Gwyneth Paltrow used GHD tongs, and the company benefited from celebrity endorsements. These helped to give it a certain exclusive cachet that then helped sell GHD products to the general public. The company claims that the iron is now used in more than 10,000 UK salons – 85% of the market. Based on this success GHD is diversifying into other haircare products such as shampoo, conditioner and styling gel, and has launched a brand called 'Nu:U', aimed at the mid-price, mass salon market.

Visit the website: www.ghdhair.com

Questions:

1 What were the important elements of the start-up marketing strategy for GHD?
2 How important is it that other elements of GHD's strategy are consistent with these? Give some examples of consistent strategies.

---

trial purchase stage by offering them free or discounted samples or trials. This is only appropriate for low-price products/services that generate repeat sales. And it is most appropriate for products/services that are only incrementally different to those offered by existing competitors. In many cases it needs to be linked to incentives offered to the distributors providing the product/service.

Price and the buying decision

While price undoubtedly plays a part in the trial buying decision, Chapter 6 alerted you to the dangers of setting your launch price too low. The pricing decision depends, in part, on whether yours is a big- or small-ticket item. If a big-ticket product or service is unique or fashionably desirable you may be lucky enough to be able to charge a premium price at its launch. This creates a certain status associated with ownership of the product or service. You might then reduce it as competition enters the market. You can then effectively lower the price later by including more features but keeping the price the same. This is the strategy used by Apple, with new versions of its products carrying new and better features. With this sort of product you can also afford to be selective about distribution, going into new channels as the product ages. So, for example, a film is shown first in cinemas, then on pay-to-view channels, and finally it becomes available on video or through download, usually with the price reducing progressively over time.

By way of contrast, it may take some pricing encouragement to persuade customers to switch supplier and make an initial trial purchase of a small-ticket item that is less unique and likely to be purchased more frequently. In these circumstances free samples/trials or special 'introductory offers' to encourage a trial purchase may be part of your launch strategy. These offers might take the form of discount vouchers or coupons, including e-coupons. They might also include loyalty vouchers that encourage repeat purchases. This approach may help you gain market share quickly, albeit at a cost in lost profit. Special 'introductory offers', rather than setting a low price, allow you to re-establish your value-to-customer price more easily after introduction. Customers will accept the removal of a discount far more easily than an increase in price.

Remember that it may be possible to adopt different launch strategies, coupled with differential pricing, for different market segments. Over time you need to establish value-to-customer prices for each segment, sufficient to make you an adequate profit overall. This might involve an element of trial and error. What is more, there may be a tension here between short-term profitability (and survival) and long-term market dominance (and higher profits). Long-run market dominance, although not necessarily associated with price competition, is likely to lead to high and more sustainable profits and can be particularly important in newly emerging markets.

Distribution channels and the buying decision

Getty Images/Fuse

Figure 6.2 (page 182) outlined the different ways of getting your product/service in front of customers through your channels of distribution. Selling through a distribution chain such as shops, agents or distributors eats into your profit margins but allows you to expand your reach, benefiting from your partners' strengths. Getting end-use customers to buy your product means incentivizing each stage of your distribution chain. While you might be able to contact distributors directly to create awareness of your product, they will need an incentive to stock it. They will be interested in the uniqueness of your product and will also react to whether customers are already seeking it out because of your customer awareness campaign (**demand-pull**). 'Demand-pull' communication strategies focus on your end-use customer, using all the communication media covered earlier. They can create awareness and demand for the product and pull it through the distribution chain. However, they can be prohibitively expensive for many start-ups and therefore restrict the available market.

Ultimately, these channels are interested in profit, so they might be persuaded to stock your product, particularly if initially it is offered on a sale-or-return basis. Indeed, they might help promote your product if you offer them an extra initial discount or bonus (**supply-push**). With 'supply-push' your launch strategy will need to influence each link in the distribution chain. However, unless accompanied by other promotional activity, such as point of sale displays and so on, this leaves decisions about promotion activity entirely with the distributor. This can lead to unintended consequences, such as distributors entering into local price promotions that are not consistent with other elements of your marketing mix. This underlines the important point that your launch strategy must be consistent with your overall strategy and should seek to coordinate 'push' and 'pull' incentives. The advantages and disadvantages of using distribution channels and a supply-push strategy are summarized in Table 7.2.

Table 7.2 The advantages and disadvantages of using distribution channels and a supply-push strategy

Advantages	Disadvantages
• Fewer buyers to communicate with: – time with buyer important – relationships with buyer important • Less capital needed to invest in direct consumer communication, distribution etc. • Potential to leverage market in line with distribution channels, gaining wider market coverage more quickly than otherwise	• High-value, infrequent purchases by buyers are high-risk: – need for detailed information about buyer – need for accurate identification of buyer incentives (product characteristics, point of sale displays, frequency of delivery, financial incentives etc.) • Lack of direct influence and control over end consumer • Buyer may have dominant negotiating position regarding price • May de-emphasize brand and not cement product loyalty with consumer

Customer feedback and evaluation

Once customers make a purchase they will evaluate your product/service against the promises you held out to them. You should be asking them for feedback. Are the value propositions you advertised real? Does the product/service meet their expectations? Is the service delivery at each stage of the distribution chain appropriate? Without a programme of evaluation you will never know where they are or where they got to on their customer journey. Remember they may decide not to repeat buy if just one element of your marketing mix, however small, does not meet their expectations in some way, and if you do not ask them for feedback you may never know what this is.

So, as well as making your first sales, you need to start obtaining customer feedback and evaluating their reaction to your product/service. You need to correct any weaknesses in your value proposition. You might try face-to-face trials, evaluation questionnaires or feedback sheets using the market research techniques outlined in Chapter 3 (pages 80–83). If you can get a customer contact address, tell them when any weaknesses are corrected, perhaps offering a free trial or replacement. It is often said that by correcting a mistake with a customer you have the opportunity of forming a personal relationship and turning them into a satisfied customer, loyal supporter and advocate. If there are no weaknesses, then these are prospective repeat-buy customers. Start to develop a relationship with them and turn them into supporters and advocates as well.

Penetrating your market

Your business will grow through a combination of repeat sales (for appropriate products) and new customers. Repeat sales will be built on the relationships you develop with customers, particularly as competitors emerge. New customers will come from a combination of promotional activity (including face-to-face selling), finding new distribution channels and using existing customers willing to act as your advocates in some way. Reputation spreads, but can take time. As your product/service attracts more customers, it will attract more attention

CASE insight 7.6

Clippy UK

Minimizing start-up costs

Calypso Rose graduated from a technical theatre course at a drama school and got a job in television production. It was while she was working in this job that she made the first see-through bag with pockets to display her collection of Polaroid photographs. She never intended to start up a business; however, the frequency of enquiries from people on where they could buy something similar prompted her to start thinking about it as a serious possibility. When her parents offered to lend her £2,000 to make the first 250 bags she decided to take the plunge, aged just 22, and Clippy was born.

Calypso Rose

Calypso decided to work from home to keep her overheads and breakeven low. Her mother, Clare, also helped with the business, meaning Calypso did not have to hire any employees. She found a UK manufacturer through Kelly's online directory, deciding that this was better than going to China to find a supplier. The UK manufacturer could turn around orders more quickly and, once she established a track record, would offer normal trade terms for payment, thereby helping her cash flow and reducing her risk.

Initial sales were mainly to family and friends – many of the people who had asked where they could buy the first bag. The official launch of Clippykit (now called Clippy) was at Olympia's Spirit of Christmas Fair in 2004. Calypso established a website, customized a large bag with a sign saying 'stop me and buy one' and took a small stall on Portobello Road in London, a popular fashion and antiques market, to see if her business idea would work. She had done everything she could to minimize her risks and now wanted to see if the bag would really sell. She sold all 250 bags in the first month. Working from home and only using the initial £2,000, she managed to build a turnover of £180,000 in the first year. In 2004, at

the age of 22, she was voted London Young Business person of the year.

Calypso was worried from the start that the idea could be easily copied – after all, it was just a plastic bag with pockets for photographs – and that a bigger company with more resources could roll out an imitation product more effectively. So the idea was to push sales as quickly as possible but also to establish a fashion brand. A major breakthrough came when the fashionable Notting Hill boutique Coco Ribbon decided to sell her bags. Things got even better when celebrities such as Helena Bonham Carter, Jools Holland and Jamie Oliver started carrying Clippy bags. The bags have even been used as a 'goody bag' at the Brit Awards and the Orange Prize.

It also became clear early on that the concept behind the bags was flexible and could be applied to other products such as make-up bags, lamp shades, wallets and umbrellas. Another development was that the products themselves could be personalized, and Calypso started offering kits to help people do that.

Calypso has been very adept at promoting the product herself. For example, in 2009, working with an enterprise organization called Make Your Mark, 650 girls in London took part in a competition to personalize a Clippy bag with an issue that was relevant to them.

The range of Clippy products has grown. With the company turnover being over £500,000, Calypso employs two full-time and one part-time staff. The bags are sold through conventional wholesale and retail markets – through about 250 independent boutiques. They are sold as fashion items and promotional products, often customized for the promotion event. However, about a quarter of sales come from the website, which shows how the products can be used, hosts competitions and has a Calypso blog. You can also sign up for a regular newsletter.

Visit the website: clippylondon.com

Questions:

1 From the information given, complete as many elements as you can of the New Venture Creation Framework.

2 Is this a 'lean start-up'? What did Calypso do to keep her start-up costs to a minimum?

3 What did she do to promote her product while keeping her costs to a minimum?

4 What are her growth options? Would you change the business model?

from competitors. They may adapt their marketing strategy and even change their product/service characteristics so as to compete more directly with you. So, your marketing strategy, including pricing, may need to adapt and change to suit this.

The appropriate strategy to adopt at this stage depends, in part, on the competitive position you find yourself in. Referring back to the new venture typologies in Figure 2.1 (page 37), the more radical the product/service innovation or market you are creating, the more likely you are to be in a dominant market position at start-up. This should reflect itself in a low level of competition for you to face.

Strong competitive position

If you are in a strong competitive position you need to expand as rapidly as possible, investing in whatever is the basis for value offering and developing your brand identity. There is a window of opportunity for you to capitalize on your first-mover advantage before competitors copy you. In terms of the generic business models outlined in Chapter 5:

- If your core value proposition involves high differentiation then you should further differentiate yourself from the competition, creating and building your brand. You will probably have been able to charge a premium price at launch and you should have been investing those profits in differentiation and branding from the start. Despite your high differentiation, as competitors emerge, your price may need to come down, either directly or, more likely, by improving the product's value in some way. Second-generation electronic products are typically better in some way (e.g. storage capacity for computers) but at the same price.
- If your core value proposition involves cost leadership (low price) then you must obtain the necessary economies of scale as quickly as possible to gain that dominant position. This involves investing in ways of keeping your costs low and, at the same time, expanding your sales through aggressive marketing, including price promotions.

So, the key to success is gaining rapid market dominance, at the same time as building those close customer relationships. To attract more customers who are willing to try new products and early adopters you need to make an intensive push on distribution. This might involve organizing frequent sales promotions, continually finding new channels of distribution, expanding into new geographic areas and so on. Customers and distributors love to sell products or services that have proved successful elsewhere. It reduces their risk. Some start-ups, particularly those that are technology-based, are international from the start. However, most move into overseas markets more gradually, starting by exporting products through independent channels such as sales agents. We shall return to the issue of international expansion in the next chapter.

Weak competitive position

If you are not in a strong competitive position then your expansion needs to be more cautious. You need to plan to combat competition from the launch, with a view to profitability. One attractive option is to find a market niche within a competitive industry. Often in these circumstances a start-up is better advised to ignore the mass market, trying instead to carve out a smaller but distinctive market niche for itself, at least in the short term. This often avoids the high fixed costs usually associated with mass markets. It also often means that a higher price can be charged for the product/service, albeit on a smaller volume which, as we saw in Chapter 6, can result in higher profits. And often that niche is bigger than the founder ever imagined. Serial entrepreneurs go on to found one business with 'limited' potential after another, often selling them on.

While competition will certainly show itself at this stage, the real battleground will come later as customers follow the early adopters. They each make up about one-third of customers and are more conservative, with slightly higher status and are more deliberate, thinking purchasers. They only adopt the product after it has become acceptable and will shop around and compare different product/service offerings. By this stage some competitors will have become established, while others will have fallen by the wayside. Those remaining will compete aggressively. This is the stage where your dominant market position and a well-recognized brand will really start to pay dividends. We shall address some of the challenges of marketing at this stage in the next chapter.

CASE insight 7.7

Jack Wills – University Outfitters UK

Low-cost marketing

Launched in 1999 by Peter Williams and Rob Shaw, the Jack Wills brand has an old-world university association. It was originally known for selling hoodies (emblazoned with the names of universities), tracksuit bottoms, rugby shirts, pyjamas and party dresses, primarily to well-off youngsters.

I had just left university and I thought the years between 18 and 21 were amazing because you've got all the independence and freedom of being adult but you haven't quite entered the adult world. I looked back and realized I didn't appreciate how amazing those years were and I wanted to create a brand that epitomised that – for the person who has an aspirational response to that 18–21 British university thing.

Using the trademark 'Jack Wills – University Outfitters', the brand has an elite 'public school' or 'preppy' image – and high prices reflect this, although they do offer a 25% discount to registered students. However, the business started life as a simple shop in the seaside town of Salcombe in Devon, a town without a university but plenty of well-off visitors (known humorously as Chelsea-on-Sea). The founders invested £40,000 in the venture, taken mainly from their credit cards, which left them little spare cash for anything else. So, they lived above the store.

Today, the founders are millionaires. And, with sales of over £120 million and more than 60 stores in the UK and some 20 overseas in the USA, Ireland, Hong Kong, China, Singapore, UAE, Kuwait and Lebanon, the Jack Wills brand is now best known for selling a modern take on traditional 'British' clothes such as men's blazers and women's tweed jackets: 'playing off the tensions between old and new, formal and casual'. These often incorporate aspects of traditional British military and sporting design. The company uses navy blue and pink colour schemes in its packaging and for some of its products. While the company plays to its Britishness, few of its clothes are actually made in Britain. They still sell sports-orientated clothing (for sports such as polo, rugby and rowing) but the shops have evolved to also sell expensive designer clothes and hats – often developed in collaboration with well-known partners like Liberty or Fox Brothers – as well as toiletries, cushions, bed linen and towels. These days T-shirts are old-hat. Instead they have given away neon yellow 'party pants' branded with different locations:

The product is amazing but if you kind of boil it down to what's really special – and what people talk about – it's the party pants … They sort of define us because it's not just a bunch of clothes, it's the best summer they've ever had, the best university experience or just the best winter trip because we're embedded in their lifestyle … There's an inherent naughty rebelliousness in everything that we do.

With many stores still located in university towns, the shops are often housed in historical buildings. Whether an old or new building, the interiors feature dark wood tables and display cases, faded Persian rugs and yellowed posters, designed to mirror the image of all things British. And products like bowler and pork-pie hats and silk headscarves help emphasize the eccentric and 'dandyish' Britishness of the brand. The company logo features a pheasant with a top hat and walking stick, known as Mr Wills.

Jack Wills' approach to marketing today can look remarkably similar to its approach when the founders opened the first shop. Back in 1999 the founders could not afford an expensive advertising campaign. Instead they gave away branded hoodies and rugby shirts to 'influencers' in the town – kids that others would admire – and would pay them to go around giving away branded T-shirts. Jack Wills clothes became 'cool'. Overt advertising would have detracted from the 'cliquiness' of the brand image. The company still employs teams of 'seasonnaires' to roam beaches, ski resorts and university campuses and spread the brand – but never to sell. They rely on word-of-mouth and social media marketing. A year before the Jack Wills store opened in Nantucket, off Cape Cod in the USA, a team of seasonnaires spent the summer 'seeding' the market.

They are the mouthpieces of the brand. They have often worked in stores and their job for the summer is to make friends, throw parties and be in the right places to seed the brand.

Peter Williams *Sunday Times* 16 September 2012

The company also sponsors certain exclusive university sports events (and related entertainment) such as polo matches between Cambridge and Oxford, Harvard and Yale, Eton and Harrow. It also hosts 'events' such as the annual seasonnaires' party and the Big Air Fashion Show. These often act as the backdrop to the numerous short videos that the company produces and places on YouTube. They also feature seasonnaires 'at play' in some of the resorts that the company targets. These videos try to capture the essence of the Jack Wills brand.

Visit the website: www.jackwills.com

Questions:

1 What is the essence of the Jack Wills brand?

2 Why has the company's original approach to creating brand awareness translated so well into a longer-term advertising/promotions strategy? What are the advantages and disadvantages of this approach?

3 From the information given in the case, use the Framework Worksheet or the PowerPoint slide to complete as many elements as you can of the New Venture Creation Framework.

4 Is the marketing mix consistent? Why is this important?

 Visit www.macmillanihe.com/burns-nvc-2e to download the Framework Worksheet and PowerPoint slide.

Sofa-bed Factory

If their business was to become a reality Piotr and Olek had to secure at least the custom of the furniture chain that Piotr worked for. Even if they were, as yet, unable to secure a sale, they wanted to get some indication of how likely the company was to place an order for sofa-beds, and at what price. That meant they had to show Piotr's buyer friend the sofa-beds they had manufactured. Piotr introduced Olek as a friend who was setting up a business in Poland to manufacture the beds and was looking for customers in the UK. They allowed him to open up a bed himself and to lie on it to test for comfort. They showed him photographs of the other sofa-beds, explaining that it was available in a range of designs and fabrics. They kept repeating the features and benefits they had decided on (without mentioning 'competitive price'):

- A robust, sturdy frame – that is easy to unfold into a bed;
- A comfortable mattress – that ensures a good night's sleep;
- Contemporary, modular design – that fits in with different styles of modern furniture.

Piotr was able to point out the weaknesses in the competitor's sofa-bed that the company was currently selling.

The buyer was impressed, agreeing that it was better – easier to unfold and more comfortable – than the ones he currently sold and asked what the price was. Olek quickly started outlining the features and benefits of the sofa-beds again but the buyer kept returning to the price. Piotr intervened to ask about volumes of orders the stores might place, and the buyer replied that with over 100 stores he would be surprised if they did not sell some 1,000 in a year – say one per store each month – but he could not guarantee this, it depended on the price. He also enquired whether Olek offered other modular sofa units that could be combined with the sofa-bed as sofa-beds were often purchased as part of a set. Olek dodged the answer.

The buyer returned to the question of price, saying the market was very competitive and that they faced high fixed costs for the stores and the extensive marketing they undertook. He could not guarantee minimum sales volumes but said, if the price was right, he could provide a month-by-month estimate of sales volumes for the year, reflecting the seasonal variations. However, he also said that the company would need at least one sofa-bed per store 'for display purposes' and that they would only pay for this display stock after three months. Customer orders would then be placed on a monthly basis and for payment the company's terms of trade with suppliers was 30 days' credit. Nevertheless it was clear that the buyer was very interested in placing an order and, after much discussion, they finally agreed that, if an order were placed, it would be at a price of €320 per sofa-bed. Olek asked the buyer to send him the monthly sales estimates and the company's normal terms of trade. Despite being asked, Olek did not concede exclusivity of UK sales to the retailer. However, the retailer did agree not to stock other sofa-beds.

It seemed like a deal could be agreed, but the truth was that the pair had yet to set up a factory in Poland, and that would take a few months. Only then could the 'display models' be made and shipped to the UK. Piotr and Olek also realized that there was a thin line between losing the contract because of delay (they had alerted the buyer to the inadequacies of the existing supplier's product) and having an unhappy customer because orders were not being fulfilled. In subsequent discussions it was agreed that 100 'display sofas' could be dispatched to the retailer in batches between October and November and that the normal ordering and delivery process would start the following January (when the company would be invoiced for the display stock). A contract would only be signed once these deliveries had been agreed. But the retailer only agreed to wait two months for that to happen.

Piotr and Olek finally realized that their dream could become a reality and they might have to give up their regular jobs and become real entrepreneurs. But they also realized that they had only just started on the planning that was necessary for all this. Could they deliver on their promises? And could they make a profit doing so? They needed to make a quick decision about whether or not to start their business.

Questions:

1 What are the advantages and disadvantages of this arrangement?
2 What do Piotr and Olek still need to do before they make their final decision?

Summary and action points

7.1 Develop a promotion strategy for your launch: Develop a staged promotion strategy for the launch of your product/service and your business: creating awareness, encouraging customers to make their first purchase, then to repeat the purchase and become regular customers.

Encourage customers to progress through these stages to become supporters and advocates of your product/service by building a positive relationship with them. You can build this relationship through face-to-face contact and through your communications strategy. You must build brand loyalty.

7.2 Develop your communications campaign: Draw up a communications campaign for the launch of your product/service and business using media such as your personal networks, internet and social media, PR and advertising. Remember that the longer-term aim is to develop close customer relationships based on shared values that reflect your brand identity.

7.3 Get PR: Try to get free PR. Write a press release and send it to appropriate local and/or national local media. The more radical your product innovation or the market you are creating, the more likely your start-up is to be of interest to the general media. However, they can also be interested in the human interest side of a business start-up.

7.4 Consolidate your marketing strategy: Ensure that all the elements of your marketing mix (product, price, promotion, place and people) are consistent and reinforce each other to form a coherent marketing strategy. Review the 'place' element by deciding how you sell to customers (direct or through distribution channels). Review your pricing strategy and consider the use of price incentives.

7.5 Identify the critical success factors and strategic options for the start-up phase of your marketing plan: Review the marketing strategy for your launch phase of your marketing plan and produce a list of critical success factors and strategic options.

7.6 Develop selling skills: Develop your selling skills. To sell your product/service face to face with a customer you need to sell its benefits: be clear about how your product/service will solve the customer's specific 'problem' and be able to demonstrate its features; be able to back up the claims you make about your value proposition with proof; be able to handle objections and concerns; and, finally, close the sale.

Workbook exercises

The New Venture Creation Workbook contains a digital version of these exercises that can be modified as your business model develops and builds into a draft business plan. It can be downloaded from www.macmillanihe.com/burns-nvc-2e.

7.1: Develop a promotion strategy for your launch

Building on the results of Exercises 5.6 and 6.2, complete the table on the next page:

(Copy the workbook if you have more than two target market segments)

1 List the ways that you will create awareness of your product/service, both directly with end-use customers and with distributors.

2 List the ways that you will encourage customers (including distributors) to make a trial purchase.

3 List the ways you will encourage repeat purchases from existing customers.

4 List the ways you will find new prospective customers.

5 List the precautions you are taking to ensure that the customer will make a positive evaluation of your service delivery and how you will monitor this.

6 List the ways you will ensure that customers work their way up the loyalty chain and how you might use them as advocates. How will you build and use a close customer relationship?

7 Estimate the costs and resources associated with the above in your first year.

	Customer segment 1	Customer segment 2
Creating awareness		
Encouraging trial purchase		
Encouraging repeat purchase		
Finding new prospective customers		
Evaluating service delivery		
Building relationships		
Estimated cost of these activities		

7.2: Develop your communications campaign

Building on Exercise 7.1, construct a communications campaign for the first three months using the table below:

1 Identify the target media
2 List your communications objectives
3 Develop your communications message and media (words and images)
4 Decide on your budget for the first three months (money and other resources)
5 Write down your communications plan (media, dates etc.)
6 Based on step 4, estimate your communications budget for your first year. This may just be four times the budget in 4. Ensure this is consistent with Exercise 7.1 (7).

	Customer segment 1	Customer segment 2
Target media		
Communications objectives		
Communications message and media		

	Customer segment 1	Customer segment 2
Budget (3 months)		
Communications plan (media, dates etc.)		
Budget (12 months)		

7.3: Get PR

Type a press release concerning some aspect of your business (e.g. the business, product/service, yourself, location etc.). It should be no more than 100 words and contain two quotes. Make certain there is some newsworthy or human interest aspect to it. Try to reflect your brand identity (Exercise 5.5) in your press release.

7.4: Consolidate your marketing strategy

Review Exercise 6.2 and, in the light of this chapter, ensure that all the elements of your marketing mix are consistent and reinforce each other. Use the template below to summarize the main elements of this strategy and identify the critical success factors. You may wish to refer back to Case insight 6.1.

	Customer segment 1	Relative importance (max 10)	Customer segment 2	Relative importance (max 10)
Value proposition				
Marketing mix ('list' elements)				
– Product				
– Price				
– Promotion				
– Place				
– People				
Critical success factors (CSF)				

7.5: Identify the critical success factors and strategic options for the start-up phase of your marketing plan

1 Combine any changes from Exercise 7.4 with the list of critical success factors you arrived at in Exercise 6.2 (5). Produce a consolidated list of critical success factors for the start-up phase of your marketing plan.

2 Reflecting on these exercises, list the strategic options for the start-up phase of your marketing plan.

7.6: Develop selling skills

The aim of this exercise is to improve your selling skills. However, in doing this you may gain some insight into your value proposition and business model and wish to modify elements of it. Review your answers to all exercises in Chapters 4 to 7 in the light of this exercise.

Team up with two other students: one to act as a buyer (end-use customer or distributor) and one as an observer. Conduct a role-playing sales meeting lasting 5 minutes.

Seller: Provide the buyer in advance of the meeting with a one-page summary of your product/ service and its value proposition (Exercises 5.2 and 5.3). Plan your meeting using the outline in this chapter. Try to close the sale.

Buyer: Make certain you understand your role. Remember you have been identified as a prospect and therefore you are interested in the product/service. However, prepare some objections that the seller will have to counter.

Observer: Observe the sales meeting and give feedback on what worked or did not work and how it might be improved.

 Visit www.macmillanihe.com/burns-nvc-2e for chapter quizzes and other resources.

8

Scalability and growth

Contents

Learning outcomes

When you have read this chapter and undertaken the related exercises you will be able to:

- Critically evaluate the strategic options for growth and understand the implications for a start-up
- Understand how to go about selling into new markets
- Understand what is involved in product development
- Use the Growth Share Matrix to communicate marketing strategies for a portfolio of products
- Show advanced knowledge of the effects of the product portfolio on cash flow and how the product portfolio can be managed
- Critically evaluate the use of acquisition as part of a growth strategy and the advantages and disadvantages of diversification

Academic insights 📓

8.1   Sticking to the knitting

Case insights 💼

Sofa-bed Factory

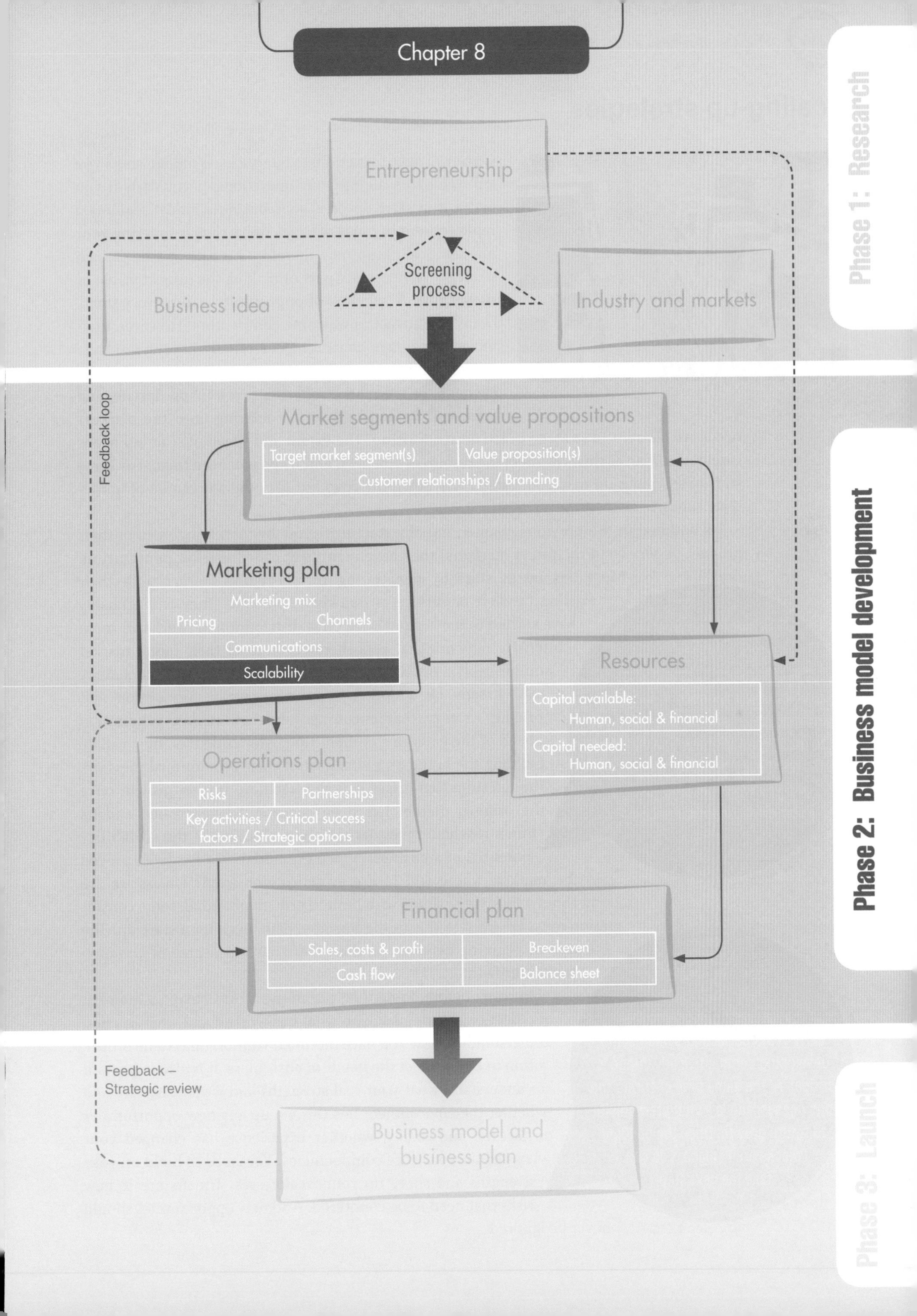
Chapter 8
Entrepreneurship
Screening process
Business idea
Industry and markets
Feedback loop
Market segments and value propositions
Target market segment(s)
Value proposition(s)
Customer relationships / Branding
Marketing plan
Marketing mix
Pricing
Channels
Communications
Scalability
Resources
Capital available:
Human, social & financial
Capital needed:
Human, social & financial
Operations plan
Risks
Partnerships
Key activities / Critical success factors / Strategic options
Financial plan
Sales, costs & profit
Breakeven
Cash flow
Balance sheet
Feedback –
Strategic review
Business model and business plan
Phase 1: Research
Phase 2: Business model development
Phase 3: Launch

Scaling-up strategies

Getty Images/ Jetta Productions

Once you have proved that your business model works you will want to scale up your operations, particularly if you had a lean start-up or if your business model requires a rapid roll-out because of a lack of barriers to entering your market. Scaling-up may therefore be part of your launch strategy – a necessary part of making the project viable or sustainable. A 'window of opportunity' can be very small. Delay can attract unwelcome competitors. However, first-mover advantage can disappear rapidly if your product/ market offering proves too unattractive or too many elements of the market offering prove inappropriate, and there can be good cause for delaying until the market's needs are clearer – a strategy called **active waiting**. The extent and speed of scale-up needs careful planning as this will affect the resources you need and when you need them. For some start-ups, scaling-up may come some way down the road but for others it can be of immediate concern.

As outlined in the previous chapter, initially start-ups grow by increasing sales of their product or service in the target market(s) they have identified, called **market penetration**. Most businesses start by penetrating their existing market with their existing product or service as quickly as possible. They will probably have started to move from a selective distribution network to a more intensive network that gets them to more of their target market and probably a broader geographic base. At the same time, they may already be adopting a more aggressive promotion and pricing strategy that encourages further market penetration ahead of the emerging competition. Alongside this, they will be building the brand as a vital part of their promotional message. The question that arises is how to achieve further growth once the original market has been successfully penetrated and its limits reached. Investors are always looking at the **scalability** potential of a business. Once the initial idea has been proved in the market, where will future growth come from? Unless we are talking about a lifestyle business with limited growth potential, some consideration must be given to this in the business plan, even for a start-up. The extent of planning depends on the time scale and degree of certainty for this growth.

However, before doing this it is always worth having a moment of reflection, looking back on what has worked and what has not, understanding how you have modified your original value proposition to better meet the needs of customers. It is also important to understand what your real strengths and weaknesses are and whether the environment has thrown up any new opportunities or threats, and finally, whether experience has changed your views about your core competencies. You need to build on your strengths and shore up your weaknesses. Threats create new risks that need to be countered. And new opportunities should never be ignored.

> **Jon Coker Managing partner MMC Ventures Sunday Times 8 January 2017**
>
> Understand what role your business plays in customers' lives and what problems you are solving for them. Knowing the answer to this helps you to grow your business in a way that makes it even better for customers and you won't get side-tracked by great ideas that nobody wants.

> **Adam Schwab founder Lux Group Business Review Australia issuu.com July 2014**
>
> Most businesses aren't overnight successes ... Spending the early years perfecting systems and developing competitive advantage is critical. At the same time ensuring the business is lean is a vital prerequisite to future growth. Once the building blocks are in place, you can take the next step.

Once the original target market has been successfully penetrated you have three options:

1   Market development – selling the existing product or service into new markets.
2   Product or service development – developing the original business idea into new products or services that can be sold into existing markets.
3   Diversification – selling new products or services into new markets. Often this option is pursued through mergers or acquisitions.

Figure 8.1 shows a simple framework for looking at these options in a systematic way. We shall discuss each in turn.

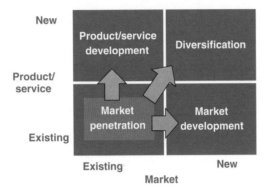

Figure 8.1 *Growth options*

CASE insight 8.1

  Invoice2go AUSTRALIA

Scaling up

Invoice2go is a mobile invoicing app available on a subscription basis. It allows small businesses to create, send and manage invoices and expenses through mobile technology, using the cloud for storage. The company was founded in 2002 by 28-year-old Australian software designer Chris Strode as he struggled to invoice clients and became frustrated by the lack of a simple, easy-to-use invoicing product:

All I found were fully-fledged accounting packages. Ninety per cent of the functionality didn't make any sense to me. I just needed to be able to send an invoice as quickly as possible.
The Australian 24 September 2014

Although always profitable, the business remained virtually a one-man band and growth was only modest in its early years. However, Chris 'bootstrapped'

(see Chapter 10) the development of a mobile, cloud-based version of the product, which was made available in the iPhone App Store in 2009. It was also soon developed for Android use. With the explosion in smartphone usage Invoice2go's simple, mobile technology and its attractive low-cost subscription business model took off. By 2011 it was ranked among the top ten business apps. The company then faced the challenge of scaling up quickly to meet demand before competitors could copy it. In 2013 Invoice2go raised US$35 million in first-round finance from US-based Accel Partners and Ribbit Capital investment, valuing it at over $100 million. While Chris remained in Sydney to run research and development as Chief Product Officer, the company then appointed former eHarmony boss Greg Waldorf as CEO in 2014. Based in new offices in Palo Alto, California, he joined Accel partner Ryan Sweeney who had been appointed to the board of directors as part of the funding deal.

Since its launch, subscriptions have doubled year on year with half the users now in the USA. In 2015 Invoice2go launched an Apple watch version of its app and a mobile payment feature powered by Stipe Connect. It also raised a further US$15 million from its existing investors to finance further expansion. By this point, Invoice2go had scaled up to over 100 employees based in four offices around the world. Now available in eleven languages, Invoice2go is used by more than 250,000 companies sending over $1 billion of invoices each month.

Visit the website: invoice.2go.com

Question:

What lessons do you learn about scaling up from Invoice2go?

Market development

Market development is the natural extension of market penetration. Instead of just selling more of the same to your existing customers, you go out and find new customers and new markets for those products or services. There are four reasons for selecting market development as a route for expansion.

> When expanding into different territories or creating new products, having a brand uniting them all under one roof is one of the best advantages a business can have.
>
> Richard Branson founder Virgin Group The Guardian Media Planet May 2015

1 To achieve economies of scale of production. This is particularly important if cost leadership is your core value proposition and it is dependent upon achieving these economies.
2 Your key competency lies with your product. For example, with technology-based products in which you have some intellectual property (IP), you need to exploit your IP by finding new markets to sell the product into within a limited window of opportunity. Most technology-based companies follow this strategy – opening up new overseas markets as existing markets become saturated – because of the high cost of developing new products. By way of contrast, many service businesses such as consultancies have been pulled into overseas markets because their clients operate there.
3 The product is nearing the end of its life cycle in the existing market and you need to develop new markets, if you can find them, to continue to grow.
4 To reduce the risk of overdependence on one market. This is particularly the case for geographic markets that might face similar economic cycles.

Any growing firm will have to find new customers, and the key to doing so is to understand the customers it already has – who they are and why they buy – and then try to find more customers with similar profiles. Many firms start out by selling locally and gradually expand their geographic base by selling regionally and then nationally. However, it is one thing to find new customers in a market that you are familiar with, but it is quite another to enter completely new markets, even when you are selling existing products or services that you know well. Nevertheless, if you want to grow you will have to do so. These new markets might be new **market segments** – the ones you originally identified but did not have the resources to target. They might be new geographical areas, often foreign markets. The low-risk option is to seek out segments in the countries that are similar to the ones you already sell to.

Trying to sell the same product or service to new market segments usually involves reconfiguring the marketing mix in some way so as to 'fine-tune' your value proposition.

Sometimes market development and **product development** might go hand in hand because the move into a new market segment may involve the development of variants to the existing product offering by altering the marketing mix or making minor changes to the product range. However, we are talking about incremental and minor changes rather than brand-new products. What is more, the move into new markets can often be undertaken in partnership with others, which reduces the risks that you face.

As we saw in Chapter 3, the structure of any new market – its customers, suppliers, competitors – and the potential substitutes and barriers to entry determine the degree of competition and therefore the profitability you are likely to achieve. Indeed the Workbook exercises from Chapter 3 can be applied to help assess the potential of any new market.

Sales agencies and franchises

One approach to market development, particularly when you need to achieve market presence in foreign distribution channels where local knowledge is important, is to appoint a local sales agent. A good agent might suggest changes to the product/service or other elements of the marketing mix to better suit local needs. Sales agents are normally paid on a commission-only basis, which means that you incur no fixed set-up costs. However, the risks you face are that your sales are not guaranteed, you have little control over the agent and you may be required to contribute to advertising and promotion. Finding an agent can be difficult enough but if, for whatever reason, they do not meet your sales targets then there is little you can do other than change your agent, if you can terminate the contract.

However, your business idea may involve you being a sales agent for another firm, selling its products/services into your geographic area, so it is worth looking at this relationship from the other side. Sales agents are self-employed and face a number of risks: insecure commission income, a time-limited and geographically constrained contract, and possible limitations on the sale of other products or services. If they do not provide you with effective promotional support or they fail to develop their product range your long-term prospects may be limited. If you are too successful, the company you deal with may be tempted to set up in business themselves. All of these things will be set out in the contract, and when the contract comes to an end, its terms can be renegotiated.

There are inherent dangers in both using and being a sales agent, particularly when there is **information asymmetry** (one party having more knowledge than another). This can make the relationship unbalanced and unstable. If the balance of power or dependence shifts too far from one party to the other, the relationship may be threatened. There must be trust based upon a mutuality of interest for any agency agreement to work effectively.

Another approach to market development is to offer individuals or local firms a **franchise** or licence to produce or sell your product or service. Franchising is a form of legal partnership. A franchise is a business in which the owner of the name and method of doing business (the **franchisor**) allows a local operator (the **franchisee**) to set up a business under that name offering their products or services. This allows the franchisee to capitalize on their local knowledge but requires them also to take on many of the business risks. Their local market knowledge and dedication are vital if the market is to be effectively penetrated. For franchisors it is a way of rolling out a business format rapidly without the need for large amounts of capital. It is popular with franchisees who are less entrepreneurial but wish to run their own business. When entering the market in another country a franchisor often appoints a Head Franchisee who will be responsible for finding other franchisees in their country.

CASE insight 8.2

USA UK

Ahmed Khan and McDonald's

Getty Images/iStockphoto/ Magone

Franchisees

A McDonald's franchise can easily take over £1 million a year. But becoming a franchisee is not cheap. It costs £200,000–500,000 – far more than most other franchises – depending upon the size and location of the restaurant, of which the franchisee must provide 25% in cash with the balance coming through a bank loan. There is also an additional one-off franchise fee of £30,000. Monthly charges include rent, based on sales and profitability

(usually between 10% and 18%), a service fee of 5% of sales plus a contribution to national marketing of 4.5% of sales. Franchises run for 20 years (most other franchises are for five), franchisees are not permitted to hold other franchises and there is a compulsory nine-month, unpaid, training programme for new franchisees. Despite the fees, the McDonald's franchise is seen as attractive because the profits earned are far higher than most restaurants and the risks are seen as lower.

Ahmed Khan left school at 18 to work in McDonald's in his home town of Southend-on-Sea. He became a supervisor and progressed until, at the age of 33, he bought his first McDonald's franchise for £240,000, using £60,000 of his own money and borrowing the balance from the bank. By the age of 44 he had five outlets in Newcastle upon Tyne:

Having worked for McDonald's, I knew what someone could achieve by owning a franchise. The most appealing thing is the near-guaranteed profits, and the potential to expand. My dream is to own 10 or 15 stores.
        Sunday Times 24 July 2011

Visit the website: www.mcdonalds.com

Question:

List the advantages and disadvantages to Ahmed of buying a McDonald's franchise.

The terms of the relationship between franchisor and franchisee are set out in the franchise agreement. Franchisors need a proven, robust business model with an infrastructure to support local franchisees. In exchange for an initial fee (anything from a few thousand to hundreds of thousands of pounds) and a royalty on sales, the franchisor lays down a blueprint of how the business is to be run; content and nature of product or service, price and performance standards, type, size and layout of shop or business, training and other support or controls. Franchisees expect a detailed operations manual and operating systems and hands-on help in their start-up. They pay all the costs of establishing the business locally. Since a franchise is usually a tried-and-tested idea, well known to potential customers, the franchisee should have a ready market and a better chance of a successful start-up. Indeed only about 10% of franchises fail. Most established franchisors are members of the British Franchise Association, which has a code of conduct and accreditation rules, based on codes developed by the European Franchise Association. Table 8.1 summarizes the advantages and disadvantages of being a franchisee and a franchisor.

Table 8.1 Advantages and disadvantages of being a franchisee or franchisor

	Franchisee	Franchisor
Advantages	• Business format proved; less risk of failure • Easier to obtain finance than own start-up • Established format; start-up should be quicker • Training and support available from franchisor • National branding should help sales • Economies of scale may apply	• Way of expanding business quickly • Financing costs shared with franchisees • Franchisees usually highly motivated since their livelihood depends on success
Disadvantages	• Not really your own idea and creation • Lack of real independence • Franchisor makes the rules • Buying into franchise can be expensive • Royalties can be high • Goodwill you build up is dependent upon continuing franchise agreement; this may cause problems if you wish to sell • Franchisor can damage brand	• British Franchise Association rules take time and money to comply with • Loss of some control to franchisees • Franchisees can influence the business • Failure of franchisee can reflect on franchise • May be obligations to franchisee in the franchise agreement

CASE insight 8.3

Flying Tiger Copenhagen (2)

DENMARK

Growth through partnership

We looked at Flying Tiger in Case insight 6.2. It is a successful price-point retailer that has added other elements to its business model. It also has both a growth and an expansion model to facilitate its rapid global roll-out. Both rely heavily on effective partnerships.

Growth model: The company's growth model envisages growth coming from four elements:

- Increasing comparable store sales growth through the introduction of new products, conducting marketing campaigns to drive up volume of purchases and the frequency of store visits.
- Increasing store penetration in existing markets by opening new stores through its expansion model.
- Geographical expansion into new markets by expanding into new territories through its expansion model.
- Increasing operating margins from scale advantage by investing in what it calls its 'corporate backbone' – its operating model – and leveraging its cost structure.

Expansion model: Tiger is owned by Zebra A/S. It has expanded by offering a 50:50 'partnership' with local partners who are offered exclusive territories that might be large cities, regions or even small countries. It stresses this is not a franchise. For example, the UK is split into four territories: South-east, Midlands, Wales and Scotland (now run by the company). These joint ventures are owned 50% by Zebra and 50% by the local partner. Zebra owns the concept and brand and supplies the products, store interior and

marketing material while the local partner is responsible for store roll-outs and day-to-day operations including staffing, training and local marketing under specific guidelines set out by Zebra. Partners are expected to have comprehensive local retail experience, know-how and networks, an ability to run a minimum of 5–10 stores and access to at least €75,000. This model has enabled Zebra to grow rapidly. It has a contractually defined exit mechanism and it is part of Zebra's strategy to take full ownership of the local operating companies when this is assessed to be more beneficial than the partner model. Some operating companies, such as the one in Scotland, are now wholly owned by Zebra.

We shall look at Tiger's operating model in Chapter 10.

Visit the websites: flyingtiger.com and corporate.flyingtiger.com/about

Questions:

1 Refer back to the Framework Worksheet or PowerPoint slide that you completed for Case insight 6.2. Using the information given in this case, complete further elements of the New Venture Creation Framework.
2 Is the Tiger growth and expansion model consistent and coherent?
3 Why is this partnership model attractive to Tiger and how is it different to a franchise model?
4 What are the advantages and disadvantages of this model to partners?

Visit www.macmillanihe.com/burns-nvc-2e to download the Framework Worksheet and PowerPoint slide.

Selling into foreign markets

Most start-ups serve predominantly national, even local markets, which is not surprising given the high proportions that are service businesses. However, increasing numbers of businesses are now selling internationally from day one. The internet has made this easier, particularly for an internet application business like Summly (Case insight 2.2), where the 'product' can be transmitted on the internet. E-commerce retailers like TruffleShuffle (Case insight 4.10) can even trade globally from inception by partnering with other firms. They use global internet retail platforms such as Amazon or eBay to sell their product, take payment by credit card and use distribution networks like FedEx.

Chinese manufacturing firms find customers and export their goods around the world by promoting themselves on Alibaba (Case insight 3.4). If your competitive advantage is based on resources located in your home country (such as cheap labour in the Chinese example), then exporting makes a lot of sense. Selling to a very small target or niche market in one country can raise issues of viability. Selling to the same niche market globally can dramatically change the equation and offer the opportunity of high profits, because of economies of scale.

There are many ways to enter a foreign market and exporting is often a low-cost, low-risk way of finding out about a market. It can take the form of spot sales – one-off sales to individual customers (TruffleShuffle – Case insight 4.11) – or partnering with other companies so as to minimize set-up costs and risk. However, if the products being sold are successful in a particular market then a greater commitment to that market will inevitably be required, meaning more costs and greater risks (see Case insight 8.4). And for businesses that need to establish a physical presence in other countries, for example, to deliver a service or product to customers, many of the barriers still exist.

Governments across the world are keen to encourage smaller firms to export. They offer a range of help and advice, including market intelligence and business opportunities in particular countries, much of which is free. They organize seminars, trade fairs and missions. Because they have their own network of contacts, government agencies can often put you in touch with potential partners or agents. Nevertheless, exporting can bring risks. It is, for example, far more difficult to recover bad debts from overseas customers. To overcome this, governments often sponsor insurance schemes that cover bad debts such as the Export Credit Guarantee Scheme in the UK. Also, if you are selling into an overseas market in local currency, there is the risk of currency fluctuations that mean the value of the transaction in your currency is not guaranteed. The answer to this is to price in your currency – something often done for small value transactions – or to 'forward purchase' the local currency, thus guaranteeing the amount you receive. This service is offered by most banks.

 Website addresses where help and advice on exporting can be obtained are included in the *Guide to UK Sources of Help, Advice, Information and Funding* on the companion website: www.macmillanihe.com/burns-nvc-2e. An additional guide for Australian readers, produced by Dr Russell Manfield, is also provided.

CASE insight 8.4

Figleaves 🇬🇧 UK

Using the internet to penetrate overseas markets

Figleaves, a UK online retailer of women's lingerie launched in 1999, has managed to penetrate one of the most difficult markets in the world – the USA. The secret of Figleaves' success when it launched in the USA was that it was already its second largest market because it sold on the internet and US women were not concerned that the lingerie they ordered came from Britain. Figleaves has negotiated a number of online marketing deals and web links to maximize the exposure its site enjoys. US deals are negotiated by a salesperson who flies out once a month from the UK. The company also has a concession within Amazon. Its 'Shock Absorber' bra was launched in the USA together with Amazon, by holding a tennis match between Amazon's founder, Jeff Bezos, and the tennis star, Anna Kournikova. One feature of the Figleaves website is the facility to purchase in a number of different currencies. Figleaves now claims to be the global leader of 'multi-brand intimate apparel e-tailers'. The website features 250 brands and more than 30,000 items of lingerie, swimwear, sleepwear, active-wear, menswear and hosiery.

Visit the website: www.figleaves.com

Question:

How important is local knowledge in penetrating an overseas market?

Another option when entering a foreign market is to form a **strategic alliance**, **partnership** or **joint venture** with another firm, whereby the partner brings different resources to the joint venture and shares the profits as well as the risks (Chapter 10). This can be a particularly effective strategy to overcome the potential deficiencies in resources and capabilities that you face as a start-up. Partners can provide vital insights into effective market entry and competitive strategies. In some developing economies, the only way to enter the market may be through a joint venture with a local firm. Used properly, strategic alliances, partnerships and joint ventures can leverage up your capabilities with limited risk.

The riskiest and most expensive option of all when entering a foreign market is direct investment. This involves the setting up of a wholly owned subsidiary which may involve simply marketing and distribution or be fully integrated into the operations of your company. Clearly this is an expensive option, normally only taken by larger companies. These different degrees of involvement in foreign markets and the increasing risk associated with them are shown in Figure 8.2. There is no prescriptive 'best' approach to internationalization and often the degree of involvement in the foreign market increases with the success of the product or service.

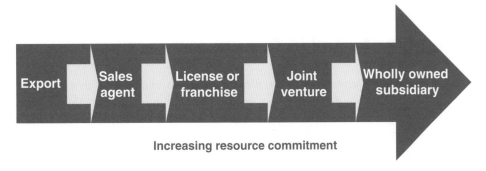

Figure 8.2 Degree of involvement in foreign markets

Zoobug   🇬🇧 UK

Exporting

Julie Diem Le was a successful 29-year-old eye surgeon with the NHS and a member of the Royal College of Ophthalmologists when she decided to start up her own business. It started when she tried to buy a pair of sunglasses for her young niece. She regularly saw young eyes damaged by bright sunshine and yet could not find a pair that provided maximum protection from the harmful rays of the sun. She also realized that few were also both fashionable and comfortable to wear. She therefore formed the idea of producing an upmarket, fashionable but ophthalmologically correct range of sunglasses for children. Having attended a government-funded start-up course in Birmingham, Julie wrote a business plan and, on the strength of the plan, obtained a £35,000 loan from NatWest Bank. She found an Italian designer to help create the first spectacles for children aged 7 to 16. A month later, in 2006, she launched her company, Zoobug, at the Premier Kids trade exhibition in Birmingham, offering the Flexibug range of sunglasses.

Within a year Julie was selling more than 2,000 pairs of sunglasses a month through upmarket opticians and stores like Selfridges. But things rarely go according to plan, and she had to adjust both her prices and target age range downwards as she discovered what the market actually wanted. Also, two summers of poor weather in the UK convinced her that she needed to sell the sunglasses overseas if she was to do well. She funded this with another £60,000 loan. In 2008 she added a range of optical frames for children aged 2 to 12 to her product portfolio, launching them at an exhibition in Milan. The sunglasses are made in Italy and the Far East. By 2009, sales of optical frames outstripped those of sunglasses and Julie was selling sunglasses and optical frames in 20 countries, eight through official distributors. France was her biggest market, ahead of the UK. In 2012, the brand was chosen to produce the official kids' sunglasses collection for the London Olympics (2012).

It was helpful that I started with sunglasses because it meant I had to look overseas for new business because there wasn't any sun in Britain. So I already had distributors in place overseas when the recession began. If we just relied on the British market, we wouldn't exist … It is really hard work. When you first approach it, it is fun and you don't really know what is involved so you go in there with a lot of bravado. When you get down to the nitty gritty, this industry is all about building relationships, and you have to fulfil your promise every time in stock, distribution and supply … I'm glad I did it. The experience has taught me a lot about business which I could never learn in a book.

Sunday Times 24 May 2009

Zoobug's website now generates 10% of sales but the company also sells in the UK through stores like Selfridges, Harrods and Igloo as well as 300 British opticians. It also sells through Amazon. Zoobug continues to sell strongly overseas and plans to further expand its overseas presence. In 2015 it joined with eye wear 'brand partners' Mondottica to help it with design and with gaining worldwide distribution.

Visit the website: www.zoobug.co.uk

Questions:

1   What are the advantages and disadvantages of exporting for Zoobug?
2   What are the problems it brings?

Evaluating potential in foreign markets

Just as with any new market, it is important to undertake a thorough market and country analysis before deciding to get involved in a foreign market with any degree of investment (anything beyond a sales agent). You are assessing the opportunities there but also the risks you will face. You need to undertake an economic analysis of the environment of the country – domestic demand, local laws and regulations, government policies, exchange rates, related and supporting industries and so on. Try using the PESTEL analysis from Chapter 3. You can use Porter's Five Forces analysis to assess profit potential but, in addition to entry barriers, you should also consider the exit barriers you face. Exit barriers can arise from legal constraints and/or high costs associated with exit. Just as high entry barriers increase profit potential (because they discourage new competitors), high exit barriers increase the risks you face because, if you do not find the market profitable, exiting it might be expensive or even prohibited.

> Managing a hyper-growth company is like putting a rocket into space: if you are off by inches at launch, you will be off by miles in orbit.
>
> Jeff Weiner CEO LinkedIn Sunday Times 14 July 2013

Every country needs to be evaluated in its own right, and not just using strict economic criteria. Cultural differences can greatly affect consumer preferences. Some of the most economically attractive countries can prove the most difficult to penetrate. For example, China is proving particularly difficult for Western retailers. In 2013 the UK's largest supermarket, Tesco, announced that 80% of its Chinese operation would be bought by the state-run China Resources Enterprise Ltd., the country's second largest supermarket chain. Earlier that year, Germany's Metro AG announced it was pulling out of consumer electronics, and in 2012 the US Home Depot Inc. announced the closure of a number of stores across China.

Product development

Product development is usually undertaken after market penetration and often alongside market development, perhaps to reflect changes in the needs of existing customers or new customers as the firm enters new markets. It can take four forms, reflecting increasing degrees of innovation.

Product modification – This involves the modification of existing products where the changes are small and evolutionary. **Product modification** might involve changes in terms of quality, function or style so as to address any weaknesses or to suit local markets. Service levels might be improved. This is usually necessary when competition increases and other firms start to produce 'better' products. This can be a particular problem if you are pioneering a product in a market with low barriers to entry, especially if the product is developing into a commodity. However, even successful products such as the iPhone need constant modification to keep up with the competition.

Product expansion – This involves developing product variations that meet the needs of different market segments. Most businesses will start to offer a range of products or services soon after launch as they spot new market opportunities. So, examples of **product expansion** would include: a soft drinks manufacturer might start to offer 'light' variants or new flavours for a successful brand, a car manufacturer might start offering sports, estate or fuel-efficient variants of a model, or a tablet computer manufacturer might offer 7 inch and 11 inch screens.

iStock.com/ picalotta

Product extension – This is where a successful brand is extended to similar but different products or services that might be purchased by the same customers. For example, a number of chocolate bar manufacturers successfully extended their brand into ice cream. The key to success in **product extension** is having a strong brand, one that actually means something to customers, with values that can be extended to the other products. Thus Timberland, a company well known for producing durable outdoor footwear, extended its product range to include durable outdoor clothing. Virgin and Saga are good examples of brands that have been applied to a wide range of diverse products, mainly successfully, linking customers and their lifestyle aspirations. Virgin, however, rarely undertakes 'production', relying instead on partners with existing expertise. On the other hand, Mercedes-Benz is a brand that has a strong association with quality, and the company has capitalized on this by producing an ever wider range of vehicles, always being able to charge a premium price for its product. This has allowed it to move into new and different segments of the vehicle market.

Completely new products – Although normally associated with the end of a product life cycle, you might introduce completely new products simply because you spot new market opportunities. They might be innovative products to either replace or sell alongside your existing product range. This is most successful when you have built up a loyal customer base and you have a close relationship with customers – a customer focus – and a good reputation for quality or delivery that can be built upon. A customer-focused firm will have an advantage in developing new products because, if it understands how its customers' needs are changing, it ought to be able to develop new products that meet them. What is more, if there is a relationship of trust, customers are more likely to try your new product, provided of course they perceive a need for it. The key to this strategy, therefore, is building good customer relationships, often associated with effective branding. For example, Apple started with computers but moved into tablets, smartphones and smartwatches as mobile technology became increasingly important.

One advantage of product development over market development is that it might be more cost-effective to increase the volume of business with existing customers than it is to go out looking for new ones. What is more, good relationships often result in customers becoming product advocates, bringing in new customers and even being willing to help with product development. However, developing new products, even for existing customers, can be expensive and risky. Product development must be grounded firmly in the needs of the existing market. Even then, if done too rapidly, it can mean resources are spread too thinly across an unbalanced portfolio.

CASE insight 8.6

Mind Candy and Moshi Monsters UK

New product development risk

Risk taking is a recurrent theme in Michael Acton Smith's life. He was almost suspended from school for organizing a betting ring on school football games. His favourite book, *The Newtonian Casino*, is about college students who tried to beat the house by having microprocessors hidden in their shoes. His first job after university was with Goldman Sachs, with whom he hoped to become a market trader. Michael always wanted to make money, as a child trying to breed chickens and koi carp, putting on BMX shows and producing a magazine.

A lot of people approach life being very afraid of risk, always erring on the side of caution, and I think that's very sad. Only by putting yourself out there and getting out of your comfort zone do you grow as a person.

Michael met Tom Boardman at university in the UK. Both started out in full-time employment but wanted to launch their own business based on ideas they had for gadgets and gifts. That did not happen until 1998 when they were both in their early twenties. They decided to raise money for their venture by taking part in medical trials for a new drug and borrowing £1,000 from Michael's mother. Working out of a rent-free attic, they started the online gadget and gift retailer Firebox.com. The business really took off when they offered a novelty chess set made of pieces that doubled as shot glasses. Firebox.com continues to sell a diverse range of obscure but 'cool' novelty products. However, by 2004 Michael was bored and wanted to develop something different. He secured £10 million in backing to set up another company called Mind Candy whose first project was an online-offline game called Perplex City – a global treasure hunt with £100,000 buried somewhere in the world and clues given in various media such as websites, text messages, magazines, live events and so on. The game received critical acclaim, being nominated for a BAFTA in 2006, but it failed to catch on and ate through money. With only £1 million left, the second project was make or break.

In 2007 he launched Moshi Monsters, an online, interactive, cartoon-based world using tiny digital pet monsters that children could nurture. Players, typically aged between 6 and 12, pick one of six pet monsters and then travel around Monstro City completing puzzles to earn 'rox', the local currency that they use to improve the monster's home. While doing this, children can chat, upload stories and share drawings. It has been likened to a Facebook for kids. It proved to be a great success. By 2012 it had over 80 million players around the world and had expanded offline into a range of spin-offs such as toys, books, phone apps, a kids' magazine, a Nintendo DS video game, a music album, membership and trading cards and many other things children can purchase. Turnover in 2012 was £46.9 million. The business model involves membership subscriptions, but it is the associated merchandise that generates around half of Mind Candy's revenue. By 2013, Moshi Monsters characters had become the most licensed property in the UK. In December 2013, *Moshi Monsters: The Movie* was released and Mind Candy was estimated to be valued at £200 million.

Both the children's games market and the online gaming market are notoriously fickle, and the question was whether Michael could continue to refresh Moshi Monsters with new ideas quickly enough. To help do this he set up Candy Lab, an ideas incubator, described as a 'cross between Xerox Park and Willy Wonka's chocolate factory with new types of toys, new types of brands and new mobile games'. Michael's ultimate vision was to 'build the largest entertainment brand in the world for this new digital generation of kids'. He believed he had a blueprint for launching new games: start with the website and then branch out into merchandising, music and video.

The bets you make are much smaller. The lead times are much shorter and the amount of capital you have to invest to find out if it's a hit or a loss are much lower.
Sunday Times 8 July 2012

However, company results were set to disappoint. In 2014 Mind Candy reported a loss of £2.2 million for the previous year, resulting from falling revenues from its Moshi Monsters licensing business – the movie had not been as successful in the USA as it was hoped – and the firm's significant investment in mobile apps. Later that year Michael Acton Smith stepped down as CEO, saying he wanted to focus on a 'more creative role' within the company rather than its day-to-day running. He became Chairman and Creative Director. Ian Chambers took over as CEO. Analysts said the company had been slow to adapt to the mobile games market, in particular the 'freemium' business model – the approach that gives away products for nothing, but encourages small payments within an app or other type of game. In 2012 Acton Smith had teamed up with Alex Tew to launch Calm in the USA (see Case insight 2.13).

Despite slashing over one-third of its staff in 2015, Mind Candy's pre-tax losses were £10.9 million and its 2015 accounts warned that its future was threatened if it was forced to repay its debt. They revealed that turnover had peaked in 2012, and had tumbled to £7.1 million, showing a particularly steep decline in licensing and sales of products such as toys based on its games (down from some £5 million in 2014 to just over £1 million). Mind Candy does not have the cash to repay £6.5 million of high-interest loans from start-up lender, Triplepoint, due in 2017, and is therefore hoping for the terms to be changed. The company is hoping for a recovery based on its new game, Petlandia, and a relaunch of Moshi Monsters, but if revenues do not come in as expected it may require a further cash injection. Candy Lab was closed in 2017. The company's future is very uncertain.

Visit the website: mindcandy.com

Questions:

1 How did the company get into the latest situation and what options are now open to it?
2 What lessons do you learn from this case about product development in this industry?
3 What lessons do you learn about financing a new or growing venture?

Developing a product portfolio

As you develop more product/service offerings (value propositions for different markets) you will need to develop different marketing strategies for each one. One of the reasons for this is that product/service offerings, like markets, have a life cycle (see Figure 3.1 on page 73) and strategies have to be modified to fit with their place in that life cycle. So, for example, McDonald's has a different marketing mix for its products in developing countries, where it is at the 'completely new' or 'emerging' phase of its life cycle, compared to the USA, where it is a 'mature' offering.

The added complexity of having a portfolio of different offerings, each at a different stage of their lives, can be handled using a technique adapted from the Growth Share Matrix. This is also known as the 'Boston matrix' after the Boston Consulting Group that developed it. Figure 8.3 shows the adapted matrix, with the vertical axis measuring market attractiveness – the growth and profit potential (rather than historic growth rate) of the market. This is more appropriate for a start-up, particularly ones entering or even creating a new market. The horizontal axis measures the strength of your product/service in this market – its sales, relative market share and so on. You launch a product/service into an attractive market (otherwise why do it?), but you are likely to be weak in the market. This is called a 'Problem Child'. Sometimes the market proves to be unattractive – then its life is very short as it becomes a 'Dog'. More often, if the market continues to be attractive, sales will grow and your market position will strengthen. This is called a 'Star'. Eventually, however, the market will mature, becoming less attractive, and your product/service will become a 'Cash Cow' – market leaders with a lot of stability but little additional growth because they are at the end of their life cycles.

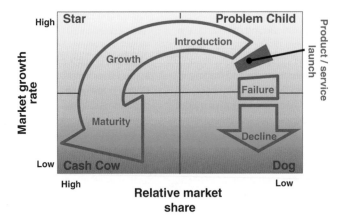

Figure 8.3 Growth Share Matrix
Source: The Boston Consulting Group (BCG). Reproduced with permission.

Different business skills are valued at different points in the matrix. Entrepreneurial skills are of most value in the Problem Child phase. Once the product is in its mature phase it needs to be managed as a Cash Cow – milked for all the **cash flow** it can generate. That means high levels of efficiency are needed, probably achieved through a high degree of control and direction. The Cash Cow is likely to be best managed by an accountant. And, if we are to characterize the management discipline needed to manage the Star, it would probably be marketing. In other words, as the product works its way around the matrix the imperatives of management change. In a one-product company this presents a challenging but manageable problem. In a multi-product firm the problem is more complex.

There are a number of measurement issues with the framework. How do you define your market so that you can measure market share or market growth? You might use just one factor on each axis or a number of them weighted in some way. Nevertheless, the problem of measurement remains. The Growth Share Matrix is therefore probably best used as a loose conceptual framework that helps to clarify complexity. Anything that simplifies complexity and therefore helps our understanding must be of value.

Marketing strategy and product portfolios

The Growth Share Matrix allows us to make some broad generalizations about **marketing strategy** for product/service offerings in the different quadrants. These are shown in Figure 8.4. If you can place the product/market offering within its life cycle on the matrix, these would be the elements of marketing strategy you would expect to see, all things being equal. But remember that while this framework reflects product life cycles, it does not reflect the **value disciplines** or **generic marketing strategies** outlined previously, which need to be superimposed on them. Nevertheless, as a product nears the end of its life and becomes a Cash Cow, it is more likely to be on its way to becoming a commodity and therefore having to sell on price.

STAR	PROBLEM CHILD
Invest for growth	**Develop opportunities**
• Penetrate market	• Be critical of prospects
• Accept moderate short-term profits	• Invest heavily in selective products/services
• Sell and promote aggressively	• Specialize in strengths
• Expand geographically	• Shore up weaknesses
• Extend product range	
• Differentiate product/service	
CASH COW	**CASH DOG**
Manage for earnings	**Generate cash**
• Maintain market position with successful products/services	• Monitor carefully – judge when to discontinue
• Differentiate products/services to keep share of key segments	• Live with low growth
• Prune less successful products/services	• Improve productivity
• Stabilize prices, except where a temporarily aggressive stance is required to deter competitors	• Reduce costs
	• Look for 'easy' growth segments

Figure 8.4 Strategy implications of the Growth Share Matrix
Source: based on The Growth Share Matrix, The Boston Consulting Group (BCG).

The Growth Share Matrix also allows us to present complex information more understandably, particularly when linked to forecasting future market positions and the strategies involved in getting there. For example, Figure 8.5 represents a hypothetical three-product portfolio. The size of each circle is proportional to the turnover each achieves. The darker circles represent the present product positions, and the lighter circles represent the positions projected in three years' time. The portfolio looks balanced as long as product C continues on its upward trajectory. The diagram can be used to explain the strategies that are in place to move the products to where they are planned to be (including the possibility of eliminating product C if the launch fails). Again, one essential added complexity relates to the generic marketing strategies. If products A and B are commodities, selling mainly on price, with low margins under intense pressure, this has implications not only for strategy but also for the cash flow available to invest in product C, particularly if this is a niche market product needing heavy investment. This might mean that rather than succeed, this product might fail and have to be killed off.

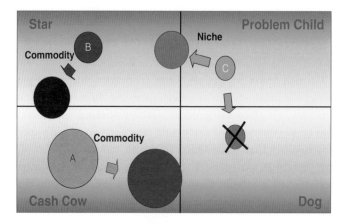

Figure 8.5 *Presenting strategy using the Growth Share Matrix*
Source: based on The Growth Share Matrix, The Boston Consulting Group (BCG).

Product modification, extension and expansion opportunities can also be represented in the Growth Share Matrix. An example of this is shown in Figure 8.6. The range of products represented as Cash Cows might be expanded or used as a basis for developing product extensions. Again, this can be a useful visual aid to understanding strategy options.

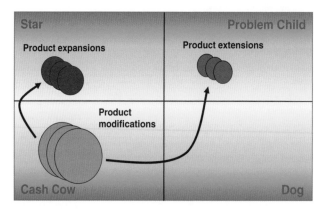

Figure 8.6 *Product development options shown on the Growth Share Matrix*
Source: based on The Growth Share Matrix, The Boston Consulting Group (BCG).

Cash flow and product portfolios

The structure of the product portfolio has implications for your cash flow. The Problem Child consumes cash for development and promotional costs at a rate of knots, without generating much cash by way of revenues. The Star might start to generate revenues but will still be facing high costs, particularly in marketing to establish its market position against new entry competitors. It is therefore likely to be cash neutral. Only as a Cash Cow are revenues likely to outstrip costs and cash flow likely to be positive. There are two kinds of Dogs. One is a cash dog that covers its costs and might be worth keeping, for example if it brings in customers for other products or services or it shares overheads. The other is the genuine dog which is losing money – both in cash flow and profit terms – and should be scrapped. It is from this model that phrases like 'shoot the dog', 'invest in stars' and 'milk the cow' came. These implications are shown in Figure 8.7.

> Fast growth normally means being unprofitable because you have to invest heavily in staff and marketing. Then there is aiming to be profitable and living within your means, which means you are not going to grow. That's the classic tightrope for technology businesses.
>
> William Reeve co-founder Loveflim Sunday Times 2 April 2017

Ideally you should have a balanced portfolio of product/service offerings so that the surplus cash from Cash Cows can be used to invest in the Problem Children. However, that situation may take many years to achieve. These surplus funds can be used almost as venture capital to invest, selectively, in new products and services. This ideal firm – if it exists – is self-financing. The problem that arises with an unbalanced portfolio is that there is either a surplus of cash (no new products) or a deficit (too many new products). If you have too many Problem Children and Stars in your portfolio (too many good, new ideas), then you will require cash flow injections which will only be forthcoming if you can either borrow the capital or raise more equity finance.

STAR			PROBLEM CHILD		
Revenue	+ + +		Revenue	+	
Expenditure	− − −		Expenditure	− − −	
Cash flow	neutral		Cash flow	− −	
CASH COW			**CASH DOG**		
Revenue	+ + + +		Revenue	+	
Expenditure	− −		Expenditure	=	
Cash flow	+ +		Cash flow	neutral	

Figure 8.7 Cash flow implications of the Growth Share Matrix
Source: based on The Growth Share Matrix, The Boston Consulting Group (BCG).

CASE insight 8.7

 Crocs™ USA

Niche product life cycles

The ubiquitous Croc can be found in most of the countries around the world. It has been estimated that about 1 person in every 500 on the entire planet has bought a pair. The Colorado-based company was founded in 2002 by George Brian Boedecker Jr. and two friends to produce and distribute a plastic clog-like shoe,

now available in all the colours of the rainbow, at a relatively cheap price. It was an instant success at the Florida Boat Show, where it was launched. It sold 76,000 pairs in its first year and 649,000 in its second year. The brightly-coloured Crocs are made from Croslite, a closed cell resin that forms itself to the wearer's feet. It is durable, soft, lightweight, non-marking and odour resistant. Originally manufactured by Foam Creations, a Canadian company that Crocs purchased in 2004, it is now manufactured in Mexico, Italy, Romania and China.

Crocs was a 'fairy-tale' entrepreneurial story, if the press were anything to go by in the early days. *Business 2.0* magazine (3 November 2006) summarized the story:

> *Three pals from Boulder, Colorado, go sailing in the Caribbean, where a foam clog one had bought in Canada inspires them to build a business around it. Despite a lack of venture capital funding and the derision of foot fashionistas, the multicolored Crocs with their Swiss-cheese perforations, soft and comfortable soles, and odor-preventing material become a global smash. Celebrities adopt them. Young people adore them. The company goes from $1 million in revenue in 2003 to a projected $322 million this year [2006]. Crocs Inc.'s IPO [Initial Public Offering] in February was the richest in footwear history, and the company has a market cap of more than $1 billion.*

The company went public in 2006 with a hugely successful $200 million stock market float (the biggest float in shoe history). Its initial strategy can be summarized as selling a relatively cheap product to as many people as possible, as quickly as possible. The company used the money to diversify and acquire new businesses, such as Jibbitz, which made charms designed to fit Crocs' ventilating holes, and Fury Hockey, which used Croslite to make sports gear. It built manufacturing plants in Mexico and China, opened distribution centres in the Netherlands and Japan, and expanded into the global market place. A foray into Croslite clothing in 2007 fell flat and was quickly scaled back. The company liquidated Fury Hockey in 2008.

And herein lies the paradox. Popularity breeds contempt in the fashion business. Arguably, the backlash started in 2006, almost as soon as the company went public, with a *Washington Post* article that said: 'Nor is the fashion world enamored of Crocs. Though their maker touts their "ultra-hip Italian styling", lots of folks find them hideous.' A blog named 'I Hate Crocs.com' followed Croc opponents. The shoes and those who wore them – from US ex-President George W. Bush to Michelle Obama and stars such as Al Pacino, Steven Tyler (Aerosmith) and Faith Hill – became objects of satire on US television shows, and by 2009 over 1.4 million people had joined a Facebook group which had the sole purpose of eliminating the shoes. The site even featured a ritual Croc burning.

Nevertheless, in 2008 Crocs was ranked by the NPD Market Research Group as the number-one casual brand in the athletic specialty sporting goods channel for men, women and children. However, having had a bumper year in 2007, the company incurred a $185 million (£113 million) loss in 2008 and had to cut 2,000 jobs. The business suddenly began to look very fragile. In 2008 the company replaced chief executive Ron Snyder, who had been at college with the company's founders, with John Duerden, an industry veteran who ran a consulting firm focused on brand renewal. He believed there was life yet in Crocs and what the company needed was new products to which he could extend the brand.

By 2009 the company was stuck with a surplus of shoes it could not sell and a mountain of expensive debt. The new business lines it had purchased – often at a premium – failed to prosper. As a result, the share price plummeted. By this time the company produced a range of different products, mainly plastic clogs and sandals but also a range called 'Bite', aimed at the golf market. The problem was that Crocs were hitting saturation point and the company had failed to successfully diversify. With a nearly indestructible product and about 1 in every 500 people owning a pair, how many more could the company sell? And the company had invested enormous amounts into meeting a demand that had seemed endless but later seemed ridiculous because the shoe's ubiquity had put off even the most ardent Crocophile. In May 2010, *Time* magazine rated Crocs as one of the world's 50 worst inventions.

But behind the scenes the company brought in Italian designers and started producing a new range of attractive Crocs, albeit at much higher prices than the original clogs, that celebrities such as Brad Pitt, Ryan Reynolds and Halle Berry, once more started wearing. These new shoes and sandals played to the strengths of the Croslite material from which the sole was made and targeted mainly beach and boat wear ('so light, they float' – 'vents let air and water flow through' – 'grooved rubber outsole improves grip'). As well as expanding their range of shoes, Crocs diversified into retailing by opening their own branded stores. And just to prove that the fashion business can be fickle, in 2011 Crocs sold $1 billion (£630 million) worth of shoes, with one-third of the revenue coming from sales of the original clogs. The 'I Hate Crocs.com' blog gave up and closed in that year. Pondering the turnaround and the ugliness of the original Crocs, *Sunday Times* (22 April 2012) said:

> *In the history of retail, has a brand ever thrived so well on adversity? It seems the more the loathers loath them, fans go wild. While for under-10s (a core market)*

they're a straightforward sell, grown-up clog wearers appear torn between love and hate.

It seems that having an ugly product polarizes opinion and this can give a brand its uniqueness. But Crocs continued to have volatile financial performance. In 2014 it announced a restructuring plan, streamlining its operations, scrapping underperforming brands, closing 100 stores and eliminating 180 jobs, half at its headquarters. As a result sales dipped but profits improved in 2017.

Visit the website: www.crocs.com

Questions:

1. From the information given in the case, use the Framework Worksheet or PowerPoint slide to complete as many elements as you can of the New Venture Creation Framework.
2. Where is the original Crocs clog now in its life cycle? How sustainable are future sales?
3. How did Crocs grow its sales?
4. What went wrong at Crocs and how was it put right?

Visit www.macmillanihe.com/burns-nvc-2e to download the Framework Worksheet and PowerPoint slide.

Using diversification to achieve market dominance and reduce risk

Diversification involves moving away from core areas of activity into completely new and unrelated product/market areas. While it is central to the process of corporate evolution, it is only something to be undertaken after very careful consideration, because it is high risk. Developing either new products or new markets is always risky. Developing both at once is even riskier – akin to another start-up. And it has been suggested that a strategy of diversification has probably caused more value destruction than any other type of corporate strategic decision. What is more, it has been shown that **conglomerates** – diversified companies with interests in a range of different industries – that are quoted on the stock exchanges create no additional shareholder value by being diversified (see Academic insight 8.1). Indeed they often trade at a discount on the value of their component parts because of their complexity.

Despite the risks, growing firms often seem to 'diversify', so the question is why? The answer probably lies in two parts. The first is to gain market dominance in newly emerging markets or industries where market and industry structures are still being formed. They do this as a way of gaining market dominance quickly by moving into related areas, often through acquisitions – simultaneously developing new products and markets. Most importantly, it is a way of defining and redefining the scope of any newly emerging industry, for example in technology. It is therefore worth considering whether your start-up involves disruptive innovation, market paradigm shift or new-to-the-world industries (quadrants 4, 5 and 6 in Figure 2.1 on page 37). The risks associated with diversification can be reduced if it is done in incremental moves, constantly bundling new products and services while extending the newly developing market.

Incremental diversification is generally into related areas, where you have some product or market knowledge and/or expertise. **Related diversification** is therefore less risky than **unrelated diversification**. However, the distinction between related and unrelated areas is

ACADEMIC insight 8.1

Sticking to the knitting

MACMILLAN AUSTRALIA

A focus on core business at corporate level was emphasized in the 1980s by researchers (e.g. Abell, 1980). A firm's core business is the one in which it has a distinct advantage by adding the greatest value for its customers and shareholders. Many studies have showed that firms that are more focused on their core business perform better than diversified ones (e.g. Wernerfelt and Montgomery, 1986). This was popularized by Peters and Waterman (1982) as 'sticking to the knitting' – not straying too far from your core competencies or customers. Although some studies were subsequently disputed (e.g. Luffman and Reed, 1984; Michel and Shaked, 1984; Park, 2002), Peters and Waterman (op. cit.) concluded:

> The most successful [companies] are those that diversified around a single skill … The second group in descending order, comprise those companies that branch out into related fields … The least successful are those companies that diversify into a wide variety of fields. Acquisitions especially among this group tend to wither on the vine.

Nevertheless, several studies have found that diversification is associated with improved performance up to a point, after which continued diversification is associated with declining performance (e.g. Palich et al., 2000). Grant (2010) suggests that diversification has probably caused more value destruction than any other type of strategic

decision. He describes diversification as being 'like sex: its attractions are obvious, often irresistible. Yet the experience is often disappointing. For top management it is a mine field.'

Developments in financial theory in the 1970s, in particular the Capital Asset Pricing Model (CAPM), also showed that conglomerates did not create shareholder value in stock markets by reducing risk (Levy and Sarnat, 1970; Mason and Goudzwaard, 1976; Weston et al., 1972). This is because diversification does not reduce **systematic risk** – that part of risk associated with how the share price performs compared to the overall market (measured by the company's beta coefficient). Shareholders can simply buy shares in undiversified companies representing the diversified interests of the conglomerate. This spreads their risk, probably with lower transaction costs. Therefore, at the corporate level diversification does not create shareholder value. Indeed, conglomerates often trade at a discount on the value of their component parts because of their complexity.

Abell, D.F. (1980) *Defining the Business*, Hemel Hempstead: Prentice Hall.

Grant, R.M. (2010) *Contemporary Strategic Analysis*, 7th edn, Chichester: John Wiley & Sons.

Levy, H. and Sarnat, M. (1970) 'Diversification, Portfolio Analysis and the Uneasy Case for Conglomerate Mergers', *Journal of Finance*, 25.

Luffman, G.A. and Reed, R. (1984) *The Strategy and Performance of British Industry*, London: Macmillan.

Mason, R.H. and Goudzwaard, M.B. (1976) 'Performance of Conglomerate Firms: A Portfolio Approach', *Journal of Finance*, 31.

Michel, A. and Shaked, I. (1984) 'Does Business Diversification Affect Performance?', *Financial Management*, 13(4).

Palich, L.E., Cardinal, L.B. and Miller, C.C. (2000) 'Curvilinearity in the Diversification–Performance Linkage: An Examination of Over Three Decades of Research', *Strategic Management Journal*, 22.

Park, C. (2002) 'The Effects of Prior Performance on the Choice between Related and Unrelated Acquisitions', *Journal of Management Studies*, 39.

Peters, T.J. and Waterman, R.H. (1982) *In Search of Excellence*, London: Harper & Row.

Wernerfelt, B. and Montgomery, C.A. (1986) 'What is an Attractive Industry?', *Management Science*, 32.

Weston, J.F., Smith, K.V. and Shrieves, R.E. (1972) 'Conglomerate Performance Using the Capital Asset Pricing Model', *Review of Economics and Statistics*, 54

> Capital needs to be deployed into areas where you are able to reap the highest returns. If a business segment isn't successful you need to be able to quickly divert valuable capital … There is no point in purchasing a business if you lower your return on equity.
>
> Adam Schwab founder

not always clear, shading into grey particularly in the areas of rapidly developing new technologies in which new markets are being created where none existed before. There are three types of related diversification. When companies move into complementary or competitive areas, it is called **horizontal integration**. When companies move into their supply chain, for example to become a manufacturer, it is called **backwards vertical integration**. When they move into their distribution chain, for example to become a retailer, it is called **forwards vertical integration**.

However, it is the speed of the simultaneous product and market development that is significant. As we saw in Case insight 3.8, five of the most successful entrepreneurial companies of a generation – Apple, Amazon, Facebook, Google and Microsoft – have adopted strategies of rapid related diversification that are probably starting to redefine their business scope – linking hardware, software and internet services. This is happening through a combination of organic market development, internal product/service development and external acquisitions. Their moves into new areas have been incremental, bundling additional services to sell to existing customers, finding out about market acceptance of their new products experimentally, a form of market testing. Often they have used acquisition to buy new customers as well as new services. Incremental, related diversification means lower risks. It is also a way of mitigating the risks of introducing disruptive innovation by using an incremental approach to test markets and obtain product/service and market information.

Typically the product/market matrix in Figure 8.1 has been used to show increasing risk as a business moves away from its core business of existing products and markets. However, there is an area in the centre of the product/market matrix where many growing entrepreneurial businesses may have a competitive advantage, facing lower risks than larger, more bureaucratic competitors because they are able to handle continuous market-related changes. This is shown in Figure 8.8 as the twilight zone of risk. It is often the way new industries or markets are created – by bundling new combinations of products with markets. This is where a good understanding of customer needs, combined with mechanisms for market testing, mitigates what might otherwise be called risky diversification.

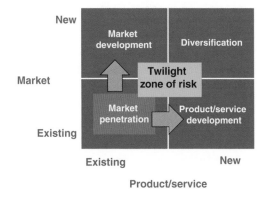

Figure 8.8 The twilight zone of risk

Brompton Bicycle UK

Growth strategies

The quirky Brompton folding bicycle was invented by Cambridge University graduate Andrew Ritchie in 1976. In 1988 he started producing small volumes of the cycle himself from a small, cluttered factory under a railway arch in West London. It became a style icon, combining practical, lightweight design, durable engineering and careful assembly. It also became a profitable niche business, selling at a price premium, perhaps because demand exceeded supply. By 2002, it still produced only about 6,000 cycles each year and employed just 24 people. That all changed in that year when Will Butler-Adams joined the firm as Managing Director aged only 28. He introduced new ways of working and budget plans, He subcontracted parts of the manufacturing process such as the manufacture of wheels and frames to other UK manufacturers, allowing more space to become available in the small factory in London.

> *The idea was to outsource the non-core stuff, so that we could then lavish more attention on the core things, and do them better. And we could make more bikes.*

Today Brompton still assembles bikes by hand in London but it has become the UK's largest cycle-maker, producing over 40,000 cycles a year and employing some 190 people. It offers seven basic models at prices ranging from almost £800 to over £2,000. Each one can be customized to suit personal requirements. Will Butler-Adams is still Managing Director, and Andrew Ritchie remains Technical Director. The company remains privately owned and all this growth has been achieved entirely organically and without outside finance.

Brompton sells bikes directly to the public through its website, where they can be customized. Brompton exported cycles from its early days (it was awarded the Queen's Award for export in 1995). Its uniqueness made it distinctive and desirable. In the UK, USA, Canada and Ireland, it also sells through bicycle retailers. In other territories, it sells to distributors who operate their own dealer networks. The cycle has been updated regularly throughout its life and has received numerous awards for innovation. Sturmey Archer gears were replaced by SRAM hubs in 2001. A long wheel base version with improved hinge joints was introduced in 2004. A super-light upgrade was introduced in 2005, featuring an alloy headset and titanium forks, rear frame, pedal bolt and mudguard stays. A new rear frame clip that allows the bike to be folded in two was introduced in 2007. The company is also expanding into other areas of business. It opened its first UK store in Covent Garden, London in 2013, adding to sites in Kobe, Shanghai, Hamburg and Amsterdam, and more recently Milan, Munich, Barcelona, Tokyo, Beijing, Chengdu and Suzhou. These stores allow it to get closer to its customers and experience what works best in selling its bikes. It also launched a bike rental scheme in 40 UK locations.

	Existing Market	New Market
New Product/Service	**Product Development** There was only one original Brompton bicycle, but the company has expanded the range, offering seven basic models at prices ranging from almost £800 to over £2,000. Each one can be customized to suit personal requirements.	**Diversification** By opening its own stores, Brompton has undertaken forward vertical diversification. It opened its first UK store in Covent Garden, London in 2013, adding to sites in Kobe, Shanghai, Hamburg and Amsterdam. Its launch in 2014 of a bike rental scheme in 20 UK locations is an example of horizontal diversification.
Existing Product/Service	**Market Penetration** Originally Brompton sold the bikes directly to the UK public, but it quickly realized that it needed to develop a network of retail outlets that stocked the bike in order to penetrate the market further. It supplied these shops directly. It still sells direct through its website.	**Market Development** Brompton exports some 80% of its bikes to 44 countries. In the UK, USA, Canada and Ireland, it sells through bicycle retailers. In other territories, it sells to distributors who operate their own dealer networks.

Figure 8.9 Brompton Bicycle growth strategies

Despite the sales growth, Will has no plans to relocate any production to the Far East to take advantage of cheaper labour costs:

> What we are doing by making the bikes in London is protecting our intellectual property. It's brilliant, and it really works. Of course we sell bikes in China, so someone could buy one and try to reverse engineer it. But it is not that simple – the complexity of our manufacturing process is such that it is not easy.
> BBC News Business 15 July 2013

Brompton's growth strategies are summarized in Figure 8.9.

Visit the website: www.brompton.com

You can see the full product range, where the bike is manufactured and view many of the worldwide Brompton events. You can also read Brompton's policies and what they are doing to achieve them.

Questions:

1 From the information given in the case, use the Framework Worksheet or the PowerPoint slide to complete as many elements as you can of the New Venture Creation Framework.
2 The bicycle is not a new invention. What role has innovation played in the growth of Brompton?
3 What strategies has the company used to grow and why have they been successful?
4 Undertake a SWOT analysis on the company. What options does Brompton have to achieve further growth? What are the risks associated with these options?

 Visit www.macmillanihe.com/burns-nvc-2e to download the Framework Worksheet and PowerPoint slide.

The second reason for diversification is the reduction of personal shareholder risk in privately owned, as opposed to publicly owned, businesses. As the owner of the business, by having business interests in a range of different markets or industries you spread the risk of a business downturn in any one. For example, the Virgin Group is a private conglomerate whose scope of business reaches into markets across the world and covers different industries from transport to media, from health and lifestyle to financial services.

However, Richard Branson withdrew Virgin from the stock market some years ago, buying back its shares. This was partly because stock markets do not value diversification. Investors can spread their risk by simply buying shares in a range of companies in different markets or industries. They do not value diversification, because it does not reduce their risk. It only adds to the complexity of managing the business and therefore publicly quoted conglomerates are usually shown at a discount. Having said that, this discount is far less when the share ownership remains largely in family hands, as is often the case in developing countries where there might be local stock market inefficiencies such as high share transaction costs and consequent low levels of share trading.

Diversification and the formation of conglomerates only adds value in companies that are owned by individuals or families where the main wealth of the individual or family is tied up in the business. It therefore remains a powerful driver of strategy for these private, unquoted companies.

Using acquisition for market and product development

Obtaining rapid market dominance can be very important for certain types of new venture. And sometimes acquiring rivals – for example Zipcar's purchase of Streetcar (Case insight 4.2) – is a way of consolidating your market position at home and buying market share in

CASE
insight 8.9

Reliance Industries

INDIA

Family-owned conglomerates

Reliance Industries is the second-largest publicly traded company in India, measured by both market capitalization and turnover. It is a family-owned and family-run diversified conglomerate that was started by Dhirubhai Ambani, the son of a poor Gujarati school teacher, who began work at a Shell petrol station in Aden. To make extra money he traded commodities and, at one time, even melted down Yemeni Rial coins so as to sell the silver for more than the currency's face value. He returned to India and started a yarn trading company in 1959 which, by the end of the 1990s, had become an integrated textiles, petrochemicals and oil conglomerate that then diversified into telecommunications and broadband, power, biotechnology, retail business and even financial services. Initially the business grew primarily through exploiting contacts with Indian politicians and bureaucrats, but in the wake of the changes caused by economic liberalization in the early 1990s, it started to do things differently – it built production sites that were competitive in global markets. Dhirubhai also popularized share ownership in India – which is where financial services

comes in – and the two holding companies now have over 3.5 million shareholders.

Dhirubhai died in 2002 and the business is now run by his two sons Mukesh and Anil. Both have MBAs from the USA and have been involved with the business for some 30 years, managing the company increasingly since their father had his first stroke in 1986 and having a strong role in forging it into the world-class company that it is today. Although little known outside its native country, Reliance has high brand recognition in India. According to a 2013 survey conducted by Brand Finance, Reliance is the second most valuable brand in India and the 2014 Brand Trust Report ranked it the ninth most trusted brand in India.

Visit the website: www.ril.com

Questions:

1 Why is Reliance such a diversified company?
2 What are the advantages and disadvantages of diversification for a privately owned business?

---

foreign markets. One of the reasons for the early success of Lastminute.com was its aggressive acquisition strategy in European markets after its launch in 1995. It purchased similar online businesses as well as a wide range of related travel and holiday firms such as Lastminute.de in Germany, Dégrif-tour in France, Destination Holdings Group, Med Hotels, First Option and Gemstone. These acquisitions helped it to quickly gain geographic market dominance as well giving it economies of both scope and scale across product categories. In this way it consolidated its brand across Europe very quickly. **Economies of scope** is the term used when less of a resource is used because it is spread across multiple activities. Also called **synergy**, this can arise when an intangible asset such as a brand can be extended across more than one product (brand or product extension). It can also arise when organizational capabilities such as sales or technological management and their related fixed costs can be extended across more products or services. The five successful technology companies highlighted in Case insight 3.8 – Apple, Amazon, Facebook, Google and Microsoft – have all adopted strategies of rapid diversification based upon product and market development alongside acquisition.

When large companies 'buy-in' product development by acquiring smaller companies it is called **corporate venturing**. It happens in a wide range of sectors from telecommunications to consumer goods to engineering, and is particularly common in the pharmaceutical industry and in the USA, where it represents a significant proportion of venture capital investment. It has been mentioned at this point because in the future this may be a way of realizing your investment by selling on your business.

We tend to be pretty adept at identifying good opportunities when they come up. We won't make an acquisition unless we know we can integrate quickly and effectively. We would never purchase a business purely for scale. It's always about profitability and return on equity.

Adam Schwab, founder Lux Group Australian Anthill anthillonline.com 22 October 2013

Clearly a growth strategy based on acquisition requires access to high levels of funding – acquiring another successful new venture in another country can be particularly expensive. It is really, therefore, only an option for high-growth businesses that have proved their business model and where economies of scale or scope are vital. It is also risky. Acquisitions have a high failure rate. The larger the acquisition compared to the acquiring company, the riskier it is because the acquired business will be more difficult to integrate. It should only be used where there is a newly emerging market and it is the only way to gain rapid market dominance in what otherwise might become a fragmented industry. An alternative to acquisition is strategic alliances and joint ventures (Chapter 10). These are less risky, do not require such high levels of funding and keep the management of each business separate. Although you have to share the profits with your partner, it can mean that you do not have to spread your management time too thinly.

Sofa-bed Factory

With one of the UK's largest furniture retailers potentially as their first customer, Piotr and Olek were better placed than many start-ups. The UK retailer would undertake the sales and marketing for them and the volumes they were talking about would take up much of the first year's production. However they realized that they still had lots of planning to undertake and that they had to make some decisions quickly. Nevertheless Piotr and Olek thought about how they might scale up the business, if it were initially successful. Their growth plans revolved around three elements:

1 Finding new retail customers to stock their products.
2 Developing an internet site that could be used, not so much for selling directly to the public, but as a sales and ordering aid for trade buyers.
3 Developing new modular units to add to the existing sofa-bed range (settees, corner units etc.), so that consumers could furnish a complete room with their sofas.

Olek also initially thought about trying to sell the steel folding mechanism he had developed to other sofa-bed manufacturers, but this idea was quickly dismissed because the mechanism was seen as one of their key competitive advantages and it might be copied by rival firms.

Initially they thought that finding new retail customers would be their absolute priority. After all, having just one customer taking most of your production was inherently risky. What happened if they switched supplier and

stopped buying from you? Having established a factory in Poland, how could you resist a demand from the customer to further cut the price of the sofa-bed (the margin was already tight)? They agreed that Piotr had to try to broaden their customer base – perhaps finding another large retail multiple in the UK but at least finding other smaller furniture outlets. This probably meant that the company had to find different fabrics to cover the sofas, so that they were not identical to those sold by the large retail multiple, It also meant that they would need to produce some promotional material and Piotr would have to visit buyers and stores in the UK himself. He could use the promotional material for trade buyers but, more importantly, also leave it for them to use in-store with their customers.

Having a good internet site was also key to this strategy, not so much for selling directly to the public, but as a sales and ordering aid for trade buyers. Piotr could use the site to demonstrate the product (particularly if they had a short video), rather than carrying a sofa-bed with him. The site could also be used for ordering, even order tracking.

However, two things were also at the back of Piotr's mind. Firstly, he had read in the industry report that, while sales of sofa-beds were increasing faster than other soft furnishings in the UK, these were more often bought as part of a set of coordinated modular units that formed suites of furniture or linked corner-units. The second thing was the keenness shown by his buyer friend in finding out whether the company produced coordinated furniture units that could be linked with the sofa-bed. Although not already developed, Olek thought that designing these sorts of units would be relatively straightforward particularly if, like the sofa-bed, they were constructed predominantly in steel.

When they contacted the buyer again, he confirmed his interest. He believed a range of linking modular units would increase the attractiveness of the sofa-beds. He indicated that if the construction were as good as the sofa-bed he would be willing to pay in the region of €250 to €300 for a two-seater unit, adding that they would still need 100 'display units'. Since the cost of producing these units would be less than a sofa-bed with its mechanical frame and foam mattress, the partners were certain that they could make a profit on this. Olek quickly produced a prototype. When he saw it the buyer confirmed his interest and, after some negotiation, agreed on a price of €270 per unit. The buyer

said that, as with the sofa-beds, he would produce monthly sales estimates. However, he also said that he needed the 100 display units on the same terms as the sofa-beds.

It seemed that in their first year of trading Piotr and Olek would have to both extend their product range and find new buyers. Then there was the small matter of setting up a factory, producing sales and promotional material and developing a website. The tasks seemed daunting.

Questions:

1   Do you agree with their growth plans? What time frame would you put on them?
2   What do Piotr and Olek still need to do before they make their final decision?

Summary and action points

8.1   Product/market development: Growth comes from scaling up your operations: market penetration, market and product/service development and/or a combination of both – diversification. Decide on the best options you have for scaling up your business should it prove successful. Reflect on the future potential and how rapid growth might affect your strategy in the first three years, and the options that you might highlight in your business plan for consideration in the future.

8.2   Develop foreign markets: Decide whether you wish to enter a foreign market within your planning horizon. There are a number of ways of doing this, each one increasing your degree of commitment and investment: to export, to appoint an agent, to license/franchise, to set up a joint venture or to set up or acquire a wholly owned subsidiary.

8.3   Strategy implications of your future product portfolio: Consider the strategic implications of developing your product/service portfolio. The position of each product/service in the portfolio has implications for the appropriate marketing strategy and the balance within the portfolio has implications for your cash flow and financing requirements.

8.4   Identify the critical success factors and strategic options for your marketing plan: If your market and product development plans fall within your planning horizon include them within your overall marketing plan, ensuring overall consistency by consolidating the critical success factors and strategic options for both the start-up and scale-up phases of your marketing plan.

Workbook exercises

 The New Venture Creation Workbook contains a digital version of these exercises that can be modified as your business model develops and builds into a draft business plan. It can be downloaded from www.macmillanihe.com/burns-nvc-2e.

8.1: Product/market development

1 Using the growth options matrix, list the strategies that you intend to use to grow the business through market and product/service development and diversification (quadrants 1, 2 and 3).

🖉 2. Product/service development	🖉 3. Diversification
🖉 Market penetration	🖉 1. Market development

2 Building on Exercise 1.2, write down your (and your group's) vision for the business.

3 If your growth strategy includes diversification (quadrant 3), jot down:

The justification for the strategy	🖉
How it will be achieved	
The time scale in which it will be achieved	
How the associated risks will be mitigated	
The critical success factors	

8.2: Develop foreign markets

If your growth strategy involves going into foreign markets, jot down:

The ways you intend to penetrate these markets over time	🖉
Any areas you need to research before deciding on the appropriate strategies	
The time scale in which it will be achieved	
How the associated risks will be mitigated	
The critical success factors	

8.3: Strategy implications of your future product portfolio

1 Using the techniques outlined in this chapter, map the product/service developments you are planning onto the Growth Share Matrix (The Boston Consulting Group, BCG).

Star	Problem Child
Cash Cow	Dog

2 Jot down the implications of these developments:

For your marketing strategy

For your cash flow and financing requirements

The time scale in which it will be achieved

How the associated risks will be mitigated

The critical success factors

8.4: Identify the critical success factors and strategic options for your marketing plan

1 Repeat Exercise 6.3 by completing the table for any new competitors you might face with these market or product development plans.

2 Repeat Exercise 7.4 by completing the template for all new market or product developments detailed in Exercises 8.1, 8.2 and 8.3 that fall within your planning time frame.

3 List the critical success factors for the growth phase of your marketing plan.

You can download the templates for Exercises 6.3 and 7.4 from www.macmillanihe.com/burns-nvc-2e.

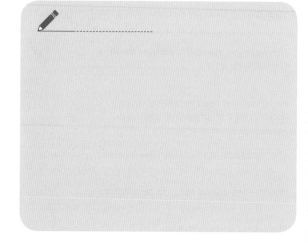

4 Reflecting on these exercises, list the strategic options for the growth phase of your marketing plan.

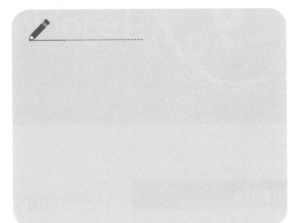

5 Produce a consolidated list of critical success factors for your whole marketing plan by combining the list from Exercise 8.4 (3) with the list you produced for your start-up phase (Exercise 7.5 (1)).

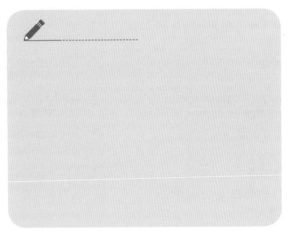

6 Produce a consolidated list of strategic options by combining the list from Exercise 8.4 (4) with the list you produced for your start-up phase (Exercise 7.5 (2)).

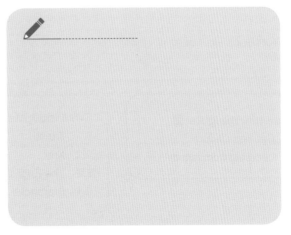

Visit www.macmillanihe.com/burns-nvc-2e for chapter quizzes and other resources.

9

Legal foundations

Contents

- Safeguarding your business idea
- Intellectual property (IP) law
- Legal forms of commercial business
- Legal forms of social enterprise in the UK
- Business failure
- Personal insolvency in the UK
- Corporate insolvency in the UK
- Corporate governance
- Summary and action points
- Workbook exercises

Learning outcomes

When you have read this chapter and undertaken the related exercises you will be able to:

- Understand the ways you might be able to safeguard your business idea
- Decide on the appropriate legal form for your business or social enterprise
- Understand and recognize the causes of business failure, the influences on them and how they interact
- Explain what options are open to a sole trader, partnership or company that is insolvent
- Understand the responsibilities of the board of directors of a company

Academic insights

9.1 Business failure
9.2 Learning from failure

Case insights

9.1 Trunki
9.2 Xmi
9.3 The English Grocer
9.4 Starbucks Australia
9.5 Alex Meisl
9.6 ZedZed.com
9.7 Cobra Beer
Sofa-bed Factory

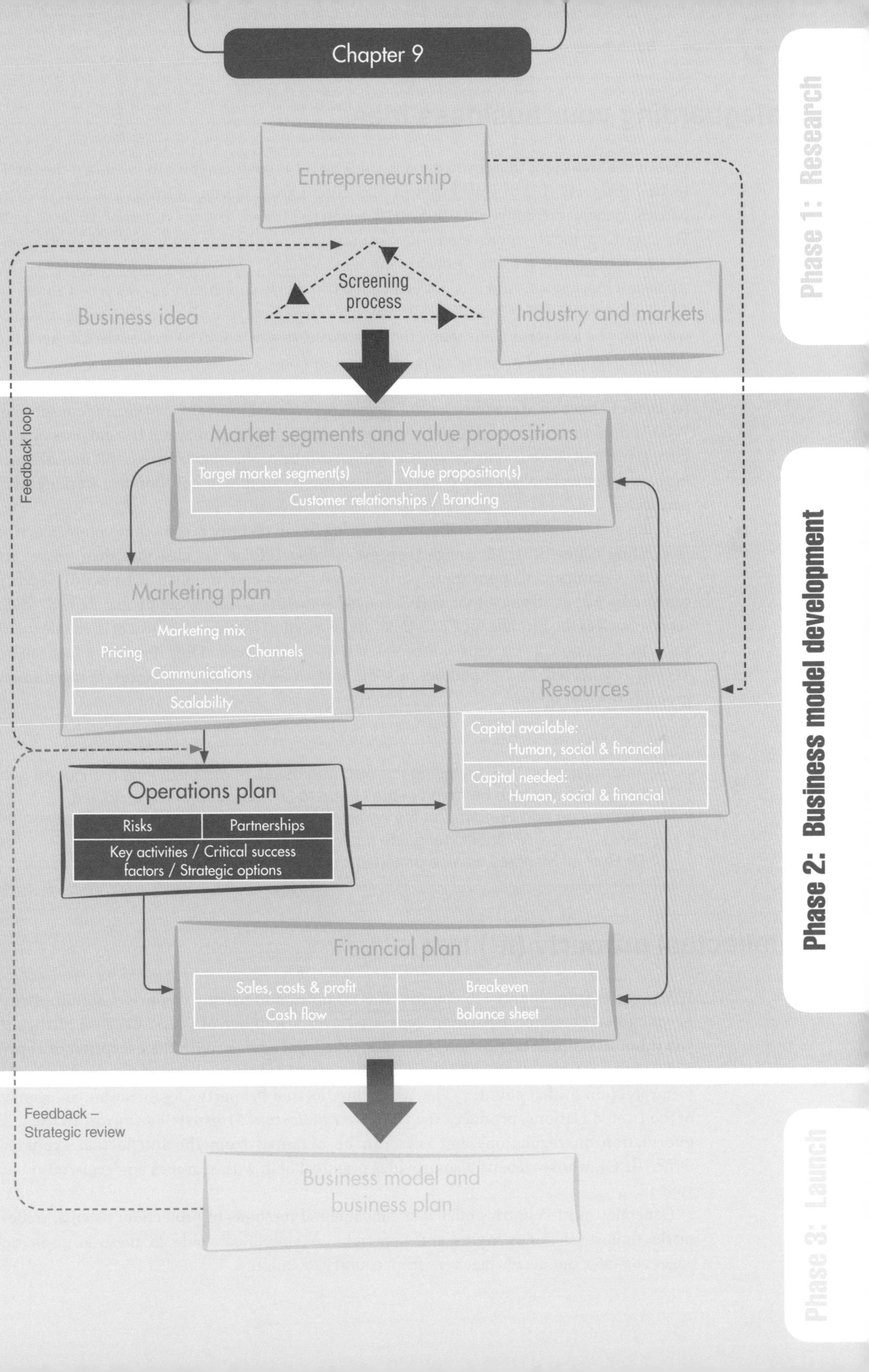

Chapter 9
Entrepreneurship
Business idea
Screening process
Industry and markets
Feedback loop
Market segments and value propositions
Target market segment(s)
Value proposition(s)
Customer relationships / Branding
Marketing plan
Marketing mix
Pricing
Channels
Communications
Scalability
Resources
Capital available:
Human, social & financial
Capital needed:
Human, social & financial
Operations plan
Risks
Partnerships
Key activities / Critical success factors / Strategic options
Financial plan
Sales, costs & profit
Breakeven
Cash flow
Balance sheet
Feedback –
Strategic review
Business model and business plan
Phase 1: Research
Phase 2: Business model development
Phase 3: Launch

Safeguarding your business idea

One of the important things you need to think about is whether you can safeguard the **intellectual property** (IP) of your business idea. There are a number of ways you can do this: patents, trademarks, copyrights, industrial design rights and, in some countries, trade secrets. For a start-up, the IP you have on your business idea may be one of the few real assets available to you, and IP remains probably the most valuable asset many technology firms like Apple or Google own. And it is not just competitors that you should be concerned about. In seeking finance for your business, you may have to expose your IP to many people, some of whom may be less scrupulous than others. In this case you would be well advised to seek the maximum intellectual property rights (IPR) you can find.

Strong IPR can also have some disadvantages. Firstly, it can be costly, not only in registering the IP but also in pursuing any infringements. What is more this can be time consuming. While your finances may be limited, those of a larger competitor may not be, and pursuing an infringement in some countries, such as China, can be problematic. Strong IPR may also get in the way for technology-based start-ups because it can inhibit collaborative working with partners.

Being first to market and establishing a strong brand identity is sometimes more effective in creating competitive advantage than establishing IPR on an idea that then misses its window of commercial opportunity, particularly for 'zero-cost' products (Chapter 6). Secrecy can also be just as strong a tool as IPR. Indeed sometimes, if they can be maintained, trade secrets, such as the formula for Coca-Cola, are more effective than any form of legal safeguard since, by definition, if you register a 'secret', it is no longer secret. Only if your product can be 'reverse engineered' by competitors in some way so as to expose its 'secret' is registration probably the best option.

> Information on IPR, including the web addresses of organizations mentioned in this chapter, can be found in the *Guide to UK Sources of Help, Advice, Information and Funding* on the companion website: www.macmillanihe.com/burns-nvc-2e. An additional guide for Australian readers, produced by Dr Russell Manfield, is also provided.

Intellectual property (IP) law

IP law varies from country to country. It is complex and usually comprises a multiplicity of individual pieces of legislation generated over a number of years. Because of this, if you think IP is important to your business, take legal advice. With the exception of copyright, if you want to protect your IP in other countries you will generally need to apply for protection in that country. The World Intellectual Property Organization, an agency of the United Nations, produces the *Guide to Intellectual Property Worldwide*. In the UK information on regulations and laws can be obtained from the Intellectual Property Office (IPO), whose website also provides practical help with searches and registration of your IP.

Generally, most countries offer four fundamental methods of protection: patents, trademarks, industrial design rights and copyright. A simplified guide to these is given on pages 267–269, but details may vary from country to country.

Patent

A **patent** is intended to protect new inventions. It covers how they work, what they do, how they do it, what they are made of and how they are made. It gives the owner the right to prevent others from copying, making, using, importing or selling the invention without permission. The existence of a patent may be enough on its own to prevent others from trying to exploit the invention. However should they persist in trying to do so, it gives you the right to take legal action to stop them exploiting your invention and to claim damages. And herein lies the problem for cash-strapped start-ups. Can you really afford the legal fees involved in pursuing such a claim? Nevertheless, the patent does allow you to sell the invention and all the IP rights, license it to someone else but retain all the IP rights, or discuss the invention with others in order to set up a business based on the invention.

The IPO says that for the invention to be eligible for patenting it must be *new*, have an *inventive step* that is not obvious to someone with knowledge and experience in the subject and be capable of being *made* or *used* in some kind of industry. If a patent is granted, it lasts for 20 years but must, in the UK, be renewed every year after the fifth year. Patents are published by the IPO online after 18 months, which makes people aware of patents that they will eventually be able to use freely once the patent protection ceases. This also can be seen as a disadvantage, and you should remember that there is no legal requirement for you to file a patent; you can always decide to keep your invention secret. This is undoubtedly cheaper but if the invention enters the public domain then you may lose your rights to it. However, in dealing with individuals, such as prospective partners, suppliers or financial backers, you can always ask them to sign a confidentiality agreement (also known as a non-disclosure agreement) which legally binds them not to disclose company secrets. You can also require employees to sign such an agreement.

The IPO lists some things for which a patent cannot be granted such as:

- A scientific or mathematical discovery, theory or method;
- A literary, dramatic, musical or artistic work;
- A way of performing a mental act, playing a game or doing business;
- The presentation of information, or some computer programs;
- An animal or plant variety;
- A method of medical treatment or diagnosis;
- Anything that is against public policy or morality.

™ Trademark

A **trademark** is a sign – made up of words or a logo or both – which distinguishes goods and services from those of competitors. The IPO says that a trademark must be *distinctive for the goods and services provided*. In other words, it can be recognized as a sign that *differentiates* your goods or service from someone else's. Once registered, a trademark gives you the exclusive right to use your mark for the goods and/or services that it covers in the country in which you have registered it. You can put the® or™ symbol next to it to warn others against using it. In the USA you can use the™ symbol without a registration process, but it limits the 'exclusivity' to your local market. To get national exclusivity for specific categories, formal registration® is required and you must prove a formal transaction has taken place within six months of registration. In all cases, trademark registration must be renewed every ten years and cannot be maintained if it is not being used on a continuous commercial basis.

As with a patent, a registered trademark may put people off using the trademark without permission and allows you to take legal action against anyone who uses it without your permission. However, in the UK a trademark also allows Trading Standards Officers or the Police to bring criminal charges against counterfeiters illegally using it. As with a patent, you can sell a trademark, or let other people have a licence that allows them to use it. In the UK, even if you don't register your trademark, you may still be able to take action if someone uses your mark without your permission, using the lengthier and onerous common law action of 'passing off'.

It is worth mentioning that registering a company name does not mean that that name is a registered trademark – company law is different from trademark law. Similarly, being the owner of a registered trademark does not automatically entitle you to use that mark as an internet domain name, and vice versa. This is because the same trademark can be registered for different goods or services and by different proprietors. Also, someone may have already registered the domain name, perhaps with its use being connected with unregistered goods or services. To search or register a domain name you should apply to an Accredited Registrar (available from the Internet Corporation for Assigned Names and Numbers).

The IPO says that trademarks cannot be registered if they:

- Describe goods or services or any characteristics of them, for example, marks which show the quality, quantity, purpose, value or geographical origin of the goods or services (e.g. Cheap Car Rentals or Quality Builders);
- Have become customary in this line of trade;
- Are not distinctive;
- Are three-dimensional shapes, if the shape is typical of the goods you are trading, has a function or adds value to the goods;
- Are specially protected emblems;
- Are offensive;
- Are against the law (e.g. promoting illegal drugs);
- Are deceptive.

® Registered design

If you are creating products or articles that are unique because they look different from anything else currently available, then you might want to protect the look by registering it as a design. A **registered design** is a legal right which protects the overall visual appearance of a product in the geographical area you register it. The registered design covers the things that give the product a unique appearance, such as the lines, contours, colours, shape, texture, materials and the ornamentation of the product (e.g. a pattern on a product or a stylized logo). It is a valuable asset that allows you to stop others from creating similar designs. It does not offer protection from what a product is made of or how it works. In the UK, **Design Right** and **Community Design Right** may also give you automatic protection for the 'look' of your product.

Registering a design gives you exclusive rights for the look and appearance of your product. This may be enough on its own to stop anyone using your design, irrespective of whether they copied it or came up with the design independently. Once a design is registered you can sell or license it and sell or retain the IP rights.

The IPO says that to be able to register a design it must:

- Be new – in the UK a design is considered new if no identical or similar design has been published or publicly disclosed in the UK or the European Union;
- Have individual character – this means that the appearance of the design (its impression) is different from the appearance of other already known designs.

© Copyright

Copyright allows you to protect your original material and stops others from using your work without permission. It can be used to protect any media:

- Literary works such as computer programs, websites, song lyrics, novels, instruction manuals, newspaper articles and some types of database;
- Dramatic works including dance or mime;
- Musical works;
- Artistic works such as technical drawings, paintings, photographs, sculptures, architecture, diagrams, maps and logos;
- Layouts or typographical arrangements used to publish a work (e.g. for a book);
- Sound or visual recordings of a work;
- Broadcasts of a work.

Copyright does not protect ideas, only how you 'publish' your ideas, for example in the case of writing, words cannot be copied. This happens automatically in most countries, which means that you do not have to apply for copyright so long as it falls within one of the categories of media that is protected, but it also means there is no official copyright register. Although not essential, you should mark the material with the © symbol, the name of the copyright owner and the year in which the work was created (e.g. © 2018 Paul Burns). Copyright owners may also choose to use technical measures such as copy protection devices to protect their material. In the UK, in addition to or instead of copyright protection, a database may be protected by the 'database right'. Trademarks can be both registered designs (for the artwork) and copyright. You can only copy a work protected by copyright with the owner's permission, even when you cross media boundaries (e.g. crossing from the internet to print).

As copyright owner you have the right to authorize or prohibit any of the following actions in relation to your work:

- Copying the work in any way (e.g. photocopying, reproducing a printed page by hand-writing, typing or scanning into a computer, and taping live or recorded music);
- Renting or lending copies of the work to the public, although in the UK some lending of copyright works falls within the Public Lending Rights Scheme and this does not infringe copyright;
- Performing, showing or playing the work in public (e.g. performing plays and music, playing sound recordings and showing films or videos in public);
- Broadcasting the work or other communication to the public by electronic transmission, including transmission through the internet;
- Making an adaptation of the work (e.g. by translating a literary or dramatic work, or transcribing a musical work or converting a computer program into a different computer language).

If you have copyright of a work you can sell or license it and sell or retain your ownership. You can also object if your work is distorted or mutilated. As with other forms of IP protection, the existence of copyright may be enough on its own to stop others from trying to copy your material. If it does not, you have the right to take legal action to stop them exploiting your copyright and to claim damages – that is if you can afford to go to court. Copyright infringement only occurs when a whole work or substantial part of it is copied without consent. However, what constitutes a substantial part is not defined and may therefore have to be decided by court action. Copyright is essentially a private right and therefore the cost of enforcing it falls to the individual.

Trunki UK

© Trunki

Registered design infringement

The Trunki is a fun suitcase that looks like an animal, designed for children. It is estimated that 20% of three-to-six-year-olds in the UK own one. It was an idea that Rob Law came up with in 1998. He protected the design through computer-registered design (CRD); however Trunki proved so successful that it attracted many imitations. In 2013 his company, Magmatic, finally won a lawsuit in the UK against PMS International, a Hong Kong company that had been selling a Trunki-style product. The UK High Court ruled that PMS's Kiddee Case breached Law's registered design rights in that the 'overall impression' created by the Kiddee Case, including the horn-like handles and clasps resembling the nose and tail of an animal, was similar to the designs underpinning the Trunki. As a result of this, Magmatic could take out an injunction preventing the sales of Kiddee Cases throughout Europe and forcing PMS to destroy remaining stocks. PMS was also liable to damages to compensate Magmatic for lost sales.

However PMS appealed against the decision and the Court of Appeal reversed the decision on Law's registered design rights in 2014. This decision was upheld by the Supreme Court of the UK in 2016. The Supreme Court found that, while the Kiddee Case had a 'number of features similar' to Trunki's CRD, it had notable differences to the original copyright such as its use of colour and having covered wheels. Lord Neuberger said he reached his decision with 'some regret' as it did appear that PMS conceived their idea as a result of seeing a Trunki. However, the appeal was 'not concerned with an idea or an invention, but with a design'. Jeremy Drew, head of Intellectual Property at RPC (a business advisory network), explained that by including specific features on the drawing for the CRD, such as dark wheels and a dark stripe along the suitcase, those elements became a core part of the specific design of the product:

Bernard Bee Trunki

© Trunki

When someone copies the case but doesn't have that contrast, it means there's one big difference between designs. You need someone to copy the product very closely to be an infringement.

Trunki had spent considerable sums of money fighting the case. What is more, the decision might have wide-ranging implications for SMEs since about one-third of designs in Europe are protected by CRD. Commenting on the decision, Law said:

We are devastated and bewildered by this judgment, not just for ourselves but for the huge wave of uncertainty it brings to designers across Britain.
The Telegraph 9 March 2016

Note: certain minor decisions reached at the UK High Court still stand. These include an infringement of the copyright in the Trunki safety notice and a breach of unregistered design rights relating to the external locking device, the method used to attach a plastic key to the strap, and the internal elasticated cross-strap and side pocket. Unregistered design rights, like copyright, are granted automatically.

Visit the website: www.trunki.com

Questions:

1 What might the implications of this case be, and how important are they for designers?
2 What do you learn from this case about protecting design?

CASE insight 9.2

© Xmi

Combating counterfeiters

Ryan Lee set up Xmi in Singapore to manufacture and sell the small, portable speakers he had developed that were capable of filling a room with high-quality music. His first product, the X-mini, was launched in 2006:

There was no other small speaker that was better than this at the time. That is why we demanded the (price) premium. Customers are willing to pay for quality.

Lee minimized the costs he faced in his new venture. Even today he operates from what used to be a bar in Singapore's central business district. He also subcontracted manufacture to companies in China, having considered companies in Indonesia and Vietnam:

Not everything can be done in these countries, and on top of that they are not even as good at assembly. So you're going to pay more for an inferior product.

Despite the high price, demand was high and the product proved successful. However, within six months Lee started receiving calls from distributors in Europe asking for a discount because they had been offered what looked like identical X-mini speakers at a much lower price. Upon investigation he found that, although these imitations had plastic casings that were identical to the X-mini, they had far poorer sound quality, different packaging and did not carry the company's serial numbers. Once he had convinced his distributors that these were fake, inferior products the problem disappeared, but it did make Lee aware that there was a black market for fake X-minis. His reaction was to change suppliers to ones with a reputation for trustworthiness. He also started to manufacture some of the highly sensitive components himself as well as splitting up components

X-mini™ CLICK 2

© Xmi

X-mini™ EVOLVE 2

© Xmi

among different suppliers. But ultimately he feels that the only way to combat these fakes is to keep one step ahead by constantly innovating and improving the product.

I'd rather throw my money to the engineers, not to the lawyers. You innovate faster than your fakes. That's how you play the technology game.

BBC News Business 25 March 2013

Visit the website: www.x-mini.com

Questions:

1 In what circumstances is safeguarding your IP through legal means worthwhile?
2 How might you combat counterfeiting through commercial means?

Legal forms of commercial business

Starting up in business is inherently risky, and how you structure your business has implications for how much risk you face personally. In most countries the three most common legal forms of business are: sole traders (almost 60% of businesses), partnerships and limited liability companies or corporations. The major difference is that only limited liability companies or corporations are legal entities in their own right and therefore offer limited liability in the event of failure. The advantages and disadvantages of these different forms are summarized in Table 9.1. In many countries a business needs a licence to operate, which can normally be obtained from the local council. In the UK certain types of business, such as those selling food or alcohol, employment agencies, minicabs and hairdressers need a licence or permit.

> ⊕ Web addresses for organizations offering relevant information on business structures, health and safety, licences and registrations, and premises requirements are in the *Guide to UK Laws and Regulations for Business* on the companion website: www.macmillanihe.com/burns-nvc-2e. This includes an interactive guide to the permits and licences you need. An additional guide for Australian readers, produced by Dr Russell Manfield, is also provided.

Table 9.1 Advantages and disadvantages of different forms of business

	Sole trader	Partnership	Limited liability company or corporation
Advantages	• Easy to form • Minimum of regulation	• Easy to form • Minimum of regulation	• Limited liability • Easier to borrow money • Can raise risk capital through additional shareholders • Can be sold on • Pays corporation tax (which can be lower than personal tax)
Disadvantages	• Unlimited personal liability • More difficult to borrow money • Pays personal tax	• Unlimited personal liability • More difficult to borrow money • Pays personal tax • Unlimited personal liability for debts of whole partnership • 'Ceases trading' whenever partners change	• Must comply with Companies or Corporations Acts • Greater regulation • Greater disclosure of information

Sole traders

This is a business owned by one individual. The individual is the business, and the business is the individual. The two are inseparable. A **sole trader** is the simplest form of business to start – all that is needed is the first customer. It faces fewer regulations than a limited company and there are no major requirements about accounts and audits, although the individual will pay personal taxes which are based upon the profits made by the business.

There are two important limitations, however. The first is that a sole trader will find it more difficult to borrow large amounts of money than a limited company. Lending institutions prefer the assets of the business to be placed within the legal framework of a company because of the restrictions then placed upon the business. It is, however, quite common for a business to start life as a sole trader and incorporate later in life as more capital is needed. The second disadvantage is that the sole trader is personally liable for all the debts of the business, no matter how large. That means creditors may look both to the business assets and the proprietor's assets to satisfy their debts. However, this disadvantage may be overcome by placing family assets in the name of the spouse or another relative.

Partnerships

Partnerships are just groups of sole traders who come together, formally or informally, to do business. As such it allows them to pool their resources; some to contribute capital, others their skills. Partnerships, therefore, face all the advantages of sole traders plus some additional disadvantages. The first of these disadvantages is that each partner has unlimited liability for the debts of the partnership, whether they incurred them personally or not. Clearly partnerships require a lot of trust. The second disadvantage is that the partnership is held to cease every time one partner leaves or a new one joins, which means dividing up the assets and liabilities in some way, even if other partners end up buying them and the business never actually ceases trading. In the UK some professions, such as doctors and accountants, are required by law to conduct business as partnerships.

Generally, if you are considering a partnership you would be well advised to draw up a formal partnership agreement. It is very easy to get into an informal partnership with a friend, but if you cannot work together, or times get hard, you may regret it. If there is no formal agreement, then in the UK the terms of the Partnership Act 1890 are held to apply. Partnership agreements cover such issues as capital contributions, division of profit and interest on capital, power to draw money or take remuneration from the business, preparation of accounts and procedures when the partnership is held to 'cease'. Solicitors can provide a model agreement which can be adapted to suit particular circumstances.

Companies and corporations

A for-profit **limited liability company** or corporation is a separate legal entity distinct from its owners or shareholders, and offers limited liability in the event of failure. It can enter into contracts and sue or be sued in its own right. It must be registered and comply with the legal requirements of a company or corporation in a particular country and is taxed separately through corporation tax (in the USA this is an election). The shareholders own the business but elect a board of directors to direct it, and they in turn appoint the management who are responsible for the day-to-day running of the business. The shares in the company or corporation can be either privately held by a small group of individuals or publicly held and traded on a stock market, in which case the additional rules of the stock market apply.

The major advantage of this form of business is that the liability of the shareholders is limited by the amount of capital they put into the business. However, banks are likely to ask for personal guarantees from the founders to get around this problem. A company also has unlimited life and can be sold on to other shareholders. Indeed there is no limit to the number of shareholders. A company or corporation can therefore attract additional risk capital from backers who may not wish to be involved in the day-to-day running of the business. Also, because of the regulation they face, bankers prefer to lend to companies or corporations rather than sole traders. Clearly this is the best form for a growth business that will require capital and face risks as it grows.

There are also some disadvantages to this form of business. A company or corporation must keep certain books of accounts and appoint an auditor. Accounts and other company information must be filed with relevant authorities on a timely basis. This takes time and money and means that competitors might have access to information that they would not otherwise see.

An internet search of *how to start a company* (or corporation) followed by the name of the country should provide you with the country-specific information you need to set up a company. The appropriate government website will give you the legislative framework, but the easiest way to actually set one up is to purchase an already registered one from the many private organizations advertising on the internet. In the UK these are called Company Registration Agents. This saves time and avoids all the tedious form filling that is otherwise required. In addition, agents will show you how to go about changing the company's name if you want to.

In the UK a company must be registered with Companies House in accordance the provisions of the Companies Acts and must file an annual return with Companies House, which includes accounts and details of directors and shareholders. Certain companies must be registered with the Financial Conduct Authority.

In the USA corporations are organized under the authority of the state as either **C Corporations** (C Corp) or **Subchapter S Corporations** (S Corp). These are broadly similar to limited liability companies. The major difference between a C Corp and an S Corp is their tax treatment. C Corps are subject to double taxation at both the corporate and shareholder level. S Corps do not pay tax; instead all profits or losses are passed through to individual shareholders. Therefore losses in a C Corp reside with the company and cannot be deducted from shareholders' other sources of income, unlike an S Corp (a limited liability company can elect for different tax treatments). Because of this, private investors tend to prefer these two legal forms if there are losses at start-up. However, most venture capital funds will not invest in S Corps because the number of investors is restricted to 100, unlike C Corps or limited liability companies, where there is no restriction. So, your planned funding structure may affect the legal framework you adopt, although a company can change its legal form later in life.

Legal forms of social enterprise in the UK

You can run a for-profit company or corporation and still have social objectives (Case insight 5.6). Many companies have them as part of their corporate social responsibility (CSR) commitments. However, many countries now have separate legal structures for what are generally called social enterprises which carry some benefits (e.g. tax or access to government funding) but equally a number of restrictions. The restrictions are usually about what can be done with the profits or assets of the enterprise and involve greater accountability.

Legislation varies from country to country. In the UK if the primary aim of your start-up is social good and *all* the profits will be ploughed back into these activities then there are six legal forms of social enterprise that offer certain advantages and disadvantages. These are summarized in Table 9.2 and details are provided on pages 275–277.

details are provided on pages 275–277.

Web addresses for organizations mentioned in this chapter and others offering help and advice on setting up a social enterprise are in the *Guide to UK Sources of Help, Advice, Information & Funding* on the companion website: www.macmillanihe.com/burns-nvc-2e. An additional guide for Australian readers, produced by Dr Russell Manfield, is also provided.

Unincorporated associations

These are informal associations of individuals that can form (and re-form) quickly – similar to sole traders or informal partnerships. They enjoy great freedom because they are not regulated. They are not registered with anybody, but they can apply for charitable status, which means they have to comply with the regulations of the Charity Commission. They can trade but cannot own assets or borrow money because an association has no legal status. However, it may be possible to set up a **trust** to legally hold ownership of property and assets for the community they are intended to benefit. Because these associations are unincorporated, each individual in the association is personally liable for any debts or loans.

Charitable social enterprises

Charitable social enterprises are set up wholly for charitable purposes that benefit the public. They must be registered with Companies House or the Financial Conduct Authority (FCA). They are regulated by Charity Commission regulations (HM Revenue & Customs in Northern Ireland and the Office of the Scottish Charities Regulator in Scotland). Charities benefit from tax and rate relief, and any surplus must be reinvested. The founder of a charity shapes its creation but not its strategic direction or operation. The charity is run by directors or trustees, who cannot be paid for their work. They shape its strategic direction.

Community benefit societies (BenComs)

Community benefit societies are incorporated industrial and provident societies (also known as **cooperatives**). The difference is that, whereas cooperatives are controlled by and set up for the benefit of their members, BenComs must have social objectives and conduct business for the benefit of their community. They are run and managed by their members, but profits cannot be distributed among members and must be returned to the community. BenComs can raise funds by issuing shares to the public and can be registered as charities. They are regulated by the FCA in the UK and must submit annual accounts. BenComs are different from cooperatives in that cooperatives operate for the mutual benefit of their members – which is not necessarily the same as the 'community' – and therefore cannot be registered as charities.

Community interest companies (CIC)

Community interest companies are essentially limited liability companies, registered with Companies House or the FCA, but with extra requirements. They can be limited by shares or by guarantee. They must demonstrate their social and environmental impact each year by issuing an annual community interest company report alongside the annual accounts. They must operate transparently and not pay directors excessive salaries. Profit distribution is also regulated; companies limited by guarantee may not distribute profits, whereas those limited by shares can do so under certain circumstances. CICs must have an asset lock, which means that profits or assets cannot be transferred for less than their full market value. People who start a CIC can steer the business as they see fit because they will be directors.

A CIC cannot be a charity. However, it is common for it to run alongside one. So, for example, it is common for a social organization to have two forms: a CIC, which runs in a business-like way while giving the community a stake in how it is run, and a charitable social

Table 9.2 The advantages and disadvantages of different forms of social enterprise in the UK

	Unincorporated association	**Trust**	**Charitable social enterprise**
Advantages	• Easy to form • Minimum of regulation • Can apply for charitable status	• Can hold assets • Can apply for charitable status	• Benefits from charitable status
Disadvantages	• Unlimited personal liability • Cannot own assets or borrow money	• Must have trust deed • Must register with Companies House • Greater regulation • Greater disclosure of information • Profits cannot be distributed	• Must register with Companies House or FCA • Surpluses must be reinvested • Trustees cannot be paid • Profits cannot be distributed

enterprise to which the CIC's profits are transferred and which decides how they are spent. This dual form can maximize tax advantages. It also means that the charity can apply for grant funding that will help to get projects up and running, while the income generated by the CIC means that the organization is not totally dependent on these grants or the goodwill of donors or government.

Charitable incorporated organizations (CIO)

Charitable incorporated organizations are a form of incorporated organization that is set up for charitable purposes and therefore reports to the Charity Commission rather than Companies House or the FCA. Like CICs they must benefit local communities and have an asset lock. They are not able to distribute profits or assets to their members. Unlike CICs which have directors, CIOs have charity trustees. CICs and charitable social enterprises can convert into CIOs.

Business failure

It may seem premature to discuss business failure before you have started your new venture but fear of failure – or more specifically a fear of the consequences of failure – can be a major influence on your decision whether or not to try out a business idea. And, as we shall outline in this chapter, there can be personal financial consequences whatever form of business your new venture takes. However, first it is worth understanding the reasons why businesses might fail and then trying to avoid those you can.

Most start-ups fail because the products or services they offer are not wanted by customers. Sometimes the founder has not researched their market adequately, relying too much on their own wants and needs rather than those of potential customers. However, they also fail because of poor execution – the founder does not have the skills or knowledge to manage the business. But there are also a myriad of unexpected external influences that cause the best run businesses to face danger. Figure 9.1 shows

BenCom	CIC	CIO
• Can apply for charitable status	• Has limited liability status • Can hold assets but must have an 'asset lock'	• Benefits from charitable status • Can hold assets but must have an 'asset lock'
• Must be registered with Companies House or FCA • Can raise funds by issuing shares • Profits cannot be distributed	• Must be registered with Companies House or FCA • Must issue annual community interest report and accounts • Profit distribution regulated • Cannot be registered charity	• Must be registered with Charities Commission • Profits cannot be distributed

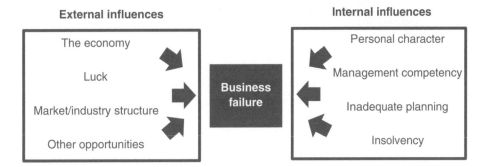

Figure 9.1 *Causes of business failure*

the main influences that can lead to business failure, gleaned from numerous academic studies (Academic insight 9.1). There are both external and internal factors that influence this, and they interact. Individually they are present in many firms, often manifesting themselves as personal or business weaknesses, but it is only when they combine and interact that the potential for failure is realized. So, timing and luck play their part.

The simple model in Figure 9.1 gives us an insight into the process of failure. What makes the small firm different from the large one is the disproportionate importance of the influence of the entrepreneur. Business weaknesses often stem from bad decisions made by the entrepreneur. These can originate from a lack of managerial competency, but they can also stem from the entrepreneurial character. However, the crisis that triggers the decline into failure is often brought about by some external factor such an unexpected change in the economy or the market place. This may lead to further bad decisions being made by the entrepreneur, for example, a decision to overtrade or borrow too much. Again this might originate from the inherent optimism of the entrepreneur – part of the reason they started up in the first place. These decisions, in turn, result in symptoms of failure such as running short of cash or declining profitability.

Insolvency – the lack of financial resources generally – is cited as a cause of business failure by many studies. However, almost by definition a failing firm is bound to have inadequate finance. Cash flow will be poor and further funding may be unavailable. However, this is usually simply a symptom of the problem rather than a root cause. The cause is more likely to be undercapitalization at start-up and subsequent overtrading (too-rapid expansion). And the root cause of this may well be the lack of management competency of the entrepreneur. Whether a cause or a symptom, insolvency (in its legal sense) is the likely consequence of business failure, and we shall return to it later in the chapter.

> A recession is essentially a time for rebalancing ... If you've got a business with either a great product or great brand or offering a great service, all that happens is a lot of things come to challenge you ... but if your business has momentum it can help.
>
> *Will King, founder King of Shaves RealBusiness 1 July 2009*

External influences and events – change generally – create both opportunities and threats. Changes in the economy can affect everyone and changes in overall consumer demand, interest rates and inflation can have a disproportionate effect on smaller firms. The recession of 2008 saw many smaller companies cease trading because of the combination of a downturn in trade and a drying up of finance to support them. However, the number of start-ups increased as people lost their jobs and were 'pushed' into self-employment. Some external influences are clearly due to sheer bad luck – 'acts of God' like a strike, fire or the loss of the major customer. A larger company might weather such events, but they can have a disproportionate effect on smaller firms. You can add to this the impact of random personal misfortune such as sickness and ill-health. But sometimes entrepreneurs make their own luck and find themselves in the wrong place at the wrong time because they decided to pursue an obviously risky course of action when they have inadequate resources.

ACADEMIC insight 9.1

Business failure

The economy – SMEs have less financial 'fat' than larger firms and have to cope with an ever-changing market and economy over which they have little control. It's little wonder then that the general economy is a major influence on closure (e.g. Berryman, 1983). Baldwin et al. (1997) found this to be *the* major external influence on closure. Everett and Watson (2004) estimated that external economic factors are associated with between 30% and 50% of SME failures.

Luck – Cressy (2006) suggested that external influences can be likened to a game of chance – an approach called **gambler's ruin** – with the entrepreneur as the roulette-wheel gambler betting resources on the outcome of each business decision they make. This model stresses 'luck' as the key determinant of the outcome, together with resource levels. The gambler with the least resources is least likely to weather a period of bad luck. This approach offers an explanation for why younger, smaller businesses are more likely to fail: they simply have less resources of any kind. It dismisses the influence of the gambler or entrepreneur and their skills and abilities on the final outcome, whether success or failure.

Market or industry structure – In reality the effect of the environment depends upon the time period, geographic area and market sector in which the firm operates. Perhaps the most significant influence on SMEs is the structure of their market or industry, called the **population ecology**, an approach originally developed by Hannan and Freeman (1977). For example, the degree of competition within an industry is influenced by what Porter calls 'Five Forces' (Chapter 3). These affect not only profitability but also, in extremis, the likelihood of failure. A small firm operating in a highly competitive market is more likely to fail than one operating in a market with low levels of competition. In Baldwin et al.'s study (op. cit.) 'competition' was the second biggest influence on closure after 'economic downturn' and just ahead of 'customer difficulties'. Berryman (op. cit.) also cited competition. Like gambler's ruin, this approach would also offer an explanation for why younger, smaller businesses are more likely to fail, but again minimizes the influence of the entrepreneur.

PhotoDisc/Getty Images

limited knowledge or education; and a resistance to advice from qualified sources.

Management competency – Much of the literature suggests that it is a lack of management competency in entrepreneurs that underpins business failures (Baldwin et al., op. cit.; Kiggundu, 2002; Knotts et al., 2003; Larson and Clute, op. cit.). In his review of some 50 articles and five books on the subject of small business failure, Berryman (op. cit.) listed a number of management deficiencies such as inability to delegate, reluctance to seek help, unawareness of the environment, inability to adapt to change and thinness of management talent, excessive drawings and pure negligence as reasons for failure. Lack of management capability and bad or untimely decision making are closely related, like chicken and egg, and both have been shown to contribute to business failure (Gaskill et al., 1993; Stokes and Blackburn, 2002). Poor financial control with inadequate or infrequent financial information, lax debtor (receivables) and/or stock (inventory) control and an inability to manage cash flow are frequently cited causes (Baldwin et al., op. cit.; Berryman, op. cit.; Haswell and Holmes, 1989; Watkins, 1982; Wichmann, 1983). The marketing problems cited are many and various, including a lack of understanding of customer needs, failure to identify target customers, and poor selling skills (Baldwin et al., op. cit.; Berryman, op. cit.; Larson and Clute, op. cit.; Watkins, op. cit.). Another major weakness cited is the typical overdependence of small firms on a small number of customers for too high a proportion of their sales (Cosh and Hughes, 1998). At the same time, some studies have shown that the wider the product range, the lower the likelihood of failure (Reid, 1991).

Other opportunities – The personal circumstances and aspirations of individuals change and other opportunities offering an attractive income, either from employment or from another business opportunity, can also persuade the entrepreneur to close the business they are currently running. This means that it may not always be the least profitable businesses that close. Gimeno et al. (1997) showed that business closure is influenced by personal factors such as the enjoyment the entrepreneur might get from self-employment, their minimum income 'threshold' and the alternatives available to them.

Personal character – Excessive optimism is a frequently cited personal characteristic associated with failure (Berryman et al., op. cit.; Larsen and Clute, 1979). On top of this can be layered the problems associated with family firms – such as nepotism (Berryman, op. cit.). These combine to produce a potent set of behavioural ingredients which might become underlying causes of failure. Beaver and Jennings (2005) found evidence of 'non-rational' behaviour contributing to business failure. Larson and Clute (op. cit.) listed the personal characteristics they found in owner-managers of failed firms. These included: an exaggerated opinion of their business competency; an over-reliance on personal opinion, intuition, emotion and other non-objective factors; inflexibility and a past (not future) orientation;

Inadequate planning – Finally, business failure has been blamed on poor planning and inappropriate strategies (Larson and Clute, op. cit.). Delmar and Shane (2003) showed that those Swedish businesses that prepared business plans were more likely to survive than those that did not. Saridakis et al. (2008) and Stearns et al. (1995) highlighted the importance of business strategy in the UK and USA, respectively; in particular, they showed that an over-reliance on inappropriate strategies such as price competitiveness was most likely to lead to failure.

Baldwin, J., Gray, T., Johnson, J., Proctor, J., Rafiquzzaman, M. and Sabourin, D. (1997) *Failing Concerns: Business Bankruptcy in Canada*, Ottawa: Ministry of Industry.

Beaver, G. and Jennings, P. (2005) 'Competitive Advantage and Entrepreneurial Power: The Dark Side of Entrepreneurship', *Journal of Small Business and Enterprise Development*, 12(1).

Berryman, J. (1983) 'Small Business Failure and Bankruptcy: A Survey of the Literature', *European Small Business Journal*, 1(4).

Cosh, A. and Hughes, A. (eds) (1998) *Enterprise Britain: Growth Innovation and Public Policy in the Small and Medium Sized Enterprise Sector 1994–97*, Cambridge: ESRC Centre for Business Research.

Cressy, R. (2006) 'Determinants of small firm survival and growth', in M. Casson, B. Yeung, A. Basu and N. Wadeson (eds) *The Oxford Handbook of Entrepreneurship*, Oxford: Oxford University Press.

Delmar, F. and Shane, S. (2003) 'Does Business Planning Facilitate the Development of New Ventures?', *Strategic Management Journal*, 24(12).

Everett, J. and Watson, J. (2004) 'Small Business Failure and External Risk Factors', *Small Business Economics*, 11(4).

Gaskill, L.A.R., Van Auken, H.E. and Manning, R.A. (1993) 'A Factoral Analytic Study of the Perceived Causes of Small Business Failure', *Journal of Small Business Management*, 31(4).

Gimeno, J., Folta, T.B., Cooper, A.C. and Woo, C.Y. (1997) 'Survival of the Fittest? Entrepreneurial Human Capital and the Persistence of Underperforming Business', *Administrative Science Quarterly*, 42(4).

Hannan, M.T. and Freeman, J. (1977) 'Population Ecology of Organizations', *American Journal of Sociology*, 82(5).

Haswell, S. and Holmes, S. (1989) 'Estimating the Small Business Failure Rate: A Reappraisal', *Journal of Small Business Management*, 27.

Kiggundu, M.N. (2002) 'Entrepreneurs and Entrepreneurship in Africa: What is known and what needs to be done', *Journal of Developmental Entrepreneurship*, 7(3).

Knotts, T.L., Jones, S.C. and Udell, G.G. (2003), 'Small Business Failure: The Role of Management Practices and Product Characteristics', *Journal of Business and Entrepreneurship*, October.

Larson, C. and Clute, R. (1979) 'The Failure Syndrome', *American Journal of Small Business*, IV (2), October.

Reid, G.C. (1991) 'Staying in Business', *International Journal of Industrial Organisation*, 9.

Saridakis, G., Mole, K.F. and Storey, D.J. (2008) 'New Small Firm Survival in England', *Empirica*, 35.

Stearns, T.M., Carter, N.M., Reynolds, P.D. and Williams, M.L. (1995) 'New Firm Survival: Industry, Strategy and Location', *Journal of Business Venturing*, 10(1).

Stokes, D. and Blackburn, R. (2002) 'Learning the Hard Way: The Lessons of Owner-Managers who have Closed their Businesses', *Journal of Small Business and Enterprise Development*, 9(1).

Watkins, D. (1982) 'Management Development and the Owner-manager', in T. Webb, T. Quince and D. Watkins (eds) *Small Business Research*, Aldershot: Gower.

Wichmann, H. (1983) 'Accounting and Marketing: Key Small Business Problems', *American Journal of Small Business*, 7.

CASE insight 9.3

The English Grocer UK

Reasons for failure

In 2006 Peter Durose decided to leave his £250,000 a year job running the fresh produce section at the supermarket chain Tesco. He was fed up with the early starts and long days and wanted to spend more time with his wife and two young daughters. The mortgage was almost repaid so he felt he could indulge his dream and open a gourmet corner shop in the village of Buntingford. He invested £100,000 of his savings in the venture, called The English Grocer, which opened its doors to business early in 2007.

The English Grocer stocked high-quality, traditional food targeted at up-market customers – good breads, hams, cheese from Neal's Yard dairy, pickles, teas, coffee, olive oils etc. Sales grew steadily, and at Christmas 2007 one of the most popular lines was its luxury £100 Christmas hamper. But starting up a

business was harder than either Peter or his wife believed. Because planning to open the shop took time and they needed the money, Peter started a small consultancy with a friend advising growers on how to find the best market for their produce. That continued once the shop was opened, leaving his wife, Marion, to work in the store.

I found it difficult to organise my time. I quickly found I was doing seven days a week again. It's easy to lose that balance and you have to stop and think – remember what you are doing here.

Things only got worse when Marion became pregnant with their third child. As she observed:

We both did a lot of work in the evening. We would put the kids to bed and then at 8.00 pm we would be sat with our laptops.

In 2008 the recession hit. At first, sales remained buoyant, but by November, just as Marion gave birth to a son, sales started to decline as families economized. Peter tried leafleting but with little effect. Customers bought £30 hampers in place of the £100 hampers they had bought the year before. In January 2009 Peter was forced to inject more cash into the business. He even persuaded his landlord to accept a 25% cut in the shop rent. But things did not improve.

I kept thinking that maybe trade would pick up when the weather got better. But it didn't get better – it snowed in March.

The final blow came when the Council started work in the high street, erecting bollards and restricting parking. The high street was closed for three weeks and when it re-opened the browsers did not reappear. In April, Peter and Marion decided to close the business. They reassigned the shop lease to a coffee shop within three weeks and sold off the remaining stock. Peter is philosophical:

I don't regret any of it, not at all … We had a lot of fun setting up the shop. I learnt more in the past three years than in the previous ten. There is something all-encompassing about starting a business … The hardest part, I guess, was that we could have carried on. It wasn't just a commercial decision – it was an emotional decision. There may be green shoots [of recovery] out there, but I am not sure anyone agrees … We found we were consistently talking about the year after next year – and for a small business that is a heck of a gamble. In our hearts we don't think the English Grocer is over for ever. Maybe, another time, another place.
Sunday Times 26 April 2009

Questions:

1 Did the English Grocer fail?
2 What part did luck play in its closure?

CASE insight 9.4

Starbucks Australia

AUSTRALIA
USA

Business failure going overseas

Many businesses fail in trying to establish a commercial presence overseas – even well-known global brands like Starbucks. Starbucks entered the Australian market in 2000 competing against established local independent coffee shops and chains such as McDonald's McCafé (Australia's leading chain), Gloria Jean's and Hudsons. By 2008, it had accumulated losses of $100 million and closed 61 of its 84 shops. In 2013 it handed over all of its remaining shops to the Withers Group, an Australian company operating the US 7-Eleven franchise, for an undisclosed sum.

Getty Images/iStockphoto/ma-no

By 2017 there were just 27 Starbucks coffee shops in Australia.

So what went wrong? Starbucks entered a market with established competitors and offered nothing particularly unique. Unlike the USA, where it grew store by store, driven by customer demand, it entered Australia with multiple store openings in numerous cities, often in low-traffic locations. The brash signage announced their arrival and Australians felt there was an element of 'cultural imperialism' being imposed on them. They also did not like the 'fancy' Starbucks 'coffee language', such as Decaf Mocha Grande, and ordering different sizes of cups. Prices were seen as too high compared to established competitors like McCafé and Australians preferred the friendly homespun hospitality and boutique qualities of the local independent shops. Whereas in the USA Starbucks picked up business as a location between home and work and somewhere to linger, that strategy did not seem to work in Australia.

It was maybe too standardised. Early on it was unique and different, but as it became a global chain the standardisation made it lose some of that coolness and edginess. It was quickly copied and lost its lustre ... [US towns] would want to have a Starbucks. Australia

was never like that. We were curious about it. We'd read about it. It was something to try. But once tried I don't know that it offered a particularly fantastic or unique experience that wasn't offered by other chains.
Michael Edwardson consumer psychologist, *BBC News* http://news.bbc.co.uk/go/pr/fr/-/1/hi/business/7540480.stm 4 August 2008

Question:

What do you learn from this business failure about going into an overseas market?

As you might expect, many of the root causes of failure can be traced back to the entrepreneur themselves either in terms of their managerial capabilities or their character traits. Table 9.3 lists some of the major managerial deficiencies cited in Academic insight 9.1. They are many and varied and, in reality, probably varied with the different circumstances facing individual firms. The safest way to read this is that a general lack of managerial capability, including a lack of planning, puts you at risk of failure.

Table 9.3 Managerial deficiencies cited as leading to business failure

• Poor planning	• Lack of understanding of customer needs	• Inability to delegate
• Inappropriate business strategies	• Failure to identify target customers	• Reluctance to seek help
• Poor financial control	• Poor selling skills	• Unawareness of the environment
• Inadequate/infrequent financial information	• Overdependence on a small number of customers	• Inability to adapt to change
• Lax debtor (receivables) and/or stock (inventory) control	• Too narrow product range	• Thinness of management talent
• Inability to manage cash flow		• Excessive drawings
		• Negligence

One of the first things I learned though was that there was a relationship between screwing up and learning: the more mistakes I made, the faster I learned.

Michael Dell founder Dell Corporation (1999, *Direct from Dell: Strategies that Revolutionized an Industry*. New York: Harper Business)

It is a paradox that the asset of the entrepreneurial character can become a liability in certain circumstances. A number of the entrepreneurial character traits that we noted in Chapter 2 can have very negative effects. For example, the high internal locus of control can lead to 'control freak' behaviour such as an inability to delegate, meddling and a mistrust of subordinates. This fear of losing control of the business can also result in high levels of borrowing – a frequently cited symptom of vulnerability – because they are unwilling to part with equity. Similarly, the entrepreneur's strong need to demonstrate achievement and receive public applause and recognition might lead to unwise overspending on the trappings of corporate life, or the 'big project' that is too risky. Their strong self-confidence can, in extremis, become 'delusional' behaviour evidenced by an excessive optimism, an exaggerated opinion of their business competency and an unwillingness to listen to advice or seek help. What is more, there is little evidence that entrepreneurs whose businesses fail learn from that failure (see Academic insight 9.2).

Learning from failure

An interesting issue is what (if anything) an entrepreneur learns from the bad decisions they make. You might expect that if they make sufficient mistakes they might realize or 'learn' that they have insufficient knowledge and skill to run their own business successfully and they decide to close it. And you might expect that they would learn from these mistakes if they go on to start another venture. Metzger (2007) found that, while German entrepreneurs who went bankrupt were just as likely to start up again in business as those who had voluntarily closed their business, they were then more likely to face closure again. It was not 'failure' as such but how they failed that was significant. Indeed, in a review of the literature, Storey and Greene (2010) concluded that the empirical evidence that entrepreneurs learn from failure was weak, possibly being submerged by their over-optimism. The reason for this may lie in the emotions generated by failure and in particular the grieving process which can interfere with the learning process (Shepherd, 2003; Shepherd and Kuratko, 2009).

Metzger, G. (2007) *Personal Experience: A Most Vicious and Limited Circle!? On the Role of Entrepreneurial Experience for Firm Survival*, Discussion Paper 07-046. Baden-Württemberg Centre for European Economic Research.

Shepherd, D.A. (2003) 'Learning from Business Failure: Propositions of Grief Recovery for the Self-Employed', *Academy of Management Review*, 28(2).

Shepherd, D.A. and Kuratko, D.F. (2009) 'The Death of an Innovative Project: How Grief Recovery Enhances Learning', *Business Horizons*, 52(5).

Storey, D.J. and Greene, F.J. (2010) *Small Business and Entrepreneurship*, Harlow: Pearson Education.

Alex Meisl UK

Dealing with failure

Alex Meisl's first company Taotalk, a telecoms business that offered a real-time internet chat and voice messaging service, failed after a potential investor had a last-minute change of mind. Alex lost half a million pounds of his own money, but found the hardest part was telling his 12 employees that they would be made redundant and would not be paid their month's salary. He felt guilty – a very common emotion.

> *I felt a huge guilt towards the staff. They had trusted me because I said it would be all right. They missed out on their last month's salary and they didn't get any redundancy other than the statutory minimum.*

When a business fails many people feel depressed and embarrassed and just want to get away from everything and everyone. However, Alex felt it was important to tell all creditors – customers and suppliers, as well as employees – what was happening, personally, either face to face or by phone. He was trying to maintain a personal relationship with creditors and keep at least some of their trust and respect, and scotch any unfounded gossip that might develop in the industry.

Alex set up his second business, Sponge, a year later in 2002. Sponge offered voice and mobile applications for agencies and their brands and media groups using a platform called TG³ which allows integration of mobile, web and email in a digital campaign. This time Alex approached things differently. Firstly, instead of going it alone as with Taotalk, he set up Sponge with an experienced business partner, Dan Parker. Secondly, they wrote a business plan together and approached every business deal more systematically. The past experience of failure had changed Alex:

It hardened me and it made me slightly more cynical, in a constructive way. If someone comes through the door and says I am sure we have got a deal with company X, I don't believe it until I have seen the signature on the bottom of the document.

Sunday Times 17 February 2008

Alex's more considered approach at Sponge brought success. The company became the UK's market-leading full service mobile marketing agency, with offices in London, Nairobi and Lagos. Among its clients it counted Autotrader, IPC, News International, Vodafone and agencies including Ogilvy and BBH. Sponge was responsible for Europe's largest mobile campaign for Walkers crisps. Alex successfully sold Sponge (twice – it's a 'long story!') to NeoMedia, LLC, a major mobile marketing company in the USA. After the sale, he remained with the company for a period, but then started another new venture, greyhairworks!, in early 2016.

Greyhairworks! is a consultancy of exceptionally experienced (ageing) industry professionals who work across different verticals, geographies and disciplines, notably retail and brand, technology and digital. They deliver help in three main ways:

- Grow businesses through opening doors, developing opportunities and refining offers;
- Support businesses in need of advice, experience and guidance;
- Launch new concepts for existing companies from inception to revenues.

The company doesn't hide the fact that these professionals have known failure as well as success – in fact they make it a selling point. The greyhairworks! website prominently states:

Let us help you with the challenges you face, let us share the mistakes we have made so you can avoid the worst blunders which we have valiantly committed. Benefit from our battle-hardened track records to bask in the glory of the right decisions we can help you

Alex Meisl

Images courtesy of Alex Meisl

make. Use our knowledge and address books to grow your business and solve your challenges.

Once again, in addition to benefitting from the vast knowledge he gained from delivering mobile and digital solutions to retailers and brands, Alex has also been able to profit from his past failures and to use them positively.

Visit the website: greyhairworks.com

Questions:

1 How do you think Alex dealt with the first failure? Explain.
2 How valuable do you think is the experience of failure?

Personal insolvency in the UK

Insolvency is the term used when an individual or a company cannot pay its debts. If you cannot pay your business debts when they fall due, or if your business assets are less than your liabilities, then your business is technically insolvent. The consequences of this depend on whether you are a sole trader or partnership – which then involves personal insolvency – or a company (company insolvency), although you may face some personal liabilities if your company is insolvent.

Web addresses for organizations offering relevant information on insolvency are in the *Guide to UK Laws and Regulations for Business* on the companion website: www.macmillanihe.com/burns-nvc-2e. An additional guide for Australian readers, produced by Dr Russell Manfield, is also provided.

For an individual struggling to pay their debts – as a sole trader or a partner or as a director of a limited company who has personally guaranteed the company's debts – there are a number of courses of action open to you in England and Wales. Most other countries have similar legal arrangements, but even those in Scotland differ and need to be checked, and the advice of a professional accountant or lawyer sought before proceeding.

Informal 'family' arrangements

This is where family or friends agree to provide funds on a short-term basis and creditors agree not to take action. However, getting other members of the family involved in the business may present other problems.

Formal voluntary arrangements

This form of **voluntary arrangement** exists when all the creditors agree to a proposal you and your advisors (which must include a licensed insolvency practitioner) put forward. This proposal will typically specify the amount (or proportion) of debt to be repaid and the timescale. If accepted, the creditors are bound by the proposal.

Partnership voluntary arrangements

Partnerships can propose this arrangement. It is similar to the individual arrangement above, but to remove the individual partners' joint and several liability to meet the partnership debts, the partners will either have to pay off the whole partnership debt or propose an individual voluntary arrangement.

Bankruptcy

If you are unable to pay your debts you can be made personally bankrupt. You or your creditors can apply to the courts for this to happen. The court will appoint an official receiver to take over your affairs (an insolvency practitioner may later take over) and sell off any assets – both your own personal assets and those within the business – so as to discharge your debts as soon as possible. Until the debts are discharged, the receiver will manage all your affairs and there are restrictions on the financial arrangements you might enter into. As a sole trader or partner your business will normally be closed down and the assets sold off. Until you are discharged as bankrupt you cannot be a director of a company. Unless you are seen as not cooperating with the receiver, you will usually be discharged from **bankruptcy** within a year; however, you may not regain full control of your own finances straight away. A major consequence of bankruptcy is that your personal credit rating will be badly affected for some years to come, which

Mark Constantine, founder Lush RealBusiness 26 May 2009

You feel a lot of shame. I had 200 staff. You feel you've let them down. [on the bankruptcy of his Cosmetics to Go business]

CASE insight 9.6

ZedZed.com UK

A personal view of failure: 'Don't pity the pioneers – envy us for our experience'

'This is a story with an unhappy ending about my dot. com company ZedZed.com, a site for independent travellers, which went into liquidation in 2000. ZedZed. com was meant to be called ZigZag.com but that name had already gone. We raised £800,000, which was no mean achievement, but it wasn't enough. In February we encountered dot.com envy from our friends. In March we were winning awards and being asked to speak at conferences in Paris. In June we achieved 1800 user reviews per week. In August we were calling in the liquidators. Mistakes are always easier to see with the benefit of hindsight, and our worst error was to believe that internet businesses should be valued by the number of subscribers rather than the transactions that they make … Today you have to be profitable or else you are not going to get funded again. They say that internet speed is fast but three months is a short period of time to reverse your whole raison d'être. I think we did a lot right too. We built a site in six weeks on a very complicated back-end platform. We chose a content management system that would make us a serious force in the market, and we successfully leveraged that asset with larger organisations who might otherwise have ignored us. We devised a very successful low-cost user subscription campaign without the help of an expensive marketing agency like so many dot.coms. We kept our non-essential expenditure to a minimum, which allowed us to return 20 per cent of the initial subscription to investors.

We employed 19 people on low salaries who genuinely loved their daily work. Being a chartered accountant, I knew where our financial position was on a daily basis and knew when the time had come to close the door. Setting up a dot.com business has been the most exciting, rewarding experience of my life, and of the lives of the team that I had around me. We did something new, different and useful to other people. Sadly for us and our investors, the capital markets have changed to such a degree that we have had to end our quest early. In doing so we are showing that there is sanity amid the madness. Don't pity the pioneers – envy us for our experience. Oh, and pay us well for them too!'

Edward Johnstone, co-founder of ZedZed.com
Daily Telegraph 17 August 2000

Questions:

1 What personal qualities do you need to see through the closure of your own business?
2 How would you feel if your business failed?

means that obtaining credit will become more difficult and more costly. Most individuals seek to avoid bankruptcy.

Corporate insolvency in the UK

For a limited liability company struggling to pay its debts and facing possible failure, there are a number of courses of action open in England and Wales. Most other countries have similar legal arrangements (again, rules in Scotland differ), but these should be checked and the advice of a professional accountant or lawyer sought before proceeding.

Refinancing

This involves bringing in new debt and/or equity finance to support the business. This may mean that the owner-manager will lose some of their equity in the business and may lose control. Refinancing will usually require the company to be restructured and may involve a pre-packaged sale of the business.

A pre-packaged sale

This allows the profitable part of the business to restart without being weighed down by the company's existing debts. **Pre-packaged sale**, or 'pre-pack', is the name given to the process of buying the assets of a business from the old failing company. 18% of US public bankruptcies in 2016 were pre-packs. Typically a new company owned by the existing management will take over some or all of the assets of the business but not the debts. This structure allows a new business to rise from the remains of the old, often referred to as 'phoenix-like', with the effect that the business and jobs are saved. Once the transaction has taken place, the old company is placed into **liquidation**.

Company voluntary arrangement (CVA)

This course of action is best suited to companies which are fundamentally profitable, or which have the potential to be profitable, but which have serious cash flow problems. The existing company continues but is given protection from its creditors. For a **CVA** all creditors must agree to either accept a longer payment term or a reduced amount, or both. A typical CVA may defer payments for between two and four years and, in England, must be administered by a licensed insolvency practitioner who will report to the court.

Administration

This is appropriate for companies that urgently need protection from creditors. Unlike with a CVA, a company can be placed into administration almost immediately by the court, if the court considers it appropriate. The approval of creditors is not needed. A company placed into administration is instantly protected from its creditors and, probably most importantly, from any pending legal action. In England, the company will be administered by a licensed insolvency practitioner, although this is often delegated to the existing management. The administration process is designed to provide protection for a limited period of time while the business is restructured and rescued.

Creditors voluntary liquidation (CVL)

A CVL takes place if the directors and shareholders decide to liquidate the company. In the UK a licensed insolvency practitioner is appointed by the directors. He then sells the assets of the company and pays the remaining funds to the creditors. The process is regulated by the court. CVL can be a relatively quick process and can provide an effective way to shield directors from the pressures of a failing company.

Compulsory liquidation

This is the final option. It is a process begun by the court at the request of a creditor. In England the creditor applies to the court for the company to be wound up, and if the court approves this it will appoint a liquidator. Compulsory liquidation is most commonly a result of action taken by government agencies to recover taxes, although it can be initiated by any creditor. A court-appointed liquidator, which may sometimes be the official receiver, will look very closely at the actions of the officers of the company and in some circumstances, such as in mishandling of tax payments, the directors may become personally liable and may face legal consequences. The company will then be sold off, in whole or in part, as a going concern, or the assets of the company will be sold off, often at a discount, to pay the creditors as soon as possible. Most companies would seek to avoid compulsory liquidation.

CASE insight 9.7

Cobra Beer 🇬🇧 UK

Company voluntary arrangements

Cobra Beer was set up in 1990 by Karan Bilimoria, the son of an Indian army general and a former accountant, to sell a different type of beer to Indian restaurants.

I entered the most competitive beer market in the world against long established brands. The product itself was innovative – an extra smooth, less gassy lager that complements all cuisine and appeals to ale drinkers and lager drinkers alike ... Deciding to import the beer in a 650ml bottle was important in positioning the product within the market and raising the profile among restaurant owners. It also promoted a new, shared way of drinking ... The brand's point-of-sale items, such as unique and different glasses, were another effective way of establishing brand awareness ... Also [the glass] is embossed with six icons telling the story of Cobra beer, from concept and production to growth and development, and this is the first time in the world that, to our knowledge, the brand has incorporated its story directly into its packaging.

The Times 23 May 2004

By 2009 the company had sales of £177 million, but there was one problem. It had yet to make a profit. Indeed, in the year to July 2007, the last year for which accounts are publicly available, Cobra lost £13 million. Instead of tracking profits, Cobra had focused on sales growth, spending £40 million on marketing since its launch. Sales growth had indeed been spectacular, showing 20% year-on-year growth in a falling market.

Unfortunately, the 2008 recession took its toll. While growth stalled, the banking crisis made it impossible to secure fresh funding. In the autumn of 2008 Bilimoria tried to find a buyer for the business, but the big brewers were not interested and the credit squeeze prevented a sale to a private equity firm. He cut costs. Four directors stood down and staff numbers were cut from 150 to 50.

Bilimoria called in the accountants Pricewaterhouse-Coopers in the spring of 2009 to work on a company voluntary arrangement (CVA). This would have given all creditors some money back, but one creditor, Wells & Young's, which brewed Cobra under licence in Bedford, vetoed the proposal. Bilimoria therefore decided to restructure Cobra in what is called 'pre-packaged sale'. In this arrangement the business was acquired by a joint venture company comprising Molson Coors, the US brewer of Carling lager, and the former owner, Bilimoria.

Molson paid £14 million for its 50.1% share. Karan Bilimoria kept 49.9% and remained as director.

The nature of this form of administration in the UK means that, while the secured creditors, largely banks, who were owed some £20 million were paid back in full, unsecured creditors, who were owed almost £70 million, got nothing. These debts included £57 million to investors, £6 million to the government in taxes and £6 million to 330 small unsecured trade creditors. These included many small businesses such as Spark Promotions UK, owed £62,018 for developing a beer pump for Cobra; Pop Displays, owed £31,129 for producing printing and packaging for Cobra promotions; and MicroMatic, another pump maker, which was owed £60,143. They were not happy:

[Bilimoria] has risen from the ashes like a phoenix while people like us, the creditors, have been burnt alive.

Brian Flanagan MD Spark Promotions UK
Sunday Times 2 August 2009

How can someone dump all their debts on creditors and then the next day walk into what is, effectively, the same business with a 49% stake?

Chris Hall MD Pop Displays
Sunday Times 2 August 2009

While the unsecured creditors may have lost out, observers suggest that Molson Coors landed a 'fantastic' deal. Bilimoria, who was made a Lord in 2007, said he lost the £20 million he invested in the firm and insists he is committed to repaying as many debts as possible:

We had no choice but to go down this route. I feel terrible about that. I feel gutted that the unsecured creditors aren't going to be paid.

Sunday Times 31 May 2009

Visit the website: www.cobrabeer.com

Questions:

1   What was Cobra's business model and what were the key elements of competitive advantage in its value proposition up to 2009?
2   Was Cobra successful up until this point? Was its strategy prudent?
3   Who has paid for the growth of Cobra? Is this fair? If not, what are the alternatives?

Corporate governance

If you decide to establish your venture as a company or corporation its direction rests legally with the board of directors. They have the responsibility of what is generally called 'corporate governance'. These legal duties and responsibilities arise out of common law and statute, varying from country to country, and may also be detailed in the bylaws of an organization.

Directors have a **fiduciary duty** – a legal duty of loyalty and care – to act honestly and in good faith, exercise skill and care and undertake their statutory duty. They must act in the best interests of the company and its shareholders. This may seem an academic distinction if there are only two shareholders (e.g. yourself and your spouse) and one of these is the sole director of the company (e.g. yourself). However, even if this is the case, you must realize that you have certain legal responsibilities. If your start-up is larger, or you have aspirations for it to grow, then your board of directors may comprise more than just yourself. It might include other key members of your executive management team, who might also be shareholders, and even non-executive directors – outside directors who are not employees and part of your executive management team. Often, if you have obtained equity funding for your start-up, one of the conditions will be the appointment of specified non-executive directors. Non-executive directors have a valuable role in bringing different skills, an independent and objective perspective and a new network of contacts that can contribute to organizational knowledge and learning. They can also act as an early warning system for potential future difficulties and a safeguard against potential business failure. They can be particularly valuable in helping to resolve conflict in family firms.

> Entrepreneurs are rebels who diverge from the norm, and the most successful are willing to tolerate in-house opposition; they realise that harmony is less important than finding the right answer … External non-executives can bring useful perspective and diverse experience. Sometimes they can see the big picture in a way that full-time executives, possibly too close to the action, cannot.
>
> Luke Johnson Chairman Risk Capital Partners Sunday Times 7 May 2017

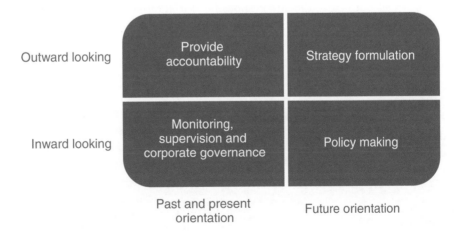

Figure 9.2 *Role of the board of directors*

The broad functions of the board are summarized in Figure 9.2, using the dimensions of inward/outward looking and past/future orientation.

- **Future orientation** – Arguably the prime function of the board is to be outward looking and future orientated – to review and guide corporate strategy and policy. This might include overall strategic planning, approval of strategies or investments in key areas, changes in the scope or nature of operations, major company decisions and so on. The board is also responsible for how these translate into internal policies for the organization such as annual budgets, performance objectives, changes in organizational structure, compensation policy for key objectives, risk policy and so on.

- **Past and present orientation** – The board then monitors performance against these strategies and policies and the ensuing risks it faces, as well as compliance with the law. These responsibilities include ensuring the integrity of the company's accounting and financial reporting systems, monitoring and supervising management performance, planning for management succession, providing proper accountability to other stakeholders in the firm, for example, by appointing auditors and approving the annual financial statements, as well as ensuring that the company complies with all aspects of the law.

While establishing corporate strategy and policy may be the most important job for the board, it is unlikely that it will be given the appropriate weighting in terms of time allocation. Most boards, particularly in larger companies, spend too much time on the other functions, particularly monitoring management performance and legal compliance.

Floatation gives a public face to your business and access to finance that is so often the key to development. But there needs to be a lot more attention to strategy.

solutions Sunday Times 23 November 2008

Elizabeth Gooch founder eg

The board becomes more important where there is separation between day-to-day management and ownership of the firm and there are multiple stakeholders. Their role therefore becomes key once a company grows to the point where it is floated on a stock market. Once this happens the board needs to function in a more formal way. For example, in Europe separating the role of Chief Executive or CEO from that of the Board Chairman is considered good practice in order to help avoid potential conflicts of interest between stakeholders and executive directors. For the same reason most of the *Financial Times* Stock Exchange (FTSE) companies comply with the recommendation that they have non-executive directors, although in small unquoted companies the proportion is much smaller. In the USA, the Sarbanes-Oxley Act imposed new standards of accountability on US public companies that made directors directly responsible for internal control, facing large fines and prison sentences in the case of accounting crimes.

Sofa-bed Factory

Piotr and Olek decided to set up a Polish Limited Liability Company (LLC) – called a Sp. Z o.o (*spółka z ograniczoną odpowiedzialnością*). The legal processes were fairly straightforward. Since 2012 it has been possible for Polish residents to set up a company on the internet within 24 hours under the 'S-24' procedure (form available at the website of the Ministry of Justice), which is just what Piotr and Olek did. The traditional method can take up to three months. The company was set up with the minimum capital requirement of 5,000 PLN (about €1,250) and the two partners as equal shareholders and directors of the company. In due course they intend to register the company with the financial authorities and obtain the company's NIP – Number (Taxpayer Identification Number) and VAT number.

They asked a friend who was a designer to develop a visual logo that could be used across Europe. They intended to attach the logo to the underside of their sofas and hoped that, in time, it might be possible to establish the brand.

Olek was keen to safeguard his design of a folding mechanism with a patent. However, the more the partners looked into this, the less likely it seemed that it might be possible. After all, Olek had just copied and/or improved on the design of other manufacturers. What is more, the costs involved seemed very high. Piotr also doubted that they could afford to pursue any legal action for infringement. All in all they decided that their capital was better spent on getting the sofa-bed onto the market as quickly as possible.

Questions:

1 Is there any way that Piotr and Olek can safeguard their business idea?
2 What is the basis for their competitive advantage and how sustainable is it?

Summary and action points

9.1 Protect intellectual property: Decide whether you wish to and whether you are able to safeguard any intellectual property related to your business. You can do this through patents, trademarks, registered designs and copyright. However, this can be expensive and time consuming. Sometimes being first to market is more effective in creating competitive advantage. You can get employees or third parties to sign a confidentiality or non-disclosure agreement which prevents them from disclosing your idea.

9.2 Decide on your legal form of business: Decide on an appropriate legal form for your new venture and the implications of this (business registrations, board of directors or trustees etc.).

Workbook exercises

 The New Venture Creation Workbook contains a digital version of these exercises that can be modified as your business model develops and builds into a draft business plan. It can be downloaded from www.macmillanihe.com/burns-nvc-2e.

9.1: Protect intellectual property

1 Decide whether you wish to and whether you are able to safeguard any IP related to your business. List the actions you need to take to safeguard it.

2 If any of the above actions are critical, make sure they are taken forward to the list of critical success factors in Exercise 10.4.

9.2: Decide on your legal form of business

Decide on the legal form your new venture will take.

1 List anything you need to do to register a commercial, for-profit business and the operating implications of this decision. If you decide to establish a limited company:
   - Decide who might be on the board of directors.
   - Decide whether you are willing to share equity in the business with others and describe the skills and competencies of those who might be on your board of directors now, and in three to five years' time.

2 If you want to establish a social enterprise, decide who else needs to be involved and what will be their status.

Visit www.macmillanihe.com/burns-nvc-2e for chapter quizzes and other resources.

10 Managing operations and risk

Contents

Learning outcomes

When you have read this chapter and undertaken the related activities you will be able to:

- Identify the key activities needed to launch and operate different sorts of business
- Prepare Gantt charts and undertake critical path analysis
- Undertake a risk management process that identifies, assesses, mitigates and monitors the risks faced by business
- Understand how risk might be reduced through networks and partnering, financial and legal structures and appropriate approaches to financing the venture
- Understand the importance of keeping contribution margins high and fixed costs low
- Identify the critical success factors and strategic options for your business

> ### Academic insights 📑
> 10.1 The benefits of partnerships and strategic alliances

> ### Case insights 💼

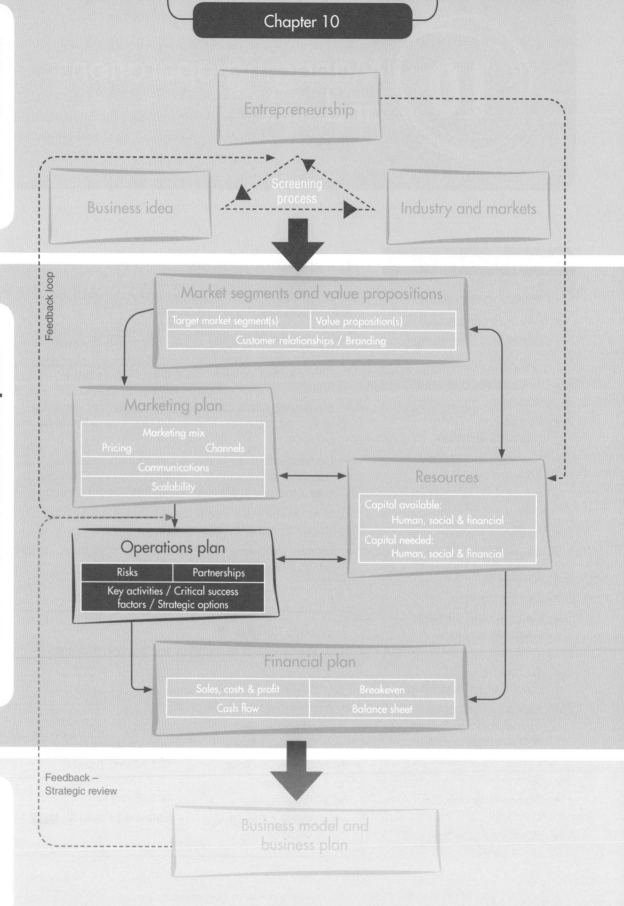

Entrepreneurship

Business idea

Screening process

Industry and markets

Feedback loop

Market segments and value propositions

Target market segment(s)	Value proposition(s)
Customer relationships / Branding	

Marketing plan

Marketing mix	
Pricing	Channels
Communications	
Scalability	

Resources

Capital available: Human, social & financial
Capital needed: Human, social & financial

Operations plan

Risks	Partnerships
Key activities / Critical success factors / Strategic options	

Financial plan

Sales, costs & profit	Breakeven
Cash flow	Balance sheet

Feedback –
Strategic review

Business model and
business plan

Managing operations

The purpose of a business is to deliver products or services to customers and that means you have to understand how to do it. If you want to start a plumbing business, you need to understand how to plumb. You need to organize and manage yourself and, if you want the business to grow, you need to manage other plumbers. Managing is concerned with handling complexity in processes and the execution of work. Back in the nineteenth century Max Fayol defined the five functions of **management** as planning, organizing, commanding, coordinating and controlling. Today, these sound very much like the skills needed to lead a communist-style command economy. Fayol's work outlined how these functions required certain skills which could be taught and developed systematically in people.

> Understanding the nuts and bolts goes a long way to reducing the risk. I want to see that the person … has a very clear grasp of what he or she is trying to accomplish.
>
> Ajith Jayawickrema serial entrepreneur and business angel *Sunday Times* 2 June 2013

Management on a day-to-day basis is about detail and logic. It is about efficiency and effectiveness. It involves being able to prioritize activities and decide which is more important than another. These priorities vary from business to business, and prioritization is a question of judgement. Nevertheless, it is vital that you are able to do this and, ultimately, compile a list of **critical success factors** (CSFs) – things that are essential to get right if the business is to achieve its mission; things that make or break the success of the strategy (e.g. getting a website up and running on time). Critical success factors are distilled from key operating activities – key things that you need to do to run the business efficiently and effectively. Not all key operating activities are critical. Which activities are *critical* is a question of judgement. It is not just about urgent tasks – most tasks are urgent for a start-up. It is not just about efficiency and effectiveness – although this is likely to be important and take up much of the working day. It is not just about identifying risks that might set you back – there will be many of these. It is about deciding which things might fundamentally affect the success of the venture.

The achievement of some critical success factors and key operating activities may be binary – simple 'achieved/not achieved' outcomes (e.g. development of website by a certain date). Some outcomes may involve degrees of achievement against which performance can be measured and judged (e.g. number of website views over a period). These quantifiable measures of performance are called **performance metrics**. They can involve the achievement of operating or financial measures (e.g. profit, resource, quality etc.) by a target date or within a given time frame. They can be inward (e.g. sales) or outward (e.g. market share) focused. Performance metrics for **key activities** are often called **key performance indicators** (KPIs). There are a whole range of financial metrics that can be used to control and measure the performance of a business (see Chapter 13). However, the metrics that might measure the success of the start-up are likely to be different to those needed to measure success in operating. You need to decide what they are and how your success will be measured, particularly if you have outside investors.

Key operating activities are derived from elements of the business model – from all the activities that need to be undertaken to deliver both your marketing and operating plans – and from the things that need to be done to manage the risks that the business faces. You will need to have completed some activities *prior* to your business launch. For example, you might need a working prototype, or your business model might have implications for the assets you need to own (licences, patents etc.), or you might need to secure key contracts with partners or customers. Some activities will be part of your day-to-day activities and your performance metrics might measure how well these are being undertaken. This hierarchy of activities is shown in Figure 10.1. This chapter is about managing operations, managing risk and providing an insight into which key operating activities might also be critical success factors for your business.

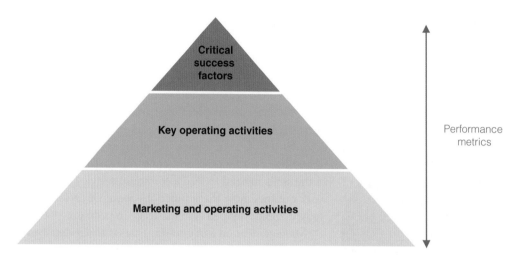

Figure 10.1 Hierarchy of activities

Key marketing activities

Some of the marketing activities you undertake to deliver your business model will be key activities and some will be critical success factors. These vary from business model to business model. They will be different for each of the three core value propositions outlined in Chapter 4 (Table 4.1 is reproduced as Table 10.1). For example, Amazon originally set out to be a low-cost online retailer of books, so it located in Seattle, a major distribution hub for several large publishers. Companies with a differentiated product, like Apple, continuously innovate while building their brand based upon what they see as their differential advantages, such as design simplicity. Companies with a strong customer focus like Virgin continually seek out new opportunities for brand extension, and Virgin does this while reinforcing its brand through the image of its founder, Richard Branson. Dell has a low-cost focus, so one of its key activities includes supply chain management. Should this focus change, as it is doing (see Case insight 5.3), then the importance of the supply chain will be reduced and other key activities will emerge.

You need to consider how the generic marketing imperatives in Table 10.1 translate into key operating activities for your business. Case insights 4.4 (easyJet) and 6.7 (Lush) give you examples of key marketing activities. For example, easyJet, like other low-price airlines, must keep its costs low, and this has numerous operations implications, from ticket pricing to luggage allowance, turnaround time to staff rostering, website design to branding. The question is whether any of these are critical to the success of the business. Critical success factors change over time, and the answer to this question will probably be different today compared to easyJet's early years. One enduring critical success factor for any airline is safety.

Table 10.1 Generic strategies and key operating activities

High differentiation	High customer focus	Low price/cost
• Understanding the basis for the differential advantage • Building on the differential advantage • Building barriers to entry • Building the brand • Continuous innovation • Encouraging creativity and innovation	• Maintaining close relationships with customers • Keeping in touch with and understanding changes in customer needs • Maintaining customer loyalty • Maximizing sales to existing loyal customers (economies of scope) • Building the brand	• Maintaining cost leadership through economies of scale • Continually driving down costs • Achieving high sales volumes • Improving efficiency • Standardization

Identifying key activities

Key activities have implications for all aspects of the business, including the resources you need. Every business has its own set of key activities upon which its competitive advantage probably hinges. Some of these will need to be completed prior to your business launch, for example, selecting an appropriate location for a retail business or obtaining appropriate licences. Others are key operating activities for the life of the business, for example, keeping an up-to-date and engaging website or maintaining service levels. These may change over time as the business develops, but they are the day-to-day operating issues that you need to get right to deliver your customer value proposition. Techniques such as brainstorming and mind maps (outlined in Chapter 2) can help you arrive at your key operating activities.

Key activities cascade down an organization and what might be important or critical for one function within a business might not be of the same importance for the business overall. Paying salaries and wages on the due date is critical to many employees but is unlikely to feature on the key activities or critical success factors list for your business. It is all a matter of judgement.

Key pre-launch activities – If you hope to sell an innovative product, you probably will need to at least have a working prototype before trying to get finance, and you certainly need to have refined that prototype and be able to deliver the product in the required volumes before you go to market. However, you do not necessarily need to manufacture or even assemble the final product, just as you do not necessarily need to retail it directly to customers yourself. Some key pre-launch activities have implications for future operations. For example, Amazon's business model requires them to have an efficient and effective web platform. This was needed at start-up, but the platform continues to be developed so the company can maintain its competitive position. Google's original business model required a working word-search algorithm. Today it needs to keep at the forefront of internet-based search and retrieval technology and developments. Dell set out to be a low-cost provider of computer equipment and developed an innovative B2C2B integrated supply chain to facilitate this. Now this is commonplace and they are struggling to differentiate themselves.

Key post-launch activities – These are specific to each business, but there are some generalizations that can be made for specific industries – retail, internet, manufacturing and service. So for example, while the location of a bricks-and-mortar retail business is a critical pre-launch decision, once you have opened a shop promotions and merchandising become more important. The effective operation of the website is a vital activity pre- and post-launch for an internet retailer. Many service businesses such as consultancies are based around some key skills, knowledge or problem-solving abilities, and training might therefore feature as a key updating activity. Production activities that underpin quality or efficiency might dominate the key activities for a manufacturing firm.

Key retail activities

Launching a retail business – a shop, restaurant, bar and so on – poses a particular set of challenges. For any retailer, the 'place' element of the marketing mix is very specific and very important. The location must provide access to your target market. If you want the casual shopper or diner, you might locate in the high street (Case insight 10.1 – Ice Cream Mama) or at a transport hub (Case insight 4.1 – MOMA!) – wherever there is high footfall. High footfall locations are called prime sites and can be expensive. However, just because there are lots of people passing a location, it does not mean that those people are potential customers for the product/service offered by your business. If you are selling something that customers will seek out and you can rely on it 'pulling' them into the shop or restaurant then you can afford to be located at a secondary site, with lower footfall. You often see stores relying on infrequent purchases (e.g. furniture, cars, do-it-yourself etc.) located in secondary locations. Secondary locations have much lower rent and rates than primary locations. However, there may be additional costs associated with 'pulling' customers into that location. Sometimes small retailers group together in areas which have lower rent and rates and establish their own customer 'pull' because of the charm the area has or because of the variety offered. Retailers offering similar products/services can also group together to establish specialist 'quarters' such as a jewellery quarter or restaurant quarter. Some of the factors affecting location decisions are listed in Table 10.2.

Table 10.2 Factors affecting the location decision of a retailer

• Size of population in local area	• Site costs
• Demographic and nature of population	• Availability of parking
• Footfall outside specific location	• Availability of public transport
• Visibility of site	• Potential for expansion
• Proximity of 'magnets' such as anchor stores or transport hubs	• Nature of legal agreement (e.g. lease term, rent reviews etc.)
• Strength of competition	
• Consistency with customer value proposition	

For any retail outlet the frontage is the equivalent of a huge advertising hoarding or billboard for the products/services sold. It therefore needs to reflect the value proposition to customers. The ambience is also very important – design, hygiene, layout and so on – and must also reflect the value proposition. It must be consistent with the rest of your marketing mix. If you are selling on price (e.g. Poundland stores in the UK) you do not need an expensive frontage or point of sale displays because it is not consistent with the low-price value proposition. On the other hand, you may still need to locate in prime sites.

Because the lease or rental cost of the premises (a fixed cost) is high for most retailers, stores need to be filled with as many customers as possible, for as long as possible. Actually encouraging customers to visit the store in the first place rather than shopping online can be a challenge. Many stores such as Lush (Case insight 6.7) and Cotton On Group (Case insight 10.2) try to bring the fun back into shopping by creating what might be called 'retail theatres', where the store is seen as a place to go offering personal contact and an 'experience'. Once in the store they try to encourage 'dwell time' – the time customers stay. This may simply be by having a small coffee shop. Cotton On do this by offering phone-charging stations, roomier fitting rooms, free yoga sessions, kiddies' play areas and even DJ decks and photo booths.

The launch of a new retail outlet needs to attract potential customers into the building. They therefore often have opening events, perhaps with celebrities or even bands, trying to generate a party atmosphere with banners, balloons, special decorations etc. Shops often have opening sales. While shoppers might just browse, drinkers or diners will want to try out the products on sale, so special opening price discounts might be offered. Rather than relying on price offers, exclusive bars or restaurants might have special opening events to which only selected people are invited, creating an atmosphere of exclusivity. And while prime-site shops might rely on attracting passing customers, other retailers will need to promote their opening event.

Even bricks-and-mortar retailers need a website these days. They can be used to attract customers, advertise products or sales promotions and order goods (click-and-collect), even if not used for online sales. While an increasing number of transactions are electronic, any business handling cash needs to ensure that there are safeguards in place to prevent theft. Staff theft is particularly problematic in bars. Increasingly, cameras are being used to supplement electronic cash registers. Cameras are also used extensively to discourage shoplifting. Table 10.3 provides a checklist of possible key activities for a retailer, based upon the mind map in Figure 2.4 on page 60. It is split between pre-launch activities and day-to-day operations.

Table 10.3 Key operating activities checklist for a retailer

Pre-launch activities	Post-launch operations
• Location • Licences and leases • Store design and fit-out • Merchandising and stocking • Internet sales and website • Sales staff recruitment and training • Credit/debit card merchant account • Launch event	• Merchandising • Stock (inventory) control • Promotions • Security (cash and shoplifting) • Service levels

Restaurants will need to develop attractive menus and make certain they have the chefs to deliver them. Waiting staff will need to be trained. Most restaurants have an online presence that can be used for promotions, and the internet can be used to offer takeaway or home delivery services. Hygiene will be an important consideration and in the UK they will need to obtain a hygiene certificate from the local authority. Any retailer selling alcohol in the UK needs to obtain a licence from the local authority. Table 10.4 provides a checklist of possible key operating activities for a restaurant or bar.

Table 10.4 Key operating activities checklist for a restaurant or bar

Pre-launch activities	Post-launch operations
• Location • Licences and leases • Restaurant/bar design and fit-out • Menu design • Chef recruitment • Staff recruitment and training • Credit/debit card merchant account • Website • Launch event	• Hygiene • Promotions • Cash control • Stock control (food and drink) • Staff rostering • Menu rotation • Service levels • Customer security

CASE insight 10.1

Ice Cream Mama OMAN

Retail location

After graduating from Sultan Qaboos University in Oman, Rami Al Lawati went to Australia to get a Bachelor's degree in accounting and then to the UK to obtain an MBA. Returning to Oman he took a job with Omantel, the country's largest telecommunication provider. He met and married Huda, who had a degree in media studies and digital technology. However, he was not happy in his job so he resigned after less than a year and decided to start a new venture with his wife using his business skills and the technological expertise of his wife. The company, called ProShots, provided high-quality photographic services, often using well-known photographers, for occasions such as weddings and birthdays, charging a high price for its services. However, the business was beset with problems. For example, it used predominantly female photographers from East Asia and obtaining visas proved problematic, creating profitability and liquidity problems. Rami decided to change ProShots' focus, targeting corporate events instead. He also broadened its scope, renaming it Pro Group with a number of 'divisions'. Pro PR dealt with social media solutions, Pro Design designed communication material and Pro Events offered events management. The company also embarked on making documentaries for clients. However, while the company was quite successful in growing its turnover, it was not very profitable.

Never daunted, Rami continued to search for market opportunities and finally decided on ice cream. This was perhaps an obvious choice for such a hot country as Oman, but the market was dominated by international firms like Baskin-Robbins and a Pakistani creamery chain called Tropical. Rami decided that, in order to be different, he would capitalize on the popularity of homemade ice cream and focus on the traditional Omani way of making ice cream. Rami's mother used to make ice cream, so he started by copying her recipe and asked her permission to name the shop after her. She refused, so instead he named it Ice Cream Mama. The first shop opened in

© Ice Cream Mama

2012, offering only two flavours: rosewater and laban. It sold out on the first day. By 2015, Ice Cream Mama had four stores in Muscat at popular locations. Huda Al Lawati said:

> We believe that Oman is one of those countries that are very rich in culture in terms of food, fashion and so many things. But it hasn't been exposed to the world in a branded way and that's the gap I found in the market, it is the first traditional ice cream company from the GCC to be branded.

One of the keys to its success has been selecting the right location. These must have high footfalls with children and younger people. Ice Cream Mama stores are located near cinemas and malls. Rami and Huda have been careful to promote a distinctive Omani brand image. To make it feel more urban, street styles, including graffiti, are incorporated into the decor. The stores are also decorated with local scarves and motifs. Stores now offer a wide range of local and international flavours, but new local flavours like halwa, date and chai karak are launched regularly with much fanfare. As a result, Ice Cream Mama has become a popular brand in Oman, particularly among younger people, and has over 28,000 followers on Instagram.

Pro Group still exists but it is now funded by Ice Cream Mama. Rami and Huda want to take the venture abroad and are negotiating with clients in Dubai, Doha and Kuwait to open stores.

Questions:

1 What are the elements of Ice Cream Mama's marketing mix?
2 Why has it been successful?
3 Will the concept transfer to other countries?

Cotton On Group

AUSTRALIA

Critical success factors

In 1988, at the age of 18, university business student Nigel Austin began selling acid-wash denim jackets at a local market in Geelong, Australia. Nigel had purchased the jackets from his father, wholesaler Grant Austin, who had imported them for his own business. Unfortunately, during his first weekend at the market, Nigel left without making a sale. Nevertheless, after talking to potential customers, he recognized the strong appetite that existed for on-trend and affordable fashion. Nigel returned to the market the following week with lower prices and completely sold out. Three years later, he opened the first Cotton On store in Geelong, where he sold a mix of casual, everyday items for men and women. Over the next 10–15 years, the business grew steadily. Its portfolio was expanded to 50 stores across Australia, followed by a significant period of growth and overseas expansion from 2005.

Today, the Cotton On Group is one of Australia's largest value fashion retailers with seven brands covering men's and women's apparel, childrenswear, footwear, stationery, giftware, sleepwear, activewear, and teen and youth fashion. It also includes a philanthropic arm, the Cotton On Foundation. With over 1,400 stores in 19 countries, a thriving e-commerce business and a team of 22,000 people, the Group is still privately owned by Nigel and his cousin Ashley Hardwick and remains headquartered in Geelong.

Recently celebrating its 25th anniversary, the Australian retailer attributes its success to the 'laser-like focus' it places on understanding the customer and delivering on-trend, value fashion 'through a world-class in store and online experience.' Customer insights are obtained through a variety of channels, including from its 22,000 team members, through sales and e-commerce data, from members of the executive team spending time in store and through its five regional support centres in New Zealand, Singapore, South Africa, the United States and Brazil. Feeding back to its global support centre in Geelong in real time, a team of trend forecasters, designers and product developers create thousands of new products each year to 'exceed customers' expectations.'

The timing of design and production are critical components in the Group's retail model. The Group implements a system of direct sourcing, which sees it work directly with suppliers, many of whom have been with the Group since day one. These relationships,

together with the fact that over 60 per cent of products are produced by the Group's top 20 suppliers, means the business is able to deliver ranges to market quickly. The turnaround time from conceptualization to store floor is four to eight weeks. In 2005, the Group also adopted an advanced replenishment system so it could deliver new styles into store weekly and replenish stock daily. This system enables the Group to track sales in real time and feed the information back to its network of 11 global distribution centres, so the product can be picked and replaced in store overnight, or sometimes even on the same day.

The Group's customer-first approach can also be seen in its global store network. Steering away from a one-size-fits-all approach, the Group draws on customer insights to determine the best location, size and format for over 1,400 stores. Fuelled by the knowledge that customers were shopping across its portfolio of seven brands, the Group opened the doors to its first megastore in 2015. This created a more accessible experience by housing multiple brands under the one roof in a larger store. The success of the model led the Group to open 90 megastores in Australia and a further 122 globally.

Typically ranging from 800 to 2,000 square meters, these megastores offer a more dynamic and convenient shopping experience. The increased floor space allows for a greater assortment of brands and categories to be combined in one place. While collectively these stores account for only 15 per cent of the Group's portfolio, they contribute to 38 per cent of its sales globally – a promising sign for a concept that did not exist five years ago.

An equally important part of the Group's growth strategy has been its focus on e-commerce, in which it invested heavily to 'create a world-class experience.' This allows customer needs to be met through around-the-clock access to its brands and products. In late-2017, the Group relaunched its e-commerce platform under the name CottonOn & Co. This website houses its five mega brands in the one destination – Cotton On, Cotton On KIDS, Cotton On BODY, Typo and Rubi Shoes.

As part of the relaunch, customers have access to easier navigation, an improved 'mobile first experience' and more accessible payment methods, supported by a host of faster and more convenient delivery solutions. While today the Group's e-commerce website accounts for 5 per cent of sales, it is confident it could grow this number 'to 20 per cent by 2020.'

The Group highlights that 'operating with integrity' has been at the core of the business since day one. This has led to the establishment of its Ethical Framework, which governs all areas of the business from design through to supply. The Group's long-standing relationships with suppliers, together with the scale of the business, have led it to implement programmes and initiatives to 'drive change within the ethical sourcing space.' In 2009, the Group implemented its Ethical Sourcing Program, including its 14 'Rules to Trade,' which guide and govern the sourcing, manufacturing and supply of its products. Over the last 8 years, the Program has expanded significantly. Today, the Group is firmly focused on 'end-to-end mapping' of its entire supply chain, together with providing full disclosure of all suppliers' details via its corporate website by the end of 2018. In addition, the company is committed to ensuring fair wages are paid to all factory workers by 2021, all harmful chemicals are removed from the supply chain by 2025 and that all plastic bags are eliminated from point of sale. The Group also joined the Better Cotton Initiative in 2016, as well as partnering with Australia's non-governmental organization, Business for Development, to establish a sustainable cotton project in Kenya. Through this project, in addition to funding the training and set-up of each farm, the Group purchases 100 per cent of the cotton lint that is harvested each year, with a view to supporting 10,000 smallholder farmers by 2020.

The Group's desire to make a positive difference in people's lives is also evident through the business' philanthropic arm, the Cotton On Foundation. Established in 2007, the Foundation was born out of a trip by Nigel to Southern Uganda following a request to fund the completion of a healthcare centre in the village of Mannya. During his visit, Nigel realised the huge opportunity that existed to make a positive difference in the community by empowering youth through quality education. Over the last decade, the Foundation has raised over $63 million through the sale of incidental items, such as water bottles, mints and tote bags, across its global store network and online. With 100 per cent of proceeds going towards delivering quality education, the Foundation has created over 5,800 educational places. Additional ongoing projects mean the Foundation is 'on track to deliver its vision of 20,000 educational places by 2020.'

Questions:

1 What have been the critical success factors for Cotton On Group?
2 How might these factors change in the future as it continues to expand internationally?
3 Why is 'dwell time' important for a retailer?

Key internet business activities

Many businesses trade on the internet, selling virtual or real products or services. Internet traders can have access to international markets almost immediately upon start-up. Selling on the web offers the opportunity to do business 24 hours a day, seven days a week – world-wide. It also offers you the chance to build relationships and develop an understanding of individual customers' buying patterns. The pure internet retailer does not require the major fixed costs of a retail business like the high-street site and the shop-floor staff. However, many traditional bricks-and-mortar businesses are now also trading on the internet, trying to offer customers the best of both worlds. At the moment, internet-based retail is most successful for branded products where the features are already understood, or for 'low-touch' products or services such as music downloads, books, airline or theatre tickets where, once again, customers understand precisely what they are buying. Almost half of all computers are now sold online, compared to less than 10% of clothing and footwear.

The key to successful trading here is a good website – one that gets people to visit and then revisit. Of course you can trade on other ready-built e-tail platforms such as Amazon and eBay. However, you may want to control content and presentation and to have your own web presence – and these platforms charge for their services. Indeed, Microsoft® software contains a basic website writing tool on Microsoft Office Live, where you will find links to free web design tools. If you do not want to build your own website from scratch you can buy skeleton sites that you can customize yourself or employ professional web designers. You can spend as much as you want on designing and setting up your own website. A basic one might cost as little as £500 but a good one could easily cost £20,000. If you search online you will find many website design services, but try asking friends and colleagues for recommendations.

Your website should enable customers to order quickly and easily. A site with a difficult sales process is likely to lose customers before they reach the checkout. It should also be easy to navigate, so customers do not get frustrated and leave without even attempting to make a purchase. Data and transaction security should also be a priority, and potential customers should be assured that their details will be kept safe. The content of the website needs to be updated regularly so as to maintain customer interest. It should also present a 'human face' and, better still, build a community of interest that encourages the visitor to communicate with you, ideally leaving their email address. You can then communicate with them directly. Just as in the real world, you should try to build a relationship with your customers, and we saw in Chapters 6 and 7 that the internet can be an important part of a communications campaign that helps build a loyal customer base around your brand.

> Calypso Rose founder Clippy *Daily Telegraph* 6 February 2009
>
> Optimize your website. Keep driving customers to your website using PR and marketing and make your site sticky. It's your portal to world markets.

You need to get customers to visit your site in the first place; just as with bricks-and-mortar businesses, you need to create awareness. Internet businesses often seem to forget this. You can create awareness of your site by using all the media outlined in Chapter 7, particularly advertising on other websites or in print media. As we have seen, services such as Google AdWords can be very cost-effective because they operate on a 'pay-per-click' basis. Social media such as blogs, chat rooms and discussion forums can also be cheap ways of getting customers to become aware of your website.

All internet businesses need to ensure that potential customers searching the web for sites such as theirs get links to their site as quickly as possible. Search engines thrive on content, and the more relevant the content with keywords or phrases, the more likely your site is to be featured on a search. However, few people searching the web look beyond the first couple of pages of results. **Search engine optimization** (SEO) ensures that you catch any potential customers searching for your type of product on search engines such as Yahoo or Google as quickly as possible. However, SEO can be expensive if you employ a company to do it. On the other hand, you can learn how to do it yourself with the help of a good book, an online course and some specialist software, which helps you monitor the traffic on your own website. Two sites that offer SEO guides and tips are: searchengineland.com/guide/what-is-seo and www.seochat.com. Google offers a free tool for analysing your website traffic: www.google.com/analytics.

Table 10.5 provides a checklist of possible key operating activities for an internet business.

Table 10.5 Key operating activities checklist for an internet business

Pre-launch activities	Post-launch operations
• Web design and navigation	• Promotions
• Search engine optimization	• Social media promotions (e.g. blogs, chat rooms and discussion forums)
• Website advertising and promotion	• 'Community' building activities
• Credit/debit card merchant account	• Website update
• Transaction security	• Stock (inventory) control
• Merchandising and stocking	
• Launch advertising and promotion	

CASE insight 10.3

Made.com   🇬🇧 UK

Business models and risk

Made.com is an online furniture store. It was set up by Ning Li, a serial entrepreneur with experience of furniture selling in France, where he imported furniture from China. Made.com works directly with designers to custom make exclusive products for customers. 'Great design, affordable prices' is the strapline the company uses on its website, boasting that it connects customers with designers and craftsmen builders, cutting out the middle men. Putting the furniture retail market online has helped revolutionize what he calls a 'dusty industry' where retailers were reluctant to take risks with new designs and designers. The internet changed that, allowing experimentation with minimal risk and improving the speed of response to changing trends.

If a new designer comes to see us with a new amazing table that looks risky, we say 'Why not?'

because the only risk that we have is taking the photo. We put it online, if it doesn't sell, we pull it off. And if it sells, then everybody wins … The internet allows us to launch products much faster than traditional business … Speed is king … The speed of designing new products and also renewing your catalogue is key… to keep people's interest… keep them coming back to the website.

BBC News Business 3 November 2011

Visit the website: www.made.com

Question:

How can the internet be used to help minimize risk for your business?

Key manufacturing business activities

There are five types of operations processes involved in manufacturing or production.

Project – This is the production of one-off, large-scale products to meet the specific requirements of a client, for example, buildings. Normally the project is built or manufactured on site around the needs of the client, because it is not practical to move it once it is produced. Operational issues include effective resource delivery to and allocation around the site and the coordination of a large number of interrelated activities. The challenge is to deliver the project on time and on budget. Because it is a one-off, specialist knowledge of this sort of project and accurate costing are vital.

Jobbing – This is one-off production to meet the specific requirements of a client, but the process can be undertaken in a factory and then shipped to the client, for example, the production of a machine tool. This would normally make the organization of operations easier. The challenge remains to deliver the project on time and on budget, and specialist knowledge and accurate costing are vital.

Batch – This is where there is sufficient volume of production to justify organizing production in the most efficient and effective way. There is a degree of task repetition, but volumes rarely justify the investment of time in task analysis. An example is the manufacture of components that go on to be assembled into a bigger, more complicated product.

Line – This is where there is a further increase in volume, with a regularity of order that justifies the investment in task analysis and dedicated resources, for example, the production of a limited range of clothing. Assembling subcomponents (which may come from subcontractors) to form the final product is usually an important part of the process. Organizing these processes in the most efficient and effective way is important.

Continuous – This is where volumes have increased to such an extent that an inflexible, dedicated process is in place to run all day, every day, with a minimum of shut downs, for example, the production of consumer durables like washing machines. This is something that a small business would not normally be involved in.

Manufacturing and assembly can be complicated and often require expensive machinery. So the first question to ask is whether you need to undertake the task yourself or whether you might have the process undertaken more cheaply, more quickly and to a higher standard by subcontracting the operation to a specialist? The answer lies in the particular knowledge, skills and capabilities upon which your business is based. If these are not based in manufacturing, then looking for a subcontractor might be a good idea.

Most manufacturing businesses require machinery and equipment of some sort. You can use trade magazines to search out suppliers. Quality control is likely to be an important operating issue and there are UK/international quality standards that may help (BS/ISO 9000 series). You will also need to source raw materials. On the other hand you may decide to subcontract all the manufacturing and focus on other more critical elements of your business model. Business-to-business directories and websites such as Applegate, Alibaba and Kompass can help source suppliers and manufacturers from around the world.

> The website addresses of these business-to-business directories can be found in the *Guide to UK Sources of Help, Advice, Information and Funding* on the companion website: www.macmillanihe.com/burns-nvc-2e. An additional guide for Australian readers, produced by Dr Russell Manfield, is also provided.

Operating imperatives in manufacturing vary considerably. Project and jobbing manufacture requires a high degree of specialist knowledge and skill and may require expensive specialist equipment. Project management skills are also important. There is the opportunity to differentiate and brand the business based upon this. Small businesses seem attracted to batch manufacturing, probably because the batches are not sufficiently large to warrant pursuing efficiencies and economies of scale. However, batch manufacturing can involve high volumes and a relatively wide range of products with different orders competing for the same processes, and therefore control can be complicated. Line manufacturing involves the ability to organize assembly and manage repetitive, routine operations efficiently and effectively. Cost control, plant utilization and economies of scale are likely to be important. Table 10.6 provides a checklist of possible key operating activities for a manufacturing business.

Table 10.6 Key operating activities checklist for a manufacturer or service business

Pre-launch activities	Post-launch operations
• Premises lease • Licences • Premises design and layout • Equipment purchase • Staff recruitment and training • Materials and stocks • Safety procedures	**All manufacturers** • Quality control • Stock (inventory) control • Safety checks **Project and jobbing** • Project management • Knowledge and skills update **Batch** • Scheduling and processing of orders • Handling complexity **Line** • Staff control • Efficiency studies

Key service business activities

The most important activity for a service business is the ability to deliver that service, and that depends upon the knowledge, skills and abilities of those delivering the service. All service businesses involve people, and their training is important. This training might reflect the specialist nature of the service – for example in consultancy and training. It might reflect the service process – for example where efficiency and effectiveness is important. Where direct contact with the client is involved, training should help develop the interpersonal skills of staff and their ability to manage client relationships as well as other staff.

Perhaps surprisingly, service delivery has some similarities with manufacturing. Larger consultancy assignments take the form of projects and require the same degree of coordination and control. A tailor-made training programme is similar to jobbing. A computer bureau that processes different clients' work is, in effect, a batch manufacturer. A fast-food restaurant has more than a passing similarity to line manufacturing. Table 10.6 therefore also acts as a checklist of possible key operating activities for a service business.

Entrepreneurs and risk taking

Start-ups are risky and it is important that the risks are managed effectively. Actions to monitor, manage and mitigate risk are likely to form some of the key activities you undertake. Some will probably be critical success factors. However, before we look at systematic ways of doing this, we need to consider the way that most entrepreneurs approach the issue.

Entrepreneurs are often seen as being intuitive, almost whimsical, in their decision making, as 'overconfident', particularly with regard to predicting a future outcome – a characteristic associated with self-efficacy and a high internal locus of control (Chapter 1). It is little wonder then that economists find their approach difficult to understand and to model. It certainly does not fit well into 'logical' economic models such as discounted cash flow. As a result entrepreneurs can often be seen as risk takers. However, while entrepreneurs may be prepared to take measured risks, there is no evidence that they like taking risks, more that they adopt a number of approaches to manage and mitigate it. These approaches to managing risk revolve around their approach to strategy and decision making and their use of knowledge and information, known as **contingency thinking**. Taken together, the approach is just as logical, but little understood.

As we saw in Chapter 5, successful entrepreneurs develop a strong vision of what they want their business to become. It is part of their motivation. Although they do not always know how they will achieve the vision because of the uncertain environment they face, they have strong **strategic intent** (*kosoryoku*) that keeps moving in the 'right' direction despite detours or setbacks. This requires a loose or flexible strategy that creates multiple strategic options so that it can be adapted quickly to suit changing circumstances. This is achieved through a continuous process of strategy review called **strategizing** – assessing the options about how to make the most of opportunities or avoid risks as they arise. By creating more strategic options they improve their chances of successfully pursuing at least one opportunity and avoiding most risks. They keep as many options as possible open for as long as possible. This is one important way entrepreneurs have for managing the risks they face. The greater the number of strategic options the better.

> Wayne Edy founder Inov-8 Sunday Times 15 March 2015
>
> As overwhelming as it might seem, if you have vision and you believe you have a unique product, then go for it. You need to take risks and accept that you will not succeed every time but that's part of the process. When it comes right, it's an amazing journey.

Entrepreneurs also make decisions differently. Research shows that they appear to make extensive use of cognitive heuristics (simplifying strategies) in decision making, a characteristic associated with self-efficacy and a high internal locus of control (Chapter 1). This entails using mental model or dominant logic as a basis for decision making. This is because in the fast-moving and uncertain world of entrepreneurial opportunities decisions often have to be made quickly. However this approach flies in the face of calm logic and can itself be risky. To combat this, entrepreneurs adopt an incremental approach to decision making. They delay decisions as long as possible, giving time to obtain as much information as possible, and then commit scarce resources on an incremental basis, only as required. It is this combination of long-term strategic intent and incremental decision making that gives them the flexibility to manage risk effectively. They find ways of reconciling these issues: ways of developing strategy without overcommitting to one course of action and ways of minimizing their investment in resources. They start with the resources they can afford to lose and then move forward (**affordable loss**) – an approach to which we shall return later in this chapter.

For example, successful entrepreneurs tend to keep capital investment and fixed costs as low as possible, sometimes renting or leasing the asset, often subcontracting some activities. They might take on temporary staff rather than taking on part- or full-time staff. They tend to commit to costs only after the opportunity has proved to be real, which may be prudent and reflect their resource limits, but then they run the risk of losing first-mover advantage in the market place – a difficult judgement call. Frequently, therefore, they will experiment with low-cost market entry or lean start-up and learn from this (Chapter 4).

The key to this approach is the acquisition of knowledge and information, often coming from the networks of close personal relationships the entrepreneurs have developed. They use these networks to form partnerships, strategic alliances and joint ventures that help them spread the risk of a venture, as well as leveraging the strategic skills of the partnership (which also helps them avoid overcommitment). They commit only limited resources to a new venture at any time – the resources they can afford to lose (affordable loss) – and take an incremental approach to decision making, assessing information and risks at each decision point.

Identifying risks

By launching your business you are inherently making a judgement – explicitly or implicitly – that you can overcome any risks that you might face. But have you really identified those risks? How will you know if or when they materialize? And have you got contingency plans to deal with them should they materialize? Anybody reading your business plan will expect that you have. Risk often goes hand in hand with return. The higher the returns your business offers, the higher the risks that it is likely to face. So, just as financiers evaluate your financial projections (and the likelihood of achieving them), they also evaluate the risks that you face and your ability to deal with them.

It's easy to take a risk when it's just a couple of founders working from a garage; risk taking is part of a start-up's DNA. When your business grows, you still need to take risks, except there's a lot more at stake. Sometimes 'betting the company' is essential, but other times the reward needs to be weighed up against the risks for shareholders, customers and clients. We take lots of risks but only when the odds are in our favour.

Adam Schwab founder Lux Group The Sydney Morning Herald 28 April 2014

Risk is inherent in business. While it cannot be avoided, with knowledge and information it can be managed – or, more accurately, identified and even quantified so that it can be managed down to acceptable levels. This might involve putting in place appropriate controls or at least monitoring early warning of potential problems materializing. These could be key activities. If risks can be avoided or options created in advance about how to deal with them, then less time is spent 'fire fighting' when they materialize.

You start by trying to identify the key risks that you face. Of course you cannot hope to predict all eventualities, but the more you try to anticipate them, the more you are able to generate both plans to deal with these risks and strategic options about the changes in direction that might result. Risk can take a number of forms. The risks associated with a particular course of action or achieving particular objectives might be identified. The corporate risks an organization faces might be identified. These risks may come from:

- **External incidents** (such as flood, fire and pandemic illness etc.) – These can be difficult to predict and the probability of occurrence might be low. However, the possible impact might be so great – for example, loss of life – that you need contingency plans to deal with them. Some of these risks will be generic to an industry; for example, the reaction of competitors.
- **Internal incidents** (such as the loss of sources of supply, malfunction of a major machine and product contamination etc.) – These can be many and varied, depending on the operations of your business. A good place to start looking for possibilities is in your key operating activities.

You can try simply brainstorming the risks you face but another approach that can be useful is scenario planning (Chapter 3). Based on the threats an organization faces, scenarios can be explored about the results of these threats materializing. Table 10.7 gives you a checklist of possible risks that a start-up might face. It is not exclusive and is in no particular order of priority. However, no matter how thorough your analysis, you can never expect to identify every possible risk. As has been said, the only two certain things in life are death and taxes, and one or two multinationals are working to reduce the latter.

Table 10.7 Risks checklist

• Pre-launch delays – are any of the pre-launch key activities likely to cause delays?	• Productivity – is it meeting targets?
• Competitors – what are they doing?	• Administration – are processes and procedures working well?
• Competitive advantage – is it being eroded?	• Brand identity – is it being established?
• Market – how is it changing?	• IP – is it secure?
• Customer value proposition – is it being delivered?	• Technology – how are changes affecting you?
• Product/service quality – is it adequate?	• Investment – do you need more?
• Customer service – are customers satisfied?	• Stocks/inventory – are they adequate or too much?
• Cash flow – is it adequate?	• Merchandising – is it under control?
• Sales – are you meeting targets?	• Debtors/receivables – are they under control?
• Profits – are you meeting targets?	• Interest rates – how will changes affect you?
• Operations – are key activities under control?	• Exchange rates – how will changes affect you?
	• Management – are the team managing well?

Mapping the risks and opportunities for your business early on can make all the difference.

The Guardian Media Planet May 2015
Richard Branson founder Virgin Group

Identifying the risks is only the start of the process because not all risks are the same. Also important is the probability of the risk materializing. If the probability is very low, is there any point in preparing contingency plans? The answer may be 'yes' – if the impact on your business would be large. And then there is the question of how the risks can be reduced or avoided and what you need to do to monitor these risks. Effective risk management is therefore a five-stage process:

1 Identifying the risks (internal or external);
2 Evaluating the probability of the risk materializing;
3 Evaluating the impact if that risk materializes;
4 Deciding how the risk might be mitigated (reduced or avoided);
5 Deciding what early warning signs might be monitored to identify that the risk is materializing.

Assessing risks

Risk management is about prioritization. Ideally the risks with the highest probability of occurrence and the greatest loss to the organization are handled first, and those with the lowest probability of occurrence and the smallest loss are dealt with last (2 and 3 in the list above). However, superimposed on this is the issue of whether the risks are controllable or not – whether they can be mitigated in some way. Figure 10.2 shows a useful way of classifying risks along these three dimensions. Any risks that have a major impact on the business are undesirable, but those which are very likely to happen pose the greatest danger (quadrant D). By way of contrast, risks with a low impact and a low likelihood of occurrence (quadrant A) pose the least risk. The third dimension is controllability. Some risks may be under your control or influence; others might be completely outside your control.

Generally, the less you control or influence the risk, the greater the danger it poses to your business. In this way the risk matrix becomes a Rubik's cube, with the greatest danger being in the cube with the highest impact, highest likelihood and least controllability (quadrant G). These risks cannot be mitigated but must be closely monitored. The risks that are very likely to happen and have a major impact on the organization but can be controlled (quadrant D) will be the focus of managerial action to mitigate them.

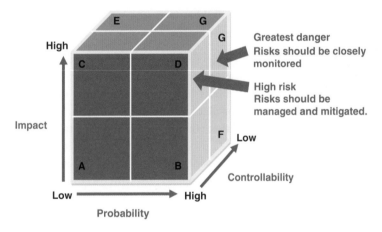

Figure 10.2 Risk classification

Figure 10.2 classifies risk probability as either low or high and risk impact as either low or high. In reality it is often very difficult to quantify the probability of a risk materializing beyond a simple low (1), medium (2) or high (3). The monetary impact of the risk materializing might be just as difficult to establish beyond a similar low (1), medium (2) or high (3). The composite **risk factor** is defined as the probability of occurrence multiplied by the impact of the risk event. Using the simple classifications above, the highest composite risk factor is therefore 9 (3×3) and the lowest is 1 (1×1). This 1 to 9 scale can then be reclassified as low (1–3), medium (4–6) and high (7–9). This is called a **risk index**. The higher the index number, the greater the impact and the probability of the risk happening. These are the really dangerous risks. The question is how might you control or mitigate them?

Mitigating risks

Once you have your risk index, you can decide what to do about the risks you face and start to develop key activities. You have four options.

1 **Attempt to eliminate the risk** – You might withdraw completely from the area of activity that generates the risk, an unlikely course of action initially for an entrepreneurial business. However, you need to at least continue to monitor these risks because at some point in the future you might change this decision.

2 **Attempt to reduce the risk** – You might increase internal controls, training or supervision depending on the nature of the risk. Alternatively, you might select strategic alternatives that are less risky. Many of these strategies might involve transferring or sharing the risk with others, for example, by partnering.

3 **Transfer the risk** – There are many useful techniques that can be used to transfer both internal and external risks (e.g. insurance, foreign exchange or interest rate hedging). For example, companies constantly 'insure' against currency fluctuations – a risk they neither control nor influence – by buying forward in the currency market. Partnering in all its forms (e.g. subcontracting, outsourcing, franchising etc.) is an extremely effective way of transferring risk.

4 **Accept the risk** – You might simply accept all the risks in quadrant D. If you accept the risk completely, all you can attempt to do is plan to manage the risk and put in place early-warning indicators of it materializing, although this might be uneconomic if the impact on the organization is small. Many industries have inherent risks that need to be accepted if you decide to operate in that sector.

The most dangerous situation in business is where you have a high likelihood of occurrence, together with a high impact – a high risk index – in a situation where you have little control (quadrant G in Figure 10.2). In this situation you might consider any of options 1 to 3, but even if you end up accepting the risk it is vital that you monitor it and then take corrective action if it materializes. Quadrant G probably represents the situation you might face with competitors if your business proves successful – and you really need to have some plans and strategic options to deal with this (option 2).

Monitoring risks

All organizations have to accept some residual risk associated with their operations. However, you will need to monitor those risks with the highest risk index numbers, particularly those that are least controllable. And this is where the information you gather by networking with customers, suppliers and other professionals is of vital importance. This can give you foreknowledge of risks materializing. You just need to be as aware of risks as opportunities and to ensure that you monitor them in a systematic way.

For those risks with the highest risk index numbers, you need to identify parameters or events that indicate an increased likelihood of the risk materializing – called **key risk indicators**. These need to be monitored on a regular basis so you can then take remedial action. To be effective, key risk indicators must be easy to monitor as part of your regular activity, highlighting when corrective action is needed and providing guidance on what action is needed. Cash flow is an obvious, simple example of a key risk indicator. The risk is bankruptcy – you need cash to pay your bills – and cash flow measures your ability to do this. Most start-ups need to monitor their cash flow on a regular and frequent basis. At the very least, it is a key activity, which might become critical if cash runs out. We deal with this in Chapter 13.

If the reaction of competitors is a major risk to your business, you need to develop a risk indicator that will measure this and put in place activities to ensure that it is monitored. For example, supermarkets regularly and routinely monitor the prices competitors charge for a typical basket of products. Without doing this they risk being uncompetitive and losing customers to rivals.

Partnerships, strategic alliances and joint ventures

One key way that entrepreneurs mitigate their risk is through networking and partnerships. These can provide knowledge and information about the risks you might face, how they might be mitigated and what you might select as your key risk indicators. They can also help you minimize your fixed costs and therefore your borrowings. Partnerships can take many forms, from the more structured ones outlined on page 312, to simple, ad-hoc, subcontracting to other firms, the use of sales agents in overseas markets, zero-hours employee contracts and 'gig-workers' (argued to be more like involuntary self-employment). The internet has made outsourcing work, even to other countries, relatively easy. Crowdsourcing can even be used to find skills and knowledge that you do not have. These are structures that shift the risk of employment entirely onto the worker, agent or subcontractor, and turn what might have been a fixed cost, into a variable one. They can find skills and resources for you that you may not have.

The manufacture of computers provides an excellent example of how partnerships underpin many of today's complex supply chains. Every element of the value chain might be located so as to provide the best combination of cost and expertise, as shown in Table 10.8.

Table 10.8 Partnerships for a computer manufacturer

Component/process	Supplier location
Design	USA (in collaboration with third-party manufacturers)
Assembly	China
Microprocessor	Designed and manufactured in USA
Graphics card	Designed in Canada, manufactured in China
Screen	Manufactured in Korea
Hard disk drive	Designed in USA, manufactured in Malaysia
Lithium battery	Japan
Logistics	Subcontracted to third parties – some local, some global
Telephone sales/support	Subcontracted to third parties in key countries

As we saw in Chapter 8, partnership, in its many different forms, can be an invaluable way of exploiting a business opportunity where you may not have all the skills or resources to pursue it yourself. Used properly, partnerships can leverage up your capabilities and help limit risk. Any partnership is usually only formed by mutual agreement and therefore where there is mutual advantage in the collaboration. The actual nature of these collaborations can vary from informal to formal, underpinned by legal contract.

Partnership – Partnering with others or organizations in setting up a new venture simplifies the operating tasks you face and mitigates your risks. Since assets are owned or contributed by all the partners, the financial resources needed and the associated risks are spread, and flexibility is increased. True partners can become part of a team pursuing a particular

The benefits of partnerships and strategic alliances

Numerous academic studies have shown that there are real benefits from strategic alliances and partnerships for organizations of all sizes. A government survey in the UK concluded that: 'in both the UK and the US, we observe that the highest growth firms rely *heavily* on building relationships with other firms, either through supply chains or through formal strategic alliances' (DBER, 2008, emphasis added). Alliances can create economic advantage by leveraging market presence (Lewis, 1990; Lorange and Roos, 1992; Ohmae, 1989). An example is Oneworld, a strategic alliance of a dozen airlines including British Airways and American Airlines whose primary purpose is to encourage passengers to use partner airlines. Alliances can also provide vertical integration and scale economies at a greatly reduced cost (Anderson and Weitz, 1992). In its simplest form this is the arrangement a distributor has with a manufacturer when they have sole distribution rights.

Anderson, E. and Weitz, B. (1992) 'The Use of Pledges to Build and Sustain Commitment in Distribution Channels', *Journal of Marketing Research*, 29 (February).

DBER (Department of Business, Enterprise and Regulatory Reform) (2008) 'High Growth Firms in the UK: Lessons from an Analysis of Comparative UK Performance', *BERR Economic Paper*, 3 (November).

Lewis, J.D. (1990) *Partnerships for Profit: Structuring and Managing Strategic Alliances*, New York: Free Press.

Lorange, P. and Roos, J. (1992) *Strategic Alliances: Formation, Implementation and Evolution*, Oxford: Blackwell.

Ohmae, K. (1989) 'The Global Logic of Strategic Alliances', *Harvard Business Review*, March/April.

opportunity, even though not part of the same legal entity. They can help you in unexpected ways and you can often leverage their capability and resources to your mutual advantage. So, just as you try to develop relationships with customers, you should try to develop them with other business entities. View your suppliers as partners, rather than just suppliers of a resource. But there are a wide range of partners and partnerships.

Strategic alliances – These are a form of partnership whereby separate organizations come together to pursue an agreed set of objectives. They can be an effective way of sustaining competitive advantage and are particularly important in relation to innovation, where the partners have different competencies that they can apply in pursuing a commercial opportunity. There are often explicit strategic and operational motives for alliances, such as gaining access to new markets. Jaguar partnered with the Williams racing team in 2011 to produce a new hybrid electric/petrol supercar. In 2012 Nokia partnered with Microsoft to rejuvenate its smartphone offering with the Lumia. Some start-ups have based their international expansion strategy almost entirely on foreign alliances.

Joint venture – A more formal strategic partnership is called a joint venture. This usually has a degree of direct market involvement and therefore needs to be underpinned by some form of legal agreement that determines the split of resource inputs and rewards. Often the joint venture takes the form of a legal entity that is separate from either of the parties involved. Richard Branson has been particularly adept at using joint ventures as a basis for rolling out new business ideas. He partnered with Deutsche Telekom to create Virgin Mobile, and Singapore Airlines owned 49% of Virgin Airlines. Some developing countries do not allow foreign companies to set up in their country, only allowing joint ventures with local organizations. The opticians and hearing-aid specialists, Specsavers, operate a contract-based, joint venture approach to retailing, tailored to professional practitioners, in this case opticians. It offers all the advantages of a franchise but gives the local operator greater professional autonomy and responsibility. Specsavers is now the largest chain of opticians in the UK and expanding rapidly in other countries.

Generic risk management strategies

There are a number of other generic strategies that can be used to manage and mitigate risk.

Affordable loss and lean start-up

Academic insight 4.1 outlined an entrepreneurial approach to management called effectuation and introduced the concept of 'affordable loss'. Entrepreneurs tend to go to market as quickly and cheaply as possible and assess market demand from that trial. They set an 'affordable loss', evaluating opportunities based upon whether that loss was acceptable, rather than trying to evaluate the attractiveness of the predictable upside. They decide what they are willing to lose rather than what they expect to make and therefore do not have to worry about the accuracy of predictions. Affordable loss can be calculated with some certainty, depending on your situation. The idea is to decide what loss is acceptable to you, should the business fail. This defines the maximum extent of your loss from the very beginning and helps shape the start-up in terms of its risk/return profile. It is a two-step process. Firstly, set your acceptable level of risk (affordable loss), then push to maximize the return this will make, as shown in Figure 10.3.

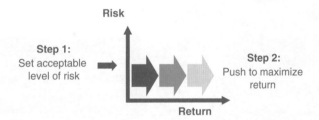

Figure 10.3 Setting risk and maximizing return

> We expanded very slowly and very carefully because in our other jobs we had some experience studying other industries, like the dot.com industry, which seemed to just sort of appear ... and then it just exploded ... We basically put into it what we could afford and we were prepared that if it didn't work out we weren't going to be on the streets.
>
> Awfully Chocolate BBC News Business 8 November 2010 — Lyn Lee founder

The approach is linked to the concept of lean start-up, outlined in Academic insight 4.4. Using lean start-up you can gain the maximum information about viability by small-scale market entry. As you gain more information, you might set higher levels of affordable loss. Lean start-up allows you to assess the viability of the business model you developed. This is part of your **commercialization risk** – the unique risk associated with developing a new product and ensuring customer acceptance. You can also help to minimize your commercialization risk through the knowledge and information you gain by networking and partnering. The challenge then is to leverage up your affordable loss through knowledge and partnerships and only finally through external finance to find a start-up strategy that is achievable.

Borrowing and bootstrapping

One way of maximizing your return is by using other people's money as well as your own. As we shall explain in Chapter 13, so long as the return you are able to make on this investment exceeds the rate of interest you are paying, then borrowing pays. However, when the reverse happens, you have to foot the bill and find the difference. And if the business should fail, it may be that you will have to repay the borrowing from your own personal funds. It all

Smak Parlour USA

© Smak Parlour

Abby Kessler and Katie Lubieski

Business models and risk

Abby Kessler and Katie Lubieski met in high school and went to Drexel University to study design and merchandising. They moved to New York to work in the garment industry but soon returned to Philadelphia to design and sell edgy T-shirts to boutiques around the country. Twelve years ago they opened a fashion boutique in the Old City district of Philadelphia, selling affordable clothing and jewellery targeted at 'fashion-savvy' women. It was successful and they thought about expansion, but the high costs and risks put them off until they heard about 'fashion trucks' in Los Angeles. These are simply box trucks that have been turned into mobile shops and follow the trend in mobile vending in the USA that was started by gourmet food trucks.

The cost of the truck is $20,000–$30,000, and it costs about $70,000 to make the truck into a shop (including air conditioning, fit-out, changing room, skylight and stock), depending on what you want. But the overhead costs are then very low. You do not have to pay for leases or utilities, only the vehicle running costs (insurance, fuel etc.) and parking permits (anything from free to $1,000 per day, depending on location). And you can take the shop to the target customers. Smak Parlour advertises its daily location to its loyal customer base on social media sites, and also visits fairs, festivals and conventions.

Visit the website: www.smakparlour.com

Questions:

1   What is the link between lean start-up and risk minimization?
2   List the ways you can minimize the risks facing your business.

comes back to the relationship between risk and financial return. Normally, the higher the risk, the higher the financial return. So, if you really want to minimize your risk, you will have to minimize your borrowings and this may affect your financial return.

> Keep your costs to a minimum. If you can work from home and do your own PR in the beginning this will give you the cash to develop the product.
>
> *Calypso Rose founder Clippy Daily Telegraph 6 February 2009*

The reality is that the lower your external funding requirement, including borrowing, the easier it is to start up, and the less you might lose if the idea does not work. The funding you need is partly determined by the assets you need to start up and your 'affordable loss' – the amount you are willing to invest in the business. There has got to be a way of bridging any gap. However, if you can minimize your commitment of resources for as long as possible, you also minimize your funding requirement. This has implications for how you approach decision making, but you also need to realize that you do not need to own a resource to be able to use and control it. Sometimes changes to your business model can help minimize your borrowings. You may be able to borrow or rent the resource or partner with others who provide it. If you do not own a resource, you are in a better position to commit and de-commit quickly, giving you greater flexibility and reducing the risks you face. In the USA, minimizing the resources or assets that you own but still use and control is called 'bootstrapping'. To bootstrap you need to tap into as wide a network of contacts as possible.

Compartmentalizing risk

A simple strategy followed by many entrepreneurs is to **compartmentalize** their business risks by setting each operation up as a separate legal entity. Should one fail, it will not endanger another. Serial entrepreneurs do this as a matter of course, partly because they intend to sell off each business at some point in the future. But other businesses, such as the Virgin Group, operate as holding companies that own (or partly own) numerous subsidiaries for less obvious reasons.

High margins and low fixed costs

As we saw in Chapter 6, high contribution margins (sale price minus variable cost) offer greater pricing discretion, which gives you the opportunity to price in different market segments differentially, thus maximizing sales volume. At the same time, low fixed costs mean lower risk of loss, should sales reduce. Both give you greater flexibility. So the two most important principles in any new venture, allowing you to keep your financial risks as low as possible are:

- **Keep your contribution margins as high as possible** – As we have observed, high contribution margins generally can only be achieved through strong differential advantage, and they allow you also to tailor prices for different market segments, thereby maximizing sales.
- **Keep your fixed costs as low as possible** – Fixed costs can come from operating costs, such as depreciation of fixed assets, or interest on borrowings. High fixed operating or overhead costs are called high **operating gearing/leverage**. High financing costs are called high financial **gearing/leverage**. Chapter 13 will outline metrics that measure these. Both should be kept as low as possible – consistent with a lean start-up. If you keep your investment in fixed assets low – and particularly your borrowings to finance them – then your fixed costs will be low.

> The ideal business has no fixed overheads, commission only sales, large volume and low overheads.
>
> *David Speakman founder Travel Counsellors Sunday Times 6 December 1998*

High interest payments could easily become a quadrant G risk in Figure 10.2. If turnover goes down, interest payments remain fixed and therefore reduce profit. Indeed, sometimes interest rates, and therefore interest payments, can go up when turnover, and therefore profit, are already reducing. This is the classic situation that is created when interest rates are increased in order to

CASE insight 10.5

Richard Branson and Virgin (2)

 UK

Compartmentalizing risk

Richard Branson is probably the best-known entrepreneur in Britain. Now in his sixties, his business life started as an 18-year-old schoolboy when he launched *Student* magazine, selling advertising space from a phone booth. His views on risk are interesting. In many ways he has been expert at minimizing his personal exposure to risk. He launched *Student* by writing to well-known personalities and celebrities – pop and film stars and politicians – and persuading them to contribute articles or agree to interviews. He persuaded a designer to work for no fee, negotiated a printing contract for 50,000 copies and got Peter Blake, the designer of The Beatles' *Sgt Pepper's* album cover, to draw the cover picture of a student. His first Virgin record shop was 'given' to him rent-free.

Today Branson's Virgin Group is made up of more than 20 separate umbrella companies, operating over 370 separate businesses. If any one were to fail it would not affect the others. Branson shares ownership with various partners. For example, Virgin Atlantic is 51% owned by Branson, with the remainder by the US carrier Delta Air Lines. Virgin contributes the brand and Richard Branson's PR profile, while the partner provides the capital input – in some ways like a franchise operation – and often the operational expertise. However, Branson is not afraid to commit his own (or borrowed) money when needed, for example when Virgin Atlantic was reprivatized.

As a result of this strategy, Branson and Virgin have seen some notable failures, but the brand has survived intact. The most widely publicized failure was Virgin Cola, launched in 1994 and closed down in 2012. Virgin Vodka suffered the same fate and was part of the entire Virgin

Drinks subsidiary that was eventually closed. Virgin Vie was a cosmetics venture that was launched in 1997 and wound up in 2010. Virgin Clothing was probably the shortest-lived venture. Offering men's and women's clothing, it was launched in 1998 but was wound up in 2000. Virginware, a venture selling female lingerie, was similarly disastrous, closing down after four years in 2005. Indeed, some of Branson's companies have themselves 'subcontracted' the brand to insulate themselves from commercial risk. For example, when Virgin Atlantic launched Little Red in 2013 – a small, UK-based domestic airline – it subcontracted all operations to the Irish company Aer Lingus on a 'wet lease' basis, meaning that they supplied the crew and aircraft, albeit in Virgin livery. Little Red closed down in 2014.

While he may tolerate risk and accept failure because it goes with being entrepreneurial, Branson continues to try to mitigate it throughout his business empire:

One thing is certain in business; you and everyone around you will make mistakes. When you are pushing the boundaries this is inevitable – but it's important to recognise this. We need to look for new ways to shape up to the competition. So we trust people to learn from mistakes; blame and recriminations are pointless. A person who makes no mistakes, makes nothing.

www.hrmagazine.co.uk 13 July 2010

Visit the website: www.virgin.com

Question:

Why has the Virgin brand remained recognized and respected, despite these failures?

---

decrease overall demand in the economy. The result is that small firms are squeezed by facing both higher interest costs and reducing sales.

There is a tension between a high contribution margin and low fixed costs. Firms with high margins are often associated with high fixed costs. For example, their high differential advantage may come from a high investment in technology or marketing. At the same time, firms competing primarily on price may be keeping their costs low through economies of scale, which are normally associated with investment in fixed assets such as plant and machinery. Because of this tension, the important factor is not the absolute level of contribution margin

Gordon Ramsay UK

Business models and risk

Gordon Ramsay is a famous TV chef with hit shows in the UK and USA such as *Hell's Kitchen*, *Kitchen Nightmares* and *Hotel Hell*. But that did not stop his business, Gordon Ramsay Holdings, from nearly failing in 2010/11 because he adopted the wrong business model and the wrong business partner. Most celebrity chefs license a partner such as a restaurant chain to use their name. They lend their name, create menus, hire key staff and undertake some promotion. In return, the chef receives a fee plus a percentage of turnover. However, the model Ramsay used was to set up and operate all the restaurants around the world himself and pay rent to the restaurant chain – potentially more lucrative but also more risky. This meant his capital costs and therefore borrowing were very high, and when the recession of 2008 hit, his fixed interest costs could not be met by his operating profits. What is more, often Ramsay committed to spend time at these restaurants – time that he did not have because of his TV appearances.

The result was a loss of £4.1 million in 2011, which meant that the company breached its loan agreements. Ramsay also fell out spectacularly with his father-in-law, Chris Hutchinson, who used to run the firm, accusing him publicly of siphoning off £1.4 million of company funds to support a secret family. After an acrimonious court battle, Ramsay bought Hutchinson's 30% stake in the firm, costing the firm some £5 million. Ramsay had then to inject £2.5 million of his own money into the company to prevent it from going into bankruptcy.

Ramsay found a new partner, Stuart Gillies, who took 10% of the company that was renamed the Gordon Ramsay Group. Many of the restaurants around the world were closed and the debt was repaid. Some restaurants were even 'un-branded' as 'Gordon Ramsay' restaurants. The business model was also changed to one that is more conventional and lower risk. The Group no longer put up capital. They take a fee for Ramsay's name and between 6% and 8% of turnover. Ramsay takes no salary from the group and his media earnings, which exceed £15 million a year, go through a separate company. Ramsay spends most of his time working on TV and books that create the brand that pulls customers into his restaurants. As a result of these changes, the profits of the Gordon Ramsay Group started growing again and the company was able to restart its expansion overseas, opening restaurants in Las Vegas, USA, and the Middle East, and returning to Asia.

Source: Facts taken from *Sunday Times Magazine*, 14 July 2013

Question:

What lessons do you learn from Gordon Ramsay's experience?

and fixed costs but the relationship between them. This is measured by your breakeven point, another financial metric that will be explained in Chapter 13.

Risk management, critical success factors and strategic options

Operating activities can be developed to monitor and mitigate the risks you face. You can apply this risk management framework to any of your key operating activities. Your critical success factors should be the key activities needed to address the risks falling into quadrants D and G in Figure 10.2 – high risk and greatest danger. If they are controllable, you need to prepare action plans – decide what actions are required, who is responsible for undertaking them and establish timelines for their completion.

You also need to prepare **strategic options** – the actions you need to take if these critical factors do not go according to plan. Creating strategic options is about contingency planning. It is about creating as many options for future courses of action as possible so as to better deal with an uncertain and rapidly changing commercial environment. The more strategic options you have, the less the likely impact of the risks you face should they materialize. This is particularly the case if you have highlighted any critical success factors over which you have little or no control, for example, with competitive reaction. Preparing scenarios of 'worst-possible' cases in advance of them happening allows you to prepare contingency plans rather than trying to react after the event.

This risk management framework can be used to highlight the downside risks facing both your launch and your growth strategies (Chapters 7 and 8). However, it can be turned on its head and used to look at business opportunities and strategic options, seeking to identify those with the highest impact (profit), highest probability (of success) and highest controllability (quadrant D, again). Once more, you need to prepare action plans – decide what actions are required, who is responsible for undertaking them and establish timelines for their completion. And what are the critical success factors? You can even use the Gantt chart technique we shall look at in the next section to help you plan this. You then need to generate strategic options, should things not go according to plan. The whole process is a continuous one that involves a concept called **strategizing** – the continuous development of strategy by assessing strategic options about how to make the most of opportunities or avoid risks as they arise.

Your success will depend on your ability to manage and mitigate both the commercialization and more general business risks you face – both pre- and post-launch. The key risks you face need to be highlighted in the business plan. How you propose to deal with them will lead to the development of your critical success factors, underpinned by detailed action plans, and strategic options. Both critical success factors and strategic options also need to be highlighted in your plan. Successfully dealing with critical success factors is a key milestone for a business. They are things to be celebrated when they are dealt with.

CASE
insight
10.7

Flying Tiger Copenhagen (3) DENMARK

Developing an operating model and identifying risks

We looked at Flying Tiger's business model in Case insight 6.2 and its growth and expansion model in Case insight 8.3. The company's ambitious growth targets are facilitated by its investment in what it calls its 'scalable corporate backbone', which aims to simplify operations and support future rapid growth. The operations model for their business units is anchored in a centralized, proactive management team that monitors and reviews the operational and financial performance of operating units. The team aims to take advantage of local or seasonal marketing opportunities and address problems of underperformance which show up. Tiger is investing substantial sums in a common IT system (using a Microsoft Dynamics AX ERP platform) so as to streamline their business processes and ensure a greater level of standardization. Not only does this increase efficiency, it also makes it easier to scale up operations quickly.

Because it operates a low-cost business model, it is important for Tiger that costs are kept as low as possible. That means it needs to have efficient supply chain operations and processes. Most Tiger products are produced by external suppliers. Tiger aims to minimize lead times from purchase to sale by making their sales forecasting process as efficient as possible. This minimizes working capital requirements as well as freeing up capital for further store expansion and future partner buy-outs. Suppliers agree to Tiger's code of conduct and often, because Tiger has a hand in the design of many of the products, work under the company's supervision. Most logistics are subcontracted to external operators, minimizing the investment in assets and making it easier to scale up operations quickly. Warehousing was reorganized in 2015 to reduce lead times to stores, minimize transportation costs and increase capacity. While the company has its own warehouse in Greve (Denmark), the warehouses in Barcelona (Spain), Raunds (UK) and New Jersey (USA) are all operated by external partners. Transport is provided by freight forwarders.

Tiger has highlighted nine areas of risk that it monitors and has put in place mitigation policies for.

1 Financial risk – mainly foreign exchange and interest rate. This is mitigated by hedging foreign currency risk for 80% of expected procurement for 12 months ahead, on a half-yearly basis. It also hedges its exposure to interest rate fluctuations by maintaining a mix between fixed and floating rate borrowings.
2 Liquidity risk – which is mitigated by monitoring its cash flow.
3 Competition risk – which is mitigated by investment in the business model. Initiatives include continued strengthening of creative capabilities within category management, product design and innovation, visual merchandising, marketing and branding as well as training of the store staff.
4 Expansion risk – mainly performance issues in local markets. This is monitored by business reviews and controls which aim to identify and then proactively address any potential disruptions in local markets.
5 Sourcing and supply chain risk – which is monitored on an ongoing basis. This is mitigated by the company's investment policy which aims to strengthen sourcing and supply chain systems, processes and capabilities so as to minimize disruption in supplies. Suppliers must adhere to the company's Code of Conduct and the company has a supplier audit programme.
6 Products, trademarks and legal risk – which are mitigated by having dedicated teams who focus on legal and compliance matters across the different legal jurisdictions in which the company operates.
7 Partner collaboration and buy-out risk – which is mitigated by the partner business model which entails a 'put' or a 'call' notice of one year. This allows the company to develop a detailed plan to transfer ownership and operations of the stores alongside the partner.
8 Infrastructure risk – mainly implementation of the company's new IT systems. This is mitigated by the strengthening of the company's project organization and project management capabilities, which is now monitored by the Executive Management.
9 People risk – which is about attracting, motivating and retaining qualified employees. This is mitigated through the work of Tiger's HR function, which supports the local operating companies and has rolled out various recruitment and training initiatives, including a recruitment kit designed to assist in local recruitment.

Visit the website: flyingtiger.com and corporate.flyingtiger.com/about

Questions:

1 Refer back to the Framework Worksheet or PowerPoint slide which you completed for Case insights 6.2 and 8.3. Using the information in this case, complete as many other elements of the New Venture Creation Framework as you can. Does this now explain Tiger's business model?
2 From all the information given in this and previous Case insights, undertake a SWOT analysis on Tiger.
3 List Tiger's critical success factors.
4 List Tiger's strategic options as it grows.

 Visit www.macmillanihe.com/burns-nvc-2e to download the Framework Worksheet and PowerPoint slide.

Operating plans and critical paths

You need a broad, 'high-level' version of the operating plan to go into a business plan. This should identify major linkages and **critical paths**, including high-impact quadrant D risks and opportunities. Below the high-level plan you will have a number of detailed action plans about things that are still important, although not to those who will read your business plan. The operations plan should produce a series of milestones – operating objectives that are measurable and time deadlines for meeting them. Behind these will go a lot of detailed planning (and hard work) that do not show themselves in the business plan. We have split our operating plan into two parts: pre-launch – the things that need to be in place before you launch the business – and post-launch operations – the things you need to get right on a day-to-day basis, including the action plans coming out of your review of risks.

Each major activity in the lists you will develop can then be broken down into more detail, showing linkages and critical paths. The activities can then be ordered, with critical and high-risk ones scheduled as early as possible. **Gantt charts** are an excellent way of showing these linkages. Figure 10.4 shows a highly simplified Gantt chart for a retailer, based upon the mind map in Figure 2.4 and pre-launch key activities checklist in Table 10.3 (assuming store location is already decided).

- Against each activity a block of time is drawn that represents the estimated length of time it will take to complete the task.
- The blue arrows show the linkages between these activities.
- The red arrows indicate the critical path along which each activity must be completed before the next begins.

The critical path is the longest path through the diagram and is the shortest possible time to complete the task, in this case opening the store. Unless the time taken for tasks can be shortened, this will take 68 days. If any task along the critical path line overruns, then the opening will be delayed. As you can see from the chart, the final three weeks are congested periods of activity when staff are joining, stocking shelves and undertaking training prior to the store opening.

At the moment there is no slack built into these schedules. An added sophistication would be to build in fastest and slowest completion times and then check the effect on the critical path time. And it is very easy to fit dates into the format. You can go on to assign responsibilities and costs for the various tasks, proceeding to identify the risks that might delay the completion of any activity. If this all seems a daunting task, there are computer programs that can help you with this sort of project planning.

You might produce a number of operating and action plans for different levels of your business. Your 'high-level' operating plan to go in the business plan would show key operating activities with their critical success factors. High-impact risks (and opportunities) would be clearly identified and strategic options developed. 'High-level' plans should be split into pre-launch and operational activities. A simplified Gantt chart for these key activities will illustrate clearly what needs to be done and when. If needed, you can write a brief line-by-line commentary. These key activities become your operational objectives – milestones in the development of your business. In our example one milestone might be to open the first store on 9 September (Day 68).

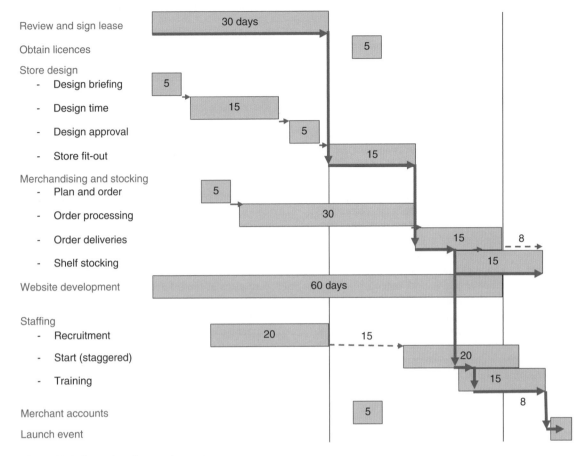

Figure 10.4 *Gantt chart for opening a store*

Kirsty's   UK

Simplifying operations and minimizing risk

When Kirsty Henshaw appeared on the UK TV show *Dragons' Den* in 2010 to get equity backing she knew exactly what she wanted. She asked for £65,000 in exchange for 15% of the business, but was happy to give away 30% because she wanted the involvement of two Dragons with experience and a network of contacts in this sort of business – Peter Jones and Duncan Bannatyne.

Kirsty was a 24-year-old mother from Preston, Lancashire, who had started her business from her kitchen less than a year before appearing on television. Her son suffered from severe food allergies and intolerances and Kirsty wanted a healthy, dairy, gluten and nut free ice cream for him but found that there was nothing available from the supermarkets. Over a couple of years, she developed two sorts of frozen dessert: Coconuka and Coconice. She invested £20,000 of her own

Kirsty Henshaw

money while holding down two jobs. Producing food for sale in the UK is not straightforward, and Kirsty took advice from her local Business Link, the Trading Standards Institute and the Food Standards Association. She had her packaging and a website developed through a £3,000 government grant. And she only started producing her first products after she had secured distribution through a national wholesaler of health foods in December 2009. She also sold her products direct to customers through her website. But these were relatively small volumes which she batch produced in her kitchen.

Kirsty knew that when she went on *Dragons' Den* looking for equity investment she would need not only a track record of sales, but also evidence of potential and plans for how to meet greater demand. She believed her products were unique and had national sales potential. But she also realized that she would face big problems with production and distribution at this scale. She therefore made two important operational decisions. First, she decided that, to really make an impact she must sell into the national supermarket chains, and, second, that the only way she could meet this sort of demand would be to subcontract production. Kirsty had no expertise in large-batch/line production and this decision would allow her to focus on two important aspects of the business where she did have expertise – product development and sales. She also realized that, if (or when) the product was successful, competitors would soon copy her; therefore it was vital that she gained market share with a branded product in the supermarkets as quickly as possible.

Kirsty's sales in the months up to her *Dragons' Den* appearance had been some 2,500 units, giving her a profit of over £2,500. But the business plan she produced for the Den showed a profit projection of £300,000 for the year. The difference was a supermarket contract. Over a period of months, Kirsty had visited buyers at Tesco, the largest supermarket chain in the UK, who tasted the product and liked it, confirming that it was indeed unique to the UK market. Tesco offered to give the product a trial in 400 stores, with each store taking 4 cases per week … so long as Kirsty could guarantee availability. Each case had 12 units and each unit had a margin of just over £1. The potential was obvious. So the next step was to find somebody to produce the product. Always thinking big,

Kirsty approached the largest ice cream manufacturer in Europe. Using the name of Tesco to the full, she persuaded the company to manufacture for her … so long as she would guarantee the volumes.

So all the elements of the jigsaw puzzle were in place, but Kirsty decided that she now needed not only some venture capital but also some commercial expertise to help put these deals together and roll out the product – which is where the Dragons came in. Kirsty was looking not only for cash but also for commercial and industry experience. Peter Jones provided the food manufacturing, distribution and retailing experience she needed while Duncan Bannatyne, through his fitness clubs, provided an opening to a health food market that she had not yet tackled.

The first thing Peter Jones did was to negotiate the subcontract deal with her manufacturer. They re-estimated first year sales at some 1.5 million units, giving a turnover of £5 million. Sales took off and the products, then known as Worthenshaws, became available in all leading UK supermarkets. However, Kirsty continued to innovate. In 2012, following extensive market research, the company pivoted from ice cream into healthy ready meals. Kirsty developed a range of gluten and dairy free meals which are now stocked in over 3,000 supermarkets nationwide under the *Kirsty's* brand name:

> We take everyday classic or exotic dishes and put a healthy and free from twist on them. We try and get inspiration from everywhere such as new restaurants and street food sellers, as well as listening to what our customers really want. A key point is whether I would eat any of these meals myself and the answer is 100% yes.

In 2015, Kirsty launched Kids' Kitchen, the first UK brand to offer gluten, wheat and dairy free chilled ready meals for children. However, Kirsty hasn't stopped there and she continues to develop new products, working with a range of manufacturers globally.

Visit the website on: www.kirstys.co.uk

Questions:

1 From the information given in the case, use the Framework Worksheet or the PowerPoint slide to complete as many elements as you can of the New Venture Creation Framework.
2 How did Kirsty go about simplifying the operational issues she faced?
3 How did she minimize the risks she faced?
4 Identify the risks the company now faces and its key operating imperatives. List the critical success factors.
5 What are Kirsty's growth options? Would you change the business model?

 Visit www.macmillanihe.com/burns-nvc-2e to download the Framework Worksheet and PowerPoint slide.

Sofa-bed Factory

Piotr and Olek were aware that they only had limited capital and that there were still a number of uncertainties surrounding their business idea, so they were keen to minimize their risks by partnering with others. Olek's current employer would manufacture the steel frames for the furniture. They would buy in cloth-covered foam and the different cloths and materials for covering the sofas. The workforce who assembled the furniture were typically paid on a piecework basis, which meant that this labour was a variable cost – no production, no cost. Delivery of the sofas to the UK would also be subcontracted. That meant that Piotr and Olek would only have to spend money on a factory, some easily sourced machinery and tools and one or two labourers (not on piecework) to work in the factory and stores. There was also the issue of the working capital they would need for stocks/inventory and to finance outstanding debtors/receivables, not least the stock of display sofas that they would have to finance for the first three months. It would therefore be best if they could delay the introduction of other units to go with the sofa-beds by a few months to ease their working capital requirements.

They reasoned that, because so much of the manufacturing was subcontracted out, they would be undertaking fairly straightforward assembly – a jobbing or batch production process. They came up with the following list of pre-launch key activities:

1 Find suitable premises – the local council had suitable factory space at €1,000 per month with a rent-free period of three months.
2 Obtain necessary local licences – this might involve a little time but the procedures were well known and, because the local council were keen to encourage employment, should not prove difficult.
3 Source equipment and materials – because so much of the manufacturing was subcontracted out, the equipment needed was just basic tools and easily sourced locally. Cloth and materials were also easily sourced and they already had a range of attractive fabrics that the retailer was keen to see offered.
4 Recruit labourers – there was a plentiful supply of local skilled workers willing to work at the going furniture manufacturing piecework rates.

Piotr and Olek concluded that none of these activities was a problem and could be undertaken speedily: in other words, these were zero-risk activities. However, as the pair thought more broadly about the risks they faced they decided that there were two problem areas. Firstly, with only one, albeit very large, retail customer in the UK they urgently needed to expand their customer base. Otherwise they could be left suddenly with no orders and, at the very least, they were in a weak price-negotiation position. Secondly, with relatively low contribution margins, tight control of both price and variable costs (materials, direct labour etc.) was vital. Although most of the materials were to be sourced in Poland, sofa-beds were to be exported to the UK and this posed two threats, both outside of the company's control: fluctuations in exchange rates (the UK is not in the Eurozone) and the possible imposition of tariffs (the UK is due to leave the EU). This prompted them to draw up a list of their critical risks and how they might be overcome (Table 10.9).

Looking at the list in Table 10.9, the partners realized that some of the highest risks they faced were out of their control and probably also threatened their competitors. It might not therefore affect their relative competitive position. Looking at the other risks, they realized how important it was to maintain a close relationship with the buyer from the UK retail chain. Without that customer the business did not exist. They therefore needed to diversify their customer base and find new distributors as quickly as possible. However, they saw that the current lack of coordinated units in their product range to sell alongside the sofa-beds was a significant weakness. They needed to extend their product range so as to attract more customers, although this would have to wait until the sofa-bed range had been successfully produced. They also realized the importance of good cost controls. Although fixed costs were very low, their variable costs were relatively high. These then would be their four critical success factors:

1 Maintain a close relationship with the existing UK customer.
2 Find new distributors to sell through (ideally not in the UK).
3 Diversify product range with new coordinated units to sell alongside sofa-beds.
4 Tight financial controls.

Questions:

1 Do you agree with this analysis? Has anything been omitted?
2 Is this a high-risk venture?

Table 10.9 *Sofa-bed Factory's risk assessment*

Critical risks	Risk impact (1–3)	Risk probability (1–3)	Risk index (1–9)	Controllable (Y/N)	Key risk indicators	Actions taken to monitor and mitigate risk
1. Customer risk (one customer taking most of production)	3	1	3 (based on current relations)	Y	• Customer complaints (product or delivery) • Retail buyer dissatisfaction (product or service) • Delays in payment • Tail-off of orders	• Maintain close relationship with retail buyer (already a friend) – regular visits • Visit stores to get local feedback ahead of retail buyer • React quickly to customer complaints • Monitor payments and orders closely • Find new distributors (retailers) • Develop online presence (later in year)
2. Product range risk (need to develop range away from just sofa-beds)	1	2	2	Y	• Lack of order growth • Customer feedback	• Visit stores to get local feedback ahead of retail buyer • Develop new range of units that link with sofa-bed range
3. Low contribution margins	3	2	6	Y/N	• Increasing costs • Decreasing price • Declining margins	• Close monitoring and control of local variable costs • Diversification of customer base • Develop and attempt to 'push' sales of higher-margin products
4. Worsening of £/€ exchange rate (sales in £)	2	2	4	N	• Fluctuations in £/€ exchange rate	• Fluctuation could be in company's favour as easily as against it • Company will hedge major currency exchange • So much of UK furniture is sourced from outside UK that fall in £ is also likely to affect competitors' prices, at least in the short term
5. Imposition of tariffs on imports to the UK	2	2	4	N	• Brexit negotiations	• So much of UK furniture is sourced from outside UK that any tariff is also likely to affect competitors, at least in the short term

Summary and action points

10.1 Identify and build partnerships: Partnerships can be very important, particularly in the context of innovation and market penetration. They can enhance your business model without requiring additional capital outlay by simplifying operations, leveraging your knowledge and capabilities and spreading your risk.

10.2 Identify key activities and related risks: Some activities will need to be completed pre-launch, and some will be ongoing key operational activities that derive from your business model. Identify the risks associated with these activities and the risks of not completing them. Put in place measures to monitor the risks and plans to mitigate them.

10.3 Identify the critical path to your launch: Identify the critical path for your launch activities, highlighting any potential bottlenecks. This can be identified using a Gantt chart and is the longest path through the chart and the shortest possible time to complete the task.

10.4 Identify your critical success factors and strategic options: Identify those key activities that you must get right to ensure the successful launch and day-to-day operation of your business. List any metrics that might be used to measure them. Put in place strategic options or contingency plans in case things go wrong. This needs to be done for both your operations and marketing plans

10.5 Identify, monitor and mitigate your critical risks: You must identify critical risks – those that are critical to the success or failure of your business. These should derive from a review of your critical success factors and the external environment. Evaluate the probability of the risks materializing, decide on the risk indictors to be monitored and then put in place actions to mitigate them. Decide whether there are metrics to measure this.

10.6 Review scale-up opportunities: The risk management framework can be applied to analysing both downside risks and your growth options or opportunities.

Workbook exercises

 The New Venture Creation Workbook contains a digital version of these exercises that can be modified as your business model develops and builds into a draft business plan. It can be downloaded from www.macmillanihe.com/burns-nvc-2e.

10.1: Identify and build partnerships

Using the table on the next page, list:

1 The areas of activity where partnership is possible and the form such a partnership might take (partnership, strategic alliance or joint venture).
2 The advantages and disadvantages of such partnerships.
3 The organizations or people that you might consider partnering with.
4 The information needed to make a decision about partnership.
5 The time scale for making these decisions.

Area of activity and form of partnership	Advantages of partnership	Disadvantages of partnership	Possible partners	Information needed for decision	Time frame

10.2: Identify key activities and related risks

Using the tables to the left, list:

1 The key activities that you need to undertake to ensure the success of your venture pre-launch and ongoing.

2 The resource and operational implications of these key activities.

3 The risks that might cause these key activities *not* to be completed satisfactorily.

4 Calculate a risk index for each key operation (impact × probability of occurrence). Identify the activities with the highest risk impact.

5 Decide on which are controllable (and which are not) and what key risk indicators need to be monitored.

Key pre-launch activities	Resource and operational implications	Risks	Risk impact (1–3)	Risk probability (1–3)	Risk index (1–9)	Controllable (Y/N)	Key risk indicators

Key ongoing operating activities	Resource and operational implications	Risks	Risk impact (1–3)	Risk probability (1–3)	Risk index (1–9)	Controllable (Y/N)	Key risk indicators

10.3: Identify the critical path to your launch

1 If you are able to do so, prepare a Gantt chart for your pre-launch activities listed in Exercise 10.2 (see Figure 10.4 for an example). Identify the critical path, highlighting any potential bottlenecks.

2 List the actions you need to take to ensure the critical path is adhered to and bottlenecks avoided.

10.4: Identify your critical success factors and strategic options

1 Review Exercises 10.2 and 10.3 and produce a list of critical success factors for your operations plan. Ensure that any bottlenecks identified in Exercise 10.3 which might prove critical are included.

2 Reflecting on the exercises above, list the strategic options that may need to be covered in your business plan.

3 Consolidate these lists with the critical success factors and strategic options from your marketing plan [Exercises 8.4 (5) and 8.4 (6)]. List any metrics that might be used to measure your CSFs. Review the list to ensure it includes all your CSFs.

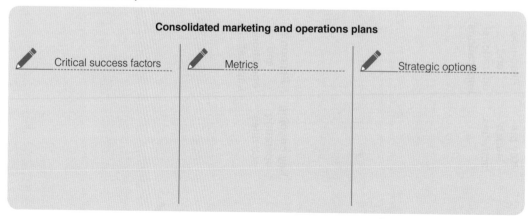

Consolidated marketing and operations plans

Critical success factors	Metrics	Strategic options

10.5: Identify, monitor and mitigate your critical risks

Using the table on the left:

1 List the nature of both the internal and external risks that you face – the risks that will cause you to be unsuccessful in meeting your critical success factors [Exercise 10.4 (3)] (e.g. currency devaluation may cause you to be uncompetitive on price because the cost of imported components goes up). Ensure that these are comprehensive – remember to include any risks you highlighted in your PESTEL analysis of this industry [Exercise 3.3].

2 Calculate a risk index for each critical risk (impact × probability of occurrence). Identify the critical risks that have the highest likelihood of occurrence and the greatest impact.

Critical risks	Risk impact (1–3)	Risk probability (1–3)	Risk index (1–9)	Controllable (Y/N)	Key risk indicators or metrics	Actions taken to monitor/mitigate risk and metrics to measure this

3 Decide which critical risks are controllable (and which are not) and the key risk indicators or metrics that need to be monitored.

4 List the key actions that you might take to mitigate these critical risks and any metrics that might be used to measure this. Ensure the critical success factors and metrics listed in Exercise 10.4 (3) are correct.

10.6: Review scale-up opportunities

This exercise uses the 'reverse-logic' of the risk index to produce a 'success index' that allows you to review your scale-up options and help you decide which are more likely to succeed and have the biggest impact. You can use this technique with any strategies that you might be considering.

Using the table below:

1 List the possible strategies that you highlighted to grow your business [Exercise 8.1]. These may also be reflected in your strategic options [Exercise 8.4 (4)].

2 Assign a growth impact score and a probability of success score to each growth option. Multiply the two to arrive at a 'growth success index'. Those strategies with the highest index score are the ones that you believe are most likely to succeed and will have the greatest impact on your business.

3 Jot down the implications of selecting any of these strategies (for resources etc.).

4 Review your strategic options in Workbook Exercise 8.4 (4) and update if necessary.

5 If appropriate, develop Gantt charts and action plans for the options you want to pursue – the ones with the highest 'success index'.

Growth strategies	Growth impact (1–3)	Probability of success (1–3)	Growth success index (1–9)	Implications

11 Managing and leading people

Learning outcomes

When you have read this chapter and completed the related exercises you will be able to:

- Assess the skills needed for your business and how these might be met
- Understand the different ways of employing people and how to go about recruiting them, including drawing up a job description and person specification
- Understand the factors that determine the selection of an effective team and identify your preferred Belbin team roles
- Creatively address how your business might be structured and the appropriate culture created, given its size, the tasks to be undertaken and the environment in which it operates
- Understand and explain how leadership style can be tailored to different circumstances, and evaluate your preferred leadership style

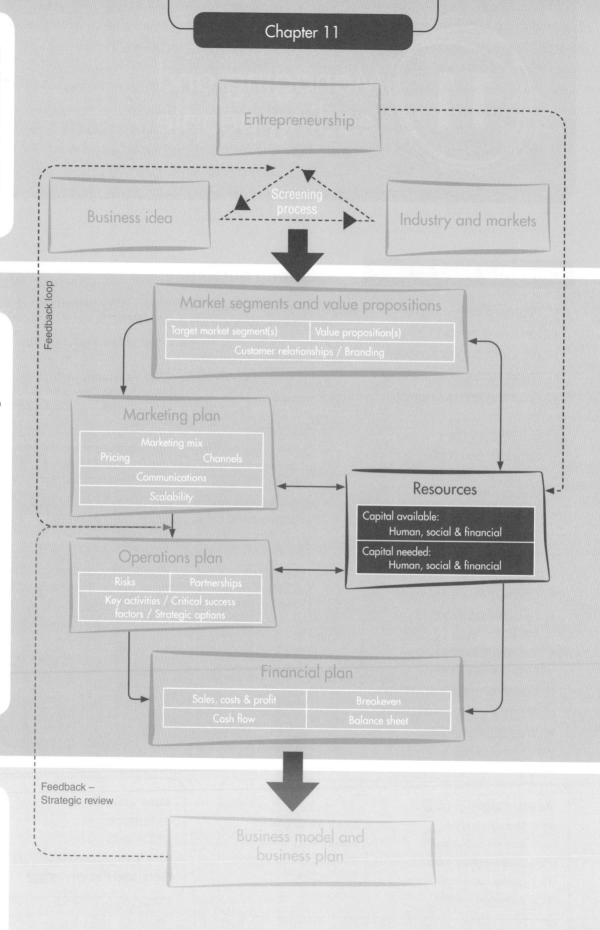

Phase 1: Research

Phase 2: Business model development

Phase 3: Launch

Entrepreneurship

Business idea

Screening process

Industry and markets

Feedback loop

Market segments and value propositions

Target market segment(s)	Value proposition(s)
Customer relationships / Branding	

Marketing plan

Marketing mix

Pricing	Channels
Communications	
Scalability	

Resources

Capital available:
    Human, social & financial

Capital needed:
    Human, social & financial

Operations plan

Risks	Partnerships
Key activities / Critical success factors / Strategic options	

Financial plan

Sales, costs & profit	Breakeven
Cash flow	Balance sheet

Feedback – Strategic review

Business model and business plan

People, people, people

> Most successful businesses are started by teams. Solo entrepreneurs certainly succeed … but they are very much the minority. Even those who we think of as great individual entrepreneurs … all had co-founder partners in the early years.
>
> Luke Johnson Chairman Risk Capital Partners Sunday Times 21 May 2017

> In the early days it's all about your enthusiasm, but very quickly it's just about people, people, people … The rest will look after itself.
>
> Ben Meldrum founder Professor Puzzle Sunday Times 7 May 2017

> The people are the lifeblood of the business. Focus on your employees and your customers and everything else will fall into place.
>
> Tom Molnar founder Gail's Artisan Bakery Sunday Times 20 April 2014

A business requires many resources such as buildings, vehicles, machinery or stock. Most can be purchased for cash although, as we have seen, there are ways of minimizing the investment needed. The one thing every business needs if it is to grow is people. Nevertheless, many entrepreneurs try to minimize the cost of people by doing as many things as possible themselves, despite the fact that this is not always a good idea as they may not have the necessary expertise. People cannot be purchased in the same way as other assets. They have to be attracted to join the business as employees or partners. Of course many new ventures do not employ anybody to start with, preferring instead to subcontract as many operations as possible. However, the only way you will grow is by recruiting appropriate staff, including managers, to deliver your product/service to more and more customers. Selecting, developing and managing staff will become a key activity, and it is something many entrepreneurs find difficult. When there is more than one founder, the issue of working with the other partners so as to become an effective management team can be just as challenging.

As your business grows you will face challenges and problems that mean you need to adapt and change. You will need to metamorphosize into an entrepreneurial leader – a leader of an organization that remains entrepreneurial. There are a number of models that seek to describe the challenges that an entrepreneurial leader faces as the business grows (see Academic insight 11.1). They all point to the danger of an organization becoming more bureaucratic as it grows. They emphasize the need to put in place an effective management team; the need to recruit reliable managers, delegate to them and control and monitor their performance. They recognize the need to become more formal, with more structure, but without necessarily becoming overly bureaucratic. They emphasize the need for the entrepreneur's role to change from tactical – involved in everyday activities – to being more hands-off and strategic. The more rapid your growth, the more difficult it will be to manage these changes alongside day-to-day operations. Some entrepreneurs even decide not to grow their business because they prefer managing an unchanged, smaller organization. This is a lifestyle decision because managing growth is difficult. It is little wonder that so few firms grow to any size.

Recruiting people

Recruiting the right people to work with is crucial to the success of your business – the bigger the start-up, the more important the team. Team members can bring a range of skills, capabilities, knowledge and networks that complement and leverage the founder's experience. Industry experience can be vital in a new venture, particularly if the experience comes from a competitor. It might take time to attract everyone you need and you might even have to launch the business with some key posts unfilled, but it is important that you recruit the best people and plug any skills gaps in other ways.

Growth models

The challenges faced by new, growing ventures have been highlighted by a number of growth models. They all chart the transition at start-up from a simple, informal organization with the founder undertaking direct supervision to a more sophisticated, structured organization with the founder delegating more and requiring good leadership skills. Some couple this with a shift in emphasis from operational to more strategic managerial skills needed by the founder (Churchill and Lewis, 1983).

Greiner (1972) was one of the first academics to develop a growth model, one that is still widely used. It offers a framework for considering the development of a business, but more particularly the managerial challenges facing the founder. In the model each phase of growth is followed by a crisis that necessitates a change in the way the founder manages the business. If the crisis cannot be overcome then the business risks failure. The length of time it takes to go through each phase depends on the industry in which the company operates. In fast-growing industries, growth periods are relatively short; in slower-growth industries they tend to be longer. Each evolutionary phase requires a particular management style or emphasis to achieve growth.

Greiner's model predicts four crises: leadership, autonomy, control and bureaucracy. Figure 11.1 shows these crises, together with the shift in emphasis needed by the founder from operational to managerial and strategic skills.

1   **Leadership** – Growth initially comes through seeking creative opportunities. However, this growth leads to a crisis of leadership as staff, financiers and even customers increasingly fail to understand the focus of the business – where it is going, what it is selling – and resources become spread too thinly to follow through effectively on any single commercial opportunity. Your challenge is to give direction by effective leadership. We return to what this means in Chapter 12.

2   **Autonomy** – Entrepreneurs have a strong internal locus of control, which means that there is a danger they will try to do everything themselves. Not only do they delay recruiting staff, partly because they are careful in managing cash flow, but when they do, they find it difficult to delegate. Your challenge is to develop an effective management team, and delegate to them.

3   **Control** – There is a danger that delegation becomes an abdication of responsibility and there is a loss of proper control. As we shall see later in this chapter, there is a balance to be achieved between autonomy and control. Your challenge is to coordinate decision making through

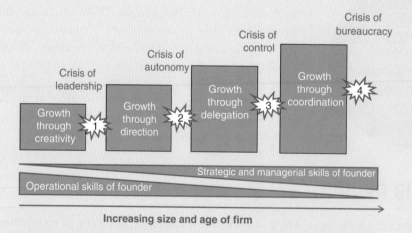

Figure 11.1 *Growth stages of a firm*

appropriate organizational structures and a culture that balances autonomy and control, and encourages collaboration.

4 **Bureaucracy** – As the business becomes larger, the danger is that it might lose its entrepreneurial drive. The challenge is to facilitate collaboration – making people work together through a sense of mission or purpose rather than by reference to a rule book.

Overall you need to develop an organization that balances the need for autonomy and control, avoiding too much bureaucracy.

Churchill, N.C. and Lewis, V.L. (1983) 'The Five Stages of Small Business Growth', *Harvard Business Review*, May/June.

Greiner, L.E. (1972) 'Evolution and Revolution as Organizations Grow', *Harvard Business Review*, July/August.

Getty Images/Caiaimage/Chris Ryan

You start by developing a **skills profile** for the business and identifying where gaps exist. You might do this pre-launch and, say, for three years' time. Your operational skills needs will depend on the nature of your business; however, you will also need to have the core functional skills of business: sales, marketing, accounting and so on. You may also be looking for specific market or industry skills or knowledge. Depending on the size of your start-up, you may have to be flexible and live with a degree of overlap and indeed cope with some gaps, at least in the short term. It is therefore useful to classify the skills and knowledge in your profile as 'key', 'important' or 'desirable'. Recruiting appropriate people with 'key' skills, particularly pre-launch, may be a critical success factor.

While you may be able to subcontract some activities or partner with other businesses, sooner or later you will need to recruit people to work directly for you. You can recruit people to work on a number of different bases.

- Full/part-time – Not all people want to work full-time and, for a start-up, each full-time employee can represent a large increase in fixed costs. So, employing part-time staff can be attractive, particularly if they are willing to work shifts and infill to meet customer demand, in which case you can specify the number of hours they work.
- Regular hours/shift work – Office workers might expect to work regular 'nine-to-five' hours, but in many industries, such as hospitality, shift working is the norm and part-time work is common. The determinant factor here is what is required to provide the necessary customer service.
- Fixed-wage or salary/commission/piecework – Employing full-time, fixed-wage or salary employees increases the fixed costs of your venture. While this may be necessary to attract the 'right' sort of person—particularly your management team – many types of jobs or even industries have different ways of working. Salespeople expect part of their remuneration to come from commission or bonuses based upon meeting their sales targets – the more they sell, the more they earn. Some workers expect to be paid on a piecework basis – they are paid for the volume they produce.

At some point you might be expected to draw up a **job description** for an employee, listing the things they have to do and what they will be held accountable for in this role. This can be problematic in a small, growing business where the nature of the tasks to be undertaken can change from day to day and over time. Job descriptions can be made flexible. However, in some countries employees expect quite detailed and specific job descriptions. For example, the Swedish home furnishing store IKEA does not give employees job titles or precise job descriptions, and this caused it a major problem when it first launched in the USA, where employees are used to clear roles and responsibilities. The resulting high staff turnover rates caused IKEA to change its recruitment processes so as to highlight the company's culture and values. Prospective employees who were not comfortable with this could therefore withdraw during the process.

Based upon the list of duties in the job description, you can then produce a **person specification** that lists the criteria on which to base selection of the person. This is an important document against which you can assess the suitability of a candidate for a post. Table 11.1 gives you a checklist of characteristics that might be included in this document. You can split these into 'essential' and 'desirable'. In most countries employees are expected to be given a **contract of employment** which outlines their terms and conditions of employment. In the UK this must be done within two months. What goes into this contract is prescribed by law. There are also a plethora of regulations and laws that regulate how you recruit, employ and dismiss employees.

Table 11.1 *Person specification checklist*

• Educational attainment	• Personal attributes (e.g. flexibility)
• Experience (e.g. retail sales)	• Personal characteristics (e.g. friendly)
• Knowledge (e.g. marketing)	• Personal circumstances (e.g. able to work evenings)
• Skills/abilities (e.g. team working)	

Attracting the right people

Finding and attracting a new venture team is rarely straightforward. Why should they join a risky start-up, particularly if they have a secure job in an established company? The answer lies in part with your persuasive power but also with the remuneration package you offer them. You may be short of cash to start with, but if you are successful there should be plenty of money to go around later on. So the answer may be to offer incentives such as target-linked bonuses, shares or share options. Most of the really successful start-ups, like Apple, have distributed shares to key managers early in their development.

Sometimes the new venture team will share the ownership of the business between them from the start. The share each has might reflect the cash, intellectual property or simply the time and effort they have put in to get the business off the ground – called **sweat equity**. The terms of a shareholders' agreement should specify how this is done, as well as anticipating future issues facing the founders. A shareholders' agreement only applies to those signing it, while the articles of association govern all future shareholders. Typical topics included in such an agreement are shown in Table 11.2. Research into what makes a successful partnership team shows that they need cohesion, shared goals and effective communication – something called **shared cognition** (see Academic insight 11.2).

> The ability to find and hire the right people can make or break your business. It is as plain as that … The right people in the right jobs are instrumental to a company's success.
>
> Michael Dell founder Dell Corporation *Direct from Dell: Strategies that Revolutionized an Industry* (1999, New York: Harper Business)

Table 11.2 Typical topics included in a shareholders' agreement

- Nature of the business
- Identity, role and title of founders
- Legal form of business
- Distribution of shares between founders
- Consideration paid for shares or ownership share of each founder (for cash or other consideration)
- Intellectual property signed over to company by founders
- Rights to appoint and remove directors
- Dividend policy
- Terms to protect minority shareholders
- Terms regulating the raising of capital (to avoid diluting existing shareholding)
- Conditions affecting founders regarding the valuation and disposal of shares, including buy-back clauses
- Other limitations on directors' and/or shareholders' freedom of action
- Resolution of disputes between shareholders

Kristian Segerstråle co-founder Playfish Sunday Times 22 November 2009

You start out with a mission or dream and then you have to work out how you are going to get there. Any time that you choose to partner with anybody you make that choice to accelerate your growth, with the impact that has in some degree on your independence.

Whatever the package you put together, you will need to seek out your potential team. Your network of contacts is always a good starting point – family, friends and professional contacts. You may need to advertise. However, rather than using the traditional media such as newspapers, an increasingly important mechanism is social media. You can use your Facebook or LinkedIn account to broadcast to friends or contacts that you are setting up a team and what skills, capabilities and knowledge you are looking for. Some companies use Twitter for recruiting. Once you have people interested in joining your team, you need to shortlist those that meet your person specification and then interview those shortlisted to assess their suitability.

ACADEMIC insight 11.2

Shared cognition

There has been considerable research into what makes a successful new venture team where ownership is shared. This has repeatedly shown the importance of cohesion and 'shared cognitions' – shared goals and effective communications and transfer of knowledge between partners. 'Shared cognition' improves collective understanding within a group, and helps individuals with different functional backgrounds to reach consensus. This can improve decision-making quality and the general performance of the business (Smith et al., 2005; West III, 2007). It can also cut down on conflict within the partnership group (Burgers et al., 2009) and increase partners'

'reciprocal credibility and coordination' (Zheng, 2012), both positively affecting performance. Conflict generally takes two forms – relationship conflict and task conflict (Jehn and Bendersky, 2003). While conflicts over tasks can sometimes be productive and beneficial, relationship conflicts are rarely beneficial and may erode cohesion within the team negatively affecting performance (Gelfand et al., 2008).

Cohesive teams have been linked to greater coordination during team working as well as improved satisfaction and productivity (Mach et al., 2010). The need for a cohesive team is particularly true for the partnership team in a new venture as it has been shown to lead to superior business performance, providing a more stable and solid foundation of interpersonal relationships that produces synergistic behaviour and improves coordination (Ensley et al., 2002; Lechler, 2001; Thye et al., 2002). These studies underline the importance of being very careful in selecting partners and basing decisions not just on task competencies but also on shared goals and good interpersonal relationships that make for a cohesive partnership team.

Getty Images/iStockphoto/Ancika

Burgers, J.H., Jansen, J.J.P., Van den Bosch, F.A.J. and Volberda, H.W. (2009) 'Structural Differentiation and Corporate Venturing: The Moderating Role of Formal and Informal Integration Mechanisms', *Journal of Business Venturing*, 24(3).

Ensley, M.D., Pearson, A.W. and Amason, A.C. (2002) 'Understanding the Dynamics of New Venture Top Management Teams: Cohesion, Conflict, and New Venture Performance', *Journal of Business Venturing*, 17.

Gelfand, M.J., Leslie, I.M. and Keller, K.M. (2008) 'On the Etiology of Conflict Cultures', *Research in Organizational Behavior*, 28.

Jehn, K.A. and Bendersky, C. (2003) 'Intragroup Conflict in Organizations: A Contingency Perspective on the Conflict-outcome Relationship', *Research in Organizational Behavior*, 25.

Lechler, T. (2001), 'Social Interaction: A Determinant of Entrepreneurial Team Venture Success', *Small Business Economics*, 16.

Mach, M., Dolan, S., Tzafrir, S. (2010) 'The Differential Effect of Team Members' Trust on Team Performance: The Mediation Role of Team Cohesion', *Journal of Occupational and Organizational Psychology*, 83(3).

Smith, K.G., Collins, C.J. and Clark, K.D. (2005) 'Existing Knowledge, Knowledge Creation Capability, and the Rate of New Product Introduction in High-technology Firms', *Academy of Management Journal*, 48(2).

Thye, S.R., Yoon, J. and Lawler, E.J. (2002) 'The Theory of Relational Cohesion: Review of a Research Program', *Advances in Group Processes: Group Cohesion, Trust and Solidarity*, 19.

West III, G.P. (2007) 'Collective Cognition: When Entrepreneurial Teams, Not Individuals, Make decisions', *Entrepreneurship Theory and Practice*, 31(1).

Zheng, Y. (2012) 'Unlocking Founding Team Prior Shared Experience: A Transactive Memory System Perspective', *Journal of Business Venturing*, 27(5).

Using professional advisors

Sometimes, no matter how hard you try, you may be unable to find the 'right person' for the role you have identified. In these cases it may be possible to 'buy in' these roles through professional advisors, at least temporarily. There are likely to be gaps in the professional knowledge and skills of any start-up. Professional advisors can be an invaluable source of this knowledge, skills and advice as well as providing an additional network of contacts for the founders. They might be persuaded to join a start-up for many reasons (e.g. as investors). They may be simply friends or family, willing to help because of the relationship with the founders. They might relish the challenge of helping a start-up. Professional advisors can also be hired or, in some cases, paid for by other bodies such as government. The types of professional advisors you might employ include:

Sara Murray founder Confused.com Sunday Times 1 February 2009

Have great advisers and listen to them. You don't have to take their advice but it's valuable to have other voices.

Accountants – Accountants can help produce your financial plan. They can then assist with your regular financial statements, as well as helping to analyse and interpret them (topics we cover in Chapter 13). Often they have access to industry financial norms that you can use to benchmark your performance. Indeed, the whole financial administration of your business can be subcontracted, including the issuing of sales invoices and collection of cash, the payment of purchase invoices and payroll administration. Accountants also offer tax advice and will handle the filing of information with appropriate bodies. They usually have a network of contacts who can help with finance and funding, from loan to equity capital. Every business needs to succeed financially to remain viable, and having reliable accounting information is vital. The more ambitious your aims for your venture, the more likely you are to need good financial advice early on.

Lawyers/attorneys – Lawyers can help with anything involving the law. They can advise on the legal requirements of establishing the form of business organization you select or the various business licences or permits you might require. They can advise on safeguarding your business idea. They can help you draw up legal contracts with staff, partners, suppliers or customers. They can be invaluable in drawing up a shareholders' agreement for the founding team. Often, like accountants, they have a network of contacts who can help with finance, from loan to equity capital, and sometimes they offer tax services. However, also like account-ants, good lawyers can prove to be expensive, so it is always best to understand how they charge their fees before they start any work.

Business consultants – General business consultants can offer advice on marketing or strategic planning. They can help you draw up your business plan. Often they can provide access to other sources of help and advice, particularly at a local level, including specialist advice on specific industries or topics such as exporting. Local consultants can also provide invaluable access to local networks of other owner-managers and providers of capital. Some consultants might be 'free', paid for by government to help small firms. Most Western countries have services offering help and support to small and medium-sized businesses. In the USA it is provided by the Small Business Administration through its Small Business Development Centres.

> Information on advice services for SMEs in the UK can be found in the *Guide to UK Sources of Help, Advice, Information and Funding* on the companion website: www.macmillanihe.com/burns-nvc-2e. An additional guide for Australian readers, produced by Dr Russell Manfield, is also provided.

Any start-up benefits from surrounding itself with high-quality advisors. They add to the credibility of the management team and can persuade providers of finance to invest. The more ambitious your start-up, the more important this is. Using advisors on a 'pay-as-you-go' basis can offer an attractive way of accessing a range of knowledge, skills and networks that a new venture might not be able to afford to employ on a full-time basis. The relationship with these advisors might be informal or formal (relying on a contract for service). Skills gaps can also be addressed through your board of directors (Chapter 9), different forms of partnership (Chapter 10) or equity investors, such as Business Angels (Chapter 12). The range of different ways of meeting your skills and knowledge needs are summarized in Figure 11.2.

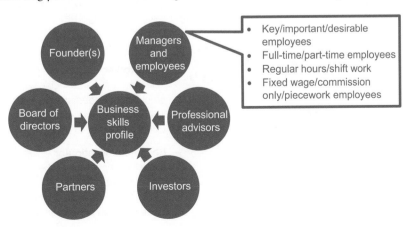

Figure 11.2 Meeting your skills needs

Selecting and developing a team

Rob Pollard Director Lightbox The Times 25 February 2014

I very much look at personality and give that more weight than skills. You can always develop ability but you can't change someone's personality.

The ability to work effectively as a team is important. Team members bring with them technical and management knowledge and experience. Selecting an effective team will therefore depend upon the skills profiles, individual job descriptions and person specifications you develop. However, research suggests that the most important factors in team effectiveness are how the team functions and their commitment to achieving overall goals (shared cognition, see Academic insight 11.2). The personal chemistry between members of the team is important. But how do you select these personal characteristics? Research into how teams work identified three 'personal orientations': Thinking, People and Action (see Academic insight 11.3). Each of these translates into three 'team roles' – functions naturally undertaken by the individual – giving a total of nine team roles:

- **Thinking orientation:** Plant, Monitor Evaluator and Specialist;
- **People orientation:** Coordinator, Teamworker and Resource Investigator;
- **Action orientation:** Shaper, Implementer and Completer Finisher.

Each team role has positive qualities but also some allowable weaknesses. To be effective a team must have all nine roles present, and individuals are naturally suited to two or three of these roles. By implication, effective teams therefore need to comprise three to five people.

ACADEMIC insight 11.3

Belbin's team roles

Based upon research into how effective teams worked, Meredith Belbin (1981) identified three 'personal orientations' that translate into nine 'team roles'. Most individuals are naturally suited to two or three roles but to be effective all nine roles must be present within a team.

Thinking orientation
Plant – This is the team's vital spark and chief source of new ideas – creative, imaginative and often unorthodox. However, they can be distant and uncommunicative, and sometimes their ideas can seem a little impractical.

Monitor Evaluator – This is the team's rock – introvert, sober, strategic and discerning. They explore all options and are capable of deep analysis of huge amounts of data. They are rarely wrong. However, they can lack drive and are unlikely to inspire or excite others.

Specialist – This is the team's chief source of technical knowledge or skill – single minded, self-starting and dedicated. However, they tend to contribute on a narrow front.

People orientation
Coordinator – This is the team's natural chair – mature, confident and trusting. They clarify goals and promote decision making. They are calm with strong interpersonal skills. However, they can be perceived as a little manipulative.

Teamworker – This is the team's counsellor or conciliator – mild mannered and social, perceptive and aware of problems or undercurrents, accommodating and good listeners. They promote harmony and are particularly valuable at times of crisis. However, they can be indecisive.

Resource Investigator – This is 'the fixer' – extrovert, amiable, six phones on the go, with a wealth of contacts. They pick other people's brains and explore opportunities. However, they can be a bit undisciplined and can lose interest quickly once initial enthusiasm has passed.

Action orientation

Shaper – This is usually the self-elected task leader with lots of nervous energy – extrovert, dynamic, outgoing, highly strung, argumentative, pressurized, seeking ways around obstacles. They do have a tendency to bully and are not always liked. However, they generate action and thrive under pressure.

Implementer – This is the team's workhorse – disciplined, reliable and conservative. They turn ideas into practical actions and get on with the job logically and loyally. However, they can be inflexible and slow to change.

Completer Finisher – This is the team's worry-guts, making sure things get finished – sticklers for detail, deadlines and schedules. They have relentless follow-through, picking up any errors or omissions as they go. However, they sometimes just cannot let go and are reluctant to delegate.

Chell (2001) suggested that the 'prototypical entrepreneur' might be a mix of three Belbin roles: plant (creative, ideas person), shaper (dynamism, full of drive and energy) and resource investigator (enthusiastically explores opportunities). She then suggested that the first team member to recruit should be an implementer (reliable, efficient and able to turn ideas into practical action). The implementer will need a completer finisher (conscientious, delivers on time), a teamworker (cooperative and unchallenging) and possibly a specialist (with particular knowledge or skills) working under them.

Download the Belbin Team Roles questionnaire from: www.belbin.com

Belbin, R.M. (1981) *Management Teams – Why They Succeed and Fail*, London: Heinemann Professional Publishing.

Chell, E. (2001) *Entrepreneurship: Globalization, Innovation and Development*, London: Thomson Learning.

> It takes real team spirit to take on challenges and win, and it also builds true camaraderie. It is this togetherness, above and beyond any other factor, that sets great businesses apart from the also-rans.
>
> Richard Branson founder Virgin Group *Sunday Times* 7 December 2014

> The best teams stand out because they are teams, because the individual members have been so truly integrated that the team functions with a single spirit. There is a constant flow of mutual support among the players, enabling them to feed off strengths and compensate for weaknesses. They depend on one another, trust one another. A manager should engender that sense of unity. He should create a bond among his players and between him and them that raises performance to heights that were unimaginable when they started out as disparate individuals.
>
> Alex Ferguson, ex-manager Manchester United Football Club, *Managing My Life*, London: Hodder & Stoughton, 1999

The challenge is to select the team and then to build cohesion and motivation. A cohesive team works together effectively because of its collective commitment to an agreed goal. In most cases building a cohesive team involves building consensus towards the goals of the firm – perhaps easier between partners – while balancing multiple viewpoints and demands. However, too great a reliance on achieving consensus can lead to slow decision making, so a balance is needed that will strain the interpersonal skills of the leader. In the best entrepreneurial firms, leadership seems to work almost by infection. The management team seems to be infected by the philosophies and attitudes of the founder and readily buy into the goals set for the firm, something that is helped if they share in its success.

Successful entrepreneurs build strong relationships with their team. Personal relationships are based upon trust, and trust is the cornerstone of a good team and an effective **organizational culture**. It is imperative that the management team trust you. This involves having a transparent vision and values, being firm but fair, flexible but consistent. It involves being straightforward – doing what you say and meaning what you say – 'walking the talk'. It involves being open and spontaneous, honest and direct – being an **authentic leader**. While always placing the interests of the firm first, it also involves being supportive of individuals and having their interests at heart. Trust takes time to build and needs to be demonstrated with real outcomes, but it can be lost very quickly by careless actions and then takes even longer to rebuild.

Building structure

Spider's web structure

How organizations are structured is a key issue, but probably only as the business starts to grow. Entrepreneurs tend to manage staff through their strong personal relationships, rather than through hierarchy and structure. They prefer informal organization structures and the power of influence rather than rigid rules and job definitions. They often persuade and cajole staff, showing them how to do things on a one-to-one basis rather than having prescribed tasks. This reflects itself in the culture in the organization.

The typical structure seen in a small-scale start-up is the spider's web shown in Figure 11.3. The founder sits at the centre of the web with each new member of staff reporting to them. This is an efficient structure that can respond quickly and flexibly to change. The uncertainty and rapid pace of change in a start-up probably mean that rigid rules and structures would be out of date quickly. In a small firm everybody has to be prepared to do other people's jobs because there is no cover, no slack in the system if, for example, someone goes off sick.

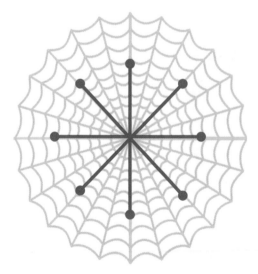

Figure 11.3 Spider's web organizational structure

The spider's web works quite well up to about 20 employees. Beyond that it becomes increasingly inefficient. This is because communication becomes more complicated as the number of people interacting increases. There is greater opportunity for misunderstanding and conflict. Then there is the tendency for a typical entrepreneur to want to meddle and do things themselves (high internal locus of control). Even when they try to delegate to a manager, they tend to meddle and employees soon create an informal reporting line to them, short-circuiting the manager (Figure 11.4). It is no wonder that this creates frustration, resentment and an unwillingness to accept responsibility by the manager. Why should they take responsibility when their decisions are likely to be questioned or reversed, or when staff supposedly reporting to them are constantly being checked up on by the entrepreneur?

Figure 11.4 Growing web structure: informal reporting lines

Hierarchical structure

The larger an organization, the more it needs some form of hierarchical structure. It creates order and allows coordination of complex tasks. Hierarchy is the fundamental feature of organizational structure for all complex systems. It gives managers confidence that they have the authority to manage and allows coordination, cooperation and specialization. Figure 11.5 shows a simple five-person hierarchical structure. Hierarchy is efficient – this has four interactions. Contrast it to the self-organizing structure in Figure 11.6, which has 10 interactions. However, while a hierarchy may be efficient it says nothing about the quality of the interactions and such a structure can discourage collaboration and sharing of knowledge.

Figure 11.5 Simple hierarchy, 5 people: 4 interactions

Figure 11.6 Self-organizing team, 5 people: 10 interactions

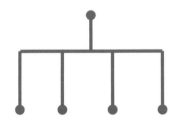

I believe in as flat a management structure as possible … in leading without title … I most certainly try to lead by example and I'm very much a big believer in making my mistakes public so that other people feel confident and comfortable to be able to air their own mistakes.

Management Today www.managementtoday.co.uk 18 July 2008 Mykindaplace and Brightstone Ventures Shaa Wasmund founder

As an organization grows, more structure can be put in place. Figure 11.7 shows a classic hierarchy involving departments (e.g. marketing, production, accounting etc.), groups within the departments (e.g. sales, advertising etc.) and individuals. This fosters stability and encourages efficient, rule-driven operation. It demonstrates a clear career path. However, collaboration and sharing of knowledge can be further discouraged by this structure. There is no one 'best' structure. Some hierarchies might have 'tall' structures, with more managers each having a narrower span of control (fewer people reporting to them). Others might have 'flat' structures, with fewer managers each having a wider span of control (more people reporting to them). Flat structures require fewer managers and the recent tendency has been to delayer – to flatten structures and widen managers' span of control. Information technology has facilitated this trend. Some Japanese manufacturing companies have only four layers of management; top, plant, departmental and section management.

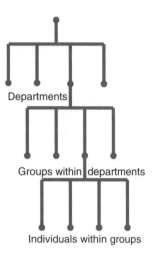

Figure 11.7 Hierarchical structure

Matrix and team working structure

A business that has multiple products, functions or geographic locations still needs to coordinate activities across all these dimensions. The organizational structure used to aid this is the matrix structure shown in Figure 11.8. In this people have multiple reporting lines – to their functional manager (e.g. accounting or sales) and their geographic or product manager. It can be combined with a hierarchical structure for some job roles within functions (e.g. the accounting department might have a hierarchy). The matrix structure is also the basis for project teams. Project teams comprise people with different skills from different departments, brought together to complete a defined project. They are seen to encourage communication, facilitate interaction and generally encourage creativity and innovation. For example, Gore, the manufacturer of the famous hi-tech Gore-Tex fabric, makes extensive use of project teams with a minimum of top-down direction. Employees (called Associates) apply or are asked by other team members to join particular teams. Teams elect their leader, decide upon their own goals and manage themselves.

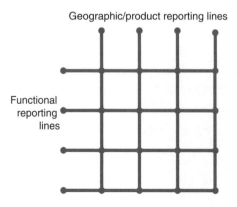

Figure 11.8 Matrix structure

CASE insight 11.1

Google 🇺🇸 USA

Team working

Google operates in a fast-moving commercial environment that values innovation and swift action. It has a flat, decentralized organization structure with lean hierarchies and is highly democratic and tightly interconnected – like the internet itself. It has been said that this comes from the founders' own dislike of authority. Each manager has about 20 people reporting to them. Google also has an informal culture with low job specialization, emphasizing principles rather than rules, and horizontal communication.

All of the staff involved in product development – almost half of Google's employees – work in small teams of three or four people. Larger teams get broken down into smaller sub-teams, each working on specific aspects of the bigger project. Each team has a leader that rotates depending on the changing project requirements. Most staff work in more than one team. Staff are allowed 20% of their time to work on new projects, with this work being monitored and scaled up if the project is thought worthwhile.

Google encourages creativity in a number of ways. Many companies that work on building successful teams or encouraging creativity are known to facilitate playful environments. The lobby in Googleplex has a piano, lava lamps, old server clusters and a projection of search queries on the wall. The corridors have exercise balls and bicycles. Other playful elements include a slide and a fireman's pole. Recreational facilities, from video games and ping-pong tables to workout rooms, are scattered throughout the campus. The site also has functional elements that aid idea generation and dissemination. For example it has enclosed, noise-free projectors that can be left on at all times and employees can automatically email meeting notes to attendees. As one newspaper commented:

To visit Google's headquarters in Mountain View, California, is to travel to another planet. The natives wander about in T-shirts and shorts, zipping past volleyball courts and organic-vegetable gardens while holding their open laptops at shoulder height, like waiters' trays. Those laptops are gifts from the company, as is free food, Wi-Fi-enabled commuter buses, healthcare, dry cleaning, gyms, massages and car washes, all designed to keep its employees happy and on campus.

Ken Auletta *The Guardian* 4 March 2010

Question:

List the advantages of working in this way at Google.

Structure and control

Most start-ups begin life with informal spider's web structures and start to develop more formal structures as they grow. The question of which structure will best suit you and your business depends primarily on the degree of control you want (or need) to have over your staff. Most hierarchical structures are aimed at minimizing risk and uncertainty and promoting efficiency and effectiveness – but often at the expense of creativity and innovation. The degree of control you exert over your staff should reflect not only your own philosophy, but also the tasks they undertake and the environment they undertake them in. These in turn must be consistent with your core value proposition.

If yours is a low-cost/price business model, then you may need to be highly efficient and controls may need to be tight. Costs need to be minimized; therefore jobs are simplified and tightly defined and controlled. Staff must conform to set rules within a stable environment, where they know exactly what is expected of them and may have incentives such as bonuses

Zhang Ruimin CEO Haier Group Strategy + Business, Issue 77, Winter, 2014

> Employees today should be encouraged to think for themselves. They should be cultivated to have an entrepreneurial, innovative spirit, and not just to implement orders.

to deliver this. There is no slack. What is needed is a highly efficient hierarchical and probably bureaucratic structure. This is typical in line and, to a lesser extent, batch manufacturing and service businesses.

The problem comes if the task you are asking people to undertake is complex and not straightforward and/or where the environment in which it is undertaken is not stable but is changing. This is typical in project and jobbing processing where the task can be complex and specifications may change. It might even be the case in batch manufacturing and service businesses where customer relations are vital. These situations require more flexibility and the ability to respond quickly to changing situations, without necessarily going through the bureaucracy resulting from a more hierarchical structure. One of the characteristics of less hierarchical structures (such as team working) is that they rely on coordination by mutual adjustment rather than control through hierarchy. Individuals within them often have multiple roles and more freedom of action.

It turns out that freedom or autonomy can be a great motivator for staff undertaking cognitive tasks where initiative and creativity are important. They enjoy undertaking something that they find challenging but psychologically rewarding and use autonomy constructively (see Academic insight 11.4). However, freedom can become licence, and with loss of control comes high accountability.

ACADEMIC insight 11.4

Control and motivation

Pink (2011) quoted a number of studies across different countries which showed that, while monetary reward was a motivator for individuals undertaking mechanical tasks, it was not a motivator for individuals undertaking cognitive tasks involving complexity or creativity. Once monetary reward was sufficient to be 'taken off the table', other less tangible factors were far greater motivators and led to greater personal satisfaction and better performance. In particular he highlighted self-direction and autonomy as important motivators if you want people to be innovative, engaged with their tasks and proactive rather than just compliant.

For employees undertaking creative tasks there were three key motivators:

1 **Autonomy** – freedom of action and self-direction, not being told what to do or how to do it, which encourages people to enjoy what they are doing (e.g. Google's 20% freedom policy).
2 **Purpose** – a reason for doing something based not upon monetary remuneration but upon a wider

vision of what the organization can achieve (e.g. from CSR policies).
3 **Mastery** – the challenge of completing a complex or creative task. Pink cites Wikipedia and Linux as initiatives that have engaged highly skilled people in creative tasks without monetary remuneration.

So if autonomy is a motivator, the dilemma is the amount of autonomy to give. Too much, and anarchy or worse might result. Too little, and creativity, innovation and initiative will be stifled. The answer provided by Julian Birkinshaw (2003) was 'balance'. He outlined the model used by BP to help guide and control entrepreneurial action: direction, 'space' or 'slack', boundaries and support. All four need to be in balance. If they are not, either bureaucracy (constraint) or chaos might ensue. This is shown in Figure 11.9.

Direction – This is the company's broad strategy and goals. Managers should have scope to develop the strategy for their own operating unit, in line with the company's general direction, values and mission. Pink agrees, saying creative people need a strong sense of 'purpose' in their work, which

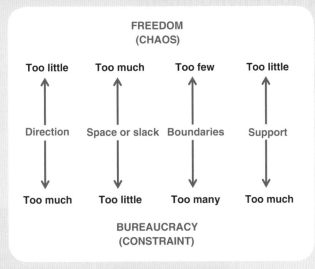

Figure 11.9 *Control vs. autonomy*
Source: inspired by information in Birkinshaw (2003)

is not just about making profit. Birkinshaw gave two pieces of advice on getting this balance right:

- Set broad direction and re-evaluate periodically as markets and the environment change;
- Let the company's strategy inform that of the unit and the unit's inform that of the company.

Space or slack – This is to do with the degree of looseness in resource availability – monetary budgets, physical space and supervision of time. In a tightly run, highly efficient organization there is no time or other resources to think, experiment and innovate. Creative organizations require a degree of space or slack to allow experimentation. 3M allows researchers to spend 15% of their time on their own projects. Google allows 20%. However, if employees are given too much space they run the risk of losing focus on the day-to-day detail of the job and it can be wasteful. Birkinshaw's advice was:

- Goal setting should be carefully managed, clear and specific, but individuals should be given freedom in how the goals are to be achieved;
- Individuals should be allowed to learn from their own mistakes.

Boundaries – These are the legal, regulatory and moral limits within which the company operates. But rigid rules that are not shared beg to be circumvented. Boundaries should come from your values – which are shared by your staff. Not having boundaries courts extreme danger, particularly if breaking them might lead to the failure of the organization. Birkinshaw's advice was:

- Identify critical boundaries that, if crossed, threaten the survival of the organization and control them rigorously;

- Manage other boundaries in a non-invasive way through training, induction, codes of conduct and so on.

Support – This refers to the knowledge transfer systems and training and development programmes you provide to help managers do their job. Systems should encourage knowledge sharing and collaboration. Training and career planning should be top down. Both should, however, be discretionary. The danger here is that knowledge will not be shared and there will be little collaboration, encouraging managers to go their own way. On the other hand, if there is too much support the manager will be 'spoon-fed' and initiative stifled. Birkinshaw's advice was:

- Put in place enough support systems to help managers and ensure they know where to go for help;
- Systems should encourage collaboration.

The broad conclusions are therefore that the greater the complexity of tasks and the more staff have to use their cognitive abilities – creativity and initiative – to undertake these tasks within the context of a changing environment, then the greater the need for autonomy. Autonomy is, however, not enough on its own. It needs to be combined with a sense of 'purpose' and the challenge of 'mastery' of that task. It can be influenced through giving individuals 'space' or 'slack' but with direction, boundaries and support. And finally it needs to be combined with a strong accountability. It is for you to conclude whether, in the light of the Deepwater Horizon oil spillage in 2010, BP followed its own model.

Birkinshaw, J. (2003) 'The Paradox of Corporate Entrepreneurship', *Strategy and Business*, 30.

Pink, D. (2011) *Drive: The Surprising Truth about what Motivates Us*, New York: Riverhead.

Structure, task and environment

The degree of control you exert therefore depends primarily on two factors: task complexity and the environment in which the business operates. The simpler and more repetitive the task, the easier it is to impose control and the less the need for initiative. Similarly, the more stable the environment, the less the need for initiative. But rigid control stifles initiative and inhibits entrepreneurship, and therefore the more complex the task, the greater the need for autonomy. Similarly, the more change in the environment, the greater the need for autonomy. This is shown in Figure 11.10.

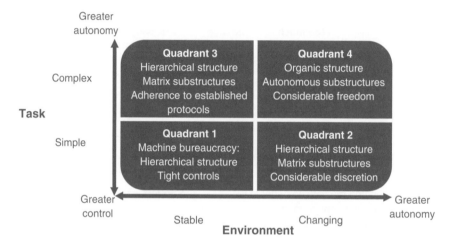

Figure 11.10 Structure, task and environment

Source: Burns, P. (2013) Corporate Entrepreneurship: Innovation and Strategy in Large Organizations, Basingstoke: Palgrave.

Quadrant 1 – A machine bureaucracy is one with hierarchical structures and tight controls. It is most appropriate where the organization is tackling simple tasks with extensive standardization, in stable environments, and/or where security is important and where plans and programmes need to be followed carefully. Well-developed information systems reporting on the production/processing activity need to exist for it to be effective. Power is centralized. It is more concerned with production than marketing and is good at producing high volumes and achieving the efficiency in production and distribution needed for the low-cost/price business model outlined in Chapter 4. It is appropriate for continuous and most line production typologies outlined in Chapter 10.

Quadrant 2 – As the environment becomes more changeable, standardization becomes less viable and responsibility for coping with unexpected changes needs to be pushed down the hierarchy. Staff are usually given more autonomy, although within guidelines. The structure needs to be responsive to change – although hierarchical, it is relatively flat with few middle-management positions. A matrix substructure (teams) can be used to tackle unexpected projects. Culture is important because the workforce needs to be motivated to make frequent changes to their work practices. It is appropriate for the jobbing and batch production typologies outlined in Chapter 10.

Quadrant 3 – Complex tasks performed in stable environments mean that it becomes worthwhile to develop standard skills to tackle the complexities. The matrix can be an effective substructure within a hierarchical organization. The matrix team can work on their complex tasks within set protocols, as they do, for example, in a surgical operation. In a changing environment the matrix team must have a higher degree of autonomy because established protocols may be inappropriate to the changing circumstances, even for the simple tasks they face. It is appropriate for the jobbing and batch production typologies outlined in Chapter 10.

Quadrant 4 – In a changing environment where there is high task complexity an innovative, flexible, decentralized structure is needed, often involving structures within structures. Authority for decision making needs to be delegated and team working is likely to be the norm, with matrix-type structures somehow built into the organization. Staff autonomy becomes far greater. Clear job definitions should never lead to a narrowing of responsibilities so that people ignore the new tasks that emerge. This is often called an 'organic structure' – one with a highly flexible, even changing structure with limited hierarchy; one which places greater emphasis on personal relationships and interactions than on structures; one in which power is decentralized and authority is linked to expertise, with few bureaucratic rules or standard procedures. In many ways, far more important than the formal organization structure for a firm of this sort is the culture that tells people what needs to be done and motivates them to do it – a truly entrepreneurial firm. It is most appropriate for the project-based production typologies outlined in Chapter 10.

While these principles may seem straightforward, their application in practice can be difficult, particularly in the context of a growing business. As with most areas of management, there are no set rules and their application involves judgement – not least in determining the 'balance' between control and autonomy. However, as a rule the less stable and predictable the environment you operate in and the more complex the tasks you face, the greater the autonomy you should give your staff, relying more on strong entrepreneurial leadership to give direction. However, with freedom comes responsibility and staff need to be held accountable for their actions. This means that your financial control system must be aligned with your structures so that departments, teams and/or individuals can be held accountable for their actions. Larger companies can have operating divisions or subsidiaries with different structures and different degrees of control, depending on the nature of their operations.

Structure and culture

We observed in Chapter 1 how the various cultures and subcultures in which you live, work and are educated affect your personal character traits. It is therefore obvious that the culture of the business you want to create will affect the people who work in it. One of your major tasks as the leader of this business is to craft an appropriate culture for people to work in. And be warned, even if you do not craft one on purpose, one will grow up anyway but it may not be the one you want. The challenge is to craft an organizational culture that reflects your values and beliefs and underpins your value proposition to customers (Chapter 5). However, this culture must also be consistent with the organizational structures that you have put in place. They must reinforce each other and convey the same messages. This means that the more formal your structures the more formal your organizational culture should be. You cannot have an informal, flexible culture within a bureaucratic structure undertaking repetitive tasks with tight control. The inconsistency is likely to lead to a dysfunctional organization that does not operate effectively because the message about how to behave is not conveyed consistently.

Organizational culture is about the web of unspoken, prevalent norms, basic beliefs and assumptions about the 'right' way to behave in an organization, sometimes simply described as 'how it is around here'. Taken together these factors form the interlinking cultural web of an organization shown in Figure 11.11. This web is crafted and evidenced by the stories, symbols, control systems, rituals and routines, power and organizational structures, that together help to both describe and contribute to the culture. The culture of your business can be more important than any formal structure you adopt because it manifests itself in the way people are *inclined and likely to behave* rather than the way they are *supposed to behave*. However, it should reinforce rather than be at odds with your organizational structures. So for example, if you asked somebody to describe working in the 'tight bureaucracy' in Figure 11.10 (quadrant 1) they might use words like 'controlled', 'hierarchical', 'regimented', 'rigid', 'repetitive' or 'prompt'. By way of contrast, if you asked somebody to describe working in the 'organic structure' in Figure 11.10 (quadrant 4) they might use words like 'flexible', 'informal', 'friendly', 'responsible', 'egalitarian', 'open' or even 'fun'.

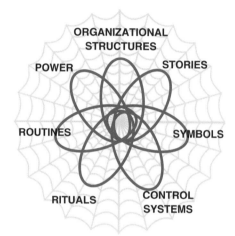

Figure 11.11 The cultural web

Shaping organizational culture

As the founder of your venture, you profoundly influence its organizational culture, either consciously or unconsciously. Your personality influences it. The way you manage influences it. Your values and beliefs – conscious or unconscious – influence it. However, the people you employ also influence it and they come with all the myriad of cultural influences we discussed in Chapter 1. Figure 11.12 shows three levers that can help you shape organizational culture: cognitive processes, organizational processes and behaviours.

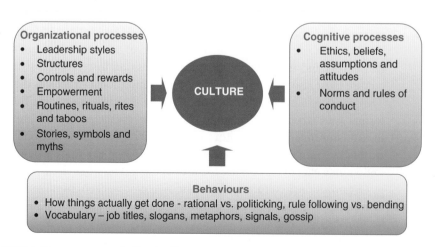

Figure 11.12 Influences on organizational culture

Cognitive processes

Cognitive processes are the underlying beliefs, assumptions and attitudes that staff hold in common and take for granted. They are embedded and emanate from the firm's philosophy, values, morality and creed. They generate norms of behaviour – rules or authoritative standards. They are strongly influenced by what the founder of the organization really pays attention to and what they actually do – not just what they say. But the important point is that they take time to frame. They do not happen overnight.

Organizational processes

These can be deliberate or just emerge, evolving organically, perhaps in an unintended way. There are many influences on this:

- Leadership styles – These send signals about appropriate behaviour. How you treat people, react to situations, even allocate your time, sends powerful signals about priorities.
- Organizational structures – Hierarchical structures can discourage initiative. Functional specialization can create parochial attitudes and sends signals about which skills might be valued. Flat, organic structures with broader spans of control and frequent use of teams encourage creativity and innovation.
- Controls and rewards – People take notice of which behaviours get rewarded (as well as which get punished) and behave accordingly. If salaries are based mainly on sales bonuses and there is a monthly league table of the best sales people, what does this tell you about the firm, its values and its goals? Criteria used for recruitment, selection, promotion and retirement are all important. Status, praise and public recognition are powerful motivators.
- Empowerment – The power to make (or not make) decisions sends defining signals. Flat, decentralized structures with delegated decision making send signals about encouraging local decision making, although sometimes informal power can lie outside formal hierarchies. The reaction to failure is an important message in this.
- Routines, rituals, rites and taboos – These form the unquestioned fabric of everyday life, and say a lot about the culture of an organization; 'guarded' or 'open' management offices, reserved or unreserved parking spaces, dress codes, methods of communication.
- Stories and symbols – Who are the heroes, villains and mavericks in the firm? What do staff talk about at lunch? Are there symbols of status that are important such as car or office size? How do staff talk about customers, other key managers and even you? These stories and symbols perpetuate a culture.

Behaviours

This is what actually happens in an organization. It decides whether outcomes are rational, transparent or the result of politicking. It influences whether the organization does actually follow rules, or is about bending them in the appropriate circumstances. Behaviour is also about vocabulary – job titles, slogans, metaphors, signals, even gossip. Language is laden with value judgements that we do not realize most of the time, but they subconsciously influence the culture of the organization. To cement an organizational culture, behaviours must be congruent with the other influences and consistent with your organizational structures and your leadership style.

CASE insight 11.2

AirAsia

Organizational culture

Former Time Warner executive Tony Fernandes set up Asia's first low-cost airline, AirAsia, in 2001 by buying the heavily indebted state-owned company from the Malaysian government for only 25c. He set about remodelling it as a short-haul, low-cost operator flying around Asia. It was the first low-cost airline in the Asian market, copying the idea from airlines in the West such as Southwest Airlines and easyJet. The company expanded rapidly from a fleet of only two planes in 2002 to a fleet of over 180 planes flying to over 100 destinations and 22 countries by 2016. It created a completely new Asian market in low-cost air travel that is now enjoyed by millions of people and claims to be the lowest-cost airline in the world with a breakeven load factor of just over 50%. It achieves this through a crew productivity level that is triple that of Malaysia Airlines and an average aircraft utilization rate of 13 hours a day, involving an aircraft turnaround time of just 25 minutes. Now with hubs in Kuala Lumpur and Singapore, it has also established associate airlines in India, Japan, Thailand, Philippines and Indonesia, and AirAsia X affiliates in Thailand and Indonesia.

An article in *The Economist* ('Cheap, but Not Nasty', March 2009) made a number of observations about Tony Fernandes' management style and its effect on the company's culture, saying:

> he came to the industry with no preconceptions but found it rigidly compartmentalized and dysfunctional. He wanted AirAsia to reflect his own unstuffy, open, and cheerful personality. He is rarely seen without a baseball cap, open-neck shirt and jeans, and he is proud that the firm's lack of hierarchy (very unusual in Asia) means anyone can rise to do anyone else's job. AirAsia employs pilots who started out as baggage handlers and stewards; for his part, Mr. Fernandes also practices what he preaches. Every month he spends a day as a baggage handler, every two months as a cabin crew, every three months as a check-in clerk. He even established a 'culture department' to 'pass the message and hold parties'.

DIGITAL VISION

Tony puts the success of AirAsia down to 'culture, focus and discipline'. His comments on his management style include:

> If you sit up in your ivory tower and just look at financial reports, you're going to make some big mistakes ... Employees come number one, customers come number two. If you have a happy workforce they'll look after your customers anyway ... You can have all the money you want in the world, and you can have all the brilliant ideas but if you don't have the people, forget it ... I look for people who have drive, who have ambition, who are humble. I've hired many people at very strange places ... Good leadership is to know when to go and you only succeed as a good leader if you've transported someone else in and the company gets stronger. Then you've succeeded as leader.
>
> BBC News Business 1 November 2010

Visit the website: www.airasia.com

Question:

In commenting on AirAsia's success, what does Tony mean by 'culture, focus and discipline'? How has each of these contributed?

Leadership and management

Leadership and management are different and distinct terms, although the skills and competencies associated with each are complementary. Management is concerned with handling complexity in organizational processes and the execution of work. It is linked to the authority given to managers within a hierarchy. Back in the nineteenth century Max Fayol defined the five functions of management as planning, organizing, commanding, coordinating and controlling. Today, these sound very much like the skills needed to lead a communist-style command economy. Fayol's work outlined how these functions required certain skills which could be taught and developed systematically in people. Management is therefore about detail and logic. It is about efficiency and effectiveness.

Leadership on the other hand is concerned with setting direction, communicating and motivating. It is about broad principles, emotion and less detail. If management is the head, leadership is the heart of an organization. It is therefore quite possible for an organization to be over-managed but under-led, or vice versa. An organization needs both good leadership and good management. In a start-up the emphasis tends to be on effective day-to-day management. But this quickly needs to switch to good leadership. However, leadership is situation specific. Some leaders are good in one situation but not in others. Leaders can have rollercoaster careers as they exhibit successful leadership characteristics at certain discrete times, in certain circumstances, with particular people, but these characteristics do not work when things change. They fail to adapt. Winston Churchill was widely acknowledged as a great war-time leader but a poor peace-time leader. Therefore entrepreneurs might be good leaders at start-up but poor leaders as the business grows. They may need to change their leadership style.

The one certain characteristic that separates leaders from other people is the obvious one that they have willing followers. Why is this? What is it about them that persuades others to follow them? The characteristics and personality traits of good leaders tell us a limited amount about good leadership. Leadership is not about who you are. It is more about what you do with who you are, and how you form relationships with your followers. Leadership effectiveness is influenced by the group, task and situation (or context) you face and leadership style can be crafted to meet these different contexts. However, while it is too simplistic just to say that leaders have certain enduring character traits, some individuals do seem to emerge as leaders across a variety of situations and tasks. This gives us some indications of the characteristics and particularly the *behaviours* needed to be a good leader. What is more, we are beginning to better understand the importance of a leader's personal cognitive abilities, motives, social skills, expertise and problem-solving skills. What emerges is a complex interaction of many factors that underlines how good leadership is an art rather than a science – and is very dependent upon the situation or context. While we can isolate the main factors that influence it and point to good practice in particular contexts, there is no magic formula.

Defining the role of leader

Our traditional view of leaders is that they are special people – often charismatic 'heroes' like Churchill – who set direction, make key decisions and motivate staff, frequently prevailing against the odds at times of crisis. They have vision – something most entrepreneurs have aplenty. They are strategic thinkers and effective communicators. They create the culture within the organization to reflect their priorities. Leadership is more about guiding vision, culture and identity than it is about decision making. If there were ever a job description for a leader, therefore, it would probably include five elements.

> The leader's story, sense of purpose, values and vision, establish the direction and target. His relentless commitment to the truth, and to inquiry into the forces underlying current reality continually highlight the gaps between reality and the vision. Leaders generate and manage this creative tension – not just themselves but in an entire organization. This is how they energize an organization. That is their basic job. That is why they exist … Crafting a larger story is one of the oldest domains of leadership … leaders may start by pursuing their own vision, but as they learn to listen carefully to others' visions they begin to see that their own vision is part of something larger. This does not diminish any leader's sense of responsibility for the vision – if anything it deepens it.
>
> Peter Senge, The Fifth Discipline (1992, London: Century Business)

Having a vision for the organization – This gives people a clear focus on the direction of the organization, the values it stands for and the key issues and concerns it faces in achieving its goals. Visions are underpinned by the values of the organization and the values are reflected in the culture of the organization. You created your vision based upon your values in Workbook exercise 5.1.

Being able to develop strategy – It is one thing to know where you want to go, it is quite another to know how to get there. The heart of leadership is about being able to chart a course for future development that steers the organization towards the leader's vision. This is what strategy is about – linking various actions and tactics in a consistent way that forms a coherent plan. There is a wonderful Chinese proverb:

> If there is a spark of genius in the leadership function at all, it must lie in the transcending ability, a kind of magic, to assemble … out of a variety of images, signals, forecasts and alternatives … a clearly articulated vision of the future that is simple, clearly understood, clearly desirable, and energizing.
>
> Warren Bennis and Burt Nanus, Leaders: The Strategies for Taking Charge (1985, New York: Harper & Row)

Tactics without strategy is the noise before defeat.

It underlines, not only the need for a consistent, coherent strategy to ensure success, but also that without it miscellaneous tactics will just cause 'noise' or arguments among your followers about what to do and why they should be doing it.

Being able to communicate effectively, particularly the vision – There is no point in having a vision and a strategy unless you can communicate it effectively in a way that inspires and motivates staff. Staff need to understand how the vision will be achieved, and believe that they can achieve it, particularly in an uncertain world. They need to understand where the organization is going and the strategies that are being adopted to take it there.

Creating the culture for the organization – The culture of an organization is the cement that binds it together. It influences how people think and how they act. Creating an appropriate culture is probably the single most important thing a leader has to do.

Managing and monitoring performance – Leaders still have to manage. You need to be a good leader and a good manager. Management may be routine, but in a start-up dealing with the day-to-day operations is about survival.

Personal attributes of leaders

A key mind-shift from manager to leader is to become a **strategic thinker**. Strategic thinkers are able to move away from day-to-day operational detail to see the broad, strategic, organizational perspective. This involves taking a longer-term, holistic view of the organization. Strategy sets a framework within which short-term actions can be judged. Leaders understand where they have come from – knowledge of the past – and how it affects the current situation, where they are going to and how to get there. They are also engaged in perpetually 'scanning' the environment, both for opportunities and risks, strategizing, considering options. They therefore become **strategic learners**. This learning may involve looking at the big picture, trying to find patterns over time and looking for complex interactions so as to understand the underlying causes of problems. Based on this information, leaders can then envision a new and desirable future and reframe this new future in the context of the organization. This is their vision and **strategic intent**. During the process they engage in synthesis as well as analysis.

Leadership is also about persuading people to follow you. As we shall see in the next section there are a number of styles you can adopt to persuade people to do this; however they all require **emotional intelligence**:

- **Self-awareness** – the ability to understand themselves, their strengths, weaknesses and emotions;
- **Self-management** – an ability to adapt their behaviour to meet different circumstances, and requires control, integrity, initiative and conscientiousness;
- **Social awareness** – an appreciation of different circumstances, both of people and the environment or context in which they find themselves, and requires empathy, sensing other people's emotions;
- **Social skills** – an ability to relate to people and collaborate with them and, above all, build relationships with them.

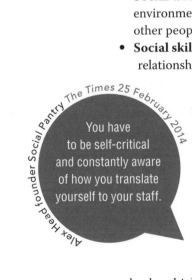

You have to be self-critical and constantly aware of how you translate yourself to your staff.

Alex Head founder Social Pantry, *The Times* 25 February 2014

A key skill in developing emotional intelligence is the ability and time to undertake honest reflection. This means that you need to check that your perception of yourself or of different circumstances corresponds with that of others. Is it real? This involves a degree of mature judgement that is not easily taught, but develops over time and can be much enhanced by having a supportive network of people around you that you are able to talk with.

Trust and respect underpin the relationship that a leader needs to establish with those they wish to lead. Followers need to aspire to the vision and buy into the strategies that will make it happen. But they also need to trust that the leader can and will deliver it, and it is easier to trust someone who has high moral characteristics or ethical values. These are the leaders who really command our respect and loyalty. They generate more commitment from staff. But ethics are not just an 'add-on'. It is not easy to adopt personal attributes that do not represent the person you really are. Eventually your guard will slip and your followers will see through the image you portray. And that will lead to distrust and resentment. To sustain your leadership, you need to be 'authentic' – to believe in and act out these ethical underpinnings (Academic insight 11.5). Trust and respect come not just from words but also from actions – 'walking the talk'.

ACADEMIC
insight
11.5

Authentic leaders

Reflecting on interviews with 125 top leaders, George and Sims (2007) talk about 'authentic leadership' coming from those individuals who follow their real values and beliefs – their internal compass. **Authentic leaders** build a support team of people with whom they have a close relationship (spouses, family members, mentors etc.) and they have a network of professional contacts to provide counsel and guidance. These are people with whom they can reflect honestly on the issues they face. Authentic leaders also have strong values and beliefs that they practise at work and at home – 'pursuing purpose with passion'. They have ethical foundations and boundaries and lead with their hearts as well as their heads. They establish enduring relations with staff because they listen to them and demonstrate that they care. George and Sims argue that, in this way, authentic leaders not only inspire those around them but also empower people to lead. But they only do this by always being true to their own principles, values and beliefs. They are authentic. And that cannot be faked.

Brubaker (2005) gives us an insight into what your staff might consider to be ethical foundations. When asked in a survey what values they looked for in ethical leaders, respondents listed nine major attributes:

1 Truth and honesty
2 Integrity and alignment of words and actions

Getty Images/ David De Lossy

3 The keeping of promises
4 Loyalty to the organization and the people in it
5 Fairness between staff
6 Concern and respect for others
7 Law abiding
8 Pursuit of excellence
9 Personal accountability, taking responsibility, admitting mistakes and sharing success.

Brubaker, D.L. (2005) 'The Power of Vision', in D.L. Brubaker and L.D. Coble (eds) *The Hidden Leader*, Thousand Oaks, CA: Corwin Press.

George, B. and Sims, P.E. (2007) *True North: Discover your Authentic Leadership*, San Francisco: Jossey- Bass.

Leadership style and contingency theory

As we have said, leadership effectiveness is influenced by the group, task and situation (or context) you face and leadership style can be crafted to meet these different contexts. The appropriate style to adopt depends upon how these factors interact. This is called situational or **contingency theory**. Three broad styles of leadership have been popularized (Figure 11.13). Each style involves different degrees of freedom or control for the employees:

- **Authoritarian** – This style focuses decision-making powers in the leader. It is most appropriate in times of crisis but usually fails to win 'hearts and minds'.
- **Democratic** – This style favours group decision making and consensus building. It is more appropriate in circumstances other than crisis.
- **Laissez-faire** – This style allows a high degree of freedom for followers. However, a leader adopting this style is often perceived as weak.

Laissez-faire   Democratic   Authoritarian

Increasing control – Decreasing freedom

Figure 11.13 Leadership styles and control

In reality there are many permutations of these three extremes of leadership styles and contingency theory states that the leader should adapt their style to suit different situations or contexts. It emphasizes that there is no one 'best' way of managing or leading. It depends on the interaction of all the factors – leader, group, task and situation or context (Figure 11.14). You may personally prefer an informal, non-directional style, but faced with an inexperienced apprentice working a dangerous lathe you might be forgiven for reverting to a fairly formal, directive style with heavy supervision. In that situation the change in style is appropriate. Try the same style with a group of experienced creative marketing consultants and there would be problems. Many different styles may be effective for different tasks, with different groups and in different contexts. Remember there is no evidence of any single leadership style characterizing successful businesses. What is more, the ability of leaders to change and adapt their styles may vary enormously. By looking at the individual elements of these four factors we can understand what style is best suited to different circumstances.

> James Cain MD Water Brands Group *The Times* 25 February 2014
>
> Don't underestimate the effect your management style has. It is not easy to motivate people because you can't do it with a large pay-packet in a small business, so you need to motivate with your vision and take people with you. Your labour turnover or attrition rate is the barometer of the culture of your business.

Figure 11.14 Leadership style

Leader and task

Leaders have to work through others to complete tasks. The degree of concern for the people they are leading compared to the task in hand will, in part, determine the style they adopt. The leadership grid shown in Figure 11.15 shows style as dependent upon the leader's concern for task compared to the concern for people. Entrepreneurs are usually more concerned with completing the task but, as the firm grows, they must become more concerned with people if the tasks are to be accomplished. Task leadership may be appropriate in certain situations, for example emergencies. However, concern for people must surface at some point if effective, trusting relationships are to develop. Low concern for both people and task is hardly leadership at all. High concern for people – the country club style – is rare in business but can be appropriate in community groups, charities or social clubs where good relationships and high morale might be the dominant objectives. You can find your preferred style on this grid by answering the leadership questionnaire in Workbook exercise 11.6.

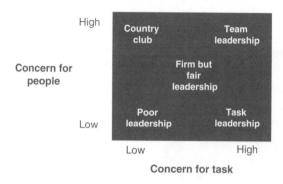

Figure 11.15 *Leader and task*

Source: adapted from Blake, R. and Mouton, J. (1978) The New Managerial Grid, London: Gulf Publishing Company. Reprinted with permission.

Leader and group

Successful leaders are likely to adopt different styles with different groups approaching the same task. Leadership style also depends on the relationship of the leader with the group they are leading. Figure 11.16 shows this in relation to the leader's degree of authority and the group's autonomy in decision making. If a leader has high authority but the group has low autonomy, the leader will tend to adopt an autocratic style, simply instructing people what to do. If they have low authority (e.g. because of past failure) they will tend to adopt a paternalistic style, cajoling the group into doing things, picking off individuals and offering grace and favour in exchange for performance. If the leader has low authority and the group has high autonomy, then they will tend to adopt a participative style, involving the whole group in decision making and moving forward with consensus. If the leader has high authority then they will seek opinions but make the decision themselves using a consultative style.

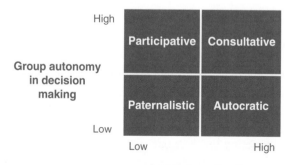

Figure 11.16 *Leader and group*

Leader and situation or context

Alex Head founder Social Pantry *The Times 25 February 2014*

> You can't avoid conflict. As well as rewarding people you need to be able to say 'that won't do'.

The weight the leader should put on these different influences depends on the situation or context they face. However, taking an objective view of any context is always problematic because we view life through our own, biased lens and we might be tempted to 'construct' social contexts that legitimate our intended actions rather than viewing them objectively. Nevertheless one situation that leaders are likely to face is that of conflict. The Thomas–Kilmann Conflict Modes instrument gives us an insight into how conflict might be handled (Academic insight 11.6). While each style has its advantages in certain situations, compromise, or better still collaboration, is generally thought to be the best way for a team to work.

ACADEMIC insight 11.6

Dealing with conflict

Often in business you find yourself at odds with others who hold seemingly incompatible views. For a leader to be effective they need to understand how they handle these conflict situations and be able to modify their behaviour to obtain the best results from others. Based on research by Kenneth Thomas and Ralph Kilmann, the Thomas–Kilmann Conflict Modes Instrument shows how a person's behaviour can be classified under two dimensions:

- Assertiveness – the extent to which individuals attempt to satisfy their own needs;
- Cooperativeness – the extent to which they attempt to satisfy the needs of others.

These two dimensions led the authors to identify five behavioural classifications which the questionnaire can identify in individuals.

1 **Avoiding** is both unassertive and uncooperative. It may involve side-stepping an issue or withdrawing from the conflict altogether. In this mode any conflict may not be even addressed.
2 **Competing** is assertive and uncooperative. Individuals are concerned for themselves and pursue their own agenda forcefully, using power, rank or ability to argue in order to win the conflict. This can be seen as bullying with less forceful individuals or, when others use the same mode, it can lead to heated, possibly unresolved, arguments.
3 **Accommodating** is unassertive and cooperative, the opposite of competing. Individuals want to see

the concerns of others satisfied. They might do so as an act of 'selfless generosity' or just because they are 'obeying orders'; either way they run the risk of not making their own views heard.

4 **Collaborating** is both assertive and cooperative, the opposite of avoiding. Issues get addressed but individuals are willing to work with others to resolve the conflict, perhaps finding alternatives that meet everybody's concerns. This is the most constructive approach to conflict for a group as a whole.

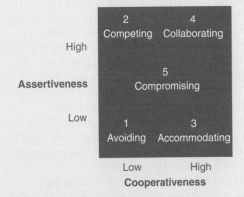

Figure 11.17 *Thomas–Kilmann Conflict Modes*

Source: Reproduced with permission from the publisher, CPP, Inc. Copyright 1974. All rights reserved. Further reproduction is prohibited without CPP's written consent. For more information, please visit www.cpp.com.

5 **Compromising** is the 'in between' route, the diplomatic, expedient solution to conflict which partially satisfies everyone. It may involve making concessions.

Each style of handling conflict has its advantages and disadvantages and can be effective in certain situations. However, management teams or boards of directors, if they are to get the most from each member over a longer period of time, work best when all members adopt the collaborating or compromising modes. A team made up of just competitors would find it difficult to get on and, indeed, to survive. A team made up of just accommodators would lack assertiveness and drive.

The Thomas–Kilmann Conflict Modes Instrument is available on: www.kilmanndiagnostics.com/catalog/ thomas-kilmann-conflict-mode-instrument

ACADEMIC insight 11.7

Leadership paradigms

Transactional leadership – This style of leadership is about setting goals, putting in place systems and controls to achieve them and rewarding individuals when they meet the goals. It is about efficiency and incremental change, reinforcing rather than challenging organizational learning. It is associated with closed cultures, rigid systems, formal procedures and bureaucratic organization structures. Bass (1985, 1998) contrasts this with transformational leadership.

Transformational leadership – This is more emotional and is about inspiration, excitement and intellectual stimulation. It is a style best suited to highly turbulent and uncertain environments where crises, anxiety and high risk are prevalent (Vera and Crossan, 2004) – which tends to describe the entrepreneurial context. Not surprisingly, this style of leadership is associated with open cultures, organic structures, adaptable systems, and flexible procedures. Transformational leaders are often seen as being charismatic, inspirational, intellectually stimulating and individually considerate (Avolio et al., 1999), and as having empathy and self-confidence (Egri and Herman, 2000). They inspire and motivate people with a vision, create excitement with their enthusiasm and get people to question the tried-and-tested ways of doing things and 'reframe' the future (Bass and Avolio, 1990).

Visionary leadership – Sashkin (1996) characterized this style as providing a clear vision which focuses people on goals that are part of that vision and on key issues and concerns. The visionary leader has good interpersonal and communication skills. They get everyone to understand the focus for the business and to work together towards common goals. They act consistently over time to develop trust and they care and respect others, making them self-confident, while having an inner self-confidence themselves. Finally, they provide creative opportunities that others can buy into and 'own' – empowering opportunities that involve people in making the right things their own priorities. (Sashkin's Leader Behaviour Questionnaire is a 360-degree assessment instrument that measures visionary leadership behaviours, characteristics and contextual effects. It needs to be filled out by 3–6 colleagues and is available on www.hrdpress.com/Visionary-Leader-Self-5-Pack-VLSQ.)

Dispersed leadership – This style draws on models of dispersed or distributed leadership which focus on leadership across all levels and in different forms (Bradford and Cohen, 1998; Chaleff, 1995; Mintzberg, 2009). It emphasizes the importance of 'emotional intelligence' in the leader and their ability to listen, empathize and communicate with those they lead (Goleman, 1996) – social skills essential to building effective relationships. As already mentioned, it emphasizes 'authenticity' (George, 2003; George and Sims, 2007) – leaders being true to their own beliefs (having an ethical underpinning) so that trust and respect can be built. The literature also emphasizes leaders as 'servants' of their workforce, acknowledging that self-interest is part of any relationship (Greenleaf, 1970) as well as 'educators' that develop organizational learning (Heifetz, 1994).

Avolio, B.J., Bass, B.M. and Jung, D.I. (1999) 'Re-examining the Components of Transformational and Transactional Leadership using the Multifactor Leadership Questionnaire', *Journal of Occupational and Organisational Psychology*, 72.

Bass, B.M. (1985) *Leadership and Performance Beyond Expectations*, New York: Free Press.

Bass, B.M. (1998) *Transformational Leadership: Industry, Military and Educational Impact*, Mahwah, NJ: Lawrence Erlbaum Associates.

Bass, B.M and Avolio, B.J. (1990) 'The Implications of Transactional and Transformational Leadership for Individual, Team and Organizational Development', *Research in Organizational Change and Development*, 4.

Bradford, D.L. and Cohen, A.R. (1998) *Power Up: Transforming Organizations Through Shared Leadership*, New York: John Wiley & Sons.

Chaleff, I. (1995) *The Courageous Follower: Standing Up, To and For Our Leaders*, San Francisco: Bennet- Koehler.

Egri, C.P. and Herman, S. (2000) 'Leadership in the North American Environmental Sector: Values, Leadership Styles and Contexts of Environmental Leaders and their Organizations', *Academy of Management Journal*, 43.

George, B. (2003) *Authentic Leadership: Rediscovering the Secrets to Creating Lasting Value*, San Francisco: Jossey-Bass.

George, B. and Sims, P.E. (2007) *True North: Discover your Authentic Leadership*, San Francisco: Jossey- Bass.

Goleman, D. (1996) *Emotional Intelligence: Why It Can Matter More Than IQ*, London: Bloomsbury.

Greenleaf, R.F. (1970) *The Servant as Leader*, Mahwah, NJ: Paulist.

Heifetz, R.A. (1994) *Leadership Without Easy Answers*, Cambridge, MA: Harvard University Press.

Mintzberg, H. (2009) *Managing*, London: FT Prentice Hall.

Sashkin, M. (1996) *Becoming a Visionary Leader*, Amherst, MA: HRD Press.

Vera, D. and Crossan, M. (2004) 'Strategic Leadership and Organizational Learning', *Academy of Management Review*, 29(2).

Entrepreneurial leadership

The academic literature provides many leadership models that describe different leadership styles. Each is associated with different organizational characteristics and each is appropriate to different situations or contexts. Academic insight 11.7 outlines just four of them. The question is whether any of these are appropriate for **entrepreneurial leadership**?

> The notion of the leader as a heroic decision maker is untenable ... Leaders will no longer be seen as grand visionaries, all-wise decision makers, and iron-fisted disciplinarians. Instead they will need to become social architects, constitution writers, and entrepreneurs of meaning. In this new world, the leader's job is to create an environment where every employee has the chance to collaborate, innovate, and excel.
>
> Gary Hamel, 'Moon Shots for Management', Harvard Business Review, February 2009

We defined an entrepreneurial leader as a leader of an organization that remains entrepreneurial, so the first question is, what is an entrepreneurial organization? The answer is one that embodies the DNA of the entrepreneur and their approach to management: an organization that thrives and prospers in this world of uncertainty, rapid change and risk taking, that encourages creativity, innovation and entrepreneurship at all levels, with or without the entrepreneur to lead it. We may therefore rephrase the question as how does a leader build an organization with these characteristics, one that is able to thrive in this context? The answer comes from the concept of **organizational architecture** – a metaphor used to describe the infrastructure an organization needs to build business processes that deliver its vision. These comprise the four building blocks shown in Figure 11.18: leadership, culture, structure and strategies.

Entrepreneurs exhibit three key characteristics in the way they manage, characteristics that have been encouraged throughout this book:

1 an ability to build a strong network of relationships;
2 an ability to mitigate risks through knowledge, partnerships and structures;
3 a particular approach to developing strategy that is better able to deal with risk and uncertainty.

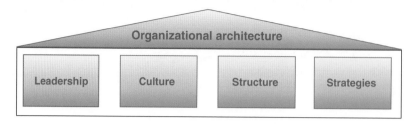

Figure 11.18 *Four pillars of organizational architecture*

Academic insight 11.8 outlines how, building on these, a larger organization might construct an entrepreneurial architecture. It also outlines the characteristics needed by an 'entrepreneurial leader' to complement this architecture. You can see that these characteristics are subtly different from the leadership paradigms outlined in Academic insight 11.7. Entrepreneurial leaders are both visionary and transformational but, importantly, they should set out to build and embed leadership into the organization – and this is more than just dispersed leadership. There is an ancient Chinese proverb that still rings true:

> *The wicked leader is he who the people despise. The good leader is the one who the people revere. But the great leader is he who the people say 'we did it ourselves'.*

To become an entrepreneurial leader you need to transform not only yourself but also your organization. You need to build an organization that is fundamentally entrepreneurial, one that embodies your DNA, as well as your approach to management. You need to build a business that is both visionary and transformational. You do this by building structures and a culture and developing strategies that combine with your leadership style to create an organizational architecture that is entrepreneurial. And instead of concentrating just on acquiring the individual attributes of leadership, you should take an architectural approach – build these leadership attributes into the organization and spread them throughout it.

However, even an entrepreneurial leader needs to remain flexible and modify their style to suit specific groups, tasks and situations. They might need to be able to adapt their style from visionary or transformational in periods of rapid change, to more transactional in periods of consolidation. This combination of influences is shown in Figure 11.19.

Figure 11.19 *Entrepreneurial leadership*

Entrepreneurial architecture

Burns (2013) explains how large organizations can be more entrepreneurial by constructing an entrepreneurial architecture through the four pillars (Figure 11.18). He paints a picture of this architecture by describing each of its elements:

- **Structure** – The best structure for any particular business depends on many factors (see Figure 11.10). However, if the business faces a high degree of environmental turbulence and if the tasks it undertakes are complex, then an organic structure that can change and evolve in different situations is probably best. This might be supplemented by more hierarchical structures in other parts of the organization, reflecting their different characteristics. Control is loose, or at least balanced, giving people autonomy but holding them accountable. There is a wide range of partnerships.

- **Culture** – An entrepreneurial culture is a strong culture, one that is underpinned by strong personal and group relationships which form a strong group identity. It views change as the norm and values creativity and innovation. It balances individual initiative and achievement ('individual' and 'masculine' cultures, using Hofstede's terminology from Academic insight 1.4) with cooperative relationships (high 'feminine' and 'collectivism' cultures). It encourages measured risk taking through experimentation, tolerating mistakes but encouraging learning (low 'uncertainty avoidance'). Information is

shared and decision making delegated down, which encourage empowerment and motivation to make decisions 'for the good of the organization'. It is egalitarian and slightly anti-authoritarian (low 'power distance') with open, informal relationships and open, unrestricted information flows encouraged through flat organizational structures. These qualities derive from and are reflected in the organization's vision, values, norms and beliefs.

- **Strategies** – Like structures, the best strategies for particular situations depend on many factors. However strategy development is characterized by continuous strategizing at all levels in the organization, underpinned by a strong vision, sense of direction and strategic intent. That vision will be ambitious but rooted in reality, creating a tension sufficient to motivate the organization. The organization is good at scanning the environment for opportunities and threats, developing strategic options, and is helped by the network of relationships and partnerships developed at all levels. Decision making tends to be decentralized, incremental and adaptive, so as to maintain maximum speed and flexibility, but underpinned by strong vision and strategic intent. Creativity and innovation will be valued and encouraged in various ways. Mistakes are tolerated and learned from.

- **Leadership** – Burns stresses that an entrepreneurial architecture may not be appropriate for all organizations. It depends on the environment it faces (Figure 11.20). For organizations facing little change, in which simple tasks are undertaken with a view to maximum efficiency (see

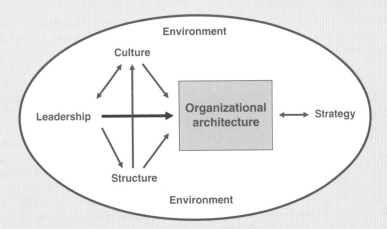

Figure 11.20 Constructing an entrepreneurial architecture

Source: Burns, P. (2013) Corporate Entrepreneurship: Innovation and Strategy in Large Organizations, Basingstoke: Palgrave.

Figure 11.10), it may not be appropriate. It is best suited to those facing rapid change, uncertainty or complexity, where creativity and innovation are essential. In these circumstances he sees the entrepreneurial leader as pivotal and needing a number of characteristics that help to build and complement the other three pillars of the organizational architecture. The entrepreneurial leader needs to be visionary, a good communicator and motivator with strong interpersonal skills that allow them to build a network of relationships. They are 'team players', able to build confidence through trust. They are strategic thinkers and learners who help clarify what others see as ambiguity or uncertainty. They share their insight and seek to build an open organization in which staff feel empowered to take the opportunities that present themselves and make decisions 'for the good of the organization', rather than just themselves.

There is a free interactive Corporate Entrepreneurship Audit tool that can be used to assess the organizational architecture of a business and the environment in which it operates available on: www.macmillanihe.com/companion/Burns-Corporate-Entrepreneurship/student-zone/Corporate-entrepreneurship-audit

Burns, P. (2013) *Corporate Entrepreneurship: Innovation and Strategy in Large Organizations*, 3rd edn, Basingstoke: Palgrave.

CASE insight 11.3

Steve Jobs and Apple (2) USA

Entrepreneurial leadership

We looked at how Steve Jobs started Apple in Chapter 1. Jobs was the epitome of an entrepreneurial leader who revolutionized three industries – computing, music sales and cinema animations. And his was the story of a Silicon Valley hero. By the time he died in 2011, Apple had become the second most valuable company in the world, measured by market capitalization, with a cash mountain of some $80 billion.

However, many of Jobs' personal character traits did not endear him to others in business. He was a perfectionist who was highly secretive and had, at the very least, what might be described as a hard-driving management style. In 1993 *Fortune* magazine placed him on the list of America's Toughest Bosses for his time at NeXT, quoting co-founder Daniel Lewin as saying: 'The highs were unbelievable … but the lows were unimaginable' (18 October 1993). Fourteen years later it called him 'one of Silicon Valley's leading egomaniacs' (19 March 2007). He was notorious for micromanaging things from the design of new products to the chips they used. In his obituary, the *Daily Telegraph* (6 October 2011)

claimed he was 'almost pathologically controlling' when it came to dealing with news reporters and the press, actively trying to stifle any reports that might seem critical of him or Apple. It went on to reveal some elements of his dark side:

He oozed arrogance, was vicious about business rivals, and in contrast to, say, Bill Gates, refused to have any truck with notions of corporate responsibility. He habitually parked his car in the disabled slot at Apple headquarters and one of the first acts on returning to the company in 1997 was to terminate all of its corporate philanthropy programs … He ruled Apple with a combination of foul-mouthed tantrums and charm, withering scorn and flattery … and those in his regular orbit found he could flip with no warning from one category to the other … Yet members of Jobs' inner circle, many of whom came with him from NeXT, found working for him an exhilarating experience. To keep them on the board, Jobs eliminated most cash bonuses from executive compensation and started handing out stock options instead.

The *Sunday Times* (30 October 2011) was just as scathing about his personality, giving examples of his bad-tempered, often rude, tantrums with staff and suppliers. He had a propensity for tears and the article cited the example of him throwing a tantrum and crying when he was assigned No. 2 on the Apple payroll and Wozniak was assigned No. 1. Jobs insisted on being 'number zero'. It cited examples of him often claiming the ideas of other Apple employees as his own and described him as 'selfish, rude, aggressive, lachrymose, unpredictable … a good candidate for the boss from hell'. It described Apple as 'a cultish, paranoid, joyless organization where public humiliations were a regular occurrence and cut-throat competition among the ranks was encouraged' (*Sunday Times*, 29 January 2012). And yet it also observed that Jobs could inspire incredible loyalty, albeit in the people he had helped to make rich.

Jobs' personal life was equally murky. Before starting up Apple, he famously paid his partner Steve Wozniak only $300 for a job he was paid $5,000 for by Atari, when the agreement with Wozniak was for a 50:50 split. At a point in his life where he was already wealthy, he denied paternity of a daughter, leaving the mother on welfare, even swearing an affidavit that he was not the father because, in effect, he was 'sterile and infertile'. He eventually acknowledged paternity. Jobs went on to marry Laurene Powell and have three more children, living in an unassuming family home in Palo Alto, on San Francisco Bay.

Writing after Jobs' death, Adam Lashinsky (2012) gives us a rare insight into the effects this must have had in generating an organizational culture at Apple. As he says: 'you're expected to check your ego at the door' because there really is only room for one – that of Jobs, who he says exhibits 'narcissism, whimsy and disregard for the feelings of others'. Jobs emerges as a short-tempered, authoritarian dictator ruthlessly pushing, even bullying, staff to complete assigned tasks. On a (slightly) more positive note Jobs is described as 'a visionary risk taker with a burning desire to change the world … charismatic leader willing to do whatever it takes to win and who couldn't give a fig about being liked'.

Central to Apple's culture was product excellence – a cult of product – where employees do not want to let the company down by being the weakest link. And if they do, they can become collateral damage because of the aggressive, competitive environment. It was work-orientated and definitely not play-orientated – long hours, missed holidays and tight deadlines were expected and encouraged. However, Lashinsky admits that 'by and large, Apple is a collaborative and cooperative environment, devoid of overt politicking … but it isn't

usually nice, and it's almost never relaxed'. In his view unquestioning collaboration and cooperation were necessary to ensure instructions were communicated and followed in this command-and-control structure. He believes that employee happiness was never a top priority for Steve Jobs. But on the other hand, employees derived pride from Apple's products and in working for Jobs' vision. Jobs appeared omnipresent, or at least visible, around the campus, despite the fact that very few people had access to his office suite.

Secrecy, mistrust and paranoia seemed to underpin the Apple culture. According to Lashinsky:

> Apple is secretive … Far from being empowered, its people operate within narrow bands of responsibility … employees are expected to follow orders, not offer opinions … Apple's CEO was a micromanager … and to an amazingly low level … Apple isn't even a nice place to work … Jobs' brutality in dealing with subordinates legitimized a frighteningly harsh, bullying, and demanding culture … a culture of fear and intimidation found roots.

Apple's organizational structure encouraged secrecy – it did not have organization charts, although Lashinsky's attempt to draw one showed Jobs in the middle of a spider's web. He describes Apple's organization as 'unconventional', with 15 Senior Vice Presidents and Vice Presidents reporting directly to Jobs 'at the centre'. Staff were frequently organized around small project teams with teams isolated from each other and operating under strict secrecy rules – 'siloes within siloes'. Staff only knew about the elements of new product development that they needed to know about. The fact there were no conventional organization charts limited the number of people employees knew outside their immediate environment – a cell-like structure.

Just like all entrepreneurs, Jobs' personality was integral to his leadership style. And he built an organization structure and culture to match his leadership style. However, it was almost the direct opposite of most successful high-tech businesses in Silicon Valley – Lashinsky frequently contrasted Apple with Google. And, at the time of his death, many commentators observed that this organization was so based upon one man, that they questioned how long it would prosper without him.

Nevertheless, Jobs had many admirers and he certainly achieved enormous things in his life. Walter Isaacson (2012) believes that you should not 'fixate too much on the rough edges of his personality'. He said of Jobs that:

> He acted as if the normal rules didn't apply to him, and the passion, intensity, and extreme emotionalism he brought to everyday life were things he also

poured into the products he made. His petulance and impatience were part and parcel of his perfectionism.

Isaacson said there were 14 keys to his success:

1 **Focus** – Jobs was always able to focus and spend time on what he considered important, often to the frustration of others trying to get him to consider other things. As he explained to the 1997 meeting of the Apple Worldwide Developers Association: 'Focusing is about saying no … and the result of that focus is going to be some really great products where the total is much greater than the sum of the parts.'

2 **Simplify** – Jobs admired simplicity, and simplicity of use was a key design feature of all Apple's products: 'It takes a lot of hard work to make something simple, to truly understand the underlying challenges and come up with elegant solutions.'

3 **Take responsibility end to end** – In his quest for simplicity, Jobs took end-to-end responsibility for the user experience, integrating hardware, software and peripherals – part of his controlling nature and drive for perfection.

4 **When behind leapfrog** – Rather than copying competitors, Jobs would always try to create something better and different.

5 **Push for perfection** – Jobs was a perfectionist and would delay production until he thought the product was 100% right.

6 **Put products before profits** – Because he was a perfectionist Jobs also wanted his products to be the best, whatever the price. He believed that if the product was great, profits would follow.

7 **Don't be a slave to focus groups** – Because Apple's products were so innovative, Jobs never trusted focus groups and market research, preferring his own instincts: 'Customers don't know what they want until we show them.'

8 **Bend reality** – Jobs' famous 'reality distortion field' persuaded people that his vision of the future would prevail. Some called it bullying and lying; others called it effective communication of strategic intent.

9 **Impute** – Jobs used the design of products and even its packaging to 'impute' signals to customers, signals that underpinned the brand identity.

10 **Tolerate only 'A' players** – Jobs' passion for perfection extended to employees and, perhaps, explains his rudeness to people who did not perform as he expected.

11 **Engage face to face** – Jobs was a believer in face-to-face meetings. His executive team met once a week, without an agenda, to 'kick around ideas'.

12 **Know both the big picture and the detail** – Jobs had both vision and a grasp of detail, or at least the detail he thought important.

13 **Combine humanities and sciences** – Jobs was able to connect ideas from different disciplines to create features in his products that customers valued (a creativity 'discovery skill').

14 **Stay hungry, stay foolish** – Jobs never wanted to lose the drive he had in his youth and always wanted Apple to keep the culture of a start-up.

So was Steve Jobs a great entrepreneurial leader? He certainly was a great entrepreneur. And under his leadership Apple certainly was extremely successful. But has he created an organization that is enduringly entrepreneurial, one that can succeed and prosper without him? Only time will tell.

Questions:

1 Review your answers to the case questions in Chapter 1. What elements of the entrepreneurial character did you spot in Jobs and what are the positive and negative aspects of these traits?

2 How important is it for the culture and structure of an organization to reflect the character traits of its leader?

3 Was Jobs a great entrepreneurial leader? Explain and justify.

4 Do you have to be a likeable character to be a great entrepreneurial leader? Explain and justify.

Lashinsky, A. (2012) *Inside Apple: The Secrets Behind the Past and Future Success of Steve Jobs's Iconic Brand*, London: John Murray.

Isaacson, W. (2012) 'The Real Leadership Lessons of Steve Jobs', *Harvard Business Review*, April.

Sofa-bed Factory

Piotr and Olek had been fairly certain about their key skills and therefore their roles right from the start of thinking through this business idea. Piotr was the person with the knowledge of sales and marketing. He had the friend who was the buyer in the UK retail chain and he had experience of the industry that made him best placed to find new customers. He better understood the whole marketing process. On the other hand, it was Olek who understood production and who had sourced all of the subcontractors in Poland. It was a natural division of labour. However, it did mean that Piotr would have to spend significant time on the road, and in particular in the UK. This he accepted. They decided that they would need two unskilled workers to work under Olek's direction in the factory. They needed a bookkeeper or accountant, but probably only on a part-time basis. Alternatively, Olek knew of a local accountant who would keep their books for them. They reasoned that, with such a small team, there was little need for any formal organization chart. They certainly did not need job descriptions and the two labourers would just have to do anything and everything that needed to be done – under Olek's direction, of course.

Questions:

1 Should Piotr and Olek have drawn up job descriptions and person specifications for the two labourers?
2 What are the advantages/disadvantages of hiring a part-time bookkeeper compared to using a local accountant?
3 Piotr and Olek are old friends. Should they still draw up a shareholders' agreement? Is it too early for them to be thinking of issues around leadership and team working?

Summary and action points

11.1 Identify skills needs: Develop a skills profile for your business – the skills, knowledge and networks that are needed to launch and operate your business. These can come from the founder(s), employees, partners, investors, professional advisors, and the board of directors. Where there are skills gaps in your existing team, they need to be filled. Draw up job descriptions and, based on these, person specifications.

11.2 Find professional advisors: Use professional advisors. They are an effective way of accessing a range of knowledge, skills and networks that otherwise you may not have.

11.3 Identify the management team roles: Assemble an effective management team – one that has an appropriate mix of skills and knowledge but also has a range of personalities that can work together as a team.

11.4 Decide on the organization structure: Decide on an appropriate organization structure. This depends on task complexity and environmental turbulence.

11.5 Decide on the organization culture: Decide on the organization culture you wish to create in your business. This is based upon values and beliefs, which are normally taken from the founder and can be created through behaviours and organizational and cognitive processes. Structure and culture should reinforce each other.

11.6 Develop your leadership skills: Leadership creates and should reinforce structure and culture. Develop the leadership skills to manage the business as it grows.

The ability to influence and build relationships requires certain characteristics in leaders – emotional intelligence, self-awareness and self-management. Leaders also need to be strategic thinkers and learners and be able to reflect. However, they also need to be able to adapt to the situations or contexts that they face.

The entrepreneurial context of leadership is one characterized by uncertainty, rapid change and risk taking. There are leadership paradigms that inform us about leadership in this context – transactional leadership, transformational leadership, visionary leadership and dispersed leadership.

Workbook exercises

 The New Venture Creation Workbook contains a digital version of these exercises that can be modified as your business model develops and builds into a draft business plan. It can be downloaded from www.macmillanihe.com/burns-nvc-2e.

11.1: Identify skills needs
Complete the table on the next page for your first year of operation.

1 List the skills, knowledge and competencies required for the business and the job roles these translate into. Make sure all skills and so on are covered by these roles.
2 Classify roles as 'key', 'important' or 'desirable'.
3 Classify roles as 'full- or part-time' and 'regular or shift work'.
4 Decide on remuneration levels and special arrangements (e.g. bonuses and incentives) for all posts, including those occupied by founders (who could be the ones working in your group).
5 Identify the roles that will be undertaken by the founder(s) and those that might be filled by professional advisors, partners, the board of directors and/or providers of finance.
6 Note any mission-critical roles and if necessary update your critical success factors [Exercise 10.4 (3)].
7 For the role gaps, prepare a brief job description and person specification. Draft job advertisements and decide how these will be advertised.
8 If your new business is a limited company, decide which members of the new venture team will become shareholders. List their goals, performance measures and targets. Draft the main features of a shareholders' agreement. Remember that you will need to ask the advice of a lawyer about this before anything is signed.
9 Repeat the exercise for each of the next two years to identify the skills gaps you will face in the future.

Skills, knowledge and competencies	Role	Key/ Important/ Desirable	Full- or part-time	Regular or shift work	Remuneration	Undertaken by founders or advisors	Critical role

11.2: Find professional advisors

Based on Exercise 11.1, list the areas where you will need professional help and advice and how you will go about hiring professional advisors to meet these needs. Amend Exercise 9.2, as appropriate.

11.3: Identify the management team roles

Complete the table below.

1 Based upon the results of the previous exercises, decide on the key roles to be undertaken by the founders and a management team with an appropriate mix of skills and knowledge.

2 Decide on the nature of the status of your management team (partners, employees etc.) and, if not already done, how you will recruit them.

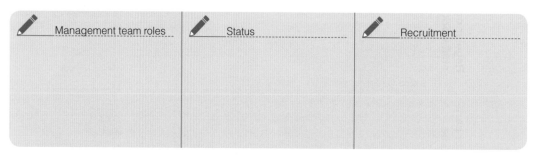

Management team roles	Status	Recruitment

3 Complete the Belbin team roles questionnaire yourself (www.belbin.com). Get other founders and your management team to complete it. Review the results and list their implications (e.g. for future recruitment, training etc.).

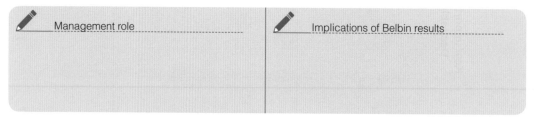

Management role	Implications of Belbin results

11.4: Decide on the organization structure

1 Identify where in Figure 11.10 your venture falls (environment vs. task complexity).

2 Draw up the organization chart for the business. Identify the key roles for founders and your management team.

Organization chart	Key management roles

11.5: Decide on the organization's culture

Based on Exercise 11.4 and using the table below:

1 Jot down a few words to describe the degree of control you wish to establish over people in your business. This may be different for different roles or areas of activity.

2 Jot down a few words to describe the culture you wish to establish in your business. Review Exercise 5.1 to ensure that your values and beliefs are consistent with the culture you wish to establish.

3 List the key actions (behaviours, organizational and cognitive processes) you need to undertake or establish to achieve this culture.

✏ Degree of control	✏ Culture description	✏ Key actions needed to establish culture

11.6: Develop your leadership skills

1 Complete the Leadership Style questionnaire.* Get other founders and your management team to complete it. For each statement, tick the 'Yes' box if you tend to agree or the 'No' box if you disagree. Try to relate the answers to your actual recent behaviour as a manager. There are no right and wrong answers. When you have completed the test, score yourself against the answers on page 478 and plot your position on the scoring grid.

What does this tell you about your leadership style?

		Yes	No
1	I encourage overtime work	❑	❑
2	I allow staff complete freedom in their work	❑	❑
3	I encourage the use of standard procedures	❑	❑
4	I allow staff to use their own judgement in solving problems	❑	❑
5	I stress being better than other firms	❑	❑
6	I urge staff to greater effort	❑	❑
7	I try out my ideas with others in the firm	❑	❑
8	I let my staff work in the way they think best	❑	❑
9	I keep work moving at a rapid pace	❑	❑
10	I turn staff loose on a job and let them get on with it	❑	❑
11	I settle conflicts when they happen	❑	❑
12	I get swamped by detail	❑	❑
13	I always represent the 'firm view' at meetings with outsiders	❑	❑
14	I am reluctant to allow staff freedom of action	❑	❑
15	I decide what should be done and who should do it	❑	❑
16	I push for improved quality	❑	❑
17	I let some staff have authority I could keep	❑	❑
18	Things usually turn out as I predict	❑	❑
19	I allow staff a high degree of initiative	❑	❑

		Yes	No
20	I assign staff to particular tasks	❑	❑
21	I am willing to make changes	❑	❑
22	I ask staff to work harder	❑	❑
23	I trust staff to exercise good judgement	❑	❑
24	I schedule the work to be done	❑	❑
25	I refuse to explain my actions	❑	❑
26	I persuade others that my ideas are to their advantage	❑	❑
27	I permit the staff to set their own pace for change	❑	❑
28	I urge staff to beat previous targets	❑	❑
29	I act without consulting staff	❑	❑
30	I ask staff to follow standard rules and procedures	❑	❑

*Adapted with permission from Sergiovanni, T. J., Metzcus, R., and Burden L. (1969) 'Toward a Particularistic Approach to Leadership Style: Some Findings', *American Educational Research Journal,* 6(1): 62–79. © Sage 1969. DOI: doi. org/10.3102/00028312006001062 Additional inspiration has been taken from Pfeiffer, J. and Jones, J. (eds) (1974) *A Handbook of Structured Experiences for Human Relations Training,* vol. 1 (rev.), University Associates, San Diego, California.

2 Complete a Thomas–Kilmann Conflict Modes Instrument (www.kilmanndiagnostics.com/catalog/thomas-kilmann-conflict-mode-instrument). Get other founders and your management team to complete it. What does this tell you about your style of dealing with conflict?

3 Review these results and, with the preferred Belbin team roles of founders and the management team in mind [Exercise 11.3 (3)], list the implications for the business and how leadership skills might be developed in the future (e.g. training, recruitment etc.).

12 Financial resources

Contents

- Selecting the right sort of finance
- Bank loans and overdrafts
- What banks look for
- Banking relationship
- Angel and venture finance
- What investors look for
- Crowdfunding
- FinTech
- The funding ladder
- Summary and action points
- Workbook exercises

Learning outcomes

When you have read this chapter and undertaken the related exercises you will be able to:

- Understand the principles of prudent financing
- Describe the sources of finance available to start-ups and small firms, and evaluate which are appropriate for different needs
- Understand how banks assess lending to start-ups and small firms, and how they monitor performance
- Understand how business angels and venture capitalists assess investments in start-ups and small firms, and how they might work with the founder
- Make a preliminary assessment of the finance needed for your business

Academic insights 📓

12.1	Sources of finance used by small firms in the UK
12.2	Agency theory and information asymmetry
12.3	Is there discrimination in lending?

Case insights 💼

12.1	Hotel Chocolat	12.8	Hamijoo
12.2	Lingo24	12.9	InSpiral Visionary Products
12.3	Solar Power Company Group (SPCG)	12.10	FarmDrop
12.4	Grameen Bank	12.11	Crowdcube
12.5	Purplle.com	12.12	TransferWise
12.6	Zopa	**Sofa-bed Factory**	
12.7	Kickstarter		

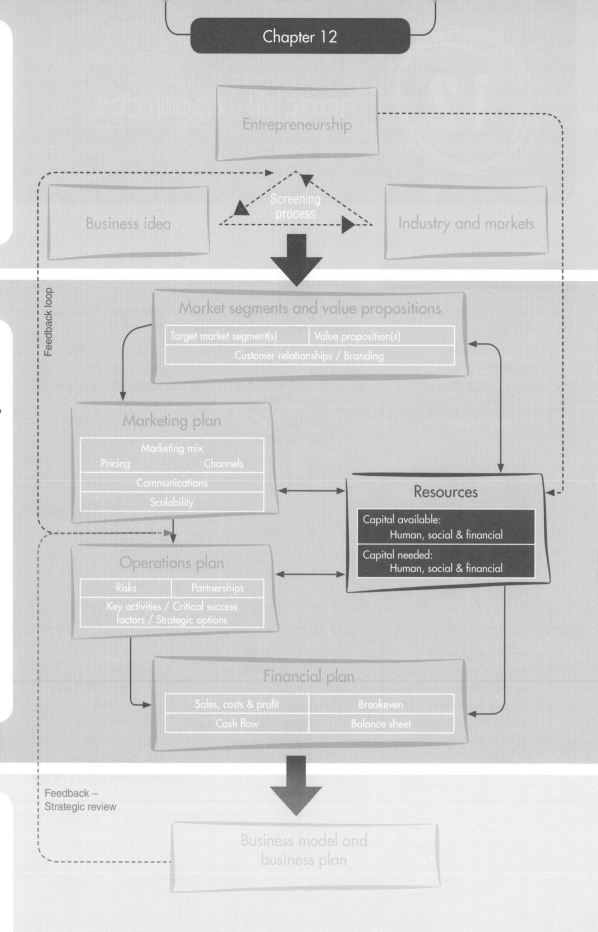

Phase 1: Research

Phase 2: Business model development

Phase 3: Launch

Entrepreneurship

Business idea

Screening process

Industry and markets

Feedback loop

Market segments and value propositions

Target market segment(s)	Value proposition(s)
Customer relationships / Branding	

Marketing plan

Marketing mix
Pricing	Channels
Communications	
Scalability	

Resources

Capital available: Human, social & financial
Capital needed: Human, social & financial

Operations plan

Risks	Partnerships
Key activities / Critical success factors / Strategic options	

Financial plan

Sales, costs & profit	Breakeven
Cash flow	Balance sheet

Feedback – Strategic review

Business model and business plan

Selecting the right sort of finance

Many new ventures require finance to get started. The more fixed assets you need, the higher your stock holding and the longer debtors take to pay, the greater your need for finance. And while a cash flow forecast will tell you how much you require and for how long (we deal with this in the next chapter), it will not tell you what sort of finance you require.

The first thing to realize is that not all money is the same. Different sorts of money ought to be used for different purposes and not all types of money are available to all new ventures. In fact many entrepreneurs, particularly at start-up, try to avoid using money at all by borrowing or using other people's assets wherever possible – 'bootstrapping'. They also use their personal credit cards, often repaying and recycling balances month by month. Where this fails, they might borrow money from friends or relatives. Friends and relatives can be flexible, perhaps agreeing to lend at a low or zero interest rate and without any guarantees because they know and trust you. They might even help with running the firm and bring valuable experience with them. However, rather than relying on informal agreements, most advisors would recommend that more formal loan agreements are drawn up so as to avoid misunderstandings and arguments later. Inevitably, however, most firms will need to obtain some form of external finance at some point in their life.

> Strangers will not invest in zero. If you can't raise 10–20% from your mates and your family first, that speaks volumes.
>
> UK Crowdfunding Association Sunday Times 14 September 2014 Julia Groves Chairwoman

Table 12.1 summarizes the major forms of finance and how they *ought* to be used, in theory. The principle is that the term duration of the source of finance should be matched to the term duration of the use to which it is put. Fixed or permanent assets, including the permanent element of working capital (stock and debtors, net of creditors), should be financed by long- or medium-term sources of finance, and only fluctuations in working capital should be financed by short-term finance, such as an overdraft.

Table 12.1 Matching sources and uses of finance

Duration of finance	Source of finance	Use of finance

Long and medium term	• Equity
	  • Personal, family and friends' investment
	  • Angel finance
	  • Venture finance
	• Long- and medium-term loans
	  • Personal, family and friends
	  • Bank
	• Lease and hire purchase
	• Crowdfunding (equity or loan)
		• Fixed assets: land, buildings, machinery, plant, equipment, vehicles, furniture etc.
		• Permanent working capital: stock, debtors (net creditors)

Short term	• Bank overdraft
	• Short-term loans
	  • Personal, family and friends
	  • Bank
		• Seasonal fluctuations in working capital: stock, debtors (net creditors)

John Elliott founder Ebac Sunday Times 10 March 2013

> To succeed in business you should never chase money. If you achieve success money will chase you. If you get too attached to the money you never reinvest. You have to treat the money in the business like it's not yours.

For a limited company the money that you put into the venture can take two forms – equity or loans. Equity takes the form of share capital. Over time the shareholders' equity grows with profitable trading. But if the venture fails then the shareholder risks losing everything, including the share capital they have put into the venture. For profitable, fast-growing businesses with a good management team there may be the opportunity to attract further equity investment from **crowd-funding**, business angels or venture capital organizations. These are covered in more detail later in this chapter.

Loans can come from many sources, but most firms will have to turn to the banks for finance at some point. Loans are serviced by regular interest payments and the capital will, ultimately, have to be repaid, depending on the duration: short-term (under one year), medium-term (up to five years) or long-term (over five years). Interest may vary with base rate or be fixed for the term of the loan. Agreeing to a fixed rate may involve a certain amount of crystal-ball gazing, but it does ensure that a small firm knows what its financing costs will be for some time to come.

As we shall see in the next section, bankers are likely to look for the security of assets to act as **collateral** against any loan and, if they cannot get this, they may ask you for personal guarantees. Personal guarantees can come from you or family or friends. Many countries have government loan schemes that offer lower rates of interest to small firms and/or guarantee provisions to replace or supplement personal guarantees. Some countries have credit mutual schemes for small firms that offer similar advantages.

There are two important ways of avoiding the need for a large capital outlay to purchase assets:

- **Lease** – This allows the firm to use assets without owning them by making regular lease payments. Because leased assets remain the property of the lessor, the company leasing them does not require collateral. Leasing therefore lowers risk and, because many leases have clauses that allow the purchase of newer, often more efficient replacement assets without penalty, they have been used extensively in industries like air transport, where capital costs are high and technology is constantly changing (see Case insight 4.4).
- **Hire purchase** – This allows the firm to purchase assets over a period of time, again by making regular payments with the assets acting as security in the event of default. Here the assets are owned by the company.

Tim Ewington co-founder Shortlist Media Daily Telegraph 5 July 2013

> We did look at securing [a conventional loan] but we quickly ended up where we are – invoice discounting ... A lot of friends run small businesses, and banks are not being generous to say the least. They're very careful – which is why they prefer to offer invoice discounting, because it's safe for them.

The main practical difference between the two methods is their tax treatment. Interest rates on lease and hire purchase schemes may be higher than on loans, but for a firm with little security to offer, they might be the only way to secure the use of assets.

Once you start trading other sources of finance become available. Most suppliers of goods and services offer trade credit terms (e.g. payment in 30 days), although they might insist on taking credit references and might also undertake a credit check. They will also place credit limits on accounts. Start-ups may have to establish a payment history to be offered credit and only gradually will the credit limit be extended. Trade credit is an important source of finance for most established firms – and it is free. It is also worth mentioning **factoring and invoice discounting** which is, again, only available once you establish a trading history. These are ways of obtaining finance against the invoices you issue (typically 75–80% of the value). You pay interest on the cash advanced, until the invoice is paid. It can be expensive and there are many restrictions but it can be a lifeline to undercapitalized, rapidly growing businesses. Your bank will put you in touch with organizations offering these facilities.

Finally, it goes without question that if there are grants or 'soft loans' available then they should be considered. Grants are 'free money', although they can involve bureaucracy and take time to come through. They vary enormously between countries and even regions, changing frequently to reflect national and regional priorities. There are often special schemes for start-ups, particularly social enterprises and for younger people.

Most new ventures will struggle to find finance appropriate for their needs. It is rarely easy. The flowchart in Figure 12.1 on the next page attempts to guide you through the process of deciding what form of finance is most appropriate and available to you.

In practice, you are most likely to use two or more sources of finance. Of course, actually persuading somebody to offer you the equity or loan finance will be more difficult. Government loans, grants and other support schemes vary from country to country and change regularly. Details can usually be obtained from appropriate government websites.

> You have to hang on to that initial money like it is gold. Look after every pound because it will allow you to get your idea right and prove it. Nobody will give you money until you can prove your idea is a winner … There's lots of money out there but only for proven concepts.
>
> Martyn Dawes founder Coffee Nation Sunday Times 23 May 2004

CASE insight 12.1

Hotel Chocolat UK

Raising funds from customers

Hotel Chocolat is a luxury chocolate maker and retailer set up in 1993 by Angus Thirlwell and Peter Harris. Over the years it developed a loyal customer base that opened up interesting funding opportunities for the business later in its life. In 2010 it raised £3.7 million by offering 100,000 members of its 'tasting club' three-year, £2,000 or £4,000 bonds, with the interest paid in bi-monthly deliveries of a chocolate tasting box. As Angus Thirlwell explained:

This was prompted by our customers asking how they could get more involved with the company. We found a way of inviting them to invest in our development plans in exchange for a return paid in chocolate. And we have been bowled over by their response. We are now in a strong position to grow

the business further using funds provided directly from our customers.

The Independent 14 July 2010

The bonds fell due for repayment in 2013 and the company re-offered them to their customers on similar terms. 97% signed up for another three years. Hotel Chocolat was listed on the London Stock Exchange in 2016 and in the same year was awarded Mid-Market Business of the Year at the Lloyds Bank National Business Awards.

Visit the website: www.hotelchocolat.com

Question:
What sort of businesses can raise funds from customers? Give examples.

Information on sources of finance and grants in the UK, including website addresses, can be found in the *Guide to UK Sources of Help, Advice, Information and Funding* on the companion website: www.macmillanihe.com/burns-nvc-2e. It also gives the address for an interactive tool that helps you decide on the appropriate type of finance for your business. An additional guide for Australian readers, produced by Dr Russell Manfield, is also provided.

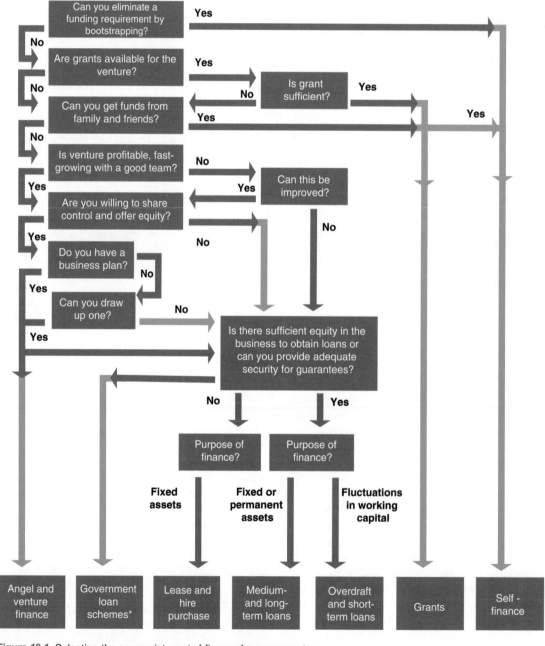

Figure 12.1 *Selecting the appropriate sort of finance for a new venture*

* These vary from country to country

ACADEMIC insight 12.1

Sources of finance used by small firms in the UK

Based upon a random sample of 160 UK start-ups (less than two years old) interviewed in 2008, Fraser (2009) found 85% used internal finance. Of these, 91% used personal savings, 13% loans or gifts from family or friends, 4% home mortgages and 4% personal credit cards. (The total is more than 100% because some businesses used more than one source.) Only 13% of start-ups used external finance, of which 94% used bank loans and 7% used grants or subsidies.

The same study looked at a random sample of 2,500 established small firms (under 250 employees) and found that they all used some sort of external finance. It found 54% used credit cards, 43% used overdrafts, 37% (free) trade credit, 21% asset finance (lease and/ or hire purchase), 16% term loans, 9% loans from family or friends, 3% used equity (which mainly came from the owner or family or friends) and 2% used factoring, invoice discounting or stock finance (again, businesses used more than one source). Citing supporting evidence from the Bank of England, Wright and Fraser (2014) conclude that bank finance remains

Getty Images/Deejpilot

the dominant element of external start-up and SME finance in the UK.

Two other interesting points emerge from these studies. Firstly, the continuing but increasing use of credit card finance, where balances might be paid off and recycled month to month. Secondly, the low use of equity finance, particularly from external sources. Indeed only 1.7% of the firms used business angels and fewer than 1% used venture capitalists.

Fraser, S. (2009) 'How Have SME Finances Been Affected by the Credit Crisis?' BERR/ESRC Seminar, March.

Wright, M. and Fraser, S. (2014) 'Financing Growth', ERC Insights, June 2014.

CASE insight 12.2

Lingo24 UK

The funding dilemma

Lingo24 is an Edinburgh-based online translation business started by Christian Arno in 2001 while still at university. It is now the 54th-largest translation agency in the world. Surprisingly, until recently this growth was entirely self-funded. In order to finance a new automated translation platform in 2013 Christian considered selling an equity stake in the business. He would have preferred to find a bank loan and was reluctant to give away equity

to venture capitalists, so he hired corporate finance advisors to help him select the right option:

I've been nervous and kept costs low at every turn to avoid the needs for funds. But now it's a pace thing. We need to move ahead quickly ... If a bank could give us a £3 million loan, I'd love it – but they'll never do that with a business like ours because of the type of assets we have. We only have our debtor book and that won't facilitate that level of borrowing ... Someone

I know had a very bad experience with outside investors. You hear horror stories of people losing control and losing the value they've built up. But with the level of ambition we have and the dynamic of the market place at the moment, we need those funds.

Daily Telegraph 5 July 2013

In April 2014 Lingo24 announced a 'seven figure (£)' investment by a consortium led by Paul Gregory, who became Chairman. In the same year it went on to be named Scottish Exporter of the Year and International Trade Best Professional Service Advisor.

Visit the website: www.lingo24.com

Question:

What was the dilemma facing Lingo24? Is there a 'right answer'?

Bank loans and overdrafts

Banks are the main source of loan finance to small firms. And so long as the return you make on the total assets in the business (see Chapter 13) exceeds the current rate of interest, then you benefit by getting an extra return on the bank's money. However, if your return drops below the rate of interest then the loan will drain money out of the firm.

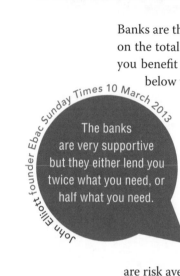

The banks are very supportive but they either lend you twice what you need, or half what you need.

John Elliott founder Ebac *Sunday Times* 10 March 2013

Banks can be reluctant to lend to small firms, and new ventures in particular, because they view them as risky propositions. And it is worth understanding why this is the case. Banks lend a sum of money in return for agreed interest payments and the repayment of the sum borrowed. They do not share in the profits of the business and, if a firm fails, they stand to lose their capital. That bad debt is expensive to recoup. For example, if banks make a 4% margin on a loan (the difference between the rate they can borrow at and the rate they lend at), then every £100 lost as a bad debt will need a further £2,500 to be lent for the sum to be recovered (£2,500 × 4% = £100). Put another way, the bank has to make a further 25 loans to cover this one bad debt. Not surprisingly, therefore, banks are risk averse and will do all they can to avoid a bad debt. Since they are all too aware of the failure statistics for business start-ups, entrepreneurs have an uphill task convincing banks of the viability of their project and obtaining a loan or even an overdraft facility.

Entrepreneurs seem naturally drawn to overdraft finance – surveys show it to be the major source of finance for small firms. After all it is flexible, once agreed you can dip into it when you need it and you will only pay interest when you use it. However, it is repayable immediately should the bank demand it, and it can be expensive if you are in permanent overdraft as the rate of interest charged is usually higher than on term loans. Term loans (short-, medium- or long-) are loans for a fixed period of time. They are usually not repayable on bank demand (but do check terms). The capital repayments are fixed and known in advance. The interest rate can vary or be fixed and is usually lower than for an overdraft.

Banks expect higher rates of return from loans that they perceive to be higher risk. New ventures are therefore likely to face higher rates of interest than larger businesses with an established track record. They are also likely to face a demand for collateral against the loan. Collateral is the additional security demanded in case there is a default on a loan. It can take many forms and is normally specified by some form of charge or guarantee in the legal loan agreement. Collateral might come from business assets but if these are insufficient then the entrepreneur (or their family or friends) may well be asked to provide personal collateral or guarantees for the loan. This can mean that the separation between your finances and those of your limited liability company is little more than theoretical.

In valuing business collateral the bank assumes that the assets will be sold on a second-hand market and this typically leads to far lower values being put on assets than you might expect. Table 12.2 gives a guide to what to expect. Given these asset security values, it is clear that the full cost of new fixed assets will never filter down to the collateral base of your business – an incentive to use lease or hire purchase.

Table 12.2 Asset security values

Asset	Typical percentage value that can be borrowed in UK	
Freehold land and buildings	70%	
Long leasehold	60%	
Specialist plant and machinery	5–10%	100% can be obtained through leasing
Non-specialist plant and machinery	30%	100% can be obtained through leasing
Debtors (receivables)	30–50%	Depends on age of debts and 'quality'
Stock (inventory)	25%	Depends on age of stock and 'quality'. In the event of business failure, raw materials will be worth more than work-in-progress or finished goods stocks.

CASE insight 12.3

Solar Power Company Group (SPCG)

THAILAND

Obtaining finance for new technology

Wandee Khunchornyakong is founder, chief executive and chairwoman of what is now the largest solar power firm in Thailand, Solar Power Company Group (SPCG). The company has created thousands of jobs and runs 36 solar farms, generating some 260 megawatts of solar power a year. Wandee is also in the top 50 of Thailand's richest people. Despite solar power being in its infancy at the time, she was so convinced of the sector's potential that she set up SPCG in 1993. But getting started was not easy. She had some experience in the use of solar energy in rural areas, and the government's offer to buy solar power from private firms when there was little provision in Thailand led her to believe in the opportunity.

Nevertheless, she could not find a single bank willing to fund her first project. None of them believed it would be profitable. Eventually she persuaded a bank that sported a green logo, indicating that it supported environmental projects, to lend her money – but only after creating a fuss, insisting that the bank should change the colour of its logo if it would not lend money for this sort of project.

The bank offered a loan for only 60% of the start-up costs and she could not find any other backers, even among friends who had invested in her previous business ventures. So she decided to use her house as collateral for the balance. Only when the first project proved to be successful was she able to secure more finance to expand the business,

By 2014 external finance reached over $800 million in leveraging finance by the International Finance Corporation (IFC) and the Clean Technology Fund which unlocked domestic funding. Wandee still owns 54% of the company and has the IFC and Kyocera among key investors. In 2013 she was named Women Entrepreneur of the Year by the Asia Pacific Entrepreneurship Awards.

Visit the website: www.spcg.co.th

Question:

What lessons do you learn from Wandee Khunchornyakong's?

What banks look for

Banks are in business to make as much money as possible with the least risk. Bank managers are employees, they work in a highly regulated environment, and they have very limited discretion. Lending decisions are heavily influenced by bank lending policies and procedures and some banks use computer-based credit scoring systems to produce lending 'recommendations' for managers – 'recommendations' that are difficult to over-turn. Generally, bank lending is becoming increasingly systematized and managers' discretion increasingly constrained. Lending decisions can therefore reflect general economic conditions and the balance of the bank's lending portfolio as much as the lending proposition itself. One bank can turn down an applicant that another will accept. But increasingly they seem to demand an offer of **personal collateral** by the entrepreneur (see Academic insight 12.2).

For a bank, the starting point for agreeing to any loan is its *purpose*. Is it legal? Is it consistent with bank policy? Is it in the best interests of the business? Next, the bank needs to assess whether the *amount* is appropriate. Have all associated costs for the project been included? Has the borrower put in money themselves? Is there a contingency? The bank also wants to ensure that interest is paid and the loan capital repaid on the due date. So is cash flow adequate? Finally, the bank will want to assess whether the *repayment* terms are realistic. To make this judgement the bank will want to understand the fundamentals of the

---

CASE insight 12.4

Grameen Bank

BANGLADESH

Solidarity lending

Professor Muhammad Yunus established Grameen Bank (meaning 'bank of the villages' in the Bangla language) as a social enterprise in Bangladesh in 1976. In 1983 it became an independent bank providing tiny loans, called microcredit, without collateral to the poor. The aim is to leverage people's skills to help them start and grow tiny businesses. It uses a local, group-based approach – called solidarity lending – to ensure that borrowers repay their loans and develop a good credit history. Each borrower belongs to a five-member group. The group is not required to give guarantees for loans to its members, and repayment is solely the responsibility of the individual borrower. However, the group and the centre ensure that everyone behaves responsibly and individuals do not get into arrears with their repayments. 96% of its borrowers are women.

Borrowers are encouraged to become savers and the bank also accepts deposits. In addition, it provides other services, and runs several development-oriented businesses including fabric, telephone and energy companies. It seeks to establish a new sort of self-sustaining rural association that reduces dependence on external finance, increases development impact and spreads risk. Funding has come from different sources. Initially donor agencies provided the bulk of capital at low interest rates but, by the 1990s, the bank was getting most of its funding from the central bank of Bangladesh. The success of Grameen Bank has inspired similar projects in more than 40 countries around the world.

Visit the website: www.grameen.com

Question:

How many stakeholders, each with different objectives, have to be brought together for this bank to operate effectively?

business – whether it is viable – and will ask for financial information. In short, the bank will normally ask for a business plan.

Within the business plan, banks are particularly keen to scrutinize the **cash flow forecast** because it shows whether interest payments can be made and what 'slack' there might be. They expect interest to be paid first and that may mean delaying capital expenditure and reducing or delaying personal drawings. They are also keen to look at the **breakeven point** and the margin of safety, which tell them about the operating risk of the business in terms of the overheads it faces and the margin it is able to command. These are vital pieces of information in assessing a loan to a start-up. Banks may also look at the projected future **gearing** ratios (particularly for larger-scale start-ups), to see whether the business might become over-borrowed. These financial measures are all explained in the next chapter. Banks are also keen to see that good financial controls are in place since this should lead to strong cash flow.

However, banks understand that most small firms are dominated by the owner-manager and usually seek to establish a good understanding of the person they lend to. They are interested in your *personal character*. Honesty and integrity are difficult to judge, but most bankers still think lending is a very personal thing and making a judgement on your character is vital. Your business track record and personal credit history are important. They will also make a judgement about your *personal ability*. How likely are you to turn this business plan into a successful business? Do you have a good management team behind you? Banks usually judge your personal character and ability by looking at your credit history, education and training, relevant business experience and proven track record. Unfortunately, with all these personal judgements, one person's objectivity might just be another's prejudice.

> Initially when I was first starting the business and approaching the big five banks for a corporate bank account, it was quite challenging. Their response to me becoming a consultant for improving financial services was to pat me on the head like a dog, saying 'there, there, little girl'.
>
> Elizabeth Gooch founder eg solutions Venture online 12 April 2007 (www.venturemagazine.co.uk)

ACADEMIC insight 12.2

Agency theory and information asymmetry

Agency theory is about the behaviour of different parties to an agreement who have different goals and different divisions of labour. Its origins lie in financial theory and are generally credited to Jensen and Meckling (1976). Agency theory is relevant when there is an arms-length relationship between a principal (such as a bank or an equity investor) and an agent (such as a small firm). It seeks to identify the mechanisms and costs that the principal has to put in place to ensure that the agent conforms to some legal agreement – such as a loan agreement. **Information asymmetry** is where these two parties do not have the same information on which to base their decisions.

Getty Images//Stockphoto/Vimverrigo

Agency theory is relevant to how providers of finance approach new ventures. By definition, a new venture has no track record, and the provider of finance has little information on which to base their financing decision. What they have may not be reliable or relevant to this specific financing decision. This is when asymmetric information favours the entrepreneur who should have more or better information than the provider of finance. This means that the provider of finance must incur extra costs in obtaining and checking the information they need in order to make, and then monitor, their decision. Many of these costs are fixed, whatever the size of the deal or the return made by the small firm. The conclusion is that providers of finance are naturally reluctant to lend or invest in start-ups or smaller ventures. This is less of a problem with larger firms because they have a track record and there is so much more public information about them, with many independent analysts reviewing this information for investment purposes.

Agency theory suggests that the natural response of a bank to these problems is to:

1 Charge higher rates of interest (which may prove unaffordable);
2 Impose conditions in the loan agreement (e.g. on use of business funds or the provision of information);

3 Demand personal collateral from the start-up entrepreneur (or collateral from the business, if it is already established).

Collateral is a property or other asset that a borrower offers as a way for a lender to secure the loan. Where sufficient collateral can be made available, the bank may feel that less information is required because the debt is more likely to be recovered in the event of default. Indeed, the bank may also feel that the provision of collateral gives the entrepreneur a strong incentive to see the business succeed. Agency theory also explains why the bank will want to be kept up to date on the progress of the business.

Similarly, the response of an equity investor is to look for higher rates of return. However, they will also expect the entrepreneur to maintain a controlling interest in the business so that, in the event of failure, they have more to lose than the other investors. This might impose a funding limit. The investor is also likely to want a greater involvement in the business so they can monitor their investment. Because of the fixed costs involved, many larger providers of equity finance will not get involved in small-scale start-ups because the return they can obtain does not cover their costs.

Jensen, M.C. and Meckling, W.H. (1976) 'Theory of the Firm, Managerial Behavior, Agency Costs, and Ownership Structure', *Journal of Financial Economics*, 3.

Banking relationship

Even after the loan is granted, banks will continue to monitor the financial performance of the business – using many of the ratios outlined in Chapter 13. They expect to see annual audited accounts and sometimes budgets for the next year. What is more, they will also monitor the bank account itself, looking out for irregularities and checking that throughput is in line with expectations. And their expectations will be based upon your cash flow forecasts.

Despite increasing centralization and the declining importance of local banking, you still need to have a good working relationship with your local bank manager. A close relationship has the potential to provide them with the information they need about your firm and thus avoid the problem of information asymmetry. Like any relationship, this must be based on two elements: trust, that both parties will honour the terms of the loan, and respect, that both parties are good at what they do. It is a personal thing that is developed by keeping in regular contact. The bank must ultimately trust and respect you, not just the business. That means visits and the provision of information. Bankers like to make regular visits. They like to feel they know the business and the individuals in it. However, bankers, more than anything, do not like surprises. Some of the things that start to make them worry that all is not well in a firm include:

- *Frequent excesses on the bank account beyond the agreed overdraft facility*: This makes the bank start to think cash flow is not being properly controlled.
- *Development of hard-core borrowing on an overdraft facility*: This makes the bank believe that a term loan would be more appropriate.
- *Lack of financial information*: If the accounts and other information do not arrive regularly, they worry about the firm's ability to produce control information and, in extremis, can become suspicious that all is not well.
- *Your unavailability*: If you are never available for a meeting or even a telephone conversation, the bank will start to believe something is wrong. Most people do not want to give bad news and avoidance is one way of not having to.
- *Inability to meet forecasts*: The bank will eventually start to question the credibility of your forecasts and your ability and understanding of the market.
- *Continuing losses, declining margins and rapidly diminishing or even increasing turnover*: At the end of the day the bank is really only interested in your ability to service its loan.
- *Over-reliance on too few customers or suppliers*: The loss of just one customer or supplier can create a disproportionate problem for small firms.

ACADEMIC insight 12.3

Is there discrimination in lending?

An issue that often raises emotions is whether bankers discriminate against certain sections of society in their lending decisions. Adequate funding is a prerequisite for business survival, let alone success, and research shows that there is a strong relationship between start-up funding strategies and business performance (Brush, 2006; Jennings and Cash, 2006; Watson et al., 2006). So is there any evidence of prejudice and discrimination causing financing gaps for groups within society?

Is there gender discrimination?

It is true that female-owned businesses tend to attract less outside funding than male-owned businesses. Studies have repeatedly found that female-owned businesses start with significantly less financial capital (typically only one-third) than male-owned start-ups (Carter and Rosa, 1998; Coleman, 2000; Hisrich and Brush, 1984). Female entrepreneurs prefer to use their own savings or to borrow money from their families, relatives or friends at start-up (Brush, op. cit., Ufuk and Ozgen 2001). They borrow less and rarely gain access to venture funding (Greene et al., 1999; Marlow and Patton, 2003). There does, therefore, appear to be a case to be answered.

However, before addressing the issue directly it is worth noting that, using financial measures of performance,

female entrepreneurs seem to underperform compared to their male counterparts (Department for Business and Enterprise and Regulatory Reform, 2008), clustering in the retail and traditional service sectors. Access to all forms of capital – social, human as well as financial – tends to be poorer for women and the female self-employed are much more likely to be part-time (Brush, 2006; Fairlie and Robb, 2009; Parker, 2009). Those who are self-employed are more likely to have family care responsibilities and to work shorter hours than males (Carre and Verheul, 2009; Verheul et al., 2009). There may be many sound personal and cultural reasons for all this; however, all these factors, especially financial performance impact lending and investment decisions.

With this background in mind, while research in the UK and USA has found differences in bank loan rejection rates by gender (in the UK: Fraser, 2006; in the USA: Treichel and Scott, 2006), it has failed to unearth evidence of a supply-side finance gap for women (in the UK: Fraser, op cit.; in the USA: Levenson and Willard, 2000). Similarly a Canadian study found no evidence of discrimination in capital availability (Orser et al., 2006). These studies could not find evidence of actual discrimination of any form by financial institutions. This suggests that other demand-side factors related to the personal and social circumstances of women are at play. Although not conclusive, other researchers broadly concur.

So the real question appears to be, why do female entrepreneurs seem to avoid external funding? Studies indicate the reasons are many and varied, ranging from risk aversion (Leitch et al., 2006) to perceived obstacles (Henry et al., 2006; Leitch et al., op. cit.; Neergaard et al., 2006; Watson et al., op. cit.) and from lack of social capital, skills and a growth orientation (Greene et al., op. cit.) to an aversion to potential loss of control (Watson et al., op. cit.). It would seem that, for a variety of reasons, female entrepreneurs choose not to make full use of the external funding that is available.

Is there ethnic discrimination?

While in the USA, Cavalluzzo and Wolken (2005) found striking differences between ethnic groups in terms of denial of credit, in the UK, there appears to be no difference between ethnic and white businesses in their dependence on bank finance, although this is significantly less for Black African and Black Caribbean business (Bank of England, 1999). Specialist banks have grown up to cater for the needs of different ethnic groups; for example, specialist Islamic banks which allow Muslim businesses to bank according to their principles and faith. There is also evidence of a strong preference for informal sources of finance among ethnic groups particularly among South Asian-owned businesses (Ram et. al., 2002). These informal sources are usually accessed from a wide network of family, friends and others within the ethnic community, thus combining social with financial capital. Many of these sources are not available to white entrepreneurs.

Although, as with female entrepreneurs, there is a strong feeling of prejudice from traditional banks, the Bank of England (op. cit.) could find no evidence of this in the UK, citing sectoral concentration, failure rates and lack of business planning for rejection rates. A large-scale study of ethnic minority businesses and their access to finance broadly supported this (Ram et al., op. cit.), noting, however, that the issue was 'complex'. It did find evidence of diversity of experience from bank manager to bank manager and between different ethnic minority groups, confirming the existence of particular problems for African and Caribbean businesses. Not surprisingly, it found that best practice was where the bank manager had built up trust with their local minority community through close contact and stable relationships. More recently, Fraser (2009) used econometric analysis on a large-scale survey of UK small business finance to look for evidence of ethnic discrimination (loan denials, interest rates and discouragement). He noted firstly that there were large differences across ethnic groups – Black and Bangladeshi businesses experiencing poor outcomes compared to White and Indian businesses. For example, from the finance provider's perspective, Black African firms were significantly more likely to miss loan repayments or exceed their agreed overdraft limit. He also noted that many from the ethnic minorities felt they were discriminated against. However, he concluded very firmly that there was no evidence of discrimination. He felt that many in these groups needed to tackle fundamentals such as a lack of financial skills and advice, and poor levels of financial performance rather than just addressing cultural differences and the effects they might have. In conclusion, academic studies in the UK and USA cannot uncover any systematic discrimination on grounds of ethnicity or gender.

Bank of England (1999) *The Financing of Ethnic Minority Firms in the UK: A Special Report,* London: Bank of England.

Brush, C.G. (2006) 'Woman Entrepreneurs: A Research Overview', in M. Casson, B. Yeung, A. Basu and N. Wadeson (eds) *The Oxford Handbook of Entrepreneurship,* Oxford: Oxford University Press.

Carre, M. and Verheul, I. (2009) 'Time Allocation by the Self-employed: The Determinants of the Number of Working Hours in Start-ups', *Applied Economics Letters,* 16.

Carter, S. and Rosa, P. (1998) 'The Financing of Male and Female Owned Businesses', *Entrepreneurship and Regional Development,* 8.

Cavalluzzo, K. and Wolken, J. (2005) 'Small Business Loan Turndowns, Personal Wealth, and Discrimination', *Journal of Business,* 78.

Coleman, S. (2000) 'Access to Capital and Terms of Credit: A Comparison of Men and Women-owned Small Businesses', *Journal of Small Business Management,* 38(3).

Department for Business and Enterprise and Regulatory Reform (2008) *High Growth Firms in the UK: Lessons from an Analysis of Comparative UK Performance.* BERR Paper No. 3, available online at: www.berr.gov. uk/files/file49042.pdf.

Fairlie, R. and Robb, A. (2009) 'Gender Differences in Business Performance: Evidence from the Characteristics of Business Owners Survey', *Small Business Economics,* 33(4).

Fraser, S. (2006) *Finance for Small and Medium-sized Enterprises: A Report on the 2004 UK Survey of SME Finances,* Warwick Business School, Centre for Small and Medium-sized Enterprises, Coventry.

Fraser, S. (2009) 'Is there Ethnic Discrimination in the UK Market for Small Business Credit?', *International Small Business Journal,* 27(5).

Greene, P., Brush, C., Hart, M. and Saparito, P. (2000) 'Exploration of the Venture Capital Industry: Is Gender an Issue?', *Frontiers of Entrepreneurial Research Series,* Wellesley, MA: Babson College.

Henry, C., Johnson, K. and Hamouda, A. (2006) 'Access to Finance for Women Entrepreneurs in Ireland: A Supply Side Perspective', in B. Candida, N.M. Carter, E.J. Gatewood, P.G. Greene and M.M. Hart (eds) *Growth Oriented Women Entrepreneurs and Their Business,* Cheltenham: Edward Edgar Publishing.

Hisrich, R. and Brush, C.G. (1984) 'The Woman Entrepreneur: Management Skills and Business Problems', *Journal of Small Business Management,* 22(1).

Jennings, E.J. and Cash, M.P. (2006). 'Women's Entrepreneurship in Canada: Progress, Puzzles and Priorities', in B. Candida, N.M. Carter, E.J. Gatewood, P.G. Greene and M.M. Hart (eds) *Growth Oriented Women Entrepreneurs and Their Business*, Cheltenham: Edward Edgar Publishing.

Leitch, C.M., Hill, F. and Harrison, R.T. (2006) 'The Supply of Finance to Women Led Ventures: The Northern Ireland Experience', in B. Candida, N.M. Carter, E.J. Gatewood, P.G. Greene and M.M. Hart (eds) *Growth Oriented Women Entrepreneurs and Their Business*, Cheltenham: Edward Edgar Publishing.

Levenson, A.R. and Willard, K.L. (2000) 'Do Firms Get the Financing They Want? Measuring Credit Rationing Experienced by Small Businesses in the USA', *Small Business Economics*, 14(2).

Marlow, S. and Patton, D. (2003) 'The Financing of Small Business – Female Experiences', in M. Davies and S. Fielden (eds) *International Handbook of Women and Small Business Entrepreneurship*, Cheltenham: Edward Elgar.

Neergaard, H., Nielsen, K.T and Kjeldsen, I.J. (2006) 'State of the Art of Women's Entrepreneurship, Access to Financing and Financing Strategies in Denmark', in B. Candida, N.M. Carter, E.J. Gatewood, P.G. Greene and M.M. Hart (eds) *Growth Oriented Women Entrepreneurs and Their Business*, Cheltenham: Edward Edgar Publishing.

Orser, B.J., Riding, A.L. and Manley, K. (2006) 'Women Entrepreneurs and Financial Capital', *Entrepreneurship: Theory and Practice*, September, Vol. 30, Issue 5.

Parker, S.C. (2009) *The Economics of Entrepreneurship*, Cambridge: Cambridge University Press.

Ram, M., Smallbone, D. and Deakins, D. (2002) *Ethnic Minority Business in the UK: Access to Finance and Business Support*, London: British Bankers' Association.

Treichel, M.Z. and Scott, J.A. (2006) 'Women-owned Business and Access to Bank Credit: Evidence from Three Surveys since 1987', *Venture Capital: An International Journal of Entrepreneurial Finance*, 8(1).

Ufuk, H. and Ozgen, O. (2001) 'Interaction Between the Business and Family Lives of Women Entrepreneurs in Turkey,' *Journal Of Business Ethics*, 31.

Verheul, I., Carree, M. and Mahuka, A. (2009) 'Allocation and Productivity of Time in New Ventures of Female and Male Entrepreneurs', *Small Business Economics*, 33(3).

Watson, J., Newby, R. and Mahuka, A. (2006) 'Comparing the Growth and External Funding of Male and Female Controlled SME's in Australia,' in B. Candida, N.M. Carter, E.J. Gatewood, P.G. Greene and M.M. Hart (eds) *Growth Oriented Women Entrepreneurs and Their Business*, Cheltenham: Edward Elgar.

Angel and venture finance

For a company with real growth potential, there may also be the opportunity to get private individuals – **business angels** – or a **venture capital** institution to invest equity in the business. Equity funding is not available to sole traders or partnerships. Equity investment involves giving up a percentage of the ownership of the business, and potentially some of the control, in exchange for cash. That means giving up some of the future wealth the business will create. Investors are paid dividends, which are only paid at the discretion of the company. While the capital invested can be sold on in the form of shares, it is unlikely to be repaid by the business unless it ceases to trade, and only then if other creditors are paid in full. It is therefore long-term risk finance.

> The beauty of being shareholder-owned and run with no outside capital is that we can make quick decisions.
>
> Adam Schwab founder Lux Group Management Today July 2014

Both angel and venture financiers might expect dividends but, more importantly, they hope to see the value of their shares increase if the firm does well. They will probably expect to realize their investment at some time in the future (normally 5–10 years) by selling on their shares in the business. Often an angel investment helps to take the investee business to a point at which it is attractive for a venture capital firm.

Business angels invest smaller amounts of money than venture capital institutions (£10,000–£1 million) and operate in less formal ways. They are usually 'high net worth individuals', often with a successful entrepreneurial background themselves. They are looking to back start-up and early-stage ventures. The typical UK angel makes only one or two investments a year. Many have preferences about sectors or stages of investment based on their personal knowledge. Many also expect to exercise some degree of directorial control over the business. Most prefer local investments, in companies within, say, 100 miles from where they live or work. Most also prefer to stay anonymous.

Angels are mainly locally based and can be contacted through local small business support agencies. Angel networks can now be found from Cambridge in England to Mumbai in India. These networks circulate business plans among the angels ahead of a physical pitch or presentation to the angels. If any angels are interested in investing, then a period of investigation and negotiation will take place before funds are committed. Often a fee is charged to the business seeking the investment and some networks take a stake in the company if a deal is successfully negotiated. Some of the networks can also provide help in raising finance from other sources and in preparing a business plan for an additional fee. In the UK many business angels belong to the British Business Angel Association (UKBAA). It has a code of conduct for its members and a directory of members is available on its website.

Venture capital institutions usually invest larger amounts than business angels (typically over £2 million). They mainly invest in established businesses (often buying out angel investments), **management buy-outs** (the management of a firm buying it) and **management buy-ins** (external managers buying a firm and normally replacing the management), but they can invest in larger start-ups. Neither business angels nor venture capitalists want to take control of the business away from the entrepreneur, and therefore usually limit their investment to less than 50% of the share capital. However, because venture capitalists invest larger amounts, they often put together funding deals that involve ordinary shares, preference shares (non-voting, with dividends at a fixed percentage of face value but with preference over ordinary shareholders in the event of liquidation) and loan finance. In the past, some of the management buy-out and buy-in deals they have structured have been notable for their high leverage or gearing. The British Private Equity and Venture Capital Association (BVCA) produces a free Directory of Members, which gives a full list of venture capital institutions and their investment criteria. A similar organization for Europe is called Invest Europe.

> We wanted to raise £250,000 to get the company off the ground and there were relatively few people who were interested in investing in three young guys without a track record and a product that was new to the UK. As the three founders were young, they had not built up a capital base and so debt was not a viable route as there was nothing to secure it on. Equity was really the only alternative option.
>
> James Davenport Finance Director Innocent The Guardian 23 October 2014

CASE insight 12.5

Purplle.com — INDIA

Early stage finance

Manish Taneja and Rahul Dash left professional jobs to set up Purplle.com, a website selling beauty and grooming products, in Mumbai in 2012. Initially they used their own savings to set up the business and establish the website but they then approached family and friends for loans and equity as well as using trade credit to finance the products they sell. Once the business model proved successful, they decided they needed more equity and approached a group of 15 business angels in Mumbai and Chennai to whom they pitched their business model. They

were successful. The investors brought not only capital but also website expertise and a network of contacts. In 2015 the company raised another $5 million from IvyCap Ventures to finance its expansion and in 2016 a further $6 million from JSW Ventures and existing investors.

Visit the website: www.purplle.com

> **Question:**
>
> What are the advantages and disadvantages of angel and venture funding?

What investors look for

While business angels and venture capital institutions may look at the same range of criteria as a banker, their perspective is very different because, unlike the banker, they are sharing in the risk of the business. If it fails, they stand to lose their investment. Consequently they are interested in both *return* and *risk*. In particular, they are interested in the return they will make on their investment rather than the security they can obtain from the entrepreneur. The return on one investment must compensate for the loss on another. They will also want to be assured that they can sell on their investment at some time in the future and realize their profit – called the **exit route** (UK) or **liquidity event** (USA). Assessing these things, inevitably, will take longer than arranging a bank loan.

Return and risk

Most investors are interested more in the capital gain on the sale of their investment than the dividends they might receive. Typically they will be looking for an annual return on their investment of 30–60%, depending on the perceived risk. Start-ups will usually be at the top end of that spectrum, but the final deal always requires negotiation. So for example, an investment of £100,000 might be expected to yield £400,000–£800,000 in five years' time – a multiple of four to eight times the original investment. And, while some may achieve this return, others will not and in that case the investor will be lucky to exit with their money intact. The business plan for a start-up is very important to an investor – they do not take guarantees and there is no track record to rely on. They will be particularly interested to see an identified and accessible market with strong growth potential. If yours is a technology-based start-up, the technology must be market ready. Investors also pay far greater attention to the quality of management – your experience and that of your management team. This is the only track record they have. And they expect this experience and expertise to be reflected in the quality of the business plan. When looking at the financial projections they will apply the full range of performance criteria, profitability and risk ratios outlined in Chapter 13. They will also pay great attention to your detailed assessment of the business risks and how they might be overcome.

Exit route (liquidity event)

Most business angels will want to realize their investment within a time frame of about five years. Venture capitalists may take a longer-term view, perhaps up to ten years. For a start-up that may be a problem because there may not be an established market for their shares within this time frame. So who might buy the shares? One option could be that you will want to **buy back** the shares and regain 100% control of your business. A management buy-out or buy-in might be another option. Angels might sell on their shares to venture capitalists. Another option for both angels and venture capitalists is to sell on their share in the business (and perhaps the founder's share) to another company, often in the same industry, by way of a **trade sale**. They might also seek an initial public offering (IPO) or stock market floatation – a listing on a stock market – so that they can sell their shares to other institutional investors or the public. This can be expensive (a trade sale is far cheaper) and means that the business will have to comply with a whole range of regulations and disclosure requirements designed to make trading in their shares fairer. It also means that the firm needs a track record of solid profitability and good growth potential. There are two 'junior' markets in the UK that ultimately lead to a full listing on the Stock Exchange Main Market. These are the **Off Exchange**

> I want to know whether it will be attractive to buyers. The only way someone like me can make money is if someone will buy me out.

(OFEX) and the **Alternative Investment Market** (AIM) and offer limited share trading. However, many entrepreneurs (like Richard Branson) do not like the public accountability and loss of control implied by 'going public' on the Stock Market.

Business angels and venture capitalists will undertake a thorough investigation of both the founder(s) and the business. They will want to be represented as a non-executive director on the board. This is their response to the issues raised through agency theory and information asymmetry (see Academic insight 12.2). Business angels, particularly, may also expect a more 'hands-on', day-to-day involvement in the business. As with bank managers, it is important to develop a close personal relationship. Ultimately they invest in people rather than businesses and, since they face more risk than the banker, they need to be convinced that the entrepreneur and the management team can make the business plan actually happen. Trust and respect are important. Since they only make money if the firm succeeds, they are highly committed to helping the growing firm through the inevitable problems it will face. They can be an invaluable sounding board for sharing both problems and ideas. Many have useful business experience, sometimes in the same business sector, and they can provide a strategic overview that helps you see through the day-to-day problems of business. They may also bring with them a wealth of business contacts. In short, used properly they can be a valuable asset to the firm.

Crowdfunding

Emy Kat/Grapheast

The 2008 recession saw bank lending contract as banks tried to recapitalize and consolidate their balance sheets. The first victims of this were those 'riskier' loans to start-ups and small businesses. However, the growth of the internet has encouraged the development of a form of funding called crowdfunding. **Crowdfunding** – the practice of funding a project or venture by raising monetary contributions from a large number of people – has a long history. However, its popularity exploded with the advent of the internet, which allowed lenders and investors to be linked directly to individuals and organizations looking for funds – a sort of finance eBay – and the 2008 recession. Crowdfunding is now a major source of finance to SMEs. Registered lenders and investors can browse through lending or investment opportunities posted by businesses and decide whether they wish to lend or invest. Being web-based, videos are used extensively to demonstrate products or services and, perhaps more importantly, the owner-managers seeking the finance. Internet crowdfunding can take a number of forms:

Peer-to-peer (P2P) lending (e.g. Zopa in the UK, Lending Club in the USA)

This can be used by individuals and businesses (usually for larger amounts) seeking loans online. Often these loans are unsecured. Applications are often assessed online using a computer algorithm to determine credit risk and interest rate. Lenders may choose which borrowers to invest in. Using P2P platforms offers advantages to both lenders and borrowers.

Lenders generally earn far more than they would if they put the money in a savings account – an average of over 9%. However credit risks are usually considered high. Borrowers who may not necessarily be approved for a bank loan might find it easier to borrow, albeit at a higher interest rate if their credit rating is low. The intermediary normally has registered lenders and charges the borrower a percentage of the funds raised. This is how they make money. As with bank borrowing, borrowers and lenders will be parties to a legal loan agreement which, among other things, will specify interest rates and capital repayment. These are organized by the intermediary. In P2P lending this can either be a partner bank (the notary loan model) or the intermediary itself (the client segregation model). P2P platforms have generally been funded by institutional investors. In 2013, Google invested $125 million in Lending Club.

Zopa was the first P2P lender in the UK and generated more than £1.8 billion of loans between its launch in 2005 and 2015. The next step was to apply for a banking licence to enable it to offer deposit accounts and overdrafts (see Case insight 12.6). Launched in 2010, Funding Circle was the first crowdfunding platform in the UK to offer P2P business lending and is now the third-largest lender to SMEs, after the more traditional banks like RBS and Lloyds. It offers loans of up to £1 million in the UK. Whole loans or portions of loans can purchased by individuals or institutional investors. Funding Circle also has its own fund to purchase loans.

CASE insight 12.6

Zopa — UK

Peer-to-peer lending

Giles Andrews had been a car salesman and had already built and sold a business that acquired failing firms in the motor industry and turned them around, when he got together with James Alexander, Richard Duvall and David Nicholson to think through the idea of a business that helped people lend to each other on the web, cutting out the middle-men. In 2005 they got the backing of some leading venture capital firms to launch Zopa, the first peer-to-peer personal lending website in the UK. It earns money by taking a margin on each lending transaction. The business was slow to take off until the 2008 credit crisis, which caused people and businesses to seek alternatives to banks. And during this time an attempt to start a similar business in the USA failed, despite the fact they raised £9 million for the launch.

We launched with a large amount of noise but attracted no business. It took a long time to gain any traction … We had a British company that wasn't growing and an American business that was doing nothing and investors were frustrated.

Sunday Times 10 August 2014

Zopa was eventually a success and has facilitated loans of over £2 billion since inception. Based in London, it now employs some 200 people and has applied for a banking licence to enable it to offer deposit accounts and overdrafts. It has over 59,000 active investors (average amount lent: £11,200) and 233,000 borrowers (borrowing on average £6,600). Andrews is now Chairman. He and the founders still own 14% and the rest of the management team 13% of the business.

Visit the website: www.zopa.com

Questions:

1 How risky was this business to start up? Explain.
2 How risky was it to finance? Explain.

CASE insight 12.7

Kickstarter 🇺🇸 USA

Niche crowdfunding rewards platform

Crowdfunding rewards sites are proving to be particularly attractive to SMEs in general but in particular specialist, niche businesses that might have difficulties raising mainstream finance. Kickstarter was launched in 2009 by Perry Chen, Yancey Strickler, and Charles Adler. It is an online crowdfunding site that focuses on the creative projects – films, music, stage shows, comics, journalism, video games, technology and food-related projects. Originally based in New York, USA, it started accepting projects based in the UK in 2012, Canada in 2013, Australia and New Zealand in 2013, and Denmark, Ireland, Norway, and Sweden in 2014. It is open to backers from around the world.

Projects posted on Kickstarter must have a set deadline to achieve a minimum funding target. If the goal is not met by the deadline, any funds offered are not collected. Funds pledged by donors are collected through Stripe. Kickstarter charges a 5% fee on the total amount of funds raised and Stripe charges an additional 3–5% fee.

By 2015, Kickstarter had reportedly received more than $1.5 billion in pledges from 7.8 million backers to fund 200,000 creative projects, several of which have gone on to receive critical acclaim. These include documentary films, contemporary art projects and music albums.

Visit the website: www.kickstarter.com

Question:

What are the advantages and disadvantages of angel and venture funding?

Rewards platforms (e.g. Kickstarter)

These allow projects to be funded in return for 'rewards' or 'gifts' such as 'free' products (rather than equity). The return to the individual is limited to the reward offered. Typically therefore, the more specific and the later the stage of the project, the more popular this type of funding is likely to be. 'Niche' projects tend to be the most successful, often arts-based (such as a new music album). Outcomes tend to be skewed, with a relatively small number of projects obtaining most of the funding and many projects being unsuccessful. There are two models. In the first the 'borrower' only receives the funding if their target fundraising goal is achieved. In the second, they keep the funding, no matter what. This usually only applies for smaller projects or ones that can be scaled down. The reward platform earns its income by charging a fee on the total amount of funds raised.

Equity crowdfunding platform (e.g. Crowdcube and Seedrs)

These raise relatively small amounts compared to the P2P platforms and, because they have little regulation, are seen as the 'wild west' of crowdfunding with big issues about information asymmetry and investor risk. They offer funding in return for equity in the company. There are two models. Some sites allow individuals to invest directly in shares, while others pool funds to be invested as a nominated agent. Typically each crowdfunding investor purchases only a very small percentage of the company. Sometimes syndicates of investors invest using these sites, thus pooling their risk. Crowdfunding platforms that offer equity funding

CASE insight  12.8

Hamijoo   IRAN

Niche crowdfunding rewards platform

Hamijoo.com is a crowdfunding rewards site for Iranian artistic and film projects that is similar to Kickstarter. Because of sanctions, in 2015 Iran's banking system remained cut off from the rest of the world and start-ups were starved of funding, not least because they could not attract funding from outside the country, even through crowdfunding. Hamijoo was founded by Mohammad Noresi, a 28-year-old biomedical engineering graduate, who had previously worked on a number of tech start-ups that failed. Despite the problems of doing business in Iran (see Case insight 3.5), within two months of start-up Hamijoo had

employed three staff. By 2015 some 160 people had used the site to fund artistic projects such as a documentary film by award-winning independent Iranian film-maker Mehrdad Oskouei and a music album by Meysam Azad.

Visit the website: hamijoo.com

Questions:

1 Compare and contrast the opportunities and threats facing Kickstarter and Hamijoo.
2 Can Hamijoo survive in the longer term?

James Davenport Finance Director Innocent The Guardian 23 October 2014

See if you can sweat more cash out of the business plan, particularly using things like cash (invoice) discounting or invoice factoring, to try and reduce the need for external cash; or look at alternative methods of raising cash, particularly peer-to-peer lending.

Jeff Lynn founder crowdfunding site Seedrs Sunday Times 14 September 2014

If you expect to post your pitch [on a crowdfunding website] and have people throw money at it, you're in for a disappointment. The more momentum there is the more others will join in; nobody wants to walk into an empty bar.

opportunities charge the business a percentage of the funds raised (typically 5–7.5%). Some platforms also accept a slice of the equity rather than a flat fee. Although still small, these sites have also seen a huge increase in activity since they were set up. The first equity deal in the UK using crowdfunding was agreed in 2013, by Crowdcube. By the end of that year these equity crowdfunding platforms had raised some £28 million (*Sunday Times*, 14 September 2014).

Equity crowdfunding investors will still expect to see a business plan. Crowdfunding is not an easy shortcut to raising equity finance. Crowdcube estimate that 30% of the offerings on their site do not achieve their target funding. The Seedrs site puts this estimate higher at two-thirds (*Sunday Times*, 14 September 2014). Nevertheless some offerings seem to be creating a momentum of their own, leading to questions about crowdfunding creating an 'auction mentality' that encourages bidding.

In many ways equity crowdfunding is the logical extension of the business angel networks discussed in the previous section. However, equity investment is inherently riskier than loans, and crowdfunding investors probably have less expertise than business angels in making this sort of investment. What is more, the issue about how and when their investment will be realized in the form of a capital gain remains even more up in the air. All of this makes this type of investment very risky, which is why each investor will only ever contribute a small proportion of the funds raised, and why the success of this source of finance – for both parties – is yet to be proved. So far, it has mainly been successful for 'quirkier' or niche businesses, often with quasi-social objectives, where investors might be less interested in risk and return than supporting the objectives of the venture.

CASE insight 12.9

InSpiral Visionary Products UK

© InSpiral

ORGANIC / GLUTEN FREE / RAW / VEGAN / PALEO

© InSpiral

Equity crowdfunding platform

Dominik Schnell and Bella Willink founded InSpiral Visionary Products in 2010. Starting life as a vegan café in Camden Town in London, the company sells organic products, including crisps made from dehydrated kale that originally sold for £3.49 a packet. In 2013, InSpiral became the first company to raise equity rather than loan finance from crowdfunding. Using Crowdcube, the company raised £250,000 from 120 investors, handing over 10% of their equity – valuing the company at £2.5 million. InSpiral paid Crowdcube a fee of 5% of the money raised.

InSpiral has used the money raised to redesign its packaging, featuring 100% compostable materials, and to sell its products online and through retail outlets. It also now produces own-label products for a number of major high-street stores. Increasing production allowed them to spread their overheads and bring down their sales prices significantly. For example, the price of kale crisps came down to £2.19 per pack, and that opened up more retail opportunities.

Visit the website: www.inspiral.co

Question:

What are the risks of investing in InSpiral using crowdfunding like this?

FinTech

The crowdfunding industry is part of what is called the **FinTech** industry (short for financial technology). The industry is in its infancy internationally but it is growing quickly and there are thought to be thousands of crowdfunding and other financial platforms. It is thought that some $34 billion was raised in 2015 by crowdfunding sites worldwide. In Europe about €735 million was raised in 2012 from all forms of crowdfunding and in the UK £1.8 billion was raised from P2P and rewards lending alone in 2015 (*Sunday Times*, 11 December 2016). This compares to estimated bank lending of €6 billion in 2011, business angel investments of €660 million in 2010 and venture capital investments of €7 billion in 2012. In the UK many FinTech

CASE insight 12.10

FarmDrop 🇬🇧 UK

Equity crowdfunding platform

Ben Pugh also used Crowdcube to raise funds for FarmDrop, a London-based company he started in 2012 which by 2017 had 35 staff. FarmDrop is a website that allows users to 'click and collect' local produce. He had a target of £400,000 to raise, but already had off-line 'commitments' of £100,000. He hit his target within eight days. Indeed he was so successful that he went on to raise £750,000 from 360 investors in the next 20 days. He parted with 27% of the company and paid Crowdcube a fee of £40,000.

We now have hundreds of advocates for FarmDrop dotted around the country in the form of our investors.
Sunday Times 14 September 2014

Visit the website: www.farmdrop.com

Question:

What are the risks of investing in FarmDrop using crowdfunding like this? Is it any different to InSpiral?

Neil Rimer, co-founder Index Ventures Sunday Times 16 November 2014

I'm not sure we're ready to declare victory on Britain being the fintech capital of the world. It is still early days. But there is a disproportionate number of really interesting fintech companies emerging. The market potential of some of these companies is limitless.

start-ups are located at 'Level39', an accelerator within One Canada Square at Canary Wharf in London. However, while it may have grown quickly in the past, there is now some evidence of consolidation, with some smaller P2P and rewards lenders struggling or even going into administration.

The FinTech industry is currently largely unregulated. In the UK, the Financial Conduct Authority (FCA) found evidence of 'potential investor detriment' in the industry. As a result it is in the process of introducing new rules and granting authorization to P2P lenders that can pass its scrutiny. Industry bodies are also beginning to be set up. In the UK there is the UK Crowdfunding Association (UKCFA) with 34 members, which collectively has some nine million investors and a European Equity Crowdfunding Association (EECA) has now been set up.

> 🌐 Information on all sources of finance and grants in the UK, including website addresses, can be found in the *Guide to UK Sources of Help, Advice, Information and Funding* on the companion website: www.macmillanihe.com/burns-nvc-2e. It also gives the address for a directory of crowdfunding associations worldwide. An additional guide for Australian readers, produced by Dr Russell Manfield, is also provided.

The funding ladder

For any start-up, deciding what assets are needed, when to acquire them and how this is to be financed are important strategic decisions where independent professional advice can be valuable. Generally, you are best advised to minimize the resources you need at each stage of

Crowdcube UK

FinTech start-up

Both InSpiral and FarmDrop use Exeter-based Crowdcube, a crowdfunding platform set up in 2011 by Darren Westlake and Luke Lang. It offers investors the opportunity to invest directly or in pooled funds with a minimum investment of as little as £10 through equity, bond or reward-based investments. Entrepreneurs with a UK registered company can showcase their business, and its investment potential, by uploading a video pitch, images, and supporting documents such as a business plan. Only if the pitch reaches its target will the business receive its funding. Crowdcube charges a commission for successful funding campaigns. Darren Westlake has high ambitions for the business:

> We've dominated the democratisation of seed-stage equity investment since we launched in 2011 and we're determined to do the same for larger businesses. We want to put the Public back into IPO.

Crowdcube already has a database of some 410,000 registered investors and has raised over £320 million in loan and equity finance for entrepreneurs since it was launched in 2011. It celebrated its first company exit in 2015 when E-Car Club (similar to Zipcar, Case insight 4.2), which raised investment in 2013 through Crowdcube, was purchased by Europcar.

Since 2014 Crowdcube has raised £3 million of funding for itself from some 570 private investors through multiple rounds of investment on its own site. £3.8 million was also

invested by Balderton, a venture capital firm. In 2015 a further £6 million was invested through a consortium led by Numis, a leading UK stockbroker and corporate advisor, and London-based Draper Esprit, with a view to later helping those Crowdcube companies who want to obtain a listing on the London Stock Exchange's Main Market or AIM. Oliver Hemsley, founder of Numis commented on the partnership:

> Crowdcube has created an impressive business model and technology platform that makes it possible for people to join together to finance pioneering businesses. Numis has a long track record of helping companies access funding for growth and this investment in Crowdcube will put Numis at the centre of the entire investment chain, from initial start-up capital all the way to IPO. We are very excited to be part of an innovative fintech solution to help the public markets evolve and connect retail investors directly with fast growing businesses.
>
> Finextra.com 30 July 2015

Visit the website: www.crowdcube.com

Questions:

1 Crowdcube is a successful start-up in its own right, but how will its success benefit SMEs generally?
2 What are the advantages and disadvantages of crowdfunding for investors and the businesses they invest in?

TransferWise UK ESTONIA

FinTech start-up

Taavet Hinrikus left his job at Skype in 2008 to join Kristo Käärmann, a financial consultant, and set up a new venture called TransferWise, an online money transfer service. Taavet and Kristo are Estonian, and had

first-hand experience of sending money back home and losing about 5% in transfer and currency conversion charges. They thought they could cut costs by using technology to match currency transfers – a form of peer-to-peer currency exchange that allows customers to wire money to one another cheaply, bypassing banks, and their commission charges.

TransferWise went live in 2011. The head office is in London – part of the UK's growing FinTech community – and technical staff are based in Estonia. The service is cheaper than traditional fund-transfer mechanisms, charging a fee of 0.5% or a flat fee of £1 if the amount is less than £200. The company has raised about £21 million in venture finance from a number of investors including Index Ventures and Kima Ventures and, more recently, Richard Branson's Virgin Group and Peter Thiel's (founder of PayPal) Valar Ventures.

It comes down to doing one thing and being the best at it … Faith in the banking system dropped significantly after the financial crisis … customer expectations changed and the time was right for financial technology.

Sunday Times 16 November 2014

Visit the website: transferwise.com

Question:

Why is FinTech such a success in the UK?

Sunday Times 2 April 2017

Get your funding strategy right and keep your investors informed. If you do that they will forgive you a lot more.

William Reeve co-founder Lovefilm

the business. Remember you do not necessarily have to own an asset to use it. You can bootstrap or partner with others. Although it is inevitable if you want to maximize the potential of your business, once you start to use external funds you start to limit your flexibility and lose control. Deciding on the form of this funding is therefore every bit as important a decision as anything else that goes into the business plan.

Most firms use a range of finance to suit their differing needs and circumstances. The advantages and disadvantages of these different methods of financing your business are summarized in Table 12.3. Getting started on the funding ladder can be difficult, particularly in a depressed trading environment. Many sources may not appear to be open to you as a start-up. Getting that first tranche of funding requires you to persuade financiers that you can make your business dream come true. They need to believe in you. You need to have credibility and to gain their trust and respect. However, a good business idea will always eventually find backing, particularly if you have a good business plan to explain it. And a good plan will help give you credibility and so gain backers' trust and respect.

Table 12.3 Advantages and disadvantages of different sources of finance

Source	Advantages	Disadvantages
Equity Personal, family and friends	• Good, secure long-term finance • No interest or capital repayment • Can be used to lever further loan finance	• Dividends may be expected • Selling shares to outsiders dilutes your stake in the business and may lead to loss of control • Outsiders providing equity may want to interfere in the business
Equity Angel finance	• Good, secure long-term finance • Can be used to lever further loan finance • Small amounts of equity available • Investment based on business plan rather than security • Investment usually made for 5 to 10 years • Often offers hands-on expertise	• Only really available to businesses with growth prospects • A significant proportion of the profits and capital growth of the business will go to the angels • Dividends may be expected • Angels will want to sell on their stake in the business at some point in the future to realize their profit • Hands-on expertise may be seen as interference in the business

(Continues)

Source	Advantages	Disadvantages
Equity Venture finance	• Good, secure long-term finance • Larger amounts of equity available – often used as second-stage finance rather than at start-up • Investment based on business plan rather than security • Investment usually made for 5 to 10 years • Can offer longer-term strategic advice • Not normally involved in day-to-day running of business • Should be able to arrange loans to go with equity investment, if required • No interest or capital repayments, unless loans are part of the package	• Only really available to businesses with very significant growth prospects and with a view to stock market floatation • A significant proportion of the profits and capital growth of the business will go to the investor • Dividends may be expected • Investors will want to sell on their stake in the business at some point in the future to realize their profit, usually through a stock market floatation • Will require very detailed information about the company • Takes time to arrange
Equity Crowdfunding	• Good, secure long-term finance • Can be used to lever further loan finance • Small amounts of equity available • Investment based on business plan rather than security	• Investors will need to see an exit route (liquidity event) – how they can dispose of their equity investment • Dividends may be expected • Crowdfunding website will expect a fee based on funds raised
Term loans Personal, family and friends	• Security unlikely to be required • Loans may be 'informal' – capital repaid as and when cash flow improves • Interest payments may not be required or may be deferred	• Interest payments may be required • Can strain relationships if repayments are not made as expected • If business fails, family and friends may suffer • Family and friends may interfere in the business
Term loans Bank and crowdfunding	• Term of loan is fixed – usually not repayable on demand (but do check terms) • Capital repayments fixed and known in advance • Interest rate can vary or be fixed and is usually lower than for an overdraft	• Usually secured against business or personal assets (collateral) • Can be refused because of lack of security • Requires good cash flow to pay interest and meet capital repayments • Crowdfunding website will expect a fee based on funds raised
Lease and hire purchase	• Guarantees not required – security is on assets purchased	• Expensive compared to rates of interest charged on loans • Requires adequate cash flow to meet regular payments
Bank overdraft	• Flexible – once agreed, available on demand • Can be cheap if you dip into and out of it – you only pay interest when you use it • Good solution to short-term financing needs	• Repayable on bank demand • Interest rate is variable • Can be expensive if you are in permanent overdraft as the rate of interest charged is usually higher than on term loans • Usually secured against business assets (collateral) and can be refused because of lack of security • Personal guarantee may then be required

Table 12.3 Advantages and disadvantages of different sources of finance (continued)

Sofa-bed Factory

Piotr and Olek were aware that they would have to find some money to launch the business should they decide to go ahead. Both were single, without commitments and they had some savings. They visited their local bank and were told that, because of their good credit history, the bank would be willing to lend to them, subject to seeing a business plan. What was more, there was a special start-up loan facility available that matched the investment that owners put into the business euro for euro. The loan was for a fixed period of three years at an attractive rate of interest and secured only on the assets of the business (which had to be a limited liability company).

Piotr and Olek left the bank realizing that their idea could actually become a reality. First they needed to work out how much they needed. They knew that the machinery would cost about €30,000 and the cost of the demonstration stock that the UK retailer was demanding would be some €32,000. Then there were the other costs they would face as a start-up that they had not even calculated. They decided that the maximum each of them could raise from their savings and from their families would be €50,000, which meant that the bank would lend them a similar amount. Surely that was enough? They resolved to prepare some financial forecasts.

Questions:

1 What are the advantages and disadvantages of taking out this sort of start-up loan?
2 What other financing options should Piotr and Olek explore?

Summary and action points

12.1 **Identify the assets you need and how to acquire them:** Minimize your start-up costs. Not all the assets you need for your business have to be purchased. You might be able to borrow, lease, rent or bootstrap them. You might be able to partner with others who have the assets you need.

12.2 **Identify your asset funding gap and how it will be met:** The asset funding gap is the difference between the cost of the assets you must purchase and the capital you have available. The gap can be met through borrowing (loans) or investment (equity). To be prudent you should match the term duration of the source of finance with the use to which it is put (long-term sources with long-term uses). External sources might include family, friends, banks, crowdfunding websites, business angels or venture capitalists. Decide how much you need and what are the best source options.

You will also need to fund your working capital and you will only be able to identify the full extent of your funding gap when you have produced a cash flow forecast.

Workbook exercises

 The New Venture Creation Workbook contains a digital version of these exercises that can be modified as your business model develops and builds into a draft business plan. It can be downloaded from www.macmillanihe.com/burns-nvc-2e.

12.1: Identify the assets you need and how to acquire them

1 List the assets you need to launch your business, and decide which you must purchase and which you might rent, lease or bootstrap.

2 For those that must be purchased, list and total up their cost.

3 Repeat the process for the assets needed for your second and third year of operation.

Assets	Buy / lease / rent / bootstrap	Cost of assets that must be purchased
		Total:

12.2: Identify your asset funding gap and how it will be met

Jot down:

1 The total cost of assets that must be purchased (from the previous exercise).
2 The capital you (and other founders) are willing to invest [Exercise 1.3 (2)]. Bear in mind your 'affordable loss' (Chapter 10) both in financial terms (financial capital plus guarantees) and in social terms (e.g. reputation).
3 The difference between the two is your asset funding gap. Consider how this might be financed and list your options.

Cost of assets that must be purchased	Capital available	Asset funding gap	Possible sources of finance

You will also need to finance your working capital (stocks/inventory and debtors/receivables) and any trading cash shortfall. You can only determine this after you have completed a cash flow forecast [Exercise 13.3]. We shall therefore return to this calculation in the next chapter.

 Visit www.macmillanihe.com/burns-nvc-2e **for chapter quizzes and other resources.**

13 Preparing and using financial forecasts

Contents

- Financial objectives
- Forecasting sales turnover and costs
- Forecast income statement
- Forecast breakeven point
- Using breakeven and contribution margins
- Forecast cash flow statement
- Forecast balance sheet
- Performance metrics and financial ratio analysis
- Evaluating your performance
- SMART performance metrics
- Controlling performance
- Valuing your business
- Go/no-go or pivot?
- Summary and action points
- Workbook exercises

Learning outcomes

When you have read this chapter and undertaken the related exercises you will be able to:

- Understand the relevance and importance of different measures of financial performance
- Develop the financial forecasts for your new venture – income statement, breakeven, cash flow statement and balance sheet
- Evaluate these forecasts of financial performance
- Understand how companies are valued
- Understand how financial information can be used to monitor and control performance

Academic insights

13.1 Entrepreneurial optimism and forecast bias

Case insights

13.1 The English Pub (2)

Sofa-bed Factory

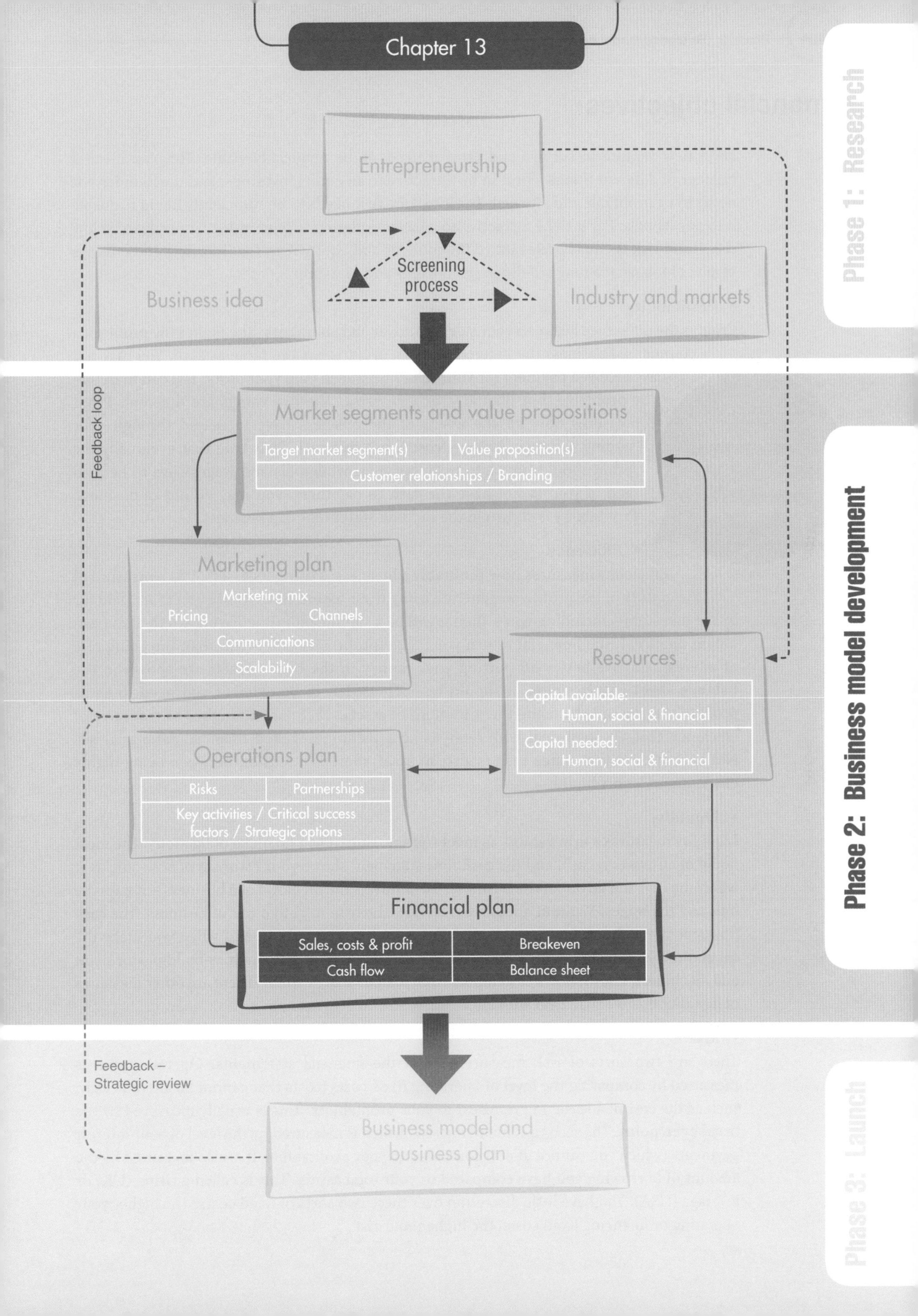

Chapter 13
Entrepreneurship
Business idea
Screening process
Industry and markets
Feedback loop
Market segments and value propositions
Target market segment(s)
Value proposition(s)
Customer relationships / Branding
Marketing plan
Marketing mix
Pricing
Channels
Communications
Scalability
Resources
Capital available:
Human, social & financial
Capital needed:
Human, social & financial
Operations plan
Risks
Partnerships
Key activities / Critical success factors / Strategic options
Financial plan
Sales, costs & profit
Breakeven
Cash flow
Balance sheet
Feedback – Strategic review
Business model and business plan
Phase 1: Research
Phase 2: Business model development
Phase 3: Launch

Financial objectives

For a new venture to survive and grow it needs to be financially viable. This can mean a number of different things. For it to be attractive to an equity investor – and the founder – it needs to be profitable and efficient. For it to survive it needs to be sufficiently liquid to enable it to pay its bills. For it to be attractive to a banker offering to lend money it needs to be low risk – and risk is equally relevant to the founder and equity investor. To assess these things involves looking at a range of different concepts and measures.

- **Profitability**

Profit is the difference between your sales/turnover and your costs. The higher the profits of a commercial business the better. However, profit is not the same as cash. You may not have received payment for your sales nor indeed paid your costs. You can therefore be profitable, but illiquid – or vice versa. The two things are different. Profit measures how *all* the assets of the business have increased through your trading activities (sales – costs), not just cash. It is true that eventually the profit should turn into cash, but meanwhile bills and wages have to be paid and, if you do not have the cash to pay them, you may go out of business. Profitability is shown in the **income statement** of a business.

> If you are going to need funding, you will need to explain how you will make money.
>
> *Sokratis Papafloratos founder Trusted Places Sunday Times 20 April 2014*

- **Efficiency**

Efficiency measures how profitably a business is using its assets. It is a measure of the *quality* of the profit you generate using these assets. Since those assets are paid for by the investors – including you – then it will be a significant influence on whether you can obtain finance. If the financial return you make (profit ÷ assets) is less than the going rate of interest, you are better off putting your money in the bank. Assets are shown in the **balance sheet** of a business. It should be obvious that to be efficient you need to be as profitable as possible by using the minimum of assets. There are a number of measures of efficiency that we shall deal with later using a technique called financial ratio analysis. Notice, however, that, since cash is also an asset, there is a tension between being highly efficient and highly liquid.

- **Liquidity**

Liquidity measures a firm's ability to meet routine, short-term financial obligations. The most liquid of all assets is cash, and the cash flow statement shows your estimate of how quickly it will come into and go out of the business. **Cash flow** is the lifeblood of a business – it pays the bills and the wages. Without adequate cash flow the firm might go out of business. The cash flow statement shows how quickly cash from your sales comes in and when you make the expenditures associated with your costs and capital investments, such as buildings or plant and machinery. It also shows cash inputs from loan or share capital. There are other measures of liquidity that we shall deal with later.

- **Risk**

There are two sorts of risk measurement in the financial statements. Operating risk is measured by comparing the level of operating fixed costs (costs that cannot be altered easily, such as the cost of a lease on premises) to your profitability. This is usually measured by the **breakeven point**. The second is financing risk, which is measured by the level of your interest payments (which you cannot affect) compared to your profitability. It is also measured by the amount of borrowing you have compared to your total assets. This is called gearing (UK) or leverage (USA). You have little discretion over these two sorts of fixed costs. The higher your operating or financing fixed costs, the higher your risk.

The financial objectives of a commercial business will usually involve being highly profitable and efficient, while maintaining adequate liquidity and minimizing operating and financial risk. The challenge is in quantifying these things and then achieving them. For a social enterprise with social objectives, profitability and efficiency may be constraints rather than things to be maximized.

The measurement of these elements of the business plan involves drawing up financial forecasts for at least a three-year period – five years for larger projects where significant commercialization risks, which are particular to this project, have not been resolved. These forecasts include:

- Income statements (including breakeven projections);
- Cash flow statements;
- Balance sheets.

How your business actually performs is measured by your historical financial statements, usually produced annually. These are used as a basis for taxing the business. Companies in the UK must submit them to Companies House, where they are publicly available. Most businesses, however, will produce monthly income statements and monitor their cash flow on an even more regular basis. They can also be used to monitor the performance of the business.

Forecasting sales turnover and costs

You can prepare financial forecasts in one of two ways:

- By forecasting your sales or turnover, the costs needed to generate this level of sales and the resulting profits (this is the most usual approach).
- By calculating the costs needed to set up the business and then working back to the level of sales needed to generate a target profit level.

Whichever approach you decide on, a number of iterations – altering price, volumes and/ or costs – will probably be necessary before a 'satisfactory' profit target is calculated. Some benchmarks to help you judge what might be 'satisfactory' are discussed later in this chapter. Monthly sales forecasts will be needed for the first year – perhaps for longer where these significant commercialization risks remain unresolved. Sales revenue in the income statement should be net, after deducting sales returns and allowances and any discounts.

Sales income for physical goods or services might come directly to you from consumers (at retail price) or might be derived from your channels of distribution (at wholesale price) – both calculated simply as price × number of units sold. Related costs will be the cost of sales (materials, labour, factory overheads), and operating expenses: sales and marketing costs (reps, tradeshows, etc.), delivery and distribution costs, administration and so on.

Sales income for virtual goods or services might also be derived from direct sales to consumers (downloads from your website), for which there will be the cost of making these sales over the web (e.g. you might use AdWords, emails or other incentives, or offer existing customers a monetary incentive for referring new customers), or through app stores, where there will be a fee (typically 30%) – treated as selling and marketing costs. Other costs will include operating expenses and product development costs (which we deal with later).

Virtual goods or services might be offered free and income derived from advertising or click-throughs. Web advertising income is typically determined by the number of page views your product generates. You might also be able to sell on your email list. Costs will include customer acquisition costs and other operating expenses as well as product development costs.

Realistic, achievable sales forecasts are the starting point for the rest of the financial forecasts so it is important that they are more than just aspirations. However, as we observed in Chapter 2, the more radical the product/service innovation and/or market innovation you are introducing in your new venture, the more difficult it will be to forecast sales. As we observed, market research is unlikely to yield an insight into demand for this kind of new product/service or market because customers do not understand it. Often the only sure way of knowing whether the idea will make a lucrative business is to try it out – launch the business but minimize your risks with a lean start-up. That means calculating the minimum costs needed to set up the business and then working back to the level of sales needed to generate a target profit level. After that it is about taking the leap of faith that Henry Ford and Steve Jobs did, but if you need financial backers you will need a persuasive argument and very attractive profit targets.

For more incremental innovations in products/services or markets your sales forecasts need to be justified by demonstrating two conditions.

1 **There is sufficient market demand** – You might be able to do this by market research that demonstrates a market need that is, as yet, unmet. This can take many forms but must be underpinned by a convincing understanding of customers, competitors and differential advantage. For example, you might be able to demonstrate from desk research that there are relatively few competitors within a certain geographic area compared to market demand, you might be able to establish the total size of the market (TAM and SAM) and should certainly be able to show market growth (Chapter 3). Alternatively, if you can identify potential customers you might decide to contact them directly to establish whether they might be willing to at least try your product or service. And if you want to open a new shop in a certain area, you might decide to measure footfall in that area yourself by field research. Another approach is to demonstrate that your share of a particular market – and this needs careful definition – is so small that you are highly likely to achieve it (your SAM compared to the TAM). While you will not be able to *prove* there is sufficient market demand, you should be able to establish that there *probably* is.

2 **Targets are achievable, within the operating and cost parameters of the business** – Your forecasts need to be internally consistent. There is no point in convincingly forecasting sufficient demand if you have not built in sufficient costs to meet the sales you forecast. It is important to establish the assumptions upon which your sales forecasts are based. That means clearly stating selling prices and volumes and ensuring that the volumes predicted are consistent with costs. Some costs are fixed costs that need to be incurred to set up the business but will not change significantly if your sales forecast is inaccurate – they do not change with the volume of activity or sales – for example, property lease/rental costs or fixed salaries. These forecasts need to be based upon a reasonable estimate. Some costs are variable costs that vary with sales volumes – for example, materials or piecework labour costs. Every time an additional unit is produced and sold, an additional cost is incurred. These costs vary with your sales forecast, and can be calculated based upon a percentage of sales.

Investors will typically pay great attention to the assumptions underpinning the financial forecasts of a new venture and, if they feel they are unrealistic, the credibility of the entire plan may be severely dented. They will often apply a range of pragmatic, common-sense tests. For example, predicted sales for a retail business could be divided by the selling space taken up. This can often be compared to industry norms. Alternatively, forecast sales per day might be calculated and divided by the expected average spend per customer to arrive at a figure for buyers per day, which can then be compared to footfall and buyer conversion rates. In a bar or restaurant you might look at the number of covers and the average spend per cover to see whether sales estimates are realistic. Remember that sales may come from different distribution channels, each with a different profit margin (e.g. for a web/mobile product sold through web/mobile channels of distribution, sales may come from your own website either directly or by referral or through an app store, and there is a cost attached to the last two sources). However you show it, investors will certainly want to know the volumes and price assumptions that underpin these estimates.

Forecast income statement

Once you have estimates of your sales and costs, you can prepare your forecast of profit or income. This is simply a case of slotting the estimates into an accepted format for an **income statement**, such as the one in Workbook exercise 13.1. The amount of detail you give is a matter of judgement, but the larger the start-up the greater the detail that will be expected.

Financial statements generally highlight the **gross profit** of a business. The **operating costs** (such as selling, marketing, administrative costs etc.) are deducted from this to arrive at the **operating profit** and financing income or costs (interest income/expense) are deducted or added to this to arrive at **net profit** (before taxes and dividends).

Gross profit = Sales/Turnover – Cost of sales
Operating profit = Gross profit – Operating expenses
Net profit = Operating profit +/– Interest income/expense

The cost of sales is the cost of the goods sold, including sales commissions. These costs can comprise both variable and fixed costs. For a shop these costs represent the cost of the items sold, which indeed is a variable cost. For a manufacturing business, as well as the cost of the raw materials, there will also be labour costs involved in adding value to the goods. If workers are paid by the volume they produce – called piecework – then this is a variable cost. However, most employees expect to be paid a regular weekly wage, which is fixed. The cost of sales will also represent other fixed factory overheads such as the depreciation cost of machinery and equipment used in the process. Cost of sales for a manufacturing business therefore might comprise material costs (variable), labour costs (variable and/or fixed) and factory overheads (fixed). To work out the cost of sales (and the value of the goods you hold in stock) for a service or manufacturing business you need to know the cost of each good or service provided. That means undertaking a costing exercise so that the fixed costs can be spread over the volume of goods *produced*, which is not necessarily the same as goods sold for a manufacturing business. (For an example of how to calculate this, see Table 13.B in Sofa-bed Factory case.) This is the basis for what is called 'cost+' or 'full-cost' pricing (see Chapter 6). If a manufacturing business fails to sell everything it produces, the cost of the excess is reflected in the valuation of the unsold stock/inventory.

> Keep your costs to a minimum. If you can work from home and do your own PR in the beginning this will give you the cash to develop the product.
>
> Calypso Rose founder Clippy Daily Telegraph 6 February 2009

For a service business, such as a consultancy, or for virtual goods or services selling through virtual channels, there are no physical 'goods'. Therefore, cost of sales does not normally apply. However, if there are variable costs that relate directly to that sale, such as commissions or app store charges, then these are the cost of sales. The major operating costs facing these businesses are labour costs, which will mainly be fixed. Cost of sales is therefore a variable cost for all other than manufacturing businesses, where it comprises both variable and fixed.

Forecast breakeven point

The **breakeven point** is an important piece of financial information. It is the point where a business stops making a loss and starts making a profit – where sales revenues are equal to the total costs. Some costs, often called overhead costs, are fixed costs – they do not change with the volume of activity or sales (at least up to a certain level of output) – for example, property lease/rental costs or fixed wages and salaries. These fixed costs are represented by the dotted horizontal line **AB** in Figure 13.1. Producing the product or delivering the service will mean incurring additional variable costs – costs that vary with volume like materials and direct, piecework labour costs. Every time an additional unit is produced and sold, an additional cost is incurred. Line **AC** therefore represents the total cost of producing the product or delivering the service – the fixed cost plus the variable cost. Over large volumes, this line may curve downwards as the effects of economies of scale are felt. Line **LM** represents the revenue generated by sales – sales volume multiplied by unit price, often called turnover. At volume **X** all costs are covered by revenue. This is the breakeven point. If your target sales volume is **Y**, this will generate the profit represented by the distance between lines **LM** and **AC** (total sales – total costs).

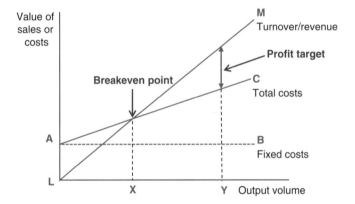

Figure 13.1 Breakeven point

The higher your breakeven point, the more sales you have to achieve before you start to make a profit and therefore the higher the risk you face. The lower the breakeven point, the less risk you face. Indeed, if the breakeven point cannot, reasonably, be expected to be achieved then a venture is probably not viable.

The breakeven point can be easily calculated without a diagram using the formula:

$$\text{Breakeven point (expressed in \$ turnover)} = \frac{\text{Fixed costs}}{\text{Contribution margin}}$$

Contribution per unit is the difference between the sales price and the *variable* cost of each unit you sell. Total contribution is the difference between turnover and your *total variable* costs. **Contribution margin** = contribution per unit ÷ sales price (*or* total contribution ÷ turnover). Usually this is expressed as a percentage. Where you are selling a range of products/services with different margins the calculation using total sales and variable costs is easier.

For example (assuming target sales of 1,000 units per week):

Sales price per unit	$10	Turnover (per week)	$10,000
Variable cost per unit	6	Total variable costs	6,000
Contribution per unit	4	Total contribution	4,000
Contribution margin	0.40 *or* 40%	Contribution margin	0.40 *or* 40%

If your fixed costs are $2,000 per week, your total profit will be $2,000 ($4,000 − $2,000).

$$\text{Breakeven point} = \frac{\$2,000}{0.40} = \$5,000 \text{ per week (or 500 units @ \$10 each)}$$

You can check this calculation:

Breakeven point	500 units @ $10	=	$5,000
Total variable costs	500 units @ $6	=	$3,000
Total contribution		=	$2,000
Total fixed costs		=	$2,000
Profit			nil

If you have more than one product or service and each has a different contribution margin, calculating breakeven can be problematic. While it might be possible to calculate it for each product/service line this can be complicated and it is likely that at least some of your fixed costs will be shared. The easiest way to approach the problem is to base your breakeven calculation on the sales volumes you predict for each line and then work out your *average* contribution margin (based on forecast total sales and total variable costs). This then gives you a breakeven point based upon that particular mix of sales. If the mix changes so too will your breakeven point.

Building on the example in Table 6.6 on page 195, if we add in the forecast sales volumes for the three products, as shown in Table 13.1, the total forecast sales is $464,000 and profit contribution is $232,000.

Table 13.1 Adding forecast sales volumes

	Product A	Product B	Product C
Price per unit (A)	$25	$32	$50
Variable cost per unit	$10	$16	$30
Contribution per unit (B)	$15	$16	$20
Contribution margin (%)	60%	50%	40%
Forecast sales volumes (C)	8,000	2,000	4,000
Forecast sales values (A × C)	$200,000	$64,000	$200,000
Forecast total contribution (B × C)	$120,000	$32,000	$80,000

The *average* contribution margin *for this mix of sales* is therefore 50% ($232,000 ÷ $464,000). If forecast fixed costs are $190,000 then:

$$\text{Breakeven point} = \frac{\$190,000}{0.50} = \$380,000 \text{ (for this mix of sales)}$$

If the mix of sales changes then the breakeven point will also change and need to be recalculated. Workbook exercise 13.2 provides you with a pro forma for estimating your breakeven point.

Using breakeven and contribution margins

We saw in Chapter 6 how useful a knowledge of your fixed and variable costs can be when it comes to pricing. The key to this is an understanding of your breakeven point and contribution margin. This can be applied to other things.

Estimating the sales needed to achieve a profit target

Once above the breakeven point, each $1 of sales contributes $0.40 (40%) to profits. If you start with a profit target rather than a sales target you can use the breakeven point to work out the level of sales you need to achieve this. Dividing your profit target by your contribution margin tells you how much above the breakeven point you need to be. The formula for this is:

Profit ÷ Contribution margin = (Target sales − Breakeven sales)

So for example, if your target profit is $4,000 per week, then your sales target would have to be:

$$\frac{\$4,000}{0.40} = \$10,000 \text{ } above \text{ } breakeven \quad = \$15,000 \text{ } (\$10,000 + \$5,000)$$

You can check this calculation:

Sales	=	$15,000
Total contribution @ 40%	=	$ 6,000
Total fixed costs	=	$ 2,000
Profit	=	$ 4,000

Estimating profitability from sales data

Once you are in business the same calculation can be used to estimate your actual profitability without having to wait for the financial results each week, month or year. All you need to know is your actual sales. Once you are above your breakeven point your fixed costs are covered and all the contribution you make is profit. The formula for this is:

Profit = (Actual sales − Breakeven sales) × Contribution margin

Using the example above, if your actual weekly sales were $20,000 the profit would be $4,000.

Profit = ($20,000 − $5,000) × 0.4 (40%) = $6,000

Estimating the additional sales needed to justify a fixed expenditure

Knowledge of your contribution margin can even help you make business decisions by informing you of the financial consequences. For example, it can help you make business decisions about whether to incur additional expenditure by telling you how much additional sales you need to generate to pay for, and hence justify, a fixed cost expenditure. It will not make the decision for you but it does provide you with valuable information to help you make a judgement. The formula for this is:

$$\text{Extra sales needed} = \frac{\text{Increase in fixed costs}}{\text{Contribution margin}}$$

So for example, if you are considering an increase in advertising expenditure of $10,000 and your contribution margin is 40%, the extra sales needed to justify the expenditure are:

$$\frac{\$10,000}{0.40} = \$25,000$$

Measuring operating risk

Even if you keep your fixed costs low at start-up, they are bound to creep up as your business grows. As they increase, your breakeven point will also drift up and what is really important about the breakeven point is its position in relation to turnover – how much your turnover can drop before you arrive at your breakeven point. This is measured by the **margin of safety**. It tells you the percentage reduction in sales needed to get down to your breakeven point, and is a measure of the operating risk that your business faces.

$$\text{Margin of safety (normally expressed as \%)} = \frac{\text{Turnover} - \text{Breakeven}}{\text{Turnover}}$$

The higher the margin of safety the better, because the firm is safer in terms of maintaining its profitability should sales suddenly decline. This reflects a number of factors: level of sales, contribution margin and fixed costs. It is therefore a simple but powerful piece of information that can be used to control a business as it grows. If the margin of safety can be maintained (or increased) as a business grows, despite the increase in fixed costs, it shows that the financial risks of the business are under control. Because it indicates lower operating risk, the higher the forecast margin of safety, the more attractive a business usually is to potential investors.

Forecast cash flow statement

Profits are important but they are not the same as cash and your survival might depend upon an accurate forecast of cash flow – how quickly the cash from your sales comes in and when you make the expenditures associated with your costs and capital investments.

Cash flow = Total cash receipts – Total cash payments, in any period

Because cash flow is often negative for technology businesses it has been called the **cash burn** for the period. Technology businesses can incur large development costs and it can take a long time before they start generating income. However, any new venture might spend cash on premises, equipment, stock (inventory) and so on before the first customer even walks through the door. The first sales might even be on credit and it can take time before debts are collected and cash received. During this time the business will have a negative cash flow. This is the notorious **Death Valley curve** of cash flow for a start-up, shown in Figure 13.2 on the next page. Without external finance the start-up in Figure 13.2 would be unable to pay its creditors and may not survive.

The length and depth of Death Valley depends on how quickly you pay cash out (e.g. to creditors) and how quickly you collect it in (e.g. from debtors). Its depth determines how much you need to borrow and its length determines how long you will need to borrow for. The shape of the valley can vary from industry to industry and the negotiating power of your suppliers and/or customers. It can also be affected by the economic cycle, for example, customers might take extended credit in an economic

> We have always very carefully managed growth against profitability. Cash is king.
>
> Eileen Gittins founder Blurb BBC News Business 11 December 2012

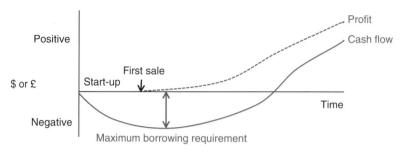

Figure 13.2 Death Valley curve of cash flow for a start-up

downturn. And the faster the growth of your business, the deeper and longer Death Valley is likely to be. In general, if the sales you actually achieve exceed your projections, your cash flow is likely to worsen and Death Valley will lengthen. So, be warned – many firms do not survive long enough to come through Death Valley.

You need to plot Death Valley's contours and plan how to navigate it – and that means preparing a cash flow forecast. Only this will tell you how much finance you might need to launch your business. By altering the assumptions on which your cash flow model is based, you can see the effects on Death Valley. A good model should allow you to understand how you might reduce the depth and length of Death Valley. A cash flow forecast lists the expected cash receipts and payments for the business in the period they are expected to come in or go out. The cash you have in any period is calculated by adding (or, if negative, subtracting) the period cash flow to the cash balance brought forward (abbreviated to B/F) from the last period. It can be prepared on a daily, weekly or, more normally, a monthly basis. Workbook exercise 13.3 provides you with a pro forma for plotting your monthly cash flow forecast.

In Death Valley you have run out of cash – your cash reserves are negative – and you will need to borrow. If you forecast a negative cash balance then you will need to seek external finance or agree on an overdraft in order to pay your bills. The consequences of being unable to pay those bills might be bankruptcy, despite the fact that you are profitable.

Forecast balance sheet

The **balance sheet** is a snapshot at a point of time that shows two things:

1 The assets that the business owns:
- Cash;
- Debtors (UK) or receivables (US) – amounts you are owed from sales;
- Stock (UK) or inventory (US) – raw materials, work-in-progress and stocks of finished goods;
- Fixed assets – things the business means to keep over a number of years such as equipment, machinery, vehicles, premises etc.

2 Where the funds for these assets came from:
- Overdraft and loans;
- Creditors (UK) or payables (US) – amounts you owe to suppliers of goods and services;
- Share capital invested in the business;
- Accumulated profits (or losses) of the business. (Remember, profits/losses measures how *all* the assets of the business have increased/decreased through trading.)

Cash, debtors/receivables and stock/inventory are called **current assets**. Overdrafts, short-term loans and creditors/payables are called **current liabilities**.

There are two sides to the balance sheet and they must always balance. If you drew up a balance sheet when you invest $10,000 capital in a new venture it would show two things: Cash $10,000 and Share capital $10,000. If you went on to purchase assets with the $10,000 of cash, those assets would be listed together with their purchase price, and the other side of the balance sheet would remain the same, showing where the funds of $10,000 for these assets came from. If you can secure more funds or credit, this would be shown in the balance sheet as a liability, with the assets purchased on the other side of the balance sheet as assets. For example, stock (the US name is inventory) purchased on credit for $5,000 would be shown on one side of the balance sheet as a creditor (the US name is payable), with the stock/inventory on the other side as an asset. Once the business starts trading and making a profit by charging a higher price for a product/service than the cost of production, the assets of the business will start to grow.

Assets	$10,000	Creditors/payables	$5,000
Stock/inventory	$5,000	Share capital	$10,000
	$15,000		$15,000

Stock/inventory will be bought and sold as part of normal trading and therefore shown in the cash flow statement and, eventually, the income statement. However, when a company purchases fixed assets – assets that it uses to create value but will last for a number of years – it has to find a way of allocating the cost of these assets to the income statement. Whereas the cash cost of the fixed asset is recognized in the cash flow statement when the cash is spent, the cost of the asset needs to be allocated, over its life, to the income statement. Depreciation is a way of showing this in the profit statement. It is not a cash expenditure, and therefore represents a major difference between profit and cash flow.

The simplest method of calculating depreciation is called 'straight-line', which writes off the asset in equal amounts over its life. For example, if the asset cost $10,000 and has a working life of five years, at which time it can be sold off for $2,000, the annual depreciation would be:

$$\frac{\text{Initial cost} - \text{Final residual value}}{\text{Life of fixed asset}} = \frac{\$10,000 - \$2,000}{5} = \$1,600 \text{ per annum}$$

The value of the asset would go down by $1,600 each year. At the end of year one it would have a value of $8,400, year two $6,800 and so on, until year five when it would be $2,000. Depreciation does not represent any cash expenditure – that takes place when the asset is purchased.

Technology start-ups often face high development costs and it is controversial whether or not these should be shown as expenses when they are incurred or as an asset that can be depreciated or written off over some timescale – a timescale that is becoming increasingly short as technological development accelerates. There are three approaches. The 'prudent' approach would be to write them off immediately. Less prudent would be to write them off over a specified time period (e.g. five years), or to try to predict sales and allocate a development cost to each unit sold (very difficult).

A pro forma balance sheet is shown in Workbook exercise 13.4. As well as listing the assets owned and liabilities owed by the company, a balance sheet highlights the total investment by the shareholders, called **shareholders' funds** – share capital plus accumulated profit. On the other side of the balance sheet this represents the net assets the shareholders own – total assets minus total liabilities.

Entrepreneurial optimism and forecast bias

Entrepreneurs are generally seen as being optimistic, sometimes unrealistically so. You might argue that it goes with the job. In a review of the literature, Coelho (2010) concludes that entrepreneurial characteristics, such as emotional commitment to the project and a belief that it is controllable, and empirical research indicate that entrepreneurs are *unrealistically* optimistic. Chen et al. (1998) argue that it is self-efficacy – a belief in their own capabilities – that motivates entrepreneurs and gives them the dogged determination to persist in the face of adversity, when others just give in. Delmar (2000) observes that entrepreneurs appear to make extensive use of cognitive heuristics (simplifying strategies) and are 'biased' in their decision making. Possibly because of this, they can be seen as 'overconfident' (Forbes, 2005), particularly with regard to predicting a future outcome, to the point of

GETTY

escalating their commitment (Baron, 1998; Gibson and Sanbonmatsu, 2004).

It seems likely therefore that this optimism will extend into the financial forecasts an entrepreneur will produce. However, since these are confidential and often commercially sensitive documents, there is little research into their accuracy. However, using data from larger, venture-backed businesses, studies have concluded that entrepreneurs' revenue and profit forecasts generally tend to be over-optimistic (Armstrong et al., 2006; Collewaert and Vanacker, 2011), although the studies are contradictory about whether this over-optimism increases over extended forecast periods. Another large-scale empirical study of the forecast performance of entrepreneurial start-ups by Cassar (2014) concluded that industrial experience improved the accuracy of forecasts, particularly in high-tech firms, but contrary to general belief start-up experience as such did improve forecast accuracy.

Armstrong, C.S., Dávila, A., Foster, G. and Hand, J.R.M. (2006) 'Biases in Multi-Year Management Financial Forecasts: Evidence from Private Venture-Backed U.S. Companies', *Review of Accounting Studies* 2006 Conference, Published online: 28 March 2007: http://public.kenan-flagler.unc.edu/Faculty/handj/JH%20website/ADFH%20RAST%20revision%20 20061106-1.pdf

Baron, R.A. (1998) 'Cognitive Mechanisms in Entrepreneurship, Why and When Entrepreneurs Think Differently Than Other People', *Journal of Business Venturing*, 13(4).

Cassar, G. (2014) 'Industry and Start-up Experience on Entrepreneur Forecast Performance in New Firms', *Journal of Business Venturing*, 29(1).

Chen, P.C., Greene, P.G. and Crick, A. (1998) 'Does Entrepreneurial Efficacy Distinguish Entrepreneurs from Managers?' *Journal of Business Venturing*, 13.

Coelho, M. (2010) 'Unrealistic Optimism: Still a Neglected Trait', *Journal of Business and Psychology*, 25(3).

Collewaert, V. and Vanacker, T. (2011) 'Forecast Bias of Entrepreneurs in Venture Capital-backed Companies (Summary)', *Frontiers of Entrepreneurship Research*, Vol. 31, Issue 2. Available at: http://digitalknowledge.babson.edu/fer/vol31/iss2/5.

Delmar, F. (2000) 'The Psychology of the Entrepreneur', in S. Carter and D. Jones-Evans (eds) *Enterprise and Small Business: Principles, Practice and Policy*, London: Prentice Hall.

Forbes, D. (2005) 'Are Some Entrepreneurs More Overconfident than Others?' *Journal of Business Venturing*, 20.

Gibson, B. and Sanbonmatsu, D.M. (2004) 'Optimism, Pessimism and Gambling: The Downside of Optimism', *Personality and Social Psychology Bulletin*, 30(2).

Performance metrics and financial ratio analysis

Performance metrics are frequently based upon financial indicators. Accounting systems usually produce this information routinely, so it is easily accessible. The performance of a business can be analysed using a technique called financial ratio analysis. This measures the relationship between two financial indicators. If we start with the usual economic purpose of most businesses ('profit' maximization) and then outline some of the most frequently used ratios, you can see that these ratios are designed to provide information for that purpose. You will also see how the ratios build to form a picture of why the company's financial situation is what it is.

Investors – and founders – usually want to maximize the return ('profit') they get on their investment. If they invest $100 and receive $10, they get a 10% return which they can then compare to other investment opportunities. You (and perhaps others) invest money in the share capital of your company and become shareholders. Shareholders in your business own all the assets of the firm and typically might expect to maximize the return they receive on this investment. Therefore, the performance ratio that shareholders expect to be kept as high as possible is the **return to shareholders**:

$$\text{Return to shareholders} = \frac{\text{Net profit}}{\text{Shareholders' funds}} \quad \text{(expressed as \%)}$$

To maximize this, operating profit should be as high as possible, interest payments should be as low as possible and shareholders' funds should also be as low as possible. And here lies the dilemma. One way of keeping shareholders' funds low is to borrow (shareholders' funds = total assets – liabilities), but this increases interest payments and reduces net profit. So the question is, how much to borrow? The answer is that it pays to borrow as much as you can, as long as you can obtain a return on these borrowings that exceeds the interest rate.

For example, the founder puts $5,000 into the business and then obtains a bank loan of $5,000 with an interest rate of 10%. If the return on this investment is 25% then they will make an extra 15% on the bank loan – a total of $750 ($5,000 × 15%). This goes directly to the founder, on top of the $1,250 ($5,000 × 25%) from their own investment, giving a total of £2,000, equal to a return to shareholders of 40% ($2,000 ÷ $5,000 × 100). The downside of this is that the financial risk of the business increases with the higher level of borrowing. The business is obliged to pay interest of $500 whatever profit it makes and, if it were only able to make a 5% return on the $10,000 it borrowed, then all the money would go to pay interest ($10,000 × 5% = $500), leaving nothing for the shareholders, despite the fact that they had invested $5,000. The appropriate level of borrowing is the classic risk/return trade-off decision – it is a question of judgement. Bankers have some benchmark ratios to inform their lending decisions, as we shall see later in this section.

As far as the business is concerned, the critical performance ratio is the return on total assets. This measures the operating performance of the business (stripping out the effects of borrowing) and must be kept as high as possible:

$$\text{Return on total assets} = \frac{\text{Operating profit}}{\text{Shareholders' funds} + \text{Loan capital}} \quad \text{(expressed as \%)}$$

where Shareholders' funds + Loan capital = Total assets – Current liabilities

However, be aware that founders take a salary, which is deducted when calculating the operating profit or income, and therefore the ratio (and the return to shareholders) can be distorted if salaries are unrealistically low or high.

In seeking to be as efficient as possible a company will look to do two things:

1 Maximize its operating profit;
2 Minimize its total assets minus current liabilities.

Financial ratio analysis can help with an understanding of this by looking separately at profit management and asset management.

Profit management

Profits normally increase as turnover increases. Therefore, looking at profit in isolation tells you nothing about the operating efficiency of a business. You need to assess the profit as a proportion of sales/turnover. The **operating profit margin** measures overall profitability compared to sales/turnover. It reflects the price you are able to charge, compared to the costs you face. The ratio should be as high as possible.

$$\text{Operating profit margin} = \frac{\text{Operating profit}}{\text{Sales/Turnover}} \text{ (expressed as \%)}$$

The **gross profit margin** reflects how well the direct costs of the product/service – the cost of sales – are controlled. It should be as high as possible.

$$\text{Gross profit margin} = \frac{\text{Gross profit}}{\text{Sales/Turnover}} \text{ (expressed as \%)}$$

Gross profit margin is different from the contribution margin – which reflects your control of variable costs. Companies often break this ratio down further by looking at ratios of key direct costs such as materials or labour, compared to turnover/sales.

Asset management

Assets also normally increase as sales increase. Therefore, looking at asset levels in isolation tells you nothing about the operating efficiency of a business. The key ratios below measure the efficiency of asset usage compared to sales/turnover. They are all expressed as numbers and should be as high as possible:

$$\text{Total asset turnover} = \frac{\text{Sales/Turnover}}{\text{Total assets}}$$

$$\text{Debtor/receivables turnover} = \frac{\text{Sales/Turnover}}{\text{Debtors (receivables)}}$$

$$\text{Stock/inventory turnover} = \frac{\text{Sales/Turnover}}{\text{Stock (inventory)}}$$

Liquidity

There are also a number of ratios that measure the liquidity of a business. The first two are of particular interest to anyone offering credit as they measure the firm's ability to repay the debt. They are all expressed as numbers:

$$\text{Current ratio} = \frac{\text{Current assets}}{\text{Current liability}}$$

The **current ratio** is expected to be greater than 1, indicating that current assets exceed current liabilities.

$$\text{Quick ratio} = \frac{\text{Current assets excluding stock/inventory}}{\text{Current liabilities}}$$

This is expected to be near to 1, perhaps as low as 0.8.

The level of borrowing is called **gearing** or **leverage**. Ratios that measure this are of particular interest to bankers. High gearing or leverage is risky.

$$\text{Gearing/leverage} = \frac{\text{All loans} + \text{Overdraft}}{\text{Shareholders' funds}} \text{ (expressed as \%)}$$

Bankers like this ratio to be under 100%, indicating that shareholders have put in more money than the banks. Frequently for growing firms this is not the case. Above 400% is considered very high risk – the business is likely to fail. However, some management buy-outs have had gearing levels even above this. Often bankers will also look at the proportion of all the loans that are short term (due within one year). They are also interested in the security of their interest payments.

$$\text{Interest cover} = \frac{\text{Operating profit}}{\text{Interest}} \text{ (expressed as a number)}$$

This measures how many times interest is covered by profit. The higher, the better.

Evaluating your performance

Ratios allow you to evaluate performance. They are useful because they measure one numerical indicator against another – they therefore allow for growth. So, for example, debtors/receivables are bound to increase as the business grows and sales increase, but what is important is not the absolute value of debtors/receivables but rather its relationship to sales, measured by debtor turnover. Similarly, there is no way of knowing whether a $2 million profit in one company is better than a $1 million profit in another unless you know how much was invested in each to achieve it.

To obtain a high return to the shareholder, a firm needs effective profit management and efficient asset management. Put crudely, margins need to be as high as possible and assets should be kept as low as possible. Systematic calculation of these ratios can give you clues about how profit might be increased and where assets might be reduced. Of course to do this you need some benchmarks. One fundamental benchmark is the rate of interest. The **return on total assets** should never fall below this value; otherwise you are better off closing the company and putting the money in the bank. All the other measures are a question of judgement, but you can assess them against:

- **Forecasts** – Ratios can be calculated both on forecast and actual financial information. Comparing your actual to financial performance in these forecasts is part of effective financial control.
- **Trends over time** – Ratios do change over time and trends can give both good and bad news.
- **Industry norms** – Industry-based ratios, often based on published financial statements, are produced by a number of organizations (e.g. in the UK, Centre for Interfirm Comparison and ICC Business Ratios). These are important benchmarks against which to judge the realism of projections. If your margins are higher than industry norms, how can you justify this? Founders and investors use these norms and ratios to validate a set of financial projections.

SMART performance metrics

Having prepared forecasts of income, cash flow and a balance sheet, you might be forgiven for thinking that the job is done. Unfortunately, actually achieving these target forecasts will involve even more hard work. These forecasts can be used to generate **metrics** against which to monitor your performance and help control the business. They provide a framework against which the performance of the firm can be judged. By comparing actual financial results to the forecast on a timely basis you can 'manage by exception', only intervening when performance deviates from your forecasts. This can free up time to concentrate on strategy or dealing with real business problems.

Computer-based accounting systems provide the financial information you need to monitor your performance, normally on a monthly basis. However, start-ups often subcontract the production of financial information, and that can mean there are delays in obtaining the information. Even if you rely on a part-time book-keeper they might provide you with so much financial information that you become 'numbers-blind' – unable to see the important pieces of information because of the detail provided. In fact, most firms can be controlled by monitoring just six pieces of information – some of which you can easily collect yourself – that tell you different, but vital, information on the performance of the business. These financial metrics are like the instruments on a car dashboard. They tell you different things about the engine of the business. Different pieces of information are important at different times and in different circumstances. On a road with a speed restriction you watch your speedometer. When changing gear at speed you watch your rev counter. When low on petrol your eye rarely strays from the fuel gauge.

There are six financial metrics that tell you all you need to know about driving the business. They apply to any and every business. They can be reproduced on a single piece of paper and provide the headline information on how the business is doing. You can calculate them from information your accounting systems produce and then monitor your performance against your financial projections. If these metrics disclose a problem, more information will be needed to accurately diagnose the cause and decide on the appropriate corrective action.

- **Cash** – Knowing your cash balance and monitoring your cash flow (cash burn rate) is vital for survival. Early in the life of a business, as you negotiate Death Valley, you will probably need to monitor cash on a weekly basis. But if you are really short of cash you may have to monitor it on a daily basis – it becomes *critical*.
- **Sales/turnover** – This tells you about the volume of work going through the business. It drives all the other financial results. Early in the life of a business you will probably need to monitor sales/turnover on a weekly, possibly even a daily, basis. The source of these sales by product or distribution channel may be important to monitor (e.g. for a web/mobile product sold through web/mobile channels of distribution this may come from your own website either directly or by referral or through an app store). If you are ahead of your forecasts, do you have the resources to meet the increased demand? If you are behind your forecasts, are there sufficient sales in the pipeline, or do you have to cut back on expenditure?
- **Profit margins** – These tell you whether your costs are in line with your sales. Your target margins will only be achieved if the sales volume targets are met, at the appropriate prices, and costs are under control. The operating profit margin, gross margin and contribution margin

each give you different information. As for sales, it may be important to monitor margins from different sources of income. Profit margins probably only need to be monitored monthly.

- **Margin of safety** – This tells you about the operating risk of the business. A deteriorating margin of safety should sound warning bells. It means you are approaching breakeven point. That could mean sales volumes are going down, contribution margins are not being maintained (prices are being discounted, or variable costs are increasing) or fixed costs are out of control. If the deteriorating margin of safety is due to falling sales, then you might try to reduce fixed costs – particularly the ones that you have some discretionary control over. This is therefore a powerful piece of information and should be monitored monthly.

- **Productivity** – For most firms the single largest and most important expense they face is the cost of wages. It therefore needs to be controlled carefully. Wages are best measured in relation to the productivity that they generate and for many firms this is most easily measured by the simple percentage of wages to sales. Often there are industry norms to compare this to. For example, in the UK licensed trade, wages of bar staff should be about 20% of sales. If higher, the bar is over-staffed, if lower, it is under-staffed – a crude but simple and effective measure that needs to be checked at least monthly. Of course, to achieve this benchmark staff need to work shifts, being brought in at peak periods.

- **Debtor (receivables) and/or stock (inventory) turnover** – Similarly most firms will have one important current asset on their balance sheet that represents over 50% of their total assets. For a service business this will probably be debtors/receivables, for a retail business stock/inventory, and for a manufacturing business it is likely to be both. You can use debtors/receivables and stock/inventory turnover ratios to monitor this investment, again on a monthly basis.

You can, of course, set up other non-financial metrics against which to measure your performance. A website business might monitor regular or active users/visitors, page views, average page views per user/visitor. A call centre might use calls answered, calls abandoned, average handling time, average waiting time, among others. The appropriate operating metrics that may need to be highlighted in projections and then monitored will vary from business to business, depending on the nature of activities. Performance metrics are not necessarily *critical*, although they can sometimes be derived from your critical success factors (Chapter 10). However, sometimes continued poor performance in one metric can cause it to become critical. For example, continued shortages of cash can threaten the survival of a business and mean that this financial metric becomes critical.

Performance metrics need to be **SMART**:
Specific for purpose;
Measurable;
Achievable;
Relevant to the success of the organization;
Time constrained.
Establishing a performance metric involves a three-step process:

1 Identify the process that needs to be monitored and controlled.
2 Establish the quantifiable outputs of that process.
3 Establish the targets against which to judge that performance. For a start-up,

Getty Images/Image Source

Mark Mason serial entrepreneur and business angel Sunday Times 2 June 2013

> My own businesses have always been very tightly controlled. I was able to sell my [first] business because the books were very clean, we had grown steadily, we never lost money and I knew where all the figures were month by month, if not day by day.

critical performance metrics are likely to be contained in your business plan as key targets.

Of course you must then ensure that performance is indeed monitored and any remedial action then taken on a timely basis. For example, if cash flow is critically poor then cash needs to be monitored daily and perhaps new lines of credit established urgently.

Controlling performance

Forecasting is not just for start-ups. You should continue to prepare financial forecasts as the firm grows because they help you control the business. Forecasts for an established firm are called budgets. They can be prepared at the department as well as company level, consistent with how you structure the business. You can use budgets to help you delegate responsibility to your management team and then monitor their performance, consistent with your leadership style. The budgeting process can then be used as a process for communicating and coordinating the activities of your management team. It can become a systematic tool for establishing standards of performance, providing motivation and assessing the results your managers achieve.

An essential element in this process of making managers accountable is that each knows exactly what they are held responsible for, and each does indeed control this aspect of the firm's operations. Responsibility cannot be assigned without authority. A clear management structure is a fundamental necessity alongside this. The principle is to make every manager responsible for the costs and revenues they control, even if they, in turn, delegate responsibility down the line.

Of course, if managers are going to be held responsible for the costs and revenues they control, they are going to want to be involved in the budgeting process. This is consistent with a dispersed leadership style where you want to involve managers in developing strategies for the business. Indeed, as the business grows, they should come to know more about the area they are responsible for than you. Involving managers in setting their own budgets means that the budgets should remain realistic. If budgets are to motivate staff generally, they have to 'buy into' them and believe that they are realistic and achievable. Once they accept the standards of performance against which they are to be judged, they will normally try hard to achieve them. Imposing budgets from above generally causes resentment and leads to a lack of commitment.

Finally, you will need to identify, monitor and put in place procedures to mitigate the risks you might face in achieving your financial forecasts or budgets. The processes for doing this were covered in Chapter 10. Internal risks might include the ability to achieve your sales forecast or your margin of safety. External risks – many of which might be out of your control – could include interest and exchange rate fluctuations. These risks and how you deal with them will be of particular interest to potential investors.

Having effective monitoring and control processes in place for your venture will help you manage it. They will help you delegate and control. They will help you achieve your targets. And they add value to your business.

Valuing your business

Valuing an established business can be difficult. Valuing a start-up is even more so because of the uncertainties involved and the lack of any track record on which to evaluate forecasts of

CASE insight 13.1

The English Pub (2) UK

Getty/ PhotoDisc

Using financial metrics to monitor performance

The founder of The English Pub was always hoping to establish a small chain of pubs and to sell them as a going concern to another pub chain or a brewery within ten years. Once he proved that his formula for filling the English pub throughout the day really worked (Case insight 6.1, page 177), his attention shifted to finding new, large city-centre sites. But he also realized that to sell on any pub chain he would have to prove that it was profitable and that it had good financial control – something that was notoriously difficult in a cash-handling business. He believed that rigorous, centrally applied financial controls were the key to profitable operation and a successful sell-on. One of the first things he did was appoint a Finance Director to provide the Board with in-house financial management skills.

As part of the emphasis on control, the company ensured that five key financial metrics were monitored on a regular and timely basis. The first four metrics were linked to targets for individual pub managers and tied into their bonus scheme. The fifth was one that the founder used to monitor the risks he faced.

- **Cash** – Daily checks on cash takings and banking, carried out by telephone and direct computer input to the company's bank account.
- **Sales and profit margins** – Weekly sales and profit performance measured within 16 hours of each week ending. Results were reviewed immediately by management and priorities for action identified.
- **Stocks** – Weekly stocktaking to ensure there were no stock losses and gross margin targets were attained.
- **Productivity** – Labour costs, as a percentage of sales, monitored through monthly management accounts, mailed to all affected parties no later than ten working days after each period.
- **Breakeven point and the margin of safety** – The founder believed that any growing business needs to monitor these two important metrics. He monitored this data monthly. Above his desk he kept a graph showing sales against breakeven point (i.e. the margin of safety). It made interesting reading, showing the gradual improvement in the margin of safety because of the higher margins and lower fixed costs as The English Pub concept was rolled out across new sites.

Within ten years of being set up The English Pub chain of licensed houses was sold to a brewer for an eight-figure sum!

The English Pub is a real company but the name is fictitious

Questions:

1 Why are strong financial controls important for a pub chain?
2 Why do strong financial controls add value to a business?

future income. However, if you are seeking equity investment then the investor will try to judge the value of the business before making you an offer for a proportion of it. It is therefore worthwhile trying to value the business yourself before going to an outside investor. This allows you to judge how much equity you might need to give away to raise a given investment.

So, for example, if an investor offers you $50,000 for a 20% stake, they are valuing the business at $250,000 ($50,000 ÷ 0.2). If you judge the amount of equity being demanded by an investor for a given investment to be too high, you are, in effect, putting a higher value on the business than them. (If you thought $50,000 was worth only 10%, you value the business at $500,000.) In this case you might be able to adjust your financial model to reduce the amount of equity investment you need, or to find some way of persuading them to improve the valuation they place on the company. For example, **information asymmetry** might result in investors being unaware of some information you have, and therefore placing a lower value on the business.

There are two widely used ways of valuing a business.

1 **Market value of assets** – Businesses that are asset-rich, such as farms or freehold retail premises, are often valued in this way. Tangible assets such as debtors/receivables, stocks/ inventory, equipment, fixtures and fittings and particularly property are valued at their market rate. For certain kinds of businesses this might give a higher value than the second approach, but for any business the asset value provides a minimum valuation.

2 **Multiple of profits** – Many firms, particularly those with few tangible assets, are valued on the basis of some multiple of net profit. For example, if an appropriate multiple of profits were 5, a company making $100,000 per year would be valued at $500,000. If the multiple were 20, its value would be $2 million. If you look in the financial press (e.g. *Financial Times*), every public company has its **price-earnings (PE) ratio** quoted. This is the multiple of net profits (from the previous year) that the current share price represents.

Companies can also be valued using a mix of both methods. Where there are tangible assets, such as property, these might be valued at market rates with an additional element of 'goodwill' based upon a multiple of profits.

While the PE ratio in the financial press is based on actual reported profits, start-ups only have forecast profits to work on. This is not an issue in principle because buyers of stocks and shares are interested in the future profits of the business and only use actual profits as a proxy measure. However, one factor that influences the size of the multiple is the 'quality' of earnings. The longer the firm's track record of profitable trading, the higher the multiple is likely to be. So start-ups, with no track record, tend to command a lower multiple than established firms. Other factors can increase the size of the multiple because they make the forecast of profit more credible, for example the experience of the management team or the existence of substantial pre-launch orders. However, these factors can work the other way, decreasing the multiple, for example if you are seen as too dependent on certain key employees or key customers. The higher the perceived risk, the lower the PE multiple and vice versa. Different industry sectors tend to have different multiples that reflect the risks that are perceived to exist in that sector. However, despite the risks they face, start-ups involved in disruptive innovations or new technologies can sometimes command very high multiples – or indeed have no profits on which to base a multiple – if it is believed that they may achieve substantial first-mover advantage by creating a whole new industry (for example, Facebook or Twitter). It has to be said that these valuations often prove to be unfounded.

The key question is what multiple of profits to use, despite projecting loss, or whether the business even has a value? There is no straightforward answer to this. It is all a matter of judgement. Just like the price of any product or service, it requires a willing buyer and a willing seller – and a company can be 'marketed' in the same way as any product or service. However, for a start-up:

- Risks are high.
- There is no track record.
- If the buyer wishes to sell their shares, there is no established market to sell them on (unlike for a public company).

These factors mean that multiples in single figures are currently quite normal for a start-up. However, if your venture is involved in disruptive innovation the multiple could be very much higher (and sometimes these companies are not even making a profit). Once established, with a proven track record, the multiple will improve for most businesses. And if you decide to sell the business, the multiple can be very high if a larger company perceives it as strategically important for some reason. For example, when Avis bought Zipcar in 2013 it paid $500 million – 34 times net profits of $14.6 million.

External factors that you cannot control are also important in company valuations. The 2008 recession saw private company valuations plunge as forecasts of economic activity were cut back. As economies emerged out of recession, valuations improved. Another factor is the rate of interest. High interest rates usually mean lower multiples and therefore lower valuations, since an investment in a company is competing against that market rate of interest. Interest rates are very low at the time of writing (2017) so future increases will mean that valuations should decrease. Nevertheless, the net effect is likely to be that company valuations will improve in the future. Accountants experienced in raising equity funding for start-ups can provide advice on the 'going rate' for multiples in particular sectors.

One way of dealing with the problem of early valuation – particularly for fast, high-growth businesses – is to delay valuation but set out the details of how it will be determined at some point in the future. The initial investor then receives equity based on a discount of that future valuation. This is particularly effective when equity funding is to be sought in tranches and valuation is easier at these later stages. For example, a new venture raises equity funding from an investor of $100,000 on the understanding that the percentage shareholding this purchases reflects a 50% discount on the value of the business in one year's time. At this point the investor is obliged to invest a further $200,000, based upon this valuation. If this valuation turns out to be $2 million, then the original investment buys 10% of the business ($2 million $\times$ 50% = $1 million, so the $100,000 investment buys 10% of the company's shares). The additional investment of $200,000 also buys 10% of the company's shares ($200,000 $\div$ $2 million), giving the investor 20% of the share capital for their total investment of $300,000.

Go/no-go or pivot?

Chapter 3 explained how you face a number of go/no-go decision points throughout the development of your business model (Figure 3.3). Business model development is a process that involves continually checking against the realities of your ability to meet genuine customers' needs. But is the business model you have developed financially attractive? Can you meet customer needs cost-effectively? Is this market sufficiently large to make a profit? Is the project scalable? The final element in this jigsaw puzzle is commercial viability, and your financial projections complete this picture. You have arrived at the all-important go/no-go decision point. Do you want to launch the business?

If you are still unsure you can go back and alter your business model using the New Venture Creation Framework in order to find ways that might improve your financial projections. The concept of 'pivoting' was outlined in Academic insight 4.4 as part of the lean start-up methodologies. It involves making major changes to your business model. For example you might:

- Increase market penetration (sales) by increasing the number of distribution channels you use, although this may affect the profit you make per unit sold (Chapter 6);
- Improve profitability by changing the value proposition in such a way that allows you to charge a higher price and, while projected sales volumes might be reduced, overall profitability might be increased (see Chapter 6);

- Improve cash flow by changing distribution channels (Chapter 6) or simply your terms of payment;
- Reduce your breakeven point by using different terms of employment or subcontracting production, distribution etc. (Chapters 10 and 11);
- Reduce the capital investment you need by finding partners to work with (Chapter 10);
- Raise more capital (Chapter 12).

There could be dozens of ways of changing your business model, so this process may involve multiple iterations before you are satisfied with the financial outcome. However, never forget that the ultimate test of viability rests with your customers. Does your business model deliver what customers want, at a price they are willing to pay? The reality is that while your planning may have been meticulous and you may have undertaken all the market testing possible, the only certain way of finding out is to launch the business and then monitor its progress. As Henry Ford said when he launched the first mass-produced Model T car, if he had asked people what they wanted, they'd have said 'faster horses'.

Sofa-bed Factory

The final thing for Piotr and Olek to do before they decide to go ahead with their new venture is the all-important one of preparing a set of financial forecasts. They know they would like to go into business and they know they can make and sell the sofa-beds and coordinated furniture units. The only thing left is to see whether the venture will make sufficient profits to make it worthwhile. They decide to produce forecasts for the first year only. Beyond this is too uncertain, particularly since if it were successful in that first year they would want to scale up their plans thereafter.

Table 13.A *Sales and production forecasts for sofa-beds and sofa units*

Sofa-bed Forecast:	Jan	Feb	Mar	Apr	May	Jun
Stocks b/f		160	120	75	40	40
+Production	260*	70	80	90	100	110
– Sales	−100	−110	−125	−125	−100	−100
= Stocks c/f	160	120	75	40	40	50
Sales value €	32,000	35,200	40,000	40,000	32,000	32,000

*includes October–December production of 200 units

Sofa units Forecast:						Jun
Stocks b/f						
+Production						40
– Sales						–
= Stocks c/f						40
Sales value €						
Total sales value €	32,000	35,200	40,000	40,000	32,000	32,000

Forecast sales and production

Piotr and Olek intend to establish their small manufacturing facility in Poland in September and start manufacturing in October. One hundred of these sofa-beds will be sent to the UK retailer as demonstration sofas in October and November but, by agreement, they will not be invoiced as sales until January (sales = 100 units). Piotr and Olek have started their financial forecasts from January. They expect to have produced some 200 sofa-beds by then and the remaining 100 will be held as stock against expected sales in the following month (sales = 110 units). The UK retailer has sent them an estimate of monthly sales for their first year and Piotr and Olek have factored into this a 10% increase from September to represent new distributors. They intend to start producing coordinated furniture units to complement the sofa-beds in June. One hundred units will be sent out to the UK retailer as demonstration sofas and the sales invoice for these will be sent to the retailer in September (sales = 100). Sales of these units represent estimates from the UK retailer only. Production and sales in August are low because of annual holidays. These sales and production estimates are shown in Table 13.A.

Forecast income statement and breakeven

Piotr and Olek need a range of machinery to produce their sofa-beds. They estimate that the total cost of this machinery will be €30,000 and that it will last some 10 years before needing replacement. Depreciation is therefore calculated at €3,000 per year (€3,750 over the first 15-month period). They have also found a suitable unit that can be used as a factory. The factory unit is owned by the local council and to encourage start-ups the first three months are rent-free. The annual lease cost for this is €12,000, including local taxes, or €1,000 per month.

It is the custom in the industry that the skilled workforce is paid on a piecework basis, but the founders intend to also employ two other workers in October. They will each be paid a fixed monthly wage of €1,200 (including taxes) – a total of €28,800 per year (€36,000 over the 15-month period). The two founders will pay themselves a fixed monthly wage of €2,000, starting in January. Their estimated wage bill will therefore be €24,000 each. One founder will supervise work in the factory, while the other will focus on sales and customer relations and spend much of his time in the UK, for which they allocate €20,000. They estimate that a part-time bookkeeper and secretary will cost €10,000. They think that they will be able to produce the new sofa units with the existing workforce but will probably need to recruit an extra person in the following year at the same time as improving their administrative support.

The average wholesale price for a sofa bed will be €320 and they will retail at about €900 (out of sale/discount periods). Piotr and Olek undertook a detailed costing exercise that showed that the average material costs (fabric, foam etc.) for each sofa-bed was €70 on top of the standard metal frame costing €110. The average variable factory overhead was €12 per sofa-bed (consumables, electricity etc.). Delivery was €8 per sofa-bed. Total variable costs are therefore €228 per sofa-bed. The average wholesale price for the sofa units will be €270

Jul	Aug	Sep	Oct	Nov	Dec	Total
50	90	60	55	45	25	
120	60	120	130	140	150	1,430
−80	−90	−125	−140	−160	−95	−1,350
90	60	55	45	25	80	80
25,600	28,800	40,000	44,800	51,200	30,400	432,000

Jul	Aug	Sep	Oct	Nov	Dec	Total
40	80	100	40	40	20	
40	20	40	80	90	100	410
–	–	−100	−80	−110	−70	−360
80	100	40	40	20	50	50
		27,000	21,600	29,700	18,900	97,200
25,600	28,800	67,000	66,400	80,900	49,300	529,200

(retailing at about €800). A similar costing exercise for the sofa units found total variable costs to be €176.

Based on the production estimates of 1,430 sofa-beds and 410 sofa units, the average costs of producing a sofa-bed and a sofa unit were calculated and are shown in Table 13.B. The fixed sales and administrative costs are shown in Table 13.C. Next the profit for the 15-month period was calculated and is shown in Table 13.D. Finally, Piotr and Olek calculated their breakeven point and margin of safety with the current mix of products, which are shown in Table 13.E.

Reviewing these calculations Piotr and Olek were very happy that these estimates show that they will make a profit of €24,354 over the 15-month trading period – particularly after they have each taken out €24,000. They were aware that they had not included any interest payments in these calculations. They were also aware that the margin they were getting on the sofa-beds (€92) was slightly lower than on the sofa units (€94). However, they are confident that they are in a stronger negotiating position with two products, and can push up the price of the sofa-bed, particularly as they find new customers.

Table 13.B *Average cost of sofa-beds and sofa units*

Fixed production costs (15 months):			Sofa-bed	Sofa unit
Factory overhead	– depreciation	€ 3,750		
	– factory lease	€12,000		
	– factory workers	€36,000		
	– founder (Olek)	€24,000		
	– other (contingency)	€10,000		
Total (15 months)		€85,750 ÷ (1430 + 410) units	= € 46.6* per sofa-bed	€ 46.6* per unit
Variable cost (per unit)				
Frame			€110	€70
Other materials			€ 70	€60
Direct factory costs			€ 10	€ 8
Piecework labour			€ 30	€30
Delivery			€ 8 €228 per sofa-bed	€ 8 €176 per unit
Total average cost of producing each unit			€274.6 per sofa-bed	€222.6 per unit

Rounded to nearest decimal point

Table 13.C *Fixed sales and administration costs*

Fixed sales and administration costs:		
Sales costs	– founder (Piotr)	€ 24,000
	– other sales costs	€ 20,000
Admin. costs	– office	€ 10,000
Total fixed other costs		€ 54,000

Table 13.D *Forecast income statement*

	Sofa-beds	Sofa units	Total
Sales	1,350 × €320 = €432,000	360 × €270 = €97,200	€529,200
Cost of sales	1,350 × €274.6 = €370,710	360 × €222.6 = €80,136	€450,846
Gross profit			€ 78,354 (14.8%)
Sales and administration costs			€ 54,000
Net operating profit			€ 24,354 (4.6%)

Table 13.E *Breakeven and margin of safety*

	Sofa-beds	Sofa units	Total
Total contribution	€(320 − 228) × 1350 = €124,200	€(270 − 176) × 360 = €33,840	€158,040
Average contribution margin	= 29.9%	[€158,040 ÷ €529,200]	
Breakeven point	= €467,391	[€(85,750 + 54,000) ÷ 0.299]	
Margin of safety	= 13.2% above breakeven	[(€529,200 − €467,391) ÷ €467,391) × 100]	

Forecast cash flow statement

Piotr and Olek are convinced that their sofa-beds present an attractive opportunity but they need to know how the opportunity can be financed, so they decide to prepare an initial cash flow forecast. Their estimates are based on the following assumptions:

1 Cash receipts from the retailer are lagged by 2 months behind sales, except for January when a payment for 100 sofa-beds (€32,000) will be received.
2 Piecework labour is paid monthly, in line with production (€30 for each sofa-bed and sofa unit).
3 Purchases of the frames, other materials and direct factory costs can be matched directly to production (€190 per sofa-bed and €138 per sofa unit). Payment for the pre-January production of 200 units must be paid in January (200 × €190 = €38,000). After that costs are paid two months in arrears.
4 Delivery costs (€8 each) can be matched directly to sales. These are paid two months in arrears.
5 Wages of the two labourers are paid monthly from October (€2,400 per month).
6 The founders pay themselves monthly, starting in January (€4,000 per month).
7 Factory lease costs and rates are paid monthly, starting in January (€1,000 per month).
8 Machinery purchased in September for €30,000 will be paid for in the following November.
9 The factory overhead contingency of €10,000 will be released in four tranches of €2,500 in March, June, September and December.
10 The sales costs comprise €4,000 for a brochure, paid in February, €4,000 for website development, paid in March and €12,000 for travel expenses for Piotr (€1,000 per month).
11 Administrative costs comprise €6,000 for a part-time bookkeeper (€500 per month) and €4,000 for postage, stationery etc. paid in four tranches of €1,000 in January, April, July and October.

Piotr and Olek produced an initial forecast showing only operating cash flows. Not surprisingly, this showed a cash flow deficit of over €100,000 during the year, with the deficit mounting quickly in the first six months as the machinery was purchased and the display stock produced. They decided to alter the forecast to show the €50,000 they had available and the matched funding of €50,000 that the bank was willing to offer, phased as needed. This is shown in Table 13.F on the next page. They thought that the occasional small cash flow deficits could be met through an overdraft arrangement.

Forecast balance sheet

Piotr and Olek were now is a position to draw up a balance sheet as at the end of the first 15 months of trading. They realized that they had assets and liabilities that comprise:

- Machinery: Cost − depreciation (€30,000 − €3,750) = €26,250.
- Debtors/receivables for November December sales: (255 sofa beds @ €320) + (180 sofa units @ €270) = €130,200.
- Stock/inventory (excl. delivery): (80 sofa beds @ €266.6) + (50 sofa units @ €214.6) = €32,058.
- Creditors/payables for the purchase of materials: (290 sofa beds @ €190) + (190 sofa units @ €138) = €81,320.
- Creditors/payables for deliveries: (255 sofa beds @ €8) + (180 sofa units @ €8) = €3,480.

The balance sheet is shown in Table 13.G.

Table 13.G *Forecast balance sheet*

Fixed assets		€ 26,250
Stock/Inventory	(from sales/production forecast)	€ 32,058
Rounding error*		€ 6
Debtors/Receivables	(November + December sales)	€130,200
Cash	(from cash flow forecast)	€ 20,640
Total assets		€209,154
Creditors	(€81,320 + €3,480)	€ 84,800
Loan capital		€ 50,000
Share capital		€ 50,000
Profit for the year		€ 24,354
Capital and liabilities		€209,154

*Rounding error due to average unit production cost calculation in Table 13.C

Table 13.F *Forecast cash flow statement (15 months)*

Receipts €'000	Oct	Nov	Dec	1 Jan	2 Feb	3 Mar	4 Apr	5 May	6 Jun	7 Jul	8 Aug	9 Sep	10 Oct	11 Nov	12 Dec	Total
Sales				32.0			35.2	40.0	40.0	32.0	32.0	25.6	28.8	67.0	66.4	399.0
Capital	5.0	15.0	5.0	10.0	5.0	10.0										50.0
Loans	5.0	15.0	5.0	10.0	5.0	10.0										50.0
Total receipts	10.0	30.0	10.0	52.0	10.0	20.0	35.2	40.0	40.0	32.0	32.0	25.6	28.8	67.0	66.4	499.0
Payments																
Materials				38.0		11.4	13.3	15.2	17.1	19.0	26.42	28.32	14.6	28.32	35.74	246.96
Wages (pwk)		3.0	3.0	1.8	2.1	2.4	2.7	3.0	4.5	4.8	2.4	4.8	6.3	6.9	7.5	55.2
Wages (fxd)	2.4	2.4	2.4	2.4	2.4	2.4	2.4	2.4	2.4	2.4	2.4	2.4	2.4	2.4	2.4	36.0
Sales/Mktg				1.0	5.0	5.0	1.0	1.0	1.0	1.0	1.0	1.0	1.0	1.0	1.0	20.0
Admin				1.5	0.5	0.5	1.5	0.5	0.5	1.5	0.5	0.5	1.5	0.5	0.5	10.0
Asset purchases		30.0														30.0
Lease				1.0	1.0	1.0	1.0	1.0	1.0	1.0	1.0	1.0	1.0	1.0	1.0	12.0
Delivery						0.8	0.88	1.0	1.0	0.8	0.8	0.64	0.72	1.8	1.76	10.2
Contingency						2.5			2.5			2.5			2.5	10.0
Interest																
Founders				4.0	4.0	4.0	4.0	4.0	4.0	4.0	4.0	4.0	4.0	4.0	4.0	48.0
Total payments	2.4	35.4	5.4	52.7	15.0	29.4	26.08	27.3	33.1	33.5	36.82	43.96	30.48	44.72	55.1	478.36
Net cash flow	7.6	-5.4	4.6	2.3	-5.0	-10.0	8.42	11.9	6.0	-2.5	-6.52	-19.56	-2.28	21.08	10.0	20.64
Cash B/F		7.6	2.2	6.8	9.1	4.1	-5.9	2.52	14.42	20.42	17.92	11.4	-8.16	-10.44	10.64	
Cash C/F	7.6	2.2	6.8	9.1	4.1	-5.9	2.52	14.42	20.42	17.92	11.4	-8.16	-10.44	10.64	20.64	

Evaluating the forecast

Piotr produced the following analysis of their first-year performance using ratio analysis.

$$\text{Return to shareholders} = \frac{\text{Net profit}}{\text{Shareholders' funds}} = \frac{€24,354}{€74,354} = 32.8\%$$

$$\text{Operating profit margin} = \frac{\text{Operating profit}}{\text{Turnover}} = \frac{€24,354}{€529,200} = 4.6\%$$

$$\text{Gross profit margin} = \frac{\text{Gross profit}}{\text{Turnover}} = \frac{€78,454}{€529,200} = 14.8\%$$

$$\text{Total asset turnover} = \frac{\text{Turnover}}{\text{Total assets}} = \frac{€529,200}{€209,148} = 2.5$$

$$\text{Debtor turnover} = \frac{\text{Turnover}}{\text{Debtors (receivables)}} = \frac{€529,200}{€130,200} = 4.1$$

$$\text{Stock turnover} = \frac{\text{Turnover}}{\text{Stock (inventory)}} = \frac{€529,200}{€32,058} = 16.5$$

$$\text{Current ratio} = \frac{\text{Current assets}}{\text{Current liabilities}} = \frac{€182,904}{€84,800} = 2.2$$

$$\text{Quick ratio} = \frac{\text{Current assets, excl. stock}}{\text{Current liabilities}} = \frac{€150,846}{€84,800} = 1.8$$

$$\text{Gearing} = \frac{\text{All loans + overdraft}}{\text{Shareholders' funds}} = \frac{€50,000}{€74,354} = 67.2\%$$

iStock.com/muzafferopuz

Questions:

1 Evaluate the financial performance of Sofa-bed Factory.
2 Do you agree with the method of financing this business? What other options might they have had?
3 From the information given in the case, use the Framework Worksheet or PowerPoint slide to complete as many elements as you can of the New Venture Creation Framework.
4 Prepare a business plan for the company.
5 Would you go ahead with this business opportunity? Explain.

Visit www.macmillanihe.com/burns-nvc-2e to download the Framework Worksheet and PowerPoint slide.

Summary and action points

13.1 Forecast your income statement: For a new venture to survive and grow it needs to be financially viable. This means it needs to be profitable and efficient, sufficiently liquid to pay its bills, while minimizing the risk that it faces. Start by forecasting your income or profit (sales or turnover minus total costs). This shows the growth in all the assets owned by a company, not just cash.

13.2 Estimate your breakeven point: Estimate your breakeven point. This measures the operating risk of the business caused by the amount of fixed costs it faces. The lower the breakeven point the lower the risk. To achieve this you should attempt to keep your fixed costs as low as possible and your contribution margin as high as possible.

13.3 Forecast your cash flow statement: Profit is not the same as cash flow. You can be profitable but illiquid, without cash to pay your bills. Forecast your monthly cash flow for your first year.

13.4 Forecast your balance sheet: The balance sheet is a snapshot at a point of time that shows the assets the business has and where the funds for these assets came from. You now have enough information to forecast your balance sheet at the end of the first year.

13.5 Evaluate your forecast performance: Once you have your forecast of financial performance, evaluate it using ratio analysis. Ratios can be compared to industry norms or used to assess trends over time.

13.6 Identify, monitor and mitigate your risks: The risks you face in achieving your financial forecasts are likely to be of great interest to potential investors. You must identify the risks that might affect your ability to achieve your financial forecasts. Evaluate the probability of the risks materializing, decide on the risk indicators to be monitored and then put in place procedures to mitigate them.

13.7 Decide on your financing: In the light of your cash flow forecast, decide on the funding you need and where this might come from.

13.8 Develop performance metrics and create milestones: Decide upon the financial and other metrics that measure your performance and put in place the controls you need to monitor your performance against them. Remember you need systems that allow you to monitor your performance against the financial and operating forecasts you have made. Based upon your financial and operating metrics, prepare a list of milestones against which to judge the success of your business.

13.9 Evaluate your business idea: The best business models–ones that generate the highest profits with the lowest risk–have certain identifiable characteristics. You should check to see how many of these characteristics your business idea has.

13.10 Review your objectives: You must decide whether or not your business is viable and whether to proceed with it. You must be happy that the business model you have developed is realistic and achievable and whether the forecast of financial performance meets the objectives you have set yourself. If they do not then either they or your business plan must change if you are to proceed with this business idea.

Workbook exercises

> The New Venture Creation Workbook contains a digital version of these exercises that can be modified as your business model develops and builds into a draft business plan. It can be downloaded from www.macmillanihe.com/burns-nvc-2e.

13.1: Forecast your income statement

1 Estimate the sales volume and value (turnover) in each month of your first year. Check that there is sufficient demand and that your targets are achievable, within the operating and cost parameters of the business. Jot down the assumptions on which this is based.

Sales	1	2	3	4	5	6	7	8	9	10	11	12	Total
Vol.													
£/$													

🖉 Assumptions

2 Review Exercise 12.2. For any fixed assets you need to purchase, estimate their useful life and calculate the annual straight-line depreciation charge [(initial cost − final residual value) ÷ useful life]. This goes on the income statement as a depreciation charge and reduces the total cost or value of the assets in the balance sheet. For more information, see page 413.

🖉 Assets and cost	🖉 Useful life (years)	🖉 Annual straight-line depreciation (£/$)
Total cost:		Depreciation charge:

3 Use the template to draw up a forecast income statement for your first year of operation. Repeat the process for your second and third years. Note: when you see Σ, you need to add up the total cost for that section.

Note: when you see Σ, you need to work out the total cost for that section.

Forecast income statement

SALES/TURNOVER

Cost of sales:

Materials

Wages

Factory overheads $\Sigma =$

GROSS PROFIT   **A**
(Sales/turnover – Cost of sales)

Operating expenses:

Selling and marketing costs

Distribution costs

Administrative and general costs

Other costs

Depreciation charge $\Sigma =$ **B**

OPERATING INCOME OR PROFIT   **A – B**
(Gross profit – Operating expenses)

Interest income/expense:

Interest income

Less: Interest expense   =   **C**

NET INCOME OR PROFIT   **A – B +/– C**
(Operating income +/– Interest income/expense)

13.2: Estimate your breakeven point

Using the template on the next page and the figures from the previous exercise:

1 Re-analyse your costs into variable and fixed.
2 Calculate your contribution margin (B ÷ A) × 100.
3 Calculate your breakeven point, before interest [C ÷ (B ÷ A)].
4 Calculate your margin of safety, before interest [(A – [C ÷ (B ÷ A)] ÷ A) × 100.
5 Repeat the process for your second and third years.

Estimated breakeven point

SALES/TURNOVER [　　　　　] A

Variable costs:

Materials [　　　　　]

...................(other) [　　　　　]

...................(other) [　　　　　] $\Sigma =$ [　　　　　]

[　　　　　] B

CONTRIBUTION
(Sales/turnover – Variable costs)

Fixed costs:

Selling and marketing costs [　　　　　]

Administrative and general costs [　　　　　]

Depreciation charge [　　　　　]

...................(other) [　　　　　]

...................(other) [　　　　　] $\Sigma =$ [　　　　　] C

[　　　　　] B – C

OPERATING INCOME OR PROFIT
(Contribution – Fixed costs)

Interest income/expense:

Interest income [　　　　　]

Less: Interest expense [　　　　　] = [　　　　　] D

NET INCOME OR PROFIT
(Operating income +/– Interest income/expense) [　　　　　] B – C +/– D

Contribution margin [　　　　　] % $(B \div A) \times 100$

Breakeven point (before interest) [　　　　　] $[C \div (B \div A)]$

Margin of safety (before interest) [　　　　　] % $[(A - [C \div (B \div A)] \div A] \times 100$

13.3: Forecast your cash flow statement

1 Use the table on the left to draw up a forecast cash flow statement for your first year of operation based upon the information you have used for Exercise 12.1. Make sure the forecast reflects:

- The salary or drawings you will take out.
- The total cost of the assets you need to purchase, but not their depreciation charge (Exercise 13.1).
- The capital you will introduce and the external finance you decided on in Exercise 12.2.

Cash flow forecast

Receipts	1	2	3	4	5	6	7	8	9	10	11	12	Total
Sales													
Capital													
Loans													
Total receipts (A)													

Payments													
Materials													
Wages													
Marketing													
Admin. and general													

(continued)

Asset purchases											
…other											
…other											
…other											
Interest											
Drawings											
Total payments (B)											
Net cash flow (A – B)											
Cash brought forward (B/F)											
Cash carried forward (C/F)											

2 Review the monthly net cash flow and cash balance C/F. How do you intend to finance any monthly deficit (cash balance C/F)? If this cannot be financed by bank overdraft consider raising more capital and redraft this statement.

13.4: Forecast your balance sheet

1 Using the template below and on the next page, draw up a forecast balance sheet at the end of your first year by listing your assets and liabilities:

- Remember to insert the capital you will introduce yourself and any loan or equity finance you need to raise. This should be reflected in the previous exercise.
- The total fixed assets cost should be reduced by the depreciation charge [Exercise 13.1(2)] to show their net 'value'.
- The 'profit for current year' figure should be your 'net income or profit' shown in both Exercises 13.1 and 13.2.
- Profits from any previous year's trading should be shown as accumulated profits brought forward.
- The 'cash' or 'overdraft' figure should be your final 'cash C/F' figure shown in the forecast cash flow statement [Exercise 13.3]. If your cash C/F figure is positive, record it as cash. If it is negative, record it as an overdraft.

2 Repeat the process for your second and third years.

Forecast balance sheet

Fixed assets:

Cost

Less: Depreciation $\Sigma =$ _____ **A**

Current assets:

Stock

Debtors

Cash

Total   **B**

Less: Creditors due within one year:

Overdraft

Trade creditors

Other liabilities

Total   **C**

Net current assets   **B – C**

NET ASSETS   **A + B – C**

Less: Long-term loans   **D**

                                                            A + B – C – D

Accumulated profits brought forward from previous years:

Share capital

_____ **E**

Profit brought forward

_____

Profit for current year

_____ $\Sigma =$ _____ **F**

_____ **E + F**

13.5: Evaluate your forecast performance

1 Calculate your forecast performance ratios based on the previous exercises and complete the table.

2 Evaluate your performance.

	Year 1	Year 2	Year 3
Performance			
Return to shareholders: $\dfrac{\text{Net profit}}{\text{Shareholders' funds (total assets} - \text{total liabilities)}}$			
Return on total assets: $\dfrac{\text{Operating profit}}{\text{Shareholders' funds} + \text{loan capital (total assets} - \text{current liabilities)}}$			
Profitability			
Operating profit margin: $\dfrac{\text{Operating profit}}{\text{Sales/turnover}}$			
Gross profit margin: $\dfrac{\text{Gross profit}}{\text{Sales/turnover}}$			
Contribution margin: $\dfrac{\text{Total contribution}}{\text{Sales/turnover}}$			
Asset management			
Total asset turnover: $\dfrac{\text{Sales/turnover}}{\text{Total assets}}$			
Debtor/receivables turnover: $\dfrac{\text{Sales/turnover}}{\text{Debtors/receivables}}$			

	Year 1	Year 2	Year 3
Stock/inventory turnover: $\dfrac{\text{Sales/turnover}}{\text{Stock/inventory}}$			
Liquidity			
Current ratio: $\dfrac{\text{Current assets}}{\text{Current liability}}$			
Quick ratio: Current assets, excluding: $\dfrac{\text{Stock/inventory}}{\text{Current liabilities}}$			
Risk			
Gearing/leverage: $\dfrac{\text{All loans + overdraft}}{\text{Shareholders' funds}}$			
Interest cover: $\dfrac{\text{Operating profit}}{\text{Interest}}$			
Margin of safety: $\dfrac{\text{Sales/turnover – breakeven point}}{\text{Sales/turnover}}$			

13.6: Identify, monitor and mitigate your risks

Using the table below:

1 List the risks that you face in achieving these forecasts (internal and external).
2 Calculate a risk index for each risk (impact × probability of occurrence). Identify your highest risk key activities.
3 Decide on which risks are controllable (and which are not) and decide on the key risk indicators that need to be monitored.
4 List the actions taken to mitigate them.

Risks	Risk impact (1–3)	Risk probability (1–3)	Risk Index (1–9)	Controllable (Y/N)	Key risk indicators	Actions taken to monitor and mitigate risk

13.7: Decide on your financing

Reflecting on your cash flow forecast and the liquidity and risk ratios in Exercise 13.6, decide on the funding you need and where this might come from. Make sure you add a small contingency. Ensure this funding is reflected in all your financial forecasts.

List the things you need to do to secure this finance and the timescales involved.

13.8: Develop performance metrics and create milestones

1 List the metrics that monitor your financial performance and the procedures you need to put in place to ensure good financial control, highlighting those that are critical.

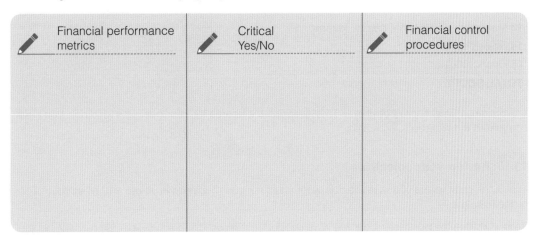

Financial performance metrics	Critical Yes/No	Financial control procedures

2 Consolidate these metrics with the metrics for the critical success factors of your operations plan [Exercise 10.4 (3)] and create a list of milestones for the business and the related metrics to measure the success of your business.

Final milestones for the business	Metrics

13.9: Evaluate your business idea

Refer back to Exercise 4.3, where you were asked to evaluate your business idea using 15 characteristics outlined in the chapter. Now you have had the opportunity to research and develop your idea, repeat the exercise. Evaluate its attractiveness on a scale of 1 (not attractive) to 5 (very attractive). Total up the score.

Criteria	✏ Score
1 Identified market need or gap	
2 No or few existing competitors	
3 Growing market	
4 Clearly identified customers and viable business model	
5 Low funding requirements	
6 Sustainable	
7 High profit margins	
8 Effective communications strategy	
9 Not easily copied	
10 Identifiable risks that can be monitored and mitigated	
11 Low fixed costs	
12 Controllable	
13 Management skills that can be leveraged	
14 Scalability	
15 Financeable	
TOTAL SCORE	

The maximum total score possible is 75. Reflect on the scores for your business idea now you have completed the Workbook exercises.

13.10: Review your objectives

This is the point where you must decide whether or not your business is viable and whether to proceed with it.

Review whether the business model you have developed is realistic and achievable. Review whether the financial results meet the objectives you set yourself in Exercise 1.2. Decide whether to proceed or not. List any elements of the plan that you want to change.

Visit www.macmillanihe.com/burns-nvc-2e for chapter quizzes and other resources.

Phase 3   Launch

Chapter 14 Preparing, using and validating the business plan

Visit
www.macmillanihe.com/
burns-nvc-2e to watch a video
interview with Paul Burns.

14 Preparing, using and validating the business plan

Contents

- Business model or business plan?
- Purpose of a business plan
- Structure and content of a business plan
- Tips for a business plan
- Using your plan to obtain finance
- Presenting your case for finance
- Validating the plan
- Undertaking a strategic review
- Harvesting your investment
- Summary and action points
- Workbook exercises

Learning outcomes

When you have read this chapter and undertaken the related exercises you will be able to:

- Undertake a strategic review
- Explain the purpose, structure and content of a business plan
- Draw up a business plan for your new venture
- Recognize the information needs of bankers and equity investors
- Be able to present the plan effectively

Academic insights 📓

14.1 Do formal business plans really help?

14.2 Entrepreneurial strategy development

Case insights 💼

14.1 wiGroup

14.2 audioBoom

14.3 Moonpig

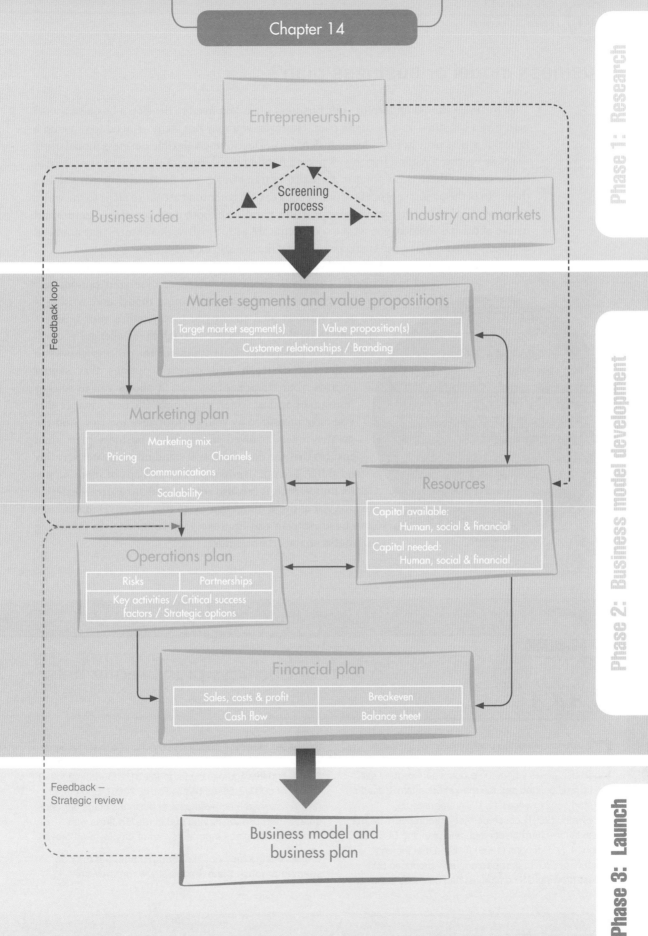

Business model or business plan?

Your **business model** underpins your **business plan**. You need to develop a business model before you can draw up a business plan. However, you may not want or need to draw up a formal business plan (see Academic insight 14.1). Developing a flexible business model using the New Venture Creation framework takes a fraction of the time it takes to write up a formal business plan. There is no point in formalizing frameworks and documenting plans unless they help in the planning process or are needed to help communicate those plans to the wider group of stakeholders in your venture. It is all a question of both the scale of the venture and nature of the stakeholders you wish to communicate with. Small-scale ventures may not need detailed or formal plans, but many providers of finance still expect them.

Nevertheless, while you may not always need to write a formal business plan you will still need to strategize – to think about the future, analyse your options and develop strategies. Developing your business model and writing it down as a business plan allows you to crystallize your business idea and to think systematically through the challenges you will face before you have to deal with them. The process allows you to develop strategies and strategic options that should improve your chances of success. It allows you to set key milestones against which to monitor the performance that you have measured by your performance metrics. And the greater detail involved in writing a business plan often ensures that the document will stand up to greater scrutiny and things are not overlooked. But perhaps of more immediate importance, it can also act as a vehicle to attract external finance. All of these things can mean that the development of a sound business plan can improve your confidence in launching into what is an uncertain venture.

https://steveblank.com/category/customer-development-manifesto/page/3 8 April 2010 (steveblank.com/category/customer-development-manifesto/page/3)

Entrepreneurs treat a business plan, once written as a final collection of facts. Once completed you don't often hear about people rewriting their plan. Instead it is treated as the culmination of everything they know and believe. It's static. In contrast, a business model is designed to be rapidly changed to reflect what you find outside the building in talking to customers. It's dynamic.

Steve Blank serial entrepreneur

ACADEMIC insight 14.1

Do formal business plans really help?

Evidence about the positive effect of business plans can be mixed, particularly for early-stage businesses where the product/service may still not be well defined and the market uncertain. Based on her study of 27 successful US entrepreneurs, Sarasvathy (2001) observed that entrepreneurs do not like extensive, formal research and planning (Academic insight 4.1). Timmons (1999) claimed that the vast majority of *INC*. magazine's annually produced 500 fastest-growing US companies had business plans at the outset. However, another study claimed that this figure was only 28% of a 'sample' of these companies (Bhidé, 2000), and this figure is closer to the 31% found in another survey of 600 US SMEs (Wells Fargo, 2006). Burke et al. (2010) asserted that the impact of business plans depends on their purpose, observing that in the UK firms with formal, written plans reported superior employment growth.

Entrepreneurs may not like formal plans, but they do seem to produce them, especially when they are needed to obtain finance. As Bygrave et al. (2007) argued:

unless a would-be entrepreneur needs to raise substantial start-up capital from institutional investors or business angels, there is no compelling reason to write a detailed business plan before opening a new business.

Start-ups may not 'need' detailed or formal plans, but many providers of finance expect them. They are needed to convince others to invest in the business – like a sales brochure. And as the venture grows and the need to communicate with more people, such as investors, suppliers, partners and prospective employees, increases then the need to formalize and document the process increases.

Bhidé, A. (2000) *The Origin and Evolution of New Businesses*, Oxford: Oxford University Press.

Burke, A., Fraser, S. and Greene, F.J. (2010) 'Multiple Effects of Business Plans on New Ventures', *Journal of Management Studies*, 47(3).

Bygrave, W.D., Lange, J.E., Mollow, A., Pearlmutter, M. and Singh, S. (2007) 'Pre-Start-up Formal Business Plans and Post-Start-up Performance: A Study of 116 New Ventures', *Venture Capital*, 9(4).

Sarasvathy, S.D. (2001) 'Causation and Effectuation: Toward a Theoretical Shift from Economic Inevitability to Entrepreneurial Contingency', *Academy of Management Review*, 26(2).

Timmons, J.A. (1999) *New Venture Creation: Entrepreneurship for the 21st Century*, Singapore: McGraw-Hill International.

Wells Fargo (2006) 'How Much Money Does it Take to Start a Business?', Wells Fargo/Gallup Small Business Index, August 15.

Purpose of a business plan

The business plan is a formal written document. It should set out what your venture seeks to achieve and how it will achieve it. There are no set rules that can be used to create a 'perfect' business plan. Nevertheless the business plan Workbook exercises at the end of each chapter should provide you with all the information you need to write a formal plan. While the next section sets out a general pro forma plan, each plan is particular to its business and will be different to others. Plans also differ, depending on the audience they are aimed at and the purpose they will be used for. Sections might be expanded or contracted and it may well be appropriate to omit or add complete sections to suit different circumstances. For a social enterprise, great attention needs to be spent on how it will achieve its social as well as commercial objectives. Because each business is unique, every business plan will be different, at least in the detail it contains. Nevertheless any business plan needs to be succinct, professional and well presented.

The complexity and length of the plan will vary with the scale of the start-up. What is more, this may vary with the purpose for which the plan was written. If it is simply for you, to help you organize the venture systematically, then it might be brief and functional, almost an 'aide-memoire' or summary plan, running to a few pages. In these circumstances the discipline of using the New Venture Creation Framework to develop a plan is probably of more value than the written plan. However, the written plan can still provide an invaluable set of milestones against which progress can be checked. And if assumptions and circumstances change, then you may have to start altering your plans. A business plan should be sufficiently detailed to give you direction but should never be so rigid as to blind you to new opportunities or threats.

Material Pleasures Sunday Telegraph 12 July 2009

Write a business plan – and get advice on doing it properly ... I needed a business plan when applying for funding and it's the most useful thing I've done.

Julie Spurgeon founder

23 February 2016 (steveblank.com/category/business-model-versus-business-plan)

Unless you have tested the assumptions in your business model first, outside the building, your business plan is just creative writing.

Steve Blank serial entrepreneur

If the plan is intended for external use, for example to help you raise finance, then it will need to be thorough, better presented and, inevitably, longer. After all, it is a document that should be 'selling' your venture to a financier, supplier or business partner. A full business plan of this sort will typically run to about 20 pages, with financial projections and other details going into the appendices. If it is intended to help you raise finance, the more money you are trying to raise, the more thorough it will need to be. Indeed, if you are trying to raise equity finance it will need to be extremely thorough and well presented. Although you might keep to approximately the same length of plan, the appendices could easily run to 30 pages and be placed in a separate document. Having said that, keep the plan as succinct as possible. Do not pad it out unnecessarily.

As we shall see later in this chapter, bankers are interested in slightly different things from equity investors, and plans can be tailored to provide them with the particular information they need. Most equity investors prefer to see a business plan (or at least the executive summary) before they meet the entrepreneur behind it and commit more time and effort. Some plans for large-scale start-ups can take the form of professionally produced brochures. However, there is always a fine balance between including sufficient detail in the plan to convince the reader that you know what you are talking about, but not so much that they lose interest. Indeed, too much focus on the operations may convince equity investors that you are product- rather than market-focused – and that will definitely turn them off.

If you are developing a completely new product or service, your business plan will need to explain what stage the development is at, and what further development is needed to take it to market. Basic ideas are unlikely to find funding. Even when there is a prototype, finding finance might prove difficult. The earlier the stage in its development, the more difficult this will prove. There is no guarantee the product will work and there is no guarantee that there will be customers for it. Even if it works, will you be able to stop competitors copying it?

Structure and content of a business plan

The typical structure and content of a full business plan intended for external use is shown in Table 14.1. This is a general pro forma and, as already stated, it may be appropriate to omit or add complete sections to suit different circumstances. The contents of each section may also need to be adapted to suit your venture. For example, location is a vital part of a business plan for a retail start-up, web functionality for an internet start-up. Your plan should read like a professional business report – succinct and to the point, and full of vital information. It must be convincing. A guide to content follows. The indicative page extent (in brackets) is based upon a typical 20-page plan – anything more should go into the appendices.

Table 14.1 Business plan structure

- Cover
- Table of contents
- Executive summary
- Business details
- Industry and market analysis
- Customers and value proposition
- Marketing strategy
- Operations plan

- Management team and company structure
- Resources
- Financing
- Financial projections
- Risks and strategic options
- Key milestones
- Appendices

Cover – The cover should include the business name and contact details. You should consider whether the plan needs to be marked 'confidential'.

Table of contents – This is a list of sections and subsections, with page numbers.

Executive summary (1–2 pages) – If you are seeking external finance, this is probably the most important section of the plan. Many equity investors will only read the full plan if they find the summary attractive. It should only be written after the full plan is complete, and then it should be written with the reader and purpose of the plan in mind. If it is to be used to attract funding, it should state what is requested from the lender or investor and how they will benefit by providing the funds. It must be a summary of the plan – not an introduction. It should highlight the nature of your product/service, target customers, value proposition and competitive advantage. It should appeal to the reader by highlighting the distinctive capabilities and potential of the business, including the financial return. If the plan is written to attract an equity investor it should state what deal you are offering; for example, '20% of the business in exchange for £100,000'. Above all, the executive summary must be focused and succinct – no more than one or two pages long.

Business details (1–2 pages) – This section covers basic information such as business name, address, legal form and ownership. It should include:

- A description of your product/service;
- Your mission and vision statement;
- Your aims and objectives.

   If this is an existing business, you should include a brief business history.

Industry and market analysis (2–3 pages) – This section provides background information on your industry sector and the market segments within it. It should take the form of a narrative informed by academic models such as a PESTEL analysis and Porter's Five Forces. You should review your competitors and their strengths and weaknesses. The more you know about an industry and market, and the competitors you face, the more confidence your readers will have in your ability to compete within it. This section should include:

- Industry size, growth, structure (macro and micro/local level);
- Industry and market trends (macro and micro/local level);
- Market segments and reasons for target market(s) selection;
- Buyer behaviour across segments;
- Competitor analysis (strengths and weaknesses);
- For an existing business – market share.

> In a well-thought-out business plan, it should be made clear that a company is attacking a big enough market and that there is an experienced team.

In most industries there are some key success factors that industry players have to have mastered in order to compete. These need to be highlighted, but judgement is required about what is important for your particular venture.

Customers and value proposition (2–3 pages) – This is the section where you outline your target market segment(s) and the value proposition(s) for your product/service. It is essential that your 'unique selling proposition(s)' are clearly and simply articulated. In doing this you should highlight your differential advantage over competitors. The more points of difference and the stronger and more sustainable these differences, the better. This is where you also set out your sales targets. If you have firm orders for the product or service, be sure to mention this.

Marketing strategy (3–4 pages) – This section provides the details about how you propose to achieve those sales targets – not only the details of your marketing mix but also the details of your sales tactics (how the product or service will actually be sold). As well as the launch strategy, this should also highlight the growth potential through market and product development, your competitive reaction and strategy for establishing your brand. It should include:

- Price, promotions, distribution etc.;
- Launch strategy;
- Sales tactics;
- Brand development;
- Competitive reaction;
- Product and market development;
- Growth potential and scale-up plans.

Investors are always particularly interested in pricing strategy because this is a prime determinant of the profitability of the business.

Getty Images/sturti

Operations plan (2–3 pages) – This section outlines how your business will be run and how your product/service will be produced. What goes into the operations plan varies depending on the nature of the venture. However, what is important is that the key activities for your venture are highlighted. The operations plan must convince the reader that you understand the operation of the business – how to do whatever needs to be done to deliver your product/service. So, issues of business control, if critical to the business, need to be covered. Also, the prospect of scalability – should the business prove to be even more successful than planned – can be addressed in this section. What are your strategic options? The content of this section is difficult to predict but might include:

- Key operating activities (e.g. manufacturing processes, business model etc.);
- Partnerships;
- Business controls;
- IP issues;
- Scalability.

Management team and company structure (1–3 pages) – This section outlines all the people involved in the venture – details of their background and experience – as well as the organizational structure you are adopting. A new venture team with an established track

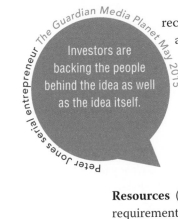

Investors are backing the people behind the idea as well as the idea itself.

The Guardian Media Planet May 2015
Peter Jones serial entrepreneur

record in the industry or with relevant experience will certainly add credibility to any start-up. Remember that investors ultimately invest in people, not products. An experienced board of directors can achieve the same result. Brief CVs can go in the appendices. For larger start-ups, an organization chart can go in this section. This section should include:

* Key people, their functions and background;
* Business organization or structure;
* Directors, advisors and other key partners;
* Skills gaps and plans for filling them.

Resources (1–2 pages) – This section describes the firm's facilities, equipment and staff requirements. It should include:

* Premises and facilities;
* Machinery and equipment;
* Staff.

Financing (1–2 pages) – This section highlights the finance you need to launch your business. External funders will expect you to contribute some capital. Lenders will be interested in the risks they face and the security they can obtain. Equity investors will be interested in the overall return they might make and how this might be realized. This section should include:

* Founders' contribution;
* Loan and/or equity finance requirements;
* Gearing/leverage;
* Timescale and exit routes for equity investors.

Financial projections (1-page summary, plus detailed appendices) – Typically financial projections for three years are expected by funders, with a monthly cash flow forecast for the first year. A very small-scale start-up might only provide financial projections for the first year. Five-year forecasts might be expected for larger projects where significant commercialization risks have not been resolved. You should provide a one-page financial summary and place the detailed projections in the appendices. Financial details going into your appendices should be as long as it takes to provide all the information required. These should include:

* Income projections;
* Cash flow projections;
* Balance sheet projections;
* Key ratios;
* The assumptions on which your financial projections are based, particularly the basis for your sales projections.

Risks, critical success factors and strategic options (1 page) – This section should identify the key risks you face and explain how they will be monitored and mitigated. You need to identify your critical success factors and the strategic options you face should these key risks materialize. Strategic options are valuable because circumstances can, and do, change. They give you flexibility in a changing environment. This section should include:

Setting some milestones for you and your team to work towards will keep you motivated and driven.

The Guardian Media Planet May 2015
Richard Branson founder Virgin Group

* Identified risks;
* Risk monitoring and mitigation;
* Critical success factors;
* Strategic options.

> I see some [business plans] where the CV is so vague as to be useless. Give me dates, give me details. Be honest about things that have gone wrong. Talk about the setbacks and mistakes and explain how you fixed them.

> What is the right plan? It's the one that helps you identify what you need to ensure success. It's the one that rallies your employees around a few common goals – and motivates them to achieve them. It's the one that involves your customers' goals and suppliers' goals and brings them all together in a unified focus.

Key milestones (1 page) – These milestones, often incorporating critical success factors and the metrics that measure them, highlight the progress needed to launch and grow the business. They might include prototype completion, formalization of partnerships, obtaining finance, securing of key customers, meeting sales or profit targets and so on. This section gives an overview of the sequence and timing of important events.

Appendices – Any information that is vital, but might impede the flow of the plan, should go into the appendix. One key piece of information is the assumptions upon which the financial projections are based, in particular the sales projections. These need to be made explicit and you can expect an investor to scrutinize them closely. This section might include:

- Detailed financial projections;
- Financial assumptions – start-up costs, basis for sales projections, fixed/variable costs, profit margins;
- Background information (CVs) on key people;
- Location information (maps, layouts etc.);
- Operations information (Gantt charts etc.);
- Details of market research;
- Details of IP protection;
- Website screenshots;
- For an existing business – historic financial statements, brochures etc.

> The UK government provides information on writing a business plan, examples for different sectors and a free pro forma download on: www.gov. uk/write-business-plan. This information can also be found in the *Guide to UK Sources of Help, Advice, Information and Funding* on the companion website: www.macmillanihe.com/burns-nvc-2e. An additional guide for Australian readers, produced by Dr Russell Manfield, is also provided.

Tips for a business plan

If used for external purposes, the business plan must convince the reader that you understand the industry, market and business you want to establish. It must convince them of the viability of the business – that you have a good product/service and value proposition, and that you know how to combat the competition. It must enhance your credibility and make them trust your judgement. They need to believe that you can turn your business idea into reality. So, when you have written the plan, get friends or relatives to read it and give you honest feedback.

Here are five very practical 'does' and 'don'ts' to watch out for when preparing your business plan:

1 Keep the plan as short and simple as possible. Do not pad it out. The plan should be sufficiently long to cover the project adequately but short enough to maintain interest. To do this you need to be able to prioritize and focus on the important things for your business. If you over-complicate your plan you risk losing that focus and the interest of the reader.

2 Keep the plan as realistic as possible. Are sales targets, costs, milestone deadlines and so on realistic? If your claims are unrealistic you will never gain the trust of lenders and investors. It is better to under-estimate and over-deliver than vice versa.

3 Make the plan clear, specific and unambiguous. Are market segments clearly identified? Are objectives concrete and measurable? Are targets and deadlines clear? Lack of clarity is often taken to indicate a lack of knowledge or willingness to be committed.

4 Check your spelling, grammar, punctuation and, most important of all, financial accuracy. Errors will damage your credibility and, if noticed at a presentation, can put you off your stride. Computers have grammar and spelling checks – use them. Using a spreadsheet package for your cash flow forecast can ensure arithmetic accuracy.

5 If you are not confident about putting the financial projections together yourself, seek professional advice, but be sure you understand how they were arrived at.

Using your plan to obtain finance

Your initial cash flow forecasts show you how much finance you need and Chapter 12 should have helped you decide on the appropriate type of external finance. External funders will expect you to have contributed some capital yourself. They will expect to see a business plan and, while both lenders and investors might look at the same elements of information from the plan, each places a different weight upon these elements. However, the reality is that both banks and equity investors ultimately invest in individuals, not in businesses or plans. The plan is just one way, albeit a very important one, of communicating with them. It must therefore reinforce the perceptions the banker or investor has of you and your team.

Before letting anybody see your business plan you need to consider whether they should be asked to sign a non-disclosure agreement, which binds the reader to confidentiality. If you are then invited to meet with the lender or investor, you need to be clear whether you are expected to present your plan or simply discuss it. If you are asked to present the plan, you need to know how long you have and then prepare a professional presentation. However, first it is worth recalling what banks and investors are looking for.

Banks

Banks are in the business of lending money; in that respect they are just like any other supplier of a commodity – and there are many banks you can approach. The thing to remember about banks is that they are not in the risk business. They are looking to obtain a certain rate of interest over a specified period of time and to see their capital repaid. They do not share in the extra profits a firm might make, so they do not expect to lose money if there are problems. What is more, the manager stands to lose a lot if he lends to a business that subsequently fails. The plan therefore needs to demonstrate how the interest on the loan can be paid, even in the worst possible set of circumstances, and how the capital can be repaid on the due date. In this respect the cash flow forecast is something that the bank manager will be particularly interested in. Where a long-term loan for product development or capital expenditure is being sought and there is little prospect of loan repayment in the short term, the plan must emphasize the cash-generating capacity of the business and take a perspective longer than one year. In addition, banks are also particularly interested in the breakeven and gearing ratios. In an ideal world, they would like both of these to be as low as possible.

Bank managers represent a set of values and practices that are alien to many entrepreneurs. They are employees, not independent professionals, and lend only within very strict, centrally dictated, guidelines. They often talk 'a different language' and are subject to numerous rules and regulations that an entrepreneur would probably find very tedious. Since they trade in money, they often cannot make decisions on their own without getting approval from 'up the line'. In these circumstances the business plan is an essential weapon in helping them get authorization for a loan. Any manager will only be able to lend within the bank's own policies, at acceptable levels of risk and with adequate security to cover the loan. However, each of these three constraints requires the exercise of judgement and can therefore be influenced, not only through the style and content of the business plan but also your credibility and track record.

Bank managers are trained to examine business plans critically. So expect to be questioned. They will ask about the assumptions that it is based on. They will ask about risks. They will always ask questions about some of the claims in the plan, so you must be able to back them up. Avoid any tendency to generalize in order to disguise a weakness in your knowledge. Your plan should seek to identify and then reassure the bank manager about the risks the business faces. They tend to dislike plans that they see as over-ambitious since they do not share in the success and see this as an unnecessary risk.

However good the business plan, bankers are still likely to ask for a personal guarantee After all, if they don't ask, they certainly won't get it. And it does make any loan more secure from their perspective. But be prepared to haggle and shop around. This is just a sales negotiation like any other and the banker is trying to 'sell' you a loan, albeit at a certain price and with certain conditions.

Equity investors

Prospective equity investors will normally expect to see a business plan before meeting you. And, while most entrepreneurs will submit business plans to more than one investor for consideration, most investors are inundated with business plans seeking finance. Fewer than 1 in 20 will ever lead to a face-to-face meeting. To a large extent, therefore, the decision whether to proceed beyond an initial reading of the plan will depend crucially on its quality. The business plan is the first, and often the best, chance that an entrepreneur has to impress prospective investors with the quality of their investment proposal. A good executive summary is, therefore, vital – many investors do not read beyond it.

Because of this and the fact that equity investors share in both the risks and returns from the business, business plans tend to be longer. They are more comprehensive, offering greater detail, and are better presented. As we saw in Chapter 12, investors want to know about the return they will make and when they will make it (the exit route). They need to be convinced that the founder and their team are as good as the business idea and they are the right people to trust an investment with. This requires a careful balance between making the proposal sufficiently attractive, on the one hand, while realistically addressing the many risks inherent in the proposal, in particular how rapid growth will be handled. To do this the plan needs to emphasize the strengths of the business, particularly compared to the competition. Behind all plans there are people, and investors, like bank managers, need to be convinced that you and the venture team can deliver what you are promising. It is often said that the single most important element in the investment decision is the credibility and quality of the firm's management.

> Ajith Jayawickrema business angel *Sunday Times* 2 June 2013
>
> I always back the jockeys because they can ride any horse. That's fundamental. I think 'If things get difficult, will they still be there?'

The most difficult aspect of any deal is deciding on the split of equity between the various partners. The simple answer is that there is no set of rules and the final result will depend on the attractiveness of the proposal and the negotiating skills of the individuals concerned. Investors will not normally want control of the business (over 50% of the shareholding) as this might affect your motivation, but they will want a sufficiently large say to influence important decisions. Key managers on your team might also want a share in the business, so you need to think through the final shareholding you will be left with. You will not want to surrender control, so you need to consider how much equity you want, not just at this point, but also when the equity investor seeks to sell their shares. You also need to think about who might buy their shares and whether they are an equity partner that you are happy with.

You need to find out how the investor operates. Some investors prefer a 'hands-on' approach to managing their investment whereby they have a non-executive director on the board, visit the firm monthly and keep in regular phone contact. Business angels can bring considerable experience and a network of contacts to the business, so do your homework on the background of your angel. Other, mainly institutional, investors have a more 'hands-off' approach, preferring not to interfere once they have invested, perhaps meeting once a year to review the progress of the business.

As explained in Chapter 12, business angels and venture capitalists expect an annualized return of 30–50%, usually as a capital gain. They also normally expect to realize their investment within five years, so work out in advance what you think their share of the business will then be worth and the return they will make. They will expect a seat on the board of directors and many angels will expect close involvement in the management of the business. You need to find out how your investor wants to realize their investment – dividend or capital gain. You should not be afraid to ask about the timescale they have for realizing their investment.

They may also have views about who they might sell their stake to. This may be an opportunity for you to increase your stake in the business by buying out the investor, as happened with Mark Constantine and Lush (Case insight 6.7, page 196). Alternatively, it may be an opportunity for you to dilute your share of the business or exit completely by encouraging a merger with, or a buy-out by, another company.

Finally, whereas a bank loan will probably take weeks to arrange, an equity investment will take months. It will involve numerous meetings, interviews and presentations. The investors, or their accountants, will undertake their own investigations into the business (called due diligence) and the production of the legal documentation will involve lengthy, detailed work. You will need professional advice.

Presenting your case for finance

At some point you might be asked to 'present' your business plan to financiers. Part of the reason for this will be to support and elaborate on details contained in the business plan but part of it will be to allow the potential backer to form judgements about you, and possibly your venture team. They will be looking for motivation, enthusiasm and integrity but, most of all, the managerial ability to make the plan actually happen.

'Presentations' can take a number of forms. A bank might just expect an informal meeting to discuss the business plan, perhaps coming back to discuss issues that might arise. Investors are likely to require a number of meetings. The first meeting might involve a 15–20-minute formal presentation of the plan, using PowerPoint or Prezi, followed by questions which could easily go on for twice as long. If this is successful you will be invited back for a second meeting to sort out the details about an investment.

The first thing to do is to follow instructions. If you are asked to make a 15-minute presentation, keep it to 15 minutes – and that means about 10 slides. Make sure a computer and projector are available. If they are not, you need to make your own arrangements – a large tablet computer can be useful if there is only one investor because it breaks down the 'us and them' feel of using a projector. Remember that what you really want is to engage in a discussion – to start forming a relationship – and you need to work to break down barriers. It is always good to bring in samples or examples of the product, service website etc., so that the audience can see and/or touch it. You need to grab their attention.

Slides should be clear and uncluttered, focusing on the main points of the topic and inviting the audience to engage and ask questions because the topic interests them. Beware of boredom by PowerPoint! Keep the slides you present to a minimum but prepare more slides than you use in the presentation so that you can go back to them when appropriate questions are asked. Remember to 'brand' every slide with your business name and ensure that they look professional. Highlights to be covered on individual slides include:

> You've got to convince your investors that you won't give up. You've got to create a vision for the backers.
>
> Martyn Dawes founder Coffee Nation *Sunday Times* 23 May 2004

- **Why you are there**: Outline the financing you are seeking and the deal you are offering. Remember that in doing this you are placing a value on the business. You will inevitably be asked what you intend to spend the money on.
- **The product/service offering and the value proposition to customers**: Explain and/or demonstrate your product or service, the problem customers currently have and how this will solve it for them.
- **Target market and opportunity**: Describe your target market segments and their characteristics (better still, name names) and explain how you will get to them (from your

communications plan). If you already have orders for the product or service this will add enormously to your credibility.

- **The competition and your competitive advantage**: They will expect you to name the names of your competitors and their product strengths and weaknesses, as well as why your product is better than theirs. They will want to know how you will react to competitors when they respond. If you have any IP, this is the point to highlight it.

- **Marketing strategy**: This is where you can sketch out how you will achieve your sales targets over the planning period. They will be interested in your sales processes and your distribution channels. Primary market research information can add to the credibility of your plans.

- **Your management team** (including board of directors): What is important is your background and experience. If you have skills gaps, explain how they will be filled.

- **Financial highlights**: These are highlights, not financial details – sales and profit, when profitability is achieved, capital investment, cash flow implications and breakeven. They will ask about the details, in particular how your sales projections and costs were arrived at, so you might want to prepare some additional slides to go back to. Remember, they will be thinking about what their share of this will be and how it might convert into business valuation.

If you have or are looking to find prospective partners then this will need to be highlighted in the presentation. If there are particular issues of control related to your industry, these may also need to be covered, albeit briefly.

The presentation is an opportunity to demonstrate your personal qualities and start to develop a relationship. First impressions are important, but an in-depth knowledge of the key areas in the business plan will go a long way towards generating the confidence that is needed. There are ways of enhancing a presentation. It is important to rehearse it thoroughly. Always stress the market and the firm's competitive advantage, rather than the product's features. Stress the competencies of the management team. In terms of style, it is important to demonstrate the product and, in Western culture, to make frequent eye-to-eye contact. You should manage the presentation with respect to any co-presenters. Finally, never try to weasel your way out of questions to which you do not know the answers. The best advice is to say you do not know but will get back with the answer in a few days.

An experienced investor once admitted that, while discussions with the entrepreneur might centre on the business plan, the final decision whether or not to invest was really the result of 'gut feel' – a personal 'chemistry' between them and the entrepreneur. At the end of the day, that chemistry must lay the foundation for a long-term relationship based, as always, on trust and respect.

Validating the plan

The first year of a start-up has been called the validation phase – when you actually prove that your business model works. No matter how good your planning it is unlikely that your business model and the plans associated with it will be 100% accurate, particularly those for a disruptive innovation. You should be monitoring the performance of the business against the financial projections you prepared, paying particular attention to your critical performance metrics. If there are discrepancies from your projections – and there will be – it is important than you are alerted to them early and you understand the underlying causes. If discrepancies are large it may be important to take early action, and, if you have major external investors, talk to them about the problems and the remedial action you are taking. Some start-ups will face serious survival problems that may cause them to rethink their entire business model as a result of this review – the process of pivoting. Twitter, Instagram and WhatsApp all radically changed their start-up business model when they found it was not working in practice. Hopefully for your business it is not the case.

For businesses that survive their start-up phase, growth can present further dangers and, without a clear understanding of what has made the business successful so far (and what has not), there is no sound foundation for the move forward. It is important that at some point after you have launched the business you take time to reflect and see which elements of your business model and plan are working, which are not and, most importantly, which can be improved. You need to be able to gauge both customer and competitor reaction to your business. New market opportunities or competitive threats may have emerged. The needs of customers or the market might have changed since start-up or the reaction of competitors might not have been accurately predicted.

Some entrepreneurs understand what they are doing, what works and what does not, as they do it, sometimes almost instinctively. Others are more reflective and need time to analyse the situation. Getting the right people and putting the right systems in place can take time, so operational problems can complicate the analysis. Once you understand the basis for your successful survival – so far – you can start to plan your growth with more certainty. So you need to undertake a **strategic review** early in the life of your new venture.

> No plan survives first contact with customers.
>
> Steve Blank serial entrepreneur 8 April 2010 (steveblank.com/category/customer-development-manifesto/page/3)

> Any plan will collide with reality and something else will emerge. People have to adjust their models to the market, the competition and events.
>
> Luke Johnson Chairman Risk Capital Partners Sunday Times 20 April 2014

Undertaking a strategic review

The process of strategic review is shown in Figure 14.1 on page 458. Central to the strategic review is strategic analysis – the process of developing strategy by reviewing the business and the environment in which it operates to determine the optimum 'fit'. This starts by looking again at your vision and mission. The question is whether they are still realistic and appropriate. These often change and evolve as you gain more knowledge about your commercial environment. Are there new, more attractive, opportunities? Have the values and beliefs on which the business is based, changed? Has the mission changed, perhaps because of new opportunities? The strategic analysis might therefore modify both your vision and mission (shown as feedback loops). However its main function is to generate strategic options and to inform strategy formulation. This then feeds into strategy implementation and entrepreneurial decision making.

Chapter 10 described the way entrepreneurs' approach to managing risk revolved around their approach to strategy and decision making and their use of knowledge and information – a form of contingency thinking. They may have a strong vision and strategic intent but they do not necessarily know how they will achieve it and are constantly 'strategizing' and developing strategic options as new information emerges. As a result entrepreneurial strategy development is often seen as 'emergent' – reactive rather than

> Have a clear strategy and don't get side tracked by activities that don't enable you to achieve this. Review your strategy constantly to ensure you are meeting market demands.
>
> Elizabeth Gooch founder eg solutions Launch Lab 13 January 2009 (www.launchlab.co.uk)

SOUTH AFRICA

© wiGroup

Mobile · Transacting · Simplified

Pivoting

Bevan DuCasse was keen to find a mobile technology-based business opportunity as he was tired of having to pull out his credit card to pay for goods and services. Africa was fast becoming the leader in mobile transacting so he thought that anything that built on this opportunity would be a winner. He launched wiWallet in 2007, a mobile transaction payment app that linked to credit cards. It was the first of its kind in Africa. However, on its own it proved to be unsuccessful, partly because of competition from existing banks and retailers and partly because it was targeting the wrong customers – the app users. At the time there were very few apps and there were no app stores.

Bevan was joined in the business by Basie Kok in 2008 and they decided to 'pivot' the business model to one offering an integrated range of enhanced benefits to a range of different customers. The company changed its name to wiGroup and developed two core offerings:

1 wiCode – an integrated platform that allows merchants to accept payments via their point of sale devices from mobile phones linked to a wide range of credit or payment providers (including mobile-based payment options such as Vodacom's M-Pesa or MTN's Mobile Money)

2 wiBlox – a card-free service that allows companies to offer customers a range of mobile-based benefits including loyalty points, rewards, vouchers, coupons and gift programmes. At the same time companies receive data on customer transactions. While many large retailers have card-based loyalty and rewards programmes, wiGroup's technology allows for this to all be integrated into one app offering payments, loyalty points redemption, coupons and vouchers.

These offerings were then targeted at four different types of customers:

- App users – who now usually download the app for free and can then use it for payments and to obtain and monitor their rewards or points status;
- Retailers and merchants – facilitating payment, enabling them to track purchases and offer promotions;
- Product manufacturers, particularly those of fast-moving consumer goods (FMCG) – allowing them also to offer promotions and track purchases;
- Banks and other credit providers – enhancing their customer service.

This change in direction meant the company had to work collaboratively with point of sale (POS) providers to integrate their systems. It also developed a small reader that merchants could plug into their POS terminal to accept payments and transactions from apps. The change also meant that the company had to sell the benefits of the platform to a range of different customers. Key to success was gaining wide market coverage in South Africa as quickly as possible. wiGroup's mobile transacting network has grown to over 71,000 POS points in South Africa and Namibia. It is used by five of the largest retail chains (including Shoprite, Checkers, KFC and Pick n Pay), over ten hospitality groups, 50-plus FMCG brands and eight mobile money issuers. wiGroup now describes itself as simplifying and improving the way the world transacts and enables everything from SnapScan to Discovery Vitality Rewards to integrate with banks and retailers. wiGroup is looking to expand into the rest of Africa and Europe, focusing on Nigeria, France, Netherlands and the UK.

See how wiCode and wiBlox work:
www.youtube.com/watch?v=RDHc53k5ooc

See an interview with Bevan DuCasse:
www.youtube.com/watch?v=OpJXumYS9HA&t=59s

Visit the website: www.wigroupinternational.com

Question:

Why was the original business model for wiGroup unsuccessful, and why has the revised business model worked?

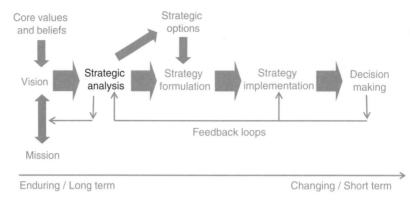

Figure 14.1 *Strategy review framework*

> Writing a business plan was a vital first step that helped me focus on the task ahead and apply a professional approach. But after a few months things had changed so much that those initial projections looked laughably naïve … What they don't tell you is that this doesn't really matter. Ditching the old plan and writing a new one just shows how adaptable you are in the face of all those 'unforeseen challenges'.
>
> *Lara Kelly co-creator of Hum Flowerpots The Guardian 12 May 2015*

> We are constantly reviewing our business plan. It is a fluid, live document … A business plan is not set in stone. It shouldn't become something that you are measured or beaten up with … A plan makes you think about what you are doing and what your goals are. If things happen along the way that will help you reach those goals faster then the business plan should change.
>
> *Alex Reilley founder Loungers Sunday Times 20 April 2014*

deliberate and planned (see Academic insight 14.2). This is a contingent approach that uses information to modify strategies to reflect the reality of uncertain situations and to mitigate risk (shown by the feedback loops in Figure 14.1).

The strategic frameworks developed in this book will help you do that by giving your thoughts structure and focus. And the New Venture Creation Framework can easily be adapted to apply to a changing environment or new product/service launches. The use of these strategic frameworks is important, particularly when engaged in distributed strategizing. If you are trying to replicate strategizing across an organization, a set of commonly known and understood techniques and processes can help – not least because they generate a common language and mechanism for communication. They help you to make the right decisions consistently. Strategic frameworks replicate good practice. They provide the link from judgement through experience to learning. They ought to be logical and common-sense. They are not in the nature of a scientific discovery. They are, to quote a colleague, 'a glimpse of the blindingly obvious' – something you knew all along but were never quite able to express in that simple way. In that sense they help organize and develop what might otherwise be a disjointed and unsystematic process.

The process of strategic analysis starts with the classic SWOT analysis of the business covered in Chapter 3, which should identify the strengths and weaknesses of the current business model and strategies as well as the opportunities and threats that it faces. The whole process of strategic analysis is an art rather than a science and there is no prescriptive approach. However, we have already explained many of the tools that can help you undertake the analysis. These are summarized in Table 14.2.

Chapter 4 explained how you can explore the effect of changes within the New Venture Creation Framework using the Framework Worksheet or the PowerPoint version with its simulated sticky notes available on the companion website, www.macmillanihe.com/burns-nvc-2e (see Figure 4.3). This allows you to explore alternatives in a structured way relatively quickly.

Table 14.2 Tools for a SWOT analysis

Internal appraisal (strengths, weaknesses)	External appraisal (opportunities, threats)
• Financial ratio analysis and benchmarking (Chapter 13) • Value chain analysis (Chapter 2) • Life cycle analysis (Chapters 3 and 8) • Product portfolio analysis (Chapter 8) • Business models (Chapter 4)	• PESTEL analysis and other idea-generating techniques about the future (Chapters 2 and 3) • Market research (Chapter 3) • Porter's Five Forces analysis (Chapter 3) • Business models (Chapter 4)

ACADEMIC insight 14.2

Entrepreneurial strategy development

This book has given you a framework for developing strategy in a systematic way and encouraged you to underpin this with a business model and plan. But do successful entrepreneurs approach strategy development in this way? Many entrepreneurs seem to develop strategy instinctively and intuitively – often they call it 'gut feel'. For them strategies evolve on an informal, step-by-step basis. If one step works then the next is taken. At the same time they will keep as many options open as possible, because they realize that the outcome of any action is very uncertain. It was Mintzberg (1978) who first coined the phrase '**emergent**' strategy development to describe the case where: 'the strategy-making process is characterized by reactive solutions to existing problems … The adaptive organization makes its decisions in incremental, serial steps.' He contrasted this with the more systematic approach which he called 'deliberate'. And there is nothing wrong with strategy that is emergent, incremental and adaptive. Burns (2013) observes that it is an approach that resonates with complexity theory, which attempts to describe how to navigate complex, unpredictable systems that are affected by multiple independent actions – a good description for today's turbulent, interconnected global market place.

However, in a study of growing firms, McCarthy and Leavy (2000) showed that strategy development was both deliberate and emergent; changing from emergent to deliberate as the firm went through recurrent crises followed by periods of consolidation (Greiner's model in Academic insight 11.1). These crises force the entrepreneur to change their preconceptions and 'unlearn' bad habits or routines ahead of learning new ones (Cope, 2005). Therefore, rather than having only one style of strategy development, entrepreneurs would seem to adopt both, depending on circumstances. In this way the well-documented process of growth to crisis to consolidation parallels a process of emergent to deliberate and back to emergent strategy formulation, shown in Figure 14.2.

Figure 14.2 Strategy formulation cycle

Burns, P. (2013) *Corporate Entrepreneurship: Innovation and Strategy in Large Organizations*, Basingstoke: Palgrave Macmillan.

Cope, J. (2005) 'Toward a Dynamic Learning Perspective of Entrepreneurship', *Entrepreneurship Theory and Practice*, 29(4).

McCarthy, B. and Leavy, B. (2000) 'Strategy Formation in Irish SMEs: A Phase Model of Process', *British Academy of Management Annual Conference*, Edinburgh.

Mintzberg, H. (1978) 'Patterns in Strategy Formation', *Management Science*.

CASE insight 14.2

Pivoting

audioBoom is the audio equivalent of Netflix. The business was launched in 2009 in the UK and has almost four million listeners. It is also quoted on the London Stock Exchange after a reverse takeover of One Delta, a shell company listed on AIM (Alternative Investment Market), in 2014. Later the same year the company raised £8 million in a share placing with a number of blue-chip institutional investors, valuing it at over £73 million.

The reason audioBoom has attracted so much attention is that so many analysts believe it has tremendous potential for future growth, particularly outside the UK in markets like the USA, Australia and India. audioBoom's strategy and business model have changed a number of times since its launch.

© Stockdisc Royalty Free Photos

Stage 1: Amateur users were allowed to record, post and share audio clips – spoken word, not music – for free. Because there was no music, audioBoom did not have to pay performance royalties. This phase attracted many celebrity users and generated a loyal listening. The problem was that audioBoom had not yet worked out how to generate income.

Stage 2: This was to persuade professional organizations to make audio content such as news, reviews and interviews available on the site. By 2014 audioBoom had developed some 2,000 commercial partners such as the BBC, Sky Sports, talkSport, Premier League and many newspapers and magazines. At the same time it started developing a new business model that would allow it to generate income. However, to enable this to happen it also had to develop a new software platform and much of the financial investment was used for this.

Stage 3: The next stage, in late 2014, was to relaunch, allowing for content embeds on the user's own website, Twitter, Facebook or Tumblr feed. It allowed users to create their own personalized feeds by downloading content that interested them. Content could range across sport, news, financial markets and entertainment. Users could select the content they wished to receive and this could be downloaded automatically at times they selected – a system called 'content curation'. In this way a sports fan could download up-to-date selected content and listen to it as the news breaks or store it to listen to on the way to work. At the same time, the original idea of allowing users to post their own audio clips via mobile devices was made easier. Just as YouTube does not pay for content, audioBoom does not pay for most audio clips and generates income by selling and inserting advertising before, during and after a clip.

AudioBoom is now the leading podcasting and on-demand audio platform for hosting, distributing and monetizing content, hosting thousands of podcasts from around the world from organizations such as Associated Press, BBC and Red FM. It has over 60 million listens per month. Content can now be shared via iTunes, iHeartRadio, Google Play, Spotify, Stitcher, Facebook and Twitter as well as users' own websites and mobile apps. The company is still based in London, where most of its users remain, but it has offices in Melbourne, Mumbai and New York.

Visit the website: audioboom.com

Question:

What lessons do you learn from audioBoom about changing your business model?

Harvesting your investment

It may sound premature to talk about harvesting your investment in a business you have not yet launched but, if it is successful the opportunity to do so will present itself quicker than you think. As you progress up the funding ladder outlined in Chapter 12, you may decide to sell off part of your equity in the business to outsiders. Indeed you may decide to sell the business completely sooner than you expect. You may come to realize that you are better at starting up than running a business and want to sell on the business as soon as it is successful. You may want to go on to set up another company, as Stellios Haji-Ionnou did when he sold easyJet to set up other 'easy' companies. And harvesting your investment can happen earlier than you might expect. Research by Nesta (National Endowment for Science, Technology and the Arts) showed that in 2008 the average life cycle of a technology start-up from its first round of funding to exit was only six years – and this had actually increased by 18 months since 2005. But not all entrepreneurs want to leave the business quickly. Increasing numbers want to take money out when the firm gets its second or third round of equity funding, only exiting some years later. They want to share in the success of the firm as it grows, without taking capital out and thus endangering its growth by relinquishing some ownership and even control.

If your business has grown to the point where it has a stock market quotation then there is a ready market for your shares. However, if you sell up completely or relinquish operational control the share price is likely to drop. If you have not reached this point and want to sell up then the most attractive option is probably to find a trade buyer – a competitor that understands the industry. They are likely to place a higher value on the business than others because they can see ways of 'adding value' through the purchase, perhaps by synergy. This is particularly the case with technology start-ups, where the smaller business offers innovation and the bigger company offers resources to take the innovation to a mass, global market much more quickly than the smaller business might be able to. In many cases the big company might be willing to pay cash, so you can walk away from the firm on the day of sale. However, if you have other equity investors such as business angels or venture capitalists it is probable that they will have to agree to the sale. Indeed they are likely to be able to help with it. Of course the business must be able to demonstrate success, usually in the form of a good financial track record and it must be able to function effectively without you. That means it must have good control systems and a good management team.

Another option may be a management buy-out or buy-in. For buy-outs, it depends on the intentions of your managers. Management buy-ins are more difficult to identify but some accountants keep confidential registers of managers searching for firms to buy into.

Finding a buyer, valuing the business (see Chapter 13) and negotiating its sale are a daunting series of tasks that really should not be undertaken without professional advice and help. Many larger firms of accountants can help find buyers, just as they can help find companies to purchase, and they can act as a confidential 'front' in the search process. They are also likely to take a more objective view on company valuation than the entrepreneur and are essential in sorting out the detail of the deal, including the inevitable warranties and indemnities that will be requested by the purchaser. Finally there is the important consideration of taxation, where planning can considerably increase the money actually pocketed by the entrepreneur.

CASE insight 14.3

Moonpig 🇬🇧 UK

Harvesting your investment

In 2011 Nick Jenkins sold Moonpig, the personalized greetings card business he had started 12 years earlier, for £120 million to the French online photo album business Photobox. He started the business with £160,000 of his own money, but had attracted other private investors including a neighbour and two friends of friends who had experience of greetings cards. When he sold the business he still owned 34% himself.

> *When you have investors they want an exit. Floating the business did not make sense. It just wasn't big enough.*

Nick had prepared well in advance for the sell-off. He had employed an experienced managing director four years earlier and had gradually handed over the reins to him. Nick's father was a director at the engineering and building firm Alfred McAlpine. Nick studied Russian at Birmingham University before getting jobs working in Russia at the time the Soviet Union collapsed. It was working here where he made the money to start up Moonpig, but he came up with the idea while doing a MBA at Cranfield. While doing the course he worked on four other business ideas: growing exotic mushrooms, running company gyms, running internet incubators, teaching English to Japanese businessmen online, but eventually decided on Moonpig. Moonpig allows you to select a greetings card and write a personalized message on it, all online. The physical card is delivered to you within 24 hours.

> *I used to buy cards, Tipp-Ex out the caption and write my own – I just thought if I could use the internet to do that, I could make a better product.*

It also proved to be a unique product, with no competition so no price pressure and high barriers to market entry once established. When he sold the company it claimed 90% of the British online card market and made profits of £11 million on a turnover of £32 million with just 100 employees. But starting a business that sold personalized physical cards seemed quite a risk in 1999, when most competitors thought e-cards would be what customers

moonpig.com
© Moonpig

wanted. Nick's MBA taught him the important things needed to lead a business.

> *My job is just to keep the business on track, the right people doing the right jobs, and the strategy sound ... It's a fun environment. I'm a firm believer that the culture of a company comes from the top. You can have an HR department saying 'we have a collaborative culture', but if the guy at the top is a total arse, it's not going to happen ... I'm a firm believer in creating enough spare time to get a bit bored to think up new things. If you're fire-fighting you don't do that.*

Sunday Times 31 July 2011

Questions:

1   Why would a larger company want to purchase a smaller one in the same industry?
2   Why might they be willing to pay a premium to purchase it?
3   If you were to sell on your business, after how many years would this be and what would you need to do to prepare for it?

Summary and action points

14.1 Summarize your business model: Summarize your business model using the *New Venture Creation Framework*.

14.2 Write your business plan: A business plan describes what your new venture seeks to achieve and how it will do this. It can be a brief document used for internal purposes or a longer one used for external purposes, particularly to raise finance. Decide whether you need to write a formal business plan and who it will be for.

14.3 Pitch your business idea: Making a short 'pitch' of your business idea is a good way of practising for a more formal presentation of your business plan. It forces you to decide on the most important elements of the plan.

14.4 Present your business plan: A business plan presentation needs to be just as good as the plan itself – well-executed and focusing on the highlights. You need to tailor your presentation to the audience and their interests. You are trying to engage with them and invite them to enter into a discussion about your venture. You are also trying to convince them of your credibility.

14.5 Remember that you need to undertake regular strategic reviews.

Workbook exercises

The New Venture Creation Workbook contains a digital version of these exercises that can be modified as your business model develops and builds into a draft business plan. It can be downloaded from www.macmillanihe.com/burns-nvc-2e.

14.1: Summarize your business model

Use the Framework Worksheet or the PowerPoint slide on the companion website to summarize the key elements of your business model. The table below tells you which Workbook exercises may be relevant to each element of your business model.

Business model	Relevant exercises
Market segment(s) and value proposition(s)	5.3; 5.5
Marketing plan	6.1; 7.4; 8.3; 10.6
Operations plan	9.1; 10.2; 10.4; 10.5; 13.6; 13.8
Resources	9.2; 11.3; 11.4; 12.1; 12.2; 13.7
Financial plan	13.1; 13.2; 13.3; 13.4; 13.5

14.2: Write your business plan

If you need to write a formal business plan, decide its purpose and who you are writing it for. Using the format in Table 14.1, write your business plan. The website contains a pro forma business plan based on this format. The Workbook exercises at the end of each chapter should provide you with all the information you need. The guide below shows which exercises are relevant to each section of the business plan. If you have downloaded, completed and saved the Workbook exercises for each chapter, you will be able to cut and paste relevant exercises into the appropriate sections of the business plan. However, remember that the business plan is a formal business document that needs to be succinct and professional, so these exercises will need to be edited – summarized or expanded, as appropriate – to produce your formal business plan.

Business plan section	Relevant exercises
Business details	5.1; 5.4; 5.5; 9.2
Industry and market analysis	3.1; 3.2; 3.3; 6.3
Customers and value proposition	5.3; 5.5
Marketing strategy	6.1; 7.4; 8.3; 10.6
Operations plan	9.1; 10.1; 10.2; 13.8
Management team and company structure	9.2; 11.3; 11.4
Resources	11.3; 12.1; 12.2
Financing	12.2; 13.7
Financial projections	13.1; 13.2; 13.3; 13.4; 13.5
Risks, critical success factors and strategic options	10.4; 10.5; 13.6
Milestones	13.8

14.3: Pitch your business idea

An 'elevator pitch' is a two-minute presentation of your business idea to a potential financier or partner, so-called because of the short time you might be confined in an elevator with them. It must be extremely succinct and convincing – designed to get the financier to enquire further about the idea, perhaps inviting you to present your full business plan.

Using the executive summary in your business plan, prepare a two-minute 'elevator pitch' for your business proposal. If you are working in a group do this individually and then compare pitches.

Your pitch should follow the framework below and, if you need it, you should use only one PowerPoint slide. You will find the lessons you learned from your selling skills exercise (7.6) relevant.

Elevator pitch framework

- What problem your business idea solves – making clear the target market and value proposition

- Your competition and why you are better

- The profit you will make and the deal that is on offer to the financier

14.4: Present your business plan

Building on your experience from the previous exercise, prepare a ten-minute presentation of your business plan. If you are working in a group, allocate sections of the plan for individuals to present. Your presentation should follow the framework below and you should use no more than eight PowerPoint slides.

Business plan presentation framework

- Your target market and value proposition – what problem is solved

- Your competition and why you are better

- An outline of your marketing strategy

- The risks you face, your critical success factors and strategic options

- Your management team – why you are able to exploit this idea

- Financial highlights for your business (not details)

 Presentation notes

Visit www.macmillanihe.com/burns-nvc-2e for chapter quizzes and other resources.

Glossary

Term	Definition	Page
Active waiting	The strategy of waiting until the demand for a new product or service is proved.	236
Affordable loss	The maximum loss you are willing to accept should the venture fail.	109, 307
Agency theory	Identifies the mechanisms and costs that the principal has to put in place to ensure that the agent conforms to a legal agreement.	383
Analogy	Connections between apparently unrelated things.	61
Attribute analysis	The features of a product/service are examined to see if they might be altered to provide the same or improved benefits to customers.	62
Authentic leaders	Leaders who follow their real values and beliefs – their internal compass.	341
Balance sheet	A snapshot at a point of time that shows the assets of a business and where the funds to purchase them came from.	404, 412
Bankruptcy	When you are unable to pay your debts and a court order is obtained by creditors to have your affairs placed in the hands of an official receiver.	285
Batch production	Where there is sufficient volume of production to justify organizing production in the most efficient and effective way.	304
Bootstrapping	Using resources that you do not own.	14
Brainstorming	A group activity that generates as many ideas as possible without criticism.	56
Breakeven point	Fixed costs divided by contribution margin, expressed in $/£ of turnover.	383, 404, 408
Business angels	Private equity investors.	387
Business imperative	The most important **key activities**. They may become **critical success factors**.	119
Business model	A plan for how a business competes, uses its resources, structures its relationships, communicates with customers, creates value and generates profits.	93, 108, 111, 444
Business Model Canvas	A generic business model that provides a pictorial structure to aid understanding and development of business models.	113
Business plan	A formal document setting out the business model for an organization.	444
C Corporation	US form of limited liability company that is subject to double taxation at both the corporate and shareholder level.	274

Term	Definition	Page
Capital	Normally refers to **financial capital** but can also refer to **social** and **human capital**.	14
Cash flow	Total cash receipts minus total cash payments, in any period.	248, 404, 411
Channels of distribution	The route your product or service takes to get to market – who you sell through.	179
Charitable incorporated organization (CIO)	An incorporated organization that is set up for charitable purposes and registered with the Charity Commission.	276
Charitable social enterprise	An enterprise set up wholly for charitable purposes that benefits the public and is registered with Companies House and the Charity Commission.	275
Civic entrepreneur	An entrepreneur in a civic organization.	9
Cognitive processes	The beliefs, assumptions and attitudes that staff hold in common and take for granted.	351
Collateral	The assets pledged against the possible default on a loan.	376
Commercialization risk	The unique risk associated with developing a new product and ensuring customer acceptance.	313
Community benefit society (BenComs)	An incorporated industrial and provident society – a legal entity set up with social objectives, which conducts business for the benefit of their community.	275
Community interest company (CIC)	A limited liability company with restrictions on its operations and profit distribution. Not a charity.	275
Company voluntary arrangement (CVA)	A legal arrangement for a limited liability company that is fundamentally profitable but is struggling to pay its debts whereby it continues to trade but, with their agreement, is given protection from its creditors for a period of time.	287
Compartmentalizing risk	Setting up each operation as a separate legal entity.	315
Competitive advantage	The advantage a firm has over its competitors, allowing it to generate higher sales or profit margins and/or retain more customers than its competitors.	37, 116, 120
Conglomerate	A diversified company with interests in a range of different industries.	253
Consolidated market	A market where there are a few, large competitors, usually in a mature or declining industry.	75
Consumer	The person or organization consuming or using a product.	181
Contingency theory	A theory that emphasizes that the appropriate leadership style is contingent upon the group, task and circumstances.	356
Contingency thinking	An entrepreneurial approach to managing risk which revolves around the entrepreneur's approach to strategy and decision making and their use of knowledge and information.	306
Continuous production	Where volumes have increased to such an extent that an inflexible, dedicated process is in place to run all day, every day, with a minimum of shutdowns.	305

Term	Definition	Page
Contract of employment	A legal contract that lays down the terms and conditions of employment.	336
Contribution margin	Contribution per unit divided by sales price, or total contribution divided by turnover, expressed as a decimal fraction, but often converted to a percentage.	188, 408
Contribution per unit	Sales price minus variable cost.	408
Copyright	A legal right to protect original material that stops others from using the work without permission.	269
Corporate social responsibility (CSR)	The combination of business ethics, social responsibility and environmental sustainability.	158
Corporate venturing	When large companies 'buy in' product development by acquiring smaller companies.	258
Cost+ or full-cost pricing	This takes the total cost of producing a product or delivering a service and divides it by the predicted number of units to be sold to arrive at the average cost, to which a target mark-up is then added.	186
Creative abstraction	The ability to apply abstract concepts/ideas.	50
Creative boldness	The confidence to push boundaries beyond accepted conventions. Also the ability to eliminate the fear of what others might think of you.	50
Creative complexity	The ability to carry large quantities of information and be able to manipulate and manage the relationships between such information.	50
Creative connection	The ability to make connections between things that do not appear to be connected.	50
Creative curiosity	The desire to change or improve things that others see as normal.	50
Creative paradox	The ability to simultaneously accept and work with statements that are contradictory.	50
Creative persistence	The ability to force oneself to keep looking for more and stronger solutions even when good ones have already been generated.	50
Creative perspective	The ability to shift one's perspective on a situation in terms of space, time and other people.	50
Critical path	The longest path through the Gantt chart and the shortest possible time to complete the task.	320
Critical success factors	The activities upon which the success of the venture critically depend.	92, 119, 295
Cross elasticity of demand	How demand reacts to changes in price.	187
Crowdfunding	Peer-to-peer, internet-based lending or investing. Also includes 'rewards' platforms.	376, 390

Term	Definition	Page
Current assets	Cash or assets that can be converted within one year into cash. Normally cash, debtors (receivables) and stock (inventory).	412
Current liabilities	Liabilities that need to be paid within one year. Normally overdraft, creditors (payables) and any loans or liabilities (such as hire purchase) due for repayment within the year.	412
Current ratio	Current assets divided by current liabilities, expressed as a number or decimal fraction.	416
Customer focus (or intimacy)	Having a clear understanding of all aspects of customer needs so that customers are satisfied with all aspects of the product/service offering. Usually involves having a close relationship with customers.	116
Customers	Those people who buy your product/service.	9
Death Valley curve	The typical valley-shaped curve of the cash flow of a business start-up.	411
Debtor (receivables) turnover	Sales (turnover) divided by debtors (receivables), expressed as a number.	416
Demand-pull	The demand of customers for your product or service that 'pulls' it through your **channels of distribution**.	181, 223
Design thinking (customer-centric design)	A loose set of holistic concepts that approach design from the perspective of solving complex problems for people, rather than just creating distinctive objects or shapes.	154
Differentiation	Using the elements of the marketing mix to make your product/service as different as possible from competitors'. When valued by customers this usually leads to being able to charge a higher price.	116
Discovery skills	Creativity skills practised by entrepreneurs: networking, observing, questioning, experimenting and associating.	53
Dispersed leadership	Focus on leadership across all levels and in different forms.	360
Disruptive innovation	Introducing radically new products or services into existing markets. See also **radical innovation**.	38
Diversification	Moving away from core areas of activity into completely new and unrelated product/market areas. Moving into complementary or competitive areas is called 'horizontal integration'. When companies move into their supply chain it is called 'backwards vertical integration'. When they move into their distribution chain it is called 'forwards vertical integration'.	253
Dominant logic	Paradigms or conventions that establish a status quo that is rarely questioned.	40
Early adopters	The second group of customers to buy a new product – people with status in their market segment and opinion leaders.	209
Economies of scope (synergy)	The term used when less of a resource is used because it is spread across multiple activities. Often referred to as '1 + 1 = 3'.	118, 258

Term	Definition	Page
Effectuation (effectual reasoning)	An approach to decision making that is not based solely on deductive reasoning.	109
Emergent strategy	Strategy development that is characterized by reactive solutions to existing problems.	109, 459
Emotional intelligence	An appreciation of yourself, your different circumstances and an ability to adapt your behaviour to meet them and relate to people.	355
Entrepreneur	A person who creates and/or exploits change for profit by innovating, accepting risk and moving resources to areas of higher return.	7
Entrepreneurial firms	Firms that are set up to grow from the start and bring innovative ideas and ways of doing things to the market.	8
Entrepreneurial leadership	Leadership that ensures an organization remains entrepreneurial.	361
Exit route (liquidity event)	The sale of an equity investment.	389
Factoring (or invoice discounting)	A form of finance where sales invoices act as security.	376
Fiduciary duty (of directors)	A legal duty of loyalty and care to act honestly and in good faith, exercise skill and care and undertake all statutory duty.	289
Financial capital	A loosely used term (sometimes just called capital) that refers to the money invested in the business. This can come from the founders, other equity investors or from loans (often referred to as loan capital).	14
Financial gearing/ leverage	All loans including overdraft divided by shareholders' funds, expressed as a decimal fraction, but usually converted to a percentage.	315, 383, 417
FinTech	The financial technology industry. This includes crowdfunding platforms and other internet platforms that deliver financial services.	394
First-mover advantage	The competitive advantage gained by being the first into a market.	128
Five forces	Porter's Five Forces that affect the degree of competition in an industry: competitive rivalry, threat of substitutes, threat of new entrants, power of buyers and power of suppliers.	86
Fragmented market	A market where there are a large number of competitors of about the same size, usually in a mature or declining industry.	75
Franchise	A business in which the owner of the name and method of doing business (the franchisor) allows a local operator (the franchisee) to set up a business under that name offering their products or services.	239
Full-cost pricing	See **cost+**.	
Futures thinking	A holistic perspective that develops a vision about the future state after a change has taken place.	59

Term	Definition	Page
Gambler's ruin	A model of business outcomes that stresses luck rather than skill or knowledge.	278
Gantt chart	A visual way of showing the linkages between different sequential activities.	320
Gap analysis	A 'map' of product/market attributes based on dimensions that are perceived as important to customers.	63
Gazelles and/or unicorns	Young, high-growth firms (usually over 20 percent per annum). Unicorns have higher growth than gazelles.	6
Generic business models (or marketing strategies)	The strategies of low cost, differentiation and/or customer focus that form the basis of developing sustainable competitive advantage. Also called 'value disciplines'.	116, 121, 249
GET test	Psychometric test of your tendency or inclination to become an entrepreneur.	18
Gig-workers/ gig-economy	Workers seeking temporary, short-term work with companies obtained by searching out opportunities on smartphone-based apps. Their status as self-employed is questionable.	8
Gross profit	Sales minus cost of sales	407
Gross profit margin	Gross profit divided by sales (turnover), expressed as a decimal fraction, but usually converted to a percentage.	416
Guerrilla marketing	Any low-cost approach to creating awareness of your product or service. Particularly associated with the use of social media.	215
Hire purchase	A form of finance that allows the firm to purchase the asset over a period of time by making regular payments with the asset acting as security.	376
Human capital	The skills and experience gained from education, training and previous experience.	14
Income statement	A document showing the sales, costs and profit of a business in a period.	404, 407
Incremental product/ service innovation	Small changes to the product or service you are offering.	37
Information asymmetry	When parties have different levels of information.	239, 383
Insight selling	Having an input to or disrupting decisions that may be made by a customer ahead of the sales meeting. This involves developing relationships with them and using knowledge gained in this way to answer or disrupt any sales objections they may have.	212
Interest cover	Operating profit divided by interest expense, expressed as a number or decimal fraction.	417
Intrapreneurs	Salaried employees of a company acting in an entrepreneurial fashion, usually to create new ventures for their employers.	9
Job description	A list of the things an employee has to do and what they will be held accountable for in this role.	335
Jobbing production	One-off production.	304

Term	Definition	Page
Joint venture	A more formal strategic partnership based upon a legal agreement, often involving a separate legal entity.	243, 312
Key activities	Important operating activities. These may become **business imperatives** or even **critical success factors**.	295
Key performance indicators (KPIs)	The **metrics** that measure performance in the **key activities**. Often used as metrics against which to judge the performance of managers.	295
Key risk indicators	Parameters or events that indicate an increased likelihood of the risk materializing.	310
Leadership	Setting direction, communicating with and motivating staff.	8
Lean manufacturing	An approach to manufacturing that minimizes costs and waste without sacrificing productivity.	130
Lean start-up	The launch of a **minimum viable product**, then using customer feedback in an iterative fashion to further tailor it to the specific needs of customers.	83, 126
Lease	A form of finance that allows the firm to use the asset without owning it by making regular payments.	376
Life cycle	Stages of life – can refer to a product, market or industry.	73
Lifestyle firms	Firms that allow the owner-manager to pursue a particular lifestyle and earn an acceptable living while doing so.	7
Limited liability company	A separate legal entity distinct from its owners or shareholders, and its directors or managers. Its liability is limited by the amount of capital shareholders have put into the business.	273
Line production	Production with sufficient volume and regularity of orders to justify the investment in task analysis and dedicated resources.	304
Liquidation (of a company)	Occurs when a company is unable to pay its debts and a court order is obtained by creditors to sell off its assets. This can be 'voluntary' or 'compulsory'.	287
Liquidity event	See **Exit route**.	389
Management	Handling complexity in organizational processes and the execution of work.	295
Management buy-ins	External managers buying a firm and normally replacing the management.	388
Management buy-outs	The management of a firm buying it.	388
Margin of safety	Sales (turnover) minus breakeven point (expressed in $/£ turnover), all divided by sales (turnover), expressed as a decimal fraction, but usually converted to a percentage.	411
Market development	Finding new customers or markets for products or services.	37, 238
Market paradigm shift	Changes in established market conventions associated with the creation of radically new markets.	38
Market penetration	Selling your original or existing product or service to the customers in the market segment you originally identified.	236

Term	Definition	Page
Market segments	Groupings of customers with similar characteristics.	144, 238
Marketing 3.0	See **Values-driven marketing**.	149
Marketing benefits	The motivations each segment has for buying your product or service.	176
Marketing mix	The 'five Ps' that define your marketing strategy: Product/ service, Price, Promotion/communication, People (service) and Place (distribution channels etc.).	116, 176
Marketing strategy	How the value proposition is delivered to customer segments.	38, 249
Metrics	Measures of performance.	130, 295, 418
Mind maps	A map of related ideas from one original idea.	60
Minimum viable product (MVP)	The minimum viable state of a product so that it can be launched and customer feedback then used to better tailor it to customer needs.	130
Mission statement	The formal statement of business purpose – what the business aims to achieve and how it will achieve it.	167
Multi-sided markets	Using different business models to sell to more than one customer.	126, 181
Net profit	Operating profit (gross profit minus operating costs) minus interest.	407
New-to-the-world industries	New industries emerging from radical innovation that creates markets that did not exist before.	38
Niche business model (or marketing strategy)	A business model and strategy that involves high differentiation and customer focus.	123
Non-metric mapping	Maps products in generic groups that customers find similar and then tries to explain why these groupings exist.	64
Operating costs	The costs of running the business and selling its products/ services, such as selling, marketing and administrative costs. Not part of the cost of sales.	407
Operating profit	Gross profit minus operating costs.	407
Operating profit margin	Operating profit divided by sales (turnover), expressed as a decimal fraction, but usually converted to a percentage.	416
Organizational architecture	Term used to describe the infrastructure an organization needs to build business processes that deliver its vision, comprising: leadership, culture, structure and strategies.	361
Organizational culture	In an organization the web of unspoken, prevalent norms, basic beliefs and assumptions about the 'right' way to behave. Sometimes simply described as 'how it is around here'.	341
Parallel new product development model	An approach in which product development and concept/ market testing go side by side.	130
Partnership	Groups of sole traders or companies who come together, formally or informally, to do business.	243, 273, 311

Term	Definition	Page
Patent	This covers how a product works, what it does or how it does it, what it is made of or how it is made. It gives the owner the right to prevent others from copying, making, using, importing or selling the invention without permission.	267
Penetrated market	The size of the served available market you capture.	84
Performance metrics	See **Metrics**.	295
Perceptual mapping	Maps the attributes of a product within specific categories.	63
Person specification	The criteria on which to base selection of an employee.	336
PE ratio	Price-earnings ratio. Share price divided by the earnings or **net profit** per share, expressed as a number.	422
PESTEL analysis	Tool to help thinking about future developments in the wider environment. An acronym for Political, Economic, Social, Technological, Environmental and Legal changes.	58
Pivoting	Changing your business model and/or strategy.	108, 130
Politicking	Rational decision-making vs decision-making based on political pressure.	351
Population ecology	The structure of a market or industry.	278
Potential market	The size of a general market that might be interested in buying a product.	84
Power distance	The degree of inequality among people that the community is willing to accept.	23
PR	Public relations.	217
Pre-packaged or pre-pack sale	The name given to the process of buying the assets of a business from the old failing company and allowing the existing management to continue trading.	287
Price-earnings (PE) ratio	See **PE ratio**.	422
Product development	Developing a completely new product or service, or modifying an existing one.	239
Product expansion	Developing product or service variations that meet the needs of different market segments.	245
Product extension	Extending a successful brand to similar but different products or services that might be purchased by the same customers.	245
Product modification	Small and evolutionary modifications of existing products in terms of quality, function or style.	245
Quick ratio	**Current assets**, excluding stock (inventory) divided by **current liabilities**, expressed as a number.	417
Radical innovation	The creation of radically new products or services, including **market paradigm shift**.	39
Registered design	A legal right that protects the overall visual appearance of a product in the geographical area you register it. It does not offer protection regarding the composition of a product or how it works.	268

Term	Definition	Page
Related diversification	Diversification into related areas where you have some product or market knowledge and/or expertise.	253
Relationship marketing	Techniques that enable companies to form loyal relationships with customers.	148
Repertory grid	A more systematic extension of non-metric mapping that uses market research to group similar or dissimilar products and to explain the differences.	64
Return to shareholders	**Net profit** divided by **shareholders' funds**, expressed as a decimal fraction, but usually converted to a percentage.	415
Return on total assets	**Operating profit** divided by the sum of **shareholders' funds** plus loan capital, expressed as a decimal fraction, but usually converted to a percentage.	415, 417
Risk factor	The probability of occurrence multiplied by the impact of the risk event.	309
Risk index	The composite risk index reclassified in some simplified way.	309
Salary-substitute firms	Firms that simply generate an income comparable to what the owner-manager might earn as an employee.	7
Scalability	The potential to scale up and grow.	236
Scenario planning	A technique that tries to assess how possible future situations might impact on a firm.	92
Search engine optimization (SEO)	An internet technique that ensures that you catch any potential customers searching for your type of product on search engines as quickly as possible.	303
Served available market (SAM)	The size of the target market segment you wish to serve within the total available market.	84
Shared cognition	The sharing of goals, effective communication and transfer of knowledge between partners in a business.	336
Shareholders' funds	The total money or equity invested in the business by all shareholders (including venture capital) plus accumulated or retained profits.	413
Skills profile	The skills needed to undertake a job or launch a new venture.	335
SMART performance metrics	SMART performance metrics are Specific for purpose, Measurable, Achievable, Relevant to the success of the organization and Time constrained.	418, 419
Social capital	Networks of friends and commercial contacts.	14
Social entrepreneur	An entrepreneur working in a social enterprise.	9
Social networks and media	Communication hosted on the internet or on smartphones, such as texting, tweeting or blogging, includes social networking sites such as Facebook, Twitter and YouTube.	214
Sole trader	A business owned by one individual. It has unlimited liability.	272
Stock (inventory) turnover	Sales (turnover) divided by stock (inventory), expressed as a number.	416

Term	Definition	Page
Strategic alliance	A form of partnership whereby separate organizations come together to pursue an agreed set of objectives.	243, 312
Strategic intent	A strong underlying vision of what a company might become.	143, 306, 355
Strategic options	Actions you might undertake if risks or opportunities materialize.	93, 318
Strategic review	The process of reviewing the business model with a view to improvement.	456
Strategizing	Continuous assessment of the options about how to make the most of opportunities or avoid risks as they arise.	306, 318
Subchapter S Corporation	US form of limited liability company that does not pay tax, instead all profits or losses are passed through to individual shareholders.	274
Supply-push	'Pushing' sales of your product or service by offering incentives to distributors.	179, 223
Sustainable entrepreneurship	Entrepreneurship where issues of corporate social responsibility, sustainability, ethics and good corporate governance are at the core of the 'for-profit' commercial enterprise. It is about meeting the needs of today through profit without prejudicing the future.	158
Sweat equity	The share of equity in a business created by the time and effort put in to get the business off the ground.	336
Switch costs	The costs of switching the company from which you buy a product or service.	86
SWOT analysis	An analysis of your Strengths and Weaknesses and the Opportunities and Threats that you face.	91, 458
Synergy (economies of scope)	See **Economies of scope**.	118
Systematic risk	That part of risk associated with how the share price of a company performs compared to the overall market (measured by the company's beta coefficient).	254
Target market segment	The key customers or groups of customers you are targeting with your marketing mix.	118
Total asset turnover	Sales (turnover) divided by total assets, expressed as a number or decimal fraction.	416
Total available market (TAM)	The size of your prospective market – those in the potential market who might be interested in buying your particular product.	84
Trade sale	Sale of the business to another company, probably in the same industry.	389
Trademark	A sign – made up of words or a logo or both – which distinguishes distinctive goods and services from those of competitors.	267

Term	Definition	Page
Transactional leadership	A leadership style that promotes efficiency and incremental change, reinforcing rather than challenging the status quo; setting goals, putting in place systems, controls and rewards to achieve them.	360
Transformational leadership	A leadership style that promotes inspiration, excitement and intellectual stimulation.	360
Trust	An unincorporated body run according to the social objectives set out in the trust deed. Trustees are personally liable for any debts or loans.	275
Unicorns	See **Gazelles and/or unicorns**.	
Unincorporated association	Informal association of individuals that can form (and re-form) quickly – similar to sole traders or informal partnerships.	163
Validated learning	Using customers to tailor your **minimum viable product** (MVP) in a **lean start-up**.	130
Value chain	The primary and support activities that add value to a product/service.	44
Value disciplines	The strategies of low cost, differentiation and/or customer focus that form the basis of developing sustainable competitive advantage. Also called 'generic business models' and 'generic marketing strategies'.	121, 249
Value proposition	The marketing benefits offered to each target market segment.	111
Values	Core beliefs.	142
Values-driven marketing (Marketing 3.0)	An approach to marketing which involves developing deep relationships with customers based upon shared values.	148
Variable cost	The cost of producing one additional unit (e.g. the costs of materials or components and piecework labour).	186
Venture capital	Equity capital invested in the business by individuals or institutions other than the founders at an early stage in its development.	387
Vision	What the business might become.	142
Visionary leadership	A leadership style providing a clear vision which focuses people on goals and key issues and concerns.	360
Voluntary arrangements	Forms of arranging the financial affairs of an individual who is struggling to pay their debts.	285

Scoring exercise 11.6

To obtain your leadership orientation rating, score one point for the appropriate response under each heading. If your response is inappropriate you do not score.

Concern for PEOPLE score (maximum score 15)

'Yes' for questions: 2, 4, 8, 10, 17, 19, 21, 23, 27.

'No' for questions: 6, 13, 14, 25, 29, 30.

Concern for TASK score (maximum score 15)

'Yes' for questions: 1, 3, 5, 7, 9, 11, 15, 16, 18, 20, 22, 24, 26, 28.

'No' for question: 12.

Total your scores and plot your position on the Leadership Grid to the left. As a guide, a score of 5 or less is low and 12 or more is high.

Concern for **PEOPLE**

| 15 |
| 14 |
| 13 |
| 12 |
| 11 |
| 10 |
| 9 |
| 8 |
| 7 |
| 6 |
| 5 |
| 4 |
| 3 |
| 2 |
| 1 |
| 0 |

0 1 2 3 4 5 6 7 8 9 10 11 12 13 14 15

Concern for **TASK**

Subject index

Author index

Quotes index